An intriguing story of horror and enlightenment… a tale of human strength in the face of meaningless suffering. This is a testimony that the African experience is very relevant in the modern world - in fact, necessary for a better understanding of our universe. This is a must read for everyone who wants to widen his or her consciousness. It is a story of humanity.

Richard Philips, Freelance journalist, Tampa, FL.

This is a brave personal story. In an age when people are running away from the psychological basis of superstition, Rahman makes it knock on our door and wakes us up to appreciate what it means for our life. This is the first time that superstition would become science, and science superstition. His life experience leaves us on the road to reconsider our views on science and religion.

Steven Dooner, Professor of Liberal Arts, Quincy College, MA.

This is a triumph for the long-discounted African experience. Not until now are the nuances of African cultural life treated credibly in nonfiction, given a real human face that everyone can recognize. It is nothing but bravery to attempt this in our increasingly scientific world.

Rudolf Okonkwo,
Columnist, Nigeriaworld.com and author of *Children of a Retired God*

On Holy Pilgrimage

RAHMAN OLADIGBOLU

Published by Oracle Publishers,
141 Memorial Parkway
P.M.B. 122, Randolph, MA 02368.

Printed in the U.S.A. by InstantPublisher.com

Cover design by Okey Okereke
Contact: 781-581-2628
617-699-1360
wolfpackprodtns@yahoo.com

Library of Congress Cataloguing-in-Publication Data
Oladigbolu, Rahman.
On holy pilgrimage: a long journey for freedom /
Rahman Oladigbolu – 1st edition.
1. Oladigbolu, Rahman. 2. African – Biography. 3. Cultural repression – Africa – Biography. 4. Culture conflict – Africa. 5. Human experience and healing – psychology. 6. Soul experience – philosophy. I Title.

ISBN: 0-9768354-0-1

For my family,
with which I share my blood;
for Africa,
with which I share my destiny;
for America,
with which I share my dream;
for Humanity,
with which I share my soul.

On Holy Pilgrimage:
A Long Journey for Freedom

Rahman Oladigbolu

THE PROLOGUES

I

The Gunshot

The neighborhood was familiar. It was Abebi, next to where I lived with my grandparents. The house, too, was familiar. My cousin's girlfriend lived there and I had gone with him this late evening to visit her. When I found myself waiting in front of the house, however, while my cousin went into the girl's room, I did not realize that there was something unusual about this moment. We always went in together whenever we visited our girlfriends together, except when there was sex or something like it on the agenda, when then we would make the visit alone.

The evening grew darker, giving way to the budding night. It was now about 11 pm and, still waiting, I became impatient. At night, the neighborhood was notorious for danger, of human and non-human causes. Muggers abounded there. And everyone was familiar with stories of demons and spirits dwelling in the Alawo River, the mysterious watercourse that cut through the area. They roamed the streets at night, a reason people shut their doors early. How much of the stories were true was a question one may ask, but to find out was at present not my idea of a good night. I would rather play safe and enjoy the stories than dare and be the story. The darkness of the night was frightening enough. So, I thought it was high time we returned home. I went inside the house and knocked on the door to the girl's room.

My cousin opened the door slightly. "Give me just a few more minutes, please," he said, almost in a whisper.

I did not know why I could not say anything more. Reluctantly, I went back outside to wait some more.

About a quarter-hour passed and my cousin was still in there. My impatience heightened. Yet, I continued to wait. When I could not see anyone outside anymore, except sleepy dogs and goats, I went back inside. It was now around midnight, already a dangerous time to walk the street; but being two of us, I hoped we could manage to reach home safely. I knocked again on the door, this time angrily, and my cousin opened it. But he gave me the greatest shocker of my life.

"I'm sorry, Rahman," he began again in his whispery voice, "I've decided to stay the rest of the night here. You can go home and I'll see you in the morning."

I could not believe my ears and I was stunned to mute. Before I could bring myself to protest, he shut the door to my face and left me out in the cold. Uncharacteristic of him indeed, but I had no time to think of what might have possessed him, whether his own mischief or one of the spirits that owned the neighborhood at night.

Facing the girl's door, I stood in the central hallway that ran straight from the front door of the house to the back door. There was no fence around the house, and what could be called its front and backyard became footpaths and clusters of houses that formed the neighborhood. From where I stood, I could see a large section of it, a layout that, in the modern sense, was obsolete, as most parts of the famous Nigerian city were. Called Ibadan, an evolved name that contrasted with its modern structure, the city was a heterogeneous mixture of old and new houses, described idyllically as a "running splash of rust and gold flung and scattered among seven hills like broken China in the sun."[1] Covered heavily by centuries-old trees that made up the Agala Forest, one of the hills lay a few yards away from the girl's house, and it was also a landscape that was as strange as the Alawo River. It was a dwelling place of fabulous creatures, real and unreal, and a haven for robbers, ritual murderers, and cultic churches.

Everywhere was night-still. The street fowls were already sleeping in their roosts. My sense of the time was frightening; it was the witching time of the night and the thought of going home alone frightened me more. I looked around. The sight was beleaguering. The nocturnal sounds chilled my bones. Everything about the time and place was sinister.

Realizing that I had no other option, I banged on the door out of fright and anger. The lovers inside ignored me. I banged harder, but suddenly stopped. I felt myself naked to the eyes of the night peeping through the wide-opened doors on both sides of me, the front and back doors of the house. Intuitively I felt the presence of a predator. Then I saw a shadowy figure move into view at the back of the house. Immediately, I sensed danger and my heart lurched, sending a creepy feeling up my spine.

It must be around 1 am now and there could not be any good-willing person outside. The figure was of a human and it had the smartness and quickness of a sportsman. He appeared like a Chinese Ninja, dressed in close-fitting, dark clothing that blended with his surroundings. I could not see his face; it was as dark as his figure. And from where I was, about fifty feet away from him, I saw or sensed he had a locally made pistol in his hand.

Simultaneously, he pointed the gun at me. Everything happened so quickly and I instinctively leapt forward to dodge the imminent shot in the small cavity that hid the girl's door about ten inches away from the wall line.

He missed. For such a gun he had to reload, and I seized the opportunity to bolt for the front door. What lay ahead of me was a jungle of houses and trees. I plunged myself into it, running as fast as I could and knocking down front-house stalls and water pots in my way. I did not look

---

[1] J.P. Clark.

back, but I felt the gunman running after me, and closing the gap between us.

After running almost blindly for about a sixth of a mile, I found myself at the base of Agala Forest. I had spent all the twenty-two years of my life in this area, but I had not ventured into the forested hill twenty-two times. And I had only gone there among dependable companies. It was more dreadful than the Alawo, with horrid tales heard and witnessed often, and everyone feared it more than the devil. One of the few times I had been there, we spotted decapitated bodies of a mother and child tied to separate trees, their heads swapped for their bodies in ritual symbolism.

Having this image of the forest in my mind, I screeched to a stop. Promptly, I glanced around in search of a better route for escape, but before I could see anything clearly, the gun went off again and hit something close to where I stood. I did not see what it was. Without further thought, I tore through the fabric of the forest. Smoke from a low burning fire filtered through the trees to greet my eyes and nostrils. It reeked of burning flesh, and the indistinct noise that came with it sounded like a song of revel, though otherworldly. I could not tell which direction the smoke and sound were coming from, but I prayed I was not running toward it. Whoever the people were, they would not mean good for me either.

Hoping that the few trees I had left behind would give a fair cover, I paused again to figure out which direction was best to run. I looked back and forth. Nothing was sure. The trees and shrubs imprisoned my sight. Again, the gun sounded off. This time, I saw it hit a tree at my side. It was very close, and I shot myself in the direction I faced, increasing my pace. The branches of the trees beat and cut into my face and arms, and the dried leaves on the ground rustled at my feet.

Twice, I lost balance and fell to the ground. I hurriedly got up and continued running. The third time, I stumbled on a tree stump. As I tried to get up, I lost balance again, but as I fell this time, I felt myself descending, rolling downward for a few seconds until a tree trunk stopped me. I had reached the hilltop and was already on the other side, heading out of it. I rose up, balanced myself and took advantage of the descent to increase my pace.

At the base, I paused to look around again, panting. The place looked like a small Greek agora, enclosed by grim-looking houses and trees that appeared intertwined at some places. Perhaps long abandoned, none of the houses looked habitable, at least not by humans. I was looking for a place to hide. If my pursuer continued to close up the gap, then I needed to find a better way out than just running. My attention went to a dilapidated two-storey house, almost hidden behind two huge trees. With quick steps, I disappeared through the opening between the trees and ran toward a shaky staircase on the left side of the hallway. I had to break through cobwebs that were almost as thick as knitting threads. The staircase and the floor of the second level were made of wood, a feature of the colonial era architecture. They creaked as I climbed and walked to the front part of the house. I wanted to find a place to be able to see the agora for signs of my pursuer.

On the veranda, I prostrated on the floor to peep through an opening in the wooden railing. I breathed heavily from near-exhaustion. I did not know where I got my energy tonight; my poor stamina had halted my career in sport, and under normal circumstances I could not have run half as much as I had done.

In a few seconds, the dark figure appeared. Strangely, he did not pause to find his bearing or figure out where I could be in the dark clustered corner of the area. He headed straight toward my hiding place, now walking with unhastened, though menacing, steps that sent my heart shuddering. His complacent gait was more intimidating than his running. Slowly and uncannily, he looked upward. Through the close apertures of the trees and the railing, he stared directly into my eyes from the distant, while I still could not make out his facial features.

Without wasting time to figure out how he knew where I was, I leapt to my feet and ran again for my life. He knew it, and he ran toward the house now. Before I reached the staircase, he was already on the ground floor, thus enclosing me up in the house. I went for the backdoor, away from the staircase. Though he did not look bigger than I was, the house made noise louder under his steps than under mine. The building shook with increasing tempest and the walls and pillars collapsed in pieces as he climbed toward me. I cut through the cobwebs further and reached the backdoor. A little relieved, I opened it and tried to run out. But there was no staircase behind the backdoor; it was a door made only to look outside – another obsolete architectural feature.

Turning around, I found my pursuer already some feet away from me, navigating his way through the dust of the collapsing house. Evidently, it was only a matter of seconds before the whole house would be down on us. Yet, he was calm, walking slowly and confidently toward me. I hurriedly turned back and looked out the backdoor again. Below was Alawo River, whose demons and spirits were reputed to be up and functioning at this hour of the night - it was their daytime. The fear of finally becoming a story in this incredible world washed over me, almost choking life out of me. Cold sweat streamed down my face and body. I turned again to my pursuer, just in time to see him raise his gun, the antiquated weapon pointing between my eyes.

I had no time to think. I had to do something or be done by something. I turned back impetuously toward the river and threw myself in the air. Down I went, until I heard the gun go off at the same time I hit the water surface.

It was a shallow and dirty river, serving as a main drainage for the city. I hoped only to duck beneath its surface to hide and crawl to the other end. But I was too late. The bullet caught me on the buttock, giving me a sharp and shattering spasm of pain that sent an excruciating tremor all over my body. I wailed out, with a convulsive pull at the muscles of my hips, delicately situated around my groin. They were extremely sensitive parts of the body and my cry of pain was pitched so high that it echoed through the entire neighborhood. At the same time, the house crashed to the ground, while the wraith-like figure still stood and walked atop the ruins.

My wailing could have woken the sleeping neighborhood, but, instead, in the strangeness of the whole situation, it woke my uncle who slept next to my bed.

"Ramoni, Ramoni!" That was all I first heard when I woke up, the accented version of my Arabic name as used by elderly people. "What is the matter with you?" my uncle asked in a terrified voice. The anguish in my voice had petrified him.

In the next instant, however, as I tried to say something to my uncle, I felt something like another shot of the gun. Without the stage and setting of the dream, I felt the same tearing of the bullet into my body, and the same convulsive pull at the delicate muscles of my groin. It was spasmodic, intensely painful, and murderous. I wailed again. And from then on, the pang came at the slightest internal or external stimulus. The slightest move of a body part, a word or an attempt of a word from my mouth, and even a breath deeper than usual would spark it off and send me gasping for life amid the choking fume of my pain. This was the strangest thing my life had ever witnessed.

The unfamiliar dream had gone back into the dream world, but the gunshot, the traumatic and mysterious phenomenon, had remained in the familiar world of reality. Then I realized that the dream had not been just a dream; it had been as real as every other event of my life. The shadowy gunman, the gun, the plot, and the setting have left me an effect that was no less real than the experiences of my wake-life. It was stranger than fiction, my uncle would later recall. Even though he thought he knew what happened, the nature of human consciousness would not stop bewildering him for the rest of his life. We realized that I had only passed through a door, from one place to another, and back, neither more nor less real than the other. But stranger things lay ahead, and this was only the beginning.

II

Marriage of Heaven and Hell[2]

Good and evil are one, (and)
God is day and night, summer and winter,
War and peace, surfeit and hunger.

Heraclitus.

The November sun was at its zenith and the temperature was roasting. Yet, I switched off the fan. It was an old noisy machine and would drown the footfalls of anyone walking toward my room. I had left two young family friends in the dining room after some discussions and I wanted to know whenever anyone of them was coming for me. It was certain that one or both would come soon, but I was tired and hoped to restore some energy before anyone would engage me in further discussion. About seven years had put the night of the strange dream behind me, but the gunshot had left my legs crippled.

For the heat, I took off my shirt and wiped traces of sweat off my body. For strength, I tried Qi gong, a Chinese breathing exercise that had lately become my habit. If only no one would come, I really hoped to catch some sleep, nonetheless. But, also, I enjoyed the kind of conversation we were having and I liked to talk some more. I was a young adult who had found philosophy as a way out of the intellectual and emotional confusion of adolescence, and talking about it had its way of further enlightenment. I especially hoped to clarify some issues that were tangled when I left them.

The two friends, a young man and woman, were majoring in philosophy at the University of Ibadan and we often discussed their subjects together. Seun Ajiboye, a second year student combining Political Science with Philosophy, had earlier in the afternoon brought up topics on witchcraft and reincarnation from a course titled African Philosophy. They were to feature in her up-coming examination and she had hoped to pick up a thing or two in our discussions.

During the interwoven session, Bolarinwa, a first year student writing a paper on evil, found my concept of evil insulting to his intelligence. For me, the devil was no longer a fallen angel to run away from, but a god that could be understood and respected. It was interesting to me that in traditional African religions, the devil was a trickster figure, a jester often raising the crucial issues of life that humans were too afraid or too indulgent to face. Hence, before the Christian and Islamic Satan usurped his image, the African devil was revered and worshipped. Bolarinwa challenged this view, and we had a complex problem to unravel. We had spent about an hour and a half on the three topics before I withdrew to my

---

[2] Reference to William Blake's poem.

room, leaving the two to go on reading their texts. I had been indignant at his argument. It seemed to me as blind, but I was not sure whether I had not been making my argument in the "I'm-right-and-you-must-believe-me" style, the blindness of the other end. Neither was a right style of argument. So I hoped to make myself better when we reconvened. Anyone could believe whatever he or she likes, so all I needed to do was to make myself clear enough. Perhaps that was the only goal within my power.

I heard no footfall when Seun walked in.

"Brother Rahman," she started out, as typically as I was now used to, using a customary 'brother' of respect rather than a religious one. Lately, many younger people, both adolescents and those in early twenties, boys and girls, had placed a 'big brother' image on me. This was a bestowment of the last few years. I did not mind it, so I tried to be there for them as a 'big brother.' I was not only helping them by being so, they were also giving me an opportunity to help myself, especially at this critical period of my life. From birth to death, life seems one long boring strip of years that needs be filled with one role or another, and the more productive a role one has in it the happier one may be.

Yet, circumstance may have forced me to accept such a 'big brother' responsibility so soon. I was just in my twenties, only arrested too early from having the typical experience of my age group. To some extent, my social mythology was still the stories of the MTV pantheon, and barely had I been weaned of my high school fantasies. Within me, I still felt the urges of youth, the carelessness of my age, while I now had to play the role of maturity and responsibility in the community.

"Where are the books you talked about?" Seun concluded as she walked toward the bed to pick up another book that caught her eye. I had promised to give her some materials to prepare for her examination. This was part of my new role. Like a librarian, books flowed through my hands to and from readers, academic and pleasure-reading books. I owned no book, yet I could barely find a space to sleep among the stockpiles in my room.

"That's not one of them." I pointed out as I tried to rise to go for the materials in my cupboard.

"I know; I can tell from the cover. I'm only curious." She looked at it for a while and asked, "What's this about, anyway?"

"It's about the title on the cover (*Mind-Body Identity Theory*). It's a physicalist theory in response to the mind-body problem (a metaphysical problem of the relationship between the mind and the body)."

"And how does it deal with it?"

"It identifies your mind, your mental state, absolutely as your physical body – as absolutely biological." I intended to make the statement duly poignant, as I believed the issue was. I had courted scholastic ideas for too long that now I sometimes could not help but sound like a schoolteacher, something I feared might alienate some friends. "That is, all you call your mind, your mental state, is merely the process of your brain - nothing more. A human being is no more than his physical body, and when the body dies, everything about him dies. He remains nowhere more - unlike religion teaches. All his dreams and hopes of paradise are no more than his pleasures at the Miamis, Vegases, and Parises of the world - no more than mere fantasy. And his fear of hellfire is no more than a mental state of ill-health, or inadequacy, treatable by medicine and psychotherapy."

"That is not true?" Seun exclaimed with disgust. "It's wrong, isn't it?"

"But the authors of the book argue that it is right." I obtained the materials I had for her and laid them down for her to reach.

Now distracted from her initial purpose, she thought the theory was outrageous. "Don't they know the nature of human beings' thinking?" She asked again, making it a topic of discussion without realizing it. I felt inclined to play the devil's advocate.

"Of course, they think they do. Just like the nature of thinking of computers, they suppose. You know that computers also think. So what they suggest is quite similar to that: a human being is no more than a thinking machine - he is as valuable and as useless as a computer." I paused briefly to await her response. When I realized she had not what to say yet, I continued, now verging on pontification. "Even computers sometimes think better, more productively, intense and, perhaps, ahead than humans. And that is what Capitalism wants. It is the modern god we worship and he doesn't care what you think or feel unless it makes a financial turnover. The world is now only a market – the capitalist shrine, and the politicians and the CEOs are the priests. All others are the worshippers, the consumers."

"But that is obviously wrong. There are certain important aspects of our mind that cannot be identified as biological as such," she continued.

"Like what?"

"For example, sometimes one may see things with the mind but which one has not known in the ordinary world before – you know, like ideas coming into one's head from nowhere."

"Like inspirations?"

"Yes. How could such a theory explain that? And it's by such inspirations that, even, computers are made. Computers are a product of human ingenuity."

"Good point. But we have to realize that inspirations (or intuition) would usually or always have a logical correspondence with our ordinary state of mind. 'No man's knowledge can go beyond his experience,' John Locke says. Remember? Your bank of experience in the world would not only have prepared you for whatever inspiration you would have; in some way, it would develop it and give it meaning to you. Unless, perhaps, for the prophetic kind of inspiration – if we can prove that scientifically, however. On the ordinary people's inspiration, it is akin to machines', and, by that, the physicalists would still have their argument strong. There are records of amazing creativity of machines and there are citable potentials."

Prophets are humans; therefore, if prophetic inspiration is logically proven, it may be a strong argument against Locke's and the physicalists' claim. I realized this, but I intended to let Seun find her way out by herself. There have been extraordinary cases of inspirations in the world that I could not believe that the physicalist theory was absolutely right. I had heard the story of Prophet Muhammad, who began to read by inspiration without learning to read or write, and of Jesus Christ, who spoke about God from his cradle and taught the Rabbis at a tender age of twelve. In a way, I believed these stories, but whether they were merely allegorical or more, our time difference may prevent a scientific verification. However, I had heard and seen of the contemporary case of a Tanzanian boy, Sherifdeen Khalifa, from whose story Jesus' and Muhammad's might be inferentially explicable. Flabbergasting people around West Africa in the 90s, the region where he was engaged to tour, Sherifdeen Khalifa knew by heart and taught both the Qur'an and the Bible from the tender age of five, and without having learned them. Furthermore, in the so-called secular arena, I had heard of cases of infant prodigies whose feats were hardly explicable in physicalist terms. There were also mysterious cases of people recovering from brain damage but who emerged with a whole new language or accent, and those coming out of surgeries with entirely new identities, and capable of doing things they had never learned.

Like the gunshot dream that had shot my life in a new and unexpected direction, these are mysteries that we might not be able to ignore in life. In a strict physicalist view, all these cases do not logically correspond to the natural banks of experience these individuals could have had in the world. Yet, in such a view, experiences are supposed to be the soil upon which trees of inspiration could only spring and strive, as the computer can only function in accordance to its programming.

Moreover, what makes the human distinctive from machines in his reality may not be the capability of thinking, perhaps not of feeling too, but that the human is unique in himself while the machine is not. Although I always agreed that the computer may have become some kind of Frankenstein monster - a creation of the human mind, but which now threatens to subjugate human intelligence – the computer still lacks the uniqueness that characterizes human beings.

I was aware of all these and many more against the physicalist claim, but it was fun to watch Seun intellectually troubled as she tried to find her way out and, perhaps, supply a new angle through which to look at the issues.

"But it is human beings who built the computers," she argued on.

"As human beings want to build human beings by cloning?"

"They haven't built one yet; besides, no one can."

"We have the potentials and a considerable degree of probability. Scientists have cloned two sheep already and that's enough to tell the world that to clone humans may not be far away in the future. Once done, the value of the created humans may not be much different from that of the created machines, at least from the physicalist perspective. They would both be claimed to be man-made. And since you and I might not be different from the clones, so might we not be different in value from them, and consequently from the machines. Then the next most important question would be, *Who made us*? *Who was the scientific genius that created the humankind*? And physicalist cosmologists and evolutionists are burning on their seats to help their colleagues out. See? And I doubt if they'll listen to Jesus on this."

Seun became spent out and confused. "But this (physicalist) theory is just not right," she blurted, "It is wrong. Human beings are much more than the physical body."

"Perhaps you are right," I eventually agreed with her, "but we cannot make a logical argument on mere opinions and beliefs. This is a logic-infested world and you are in a logic-oriented discipline. What the priest can get away with in church, you cannot get away with it in your class. It's your *whys* and *hows* that'd get you wherever you want to go. These theorists have stated their *whys* and *hows* in the book and they've gotten their recognition as philosophers and scientists, even if they're not right, or not so right enough. And in our modern world, it seems it is the logical that is most meaningful. Even when illogical and unreasonable are the most meaningful, they have to be logically and reasonably presented as illogical and unreasonable."

"So you agree with me that they are wrong."

"Yeah, I believe they are wrong. I think I do. But I also believe that in every wrong thing there is always an element of rightness, and in every right thing there is always an element of wrongness. And perhaps we would be better to always keep that in mind."

We dropped the topic as I showed her the materials she came for, a book on reincarnation and some essays on witchcraft, and as Bolarinwa walked in to continue our previous discussion.

Earlier, enveloped in local experiences and beliefs, Bolarinwa had recalled and mentioned the many cases of witchcraft in our environment. He had mentioned what he called the healings of witchcraft victims, confessions of witches, and exorcism of witchcraft in many churches, and had wondered how anyone could be right to say there was no evil in the world. "What is all that?" he had asked in utter dismay at my claim that there were perspectives from which one can view the world and see that there was no evil in it. The idea I was trying to show was that of relative perception, perhaps constructivist, by which every individual may be said to determine the nature of what he or she believes. If beauty is in beholder's eye, as most people readily agree with Shakespeare, then ugliness must also be in beholder's eye. That was my point.

But my friend and I still could not resolve the issue and we had to leave it again for another time. I brought the fan back to life after they had finally left the house. I wanted to lie down and catch some sleep, but I could not. The arguments of the day remained on my mind, like pieces of information on the memory stick of a computer. Something in me wanted to write it down, but I felt weary from the eight hours I had already spent writing in the day. Nonetheless, I got up, walked over to my writing table without thinking twice. I must have made up my mind, or my mind had made up itself to write. I was now the only one in the huge house and I could continue writing for as long as I pleased. But I did not write it, at least not then. The sound of someone knocking stopped me and I went to open the heavy fortress gate.

Situated at the outskirt of Ibadan, the house was a magnificent modern castle that had made my uncle broke. Uncle Tunji, one of my mother's younger brothers, had spent half his fortune to build it, and one of the people he would not like to see near the house was the woman at the gate. She was a long-time tenant from my grandparents' house, and part of the past that my uncle would like to shield from his present life and from me.

I offered her something to drink. She refused and went straight to the reason of her visit.

"I have come to apologize," she said from across the table of the living room, staring directly into my eyes to show the seriousness of her mood.

At a loss of what to say, I chuckled, but said it was all right. She was such a good woman that people could not hate, apparently unassuming and generous. For years she ran the same petty trade, from which people bought their little needs. Yet she was feared for being a strange woman, from whom many wanted to keep a distance. Once, she was openly accused of witchcraft, but the accuser muffled his words in her presence during a community trial and there was no concrete evidence against her.

Like my uncles and aunts, I had also wanted to avoid further contact with her, even though many people were not sure of the stories they heard about her. My grandmother warned me fervently, "If you love me, Rahman, and you want me to live long, please stay away from [that woman]." Perhaps I was only being foolhardy, but to avoid her was no longer my priority. I saw a picture larger than what people talked about. Or I thought I did. So, when I said to the woman that it was all right, I meant it, though I did not know whether she believed me.

She had her reasons for coming clandestinely to apologize. Without mentioning it, she knew that I knew what it was all about. What she did not know was why I had kept it a secret from my family and everyone living in the house. Hence, her apology was also a show of appreciation for my reticence.

I now saw her as a victim as I was, a character in a larger story, which neither she nor I could fully understand. For me, I have found joy and contentment in the story and I would not look back to apology. I wished I could tell her. I wished I had courage enough to tell her. I wished there was time enough to explain to her. I wished she would understand, at least as much as I thought I did. But I could only wish, and she was only a few weeks to her grave. Perhaps that was also a reason she had come. Realizing that the curtain that would fall over her stage had started dropping, she had wanted to put things right for her soul.

Every life is a story. This story had placed me at the center of attention for too long, and all I now wanted was to step out of it and live a different life. Coinciding with the gunshot dream, now known to everyone, it had been a rough and precarious period in my life, with many evil events at which people shook their heads in pity and dread. To Bolarinwa, it was an experience that made me a least likely person to think there was no evil in the world. To the people who knew me, and those who heard about me, I was a classic victim of evil concocted by witchcraft. Yet, I rarely used the language of good and evil. Now I only wanted to put this behind me and move on. Even though life may only be understood backward, it must be lived forward.[3] I have embraced death as the only inevitable; good or bad, it is the only human goal that never fails, whether we aspire to it or not. Before it comes, my only dream now was to do something important with my life, and my only hope toward this was America.

I had an arrangement to arrive at St Luke's hospital in Massachusetts for a surgery that would restore my legs, but the American consulate refused me an entry-visa. After three futile trials, I was left to moan under the burden of our modern world. Sometimes, one may wonder whether America and Europe were justified in the business of visas held over the so-called third world countries. From whom did they seek or get visas in the past centuries, one may ask, when the rich resources of Africa were their dreams? The diamonds of South Africa; the gold of Ghana; the diamonds and rubber of Congo; the antique artifacts of Benin, of Mali and other places; the cuddle of the tropical climate; the preciously natural scenery; the wild life; and, most importantly, the great sons and daughters, those ferried across the ocean and those left behind, whose fates were turned grueling and gruesome. The sons and daughters whose sweats, tears, and blood, together with their treasures, their birthrights, were immensely sacrificed to build a dependable infrastructure for a profiteering and developing West. In those centuries, these were the bounties that were the most promising desires of their hearts. And all they needed to do was to choose to come, regardless of what the Africans thought. Now, Africans have to be packed into lines like soldier ants to beg for American and European visas - almost like they were packed into ships in the ugly slavery past. Sometimes, civilization seems only a ridicule of humanity.

However, America's apparent concern for the good of the world may be enough for me to absolve her from the blames. America gives financial aid to poor nations, intervenes in political conflicts, promotes democracy, and is inclined to embrace embattled exiles. Yet, whether this absolution was by reason or sentiments, good judgment or one blinded by my predilection for America, my self-criticizing conscience dandled for conclusion. I could not ignore the situations and feelings of other peoples around the world, many who felt oppressed by America's giant strides. Perhaps, then, America has not always altruistically loved the rest of the world as it

[3] Christian existentialist Soren Kierkegaard.

appears. Perhaps the rest of the world has only been benefiting from America's generosity because America loves only herself – which, if so, she did not seem to be doing cleverly enough. In the philosophical circle, it has always been a debatable question whether altruism is really selflessness or only an informed egotism. As long as the debate goes unsettled, perhaps America may rule freely over the rest of the world as imperially as she likes.

Nonetheless, I loved America. Rather than being a nation held in contempt, I believed America could be a place respected and protected by the rest of the world, and whose potentials could be harnessed for the unity of the world. I saw America as a great nation - at least the people of America, because the people of a nation are usually not the same as the government of the nation. While it is blood that runs through the veins of the people, policies run through the veins of the government, and sometimes virulent policies obscured to the often schmaltzy people.

Ever since the beginning of the historic period, certain nations, usually one at a time, have been known to be the center of attraction to the rest of the world. They are nations where men and women migrate to achieve their goals, economical, professional, political, spiritual, and social goals. In the pre-Classical age, it had been Egypt, it had been Mesopotamia. In the first Classical age, Athens was that nation. In the Hellenistic age, it was Alexandria. In the subsequent Classical age, it was Rome. In the second half of the Middle Ages, it was the Ottoman Empire. In the beginning of the industrial age, it was England. And now, in the expanding age of industrial technology, the age proudly called the Information Age, the United States of America is that nation that leads all nations, the nation that attracts all peoples and that gives hopes and fulfillments to their aspirations. From the most known and respected persons to the least known, America has offered political and economic sanctuary.

Starting with William Penn in the 17th century, this is a nation that has taken and cushioned the landing of people like and unlike the Nobel-feathered Albert Einstein and Wole Soyinka, when threatened out of their birth lands. It is a nation that has been home to the various conflicting parts and ideologies of the world: the Arabs and the Jews, the German and the Jews, the Catholics and the Protestants, the Indians and the Pakistanis, the Japanese and the Koreans, the whites and the blacks, the religious, pagans, and the atheists, the soldiers who fought themselves angrily in the bitter battles the world has suffered in recent times, the world religions, which, elsewhere, want not to see themselves, all there on the American soil, living for the same goal, the same hope for humankind: freedom.

To imagine all these conflagrating diversities of the world living together in relative peace in a single country has always been intriguing and inspiring to me. And even though it seems to me ridiculing to the entire people of the world, including of course the people of America, I still found this mystically interesting. The first time I saw "The New Colossus", a poem written by Emma Lazarus and inscribed on the plinth of the Statue of Liberty, I found myself memorizing it right away, and it has been one of my favorite poems. America; this is where I wished to live, if only for now, among this people of peoples, in whose hands tomorrow lies, more than in any other's, waiting to be born, like many of it has been, and like many of it has never been before. At least, if the consulate would give me an entry-visa.

PART ONE

The American Dream

When life lows and crawls

clouded around by flameless smoke
and tending to rot and melt away
dreams are the tufts of wings
that make men borne as pretty aves
fluttering high among the joyous wingeds.
Once grown out of his dark smoke
he soars and soars
and till he reaches the silvering sky
no aught does his wings know
'xcept to fly and fly,
beyond the doomning smokes

"Dream," Rahman

ONE

Different Strokes for Different Princes

I

Sometimes I wished I were Akeem, the adored African prince of Hollywood fame.[4] Or, at least, a prince like him. But I was not Akeem, and neither was I like him. I had my own name and destiny unlike his. By virtue of our births, we only shared the same birth-term *prince*, and of kingdoms in Africa. Akeem was a wealthy prince of Zamunda. I was a broke prince from Oyo, though one of the most historically significant kingdoms of Africa. At age twenty-one Akeem already had so much in life that he had a money bill carrying his name and picture. At the same age, I had no more than my birth and school certificates carrying my name - which perhaps nobody cared to see, not even myself - and a signature that would pull nothing but dusts and end up in some trash. This was a characteristic difference between the ancient glory of African kingdoms, represented by Akeem's opulent life, and that of modern era scorched by the flame of slavery and colonization. I represented the latter.

If I were like Akeem, however, perhaps I would not have a story to tell. Nonetheless, I envied him. He decided to go to America and, a week later, he was walking on a New York street. How I wished I were like him. When I made a decision to go to America, I did not think that hundreds of weeks later I would still be here, trapped in the crannies of our streets by seen and unseen hands of nature. A lot of water has passed under the bridge, as the saying goes, but I was just not like him. While Akeem's ball was at the guardless goalmouth, mine was a mile and a half away from it,

---

[4] Reference to Eddie Murphy's 1988 movie, *Coming To America.*

and I had dozens of opponents still to tackle. But one thing is always true: no race is more interesting than a steeplechase, and none more dangerous and uncertain. By the time this story of my life was unfurled, not even Akeem remained in doubt that we had to be so different. It was an adventure of a lifetime, and it was my destiny to take it.

Many of us have heard Roberts Schuler's famous words of encouragement, that *one who has a dream has everything, including an awful lot of problems*, but I do not think that as many have paused to realize that how much 'awful', or awfully lot, one never really can imagine. This may be one of the problems life belies as it smiles seductively at us, tempting us to feel free to dream and aspire. My father often told me that this was a quality that made God different from humans: God sees everything - yesterday, today, and tomorrow, all at once - while we see but a little. Still, I sometimes think our inability to know what tomorrow has in stock may be part of the thrills that life holds for us - some fun in stock. In the pod of sorrow does joy breed, and perhaps one that never had the sorrow of life never can have its joy.

***

One Sunday in the ninth month of the year 1992, I woke up as usual at five o'clock in the morning, but with an unusual mood. In our house we woke up around this time to observe the early morning *salat*, the *subhi,* the first obligatory prayer-worship of the day. I lived with my maternal grandparents, both assiduous Muslims and title-holders in the Muslim community. My grandfather's cardinal goal was to inculcate the virtue of *God first* in us. Though I observed the salats almost regularly, it was primarily because of my grandparents, and an unconscious motive of the wonders of religion. I had heard so many stories of miracles that I had become eagerly aware of its insinuation: how problems could be solved through prayer. Since human life is one long chain of problems, my chief concern was to assuage whatever problem that made up my present life. I longed for the magical hand of religion to crush the myriads of problems I perceived as I was growing up. I wanted God to bestow upon me the material good of life and assist me to live happily forever. Preachers talked about Paradise and Hell, but, even though I preferred Paradise to Hell, I never was ready to hear of either, for I never was ready to leave this promising and alluring world. It was the only world I knew, and the only one I was sure of; the best that preaching of afterlife did was to frighten me of losing it.

Although I had a natural inclination toward religion, or toward an unseen reality on which I knew this world might be dependent, I also had a natural outer disinclination against religion. But sometimes, this disinclination was against Islam, or my perception of Islam, which, unlike Christianity, was not catching up with our fanciful modern civilization.

This was not that I liked the God of Christianity better than the God of Islam, however; it was the general fashion of Christianity that I liked better. Islam had entered our part of the world several centuries before Christianity, and it has so much become part of the local culture that it was losing its trendiness to the Western-cultured Christianity, as our entire traditional culture was doing. The way of the West was the trend and it was what Christianity was modeled after. People wore coats, shirts, belted pants, and various modern outfits to church while we wore local clothes, which I did not see as fashionable. In church they often preached in English while we used Yoruba, a local language considered as the uneducated language, as all indigenous languages. Speaking vernacular was an offense in many schools.

My grandparents may be credited for the endeavor I put into my religion. Perhaps the only person who would care to see what my signature and certificates looked like was my grandmother who could not read. We called her Alhaja - the female title for someone who had performed the Hajj, or holy pilgrimage to Mecca. Every morning she would wake me up, knocking on my door that only needed the slightest help to make the noisiest noise. With so much trouble to my sleep-laden body, I would dress up, grab a jug of water for my ablution, and climb the stairs up to the fourth floor of the house, naked to the watchful eyes of the sky. Waking me up at this hour was like stopping a pleasurable free flow of urination halfway to the finish, and from a bladder that was excessively full before going into the toilet. Though it was called early morning, to me it was nighttime, for it was still dark and I was still sleepy. The rituals of Islam are geared toward self-discipline, but, at my age and state, 'discipline' was the least reasonable word I knew, one that even older people employed to subdue your freedom.

On this Sunday morning, however, things were different. I woke up without my grandmother's help, and with no residue of sleep to slow my actions. I was happy with God, I was happy with the world, and I was happy with myself. My mind was loaded, like passenger vessels of the peak migration era bound for the American shore, hoping to unload in the land best known for her freedom. It was Nigeria's age of exodus, and, in my own way, I was caught up in the frenzy.

This morning I was to go and make a phone call to America to tell my uncle to send me a flight ticket to America, or, at least, the money to buy it here in Nigeria. Uncle Jibola had promised to send the money whenever I was ready to use it. Now I was ready to use it, and because of this, it was as if I did not sleep in the night. I was excited. One Mr. Okunwole had made the deal to procure an American visa for me and he had asked me to buy the ticket and be ready to fly. In a long time I had never had any news so good. Even though the visa was not ready yet, I was as eager as the passengers on those old-time vessels to the New World. Now it was my New World.

I rose up briskly and went for my ablution. With my luminescent rosary hung around my neck, gleaming in the semi-dark morning, I headed to the in-house mosque that was set up on our veranda. My grandmother smiled as I walked into the mosque, happy that her boy was on time today.

On a typical day, whilst various muezzins' calls in our neighborhood pierced the half-night, I would sit down lazily on the fourth floor, dozing with my jug of water in front of me, until everyone would be lined up for prayer. My grandmother did not like this and she would dash out of the prayer ground to call out my name angrily and threateningly at the sky. "Ramoni! Ramoni! Won't you come down quickly? You must not miss the prayer." Sometimes she would threaten me with punishments, "There would be no food for you if you missed this prayer." Some other times she would swallow her anger and call me "*Akehinde gbegbon,*" which means something like "the last to come only to lead."

Even though this last statement was always said affectionately, I did not like it. It was a common phrase, perhaps originated among Yoruba Muslims, and used adoringly for Prophet Muhammad as the last and leader of all prophets. Whenever I heard this, I wished she had not said it. Discomforted, I would rush up the ablution to join them in the prayer so she would not have to repeat it.

With my little experience of polygamy and extended family, as our home was, openly calling your child the leader could sound taunting to the other wives and their children, even though my grandmother's intention was different. In such a complex living situation, suspicion, jealousy, and hatred were usually part of the game, and some wives often turned to sorcery and witchcraft to fight or defend their side of the feud. Though I did not like to raise such discomforting sentiments in the family, my feeling was not of a feared consequence as much as it was of my natural dislike for seeing people jealous, hurt, and unhappy. Yet, it was in this polygamy that the seed of my troubles would be planted – if not already done.

This morning I was not the last to come. Rather than the self-discipline of our religion, the bright bulb of hope shining in my heart was all the energy I needed. America was the land of my dream, the land of a new beginning for my life, a new beginning with plenty of promise, plenty of excitement. This was what I had been hoping and working toward in the last few months.

***

More than a year earlier, I made up my mind to go to America. Unlike Akeem, I was not going in search of a princess. The lucky prince already has his life secured while I had not even had mine established. He has his image beautifully emblazoned in the national psyche; dozens of half-naked girls bathe, massage, and wait on him; the throne incontrovertibly warming up for his behind; and the national coffers yawning for his royally manicured fingers. I had nothing like these to make me feel ready for a princess. I was going to America in search of life, a strong and admirable life that would engrave my image in people's hearts and build a treasury inexhaustible in my lifetime. I was going to America in search of my

"American Dream."

Though I had a few relatives living in America, the only person I could turn to for my goal was Uncle Jibola. He is one of my mother's three full younger brothers and he had been living in America for about four years. My mother also has a full younger sister and several other brothers and sisters from her father's polygamal marriages. I believed I could count on Uncle Jibola as my resource to make my dream come true. Not only because he was in a relevant position by being in America, but also because, despite the thousands of miles that separated us, he had remained by my side more than any other person I could easily recall. I had grown up in the Piagetian[5] mindset of *you-exist-when-in-sight-and-not-out-of-sight*. Once a brother, sister, or any family member was not around, I did not have any reason for correspondence between us. This infantile psychology was one of the unfortunate realities of polygamy and complex family structures, but Uncle Jibola saw beyond this and his actions became a lesson for me.

From the time he left for the United States in 1988, Uncle Jibola had continued to maintain correspondence with me. Because I attended the same school with my namesake uncle, whom we sometimes called Raymond to distinguish him from me, Uncle Jibola always wrote us together. In his letters he would ask about our progress in school and urge us to write him back. This showed us that, despite the distance, we still mattered to him. Even when we did not write, he wrote. He was someone who had a room in his heart for everyone he knew, and he had always been an important figure in my life.

I always looked forward to his mails, especially because of the magazines he packaged in them: *Ebony*, *Jet*, and sometimes *Essence* magazines. These gave me my first contact with the outside world and ignited my fascination for America. The magazines made America prominent in my mind and a spontaneous place of my reference. Regardless of this, however, I did not then think of going to America. America was a story; Nigeria was the real world I knew, and there was no reason to leave it for another. I was content with my uncle sending me the magazines and some occasional dollars.

One interesting thing about my picture of America was that the seven-letter noun was etched in rich ebony black. My mind was awash by the black magazines, the much adored Hip Hop and R&B artists, and the 1980s Break-Dance culture that almost broke my bones. I often did not think of America as a black and white country, but as a black man's land.

When I finished my West African School Certificate (WASC) examinations in 1989, I had nothing other than the delusion of the after-school pseudo-freedom to play around. My father wanted me to get a job at a Local Government Secretariat in Oyo, where I had my secondary school education. This was not my idea of after-school life. Enjoying the

[5] Psychologist Jean Piaget's concept of object permanence in babies.

freedom of no-school, no-lectures, no-teachers, no-time rushes, and no uniform clothes was all I had craved for. Even if I would work, I did not want it in this town. But my father forced me to stay to look for a job.

Oyo was boring to me. I had no enthusiastic friend with whom I could enjoy my freedom there. My alma mater, Olivet Baptist High School, had hostel facilities that allowed for children all over the country to attend the school. Because of this, most of my friends while in school were boarders from other cities and states. Moreover, I had known so much excitement in Ibadan, a metropolitan city, and Oyo could not appeal to me. Oyo was an ancient town, where even the few resident friends I had did not feel cool to live. The best thing to do was to go out and enjoy life outside.

I waited in utter displeasure for my father to secure the job while I prayed for him not to succeed with it. My daily chores were limited to my house and they were droning and stultifying. It was as if my brain was freezing up. After a few months, I left the town in an inevitable trip. I had to go for my month-long General Certificate Examinations (GCE) at Ibadan. Honestly, I did not think much of the exams other than their being my salvation from Oyo. My father expected me to return immediately after the period, but I only laughed at him as I rode out of the town. This was my chance to stay away, and, after the exams, I did stay away.

Ibadan, one of the largest cities in Africa, was where my maternal grandparents lived, and I spent the most of my childhood with them. I had been so used to their place that any restriction to keep me from there would be close to a capital punishment. Even when my father lived at Ibadan, I did not live with him. He changed my school to Oyo when he “returned home,” and it was only because of this that I had spent my school periods in the town. Still, I always returned to Ibadan during holidays.

My most important tie to Ibadan was my grandmother. She had been mothering me from my birth and I only left her presence during the school-sessions at Oyo, and during a few holiday periods that I spent with my mother in Ilorin. Life existed nowhere else except in my grandmother’s presence. This was one reason that my father wanted me to stay and get a job at Oyo after my secondary school. He believed that I had been spoiled by my grandmother's pampering, and that I was not making my father's home as my pivot-home in my life. "This is your father's house," he often said to me. Our patrilineal culture dictates that the father owns the child, and that his home is the child’s primary home. But neither this nor my father’s words made any sense in my juvenile understanding. All that mattered was my grandmother’s presence and the fun-full environment of Ibadan where I had dozens of friends.

My mother also believed that her mother was spoiling me, and that living in her parents’ house might be altogether dangerous for me because of the polygamy of the house. But I sometimes thought she and my father were only jealous because I loved neither of them as much as I loved my grandmother. My grandmother raised me in a princely lifestyle, giving me a little taste of what life is with Akeem. She had many female apprentices, and loving and taking care of me were the unwritten first rules for their success. Growing up, the only thing I did for myself was to eat, play, and decide what I wanted - if that was *spoiling*.

Both my WASC and GCE results came out poorly and I had no great concern or compunction over them. Not that I was not school-smart, I only subordinated school to other things. But peer pressure later changed my attitude.

Eyeing campus life, I thought about making better results for university admission. However, I had created an obstacle for myself. Now, my father did not think it necessary to waste any more money on my examinations, especially when I was being recalcitrant and he was broke. My mother had paid for the GCE exams that I failed, and an earlier one that I did when I was still in school, which I also failed. No money, I was sure, would come out of her purse, especially when she was also cash-strapped and I was being "unserious", as she thought. She warned me not to come to her for exam fees anymore. "... Now, where is the money that you want to be wasting?" she had said angrily at me. Besides, she thought my father was the one to take care of my education, and her part was only to be subordinate. "He paid for your older brothers and sisters, so go to him."

With no dream for the future, I ignored all these and plunged myself into the rollicking social stream. There were always parties, girls, friends, and street-hustling to do. Nonetheless, I had a glimmering fear at the back of my mind on how my future would be, a faint feeling that my present life may be heading nowhere promising. But, typical of adolescence, it was not yet strong enough to shake me out of the fantasy of childhood consciousness. I was blinded from the reality of self-responsibility.

One day, Uncle Jibola learned about my situation and called to talk to me about it. He did not like what he heard. He believed in the value of education and he immediately paid for me to reapply for another set of examinations. I reapplied and, this time, the results came out in flying colors.

"The naughty boy has the brain," one of my uncles commented, "he had only been lazy." I was brilliant as a kid, making the top grades without trying hard. So, when my previous results reached them, they believed they were due to a developed bad attitude.

Then, the results changed my life. I started thinking of moving forward. The next thing was to sit for the Joint Admission Matriculation Board examinations (JAMB), which would place me in a university. But this was another problem. JAMB was a menace to many students. I wanted to be admitted into a university for a program of my choice, but that was a luxury for only a few students. Few students of which, probably, less than half would be by merit; admission for programs of choice was usually by naira, the Nigerian currency. This often forced many students into programs they were not interested in, sometimes reducing the spirit of their promising hearts.

Together with other ills in the society, this practice predisposed people to celebrate mere certificates as the god and end of education. Once admitted, a large number of students did all they could only to obtain the certificate, thereby plummeting proficiency to a state of lowest concern, as some people now complained about. And there were many ugly ways to get the certificate without getting the education.

Now, I faced the same problem. I developed interest in Medicine and I garnered the necessary emotional preparation to face the challenges of the College of Medicine, but its JAMB pass mark made it a program reserved only for the exceptionally brilliant and the exceptionally cunning. I did not see myself as either. To belong to the latter required money, which I did not have, while to belong to the former required so great an effort, and I thought I did not want anything to do with the secondary school books I had studied through four times already.

Nonetheless, I applied for the JAMB and enrolled in an extra-mural lesson, hoping that my effort could get me somewhere. But I had not completed the session when a new air breathed upon me and transformed my idea of life. I became doggedly resolved on career and ambition.

In the secondary school, I periodically dreamt of pursuing various careers. Year after year, I dreamt of being an accountant, a computer scientist, an electrical engineer, a computer engineer, a chemical engineer, a medical doctor, and so on, but none of them had grown up with me. This is the beauty of the modern civilization, disposing us to a wide range of options in the choice of what life we want to live. Ironically, though, it increasingly leaves the modern man more alone in his world, forcing him to turn inward into himself. Most of us are not internally developed enough to accommodate the multiplicity of options, and we end up in confusion and dissatisfaction and anxiety.

One interesting thing about my secondary school dreams was that I never thought of going to university for them. The legend of the university in my mind was that it was a place where all were books and straight faces - the most boring life I could ever think of. In our environment, there were more people without university education, and the predominant attitude toward it was of awe. University graduates were treated as gods, and it seemed to me that to make a god was not an easy task. I wanted to be a god, but I did not like to go through such a bore. Growing up, there was almost no one to pay attention to what I thought, what I felt, and what real things I should know. They thought I was brilliant and that I could handle things for myself. Their only concern was my naughtiness, for which everyone was ready to flay me.

Now I began to dream of filmmaking and I had a strange and strong feeling of wanting to achieve it by all means possible, even if I had to go through ten universities. Everything I thought and felt pointed toward or revolved around it. I had great pleasure in imagining myself as a filmmaker and I desired to begin as soon as possible.

I realized that there was not much fun for me in traveling down a road already traveled or anticipated. My fun lay in challenges, exploration, experimentation, innovation. There were doctors, engineers, accountants, pharmacists, lawyers, and almost every other professional in my combined family, and all expectation of me could not be outside this spectrum. Yet, being a medical doctor everyone already knew I would live the rest of my life wearing the white coats, prescribing medicines, writing in cursive, and, perhaps, cutting into human bodies; being a lawyer I would wear the middle ages scholar gown with a peruke like that of Isaac Newton, and I would be going into courtrooms to manipulate truths.

I wanted to live digging things from the mine of my soul to make people wonder; perhaps to shake and thrill the world out of its slumber, out of people's everyday indulgence and delusions. I saw nothing but filmmaking promising me this. There may be a million movies a year in the world, but every single movie has its own life, especially in the mind of the maker, and each one born well lives forever in the world, doing again and again what its maker initially intended, and more. This was my newly discovered bride, my fascination, turning me into someone like Goethe's Faust, fortunately or unfortunately. For new frontiers my heart yearned, feeling less content with a life regular in rhythm. Of course, not long would someone like me make a deal with the devil.

There was almost no film production in Nigeria, or in the entire Africa, and I hoped to be among the front-runners. This was how I landed on the decision to go to America. America was the hub of film production in the world. Learning and making movies in America was as living next door to Jesus Christ would be to a Christian minister. For ages, artists have been migrating around to places that suit their creativity. From Macedonia Aristotle moved to Athens to join the Academy; Da Vinci moved from Vinci in Florence to Milan, and then to France; Shakespeare from Stratford-upon-Avon to London; James Baldwin from Harlem to France. Without a conscious awareness of these precedents, I was following the paths of my call.

II

I began to send letters of persuasion to Uncle Jibola. At first, his response was, "Get your Bachelor's degree in Nigeria, and coming to America could follow." When I told him I wanted to study film and there was no film school in Nigeria, he tried to reason with me, and with his fears for such a career.

"Do you think making films in America is as easy as you are thinking?" he asked on the phone, "Even it is difficult for the blacks here. Spike Lee and the few blacks who have been lucky to get into the industry know what they have gone through, and what they are still going through to remain in there."

"I'm ready to go through anything to make films," I had replied, as innocently ignorant as I could be, and as stubborn.

Growing up, there was something I repeatedly experienced in the lives of people around me and I could not help but reckon them in my hope in life. I had seen many people pursue one goal or another for happiness: marriage, university degrees, a particular business, task, or living status, but only to become unhappy again after achieving the desired. They only came to find out they had not seen beyond the goal for its stability, or to find out that there was more to their happiness than they had imagined.

This strongly presented to me the reality of an uncanny boredom and misfortune that seemed to underlie all stages and aspects of life, and perhaps it made my thinking and desire for happiness as for long-term. I did not want to be happy at a particular time in my life, or at a particular achievement, only to be unhappy sometime after. I was afraid of this about life and about my life.

Now I thought going to America to join the filmmaking industry would help me over this hole of life. I thought making films would give me eternal joy and I did not care about anything I might have to go through to get it. This was one of the reasons why I believed in the reply I gave my uncle, a reply that I gave eagerly without really knowing all what happiness meant and all it needed to be stable and eternal. A reply that I gave without the foggiest idea of what I was really going to go through. Because my pursuit might have been that after the horizon, the greatest land God ever made, perhaps where no man can reach, no matter how far he goes.

Life was not a free lunch, they say. But I had no idea it was not. For my vision, I thought I was ready to go through the difficulties that I foresaw to get my films to the theaters in America. I had read different difficulties encountered by various black filmmakers in the *Ebony* magazines and I thought I could go through anything that came my way. What I did not think was how much life was going to ask to serve my lunch. This was the destiny I had to live. I may have had the same goal as Spike Lee and John Singleton, but I was not Spike Lee or John Singleton.

My uncle agreed after due consideration and advised me to go to the office of the United States Information Service (USIS) to obtain the necessary information needed to get into an American school. Although he was still a student who worked part-time to make ends meet, setting a limit to the financial help he could give, he was always willing to go an extra mile to do what he thought he had to do.

My life was illuminated. The last time I was as happy was about seven years earlier when I finished my primary school education and was admitted into Olivet Baptist High School. In the two-month period between the date I finished my entrance examinations and the date I received the news of being admitted into the new school, I had been deeply worried, as if I carried the universe on my head. There were dozens of schools in Oyo, but I wanted no other school. Olivet was the leading school in the town, often attracting candidates nationwide, and competition to get in there was higher than for any other school in the town. I chose Ladigbolu Grammar School as my second choice, a school named after my great grandfather, a former king of Oyo, and I chose St Bernadine's Secondary School as the third choice, a missionary-founded school like Olivet. But I had made these other choices only to fill the blanks in the application form. Although, I was considered one of the top students in my primary school, I was ill on the day of the entrance examinations and I had a very bad time with the question papers. This made me so anxious that when the result came out I was overjoyed. Along with a few students, I scored the highest mark in the town.

I obtained the information at the USIS I had to sit for Test of English as a Foreign Language (TOEFL) and Scholastic Aptitude Tests (SAT) and I had a list of about thirty-three universities to choose from. I applied for the two tests immediately and my uncle paid for them. I mailed applications to all the schools on my list and waited impatiently for their response. When replies came, it was then I knew how expensive education was in America. I had to choose the cheapest school on the list, and, even though its film program was not satisfactory to me, the price was still more than my uncle could afford. In this case, he thought it would be better to reach America first and then look for an affordable school.

What next?

"Try and get a visiting visa," my uncle advised, "and when you are here, getting a cheaper school would be easy, and you can then change your visa to a student visa."

This was the point where a prospective migrant began to realize what task he or she had ahead. Sometimes, it seemed visas were more precious and harder to get in the market than the Holy Grail, especially, the visa emblazoned with a giant bald eagle, donned in *stars and stripes*, and showing the strength of the nation it represented. Anyone who had had the fortunate or unfortunate circumstance of seeking an American visa in Nigeria would understand how physically and psychologically rigorous the endeavor was. The media called it the *almighty visa*, and a person in possession of a valid one was like a person in possession of a winning lottery ticket to some million bucks. He or she was the person whose future was believed to be bright and secured. Hence, pursuing an American visa was a dangerous, risky, and elusive game. It was a career on its own.

I journeyed one day to Lagos to see what the visa factory looked like and to feel close to the ticket to my dream, but what I saw did not make me feel as close as I had hoped. The embassy looked so intimidating that I could not imagine anyone or anything dwelling in there as other than an almighty. Right there I reached a conclusion that I would never try my luck at the consulate by myself. Against something so intimidating, I did not trust my luck enough. I decided I was going to look for help or, at worst, buy it.

There are so many ways to kill a rat, as the saying goes. The American visa was a rat you could try killing in more than one way, legally or illegally. To the consulate, buying the visa was clearly illegal, but all I wanted was the visa, and I had no eyes for legality. In most cases, what the

American immigration service would call illegal was not illegal to many of us in Nigeria. The legality of a traveling document, in our terms, depended on whether it could get the traveler to his or her destination. Perhaps laws are broken sometimes not because the individual is morally inadequate, but because the system is provisionally inadequate. And what is legally right or wrong may not always be morally so; or who would blame a poor boy for seeking to improve his life when he is not intending to harm anyone?

Nigeria was almost in a frazzled state. The rulers were busy satisfying their greed, and corruption ran from head to toe of the government. The country had only two classes: the rich and powerful, the minority called the *oppressor* class. The other class was the poor and weak, the *oppressed* and majority class. To belong to the former group, one had to be *connected* and accept the lies and evils of the rulers as truths and righteousness. Then one would be rewarded with job positions of good pay with no work. Or one had to display self-evil qualities that would bring money. Among the limited chances of survival was to travel out of the country.

The cost of *checking out*, as traveling out was often called, was in itself an end to most Nigerians. For this, some people worked out their heads to come out with fraudulent ways of making their pastures green and lush on desperate *out-checkers* or *Andrews*. These fraudsters were colloquially called *419ners* or simply *419*, a term that originated from the anti-fraudsters' law, in section 4 subsection 19 (4 -19) of the Nigerian criminal code.

People were *checking out* to various economically better places across the world. The United States and Great Britain topped on the *to-go* list, with the British visa second to the American visa, and they were the goldmines for the 419ners. Although the American visa was more difficult to obtain, many people preferred America to Britain.

The United Kingdom was sometimes seen as inordinately oppressive on Nigeria. The British government had been partly responsible for the current situation in Nigeria, as we were once a colony of the British Empire. Also, Nigeria was a member of the Commonwealth and Nigerians were theoretically not supposed to need entry-visa to any other Commonwealth nation, from Europe to Canada – which could have helped business and development in Nigeria. But, out of political malice, the visa-ban was imposed on Nigerians in the 1980s. This was one of the reasons many thought the West was treating Africa unjustly. In direct and indirect ploys by Western leaders and institutions, African resources were siphoned to the West; yet, they victimize Africans for the problems they themselves partook in creating.

Since Nigeria received her so-called independence in 1960, the decision of who ruled the country had always been made largely by the British government, not by the Nigerian people. And their primary goal had not been to improve the situation of Nigerians as independent people, but to perpetuate their situation as factory workers to keep the reign of England going. England was the "extraordinary gentleman" who sought his immortality not in the blood of the Anglican Jesus, but in African oil and other resources.

It is funny then that people have been calling the previous situation as colonization, and referring to Nigeria as one of the colonies of the empire. Whereas Nigeria had only been a company owned by the British government, and the independence had only been an incorporation into the hands of their stooges. This was the reason the nation had not faired better under incorporation than under sole proprietorship. The previous sole owners still owned all the shares and constituted the board of directors - without the mandate of Nigerians.[6] They selected the CEOs; and once the CEOs have got it going to feed the greed of the board of directors, no matter how corrupt they were, it did not matter whether the poor company workers were denied their rights to freedom and life. The workers could always go to hell.

To avoid this hell was the goal of many Nigerians when they pursued one thing or another, of which traveling to the West became significant.

I started to look for a visa, wishing I were like the prince of Zamunda. There were so many back-door visa dealings, trustworthy and untrustworthy, and all joined seamlessly together. It was difficult to know which to trust. The trustworthy ones, still, could be stuck in process due to an unforeseen reason, often without refund of one's pre-payment. The process thus became a game of the Russian roulette. I knew many families and individuals that had lost their fortunes in the game, yet I wanted to try my luck this way.

One thing the Western governments did not realize was that it was this difficulty in the visa business that made immigrants stayed longer than necessary in their countries. Many Nigerians, for examples, preferred life at home and close to their families, and they would prefer going anywhere in the world for short business interactions to better their lives at home, and not to drown in the c*old water* of foreign lands. By the time some people survived the visa-quagmire, perhaps after selling their family assets in the struggle, they became so desperate that life became a do or die affair wherever they went.

At such a stage when people were faced with the prospect of seeking for visa, those who believed in God would go to Him, or back to Him. No situation makes humans more susceptible to religion than one of uncertainty and fear. For me, even though I may have been indulgent, God had always been lying around somewhere in the darkness of my heart, and this was the time I picked up a flashlight and seriously looked for Him. Before my uncle consented to my request, I had been prayerful to the best of my capacity, begging God to open up the Heaven and provide me with an American visa. Our Imam at home had begun to see me as a good boy,

---

[6] Africa was "partitioned" into "real estate property" by and for the Europeans at the Berlin Conference in 1884-85, and Nigeria, allocated to Britain, became the "Royal Niger Company Territory". It's not surprising that the first governor to govern Nigeria was hired by the company.

sticking it out at every prayer and religious activity. I wanted not to leave any stone unturned, and if there were wonders in religion, which I did not doubt, I wanted it in my favor in the battle for the almighty visa.

One day, I remembered Mallam Ali, a Hausa priest from northern Nigeria. We simply called him Alfa, from the professional name *alfa* often used for Muslim clerics. My father met him sometime in 1987 and brought him home to live with us and to offer special prayer for our household. Alfa, who now was in Lagos, offering prayer service for a client, was a plain man. He was as simple as he dressed, down to earth, kind, and spiritually powerful. People in the town knew this and they always sought his spiritual assistance. In Nigeria, people trusted in spiritual personalities, alfas, pastors, and *babalawos*,[7] and they consulted them on almost all of their affairs.

Like Indian gurus of ancient fame, and Christian saints of medieval Europe, Alfa had lived in seclusion for many years, praying and fasting to acquire immense spiritual power before my father met him. He memorized the whole of the Qur'an, and, for special prayers, he would read it A to Z, three times daily, without opening the book. That was more than a thousand pages of scripture, one hundred and fourteen chapters, six thousand six hundred and sixty-six verses or *ayats*, and approximately seventy-eight thousand words. That never ceases to amaze me.

With the awareness of how difficult the American visa was, I went to Alfa in Lagos to ask him to make special prayers for me. He did not just hear of my plan, however. I had briefed him one day when I went to Oyo during the Ileya festival to tell my father about my plans and to have his consent. In an effort to resolve an issue, Alfa called me aside and told me I was not in good terms with my father. As he stated, this was because I did not heed his advice on securing a job in Oyo after the completion of my secondary school. Alfa was more than just a prayer person for our family; he was also like a family counselor. I implored him to settle the disagreement and he did. In the Yoruba culture, fathers were like gods; always right, pure, and perfect. Especially, my father. By virtue of his birth and personal achievements, he was highly respected by everyone, almost worshipped. So, I did not want the wrath of the god. Rather I wanted his blessings.

After the misunderstanding was settled, my father gave me his blessings and promised to be on the lookout for visa for me. I breathed an air of relief on this day. When one wants something, one wants everything tangled in its way to be resolved. And in African and Islamic philosophies, how the parents feel about a child is crucial to his or her success.

[7] Literally meaning the "father of mystery," a babalawo is a traditional priest of Ifa religion.

III

My namesake uncle, Raymond, was also in the struggle to get an American visa and we shared ideas to help each other. One may think this had an influence upon my decision to go to America, but I did not think so. Perhaps, though, it helped to reinforce my confidence in my endeavor. At this stage in my life, friends had influence on me more than my family, though I quickly realized I had to abandon such influences if I wanted to achieve my goal. My friends were up to things similar to one another, but different from mine. Although many of them would later pursue traveling out, most of them currently wanted admission into one Nigerian university or another, and, while I was still waiting for admission to America, their wishes were granted. Hence, in my circle of friends, I was alone in my pursuit.

At first, I assumed that rolling with my friends on campus would be an opportunity to occupy myself so as not to allow the lonesome search for visa to drown me. I did this for some time, but I feared I might become too absorbed in the fun of the campus to focus on my own career. Also, going about with them was somehow embittering to me. They had got what they wanted while I had not. I thought I needed to go to places that would benefit me by encouraging and widening my consciousness in my chosen path. I thought myself almost an odd one out among them. Together we talked about our joint interests, but filmmaking was not of so much interest to them, and they could not offer enough encouragement.

I decided to find my own way. I did not stop being friends with them, but at this stage I realized that we could not always flock together anymore, because we were not hunting for the same kind of prey.

There was one occurrence that further tore me mentally away from my friends. It happened one Saturday evening when four of us were going to a party. Though sometimes we were five to six in the circle, and often had access to three to four cars, but that evening there was only one car. This meant that the one who owned the car would pick the rest of us one by one for the party and drop us off in the same manner.

He had already picked two of us, and we were about to leave the last boy's house when his father came in. Impressed by our association, and trying to ascertain his son's friendship character, he engaged us in conversation. One after the other, he asked about the school we were attending and the program we were doing. I was the last to respond, and having heard each of the others tell him of a university and an academic program, I was confused on what to say. I was not in any school and I was aiming for a program that, apparently, majority of Nigerians then did not see as promising. Even though most people liked Nigerian films, filmmaking in Nigeria was neither an academic nor a lucrative business.

"I'm traveling out," I replied modestly, though I realized it was not a good response still.

And I got it.

The elderly man's reaction was sneering and I felt embarrassed. A common ruck with the dollar-rush craze, he seemed to think.

With great effort I bore it. It was not his fault. The phrase "I'm traveling out" was like the phrase, "I'm a "gold prospector" in the 19th century Western hemisphere. Events happening around had made the aspiration a suspicious symptom, one of a moral morbidity commonly called *get-rich-quick* syndrome (GRQ). Many youths *checked out* of the country with the desperate desire only of making fast money and coming back home to flaunt the wealth. Some so desperate that they did not care where the money came from, especially when they found themselves in the reality of *earn-what-you-get* situations of the labor-driven economies of the West. Whereas they would have *checked out* on the fantasy of *pick-money-on-the-street*, the common story of life abroad. Like this, they tagged a bad name to their motherland, a name really shared only by the proportionally few.

This was how our so-called leaders have messed up our values, making us obsessed with the pursuit of opportunistic abundance and pleasure rather than meritorious achievement. Many of us wanted plenty windfall but no sweat drop – because the rich we saw among us sweat nothing to be so wealthy. Vice had thus become the modern virtue, and an honest person may simply be a foolish one. In the international eyes, an average Nigerian was now a likely drug trafficker, a fraudster, or both, and is often treated as such. Of course, it may not entirely be the faults of those who looked at us this way. International perspectives may be blind to the fact that every human being is a potential criminal, and that it is only the various circumstances of the people that vary the manifestation of the criminal potential in the different people. Nonetheless, our sybaritic administrators had made the criminal potentiality in many of us more profound and frightening in the world that we hardly had any voice to protest the international prejudice that, in effect, often violated our human rights. No sound education for us, no employment, no finance for entrepreneurship, no regular or sufficient wages for diligent workers, and no protective plan for naturally wanting conditions such as accidents, old age, disability, sickness and so on. Like beasts in the jungle we were left on the streets to fight to survive.

Yet, many more youths still wasted valuable times of their lives pursuing the dream of *checking out* until a time too late, while they could have been useful to themselves and the society in other ways. In truth, money catches almost everyone's eyes. Though an invention of humankind, it is now an important determinant of life and we naturally tend to pursue it. But many tend to rush their lives solely for its acquisition, while a few people who, with a different kind of understanding, believed that such a rush was a waste of valuable human time and resources. However desirable money might be, it was not the ultimate element for happiness, and a craze for it was a crazy life. They saw this delusion over money as what made *checking out* a common anthem in the mouths of many Nigerian youths.

My friend's father was among these people who constituted islands of integrity amid the ocean of corruption-stormy society. He thought traveling out was a ruse to avoid school, struggle, and endurance, the stoic-lot of many hard-working Nigerians, and he saw me as falling for the craze.

Really, I did not care about this kind of upright thoughts. It was my belief that the state of the nation was bad enough to make any attempt to travel out a justifiable one, even though I agreed that what many did for money might be unjustifiable. But I was disappointed that my friend's father had been too presumptuous of me. I hated to be thought of in this manner - as someone with a base and vulgar desire. This was not the reflection of myself I liked to see mirrored in people's eyes.

I liked to have money, of course. It could solve many problems and make me live comfortably. It could give me seductive automobiles and fame, for which my youthful heart had an appetite. But I was not dead-hungry for these; at least not as hungry as for the realization of myself. In America, film successes meant wealth, and my desire for films was to make them successful. But, deep within me, it was not just for the money and fame. Satisfaction got from a man's dream-activities is an achievement too expensive for money to pay for. He that is well satisfied is well paid.

I realized that this was a gauntlet I had to run. My friend's father was only one of many I knew whose eyes I felt scorching on my back. Some of them were members of my family who saw meaning only in academic life and *checking out* as an evasion of school. One of the gold of adolescence is for the individual's becoming to make sense to those who make sense to him or her. For this pressure, I could have changed my mind and entered a school here in Nigeria, but I also realized that this would be a fatal imbecility, as I would not be making sense to myself. What is life worth if one cannot pursue one's dream? It will not be long, I always assured myself, and the gauntlet will be over. I needed to make sense to myself to prove myself.

Hence, I was determined to go to America to pursue my career, no matter what anyone thought about me. With my dream in my head I became a similitude of a possessed man, whom no amount of jeering would make leave the street to play sane. To him, insanity is sanity.

Nonetheless, a fear of failure lurked at the back of my heart. I was taking a long shot and I could not help but to feel that if I missed, it would drag me far behind my peers and worsen my situation in life. In my experience so far in this environment I had never seen a pursuit so precarious and time-wasting as one to *check out*. People often did not realize it until plenty of water would have passed under their bridge, running dry, while they were yet to get a single cup to drink, not to talk of to wash. Then they would find themselves dirty and odd among their peers, and spending their days trying to catch up. I could not help but to imagine the poking eyes that would then round me up, yelling, "Didn't we tell you?"

I knew I had made a decision of make or break, a decision of yield or die. I had embarked on a walk across a tightrope hundreds of yards above the ground. If I made it to the other end, everyone would praise me, but if I fell, they would flay me. Although it appeared as a situation of taking a risk, I tried to look at it only as a way of life – my way of life. And I could not stop living it.

One day, I decided to check on a next-door neighbor who was our family friend. He studied film and television production at a university in New York and I thought getting close to him would help me. We called him Uncle Segun. He came back to Nigeria late in the '70s with the hope of putting his foreign and costly acquired knowledge to good use for his motherland. He was passionate about partaking in building the nation's film and television industry. "American film industry has reached the top," he would repeat often to me, "and there's nowhere else for it to go other than stay at that top, or fall if care is not taken. But Nigerian film industry is still in the womb and needs to be born and nursed to full growth."

Uncle Segun played a pioneering role in the creation of the New Day television station, a state-owned station now called Broadcasting Corporation of Oyo State (BCOS). But Uncle Segun was later trapped in the dirty game of the old-time Nigerian politics and he lost his much-adored job to the game he had nothing to do with. Since then he had been planning a comeback onto the scene, for so long a time that people had been thinking he might have lost his sanity. Assiduous in his planning, he transformed a cabin at the back of his house into a writing studio and he seldom came out into the public.

Government's shortsightedness, instability, and favoritism were major problems plaguing professionalism in Nigeria. Many noble ideas were in the garbage cans and competent people lived on the fringe of the society, while friends and families of people with guns enjoyed the country's bounty. Frustration was written boldly across the land, making people feel that their fate was out of their control. Consequently, they depend on the idea of random luck or chance, hoping and praying more than faithfully working for their goals. Already there were very few cues for anybody to so work on, and people only worked to survive from day to day. Even though Africans were originally spiritual, this might be a reason many Nigerians now strictly adhered to religion. We believed that the spinning of the Wheel of Fortune was done by the Father up in heaven, and He did it as it pleased Him. Therefore, all we had to do was to ingratiate ourselves into His favor, a process apparent in people's reliance on alfas, pastors, and babalawos, and appearing as if proving the Marxist criticism of religion.

Uncle Segun became an encouraging figure to me. I visited his cabin often and he always fed me with relevant information about filmmaking. I learned about the division of labor in productions and discovered where I could fit into: directing. Even though I saw directing, then, with little or no fame, the art intrigued me beyond description.

Uncle Segun gave me books on filmmaking and allowed me to read a few of his screenplays. His were the first I ever saw, showing me what constituted the art of screenwriting. He advised me to start going to the two foreign libraries in Ibadan: the USIS library and the British Council library. The British Council library just opened a branch in Ibadan that year, while the USIS had been in the city for close to thirty years, or more. Uncle Segun used the library before he traveled to the United States in the late sixties. The most encouraging of its stocks were the film and television magazines: *American Cinematographer* and *Broadcasting*. Through these, I learned about filmmakers and film equipments, and about various film techniques directly from the filmmakers. They were the most inspiring things I had ever known.

I came closer to the images and minds of filmmakers like Spike Lee, especially when he was working on *Malcolm X*, and I was almost thrilled out of my skin. The way Robert Townsend broke into the industry with *Hollywood Shuffle* was something of marvel. I became acquainted with Quentin Tarantino when he was working on *Reservoir Dogs*; the Hudlin brothers on *House Party*; Ayoka Chenzira; Francis Coppola when he was working on *Dracula*; and Romano Coppola, as he handled the second unit production of *Dracula*. Romano thrilled me more than his father - a young chap like myself! I always wondered. And then I read of John Singleton when he was working on *Poetic Justice*, and a few other young people like myself.

The libraries became my second homes and books became my friends. Not just film and television books, but all the books that caught my fancy, and from which I could learn. I was also learning America. I thought I should know about the country I was going to make my home, and I began to learn her history, culture, and language. I began to like the American culture and language. Already, American movies and songs had been making the culture-campaign on me, as with many others around the country. It was common to turn on the radio and hear the DJs talking like Hip Hop rappers. It seemed to me that by the consciousness of cultural liberty, which America apparently represented in the world, Americans freely chose to enjoy a degree of poetic license in their language. Yet, the more there was human migration into America the more there was lexical migration into the language, all enriching the culture. At this period I began to watch the local television airing of Reverend K.C. Price's church services, as more a language program for me than a religious session.

Magazines were also good materials to learn about American culture. In the magazines of a nation, one could get at the character of the nation and her people – although things look glossier in magazines than in reality. Many things may have eluded my grasp beneath the gloss of the magazine pages and the novelty of my perception, but I was learning of life in America and I was eager to live among the people. In the world, American politics may somehow be repulsive, American culture is attractive, perhaps seductively attractive. I was learning the people's way of thinking and feeling, their prides and, painfully, their prejudices.

The most intriguing thing to me about America was her cosmopolitan population. This is the true strength of the nation, and not her material wealth or military might. I cuddled the desire to get closer to other peoples from other parts of the world. I learned that this cosmopolitan nature of America was the gene that evolved Hollywood to its present status of global acceptance. The smart moviemakers in the early 1900s had been faced with the task of making movies to satisfy the various immigrants of various cultures, and their success became the foundation for the success of the American film industry.

With all the preparation going into launching my career, the biggest question in my life now was how to get to America. It increasingly grew prominent in my mind and I was beginning to have sleepless nights over it. How will I get to America?

IV

My mother had been struggling with a tough life before I knew her, a reason I had had to live with my grandmother since I was only a few months old, when she broke up with my father. Absolving himself, my father often cited her impatience as responsible for the divorce and her subsequent problems. But, having divorced the second time, her single marital status became the factor for her troubles, and she always blamed it all on my father.

Her second marriage was long enough to bless her with two beautiful daughters, after which she lost her trust in men. The men in her life had been too predatory for her inner needs to be mutually nurtured. Yet, to her disadvantage, she was irascible and perfectionistic, always seeking justification for every wrong, and always coming into contact with what she saw as wrong. This always put her in more troubles. She continued to live unmarried and unsettled, moving from place to place, and with financial leeches on her back. Sometimes she had money and met of hers and her children's needs, and other times she had no money and had to pawn or sell her things to eke out a living.

At this time, my mother lived in Ilorin, the capital city of Kwara State. Because of the way our relationship had begun in life, we did not feel comfortable in each other's presence. She did not get over the problem of her relationship with my father, and hostility toward me was her way of avoiding the reality of my existence. Though she saw in me a son and a hope for a better future, she also saw the painful past of separation, a reminder of the loss of the life she thought she could have had. We had a long list of quarrels. During my school days, I loved to go to her place for vacation, but she often found faults with me and booted me back to my grandmother within two to three days of my stay. Everyone at Ibadan was so aware of this that whenever they saw me returning, and before I could say anything, they would jeer at me, saying, "Your mother has kicked your ass out." They thought it was funny. Though there was love for little children in those days, and there was love for me especially because of my grandmother, but there was not enough understanding of the feelings of little children for them to know they were laughing at my pain and making it worse.

My mother was a strict and impatient disciplinarian, and, because of her trying social and economic situation, she always restricted me within her apartment whenever I was there on holidays. "Don't dare step out of this house whenever I'm out, or I'll *show you pepper*," she would threaten me every morning when she was going to her shop. Sometimes she would be a little explanatory: "I don't want anybody nosing into my life, so don't go and bring them, all right? Stay where I put you, or else I'll beat the hell out of you. There are books in here for you; I bought them for reading and not for decoration; read instead of playing around the neighborhood."

My mother really knew how to *show pepper* to a stubborn child, and she had books and magazines that could take me years to read without stopping to pee. To keep from being kicked back to Ibadan, all I had to do was to read and read, many times more than my fun-seeking sense saw necessary. Her house was a jail to my frolicking spirit; though, unrecognized by me then, it was doing something good to my intellect, the more inner and neglected part of me bordered and obscured by my emotions. Without my intention, this brushed up my reading habit, a habit engendered by my unlettered grandmother.

Long before I entered the nursery school, my grandmother enrolled me in lesson programs and always tested my ability by asking me to read to her what was on every billboard on the streets. She bought me English and Yoruba alphabets and words books to learn how to read before I was taken to school on my third birthday. After I had started the nursery school, she continued to buy me English and Yoruba story books, almost as she bought me food and toys, and she would ask me to read them to her whenever she felt like. Despite being in a society in which the relationship between Muslims and Christians was tensile, one of the books she had bought for me was *My Book: The Bible Stories*, a children's illustrated Bible, from which I often read to her. She loved to be thrilled by my early-developed skills, and by the time I reached primary one on my seventh birthday I was far ahead of my class in reading and general school work, even though my school brandished of the brightest students in the city. It only happened that the qualities came to be nipped in the bud in my third year in the primary school when I changed cities and schools.

It was this strict condition and its accompanying monotony at my mother's place that eventually quenched my appetite to go there. I did not see myself as a bookworm who would do nothing other than to eat down all the pages in her house. I needed adventures.

Incidentally, however, it was during one such occasion when I had nothing else to do other than to read of her stacks that my dream was born. I was nineteen years old and was reading a novel from her shelf when I found myself fallen in love with the book, so much that I had an urge to share the story. I liked to share every book I enjoyed, and I subsequently had an idea that the story could be made into a movie for a wider sharing.

This was not a new experience to me, however. I had often thought for every good story I read to be made into a movie. But now, as it had never happened to me before, I thought I could do it myself. Yes, I could do it myself! I could make the story into a movie. My body and soul immediately accepted the idea without question, and I felt a kind of elation I had never felt before in my life. In the next moment, a new self-image emerged in me, one with a dream, a goal, and an inexorable desire to accomplish.

The American magazines from my uncle may have played a role in this transformation, already predisposing me to the art of filmmaking and the possibilities it offered. I had read of many black filmmakers, from hustles to glories, and, although I had not yet thought to be like them, I had unconsciously developed some fearlessness toward being like them. The magazines bridged a long-standing gulf between the people of the movie world and me. I had always thought that the people in the movies were absolute screen people whose dwellings were in the mythical far-away *screenland*, almost like the land of gods and goddesses.

Now, I did not think I could not reach the *screenland*. I did not think I could not become one of the gods. I always had Eddie Murphy's *Coming To America* in mind. I liked the movie and I liked Eddie Murphy's role in it. I wanted to make my film adaptation of the novel like it. Although the leading character was not much of a hero like Akeem, I wanted to play the role. I thought I could do it and I bought my own copy of the book, unbound it, adapted it into screenplay format, began the process of obtaining legal rights to it, and I had given it the most befitting title that I could imagine: *The Prodigal Son*. It is about a wealthy but compromised family, whose wealth and condition nearly ruined the life of their only son - somehow the way the wealth of the oil-rich Nigeria had been ruining the life of the young nation.

***

With the burning desire to go to America now, I went to my mother in Ilorin to tell her about my visa search. She had heard about it before I reached her and she was only waiting for me to come to her. She had something ready for me. She had told a friend of hers and the friend had assured her that visa was a small problem. The friend was an international businesswoman, and for such people, as it was generally believed, obtaining visas was a small problem – if one was important enough to them. They knew the right people and the right ways to go. My mother's friend had boasted, as my mother explained to me, that she would get the visa for me in a flick of her fingers. "Send him to me and forget the rest," she had assured my mother.

One of the things I genetically inherited from my mother was an easy susceptibility to trust friends or people around me for what they appeared to be, or what they told themselves to be. The other things that I know of were a little of her looks and perhaps plenty of her temper. When I rushed to her friend's place in fine fettle, thinking that I had at last found a way out of the confusing visa search, she turned out to be one in a series of dead-ends I would encounter, starting out with rising hope and enthusiasm but ending in disappointment.

***

I phoned my father one morning to inquire about his promise to look out for visa. He had two pieces of news for me, one bad and the other good. He gave the bad one first. "Alfa has died," he said. I almost dropped the telephone receiver. How? When? Where? Why? I could only read in my head but not put into words.

"What happened to him?" I managed to ask.

"He just died," my father replied and continued with the other news, which I was now hearing coming from behind the image of Alfa on my mind. He had found "a good way of getting the visa" and wanted me to come for the detail. My father had ways of making serious matters seem unserious to ease our hearts. When I tried to cut him off to express my sorrow, he said, "It's God who created him, and He took him back. So what do we do about it? Just thank God for his life and pray for his soul."

I prayed for Alfa's soul and bore the loss. Sometimes I could not help but mourn my ill luck with his kind of help. About a year earlier, I met a huliyy in whom I so much hoped upon for beseeching the Heavens for my sake. Nigerian Muslims believed that huliyys were a few selected alfas that God endowed with special spiritual powers. They saw beyond the present and had a special authority of prayer. Many were conscious of their endowment, but some were not. I talked to the huliyy about my wish to go to America and he assured me that "it shall be done." I took his home address, hoping to visit him someday if need be, but by the time I thought I needed him, I reached his house only to find that he had died a few months earlier. My awareness and belief in wonders of religion was so strong and superstitious that the death gave me a nagging feeling that perhaps God did not want me to get to America and was cutting off my links to Him.

And now this also happened. I did not know any alfa in whom my fastidious mind could have full trust. But I was stubborn, as I always was whenever I wanted something. Sometimes such was what kept me strong and going, and I remained committed to my American dream.

The *good way* of visa my father found was through a businessman in Ibadan. Mr. O. A. Okunwole, a bald and extraordinarily dark man in his fifties, had a business consulting firm called "Anthony George and Associates." With the sparse growth of spike-like hair on his vein-striated arms, he had an appearance of a man who had been living a hard life. He had on a gray safari suit, commonly called "conductor", made of a strong cotton material intended to last more than the owner's lifetime.

Mr. Okunwole had an honest look and plan. In a manner that told me he had been cracking his old, baldhead to make big bucks in a long time and had just come by a sure legitimate one, he tabled all his cards for me to see. According to him, he contacted an American university, which would confer honorary degree awards on financial donors to raise money for the school. It was supposed to be like a simple transaction: pay and get honored by an American university. There were plenty of moneybags in Nigeria who would want this for status symbol. And, as I was to learn, there were many Americans who would sell anything for money, even nothing, as long as there were suckers to buy.

Perhaps judging such buyers as suckers was wrong, however, for there are some *nothings* that are sometimes relative *somethings*, and, once in a while, every one of us buys one.

I had never heard about such a transaction before, but so had I never heard about a lot of other things. Nonetheless, I did not doubt him. Whether his intention was to make his 'bucks' by taking advantage of status-conscious moneybags or by fooling *Andrews* like me, I could not tell. He claimed he had contacted six rich men who had agreed to pay for the award. He was like a middleman. These six men would go to the United States for the conferment and would be allowed to take along six people each to celebrate with them. Knowing the rich men would rarely want to waste more money to take up to six persons along with them, he said he planned to slot in names of prospective U. S. immigrants in this quota, from whom he would collect N10, 000 each. The rich men, he said, with whom he would have to send the prospective immigrants' passports to the consulate, must understand this.

"When will this ceremony take place?" I asked.

"November, and you'll have to pay half of the money before I send your passport to the consulate," he replied, and added that he had found a good number of prospective immigrants to commence right away.

This sounded good to me, and the proximity of the date was also appealing. Already, we were in September, and that meant I could be in America in two months time.

"There is no time to waste any longer," he said, "I'll send a copy of your names to the consulate and a copy to the university for endorsement. In a few weeks, your passports have to appear at the embassy, with your tickets as proves of your readiness. So, get your ticket ready."

There is a saying that someone who is too careful to buy falsehood would never buy truth. In human affairs, falsehoods and truths sometimes or often wear the same color that if one does not go ahead to buy something, one would eventually buy nothing. Another one says that if one closes his eyes for evil people to pass by, so as not to see evil, one would miss the good people as well, because one would not know when the good people also will pass by. Therefore, if I wanted to buy truth, I thought I must go ahead and buy something. If I wanted not to miss the good people passing by, then, may be I must not close my eyes to what lay in front of me. I accepted every word Mr. Okunwole said. In fact, they were convincing.

The process commenced. To deposit the upfront money requested, I went with Baba, my maternal grandfather who was now in his late eighties. Since elderly people traditionally occupied a position of respect, I thought that Baba's presence would make a difference - to make Mr. Okunwole think again if he was thinking of cheating me. Baba was the first hero in my life. I adored him and he never let me down. Since he learned about my plan, he had been giving me all the assistance he could offer: persuasion of my uncle, prayers, blessings, and counsel for the life ahead. And now, also, he wanted to be sure I was not duped. Despite his much concealed senility, Baba climbed with me the stairs that seemed to run into the sky at Mr. Okunwole's office.

The next step was to have the ticket ready and Uncle Jibola had promised this. At the time, it was about N32, 000, which was around one thousand dollars. One Sunday morning in September 1992, I went to call Uncle Jibola at a commercial phone center to remind him. He promised to send it soon through Uncle Razaq, his half-brother who worked at a bank in Lagos. I did not know which day the money would come, but I was already happy, reveling in the anticipation of going to America. Apart from the expectation for my career, the thought of living in America hypnotized me.

To steer my mind elsewhere so the anticipation would not consume me, I visited the libraries more frequently. Before, I had been going more to the construction site of Uncle Tunji's new house. Uncle Tunji is my mother's younger brother, older than Uncle Jibola. He assigned me the task of keeping watch over the workers to make sure the work was done well enough. Uncle Tunji worked at Lagos, while the site was at Ibadan, and he only came to Ibadan to spend the weekends with his family. So, all weekdays, I was the lord of his construction site.

Because there was now less work at the site, I had more time I could spend at the libraries, especially at the USIS library. Though I still visited the British Council library sometimes, my membership card had expired and I could no longer borrow books from there. Normally, members were not supposed to be allowed in any longer than the expiration of their membership, but my surname, a royal name, did the trick. The day I registered at the library, I registered my name not only in their system, but also in the registrar's heart, a young lady in her late twenties. As I mentioned my surname *Oladigbolu*, she paused and looked up from her computer. Leaving the long chain of people behind me grunting, she said, "[From] Oyo?" It was more a statement than a question, and I replied in the affirmative, with a self-satisfied smile, reveling in the pride of being recognized as of noble descent.

But that was only a momentary reaction at the opportunity of polishing my ego. As the name did not seem to mean too much to me than its royal lineage, the lady's action came a little as a surprise. Except, perhaps, in the local towns less invaded by modernization, Nigerians no longer seemed to care what anybody's name was. They now cared more about what your power was, or what power was contained in your name. And that power was usually money. After the incursion of the white men in Africa, not many royal names still remained with such a power, except those of a few incumbent kings and their immediate families. By virtue of history, though, the family into which I was born was one of these few. However, because my immediate family was not the incumbent first family of the traditional pride - or not yet as my father would rather put it - I did not think I had a name that powerful in the evolving world. I did not see myself out of the ordinary. The prince of Zamunda may have been awed and admired not so much because of his royalty as of his affluence, and so may have been the princes of England and their other European and Arabian counterparts. In the emerging world, it seems it is only money that talks, and my family no longer had much of it.

But I was wrong. The mythology of nobility still held sway over people and I had the good fortune of being part of the pantheon. I may not have had money in the bank, but I was born with a name whose reality I was forced and proud to admit. Due to the royalty, I was not always seen just as anyone on the street. The exclusivity of the name, and its cultural and historical significance, marked me out. Coined and first used by Alaafin Siyanbola, it was a name to designate the union of two royal families in marriage. Alaafin Siyanbola had been born of the marriage between the king of Oyo and the daughter of the king of Iwo, the Lamuye of Iwo. Now it is a name that has become part of the history of the Yoruba nation, and synonymous with the royal head of the people. In literature and history classes in which prose and poetry about Oladigbolu were taught, fellow students often turned toward me with expectation of learning more on what the teachers were talking about. And a panegyric poem in our textbook, a mixture of ode and elegy made for Siyanbola, was often sung to tease me in the school playground.

Plutarch[8] may think the glory belongs to our ancestors, but I found that the glory is as inheritable as any other property. Oladigbolu has become an indelible traditional figure in the Yoruba and African history, and I happened to be his great grandson, I increasingly assimilated. I happened to be heir to a great African past, a symbol of cultural pride, and I felt it was great. Although I was not looking for it, but if someone was going to feed me with it, I was darn well going to eat it, and feel good at eating it. It is a privilege money cannot buy, as my father's siblings often said.

Through the British Council registrar, a respectable image of me was created for the guard that checked in the library users. His geographical position was close to the lady's table, and he always saw how the lady, his superior, beamed reverentially at me each time I walked in there with a

---

[8] Plutarch was a 1st century Greek biographer and author.

graceful manner I reserved for the special effect. This made him ignore the routine checking procedure for me, and when my card expired, I still walked into the library as a dignitary. For the time, I was like the prince of Zamunda, and it felt good.

***

Lagos was less a place of interest to me now. Gone were the days when I was eager to go there to see places. Now I was eager only to collect my money from Uncle Razaq.

Unlike Ibadan, Lagos State, a conurbation of a place, was a rough and tough place to live. Everyone in Lagos seemed to be in a rush for one thing or another. Named by the Portuguese explorers, the first Europeans to arrive in the area late in the 15th century, it was now to Nigeria as New York was to the United States. I had never seen a place where survival was so overtly the game people woke up every morning to live as in Lagos, and the no-nonsense attitude of Lagosians fascinated me. This was why the epithet "the land of wisdom" was used for the land, with the word 'wisdom' meaning survival savviness. If someone grew up in Lagos but was not smart, people often said, he could never be smart anymore in his life. Perhaps this run-for-survival of Lagos started in the centuries when it was the leading slave market in West Africa, with people trying to elude the grasp of the European slave traders and their African collaborators while still maintaining a living for their family.

Whenever I visited Lagos in the past, I went about like a tourist, savoring every step I took and enjoying the haste of the city. I enjoyed the often-overcrowded public buses called *molue*, with their obdurate and insolent conductors. Even when I had money enough to travel in taxis, I would still cramp myself in the molue.

Now there was little or no time for tourism for me, and the rush-rush of the city suited me more. I wanted to quickly reach where I was going, collect my money and leave. But my money had not come and I left back for Ibadan with Uncle Razaq's promise to send it to me as soon as he received it. I was almost impatient as I ran around to hold the course of events in my way, but the best way to play this, I realized, was to continue to divert my mind.

My namesake uncle Raymond left for Canada in the week, leaving me in hunger for the time mine would come. But the date Mr. Okunwole set to go to the embassy changed and it created more need for my mind diversion.

V

I spent the following Saturday morning at the construction site of Uncle Tunji at Agbowo. I always met him there on Mondays and Saturdays, and sometimes on Sunday I visited him at his residence at Oke Ado. The house at Oke Ado was my grandmother's house, though she did not live there. She rented out a large part of it and kept the remaining part for family needs. I spent Saturday and Sunday evenings at REC club, a recreation club at Sabo, where I eased off the burden of the ending week and refreshed for the new one. It was my weekend diversion.

This Saturday morning, my meeting with Uncle Tunji was brief and I left early with him. I liked to have a ride with him. The road and the distance to the nearest bus stop were sometimes a challenge. In addition to the sweltering sun, the road was so bad that it had no mercy for shoes. In a short time it would give the heels of a new pair of shoes a shape like Bobby Brown's *Don't Be Cruel* hair style: one side up and the other side down, and soon one would be walking with a side of one's feet kissing the stones. The road never heeded Bobby's advice not to be cruel.

When Uncle Tunji assigned me to the work, and I walked the road for a week, I purchased a second-hand pair of walking shoes that must have been made specifically for quarry-work. When I walked with the shoes the first time and heard the hard dry sound of rock and sole in conflict, I knew the shoes would save me a lot of money.

I got off at a bus stop and Uncle Tunji gave me some extra pocket money. This was another advantage of riding with him. For this, I especially liked him. Before, I did not like to get close to Uncle Tunji because he had a brusque disposition that kept people at a distance from him. But since my grandmother persuaded me to take it as his nature, and not an intention of malice, I resorted to finding a balance in his openhandedness. At least, he gave me what he had. Money was the only vehicle through which Uncle Tunji could convey affection to others, and he gave it generously. Because of my high expenses, however, his generosity was only enough to take care of my needs. I spent my money on transportation, running around for my dream.

Sometimes I tried to spare a little of my income for girls, but for the reason that I did not want to be distracted from my goal, I often had little mind for girls. I was always seeing a girl or another, but I was never in a serious relationship, sometimes out of fear for the girls. I was aware of the hypnotic effect of America on people; the still burning flame of Lady Liberty glowed beyond the American shore and dazzled people all over the world. In Nigeria, another name for success may have been America. It was the best thing a mother could wish for her child, and going to America was perhaps like going to paradise - having no problem anymore in the world whatsoever. Hence, just for me to tell a girl of my ongoing process to go to America may make her become all mine. I could always have more girls on my arms than I could handle. However, I did not think I had a place to safely keep a woman's heart, afraid that my hustling and bustling might let it drop and break, which I could not stand. I did not know what would happen in the far away land I was going. Tons of girls must be waiting on my path, as I fantasized, and to tie myself to someone in Nigeria was unreasonable. I had seen beautiful girls on the covers of the magazines and school brochures sent to me and I had been yearning.

Dating a cover girl was a dream.

About a year earlier, I had tried repeatedly to date a famous girl, and it would have boosted my rating among friends if she agreed. Now, after hearing that I was going to America, she wanted me earnestly. At first, I jumped at the opportunity, but later quit for fear of eventually leaving her heart-broken. Besides, the new state of the game was less challenging to my adventurous ego. I was a kind of animal who would rather hunt his prey than find it lying dead at his doormouth.

At four in the evening of this Saturday, I headed for REC club but got off the taxi at Mokola Roundabout, about half a mile away from the club. I liked to walk the rest of the way to prepare my body for the swimming pool at the club. Dozens of moneychangers cried *"dollars!" " pounds! "deutschmarks!"* hoping I was a prospective buyer or seller of hard currency. As a business of the Hausa settlers from Northern Nigeria, Sabo was the central money black-market in Ibadan.

I arrived at the club with sweat trickling down my body. There were many people at the pool. Some of them were boys, but most of them were girls, half-naked in bikinis, seductively cat-walking back and forth. I stripped off my clothing and dived my longing body into the cold, waiting pool. On Saturday evenings, the swimming pool section was always full of activities, and, since I started visiting the club about a year earlier, swimming had become my favorite hobby. On my first time, I came with three friends who introduced the place to me. Among them was Dotun Adigun, whose father was an influential member of the club. Children of members were automatic members, and as Dotun's friends, the rest of us were allowed in - saving us the cost of the one-time pass. Since then I had become a habitué of the club. After about three weeks, my friends stopped going, but I continued as a lone ranger and I had been enjoying it, except for one problem I had at first.

The club was an exclusive one for the rich. Though I only needed its swimming pool, and sometimes the wealth-sculpted girls, I was required to pay the exorbitant annual membership fee to continue in the absence of my friend's influence. Otherwise, I was to buy the overpriced one-time pass each time I visited the club, and pay twice as much as members for swimming tickets. It was not long when I found a way around the ticket problem. The lifeguards, who were supposed to check swimmers' tickets to confirm payments at the front desk, colluded with me and a few other guys in similar situation. Now, I needed not to buy any ticket; just give them half the price to pocket for themselves and swim on.

I left the club early today, just around 6 pm. I reached home some minutes before seven, with little time before the *magrib*, the late evening prayer. I went first to greet Baba as we always did. He was resting in his bed and I was leaving his room when he called me back. I turned around and waited for what he had to say. But rather than talk, he dipped his hand slowly beneath one of his pillows and brought out something. It was a slender bale of dollar bills.

"Count this money," he said gently.

My excitement began to gather. I knew immediately that it was my money. I counted it. "One thousand eight hundred dollars," I reported to him.

"Fatai said we should give it to you." Fatai is Uncle Jibola's Islamic name, and it was the name Baba and my grandmother called him.

I did not know what to do in front of Baba. Do I jump up and hit my head against the ceiling or prostrate to thank him, as our tradition demands? I knew I needed both. I left his room, frantic with joy. My uncle had not let me down.

My dream was now taking more form in reality. How sweet the world is when things go our way. It was around the time the current Nigerian head of state, President Babangida, formed a transition government headed by Ernest Shonekan and I quickly changed the money to naira. Shonekan was the retiring CEO of United African Company (U.A.C.), the largest business venture in Africa owned by the British and Africa. The reputation of the members of the transition government as reliable economists made me conclude that the economy would improve and the naira would appreciate against the dollar. If I had been wise enough to see that Nigeria's problems were beyond lack of professionalism at key administrative points, but fundamentally that of military conspiracy and civilian sycophancy, I would have known that I had made a wrong conclusion.

TWO

War of the Roses

I

Basheer Alabi was born into the ancient Oyo dynasty. His father, Aleem Agboin, was the son of Siyanbola Oladigbolu I, the king who ruled Oyo for 33 years early in the 20th century. Oyo was the power center of the ancient kingdoms of the Yoruba people, a large tribe that spread from the southwest of present Nigeria to Dahomey, the present day Republic of Benin - a land area of about 95, 000 sq miles, approximately the size of the United Kingdom of Great Britain and Northern Ireland and about six times the size of countries like Denmark, Netherlands, or Switzerland. The Oyo dynasty thus was the direct, and - after the fall of Old Oyo Empire - later indirect, ruling family of the entire Yoruba nation. The nation became one of the three nations of the Northern and Southern Protectorates amalgamated and named Nigeria by Her Majesty's government in 1914.

Before the intrusion of the Europeans in Africa, the Yoruba people had a remarkably advanced civilization, with flourishing kingdoms and culture far back into early history. The common story of the tribe's origin often told has always been one wrapped in myths and legends, as with all ancient tribes of the world. However, prying into oral traditions and investigated scholastic histories may reveal a probably more accurate history of the tribe.

A section of the present Yoruba nation may have grown out of two spiritual cities, Mecca and Jerusalem. The current rulership families are progenies of Oduduwa. Oduduwa was either Lamurudu or the son of Lamurudu, the Yoruba variation of the Arabic Namruud or the Hebrew Nimrod, and who was said to have hailed from Mecca and journeyed down southward to a town called Ile Ife. A story has it that Lamurudu was a king of Mecca - or a member of the royal institute of Mecca - perhaps deposed by the homecoming of Prophet Mohammad in the 7th century, or earlier.

One thing that makes this probable was a tradition that shows that the people in this part of the world would not accept anyone other than a royal blood to rule over them, unless by a warrior when forced through conquer. In history, Oranmiyan, the first king of Oyo, was a prince of the Oduduwa clan from Ile Ife, and he was allowed to rule over the people of Benin where he first migrated before he finally settled down at Oyo, where the same kind of acceptance was repeated. It was in the same way that all of his six siblings assumed the rulership of the six other kingdoms that constituted the Yoruba nation. They were all accepted to rule because of their royal blood.

The emergence of the Yoruba tribe in recorded history of humankind may be traced as far back as around the period of the third king of Jerusalem, King Solomon. Scriptural accounts, the Holy Qur'an and the Holy Bible, tell of how King Solomon fell in love with a queen of a southwestern Arabian land called Saba or Sheba, whom Jesus Christ also notes as from the south of the world - Africa. The history of this majestic woman seems the missing link between the ancient people called Jebusites and the Ijebus. According to the Bible and the history of the Middle East, the Jebusites were the original owner of Jerusalem before King David and his army invaded the city and drove them away. The Ijebus were a group of people who later emerged in Western Africa and are a large section of the Yoruba race. The name "Ijebu" becomes apparently etymologically arguable as a variation of the name "Jebusites."

According to the preserved oral tradition of Oke Eri, a sleepy village owned and inhabited by the Ijebus, an Ijebu princess, several centuries ago, had traveled widely across Africa and the Middle East, and specifically to Jerusalem. The story tells the name of the princess as Bilikisu Sugbo,[9] the same name the Qur'an gives as the name of the queen of Sheba, Bilqis. After she must have created the royal family of Ethiopia by the son she had with King Solomon, Bilikisu journeyed back down south, died and was buried at Oke Eri at a magical site that has for ages been a holy tourist center.

In Persian folklore, Bilikisu was known as being born by a Chinese king and a peri, a supernatural being descended from fallen angels. Recent archeological findings at Bilikisu's burial site at Oke Eri revealed the remains of her kingdom, found to be one of the largest known African monuments, and built of bricks likened to those of the Egyptian pyramids.

The slave trade of the past centuries did not leave the Yoruba nation untouched; it ended after a large part of the people had been bought and stolen to Europe and the Caribbean, and to North and South America.

[9] Bilikisu Sugbo, Bilkis of Sheba; Sugbo may be a Yoruba variation of Sheba.

According to the current spiritual leader of the tribe, the Ooni of Ife,[10] there are now about a hundred and forty-three million Yorubas around the world, of which only about a third live in the Western part of Nigeria known as the Yorubaland. From Brazil to Argentina, Cuba to Haiti, Benin to Sierra Leone, and in the United States of America, the Yoruba people spread across the world, carrying along all they could of their cultural identity, and making it the largest black tribe in the world.

This does not mean, however, that the Yoruba tribe, a part of black Africa, has its origin only in these two Middle Eastern cities rather than in Africa, the cradle of the world and the seat of the black people. In the days before the dawn of written history there had been dispersions of black people from Africa and into the vast spreads of land beyond Africa. This had brought about black settlements in various parts of the world long before the time of the slave trade, some losing their color and identity to the new environment and its characteristic experience. In addition to their part in the discovery and creation of the New World, the black people were well known to the Greeks and the Romans of the earliest historic period. It is interesting to note that these black Africans were the ones asserting racial supremacy by the fact of their being the inventors of the then civilization, though as a pride rather than prejudice. There are archaeological evidences that suggest the ancestors of the Yoruba tribe to have existed in the same area of Africa since prehistoric times. Therefore, even though they have spread around the globe, they have maintained their original place in the world.

Sometimes, however, I wonder whether the peoples to the east and west of the Red Sea had not really been one people, and whether the modern continental division had not brought a little confusion to our understanding of races. It is not surprising that parts of the Jewish tribe are found in Africa today. And the Quraysh, the tribe of which prophet Muhammad was born, was of African and Mesopotamian origin – Hagai and Abraham respectively.

Permanently situated in the west coast of Africa, the Yoruba tribe now has its central spiritual root at Ile Ife and its central government at Oyo, under the rulership of the Alaafin. 'Alaafin' is the title of the king of Oyo, a throne believed to be an authority second only to the gods. Oba Siyanbola Oladigbolu was the Alaafin of Oyo during the event of the amalgamation of Northern and Southern Protectorates and was still the king during the birth of Basheer Alabi. With the intrusion of the British government, the course of the Yoruba history was altered and erosion of power from the traditional rulers began. The kingdom of Oyo, once a large empire, has become only a part of a state named Oyo State. The state has its capital city at Ibadan, and has had many towns slashed away into some other Yoruba states created so far.

In the past, it was the custom of the royal family, for morality purposes,

[10] Oba Okunade Sijuwade

that the princes and princesses of the Alaafin be raised outside the palace. Immediately after they were weaned, they were transferred to the care of the king's servants living outside the palace. Sometimes, some princes and princesses had the opportunity of living with their maternal family for a while before finally moving to the assigned servants' place.

The office of the servant of the Alaafin was not one that could be looked down upon, however, as the term 'servant' may suggest. It was a revered office, usually subjected only to the Alaafin. In those days, when there were no photographic media to acquaint the king's physical identity to the public, Kudefu, the head of the servants, was oftentimes mistaken for the Alaafin. In the palace the Kudefu lived in majesty similar to that of the Alaafin, with his own chain of servants. Sanctioned by the Alaafin, he often acted as a double for the king to perform various royal functions, one of which was presiding over the royal court.

On September 30th 1936, Sabityy Tolani, the pretty young wife of Aleem Agboin, gave birth to Basheer Alabi at the house of the servant who raised his father, and he was taken to be blessed by the patriarch, the Alaafin, as the custom demanded.

Reincarnation was a traditional belief among the Yoruba people, and, on seeing the baby, the Alaafin saw in him traits of his own brother, an older prince who had died earlier and who also was believed to carry the traits of their father, an earlier Alaafin. By this he recognized the baby as the reincarnated soul of these two persons believed to be a single soul. He loved and missed the two, and therefore transferred the love onto the new baby. For this reason, he named Basheer as Mamadelo, a name signifying reminiscence of the two persons, and hope for the soul not to leave him this time around and to live the glory of his birth as a future king. The king was often reported to have said, "You came as my father; you left me. You came as my brother; you left me. Now you came as my child; you are not going to leave me again."

Then he ordered that the first born - also the only son - of Sabityy Tolani be living with him at the palace instead of at the servant's house, bending the long-standing tradition for his wish. The new mother was required to come every morning to the palace to take care of the baby during the day. Like this, Basheer started out his life under the nose of the Alaafin, an advantage that would influence the rest of his life. The Alaafin bestowed on him royal privileges that no other prince had access to, except the Aremo, the immediate heir to the throne, and whose privileges were by virtue of primogeniture. Yet, the Aremo also did not have the opportunity of living in the palace.

Like Charlemagne, the Carolingian Roman Emperor who loved his daughters so much he was afraid to give them out in marriage, the Alaafin was afraid to allow Basheer to go to school when he reached school age. He could not see his grandson ruled over or hurt. Even in the palace, when away from the king's direct presence, bodyguards working on shifts accompanied Basheer around, one of whom was punished one day when the boy hurt himself at the playground.

Everyone knew Basheer with the king. In a Daimler-Benz limousine custom-built for the Alaafin, the British government, in its effort to continue to placate the king, built in a special baby seat to accommodate Basheer in the car. But this Zamundan royal lifestyle did not last for long. The Alaafin ascended into the firmament of royalty,[11] where his ancestors dwell, and where they are silent but speaking, giving valuable advice to incumbent kings. Alaafin Siyanbola Oladigbolu transited in 1944 and Basheer Alabi Oladigbolu, now an eight-year-old boy, had to begin a new life.

There were two royal lineages in Oyo: the House of Oladigbolu and the House of Adeyemi. This called for shifting between the two in the ascension to the throne. Although the lineage was only recently split into two, they both originally had been one; they were of the same dynasty. The split occurred when, after the death of a king sometime late in the 19th century, a brother of his who was still eligible to the throne was alive. Then there happened to be two persons eligible to the throne: the Aremo (the heir of the passed-away king who perhaps was underage) and his uncle, the king's brother. The throne was conceded to the brother, whose name was Adeyemi, and who became the Adeyemi I, opening up the Adeyemi lineage. When Alaafin Adeyemi I passed away, he left behind an Aremo who, by that virtue, was as eligible to the throne as the former king's Aremo. The former Aremo ascended the throne, while the latter waited for a turn, and the alternate shifting of the throne continued until present time. Now, after the passing away of Siyanbola, the throne was occupied by Adeyemi II, the second king under the second lineage. Nonetheless, the two Houses are still seen as one by most citizens.

Children and relations of previous kings lived almost like normal citizens after their central father-king passed away. Although they had privileges, the privileges were now only a little more than the prestige and honor of being members of the royal family. This was partly due to the very large polygamies of the kings. It would not be easy for an incumbent king to cope when he would also have his own chain of wives and children. Unlike in the Roman Empire, however, where such other princes, after the heir, turned into brigands for the survival of their opulent lifestyles, the system of raising the Alaafin's children in working-class homes gave them the opportunity of having a career and a life of their own. Basheer was taken away from the palace and placed in the household of the servant who fostered his father. He started school and continued until late adolescence when he went to work with his father as a cloth-weaver.

Usually, the princes and princesses were content with their prestige and honor. It was generally believed that the ultimate goal anyone could aspire

[11] We do not use the word 'death' for the kings, because we believe they do not die; we say they ascend into the firmament of royalty, where they keep watch over the kingdom.

to in the world was to be recognized and honored by the people. “Someone who is looking for money, but found prestige,” a proverb says, “has found what he is looking for.” For a typical Yoruba man or woman in those days, the best thing money could buy was prestige and honor, though it was also believed that money was not enough to buy it if not combined with character. Yet, the royal prestige was a natural privilege that no amount of wealth could buy; you only have to be born in it.

Basheer had the choice of following his father’s business, but the encroaching modernity had begun to widen the professional horizon and he ended up choosing a different path. Leaving behind his older brother, Tiamiyu, born of his father’s first marriage, Basheer moved to Ibadan, the rising metropolitan city where he first dealt in merchandise and later started a cab service business. In addition to Basheer and his brother, their father had four daughters: two by Basheer's mother and the others by two other wives.

Basheer married and had his first child, a boy named Gbolagade, but he was destined for polygamy like his *fathers*. As his social and economic status rose gradually, the number of wives and children in his household rose along with it. Divorce, a common event in polygamy, came into the scene and women came and went in his life. However, he liked children, so much that he would not let departing wives take their children with them. "They are my children," he always said - a traditional view that may seem male-chauvinistic. Mama, as his mother was now called, together with incumbent wives, took care of the children.

Basheer moved from one apartment to another to meet his growing family, and his business grew even faster along. By the time he came to his last rented house, he had acquired a chain of taxicabs, his influences in the city increased, and he had established for himself a new princely lifestyle reminiscent of his early life. The house was at Oniyanrin, Ibadan, and owned by a civil engineer who was a native of Ejigbo, a Yoruba town now in Osun state. Alhaji Aliyu Gbadamosi Ilupeju, the landlord, was a man of eminence and moderate riches. He also had a large polygamous and extended family, with many of the members living in the mammoth house at Oniyanrin.

Polygamy was a strong cultural element in the days, and the very few people who did not practice it were of those with European education. An average Yoruba man's idea of women in those days might have been the model for the American novelist James Haedley Chase's. They believed that women were innately mischievous, and dangerous if not checked. Perhaps, this was a typical idea of many American men as well, as Chase might not otherwise have been predisposed to write thus. In Chase's world he did not see a remedy, but the Yoruba man believed that when women were multiplied in marriage, their dangerous instincts would be redirected toward one another through the natural vehicle of jealousy. Hence, as rivals, their goals would become taking care of the husband in attempt to out-do one another to win his love, rather than trying to hurt or murder the husband as typical of Chase's female characters.

The Yoruba family, therefore, sometimes became a large body of competing units under a patriarch, rather than a warm place to nurture children. With badmouthing, conspiracy, and voodoo, the women often ended up hurting one another and one another's children in attempt to destroy their competition. For this, Basheer took an extra measure. By trying not to have his women under the same roof at the same time to prevent the bitter feud, he made divorce an easy option. Draping over his sexual love for women, he always argued that to let the women go was good for the safety of his home from the devastating feud of polygamy. But one thing he did not realize was that, as he was running away from one trouble, he was taking cover in another.

It was at the Ilupejus' house that Basheer found his sixth wife who bore him his eighth child – the fifth son. The new wife, Silifat Funmilayo, was one of the many young daughters of the landlord, born to him by Alhaja Asanat Ilupeju.

During the military regime of General Yakubu Gowon, about a year and a half after the civil war that took about a million lives, God gave the baby as a blessing to their union. Everyone appeared to be happy over the birth; although, as the life story of the baby would later reveal, not everyone really was. In the polygamal rivalry of the Ilupeju's house, the goals of the women had been to marry their daughters to the prince, who had also become so materially successful. Though also born into his father's own polygamy, these became the forces that would play influential roles in the life of the new child.

Born on the day of the full moon, with a full body and a full mind, and leaving behind a world he could remember nothing of - or perhaps a world of nothingness, as some thinkers would say - the baby was the one from whom the story of my life started out. He was the beginning of my destiny. The baby was I.

I was born on a church day, the day of the ancient sun god, when also God reached the peak of His creativity in the prologue to the story of the universe. It was the fifth day of September 1971, at a time when the sun was strongest in the sky, and I was first named Islamically as AbdRahman, from Al-Rahman, the first of the ninety-nine Names of Allah. Three other names, Ademola, Abimbola, and Olasunkanmi, were given me, representing my family and tribal origin. And Ayinla was given as my traditional panegyric name. Of all the names, AbdRahman was stuck on me, but it was shortened as Rahman and often pronounced by the African tongue as Ramoni.

Before me, my father had four sons and three daughters: Brother Gbolagade, Sister Toyin, Brother Isiaka, Sister Saudat, Sister Ramota, Brother Akeem, and Brother Fatai respectively, and they were all living in the house at this time.

There was a drama that came about by my birth. A disagreement erupted over where I was to be named. Because my maternal grandfather was a man of muscle in his own world, he and my grandmother wanted the naming ceremony to be held at their house at Oniyanrin, while my father wanted it to be at his own father's house at Oyo. Having being born at Ibadan, taken home to Oniyanrin from the hospital, the advantage already lay on the side of my maternal grandparents.

Then, my father remembered the muscle of his own family and he tried to exploit it. Nine months before my birth, a new Alaafin had been crowned: Oba Lamidi Adeyemi III. Having lived together in the same compound, my father and the new king grew up with a rapport between them. My father supported him over his older brother during the family tussle to select a new king. Single-handedly, my father had played a significant and dramatic role of safeguarding him from the anger and assaults of the opposing camp until he was crowned as the new king. Now, in his own tussle against his influential in-laws, he went to the king for help.

Because my father did not want to look into the eyes of his in-laws in disagreement, he stepped out and left the affair in the hands of the Alaafin. In a royal convoy, the Alaafin sent his envoys with his scepter and the palace's music band to bring the baby to the palace. With the famous palace conch blaring into the air, announcing the passage of the royalty through the city's streets, they came to my maternal grandparents' house at Oniyanrin. They laid down the music band and played the presence of royalty in the neighborhood for hours long into the night, greeting my birth and asserting the Alaafin's message. Music always an accompaniment of all royal activities, and the envoys and scepter of the Alaafin were as respectable as the Alaafin himself.

The king must have his way, and my grandparents released the baby to the king's emissaries. The eighth day naming ceremony was finally held at Oyo, at both the palace and my father's house, and the king named the baby Omogbolahan, implying that the child carries the wealth and prestige of the family to a new height. Though the disagreement was buried in the past, it left behind tensions that made my father and his in-laws treat one another with delicate caution, and it was to haunt me for a long time.

Shortly after my birth, my father moved to his newly built house, indirectly behind his in-law's house, but on Abebi Street, a street separated from Oniyanrin Street by a bridged mysterious river called Alawo River. After a few months, he had a divorce with my mother. She remarried and I was left with my maternal grandparents, in whose house I continued to live.

My father married more wives, continued to have more children, and his wealth and influence soared. He bought more taxis for his business and built more houses. By the time I became self-conscious, he had entrenched himself in the status of a successful transporter. My siblings and I thus found ourselves as children of a wealthy man, loved and respected by the people as princes and princesses as we were called. In my grandmother's neighborhood, where she ran a pharmacy, the people loved to call me as

"Alaafin," invited me into their shops and houses, and treated me with palpable fondness.

This was the splendor from which I started out in life. Nonetheless, due to the circumstance, the 'father' and 'mother' designation for my parents seemed only ceremonial. Even though both my parents contributed directly to my well-being, I saw my grandparents instead as my father and mother. Because my grandparents' home was a large extended family home, however, I rarely came into direct interaction with Baba, my grandfather, until I was about fifteen years old. My grandmother, hence, became everything to me, mother and father. I sought everything I wanted from her and she lovingly gave me as much as she could.

By his foresight, my father had great pride in giving qualitative education to his children and he put us all in the best school in the city. When I was about three years old, my father enrolled me in a nursery school called Alaafia Nursery and Primary School. His vision and investment began to yield dividend in me almost immediately, though with a trace of my prankish character.

Perhaps due to the reputation of my school, I became popular in my father's neighborhood as a kid with an amazing proficiency in English language. It was a pride that I took pleasure in. Almost no pupil in the neighborhood could speak English at the time. Once in a while, people would gather in front of our house, including many older students, to ask me to speak English, and I would stand on a raised patio where they could all see and hear me. But they were too early in their expectation. I did not know as much as they thought I knew, and their complete lack of understanding of the language made them an easy prey, gullible to my pranks. A true Englishman would have thought I was speaking Sanskrit to them while an Indian would think I was speaking an extinct language. I would stand on the makeshift podium, like our unfaithful politicians during campaigns, and gibbered away the afternoons. It was too early for me to speak at length in English, and especially when I had nothing in particular to say, but not too early for me to feel the pride and joy of being marveled at and praised. I loved the celebrity attention.

Being the type of person who did not like leaving his children, my father liked the idea of my school being something to tie me back to him. Nonetheless, I still did not live with him, and he did not like it. He wanted me to grow up with my brothers and sisters under his roof. He wanted me to see his home as my primary home. Though our houses were very close to one another, about a hundred yards apart, but due to the Alawo River that ran between them we had to walk about two hundred yards from one to the other. It was also the river that put the two houses in different neighborhoods. Every morning I went to Abebi to have my father or his chauffeur take me and my brothers and sisters to school. And on returning from school in the afternoon I went back to my maternals' place, the place I saw as my home. This contributed to the tension between my father's house and my mother's house, and it was to play a hand long in the story of my life.

During the annual Ileya festival, the Islamic Eid-el Kabir festival, about Abraham's attempt to sacrifice his son for God, my father liked to go home with his children and wives to his father for celebration. He always wanted me to go with them, but my mind was strongly attached to the festivity at my maternals'. This did not suit him and, on one occasion, he put pressure on me to go with them. I was about seven years old and, really, it was fun in the town. We visited people and toured the ancient town. We visited the quaint palace, met with the king, viewed the traditional beauties of the palace, and listened to genealogical and historical songs from the palace griot. But after all this, I still determined never to go to Oyo again. First, my mind did not leave my maternals' place, and then Oyo seemed to me as rural, unsophisticated, what we called *local*. On the night of the festival, an experience further alienated me from wanting to come again.

I had eaten too much during the day. We ate childishly everywhere we went, while our house was also filled with food. This was typical of Ileya festivals. It was a cornucopia, with plenty of food through the horns of the rams killed to symbolize the ram God substituted for Abraham's son. I woke up in the middle of the night from an upset bowel and rushed for the toilet, which had only been pointed out to me during the day. There, I met a shocker. The house, built a long time ago, had no toilet seat; it only had a small hole at the center of the floor and a flat slab lay by its side. I had never seen a pit latrine in my life and, terrified I would fall inside, I ran back outside, faster than I had run in. But while I was looking for where else to ease myself, it came accidentally on my body. I was transfixed to a spot, confused for several minutes before I finally cleaned myself and sneaked back onto my mat.

This left a strong impression on my psyche. I was always afraid something would pull me into the pit latrine if I went near it. And from that night I made up my mind never to go back to Oyo again, no matter how much pressure was put upon me.

***

My father's business continued to grow, and his reputation in Oyo and in the city where he lived increased accordingly. Among nobles in the town, dissatisfaction bred against the Alaafin's rulership and it ultimately brewed controversy in the kingdom. Some factions, including kingmakers, consulted my father and persuaded him on taking over the throne. In a series of events that would change our family forever, my father, already in some disagreement with the king, eventually agreed. He began to see himself as having a destiny to fulfill: the destiny of a crown prince of Oyo. This, he believed had been born with him and laid down by his unique childhood at the top of the royalty.

Since it was from the Oladigbolu side of the family that the next king was to be chosen, my father accepted to carry the scepter for the change in the kingdom - or, at least, to clear the path as a legacy to be left behind for any of his sons to walk, if fate so twisted, as he sometimes feared and stated. He had a foreboding he was walking into the most crucial struggle of his life. His decision quickly withered the decades' old cordial relationship between him and the king. It engendered a new cold war era within the entire family, a new War of the Roses.[12] The town was split into two, and all the power-holders contended, using political, voodoo, and all other possible powers in the struggle.

Though anxious about fate, my father nonetheless did not lose faith. He believed he would attain the throne of his fathers as the head of the Yoruba nation. For this, he built a big modern house in Oyo in 1980 and announced his intention to return home after twenty-seven years in Ibadan. The house became his fourth house in the town. My father loved and respected his parents so much that two of the houses were for them. The first house he ever built in his life was for his father. And with his wealth he bestowed upon them all the great things in life they could not get for themselves. Overtly, he often claimed it was his father's wish that he returned home and he wanted to please him. However, his ambition may be the covert reason for the decision; he wanted to be at the battlefront.

My father wanted all his children to go back with him to live in Oyo, and by this a big change in my life came in the offing. By this time, I had had four younger siblings in the family: a boy named Bili, and three girls, Ganiyat, Adejoke, and Temilade. With all my brothers and sisters, I was slated to move to Oyo, a move I had neither heard of nor wanted.

Knowing I had not changed my mind about the town, and still avoiding confrontation with my grandparents, my father left my older brothers to handle the job of getting me to go. The duty was not new to them, however. They knew that mere order from my father would not make me pick up my baggage to go and drown myself in the latrine, and they were already familiar with tricking or forcefully carrying me to my father's place at Abebi whenever I was needed. One of such occasions was haircut times. Every month, my father hired barbers to come to the house to cut our hair. But I disliked haircuts. I thought it made me look ugly, and I was conscious of the girls in my class and neighborhood. So, it was my brothers' task to hunt me down and get me there to the barber's chair. They did not always succeed, however. Sometimes I would disappear into the huge and puzzling structure of my grandparents' house, which could be a labyrinth to strangers. They later became wiser and sometimes came to the house stealthily before I would be aware of them.

There was an occasion that they closed in on me without my awareness. I looked around and I saw big boys looking down on me, with hands waiting to carry me forcefully if I refused to go gently with them. I did not

---

[12] Though a similar historical event in a lot of respect, the use of the term "War of the Roses" is here metaphorical, and not a literal adaptation from the 15th century dynastic civil wars between the English Houses of Lancaster and York, which was so named for the rose emblems of the two Houses.

stand a chance, so I pretended to be a lamb. Everyone thought I had become a changed boy, following them without a protest. By the time it was my turn to have my hair cut, they had all relaxed, fooled by my pretense, while I had been looking for an opportunity to escape. But I did not get it until the barber took the first chop off my hair. The door was ajar and no one was near it. I swiftly leapt for it and bolted for my grandparents' house. My brothers jumped up and chased after me, but they were not quick enough to close the gap I had created. And once again, I disappeared into the labyrinth of our house.

The chop in my hair was circular, like the scrape on the head of someone with ringworm. That was what my classmates thought I had, and they mocked me until I realized it was better to look ugly for a few days than be mistaken for having ringworm. I went to a barber of my grandmother's choice to cut the rest of the hair to make it all even.

The movement to Oyo was to be gradual. We, the children, were to go first during the next school holiday to get used to the new house and for our new school to be arranged. The day we were to go was the day I first heard of the plan, and even of the new house. Two of my brothers came for me and employed persuasion. They started out by telling me of the new house and asked me to follow them there for sightseeing. That was not interesting enough to take me away from Ibadan. Even if there were five new houses, I would not be impressed. Although our neighborhood at Ibadan was filled with senescent houses, it gave me so much fun and I was not ready for change.

They continued the persuasion, telling me that the house was equipped with flush toilet systems. That brought us to an equal ground; but though I knew I would not fall down a latrine, it was not yet enough to convince me to leave Ibadan.

They stepped up their salesmanship, enticing me with fascinating things that were built in the house, and those I had never seen before. Its modernity and sophistication were their best bet. They told me we had our own living room separate from my father's, and equipped with our own telephone.

That was a good one. Telephones were yet a thing of marvel to us. Even though the Nigerian telecommunication company had a station in our neighborhood at Ibadan, where the towers that served the entire city were only a few blocks away from us, one could count the number of phone lines in the neighborhood on one hand. For me, it was only in my father's house at Abebi that I had ever seen a telephone, and it was only in his room.

Then, my brothers went in for the kill. They told me that the bathrooms had "phone" shower sticks, with water coming from the mouthpiece ends.

This was unbelievable. I must see it. If true, it would make a good story for my friends at Ibadan, thereby making me a hero who had seen what they had not. I agreed to go to Oyo, but with a condition that only if I would come back the same day. "Nothing surer than that," my brothers lied.

I ended up spending a week in the house, though I eventually thought it was fun. I enjoyed it not because of any beautiful things there, but because of my brothers and sisters. They were fun to be with. We had the house to ourselves; no father, no stepmother; all excitement in the new, big, and beautiful house. And this made me eventually agreed to go to school there.

The house was located at Kosobo, a quiet and modernly laid out residential area that gave me a new picture of Oyo.

II

Before this time my father had opened an automobile dealership at Ibadan, a big city that was more a commercial place than Oyo. Hence, he was to remain commercially in the city for some time. We, the children and his two new wives, all moved completely to Oyo by the end of 1980. It was a period shortly before the famous "Maitatsine War" of 1980, Nigeria's most gruesome religious crisis between Muslims and Christians. An event that occurred in the northern state of Kano, it claimed over four thousand lives, including that of the leader of the rampaging Muslims, Mohammad Maitatsine.

Even though this new development allowed me close relationship with my siblings, I did not enjoy being away from my grandmother. With the school, I had now been tied to Oyo and I could not change it. I thought of my grandmother often and I wept silently and alone the often. I could only spend the holidays with her, and these were three months apart, too long a time to stay away from her. Most of the time I felt homesick - homesick while at home. This was worsened because, at Oyo, I was an individual who had to be in confrontation with domestic issues. I had to wash my clothes by myself, I had to wash dishes, and I had to undertake a share of the general housecleaning. Whereas at Ibadan my grandmother had people who took care of my domestic needs.

Also, Oniyanrin was a lively place. There were always interesting things going on. Staying in the house and doing nothing in particular was fun enough. Yet, there were friends outside, with various games to play. I could not but remember the kite-flying and the table-soccer, the real soccer and wrestling matches, and occasions of discussion of late-night movies, often in hyperbole of our fantasies. The traditional festivals in the city were memorable. I remembered the *Oke Ibadan* festival, the traditional celebration of profanity, with its obscene chanting; the *Egungun* or masquerades festival, with its dances and ritual whip-fights; the ram fights tournament during Ileya festivals; the firecrackers at Christmas and New Year celebrations; the activities at our Boy Scouts organization, in which I was about to be promoted. Ibadan was just exciting, and these I missed and always looked forward to.

Oyo was not devoid of things to look forward to, however; it was just that Ibadan had the great charm over me. The things that were new and fascinating at Oyo were the adventurous hunting and fruit gathering. There were plenty of unoccupied and forested lands in Oyo, and it was a miracle that I survived into my adolescence. Many evenings and weekends I would go with my siblings and friends into the deep, dark forests, searching for fruits or animal game. Fearlessly, I would climb centuries-old trees, halfway to the sky, and which were home to wild bees, snakes, and various wild animals. Oyo also gave me a new experience of termite eating. In the rainy season, the termite *alates*, the winged princes and princesses of the termite kingdoms, would fly out after a downpour to mate and seek places to set up new kingdoms. They are the reproductive breed carrying on the reproduction of the termites for more than a hundred million years. Naturally they are nocturnal creatures, flying out in darkness to fulfill their destiny. But the sophistication of their human counterpart now influenced their culture. Once they were out of the protection of the sterile soldier-termites, the resplendent lights in front of close-by houses attracted them, distracted them, and made them change their course. Then we would gather them in bowls of water, which de-winged and made them weak. Perhaps, a story symbolic for the human culture under direct influence of the sophistication. When roasted in their baste, with moderate salt, the high-protein creatures were a delicacy.

Although I often ate some kind of grub worms in vegetable soup, I first thought I could never eat termites - perhaps because I had seen them alive and creepy. I had missed plenty of it before one of my sisters, Sister Saudat, finally convinced me to eat a piece one evening to see if I would like it. That night, I ended up eating several spoonfuls of the roasted termites, and I started leading in the efforts to gather them.

My first days in my new school at Oyo were unforgettable. Bili, Ganiyat, and I were first taken to a school near our house, but we rejected it on the basis of hygiene. The school was too dirty; classes were juxtaposed to a lengthy refuse dump that partly served as a sewage dump. We were then taken to Saint Andrews Demonstration School, about two miles from our house, and we were enrolled in Primary Three classes, although we were supposed to be in Primary Four.

When I was a kid, people often said I was stubborn, and maybe that was the reason I stubbornly left class 3A for class 4A, where I thought I belonged. It was break-time and the 4A class boys were having wrestling matches as the girls sang to give soundtrack and motivation. The class was spirited, noisy and almost frenzied, and I loved it.

I did not have the school uniform yet and was clad in a white long-sleeved T-shirt striped with brown lines, a pair of Emos blue jeans, and a pair of ox-blood shoes with gold chains laced on them. I looked like someone going to a party, and odd among the pupils who had on the institutional green uniform of short pants and short-sleeved shirt. The girls' uniform was made into a gown down to their knees.

A big boy was the champion of the wrestling matches. He was the strong boy throwing everyone that went for him in the fights. When there was no one left to face him, he jumped up and danced to the victory songs from the girls, given beats by some other boys. This kept the class in rollicking gaiety. The girls hailed him in their songs; they liked him, a thing of envy to other boys. The boy, called Bimbo, was also a funny character to watch; he danced around in a comic manner that made everyone laugh. He was the darling of the class, and, as I would soon learn, he was a darling of the school, endeared even to the teachers.

Then I went for him. Although I still liked girls, as I did three years earlier when my only motivation for school was the girl with whom I shared the school's typical double-seater, and I coveted Bimbo's girl-famous position, but I went for him primarily because I wanted to have the fun of the game. I loved wrestling.

When we began, everyone was still screaming Bimbo's name, hailing him as the champion. They did not see me as a threat to his title. They were sure he would throw me without much trouble, since he was about twice as big as I was and, more importantly, since I was a *butter*. Sometimes fully called *aje butter*, it literally means *someone living on butter*, with the word 'butter' signifying Western foods, seen as sophisticated foods. It was believed that children raised on Western foods and manner were of artificial upbringing and had less strength and less natural intelligence than the ones raised on natural local food and manner. My dressing and everything else about me led them into thinking I was really a *butter*, whereas in the full sense of the term I was not. Rather, I was like them, a natural *local*, only a city boy. At Ibadan I belonged to a group who also used the term for certain other people. However, I recognized that being a city boy still distinguished me from them, and this distinction could make them contemptibly call me anything enviable to them. I was everything they would like to be.

The ideas of *local* and *butter* usage, therefore, had some class undertone. Most of the people here were those we regarded, by city perspective, as rustics, an additional meaning to our use of *local*, as Oyo was not urban. In the class of kids I belonged to in my neighborhood at Ibadan we would not call ourselves *local* because of the rusticity undertone, but neither would we call ourselves *butter* because of the connotation of artificiality and refined weakness, though we envied some aspects of the *butter* class. However, the class I belonged to in school, by the virtue of the high-brow school, would call the one I belonged to at home as *local*, for it was the one my home class would call the *butter* class, even though many of them might not call themselves *butter*, because they understood its connotation. So, I may be said to belong to multiple classes, but identifying me with any single one would miss the truth. In the various diversity of life, this was a characteristic that would stay with me for a long time, perhaps for the rest of my life.

Bimbo and I began the fight. We struggled back and forth, looking for an opportunity to throw one another. My white shirt was subjected to a shameful experience, but I did not care. I liked this better than clothes.

After a little struggle, I threw Bimbo, sending him crashing like a shot elephant. He gave a loud groan, like the elephant, especially when the bullet hit its balls. Quickly, I posed for the second round. The number of times one threw his opponent, the greater the value of victory. But Bimbo did not get up to my ready hands. At first, I thought he wanted to accept defeat so soon, but after some time we found out he had broken an arm. I had broken his arm. On my first day in the school, I had broken the arm of one of the school's most popular students, a great sin against the student body.

At first, everyone went silent, unbelieving that their champion was down. They did not hail me. Then they became shocked when they realized what the situation was. They were afraid for the unfortunate boy, and, reputable or disreputable, they wondered at what kind of person I might be. Some feared me. Some hated me. And some felt pity for me, of whom a few chose to inform me how dreadful the school headmaster was with a cane. If the headmaster did not feel like flogging me himself, they said, the worse was the case, as his closest aide in punishment called Mr. Komolafe was more dreadful.

But the headmaster and the teachers instead were confused over what happened and they did not know what to do with me. On the first day a student was admitted! "Just come with your father to school tomorrow," was all the headmaster could say. I was returned to class 3A and I could not complain or reject it anymore.

That event was enough to tag me as formidable in the school. Throughout my four years in the school no one wanted to wrestle with me anymore. I was someone who could break their bone. It was an unfortunate label for me, as I was to miss the pleasure of wrestling. I only ended up finding close friendship with the Indian students, Krishna, Rupal, Kumar, and two brothers called Raul and Ashes Bindra. With them and the prominence of Indian movies in our society, I learned a few Indian sentences. With the exception of Kumar who understood Yoruba, so much that he often led his Yoruba language class, all of them sought translation of the language spoken by other students. They often wanted to know the meaning of the curse words thrown at them by many other students, especially junior pupils, most of whom did not speak English for lack of understanding or fear of mistakes. To their benefit, we communicated well in English, and it helped me as well to maintain my spoken English, learned from my previous school.

By the white color of their skin, and the lack of the sense of non-black ethnic differentiation of the school pupils, my friends were not seen as Indians but just as whites, *oyinbo*, like other white people they knew. One may then wonder how the term "white" could strictly be patented to a particular race while there were other races with the same skin color.

Being of the few white-skinned kids in the town, the younger pupils saw them as things to play with, like toys, and in a way that appeared molesting to my Indian friends. They always tried to put the pupils off, in a way that appeared to the pupils as disgusting. How could white *butter* kids ride over us, they always seemed to feel as they made out to fight the Indians. It was believed that white people were fragile people, by which the term *butter* was coined. However, by the legacy of colonialism, they still looked up to the white people as superior; they envied their skin color, in which they saw admirable but black-unattainable amount of possibilities. And to beat a white boy was an interesting experience for the kids, as much as toying with them, or more. It was cathartic, an unconsciously way of dealing with their inferiority complex in the presence of the white color, and to assert a consoling idea of equality, of which they were not really sure. Therefore, misunderstood as *oyinbo*, the Yoruba word for white people, they threw things at my Indian friends, pulled at their curly hair, and sang the puerile gibberish at them: "*Oyinbo pepper, yukuyuku pepper*."

In this, also, the Indian boys found me a valuable friend. When around me, no one could toy with or fight them. They were safe with me, and this put me at an advantage over them. I dominated them. I ruled whenever we were at odds, and they oftentimes bribed me with their spicy Indian cuisine to keep my friendship. Nonetheless, we were honest friends most of the times.

All this gave me a reputation: master of the white folks. But this was more in the eyes of the junior students who were more remote to the white guys, and those yet to be de-mythified of the common white myth or *oyinboism*.

For some of the local students who were lucky enough to be admitted into Olivet Baptist High School, the *oyinboism* was to be slightly demystified by an old male teacher who hated white people so much that he would double the punishments for white students for offenses committed by both white and black students. He had lived for many years in America in the days of heightened racism and he had been so victimized, as the stories went, that he came back to Nigeria with his anger. There was a story that he was once jailed simply for defending himself against two assaulting white racists.

***

A few weeks after the notorious event of my first day in school, I had a boost to my reputation as a tough boy when I had a real fight with a domineering boy in my class. Feared for his toughness, he was the virtual leader of my class as I met it. He could have been the official class captain, except that he was not doing well enough in schoolwork. Instead, Saibu ruled only as a kind of open cult leader, and worshiped by the rest of the class. Everyone danced to his tunes, and even the official class captain would not dare to fall out of his grace.

During lunch breaks, the longest break-time of the school day, we liked to play soccer. However, no one must touch the soccer ball until Saibu came out of the class to do so. The ball would be placed at the center of the field while all the other boys surrounded it, waiting for Saibu, who liked to enjoy the pleasure of his reign by staying away a little late. On finally reaching the field, Saibu would juggle up the ball and call out "Goalie 1, Goalie 2," to select the goalkeepers, the two students lucky to respond first. Then the goalkeepers would select their teams in alternate picking, with the precedence privilege to goalie 1. And, as a norm, the goalie 1 must pick Saibu first or lose his opportunity of participating in the soccer match for as long as Saibu pleased. It was like a religious ritual and everyone strictly observed it.

Though I was not oblivious of Saibu's rulership, I did not at first notice the soccer field tradition, because I had always come out later than Saibu. Then, came the fateful day when I was earlier and found the boys staring at the sacrosanct ball. I went to the ball and desecrated its position. I had started to juggle the ball when the boys warned me of the consequences if I did not put it back in its spot. They all still admired me as a city boy and did not like to see me in trouble with the god. If it were someone else, they would instead have waited eagerly to report him to Saibu and enjoyed the show of his wrath, as we often enjoyed those of God's told in the Scriptures. But their warning only seemed to me as a joke and I rebuffed them. Now I was a disrespectful demigod waiting to be punished by the god.

Saibu came and trouble, truly, came. First, he turned toward the other boys who returned that they had warned me. Then he asked me to put the ball down. I refused and called for "Goalie 1, Goalie 2."Nobody responded. Again, he asked me to put down the ball, and, this time, he threatened that he would not ask me the third time. Again, I refused. Suddenly, he charged forward and pushed me at the chest. From where I came I was a deity in my own right, and only the daring would do that to me. I pushed back at his chest with a stronger force and waited for him to make further charge. But, instead, he gave a sardonic smile and said, "If you're sure of yourself, city boy, meet me in front of the toilets after school hours."

The toilets were at a far end corner of the school. It was a popular out-of-the-way fight center. The place was as silent, obscured, and canopied upon by trees like in a jungle, which would make our fight seemed a rumble in the jungle. I was a fearless kid, always happy whenever there was a fight.

"That's fine," I agreed.

The other students looked at me as if I was a misguided dog trespassing into the domain of a jackal, and they tried to warn me off. I told them that the tradition either stopped today or I be seen as an exemption to the rules.

Saibu was almost the same size as I was. He was bald-headed, had tribal marks on his face, and usually dirty and unkempt. His worn-out uniform was sewn like a local *buba*, with buttons at the shoulder, untypical to the more common front-lined buttoned shirts. His was like a prison uniform, like that we often saw on Gboko prisoners going out to work.

Because of my reputation Saibu was not sure of himself against me, and my meeting his charge with a stronger force heightened his fear. Yet, he had to show the class he was up to his claims. The students knew they were going to be treated to a big and tough fight and the news spread across the school. For them, this was the real rumble in the jungle. It was like a fight in the IWA (International Wrestling Federation) between Mighty Igor and the Bulldog. Nonetheless most of the students seemed convinced that I was the one going to be beaten, sacrificed at Saibu's alter of bully-dom. I still looked like a *butter* to them, whereas Saibu looked fearsome, especially with his raggedness. His tribal marks that looked angrily cut added a fierceness and badness to his look. Like the ridiculous joke we often made of kids with tribal marks, he seemed as someone who had fought a lion - from whose claws he had got the marks. But I was a kid who would dare a fight with a lion. At my age, I feared nothing except the spooky.

Bili did not say anything about the fight, even when some students advised him to warn his brother off the fight. We liked each other as brothers do, but we did not think to interfere with each other's fights was part of showing it. Perhaps his own reason was his gentle character, but my reason was primarily because I was a kind of person who liked not to be misunderstood as favoring my sibling in such circumstances. I liked to be neutral. Also, I secretly wished to see Bili fight. He was so gentle that he never got into trouble with anyone as I often did. And because of this, other kids in my neighborhood liked him more than they liked me and, even, thought he could beat me in a fight. For this reason, I sometimes wanted to see him fight and beaten so I could laugh at him and the other kids. But it never happened. Bili was the gentle and unadventurous brother of the prodigal son; I was the one with the Faustian obsession to expend my resources, and I troubled and fascinated everyone by my energy. One of my father's tenants always told everyone that I was a "monkey, only covered in human skin."

Dozens of students assembled in front of the toilets after the school's closing bell rang. We began the fight, just like in the IWA ring much shown on TV, but we had no canvas-laid ring, no referee, and no time limit. We moved slowly toward one another and started throwing punches until we were in each other's grip. We held on tightly and struggled back and forth, each seeking an opportunity to throw the other. For some minutes, the struggle went on, with suspense-filled silence from the crowd that circled us up. A few times we broke off and re-gripped each other, but in the end I threw him to the ground. He landed with a bang and I was on top of him. This was not a fight of counting the number of throwing; the winner had to give a hands-down defeat to his opponent.

Saibu tried to free himself, but my grip was too tight for him. I punched, kicked, and head-butted him to the ground, knocking out his breath and strength. I was not gaining my breath either, but my victorious side of the fight spurred me on and I went on to put my signature on the victory. I dragged him to a wall and, for about five or six times, hit his head against the wall, with the spectators counting out loudly. Then I threw him back to the ground and filled his mouth with dirt, a typical signature of winners to attest that I did not win by chance, but because the opponent was not my match. Thus, I had killed the god and eaten his flesh - perhaps a more violent variant of the communion. I had become the new god, except that the celestials did not seem to me a fun place to live, and I only demolished the throne from anyone to ascend.

***

After about three years in Oyo, my father married a young lady called Sheri and built a new house for a new life with her. Around the time of another religious war[13] between Muslims and Christians in Kano, which claimed over a thousand lives, the house, a magnificently modern, marble-floored mansion much talked about in the town, was completed at the outskirt of the town. With a lavish launching and marriage ceremony, he celebrated his movement into the house with his new wife. And after their honeymoon, so to speak, we joined them, against his initial plan, one after the other until we all left Kosobo for the new house.

III

The military coup of December 1983, which brought an end to Nigeria's second Republic, brought an end to my father's business as well. The military leaders, intent on destroying merchants' hoarding of goods, took freedom away from the market and, with force, they led the bull of a lot of businesses to the slaughterhouse. They set prices and, with armed soldiers' presence at trading places, they forced many businesses to sell their goods at bankrupting rates. My father's auto business crashed in the process. He switched back to transportation and added wholesale distribution of Coca-Cola and 7Up products to struggle for business survival and save his pocket from the economic decline.

Yet, his business did not improve. Coupled with other problems, it eventually collapsed after about a decade of struggles. The beverage distribution went first, and one by one the cars and trucks in his fleet followed. Financial figures closed in on our family until it became skintight and suffocating. It was not a good experience for us, especially in the eyes of people outside. Many of the people, including my older brothers and sisters, blamed it on his decision to come back to Oyo – to wrench the throne from his cousin. Although he was already a high-spender, but my brothers and sisters believed that he was spending too much for this dream.

My father ignored these views and, despite the fears in our household, fought on in the struggle that continued to wax stronger. Success stories of

[13] Religious conflict of Kano: February 1984.

goals as his in the history of the family made him see his as attainable. Alaafin Gbadegesin, the second king with the name Oladigbolu, had fought for the crown against tides that appeared insurmountable. The second Adeyemi - the father of the current king - was already on the throne; the Aremo of the first Oladigbolu, Gbadegesin's older brother entitled to the throne by virtue of primogeniture was alive and waiting for his turn; and most of the town's people did not like Gbadegesin, an unrepentant hedonist. Yet, contrary to traditional logic, Gbadegesin believed, ever since he was a little boy, that he would rule the kingdom, and he fought with everything he had until Adeyemi II was dethroned and he was crowned over his older brother's rights and against people's disgruntlement. What would later characterize Gbadegesin's reign was his winning over of the people of Oyo, though he maintained behaviors that further alienated some of his enemies.

Also, some events in the past and present times of the family, and continued supports from a sizeable chunk of townspeople, chiefs and elders, egged my father on, while the financial edifice of our house fell and broke like eggs. The fear within our family grew from trickles to flood when one of his informants in the opposing camp reported his adversaries as vowing to send poverty by voodoo into our household to weaken his fighting ability. Now, events seemed to be proving this. The voodoo warfare was one of our major fears.

During the dry season one afternoon, when rain was months away from the sky, a strange thunder struck over our house, shook it to its foundation and sent everyone scrambling for safety. Using thunders as warfare, though a common knowledge, was a rare occurrence in the society. In the middle of one night, another thunder vividly shot and circled our buildings, enveloped our compound in its flame, and finally knocked down trees in front of the house. Its stone was recovered at the base of a tree the following day, with the warning for my father to desist. This was when we, the children, knew we were caught up in a serious conflict of the powers that be in the kingdom. What our father's camp was doing to the other camp, we could not know; it was what we knew that tormented us.

On one other occasion, a dog carrying charmed rings around its neck was knocked down by a car as it tried to cross over into our compound one afternoon. Surprisingly, controlled by voodoo joystick, the dog still struggled, dragged its crushed hind legs, and tried to sneak into the compound to drop the rings. It managed to get into the water drainage passing through our compound, but was drowned by the evening rain before we discovered it, still carrying the rings around its neck.

The menace of internal conspiracies also dogged our lives. Often we had people decamping back and forth between the two factions, and, many times, royal sons who had been on my father's sides clandestinely rose up to the opportunity of taking the throne for themselves. One day we would have someone dining with us, the next day he or she was taking orders from the other side. We hardly could trust anyone anymore.

Our worst fear came on November 26th 1992. In a mysterious conspiracy, the Asipa of Oyo, an arch-supporter of my father, was gruesomely murdered. Shot several times but unhurt, he was finally killed with acid compound forced down his throat. The hired assassins had anticipated his use of voodoo bulletproof, called ayeta, and had come with the second plan of the acid. After this, many similar attempts on my father followed, though foiled. The Asipa was the traditional leader of the people of Isale Oyo, a large section of Oyo town. The people of Isale Oyo were the original people met on the land by the migrant Oranmiyan, the first Alaafin of Oyo, after he had handed over his inherited kingdom of Ile Ife to be looked over by the chief priest, the Ooni, and after he had established his son Eweka as the king of Benin. Ever since, the progenies of the Ooni, Eweka, and Oranmiyan have been the ruling families of Ile Ife, Benin, and Oyo respectively. Asipa's death embittered and enraged people across the country, but no one, not even the vocal newspapers, could point a finger at the direction feared for its conspiracy.

I knew of the financial decline in the family not exactly by what was going on, but by the dwindling glory of our kitchen. First, the meals began to come late, and then lesser in quality. Then we began to skip meals. Thus, I grew up not into a financially robust home, but into a trying environment of financial skeleton, unlike that of the prince of Zamunda. We were only lucky that my father had built more houses over the years, on which he collected rents. This helped to keep our plates warm in the cold times. Even though the presidents of the town's banks still converged at our house for drinks and chatters, my father did not have the need to use his bank accounts anymore. We fed from pocket to mouth, living at subsistence level, although with hope. That, my father always had.

Really, his houses were many enough to gross revenues big enough to be a fortune to many a man's dream. However, the extent of his spending in his robust times had left holes to be filled around him, and such revenue could not take him beyond the subsistence level. One of the holes was the large number of mouths he had to feed. In the good times, he had added more kids to the family - although the number of wives cut down to the last one. Now he began to experience one of the realities of polygamal burden that his earlier fat pocket had camouflaged as an illusion to him. Yet, there were many other relatives that depended on him, whose needs a share of his income must service.

However, he was able to keep the problem relatively within the family. Although people knew that things were no longer the way they used to be, what they did not know was the extent of the financial decline. To many, we were still a wealthy family. Whenever they came into our house they saw the exclusive marble floor, the exotic wood paneling on the walls, the lush furniture, and they saw the royalty and its effulgent prestige enhanced by my father's once-had wealth. I was embarrassed one day when a classmate visited me. He looked around my room, which I had made appealing especially for girls, and self-consciously remarked: "Rahman, I envy you." I was taken aback. Even though I could see it in people's eyes sometimes, I had never seen myself in a position out of the ordinary. Then he made it worse by adding, "My father's living room is not half as good as this!"

When people saw the broken-down seats in our living rooms, they only thought my father was being carefree, as they knew him generally to be with material things. In the old days, he would use a posh car in his fleet to transport coal and firewood for our various parties. And on special occasions, when everyone was looking preen, my father would use his expensive clothes to clean up the dirty face of a little kid's whenever he saw one crying. To him, even though he spent his wealth on the best of things in life, material things were to serve human needs rather than be worshipped. And essential among the needs were food in the stomachs of little children and smiles on their faces.

Nonetheless, we knew the extent of our problem and we felt it. But, to my respect, my father was strong. He smiled in the face of suffering. His case was one that would strike Aristotle's sense of tragedy, but still he remained stoic and strong in hope. One of my brothers said of him one day, "Only God knows with what he is made." He beamed and waved while he had fire burning inside him. A long time afterward, I was to see him go through more difficult conditions that I could not have believed a man of his status could endure. When other royal sons tempting the opportunity were falling, my father kept on the struggle undaunted. When he put his hand in his pocket and came out with nothing to feed his children, he made jokes and laughed about it. He was always happy in himself and to the world, always courageous, determined and hopeful, even toward what seemed to his children as a hope of apple fruits from a rock. And I always said to myself, "Even if this man had nothing more to give me, this is enough a legacy for me."

Whether the pursuit of his goal had caused his home's problems or not, one other thing he achieved is a place in the history of the kingdom. Like Alaafin Gbadegesin Oladigbolu, he had stood in battle for the crown with an incumbent and he had held the breath of the town for so long.

We, the children, often divided ourselves into generations. The first generation was that of my older three sisters and four brothers, who all received a fleshy cuddle of his fathering hands. The second generation consisted of Bili, Ganiyat, and myself. Adejoke, who was much younger than the three of us, but much older than the next generation, hanged between the second generation and third generation, which consists of three girls and a boy. She switched back and forth depending on which satisfied her current need. And the fourth generation is of the five children of his last and current wife. Of all the first three generations, only the first one was well taken care of, partly because they had all almost grown out of his care by the time his fortune changed. In my generation, Bili and Ganiyat had to drop out of school, with his expectation of me to follow suit. The good fortune of the last generation could be credited more to their mother, though at the expense of the second and third generations.

This was still the situation of our home when it became apparent that Mr. Okunwole could not obtain the American visa for me. I asked for the refund of the payment I had made, but it was not anymore available. He only promised to pay it every following month - the common story in visa business. I was afraid I had fallen a victim, bruised in the heart and knowing not what next to do. My life seemed crumbling; the heavy world seemed to be on my head and I was buckling at the knees. But I had to get to America, I always thought. I had a dream, and it goaded me on. Maybe I got that from my father, but I had the hope.

In the days that followed, a new idea of obtaining the visa came up in my mind and I decided to give it a try. Nothing comes into the world, but from an idea.

THREE

Chief Bankole Bernard

I

Ahead swings my lofty venture,
Clinging my affections to my hopes abroad;
Where my dream lies, there my heart dwells.
With my wit I chart the course,
And my spirit I swell the sail.
In a boat of my wishes' make,
I hope someday I reach my dream.

I row and row along the river bedding,
Slept upon by smoky currents,
And hooding my sight to vision beyond,
Where always the unknown lie,
Waiting patiently for their time to come.
But till I reach my Golden Fleece,
No slumber would my oars know.

"Dreaming," Rahman

Sometimes, putting one's eggs in more than one basket pays. Before Raymond left for Canada, an elderly family friend introduced him to a man believed able to secure an American visa for him. Raymond's Canadian processing was costing him too much money and time, so he wised up to splitting his hope on the two lines, hoping to go with whichever came first.

Chief Bernard Bankole planned to visit America in December for the wedding ceremony of his daughter. Although, he was reputed to have the opportunity to obtain British and American visas with little effort for prospective migrants, he planned to use the chance of his wedding trip to get Raymond a quick American visa. Chief Bernard did not just do it because of the money he collected from prospective travelers, but to help people he believed were of good intentions and promises, according to the family friend that took Raymond to him, a painter employed at my grandfather's construction projects. He collected money only to process the visas for them – for official visa fees and other expenses. Raymond gave the Chief his passport and promised to come back with money for the processing. But his Canadian traveling documents came through and he left for Canada, forgetting to let the Chief know. Chief Bernard, angry that he had been disrespected, left for America early in December and came back a few weeks later.

In January, I decided to try Chief Bernard for my visa. I had heard how well the elderly painter praised him. "He was the one who helped my son to London," he had said to Raymond in my ears, "and he even allowed him to stay in his house in London until he became economically stable enough to rent an apartment."

The painter was a man in his late 40s or early 50s, but, from his heavy drinking habit, he looked older than his age. He lived at Basorun and he painted the Chief's residence in the same neighborhood. It was a mammoth house with an average size shopping complex on its right side and the Chief's office on its left, all in the same compound and color. I asked the painter to help me talk to Chief Bernard.

"I don't think he would agree," he said to me, with his coverbal language telling me he wanted to do it but was afraid of the Chief. "He was very angry when Raymond failed to turn up in the first arrangement. He flung his passport at me in anger. He thought we were only wasting his time while he could have helped someone else." The painter concluded and expected me to accept the situation like that.

"But you could still try him; he may have cooled off over it," I said back to him.

He did not like to go to face the Chief with that again, but he wanted to help me. "Okay," he said at last, "I'll try."

He tried, but the Chief did not want to hear of it. He was still angry at the way he thought my uncle had ignored him. He felt insulted. Nonetheless, I still insisted that the painter try again. It was like a dilemma for him, afraid to face the Chief and afraid to let me down. I had an advantage over him; he was currently working on a house for Baba and there were more houses, especially Uncle Tunji's house, of which he knew I was partly in charge. I did not directly use these, but it was clear enough for him to reflect by. I was now like a manager in Baba's affairs and I carried duties and powers that Raymond, the previous manager, had left behind.

Moreover, the painter was a little high on liquor when I asked him again and he could not argue with me. He went once more to talk to the Chief, and this time the Chief agreed and asked me to see him. Immediately, I went to the Chief's house. I was directed to his office where I had to side-step two fiercely built dogs.

Born a Togolese, Chief Bernard had spent a lot of years in Nigeria, by which he had been honored with a Yoruba name, Bankole, and a chieftaincy title. He was an elderly man that must have been in his early or late 60s. He was light skinned and good looking. He had no mustache and wore his gray hair and beard finely combed. When I was told he had been a university professor, I thought he looked a well-paid one. He had on a pair of black pants, a black and white striped silk shirt, and a pair of black shoes. He had on a gold wristwatch on his left hand and a chieftaincy bead-band on his right hand. I could see a preppy taste behind this, a characteristic taste I admired more than the clothes. His dressing had not created an image for him; it had described his self-created image, reflecting the man beneath, an academic and wealthy man, potentialities for the enjoyment of the best of both worlds.

"So, where do you want to go?" he asked, after exchanging greetings with me and after he had told me how the previous case had warranted his earlier reluctance.

"America," I replied, as I sat opposite to him, awed by his presence.

"What do you people see in America that every one of you wants to go there? Britain is more peaceful."

"I like America better. Besides, it's where I have someone to help me."

He shrugged. "Do you want to school there or you're just looking for work?"

"I want to go to school first." I expected that to make an impression, knowing the kind of person he was said to be - a professor.

And I knew it stuck when I saw him nod his grizzled head in agreement and said, "Fine. I don't like young people going out there only to find money without good education. They waste valuable time on worthless things." He flipped through my passport. Satisfied, he put it on his table and looked up at me. "It's N12, 000 for an American visa, and you'll give me a few weeks."

I nodded in agreement. He acknowledged my consent and said, "So, when you bring the money, I'll start." It was with a tacit conclusion that told me the meeting was over and the rest was up to me.

I was happy, but I did not forget a visa business tactic. "I'll bring half tomorrow sir, and when..."

"What?" he cut in angrily. " What do you mean half? What kind of person do you think I am? You think it's my work to get you visa for a fee?"

"I'm sorry sir," I managed to say. I was afraid and I did not know what to say. It was as if I was looking at the visa slipping out through my fingers, and because of my folly. "I'm sorry sir," I repeated at his apparently insulted glare, and only became a little relaxed when I saw his anger simmering.

"I have my own work, and this is not what I live on. It's because of the painter that I agreed to help you; if not, I wouldn't touch your work from what your uncle did. I only help people with it; it's not my business. And do you expect me to use my own money?"

"I'm sorry sir. I'll bring the full amount tomorrow."

He dropped my passport carelessly back on his table; he had angrily picked it up in an attempt to give it back to me.

"I'll definitely bring it tomorrow, sir. Thank you, sir." I almost drowned him in 'sirs'. I rose up and walked out, thanking God that he did not throw me out with my passport. I must have been foolish to say that, I thought. Could I not see how elderly, rich, and reputable he is? I chided myself. The street on which he lived was even named in his honor: *Chief Bernard Bankole Street*, the sign read. And I knew he had his own work. He imported laboratory chemicals and, perhaps, some other scientific materials into Nigeria.

Nonetheless, all that did not mean someone would not cheat in the Nigeria of the day. Although I trusted him, even alone from his appearance, but I ended up telling myself that I had not done anything wrong, perhaps I had only done it at a wrong place. And who in my place would have known otherwise? But I was happy I had got a good place at last, with a moderate price compared to what people paid elsewhere. This also showed me he was not doing it for profit, as he said. Where they did it for profit, the charges were mostly between N25, 000 and N40, 000, and more in some other places.

Again, Baba thought his presence at the payment would make an impact. We went there together the next day. Everything went smoothly to my delight. Having lived in Togo, among many other countries, Baba spoke freely in the Togolese language, among his many languages, and he spoke it with Chief Bernard to his pleasure. There, they became friends, and he showed a renewed eagerness to help me. "Check with me in two weeks," he said at the end of the meeting.

II

With excitement I started out on a Monday morning, hoping to see Mr. Okunwole about my money and Chief Bernard about my visa. They were at opposite ends of the large city, but my enthusiasm masked the distance.

At Mr. Okunwole's office I joined a group of people already waiting to see him. I wondered what each one came for. The man was not a man of one trade. He seemed to be putting his hands into everything that could bring money, though money did not seem to be coming his way. As I had feared, he did not have the money for me, and he only set another date to come back for it. The many thoughts of fraudsters in the visa business gave me fears of having being swindled. Could he have set up the plan just for the money he was hoping to scrape from people like me? I began to think. But I did not want to think of it like that. I had paid because he was convincing. Besides, if I did not learn to buy something, I might not be able to buy anything. Falsity and truth were probably most difficult to tell apart in such transactions.

The news at Chief Bernard's place offset the disappointment. Though it was not yet the ultimate story I wanted to hear, it was promising. Before I met him, I waited first in his secretary's office, a small room that contained two typewriters and chairs. On the wall behind the secretary was a large poster with an inscription that suggested that Chief Bernard drank with a free conscience. It read:

HE WHO DRINKS GOES TO SLEEP.
HE WHO SLEEPS DOESN'T SIN.
HE WHO DOESN'T SIN GOES TO HEAVEN.
WHY NOT DRINK AND GO TO HEAVEN?

A funny fallacy, I thought at the time, though later reflected that he might have had a point, one crucial to the beauty and joy of life. Many of us drink one thing or another to go to Heaven.

The passageway to Chief Bernard's office was like an alley of ruins in a war-torn city. Strategically situated on the sides are glass cases that housed skeletons of different kinds of animals, big and small. Perhaps this was to exhibit the function of his chemical merchandise.

"I have submitted an application form for you," he said after he asked about my grandfather. "So you can relax now. We will wait for them to check on it. A letter will come from the U.S. to us and to them, clearing the way for your visa, and then I will go in and collect it for you. That's the way I do it."

I looked at him the way the Israelites must have looked at Moses when he was delivering them from Egyptian bondage. This was promising news.

"Come in another two weeks to check the status."

"Thank you, sir," I said, musing over my luck. I could read from his face that it was neither a difficult task for him nor something for me to worry about anymore. It was time to begin preparation to cross my Red Sea.

III

It was jacket-weather in America. I saw a corduroy jacket at Sango market and I thought it would be suitable for my journey. I had first seen the jacket about a year earlier but I could not afford the N200 price tag then. Besides, I thought that was too much for a 'tokunbo' that it was, a ridiculous price that must have kept buyers away for twelve months. Literally, 'Tokunbo' was a name for a child born abroad, but in this context it was adapted as a colloquial term for second-hand foreign goods. Now I needed the jacket and I had N200.

It was a little shop-worn, proportionally to the one year period, but still in a good condition. I asked for the price, hoping it would have been cheaper, but the same retailer I met the last time told me it was N500.

"Five hundred naira!" I exclaimed. "Are you out of your mind? I had been here before and you said it was N200." I talked in a defensive but pleading manner.

"That was before; this is now," he replied. "Things have changed." He looked as if he did not care if the jacket rotted on his rack. It was a shrewd business tactic, but, whether I was certain it was or not, I could not dare him.

The bulky jacket was black and velvety, so attractive that I could not turn from it. Although it was not a famous designer's job, a vanity of my youthful mentality, and I could not hide its second-hand appearance, as I would have loved to, it would still make my friends drool. For the second-hand nature, everyone knew how tough things were increasingly becoming in the country; people no longer were able to afford new foreign goods, with which our earlier all-consuming economy had spoilt us. After a long haggling, the retailer cut one hundred naira off the price. At home I showed the jacket to my grandmother and told her my purpose for buying it. "I will see you wear it to America by the grace of God," she prayed.

At this point, I needed plenty of the prayer. As the old saying goes, that which is promising is as wanting of prayer as that which is bleak – even if only to sustain the promise. I moved closer to God and prayed as much as I could over my situation. Once in a while, when there was an opportunity of anyone I thought was spiritually powerful, I sought his help in prayer. If not that I could not afford it, I would have asked many of such persons to be praying on my project all the time, so we could bombard heaven with my request. That would tell the angels how serious I was about my dream and would make them give my file a priority on God's big desk. But prayer people's time was money. In Nigeria, like in Martin Luther's Europe, even paradise was for sale; the only difference was that the trade was a free market in Nigeria, and not monopolized by one institution.

Sometimes it came into my mind, challengingly, that it was when I felt incapable by myself and needed God's assistance that I began to get nearer to Him. I had always been an irregular worshipper, but now my daily salats were always complete. Am I not being chaste like a dog whose chastity came when he saw the bitches were out of reach? I often asked, shamefully. But I always found an absolution by reasoning that one could go to God at one time or the other. Perhaps, the most religious people in the world, either rich or poor, are religious because of one sense of incapability and insecurity or another. Perhaps the human specie evolved the sense of faith because it developed the sense of fear – an evolution that may be a symbol of the ineluctable limitation of human reasoning, either scientific or philosophical. Perhaps it is simply the nature of human beings to seek a higher power when we feel our problem as beyond our control. Perhaps the higher power also throws such fear at us so we could remember and go to Him. Then, may be what matters is just to go to Him, no matter when one does it. It was when things become sour that the Prodigal Son also remembers his father. Yet, his father does not mind; he is even happy and he kills a cow to throw a welcome feast.

In addition to my regular prayer, I now regularly observed the obligatory fasting, the fourth pillar of Islam, covertly hoping to be a good servant of Allah deserving to be thrown a feast for. Honestly, I did not need a fatted cow; all I needed was an American visa. No matter how intimidating the American embassy was, I did not think the visa could be difficult for God to obtain for me. All I thought I needed to do was to be good in the Eye of the Father Who art in Heaven.

Last year's Ramadan was my first honest and complete fasting period. Before, I only hovered between seven to fifteen days of sincere fasting in the 30-day period and pretended the rest of the month. There were special rations of food at break time for those strong enough to fast and I could not take anything less and be seen as a weakling. It was a ration of appreciation from our parents and of respect among ourselves. Hence, if you could not fast, you faked it.

I devised many ways of filling my stomach secretly during the day. Sometimes, I would stroll out to an out of the way restaurant. And sometimes I would smuggle food into my room. But my grandmother always knew whenever I broke my fast and, because of this, she did not even believe I ever had one honest fast. She would look at me inquiringly and say, "You don't look like someone fasting." Yet, she would give me the special rations, as for those fasting, since she could not prove otherwise.

Now I had stopped all that. I had accepted that my fasting was for my own benefit. It was one of God's requirements of us, and, trying to be good in His sight, I realized I needed to do His wish. Fasting times were trying times, however. To abstain from food, sins, and immoralities – which were the pastimes of youth – was not an easy thing for me. Yet, fasting times seem to give more daunting challenges than ordinary times.

At my age and environment, girls were our chief pleasure, but preachers were fond of calling it fornication. Though it was difficult to listen to them, but at fasting times I had to heed the warnings. It became a dilemma: I could not dare God, whereas the girls were also hard to ignore, especially in their suggestive dressing styles, the symbol of modernity. In modern times, religion seems to be in an unfriendly world. With our free society and its exhibitionist and voyeuristic culture, one may wonder whether we would not choke the innocent thing. Yet, religion seems to be so enduring an unwanted pal, still sticking its head out to be friendly at every opportunity. Sometimes, however, I wondered whether religion was really as innocent as it appeared, and that Nietzsche's[14] dead God may have had a hand in His own death, perhaps for a purpose. That is, God may have actually committed suicide, so to speak. In modern times, then, maybe the Paradise of those who could refrain from what religious preachers call fornication and adultery would need to be better and greater than those in the past civilizations. The reason is obvious: we have more hurdles to scale over in this seductive civilization. But maybe not - who knows what the big Judge's yardsticks are.

In the previous year, when I made up my mind not to fake my fasting anymore, I met with something I did not expect. It was an unsettling challenge on the first day of the Ramadan month - the first day of a true

[14] German-Swiss philosopher, Friedrich Nietzsche

and sincere fasting month in my life. I had met Taiwo Tomato, a voluptuous and show-stopping girl. For the kind of relationship I had had with the girl, meeting her was a disaster in the holy month.

More than a year earlier from the fateful holy month meeting, I had tried to date Taiwo Adeolu, a classmate at my extramural lesson center, but events turned out to mock my wish. Taiwo was an epitome of beauty; slimly built and sexily shaped. She had a dulcet voice with an undertone that sounded as officious as of a beauty queen giving thanks and humanitarian vows at her crowning ceremony. Her mulatto-light skin earned her the nickname Tomato, and we only called her Taiwo Tomato.

Initially, I did not want to attempt to date Taiwo Tomato. I was afraid of the tough competition among boys at the lesson center, and, turning to the wisdom of game theory, I turned my efforts to other girls at the center. The advantage was that there were many beautiful girls at the center; most of them were from the upper class area of the city and could afford good looks.

However, Taiwo was an outstanding girl whose beauty would make one think, think, and think again, and whose amiableness would make one assume that one's chances were high. By the time I realized that Taiwo was not only an irresistible date for me, but also an achievable goal, the lesson year was only a few days left on its calendar. It turned out that, as I was afraid of attempting to date her in the face of competition, so were all other boys in the circle around her. Thus, we had created an illusory competition that scared everyone off. But by the time I realized this, it had become real. A close friend of mine, Femi Ayinde, had also become disillusioned and we contended over dating Taiwo. I persuaded him to let me have her, but he also persuaded me to let him have her. Then we concluded that she went to the faster of us. When there were many other girls at the lesson center, one could only imagine why neither of two good friends would leave Taiwo Tomato for the other. Taiwo was a religion for the eyes of men to lay on in worship, and their hearts to kneel in prayer, except the eyes and hearts of men who were aesthetically pagan.

Valentine’s Day was about a week away, and Femi was famous for his dating skills. To out-play him in the game, I contrived a trick. With a feigned joy I told Femi at the end of the day's lesson that Taiwo had agreed to be my date on Valentine's Day. He fell for it, and that left me plenty of time to relax, plan, and rehearse my move. It took me the next two days to finally ask her out for the Valentine's Day and she agreed, though tentatively.

I arranged with another friend in my group to get a car to pick up my girl on the Valentine’s Day. None of them in the group had a date for the lovers’ day and I arranged that they would drop us at a fertile spot in the city. When the day came, we went to her house. But by the time we got there, she had gone out.

This threw me in agitation and I inquired on how to locate her. When I was told she had gone out with a guy, I knew someone else had climbed over my head. I felt hurt to the marrow, but there was nothing I could do. I was sure the guy would not let loose of her until the day and his emotions were exhausted. No guy in his right pants would. I could only go back to my friends and be mocked.

The lesson center had already closed and, for some reason, I did not see Taiwo Tomato again, until this day, the first day of my honest Ramadan. That fasting morning, I had slept till around ten in the morning after the *sari*, the twilight opening meal. I felt good, fresh, and pure, more than any other normal day, as though I was sure I was a beloved of God already.

I set for the U.S.I.S. library, my first and main occupation of the day. At the last bus terminal to the building, I came down and was walking the rest of the way. The road was a slope and it gave an added bounce-off to the pride of my pair of sneakers and the vigor of a spiritually fresh outing. I reveled in them all.

Favos building was to my right as I walked, a famous supermarket in the area. At its end was the turning that led to the U.S.I.S. building. And to my left were other buildings that I never cared about, but for an alley there that led to a building that was of occasional interest to me. It was the site of another extramural lesson center. Such lesson centers connoted fun. They were private education institutions with less restriction than in traditional schools. For boys, they were places of plenty of girls.

As I walked down the street I noticed a stream of students at the mouth of the alley, murmuring, but I tried to ignore them for fear of putting my fasting in peril. There must be plenty of girls there, and with the kind of clothes many of them would have on, I might be forced to take a second look and probe with my eyes. A second look was sinful, as the Prophet was often paraphrased, and especially hurtful to fasting.

Then, suddenly, above the murmurs weakened by distance, came a soft dulcet voice sounding off someone's name. It was clear. "Rahman, Rahman, Rahman." The voice could stir a music producer to dream of Platinum. But it stirred me instead to displeasure with my luck. Before I could identify the voice, the owner had shot out of the crowd and was running toward me. It was Taiwo, the Tomato of my lesson center, so hotly dressed she was already filling me with sin.

Then, temptation came. With joy she jumped to hug me, but I tried to prevent it while I tried not to bruise her feelings. The mind determines the mood when two people wrap up in a hug. And in clothing so skimpy that even a priest would be inspired, the boundaries of that mind may be as vast as the sky. With me conscious of how and where we left our story, and with her closing me up as she was coming to do, body to body, chest to chest, I did not think she would leave my fasting as honest as she would meet it. If it were one of those past fasting times, I would not have thought twice before I would throw the poor thing up in the air and enjoy a munificent hug. 'God will understand,' I would assure myself as I always did, giving up to the lure of my senses. And I would have been thanking my stars, knowing there was bucks in my pocket, cool joints around, and eagerness in our spirits. The sky might find it difficult to be the limit.

But now, I was cursing my stars. I held both her hands as I expressed my excitement at seeing her as well. Although, I tried to disguise my acts of preventing her from hugging me, I did not kid myself that she was kidded. The place was too open and we had attracted all attention. Nobody would think I had done that for religious purpose, and for that she was embarrassed.

Some other kinds of challenges during Ramadan were the rare and special meals at Christian friends' houses, the much talked about parties in town - sometimes bikini parties at the swimming pool, and so forth, all luring and tempting toward participation. However, now that I wanted America, I did not like to joke anymore with my fasting, and I always tried not to mess around with God.

***

On the day Mr. Okunwole promised, he only promised another week away. I also went to Chief Bernard on his date, but he also gave me another two weeks away. One week, two weeks, one week, two weeks, and time stole its steps into the road ahead, while it bundled me along on its head, and chewed on my hope. In such a situation, one feels helpless, and only could peek back on the trekked road and shudder at the amount of footprints time has left behind, and the amount of cud it has spat. To my frustration, I always peeked back, and I prayed for God to answer my prayer quickly.

FOUR

The Pandora Box

I

I lay in bed with two layers of socks on my feet. The weather was warm, yet I wanted as much warmth as I could get. I had on a pair of jeans. Underneath my corduroy jacket, buttoned down to trap in heat, two layers of shirts drank my sweat. And I swaddled myself in a blanket, feeling the burning of the mentholated balm rubbed on my right arm. I woke up in the morning with pain in the arm, and I had remained in bed since then, nurturing the arm. Called 'crisis', it was a pain characteristic of my genotype, which carried the sickle cell trait.

This was my condition on the April morning when one of my brothers from Oyo walked in unannounced. It was Brother Isiaka, nicknamed Sico, though I was not surprised to see him. He was in the habit of checking on me whenever he was in town.

In my family, I had individuals representing ideals. Sico was an embodiment of endurance, boldness, enterprise, and courage. He was like an eagle, always willing and daring to fly. "What's the matter with you?" he asked, looking uncharacteristically worried.

"I'm having pain in my arm." My voice was thin with illness. To my annoyance, the pain usually came with fatigue, which caused me as much trouble as the pain. Sometimes I could completely ignore the pain, while it eased off, but I could not ignore the fatigue. It was worse.

"Sorry," he said, as he checked my temperature with the back of his right hand. "Have you taken any medicine?"

"Yes, I'm only waiting for it to relieve me. It shouldn't take much time," I replied, as if I had had a private discussion with God and He had assured me.

Sico stayed with me a little, and then went outside to the veranda. After a little while, I got up and joined him. He leaned his body over the rail and I did the same by his side. The pain was still in my arm, torturing me, but I felt like talking with him. Besides, I did not like to be seen down, sick.

I noticed that Sico looked low in spirit. Although he was naturally gentle, this was unusual. He would have been chatting away with one or another of my uncles or aunts, or even with Baba. Baba liked him and liked to talk with him. One other thing he was always respected for was his wide knowledge of current affairs. He knew what was going on in all parts of the world, he knew who was the leader of where, and it was from him many current affairs arguments in the family were often resolved. But here he was, keeping to himself like a xenophobic stranger. I knew something was wrong, but I guessed it was one of his economic problems. The wings of his eagle had been lacking in oil lately. I tried to chat with him.

"What's up with you?" I asked.

"Ganiyat is gone," he said in a low voice.

In the next moment I became paralyzed. The pain in my arm stopped, or I forgot it existed. I stared at him, wanting him to say more, but he did not. I understood him all right. My sister Ganiyat had died.

"When?" I finally asked in shock.

"The day before yesterday. They brought her home yesterday evening and she had since been buried."

"What caused it?"

"They said she complained of stomach discomfort and she was taken to the hospital where she later died. You should come with me to Oyo; I don't see why anyone of you should treat even a minor ailment away from home anymore."

I understood him. He wanted me to come home with him for treatment in the traditional way. My father knew a lot of traditional medicine men. Traditional or alternative medicine was gaining strong hold in Nigerian healing community, and it appeared that the poor economy was making the expensive mainstream medicine lose the hold to it.

"Did you come to pick me?" I asked him.

"No, I came to fix my car, so I decided to let you know, because I knew you wouldn't have heard. Everyone has been so shocked at home that no one is remembering anyone anywhere."

I went with him.

Ganiyat's death was a big loss to our family. I did not know what to make of the news; I just sat there in Sico's Peugeot 504 station wagon that had seen the last of its good days. The car looked ready to fall to pieces at the smallest collision. It was like an old woman who was living her last days and must always have a nurse. Sico was the nurse. He was exceptionally good at driving and caring for automobiles, but this was not what made him stick to the old hag. It was his endurance in the face of the country's battered economy and poor financial stand of the family. His strong will and enterprising spirit made him believe he could rise up to a good business by running the car commercially.

Many times I had looked at Sico and pitied him. Once very famous in the town, he was someone who had always been making love to brand new dream cars of my father's fleet and stock. Now he only masturbated with an old, sickly one. But as we drove home, I only sat in the front passenger seat, uncaring of anything in the world and gazing into the face of my sister through the windshield. I remembered her in her family-famous extraordinarily gymnastic body, her dark chocolate color, her gentle but firm character, her forehead and beautiful eyes. As the sun baked me through the windshield, I said to myself, "She's gone, and I will never see her anymore."

On our way Sico kept talking to me, telling me how he would revamp the car against all odds. He wanted to take my mind off the event, but I was not anymore in the mood to talk. I only nodded or shook my head as the situation alternately required. It was my turn to be unusually calm. It was an unusual situation, so painful that I did not remember the pain in my arm until late in the evening.

***

The past months had been a struggle. I had been going to fulfill appointments with Chief Bernard only to be given another one. The painter had told me that the most time it could take him was about a month, but more than three months had passed and I had not seen any visa.

Still, I was assured by Chief Bernard's personality, confidence, and words. Although he sometimes appeared a little concerned about how the process was taking so long, he was never in doubt about getting the visa. Playing the waiting game may be nerve-racking, but all I needed was to keep myself going, attuned with the waiting. The extra time may not be too much a price to pay for something that meant the rest of my life, I often counseled myself. I had already been waiting for about twenty-five months, then three or four months should not be my waterloo. When preachers said we should be patient as we prayed and worked toward our goals, I found strength in their teaching, although the famous addendum "God's time is the best" made me a little uncomfortable. While I believed the maxim, I did not like to reference it to my situation. It made me feel as if it might not yet be God's time for me, while I wanted the American visa right now. "God's time is the best and God's time is now," I always said to myself whenever the thought came into my mind.

Uncle Jibola called and told me he might visit Nigeria in November if he got his Green Card, and that if I had not got the visa by then, he would find something to do about it when he comes. With a better immigration status, he thought he might be able to clinch it for me. But I always believed I would have flown across the Atlantic Ocean by then, and never liked to think myself as hoping and waiting that long. Soon, I would be there with him, I always thought, very soon.

***

It now appeared that Mr. Okunwole did not want to give back my money, but I was determined to collect it. I got there one morning and met about six clients waiting for him in his secretary's office. There was hardly a space for me to sit, but I finally cramped myself somewhere. Someone was in his office and we waited. Everyone looked on their own, not even caring for any other's business. I wondered how many of us hoped to collect valuables from him; visa, money, anything.

Suddenly, a woman burst out preaching. This was not a time for that, I thought. No one seemed interested, yet she continued. Although they were increasingly becoming a nuisance, sometimes I gave credits to the evangelists who preached in public places. In most circumstances people wished they would shut up, still they preached. I was too shy to make a public speech, not to say to preach religion.

As one person came out of Mr. Okunwole's office, another entered. Soon it would be my turn. I no longer trusted the man, at least not any more than a cat worshipping in the kitchen. He had lied several times, and I knew he was still going to do it today. But I was boiling inside and determined to erupt on him like an angry volcano. I was determined to stop his game today. I had only been respecting him for his age, as custom required, but his character had withered that out.

The preacher really meant business as she continued with fervor, pouring out what she called the Word of God. I sat directly opposite her and she was looking into my face more than any other's, now using the wretched state of Nigeria to preach. The high prices of everything, the corruption, and every economic disease that was ailing the nation, all became tools for her preaching. She wrapped them all together and called it a sure sign of the end of the world.

Some people do not see beyond their noses, I thought, wondering at her argument that was not making any appeal to me. "Do you know there's someone who can save us out of all these problems?" she then asked. Maybe the question was for no one in particular, but she was staring into my eyes, with a self-righteous smile on her face - a good oratorical trick to send home a message. I did not disappoint her. I stared back in a manner that told her I was attentive. But she did not know that I was listening to her not because I wanted to hear her words but because I did not want to make her feel ignored. That, I often did for the preachers that had come my way. I listened to everyone not so much for their preaching as for their humanness, their being humans like I was, wanting to share and wanting attention when they talked. I always cared about others' feelings.

I knew what answer she wanted from me, but I did not want to make it a sitting duck for her. To me, she had not preached reasonably enough to deserve her expected answer. All the problems she mentioned were economic and political. If our economic and political woes meant the end of the world was near, then the world must just be beginning or reaching midday in countries like the United States, Japan, Britain, and the other high-income nations. The economies of these countries were impressively booming, hence Nigeria and other troubled nations must be the only target of her God's apocalypse. That was not a logical preaching to me and I was not going to let her get away with the shallow thinking.

"My dear brother, who is this savior that is going to save us from these troubles?" she asked again, with a typical smug expression lining her face.

I tried not to laugh as I brought myself to reply her. "Abiola. Chief M. K. O. Abiola."

Everyone in the room burst out laughing. We were close to the much-expected June 12 presidential election of 1993 and Abiola was my candidate. The preacher, also, could not help but laugh. For her as well, and everyone there, Abiola was the candidate of choice for the nation's first office - the only ' Hope '93 ', as often referred to.

"Yes, yes. I know that Abiola could help us in all these problems, but there is a more superior savior that I mean and he is Jesus Christ," she explained.

I considered reminding her that Jesus Christ was not in the presidential race. She preached on and on until it reached my turn to go in to meet Mr. Okunwole.

After the usual greetings, Mr. Okunwole dabbled into his usual stories. He looked sickening to me now. His countenance no longer appeared honest; every twist of it read *deception* to my eyes, and his teeth-showing smiles ran the word into my head.

I became angry, and, with ice in my voice, I interrupted him and uncompromisingly demanded my money. I refused to leave his office if he did not pay me back my money, and I succeeded in making the situation so intense that he paid me half the money.

Later in July, he gave me a check for the remaining half, but it bounced. By the time I stormed into his office, he was out of the city. The chance of getting back the remaining of my money, thus, became unstable, and eventually lost - lost forever, because I did not go to him anymore. It was not that I did not want to go there, however; it was that before he could return to Ibadan, the story of my life had turned around and made it unnecessary to go there anymore.

***

For Chief Bernard, it was an increasing struggle to continue going to his place every fortnight, though I still believed something would come out of it, and it would be an American visa. I took it as a war. There is no victory when there is no war. I wanted victory, so I urged myself on and fought on. But I was not totally relaxed. A sense of uncertainty clouded over my head and sometimes frightened me. However, whenever the worse tended toward the worst, I calmed myself with November. At least, Uncle Jibola would come in November, I always thought. If I have not got a way by then, he would save the day. I looked at November as my last resort.

***

On the 12th of June I went to perform my duty to vote in the presidential election. The modern life of Nigeria had been too much lived through horrible roads than for young people like me to ignore the right thing. Coup de tat, counter coup de tat, civil war, ethnic wars, religious wars, corruption, neglect of the masses, and so on; these were the inglorious events that largely made up the history of the young nation. If Chief Abiola became the president, people believed the pressures on Nigerians within an outside the country would reduce, as Nigeria would become a better country. For one, the foreign countries and their embassies would have more respect for us and less suspicion for our visa applications.

My spirit was up with the Social Democratic Party, SDP, the party of Chief Abiola. In our neighborhood I often engaged in heated debates with the representatives of the main opposing party, National Republican Convention, NRC. I did not want them to take people in our neighborhood away from SDP. There was high hope in the air. The price of Volkswagen Beetle was expected to come down more than five hundred percent, and I had been priding myself to be worth about five Volkswagen Beetles in the coming weeks. In the few days after the election, when it had become obvious to everyone that Chief Abiola had won, the prices of many things plummeted and faith in Nigeria as a country with great destiny began to germinate in people's hearts.

Then it came as a shattering shock when the self-made military president, General Ibrahim Badamasi Babangida, conspiratorially annulled the election. For the first time in my life, I regretted being a Nigerian. My hope in the country wavered. I wished I was born anywhere but Nigeria. I loathed the military and I wanted to support a secession doctrine that would cut off the Hausa people. It was as if it was the northern tribe against the rest of the country on the issue of the seat of power. The British favored the Hausas because they offered little resistance to colonial rule. Hence, in the hope of using that as a British asset toward a continuing, though stealthy, control over Nigeria, they left behind an ethnically imbalanced federal government that divided the country. However, I regained my foothold properly when I realized that it had become only a conspiracy of a northern clique, and not of the entire northern people. Since the first Nigerian coup in 1966, which the Hausa leadership interpreted as an ethnic one by the Igbos, the clique had been caballing to keep the power to the north, which was where the colonists' conspiracy left it. Majority of the Hausa people were as much victims of the current situation as the rest of us, even though many of them had come to view it their ethnic pride to produce the leadership of the country, democratically or militarily forced. Now, realizing that the pride was not the same as progress, most of the Hausas also voted for Chief Abiola, a Yoruba man, and against a Hausa candidate. This landslide decision trimmed off our ethnicity and redefined us all as Nigerians. Regrettably, many people did not look at it this way. During the protest against the government that followed, there were bloody clashes among the tribes in the southwest, by which I almost got killed by angry Hausas.

I took to the streets along with thousands of youths in protest of the outrageous annulment and had a little taste of how a nation could be in wartime. Rampaging youths were everywhere; bonfires, roads emptied of vehicles, unfriendly smoke and tear gas seeping through our nostrils, lethal bullets flying sporadically in the air, and angry songs like soundtracks filling our ears. It was horrible, and it claimed many lives before people strangely and unexpectedly became tired of protesting. Ibadan, one of the liveliest cities in Africa, became a ghost of itself.

Perhaps Babangida was the most cunning of all the Heads of State Nigeria had ever had. It was surprising to see the protests go down as it did, after it had begun promisingly as the Philippines' protest that ousted Ferdinand Marcos about a decade earlier. We would have used the power of the people to oust the clique that fed ironically on our support, a support made up of our anger and rejection for the government but leashed by our fear and greed. I was later to know that the self-proclaimed evil genius of a president had punctured the protesting strength of the people by dispatching gifts to the various key mobilizing positions among the people. The labor force's organization and its leadership were thus divided, with government cash flowing to its key players. The leaders of the transport workers, a key mobilizing unit, rode in beautiful official cars given by the president; and they all eventually saw no more need to protest against the subversive government. I saw this country as goddamned and my regrets of being born there persisted a little longer.

With a strong fear of another civil war lurking in our hearts, we waited to see what would become of August 27th, the date the military government proposed to handover to a civilian government. The masses were tired of Babangida and the entire military rule, and we waited in anger and fear. Among the youths in my neighborhood a funny fear was making the rounds. We might soon be forced to Ghana as refugees, where we would become itinerant shoe repairers and shiners called *so bata,* as the Ghanaians had come to do when they were in their own political troubles more than a decade earlier. It was that bad, and I only wondered whether Ghana would allow us after the brutal act of forcing them back home by our previous military government. Although the Ghanaian government started the xenophobic madness between the two countries, I thought that as one good turn deserves another, one bad turn may continue to bring forth another. Regrettably, as it is the ordinary people who suffer their government's crazy policies, it was we who would have to suffer it, if it came. For me, it would only be a second-time suffering. From my primary school days to my early secondary school, my friendship circle had been made up of Indians and Ghanaians. But they were both the peoples targeted by the cruel laws, and I was left all alone and to look for new friends when they were all forced out of the country. I do not know why we could not be left alone to live wherever we liked in the world.

II

In August, General Babangida finally 'stepped aside' from Aso Rock, the federal State House, and instituted an impotent transition government. Also, I spent two nights in a hospital bed for fever. I cannot remember the last time I was at a hospital. It had been a long time, and a longer time that I had last been admitted - sometime over a decade and a half, perhaps.

The waiting game was now becoming a big problem for me. Going to the libraries and the construction site could no longer comfort me enough. I needed more engagements to ease my mind from worrying over my situation. For the weekends, I indulged in my club, going every Saturday and Sunday to give myself completely to its romance. Whenever I was angry or bitter, swimming was the treatment I turned to. And sometimes, when there were a lot of people at the club to make friends with, the club offered a good hiding place from the world's troubles. Once in a while new people came for fun, and, especially, to learn swimming. We, the regular club boys who knew how to swim, were always enthusiastic to teach them, especially the girls.

It was fun teaching the girls to swim, and anyone of us who had the good fortune to teach a pretty girl had the envy and respect of the other boys. He would feel on top of the world as he went about his duty, and would take sly glances at the coveting eyes of the unfortunate ones to prink his ego. We did not do it as a duty, or out of goodwill, but for our own pleasure, and the slower a girl learned the better for us.

Sometimes, there were new boys who could also do with some help. Not only did they have unwilling teachers, most of them also did not like to be seen as unable to swim. Boys' ego, one may say, especially when girls were around. They would go on breaking the rules meant to restrict amateurs, unwillingly taking in swills of water, having red eyes, and incurring the scolding of the lifeguards who had the difficult task of watching over the swimming multitude. The lifeguards' task, sometimes, also brought insults upon them, as naughty boys who felt themselves embarrassed sometimes rebuffed their warnings and scolding. All these made the swimming pool side of the club interesting, and a place for me to let out the troubling emotions of my increasing frustration.

I also did not know how to swim when I began using the club and I did not want to be viewed as such. So, I did not want anyone to teach me while the many others looked. Instead, I arranged and paid one of the lifeguards who taught me on a weekday morning when there was no one at the swimming pool. It was only he and I, and he spent an hour teaching me to swim in the shallow side of the pool. He wanted extra money for the deep end, but I refused him.

The next weekend I stubbornly tried to swim over and across the deep end. I had learned to float and swim at the shallow end and I thought I could transfer it to the deep end without any problem. I moved close to the deep end to start, so I would have enough breath to swim across and far to the other side before I would stop. It was a careful decision and I launched myself ahead.

All was well until I reached the middle of the deep end. Realizing that I was on a surface with a bottom beyond the reach of my feet, a place where I had no control of myself, I panicked. I knew it was purely psychological, but I could not keep it only at that. It became physical, and in the next moment I was struggling for my life as I felt myself going down. I remembered an old classmate who died in the same pool less than a year earlier and I feared for my life.

I tried to hold on to the sidebar that guided the pool's gutter. I had been cautious enough to try my experiment close to the sidebar so I could save myself if things went wrong. Now, things had gone wrong and I was trying to use it to save myself. But it was not easy.

There were plenty of people at the pool and, to make it worse, there were plenty of girls there. It was like the whole of the city was there. There were some boys who had more mischief in their heads than places to enact them. We called those boys *monkeys*, because they were as mischievous as monkeys. My current situation was a golden opportunity for them, and they would play it to the extreme if they saw me. Because of this, I wanted no one to see me, and yet I did not want to die there.

I went some feet down the water and got one inevitable swill down my throat. I floundered about. Then my head resurfaced above the water level. I saw that I had drifted a little away from the sidebar. I further struggled to grab the bar, and as I floundered I saw one of the lifeguards hurrying toward me. He knelt close to me and stretched out his hand into the water to help me out. I knew he would pull me out ridiculously that all the girls would see me, and the *monkeys* around would amplify the embarrassment. I ignored his hand and tried further to grab the sidebar by myself.

But I went down the water again. I kept on the struggle, with fear in my heart - fear of drowning on the one hand, and of ridicule on the other. I struggled and floundered. Then the water surged me up again, and this time I was lucky. I reached the sidebar and used it to drag myself out. While I tried to catch some breath, I looked around for mocking faces. I did not see any. I thanked God they missed the show.

"I have warned you not to come to this side..." The lifeguard said to me in a low but angered tone. He could not shout at me for his own reasons. I had been his illegal client. Though he was the one I paid to teach me how to swim, he collected money from me in place of the official tickets.

I waved him off stubbornly so he would not attract undue attention. He could not protest against my insulting attitude; he had sold his right for my every day one naira. But I was only insulting out of the fear of shame for my face. I had hardly relaxed when two guys came up to me and told me they saw the whole drama and that I was lucky no one else saw me or really knew what was going on. They were not of the *monkeys*. They offered to show me how to swim at the deep end and I accepted.

"First, you need to know how deep this end is and it will take away your fear," one of them said, and they held my hands on each side and pulled me down to the bottom of the pool.

It was not much of a depth, I discovered – only about ten feet deep. They pulled me out, and then we went down again. This time, we sat down on the floor of the pool, as we had agreed to do. When I needed to breathe, I pinched them, as prearranged, and they pulled me out. This exposure trick took away my fear. They taught me how to swim and I became a master of the pool, although not enough to try the Olympics; only to enjoy myself and to catch some sensuous swimming contracts. This was how I enjoyed my weekends.

However, the weekdays became increasingly boring. Idleness is the font of boredom, they say. There was not much to do at the construction site anymore, and everyday I spent more hours at the U.S.I.S. After that there was nothing else for me to do and I loitered around. I needed to get to America. I needed to get a life started.

The unfolding frustration was creating a dam to my emotions. Sometimes the pressure was so strong that I would feel like wriggling out and onto one of the American streets I had seen in movies, the way one would wriggle out of a horrible nightmare. I began to feel that the way life was treating me was not fair.

III

It may be that I shall fade, fade and die,
I, the young corn stalk…
A song of the Aztec god, Xipe.

Finally, I began to spend away some weekdays at the Student Union Board building, S.U.B., at the University of Ibadan, sometimes alone, but many times with my on-campus friends. I had backed away from them at first because I wanted to concentrate fully on my dream, now I came back so as not to dream my head off in my waiting.

Perhaps this was a wrong step in my life. Perhaps, not. But if I knew what was waiting there for me, I might not have taken the step. I might have consciously chosen a different destiny. It is funny how life is. When we are not consciously making decisions, we seem to be making them unconsciously, and even when we are consciously making them, we still seem to be making them unconsciously. And how are we to know? Mortal little humans, we are.

One day, I was at the S.U.B., spending the afternoon away. The S.U.B. was a big building with an open space sandwiched between the building and a hall. It had a few shops and stalls around the open space for petty traders, and it had some eateries and bars alongside. There was a pool table that made the place lively, and music came loudly from one of the bars. As always, the place was bubbling, like a rollicking school party. Boys and girls went about their leisure activities, among whom were humans and beasts. Cigarettes smokes mingled with the sound of Hip Hop, and they danced together in a modern Carmina Burana.[15] This was what made school fun.

By *beasts*, I mean members of the secret cults who terrorized other students on campus. Secret cultism was a major disease in Nigerian universities. We felt them in the air, but hardly knew the members. They lived like the Mafia, and the few we knew, or thought we knew, we feared. In later years they would become worse than beasts. But, right now, they were the least of my worries. I sat at a table in a far corner, enjoying the shade of the lone tree in the place. Surprisingly, I had a cigarette burning between my fingers.

This was surprising because I had only just picked up the habit again recently. My despondent situation had been draining my self-worth, and I thought I needed this to give me the required hardness I thought I needed to become part of the campus community. Most students smoked cigarettes, and many even smoked marijuana. Now I smoked cigarettes whenever I was at the S.U.B.

I had first picked up the habit in my final year at the secondary school, but when I realized I was not gaining anything from it, and that I was only being a copycat, I dropped it. I hated to see myself copying anyone. Now I was enjoying it. Not for any characteristic taste, though - just enjoyment. May be it was only psychological, but, of course, psychological events do have remarkable influence on human lives. Sometimes I thought that if I were given a mere folded paper, without knowing, it probably would have given me the same pleasure. Perhaps there was a little tinge of substance excitement lost in the play of my mentality, but holding and pulling at the cigarette was enough. For the fore and middle fingers to hold the stick was itself fashionable.

On this evening, I was enjoying my smoke when two of my friends joined me at the table. They were among the closest friends I had on campus. Segun Adekunle, lean and tall with a windbreaker that seemed born with him, sat beside me. He ordered drinks for the three of us and cigarettes for him and Kehinde Akintunde, who was also of the same stature.

"Roth," Kehinde said to the bar man, to be clear on their favorite. Although I also smoked Rothmans, I did not think I felt any difference in all the cigarettes. And that became the topic of the moment.

"Why do you always take Roth?" I asked Kehinde.

"Roth gives you the thrill," he replied.

"I don't feel any difference in all of them," I said, "They don't move me.

---

[15] In Medieval Europe, Carmina Burana is a form of students' music of profanity.

It's like I take nothing, sometimes."

"Maybe your system is too strong for it. But if you try Moore, you'd feel it." Segun put in.

I had tried that too and I told them. In a way, I was maneuvering myself back to a complete acceptance of the fact that I was gaining nothing from cigarettes. This would finally make me drop the habit again. The maneuvering was not something I had been contemplating before, however; it just sprang out there and then. But it was out of my self-criticism. I was someone who internalized his experiences for self-scrutiny. Oftentimes, when people would say, 'they like this', 'they like that,' I would say I like it too, but to later realize I did not really like it. So, I wanted to be learning to know myself, and be myself anytime I did or said anything.

The only time that tobacco had excited me was when I smoked raw tobacco leaves during the month of my school certificate examinations. The tobacco had been part of the specimens we were required to identify as part of the testing in the Agricultural Science exam. After the exam, I kept mine in my school bag, and even went back to the hall with some friends to collect the other students' specimens after they had left the hall. It really did excite me; one puff, and my head was already dancing and my crotch tingling.

But these cigarettes did not do that to me. I realized I was the one actually stimulating myself, and the cigarettes may only have been destroying my health.

"There's a cigarette over there," Kehinde said, pointing at a variety stall. "It's not longer than this," he described on his finger a size about half the normal cigarette size, "and one stick will definitely hook you, no matter how strong you are."

"Then, let me try it and see," I asked.

We bought three sticks, and, at Segun's request, we proceeded toward Agbowo, the neighborhood opposite the campus. He hoped to meet his new girlfriend at my uncle's site and we waited to try the cigarettes there. The girl's house was on the same street as my uncle's site, and about a stone throw apart. I commanded respect in the neighborhood and Segun hoped to use it to his advantage over the girl. There were two other girls in her group, all of whom I had an impression on. They saw me as a cute and well-dressed guy, and I was building the most impressive and expensive house in their neighborhood, a modern house years ahead of the rest there. Though, they knew it belonged to my uncle, still it was easy to deceive them that I also had something going, especially when aided by my fine apparels and mastered manner.

After the girls had left us, we lit the dwarf cigarettes. Still, it did not excite me, or I thought it did not. I dropped the butt contemptuously and laughed, as if mocking my friends, who seemed to have become bent upon exciting me with the substance, perhaps to make me appear less unique. By this time I had lost count of the number of cigarettes I had smoked that day. But it did not matter to me. I had been a chain-smoker in the last few weeks.

"You need to take weed to get *shacked* (excited), then," Segun said.

"Yes, *efo* will definitely *shack* you," Kehinde added, using another name for the same stuff. "Should we go for it?"

Literally, *efo* means vegetable, the kind used for a variety of soup, but, as here, it was one of the slang-names for marijuana. Some people also call it *Nigerian hemp*, a name that Fela Kuti gave it in place of "Indian hemp," because, he said, it was not grown in India but in Nigeria. I believed weed could excite me, and I might not really need to take it, but I felt like experimenting. I knew my two friends were not new to it. They had mentioned it a few times before, though I had never given in to its lure or their persuasion. But now, my despondency in the face of my visa search had left me drowning in my mind, and my moral fibers were no longer strong enough to hold the little rectitude I had from going down with me.

The closest I had ever got to marijuana was at Kehinde's birthday party earlier in the year, yet I did not take it. After Kehinde's mother was done with the party's cooking and out of the kitchen, Kehinde and Segun mixed marijuana and alcohol in the fruit punch she made. Everyone who took it went sky-high and the party became as wild as they had hoped.

"It would make the girls forego all their inhibitions and respond very well," Kehinde had boasted to me before the party. "Guys now use it at parties. You'd rock and lay a girl who would snob you on campus the next day when sober."

It was an *easy rock* and *easy lay* concoction that most of the girls did not know about. They only jumped at a sweet punch at any good party and walked into an emotional elevator. Guys would then seize the opportunity to have what we thought as real fun with the weed-made zombies, sometimes singing humorous puns made from music lyrics. "Hip Hop Hurray" by *Naughty by Nature* was a favorite; the chorus made a good obscene pun when phrased into vernacular, spreading the message among boys that "these are free *lays*, so don't waste the opportunity." We would recite it so fast that the girls, who were already dope-crazy, would miss the message. Perhaps we are all truly naughty by nature.

That day at Kehinde's party, I had meant to take the *weeded* punch for experimentation and deliberately to lose my individuality in the orgiastic frolic, hoping to get into the fun, but I wanted to wait until after the *asri* salat, the third obligatory prayer of the day. It was around the time I was becoming more religious and I could not pray with alcohol and weed in my blood, as preachers warned against. Besides, one could stumble, as I had seen one of my cousins did at salat after being drunk one evening. He almost rolled over when he bowed to touch the ground with his forehead.

Kehinde's father had a mosque at their house and I decided to have my salat in there. Although, preachers said it was better to observe the prayers at their appointed times of the day than to repay them later, I even saw it burdensome to miss the time and have to lump them together at night.

This was what I wanted to avoid by observing asri before I took the weed. It would trim the obligations down to the last two for repayment later in the night at home. Two would be easier to repay, I thought.

But I did not take the punch after the worship. I realized I would not be able to observe the remaining two until I had slept off the substances in my blood, by which I might lazily end up not observing them at all. This was the worst attitude to salats, so I further decided to delay taking the punch until after the last two salats of the day, which I completed at about 7:30 pm.

The party was still swinging in full motion by the time I finished all the prayers. Everyone was slaphappy. One would think that the girls' boobs and bums would fall off. They were all high and doing extreme justice to the Raga and Hip-Hop songs, except for two gorgeous girls that remained on their seats. One of them was Kehinde's girlfriend and the other was her friend. Kehinde had told his girlfriend of the weed in the punch and they stayed away from it. The two girls liked the idea of a calm-headed guy to keep their company as I had been doing before I completed my salats. Kehinde's girl and I had a lot of respect for each other, so I granted their request to stay with them clear-headed till the end of the party. Because of this, I eventually could not take the punch. Afterall, what could be as high as the company of two cool-headed, beautiful girls, hotly dressed, especially, when one of them was free of a date and thought I was cute. With them, I enjoyed the night, although I could not completely take my eyes off the shaking rumps that surrounded me. African women were best in rump-dancing, and the men liked them big, supple, and able to roll to beats; that way we thought them healthy, and not when anorexic. In the olden days they would wear beads around their waist so that it added to the music as it rocked to the drums. By this, the Yorubas often appraisingly called a so-blessed lady as "*idi ileke*", that is, "the beaded behind."

Feeling like experimenting on this day at the site, I agreed to go for the weed. They were enthusiastic. The more people you have around you doing a thing with you the more confidence you have doing it. That was what their psychological state seemed to be craving for, wanting me to join their marijuana-smoking club.

We headed for Bodija market where they said the best stuff was. A small voice rang in my head, telling me not to do it, but another, to which I readily submitted, persuaded it along. It made it fair-seeming to the first by repeatedly telling it that it was just on experimentation. However, I still had to drag the part of me that belonged to the first voice. Sometime later in my life, with a little more knowledge of human mental activities, I came to wonder which voice it was that advised me not to go and take the hemp: an intuitional voice from my soul or a voice of an internalization of my parents and society's value? But I was sure the other voice was an experimenting emotion with youthful limitation and vigor, like the one that drove the Prodigal Son, and which seemed ruthless to seemliness. And it was stronger.

Coming off a bus, we crossed the road and walked on to the vast space of land in front of the market, where there was an incessant stream of people to and from the market. I hoped not to meet anyone who knew me around the place. My guilty conscience was concerned. We did not take the main entrance to the market. Instead, we walked a little up along the wall of the cattle section and took the turning at the cattle stalls. It led into the inner side of the market that I had never before been, and, as we walked on, something happened.

We met a stall on our way, owned by a woman in my neighborhood. The woman was there with her daughter, a friend of mine, and they both saw me. I greeted them as we passed by, a little worried, but I tried not to think too much about it. Something pulled me to where we were going. A dog that would stray in the forest would not hear the call of his hunter-owner. He would not listen.

We reached the far end corner of the market where the prohibited stuff was sold. It was a secret world, all right - a hell of a place. Although, it remained a part of the market, it had drifted, hidden away from the main market. The kind of people who littered around there were obviously initiated people of the forbidden world. It was filthy. I could not distinguish the odor of marijuana from that of a refuse dump of rotten animal flesh. The cattle division of the market had an abattoir and this place was the dirt-dump corner of the market. Moreover, it also stank of something rotten in human nature that made me uncomfortable.

About five young men hanged around the place, startled on sighting us. Segun calmed them down, telling them that we were from the campus.

"I thought you were law guys," one of them with dark goggles said. "Those finks never let us rest here. They don't mind their fucking business."

Girls of their sort hanged around, coming and going as some of the men rubbed their hands on their bodies in sex-solicitous manners. The one with goggles was the most sex-hungry. His goggles were as black as a moonless night sky. And as threatening. The girls shook off his hands like he was a debtor they knew would not pay for the service. There was smoke of marijuana in the air, as they passed some sticks among them.

"Give us N2 worth," Segun said to one of them who lay on a table, as if on a hospital casualty bed and drawing his last breath with an almost unconscious effort. He was the one selling the weed. Like the others, he had no shirt to cover his dirty and skinny body. The weather was hot and he was *stoned* out of all his senses, except a tenuous one that sold the hemp and ready to pick up signals of approaching cops, if they came. His eyes were shiny under their drooping lids, which he must be having a tough time to keep open. His hands trembled as he fumbled for the bhang in his pocket. In an irritating way, he seemed to me as not of this world.

I looked at him and wondered whether it was true as they said that weed gave strength. It had taken away all the strength in this goblin in front of me, and he looked as if he was begging nature to live. If I was a doctor, and he my patient, I would not have any hope for his survival and I would send him to the mortuary to save the cost of treatment. To keep me at ease, my friends assured me that he must have taken the hemp many hours before and he must have taken too much.

"How much?" He asked, croaking out his words as if he had an anguished toad in his throat.

"Two naira," Segun repeated. If there had been life in is eardrum, he would have heard Segun the first time. With a trembling hand, he handed the bhang to Segun who expertly rolled it up into a stick, lighted it, and handed it to me. I pulled at it, a few tokes, and gave it back to Segun, who also took some tokes and passed it on to Kehinde. Kehinde remarked that I did not inhale it properly, and, by a toke, he showed me how the smoke I exhaled had been thick instead of being thin as his own was. Virgin lungs, mine were.

I knew how I took cigarettes; it was a slight fear that hindered me at first. Then I inhaled it again, and the smoke that came out of my lungs this time was thin. Being the one on experiment, I was left to take about half the stick. My friends took some of the remnant and offered the remaining to the guy with dark goggles. He snapped at it as fast as a lizard snaps at a fly, and from the way he burned it down, it was obvious that my friends were only amateurs.

When we reached the stall woman from my neighborhood on our way back, she offered us some *Tom Tom* peppermint candies, well known as a choice for smokers and drinkers trying to cover up their breath. We thanked her and walked on toward the main street.

We were halfway to the street when my mind began to reflect on her decision to give us the *Tom Tom*, and I thought she must have known why we were there. Though I had lied to her that we were going to see someone in there, I realized that since she had been selling stuff here for a long time, she must have known about the marijuana joint at the back of the market. She must have been seeing campus guys like us going there everyday, passing by her stall. She might have been suspicious of us. Then, she gave us the *Tom Tom*, of all the various candies she was selling. I concluded that she had not been fooled. Growing up among market women around my grandmother's shop, I had learned that they were so smart they often did not pass messages directly among themselves; they spoke with their eyes, manners, gestures, and actions. Thus, I thought this woman might be using the candies to make the statement that "I know why you're here, boys."

I tried to point this out to Segun and Kehinde as we walked on out of the place, but they did not see my point. They thought the weed was already taking control and I was beginning to think as in smoker-madness. They already had the candies in their mouths and I could see the bulges on their cheeks as they mocked that I have begun to talk too much. I felt ridiculed.

"I'm not feeling anything from the weed yet," I said angrily. "Can't you use your head? Why did she give us *Tom Tom* of all the candies on her shelves?" I asked as I walked angrily past them. They did not reply me. When I turned to look back at them, to imply that I required a reasonable response, they were still engaged in their mockery, and were now laughing conspiratorially.

I became angrier and yelled at them, "Why this rubbish, you dummies?" That made them laugh more, infuriating me. I hated the sight of them and I thought they were more than just dummies. They were foolish dummies. The sight of them looked strange and sickening to me now; they made me feel like something was wrong with me and I turned to walk away from them.

Then, suddenly, I had a vertiginous fit. I felt as if my consciousness had just come back into me, renewed, and as if from a kind of state of stillness in nature. When did it leave me? I could not ask myself and I could not even know, but I knew there was fluctuation in my consciousness at that moment and there was a time lapse. Then I became frightened. I became frightened for my life and of my life, as well as angry with my friends. Out of this confusion, I yelled more angry words at them and trudged on to the main street, almost aimlessly. I was now unsure of what would or could happen next, and I was terribly frightened.

In the moment, I had lost my natural sense of security. It was as if I had become hyper-self-conscious. I became more conscious of my individuality, and it brought upon me an accompanying mental responsibility for my security. Now aware of my mental limitation at maintaining such an individual security, it became a sense of vulnerability. I needed to reach home quickly, to get away from the scene. But I was apparently so shaken that I did not have a clear mind of how to go about it. The existence of the sense of security in the human psyche, which maintains our psychic integrity, was one I had never been aware of; neither did I realize of what value it was until this moment when I lost it. I was no longer in control of my composure. I was no longer in control of my life. I seemed too alive than I could handle.

My friends were now certain that I was *stoned* and they ran after me. They had to help me. Kehinde grabbed me first as I hit the main road. I did not realize I was walking into the paths of fast moving trucks. I had become morbidly excited and I felt the vertigo persisting.

"What's the matter with you Rahman?" Kehinde barked at me. "You're going to get yourself killed. You got to calm down."

At this point, I became hysterical. I was miles away from calmness, sweating profusely in the heat, and I was badly in need of fresh air. I wanted my shirt off, yet I did not anymore have the slightest patience to unbutton it. I tore wildly at it, but its material would not easily give way to my madness. I only succeeded in breaking a button. One of my friends quickly unbuttoned the rest. Compunction swept over me, overwhelming me, like little stones on an angry seashore. My heart beat very fast and the society's morality took over. The various voices of warning against marijuana flashed in my head and I felt guilty and regretful of my action.

"I shouldn't have taken it," I said bitterly as I sank my head in my palms in anguish and remorse, dropping to the floor.

"Calm down. You'll get over it soon," one of my friends said.

But I could not calm down. I remembered stories of marijuana driving people crazy and feared I was going crazy already. I'd rather die, I thought. I'd rather not see such a day dawn in which, instead of my ebony hair, my head would be growing out my brain for people's scorn. Neither would I live to see myself walk around the streets with days and weeks and months of filth caked around my skin, as the uncared for crazy people in this part of the world did. I'll have to kill myself.

Yet, the thought of death also overwhelmed me on its own. It shifted from my thinking of killing myself to an idea of the possibility of being killed by this cause. And I trembled. Perhaps it is easier to face the thought of killing oneself than to face the idea of being killed by something else. In the former one has the sense of control, by which, of course, one could eventually stop it. The loss of the sense of control then seems to be the main factor behind all human problems.

I should not have taken it. Something they have been warning me against everyday of my life, I have taken it. I have thwarted all of my family and society's values and warnings, and now I am bearing the cross. I looked back on the years I had so far lived in my life and they seemed all like yesterday. No matter the amount of years one has spent in this world, our Imams always taught from the Qur'an, after death, one would think one had only tarried a few days or hours. In the jaws of death that I felt hold me here, I now saw my twenty-two years as like twenty-two minutes. I'm too young to die, I cried in my heart. My spirit begged for more years, more opportunity.

"Oh, my God, help me out. I don't want to die. I don't want to go crazy." I begged as the jaws of disaster tightened around my head, waiting to feed on me.

"Have I not wasted my life like this?" I was crying out now, tears streaming down my face. "All my hopes, all my dreams; have I not smoked them up in that fucking weed? Have I not smoked up my life away in that devil stick?" My friends kept trying to calm me, while I remembered an oft-played song by Funmi Adams, in which she warned youths against hard drugs. For the first time in my life, the song became precious. I wished time would reverse for me to take heed of the warning now, but the song kept playing in my head, like a soundtrack to intensify my misery. And it had a disturbing message: *Didn't we tell you? Now it has happened, and it couldn't unhappen.*

Suddenly, in the midst of the chaos, I became hungry. Perhaps this was because I had often heard that weed made people hungry, and I feared such hunger might aggravate my condition. I quickly told my friends I was hungry.

Promptly, they dragged me to a nearby restaurant a few meters further away from the main road. We had made a show on the street while people watched, and, to my friends, we could not remain there any longer. They cared about people's eyes. Life sometimes is ironic, as one of our fathers' sayings goes: "The source of sorrow for one person is but of laughter to another." What is funny to people about a crazy person's acts in the street is what makes his or her family sob in their rooms. The story of tragedy in one house is often an interesting thriller in another. For me, my life was the one at stake and I could not care for shame as my friends did.

I took a spoonful of rice from the dish placed in front of me. I had hoped to assuage my excitement, but the fright was too much for food and I had problems swallowing the spoonful in my mouth. I became sick of the food and I pushed the plate away.

"Let's take him to Good Life," Segun said, suggesting a motel at Bodija. "We could rent a room and let him sleep it off."

"No," I retorted. "I'm not going there. I'm going to our family doctor."

They became frightened. I was going to blow this thing into the open, they thought. They began to persuade me that it was going to be all right after some rest and I needed not expose the secret. Exposing them would have come easily. My grandparents would want to know the friends who took me there and to talk to their parents. All I would need to do was show their homes and my grandmother would put the blame on them. She would blame a mosquito for stinging me.

Finally, I agreed and we chartered a cab to take us to Good Life. But the receptionist noticed my condition and was scared off, especially seeing three young men asking for a room. Everyone was afraid of the secret cults, and our request could hint anyone of the danger. He declined to give us a room.

Monad Motel was close by and my friends decided to try our luck there. It was a walking distance from Good Life, so we walked. There we had to try harder to get a room. It was difficult for me to play along with them, but I managed. My mind was filled with morbid imaginations. On our way there, we climbed over a bridge and my mind strongly urged me to jump into the steep river beneath and end it there. It was a great effort for me to keep straight on the girder.

Kehinde asked for gari and the receptionist gave us a small cup of gari. He claimed it would calm down the effect of the marijuana, so I drank it.

As I lay down on the big bed, I closed my eyes to summon sleep, but I could not sleep. Instead, my mind dwelled on my condition. I saw the years of my life hewing down into worthless shreds, its edifice crumbling into shards. I saw myself spending my last days on earth, if not my last hours. I felt terrible about myself. How could this be happening to me? How could this be happening to my father this same year? He just lost a daughter, and here I am now lingering on the border of life and death. I remembered how my father loved his children.

My friends began to tell stories of how, sometimes, weed does on first-timers like me, but I was not with them as much as they thought I was. As never before, life became precious, so precious that I now recognized that it was also fragile. But why should something so important be so fragile? Why should something so fragile be so important? I thought I had not spent anything in my life; I was just beginning, and it would not be fair if I wasted away like this. And even, if I am going to die, this is a shameful way to go, shameful to myself and to my family.

I remembered my mother. As troubled as she was, how more troubled would she be to have her first and only son smother out of existence? Tears welled up in my eyes. I tried to force it back. I wished God had not created death and insanity. I wished He had not created weed; my life would not have been botched like this.

I did not come close to sleep. Staring blindly at the ceiling, I half-heard the stories my friends were telling. Kehinde was now talking of a boy who grabbed a machete after smoking his first weed. He said they were about five boys in a locked room where they were secretly smoking marijuana. Then the boy became *stoned* and threatened to butcher anyone who dared touch the door. No one could go out, not even to the toilet. They both laughed at the story, but I did not. I could not. I was too far away to find fun in anything. My mind drifted on to my grandmother.

Now she is at her shop, I thought on as I closed my eyes to see her more vividly in my mind's eyes. She knows nothing about what is happening to her grandson now. If these were going to be our last days together, how is she going to take it? I remembered how she had quarreled with some of our family members only for coming late to visit me at the hospital when I was admitted for fever in August. How then would she feel now if I died? I remembered a lot of things that evoked in me her empathic love. Tears flowed down my face as I tried to hide it from my friends. Oh my God, my grandmother could not live to see me crazy or dead.

I wanted to live, but I felt as if death wanted me so much. It was a distraction from life in the presence of my attraction to it, and I was sure one of them must prevail. Yet, the force of my attraction was weak. I thought life should not be this cruel to me. It should not be this cruel to my family. Sometimes I wished I did not have a family; I might not have had to worry this much.

This made me realize that people could allow themselves to slip into this hole of hard drugs and underworld because of absence of family love and security in their lives; no comfort and duty of love, therefore, no security. Then, instead, they develop lust, filling the vacuum left by love, left by the communality of love. Becoming overwhelmingly aware of their isolation, they feel socially insecure and seek security in the world outside. With this as their makeup, they become vulnerable to any damning influence out there. In a sense, Machiavelli may think that fear was a stronger emotion than love, but, in another sense, I think love is the only master that could tame out all the fangs of fear, and it catches them better when they are young. I remember an old-time friend of mine who, after his secondary school education, vowed his life to the underworld. He had grown up with no love around him, but lust, dislike, and distrust. Someone who has nothing loses nothing, he often said of himself. But for me, I had not 'nothing' to lose. I had my loving family and I had my career-dream; these made me know I had myself, something to lose, and I did not want to lose it. I did not want to be lost to my family.

FIVE

Bermuda Triangle

I

I needed to inspect something at Uncle Tunji's site, but I still slept again after I woke up for subhi. If not for my grandmother, I wished to be left to sleep during the salat. Later in the morning, I set out for the site. The events of the previous day flashed through my mind, as an evil day, and I hoped it had gone as it had come. I did not want to remember it anymore and I promised myself I would never go back to that thing again in my life. Marijuana was not meant for me.

Off the bus, I began to walk the rest of the way to the site. But I was half way there when I felt a swim in my head. Suddenly, I had another fit of vertigo and, again, it was as if my consciousness had just come back into me, from a place I knew not where, and a time I knew not when. Yet, I could swear it had not left me in the first place. Perhaps, somewhere, the time lapse was hours and hours long, but here it was not more than a fraction of a second, too small beyond my conscious notice. Nonetheless, it threw fear back into me.

This was how it began the previous day, I recalled, except that I had not taken anything this time. Then I feared that this thing really might have stubbornly come to make me crazy and die. But I did not want either and I tried not to dwell on it.

I pulled together some determination and walked on. It was a lot of an effort, and when I finally reached the site, I went in and just sat down. I could not get myself to do what I had come to do. My mind dwelled on the fear for my life and I wondered what all this could be about. I did not know exactly how studies on marijuana smoking had been claiming this kind of experience as one of its adverse effects, but I knew the weed had something to do with my present experience, as with yesterday's.

However, I remembered something else. The experience was similar to one I had had about six years earlier, whereas I had not taken any marijuana then - not even a cigarette, or a paper simulation. Then, this brought a confusion that became part of the problem, and a problem on its own. Could the marijuana have caused this? I began to wonder. Or is it something else?

I was only sixteen years old, in my third year in the secondary school, and we were having our school Inter-House sports games. At the end of the games we gathered at the school's pavilion for the results, and then I had the fit. I was in the midst of a noisy crowd, whose stampede shut up dust into the air. Then I had the strange feeling as if I was collapsing, and a sensation as if regaining my full consciousness, which I initially did not know I lost or was losing. At this weird feeling I became frightened. Thinking I was going to die, I ran out of the crowd, not stopping until I reached home. Everywhere I looked spun in my sight and I knew things were no longer the same for me.

At home, Mama, my father's mother, got me some traditional medicines that I used and became well. For about a month after the day, I felt my eyesight altered, though unlike on the first day, and I had a little nagging fear that I might die. But I did not worry over it as I now did. The paradise of little children had not yet been taken completely away from me and I did not have much cause in the world to worry. Without my notice, the entire feeling faded away. Until this day at the site, six years later, I never even remembered the event.

Now at the site, I tried to believe that my present experience was the same as this teenage one. My burden could be easier to bear this way, realizing that the first one had not been caused by weed and that it had eventually fizzled into oblivion. I wished I had not taken the weed, and wondered whether this would still have happened today. Of course, it happened to me six years ago when I did not smoke anything, I challenged myself. But a large part of my mind kept thinking that it would not have happened if I had not taken the weed. And, by this, panic and regret jumped back into me. I was afraid I was really going to go crazy and die. I blamed everything on the previous day, now seen as the *evil-day*.

I could not stay alone any longer. My sense of insecurity was washing over me. Without doing what I came to the site for, I quickly headed for home. If I would die, I wanted it to be at home, and not here or on the street.

At home, I felt a little better, until the evening when I tried to go out again and discovered I still felt insecure. Agoraphobia. The experience of the *evil-day* seemed to have conditioned this emotional response to the outdoor, but I also realized something was wrong with my eyesight. It was now blurry, and the intensity of daylight was too much to bear. I decided to stay home, feeling it would all clear off by the following day.

***

The following day, I had to meet Uncle Tunji at the site, but the feeling did not clear off. For about an hour or two, I tried to prepare myself. I built a mental fortification, gathered mental momentum, and hit the road for the bus stop. Still, my mind entertained the phenomenon and my fortification was collapsing. I tried to think it was just a product of my imagination, but as I entered the bus, and as it rode on away from our house, I realized I was not going to make it.

My eyesight whirled in my head and I rubbed at my eyes frantically in an attempt to focus. Everywhere I turned to was the same. Then my consciousness began to flicker. I stopped the bus, came down, and hurried back home.

This thing was now becoming too disturbing, preventing me from functioning normally. I was not half as troubled as this during the teenage episode. I had felt only the blurriness in my eyesight, but neither had I had agoraphobic tendency nor any consciousness freak like this. Perhaps this was because, cognitively, the world meant more to me now than then. I must have lost my childhood paradise completely. Now I wanted many things from life. Wherever there is desire, there is always fear.

Nonetheless, I still struggled with the thought that the accursed event of the *evil-day* had not caused this, despite that it seemed too obvious that it had. I tried to believe it came on its own, and that it only took the opportunity of the *evil-day*. The fact that it had happened before was helpful, but I still thought it might not have been this exacerbated if I had not taken the weed. Thus, a conflict of views engaged my mind. The Pandora box had been opened and all I had from inside was trouble. The *evil-day* was now a stubborn and vindictive ghost whose death I had been guilty of. It haunted me. In spite of all my efforts, the *evil-day* haunted me. I continued to have the strong and bitter feeling that it would claim me in the end, and my days on earth were now numbered not more than in days. The rope of anxiety was winding around my life's limbs, and in captivity of my fears I was groaning. Yet, I struggled for an escape.

I stayed home all day, and in the evening I had an experimenting stroll outside with one of my cousins, hoping to expose myself to the feared experience under his protection.

My eyesight was still blurry and the consciousness freak, though less, was still there. But nothing bad happened to me. I did not go crazy or collapse on the street. I concluded that this meant I could go out, but perhaps only in a company. Who would not live his own life and be my escort? Then, I still was in a problem. If I had not been too troubled to remember Akeem as a fascinating person I might wish to be, I would have wished I were the prince of Zamunda whose servant was always by his side.

What an unfavorable coincidence. Why in the world did I take the weed? I should have listened to the other voice on that day. Now it has happened, and I would only have to find something to do to it, or it would find something to do to me.

Perhaps, I need medical help. Perhaps, my family doctor could explain my confusion. But now I shrank away from the thought. If it was the marijuana that caused my problem, how could I keep it away from the doctor and still receive a fitting help. And, with the secret spilled, how would I appear in his eyes and in the family's eyes. Weed smoker? That was one of the worst names you could get in our house. I discarded the idea and decided to wait and watch it for more days. Perhaps, I was even merely being hypochondriac.

I lived the next few days in extreme caution, yet the condition persisted. I went about my activities in the house with my life burning within with anxiety, but nobody felt it with me. How alone man is in the world, I often thought. I no longer enjoyed any fun in the house. Although, there was not any agitation enough to be expressed, the condition was enough to trouble me inside. I constantly thought I was going to go crazy and die. Sometimes, alone in my room, frustrated, I would tell myself, "O.k. go crazy and let me see." I would demonstrate some madness as David did when he learned that he would become a werewolf in John Landis' 1981 movie. But I never went crazy, and I would tell myself, "You are just a fool; nothing is wrong with you, and you're only imagining things. Forget it and live on, boy!"

But I did not forget it. The devil haunted me and I lived on with trepidation. Perhaps, I need to see a psychiatrist, I thought at one time; but I knew no psychiatrist. I had never met one in flesh. There could be some at the University College Hospital, U.C.H., but I thought that would take too much unnerving protocols and it would be too expensive for me. This might not entirely be the case, however. I had a phobia for U.C.H. and any small excuse against it, real or imagined, would win my will. Besides, remembering the event of a psychotic patient taken to a psychiatrist some years back in my neighborhood, the label that visiting a psychiatrist might bring frightened me.

No, I told myself, I cannot go there. I am not crazy. What I need is just a mental health expert to hear my story and tell me I am not going crazy and not dying. That's all. I wished I had the opportunity of making a telephone consultation, as in some high-income countries. Stories had it that they had that in America and I wished I had been there already. Perhaps the joy of such fulfillment in my life alone could even do the trick for me.

Things got worse and life was increasingly losing its flavor. I realized that I was losing my curiosity to live and to achieve. Faith and fear seem but a single force, one and the same, only pulling in opposite directions. With faith comes security and reason to live; with fear comes the opposite. Although I wanted to live, but there was hardly any excitement in living anymore. My present and my vision of the future were haunted mansions in which I wished not to live, and my past became a precious but inaccessible property. Looking back into my past became the only gratifying vision of my present life; in it I saw my past self who had a dream, hope, and verve to achieve, only that he was a dissociated figure of envy to me now, someone I would wish to be. But that past always ended up ruined by the thought of the *evil-day,* and I would end up wishing not to remember anything of my past anymore. Hence, the past, present, and future were now angles of a triangle, a Bermuda triangle, waiting smugly to swallow me up. I did not want to die, yet I was afraid to live, and the imagination of living on like this between the two was dreadful - the three sides of the triangle within which I struggled to stay afloat.

This was the problem I was degenerating into. One may pretend to know the value of something; one may even really know, but one never feels the value of anything until one has lost it, or on the brink of losing it. I knew now how important curiosity is in human life. It may have killed the proverbial cat; through the opening of the *Pandora box* or the eating of *the fruit* in Eden, it may have let loose of evil into the world, but now I knew it was just a fundamental need for human life, almost as breathing was. And, as with life itself, we do not really know or feel its value until we lose it – when, then, we feel the need for it. The sense of curiosity is a vital spirit of life, but I was increasingly losing mine.

The lived years and accomplishments of old people became sources of envy to me. I wished I could only have the opportunity to make one movie before I die. Not necessarily for the world to remember me by, but for me to have a taste of the creativity before passing on.

As life increasingly became unbearable, somehow I still thought I could fight. Cornered like this, I would not lose anything by fighting. And who knows, the God of Moses may still be reachable. The key that opened up the Red Sea may still be available and have some magic for me.

I forced myself to go to places alone. Because I spent too much energy trying to keep my mind focused, I could only go to necessary places. In addition to the *evil-day*, the visa burden weighed on my mind, but each time I went to Chief Bernard's place, I returned home only with frustration. I often felt as though I was in a nightmare from which I could not wake up, in spite of how much I tried. As much as I wriggled, it was only getting increasingly sickening.

Although, I was not really thinking about it this way, but this gave me a sense that the control of my destiny may not be in my hands. Because of my uninspected faith, I thought it was in God's Hands. But it was disconcerting to feel that He did not seem to be helping me about it. Now I could feel what, I believe, made many Nigerians think of life and its success as of random opportunity or luck. A thousand times in a thousand days you came face to face with the realization that you could not do or get what you wanted when you wanted, and that you may never do or get it. What a life we lived. We were oppressed both from within and outside the country, and yet God seemed to ignore us. We no longer seemed human enough to enjoy the basic privileges that are supposed to come with being alive. I could not even choose freely to migrate and do it!

Perhaps fate did have favorites, afterall. The children of the rich did nothing and sweated nothing, yet they traveled back and forth between Nigeria and America, as if America was the backyard of their house, making one to wonder if the world was thus fair. If it was fair, then it was not as it appeared to be. Learning physics as a science student in my secondary school, I knew 'load' was always proportional to 'effort.' But here in living science, it seemed not. Many times, many of us put plenty of honest effort into something but received little or nothing for it, while some put little, nothing, or corrupt effort and received plenty. And often the latter were the wise and the great in the eyes of the world, while the former the foolish and lazy. Yet, preachers talked about God as just. The real situation seemed more like the Darwinian survival of the selected fittest, a selection aided by a mere natural chance. Or, at least, by a supernatural chance in the hands of a God practicing not what He preached, as our religions sometimes implied without realizing. Whether the natural or the supernatural, this chance was not fair enough.

But I was always afraid and I would not want to think this far. I would not want God to get angry with me. Without His anger, already, I was suffering enough. I had been praying and struggling for years and it all just seemed like I had only been spinning and burning my car wheels without getting anywhere. I would rather stay in the religiously submissive way and hope that one day would dawn when He would hear me and give me my chance.

Perhaps the chance was already around the corner. With my uncle arriving in the country in a few weeks' time, as promised, I hoped this would be the time for my selection into fate's American 'favorites'. Whether my uncle would use his new American immigration status to get me a visa or find another way, this November may be my time. And while my psychological troubles persisted, I waited and prayed.

II

The U.S.I.S. library was moderately populated and I sat at the center of the reading space. It was a few days before General Sanni Abacha, the new dictator, would terminate the transition government left behind by Babangida's government, and about two weeks after the *evil-day*. Though I had been going through my internal tortures intermittently, the last few days had been relatively calm and I was happy, hopeful that the emotional disturbance was finally leaving me.

Twenty-Five African Film Directors, a biographical book about the fathers of African film, absorbed my attention. The story of an African film prodigy caught my interest first. An inspiring figure who started out telling stories by using lights and shadows to create moving images on walls.

There was also the story of Ola Balogun, the first Nigerian film director, trained in France. His return home engendered the Nigerian film industry, and his first work *Ajani Ogun* was the first Nigerian film and the first African music comedy. He directed some of the treasure films created by Chief Hubert Ogunde before the baby industry was suffocated by its various problems.

I was reading the story of Ousmane Sembène, the Senegalese maker of the first African film, when I found myself in one of the fits again. It was around noon and I felt my consciousness flicker. Suddenly, I felt myself depressed at feeling the recrudescence of the illness. I rubbed my eyes and shook my head to re-energize my eyesight and refocus my mind. I turned to other directions, but they were all the same. Everything I looked now tilted around in my eyesight. Simultaneously, my excitement rose to a fever pitch, the level of the *evil-day*. I became horridly sick of the book I was reading.

I tried very hard to be calm. There was no friend around to help me here and I did not want to cause a scene as on the *evil-day*. I rose as gently as I could, with the earthquake rumbling inside me. I managed to give solid and mirthless smiles to the librarian and the guards as I walked out, gently. At the stairway, out of sight of the people, I hurried down and onto the street.

Overwhelmed in obsessive insecurity, my only thought was to get home quickly. I feared going crazy or collapsing on the street. I dreaded the humiliation, though that would only be if I did not die, by which the story would be worse. Goats' carcasses on the streets received better treatments than human corpses. A dead goat on the street would have people who needed it carry it home to cook or to food stalls to sell, while a dead human body would rot there on the street if not seen on time by his people. By the state of the economy, it was sad that it was humans that were now carrion crows, preying on roadside dead animals. The thought of being on the street for days and rotting under the eyes of passersby frightened the heavens out of me, and I thought I had to get home quickly if I was going to die.

I crossed the road to look for a taxi. My restlessness increased, so much that I could not believe I would survive every minute that came by. I was giddy, with my eyesight dimmed and stretching for a clear focus. Everywhere appeared as if a dream scene. I felt alienated from the objects of my eyes and from my entire environment, as if my soul was falling inward, as if a powerful and otherworldly force was trying to exclude me from life around me. Everywhere shook to a blur, then to disappearance, as unreal things in a nightmare. And I had a horrible feeling of being about to be shaken along into the blur, in to the nothingness. Terrified, I repeatedly shut my eyes, even when crossing the busy highway.

The first taxi did not pick me. It was a long time before another came along, while my nerves made it seem even longer, as I prehensibly held onto my life to reach home before it was extinguished. Likewise, the second taxi did not pick me.

Like the biblical Job, I could curse the day that saw my mother kneel in my labor. Perhaps, it would have been better if I had not come at all than to come and cause so much grief to myself and to my people. Now, the grief was imminent, for as I lived, I knew no joy, I knew no peace, I knew no rest. Why I lived, I did not know, but why to die, I could not admit. In my misery I hung onto life, waiting to die and hoping to live.

I waved down the third cab and called out “Roundabout.” That was my first destination, a stopover destination, because I could not get Oniyanrin straight from where I was.

The driver paused for a little while before responding, looking as if he did not want to go that way. "Ten naira," he spurted with a take-it-or-live-it look on his face.

That was five times more than the normal fare. "What? Why ten naira?" I asked, surprised. I had about one hundred naira in my pocket and I did not care how much it would cost to get home, but I asked only because it was an extraordinary price. Already, I was getting into the car as I asked the question.

"Haven't you heard of the fuel price increase that the government is now talking about?"

I had not heard and I did not care. I just talked. Talking, I thought, could help me in my effort to hold onto my life. "You said it's just being talked about, not yet implemented, why have your fares increase this soon?"

"The petrol stations have shot up the price already," he replied, waiting for my word on his price.

"What are you waiting for?” I cried, “Please, get moving." I realized I was alienated from my words too, as if the words came from somewhere else, or as if I was too far away inside my body to hear it as spoken by my own mouth.

The driver talked on about the timid and illegal government and the unscrupulous gas station owners, but my mind was not anymore with him. Because of my strange ventriloquism, I had become afraid to talk.

At his mention of the current rulers my mind went on to imagine that they would serve their time with me dead and buried. Then I began to wonder about the grave. I had always dreaded the grave: the loneliness and the breathlessness, made worse by the heavy sand dumped upon the body. According to a tradition, they might not even use a coffin for me. But maybe that would be better. Coffins were so expensive that for death to rob a family of a child and still be allowed to gulp the family’s scarce resources may not be a fair game. That would be too much an honor for death, and it would not even know it has done a wrong thing.

I would not be buried at Ibadan, I continued to ponder. They would send my body to my father in Oyo. The father owned the traditional right to bury his child. Now, I wondered how people in the neighborhood would look when my corpse is being carried out of the house at Oniyanrin. I remembered an event imprinted on my memory since I was a little boy, how they had carried into the house at Oniyanrin the corpse of one of Baba's wives who died in Lagos. I then visualized how they would carry my own out of the house. Then, like it had always happened to me, the little kids would be thrown into fear of seeing my ghost at night. They would be afraid of dark and lonely places in the house, the places where we thought ghosts and uncanny things lurked.

I did not think dead people were happy people and I feared how sad I would become. Almost all the ghost stories I had heard and watched did not portray dead people as happy as the living people were. They always had a cloud of gloom hanging over them, hinting that they were painfully experiencing the loss of the precious world, and wishing they had not died. Ghosts did not make friends, party, go to the movies, or smile. They were often lonely and unhappy, and even crying, sometimes. These frightened me about death. And now, they frightened me to my underpants as I fought back tears from my eyes. Leaving a bright and spirited world for a doomed and gloomy one; leaving a happy house for the dead-boring graveyard; and the bright world places and stages for the dark uncanny corners to live and lurk; this was the future I only could see for myself. How sad the journey of life could turn; how sad the journey of my life has turned, just by a few tokes of *weed.* What a price to pay. I cried inwardly.

If You would spare my life, I began to bargain with God, and give me a second chance - by what I could only believe would be a miracle - I swear I will never touch that devil of a stick again in my life. I swear I will be a good boy forever. With such a tragic end and a gloomy afterlife, life appeared meaningless, though it was nonetheless not a place one would want to give up so easily and so cheaply. Besides, if life in heaven was going to be eternal, as preachers cried, there was no point in going this early. I am just twenty-two, for God's sake! The punishment does not fit the crime!

I wished God would rewind my life back to the morning of the *evil-day* and allowed me to listen to the other mind that warned me. I wished I would go to sleep and wake up two months earlier in my time. I wished I could turn back the hands of time. But a voice screamed in my head, *you've had your only chance, and you've screwed it*. I could only hope my head would not ditch me at this moment.

I was still floundering in my thoughts when I spotted U.C.H., far away to my left, and I flinched in my seat. Could the hospital solve my problem? The question jumped at me. Could it hold the magic or the miracle? But, I thought, if I would go to the hospital, it would not be U.C.H. I would rather go to my family doctor. I dreaded U.C.H. so much that merely passing by the place made me uneasy. It was a phobia I developed since one day in January 1992 when I went there with a group of friends to collect the corpse of another friend who died there.

Hagler, nicknamed after the boxer Marvin Hagler, was involved in a small automobile accident. His taxi hit a roadside wall, though with nothing serious than a scratch to the cab and the wall. He was the only one affected, but with nothing apparent. And it was only after he collapsed on his way home that he was rushed to U.C.H. Stripping his clothes, the doctors found his letter of admission into the College of Medicine, of which U.C.H. was its teaching hospital, and with an intention of helping a future colleague, they keenly attended to him. Hagler had just received the letter of admission a few hours before the accident and the accident had occurred during his jubilation over the long-sought success. Unfortunately, the doctors could not help him. He died a little while afterward.

Unknown to his family, they searched around the city for about two days before his body was identified at the morgue. The next day I was at his house, among a multitude of relatives, friends, and neighbors, all in somber mood, and too shocked to talk or cry.

I went to U.C.H. with some other friends to bring home his body, and that was when the whole neighborhood burst out their pent-up emotions. They reeled with tears and lamentation. *Why does he have to go this way - at this prime and crucial time in his life? Why does he have to die in such a condition despite his good nature and fortune? Why does he have to die now? Why? Why? Why?* But my friend only lay in his coffin. He did not give us answers and neither did his God. In a dirge tone, the old women counseled his soul to choose a better destiny if given a second chance – a foreshadow of the traditional African belief in reincarnation, despite the silence and denial by our Islam and Christianity.

The atmosphere in the neighborhood was funereal and it was as if the city was mourning Hagler. It was an unforgettable day for me, especially when there was no answer why life sometimes was so unreasonable.

It was this event and many stories of death and terrible sicknesses at the hospital that gave me the morbid imagination about U.C.H. Being a superstitious person, so to speak, the hospital always reminded me of death and the gloom that surrounded it. It seemed to me a place where people died more often than healed. I passed by the place about three times a week but I always looked away from it, as I now did when my taxi drove past it.

Whether I could stand up to meet what I thought was coming or not, I could not tell, and neither could I imagine. As I reached home, I only tried to go about what I needed in the house and to wait for whatever was to come. I prepared some gari and groundnuts and tried to have something in my stomach. But when a surge of anxiety flooded outward from somewhere within me and shot off my appetite, I pushed the food away. Its sight alone now sickened me. I got up and, panic stricken, paced up and down the room, lost for what to do, lost for a remedy.

Then, a thought propelled me to go and deliver myself to my grandfather. The thought was from fear. I did not think there could be a solution from him, neither did I think a solution existed anywhere. Automatically, I only thought I should go to him. I found him in the living room but with a visitor. I almost cursed and I hurtled into my grandmother's room. I needed some diversion, but she was not in the room.

Two large cupboards occupied about one-third of my grandmother's room. A bed and a large wardrobe occupied a second third. On the outer side of the wardrobe's main door was a giant mirror that faced the bed. More than half of the room reflected in the mirror, and I could see the bed behind me as I stood in front of the mirror.

This was my habit from my childhood days. As a child, I would watch myself perform clandestine gymnastics on my grandmother's bed. As I grew older, the mirror became the magic screen from which I sought and conversed with myself. I would welcome myself back home in front of it whenever I returned from a distant journey; I would watch and console myself in it whenever I was sick and in the bed; and I would congratulate myself in it whenever I was happy. Once upon a time, when my first teenage heartthrob gave me love cards for the first time, initiating a relationship I had been too timid to ask for, I had posted them on the mirror. And each time I entered the room, I would wink at my mirror image beside the cards, giving myself the thumb-up and saying, "Lucky you."

There, again, I now stood. But this time I thought myself unlucky, shaking my head for my poor self. Mouth closed, I began to talk to the man in the mirror. Trying to think the problem was not there, and that I may only be imagining it, I asked, A*re you truly going crazy or are you just imagining things?* When the image would not reply, I added, *Okay, go on, go crazy and let me see*.

For a few minutes I remained motionless, staring at the silver sheet with a crazy readiness for whatever it was that would happen. Then, I distorted my face and gave a deep guttural sound, "Ahggrrr!" as if I had taken a lycanthropic rather than a psychotropic substance and was now transforming into a Landis' thing. *That's monstrous, you fool. Or are you turning into a werewolf?* I must have seen too much of the movie. I immediately reproached myself.

I remained still for a few seconds while nothing happened. At that moment I remembered an argument about the reality of ghosts that one of my older brothers often made. "No one actually sees ghosts," Brother Akeem would say to me whenever I was afraid of ghosts in the house, "it only appears so when they are awash by their fear of ghosts. It's their imagination running riot." In other words, it is when someone's fear of ghosts has grown so much to overwhelm him that his imagination creates one for him. Therefore, ghosts are not real.

Because Brother Akeem was someone by whom I was especially fascinated, whatever he said was the truth to my puerile sentiments. But the statement was now a good one to me and I wished I could believe its transference on my present condition. Continuing my conversation, I asked, *Is your imagination running riot? You may have supplied too much emotion, by undue concentration to burst up yourself into this state.* There was a pause, a long pause in which some debates went on within me. *No, I hadn't been thinking of any such thing; it just came by itself. This couldn't be only a product of my imagination.*

Then I opened my mouth and said somberly to myself, "Nothing is going to happen to you, Rahman, JUST CALM DOWN." Despite that it was too prominent in my mind to be a mere imagination, and it had started today without my thinking about it, I wanted to believe it was my imagination "running riot." I wanted to believe that there was no real ailment troubling me, no real ghost of the *evil-day*. But I could not. It seemed too real: my eyesight had been affectedly blurred and the panic was obsessive.

Later in my life I came to believe my brother's statement reasonably. One usually projects one's fears of ghosts upon a circumstance and mal-registers innocent objects as ghosts, or sometimes creates illusory ghosts. But I also came to believe that it is not an absolute explanation for all circumstances, as my brother claimed. Sometimes, I think, real ghosts do appear, although they may need not be feared, if one is innocent of their death and if one has not trespassed into their affairs.

However, I had not been innocent of the death of the *evil-day* and I could not have been helped by my brother's philosophy.

III

The visitor was coming out of Baba's living room when I went back to check. He was an alfa who had been visiting Baba often lately. Baba always welcomed everyone who talked about God, indiscriminate of sect, age, class, or intelligence. He listened to everyone, and whenever he saw anything impressive or improper in the conducts or teachings of the visitors, he would point them out for us to learn by. Also, people visited Baba because he was an elderly man. He was in his late eighties or early nineties, and elderly people were customarily respected, almost as gods. Their tongue, their caved-in eyes, and their gray hair were things of reverence; they have said plenty, seen plenty, and gone through various kinds of weather. And they are closer to the grave, the world of the spirits, believed to hold more truths about the human world.

I hastened to Baba's side. I had become freer with him in the last few years. He would call me and discuss life with me. He would use my uncles and aunts as examples; what went right or wrong with whom, at what time, and who heeded his counsel or did not. He was the only parent who understood and stood by my dream. He believed in me and he prayed and waited to see me realized. And, for all of us, he often sat us down and told us about himself, his mistakes, his problems, and his successes in life, all to make us learn the world. "You got to be strong," was Baba's favorite line, "Life takes strength, mental strength. You will fall down, but you have to learn to always rise up again."

Now, I thanked God for this way he had prepared. As a little kid, he had seemed to me an unapproachable patriarch, and it might not have been easy for me to come to him this way now.

"Baba," I said, gently, "I don't know what's the matter with me. I'm feeling frightened from within. I don't know why, but I'm just frightened."

I did not miss his sudden change of composure. He was alarmed. He winced at my words, and that hinted me he knew what sort of thing it could be.

"Sit down right here," he said agitatedly, "Don't talk; don't say a word; just sit down."

In his whole aged frame, Baba hurried toward the veranda, nervous, and sent for the alfa that just left him. I was happy for my good fortune. Knowing that someone, especially Baba, knew what my problem was all about was relieving. How good for one to consult elders on problems. I felt a spark of courage to beat my problem in the battle.

The alfa came and sat down.

"Tell him what you just told me," Baba said to me, and I repeated what I had told him.

The alfa brooded for a little while. "That's no problem," he finally responded, "God will take care of it."

Then he asked me to follow him home. All this time the panic was still strong, and nothing but my life mattered to me. Though I now had a spark of courage, my natural predisposition did not afford me a speck of hope in the alfa. I often approached things like this with skepticism, especially because they were meant to help me. I tended only to see as real whatever was against me, prompting me to build courage only against my thoughts, against myself. I often would not stress over invaders from outside – external problems – perhaps because something in me saw them as the easier enemies. I would believe in ten miracles predicted for ten different people before I would believe in the possibility of one for myself; hence, I would build the courage to fight my own battle. Even, in our religious teachings, I doubted what otherwise might be true, simply because it was meant for me to believe.

This characteristic feeling, which I sometimes called my contra-ego, made me wait to see what this man would do. I did not think he could not help me, neither did I think he could. I was only sure that I was in a problem, a serious one, and the feeling made the larger part of my imagination see me possibly as hopeless against it. I could not keep from imagining that I was doomed to be wasted away by what I thought was strange and incurable.

Nonetheless, the spark of courage fanned the little light of hope, and I thought that perhaps somewhere, sometime, my problem could be taken care of. It was the irony of my characteristic despondency. I often felt strong to struggle only when I saw the tides against me. And I would not imagine solution as near until it reached my hand, even when they might be apparently near. Now, even though I did not know surely whether my solution was near or not, I was going through the motion and thinking it might not be near. I always wanted what was difficult for me to have, and I always felt my best in the face of the struggle for it. This made life as an adventure rather than a lounging couch. Perhaps this was what my soul wanted, but at this point in my life, with no understanding of such self-analysis, I only lived in my feeling, and it was painful.

The alfa's house was only about a fifth of a mile away from our house, and it was one I knew so well in the neighborhood. I knew before he told me that he just moved into the house. Still incomplete as I had ever known it, it was a two-storey building with no railings on its stairways and porch. By Nigerian economic standard, it was nonetheless inhabitable. It was fitted with a functional roof, windows, doors, and a water-well, and it was fully occupied by tenants.

With one of his sons, the alfa occupied only a room on the second floor. He was a man in his sixties and we simply called him Alhaji Ibrahim. He was short, thickset, and potbellied, with tribal marks on his face. He walked as slowly as he talked. In his room he had a small comfortable chair for himself, a less comfortable one for visitors, and a double-sized bed. A table at the center of the room contained bottles of different herbal concoctions. At the foot of his bed was a space big enough to take his praying mat, surrounded by slates for scribbling Quranic words. The words were either learned by students of the Qur'an, washed into a container for spiritual purpose, or both.

He gestured for me to sit on the chair reserved for visitors. Then he asked me how exactly it began and how exactly I was feeling at the moment. With fear of death in my mind, I thought I should tell him all the truth. If he could help me to live, he would need all the facts. I told him everything from the smoking of the *weed.*

He gave a long smirk, and it took some time before he talked. When he finally did, it was far from what I expected to hear. He said that my smoking marijuana might have played a role, but it was only a smokescreen, and that I was actually bewitched. Then he went on to tell a short story.

"An amazing animal, bestowed with gold, diamond, and many great things to beautify and adorn his world, was cornered and torn into pieces by jealous wild animals who did not want him to achieve his destiny. They took the pieces of meat home hoping to eat it, but God cast forgetfulness on them and they could not eat the meat until God gathered them back and put them back together. Like the Phoenix bird, the animal rose from its ashes, more beautiful and more bestowed than before its earlier death.

"Keep this story very well, along your life you will understand it better. The evil ones are always out to spoil good things. They have seen your destiny and they want to hinder you from achieving it. But you need not worry anymore. Your God is with you, and He is more powerful than anyone."

I had been taking traditional and spiritual treatments for as long back as I could remember, but I had never been told such a thing before. Although I had never gone to traditionalists or spiritualists by my own will, and I had never taken them seriously, but I had never been told that I was being attacked by a witch. Still, I did not worry. I could not imagine anything in me for some witches to worry about. When two different psychics told me that certain persons using voodoo were obstructing my progress, I did not think of them as witches. One of the psychics was a ragged-clothed, fortune-telling tinker who walked into our house one day, perhaps a gypsy or a northern African nomad. He met me alone in the house and begged for clothes. Moved with pity, I gave him some clothes, and in gratitude he made an unsolicited divination and advised me. Despite some magical feat he performed to prove the potency of his art, and which amazed me, I still doubted him. More than half of what he told me seemed implausible, and he was too eager to get more clothes to appear genuine.

He knew what he wanted, I concluded about him, and he knew a way to get it. A lot of people thought a witch or an evil-minded person was after them with voodoo. And how else can one exploit the people better than through their fears.

Although, I did not try to ignore the possibility that such things might be going on among the people. Our schools may be teaching us what the European-founders wanted us to know, that the culture we inherited from our fathers was a bunch of illusion in the minds of ignorant people, but I could not think they were absolutely true. The awareness of voodoo was part of our environment. I watched TV, read magazines, listened to radio, and I was aware of the complex and invidious structures of families, especially polygamous families, of which majority of our families was. Yet, I often did not like to look at these experiences as more than a possibility. Even though I have had some direct experiences, like those in the on-going conflict for the throne in Oyo, I still was not crystal sure which to consider the truth – that witchcraft was real or an illusion. Perhaps, I was only afraid to admit what I knew, but my sanctuary was to treat all my experiences like the fabulous stories we heard everyday. And fabulous, really, they were.

Sometimes I thought the big witch-group causing or aggravating all these problems was our political group, both military and civilian. They kept the chances of frustration high enough to make people's minds susceptible to suspicion, jealousy, and hatred. And they kept idleness high enough to make others' minds accommodating to the devil.

Since the facts of causes could be confusing in this kind of situation, especially to my Western-educated mind, I usually cared for remedies rather than causes. Even if such remedies would only be like placebos, making my actions appear as superstitious, I still preferred to do it to dissipate all the worries. It is better to be safe than sorry. But I also knew I had to be careful in pursuing the remedies. There were charlatans who would deceive people by their inaccurate and false divinations. They would even give false names and descriptions of the attackers and cause malice and quarrels in innocent relationships, if the names and descriptions coincided with real persons that one knew.

This was something I always remembered along with my doubts. Desperate people could do desperate things to get money, and it is other desperate people who would fall victims. Although I could not prove the tinker wrong, as I could not prove him right, but I was not desperate enough to believe him and I quickly forgot about him.

Now, I faced another spiritualist, in such a dubious but hard-pressing circumstance, and I would have to decide whether he was to be believed or not. But at the moment, this was not my priority. I was eager for help, and I was impatient to see him do whatever he could. I was desperate, but still afraid to trust a fate that was behind the curtain.

The alfa pulled out a bottle containing a green potion and poured me a tablespoonful from it. It looked like animal bile, but tasted slightly differently.

To my surprise, and delight at the same time, the panic was washed by the passage of the medicine down to my stomach, as water washes down a nasty bolus of food that stuck to the throat. With the tablespoonful all my troubles went down, and there remained no sign of panic in my heart.

This was a miracle! I could not have believed that anything in the world could take it out like that, and I now looked at the alfa with different eyes. So, he is this kind of a traditional medicine man, I thought. Could he then be right about the witches' stuff? This brought me closer to believing him. He stared at me and smiled smugly and wryly, confident of his medicine's work, and as if he knew what was gong on in my mind.

"I'll make you some soap," he then said to me, "You'll bathe with it everyday, and it would ward off the evil spell laid on you completely." I listened intently with all my body now - eyes, arms, and legs, as if they were my ears. He asked me to get a white plastic bowl and some black soap for him to make the bathing concoction.

Then he began to ask random questions about some people in our house. He appeared ordinarily curious about them, and not necessarily in relation to my problem. He got to a particular woman, and to his question, I told him who she was.

"I know her," he said, as he brandished a loaded smile. "I've known her in a long time." He continued, gathering a kind of momentum that hinted me he was going to ask more about her. I thought within myself that this was none of my business, but, since he was my business, I had to mind him entirely.

"When you get home I want you to tell her that I know her," he continued, "and ask her if she knows me or not. She knows me all right, though, and she cannot deny it. But just ask her." He concluded, with a special emphasis and a smile that reminded me of sexual indiscipline in men. His looks and words had some dramatics that I did not quite fathom, though I thought I did. I thought the title of his acts was lechery, because I knew the woman was married. I knew he had some knowledge of something between both of them, which the woman must also know about, which he knew I did not know, but enjoyed having me in its dark. This was sometimes the way older men talk about such relationships. But my business was to get well, and that was what I had to mind.

I told the woman about him and I asked if she knew him. Her reaction surprised me and made me believe my theory further. "Who is he?" she had asked me in obvious pretense, and I told her who he was. "I don't know him. He must be crazy. Foolish man. He'd better face what he's asked to do. To hell with him." But I knew she knew him and understood the implication of the message. When people resort to using curse words and vulgar language, it is often a conscious or unconscious reaction to sensitive issues in their psyche, like a defense against a resurfacing past dirt.

However, it was a different message the alfa was trying to pass across to me, but it was not until after some years before I got it. Then, perhaps, it had become too late for me, for all havoc had been wreaked.

IV

After the last salat of the day, several hours from my meeting with the alfa, I settled down for supper. Because I thought things had calmed, I had told my grandmother of the problems of the day, how it had begun and how the alfa had helped me out, though leaving out the marijuana story. Yet, she was worried, and I had to try to allay her fears. "It's been taken care of and now I'm fine," I assured her.

I had not been able to eat well enough since the morning and my grandmother prepared my favorite dish to help my appetite. But, alone in my room, I had not taken more than three spoonfuls when the anxiety surged up in me and I lost my appetite again. For God's sake, what kind of thing is this? I thought, with fear rising back in me. I dropped the spoon and almost capsized the plate. This time, I was angry, and with the fear for my life, the anxiety increased.

For distraction, I went to the living room to join people watching a movie. I took a seat and stared at the TV screen. I could not concentrate. My constant effort was to suppress my anxiety so no one would notice. The movie, an Indian picture titled *Sholay*, had always been an inspiring movie for me, but this night it was a flat show. Sick of the whole phenomenon of the anxiety, I tried to occupy myself with the random discussions people were having on the movie, yet I succeeded only in keeping the anxiety away from them. The fire burned within me. Amidst the people that crowded the room, I felt alone, dying alone. Inside, I wept for my plight, perhaps also for the plight of the human specie. *How alone man is, / Journeying through the harsh ocean and deserts of life, / all alone is he*.

For a while, I stared at myself in my grandmother's mirror. I appeared healthy; yet, internally, I was a wreck. How hopeless the physical body is when the mind is sick or lost. I hoped the morning would come quicker so I could go and see the alfa again. I put my hopes on the concoction, though

I began to wonder whether this was how I would drink up the whole bottle, spoon by spoon, if this thing relapsed again and again. Unless the problem would have gone by the time I finished the concoction and the soap. This was a hope, and I hanged on it like a stole on a rack.

Everyone went to bed at around eleven o'clock. Wasiu was my cousin with whom I shared a room, and we slid into our separate beds after light-out. If I had known sleep would not come, I would have taken a dose of trusted sleeping medicine. The more I tossed and turned the farther I got from sleep. As if that was not enough to give me a bad night, my morbid panic grew, as if I was going to burst open. And this time, more than it had ever been before. My chest pounded faster and heavier. My liver, intestines, and lungs trembled as if I was in intense cold. Yet, I sweated profusely at the same time as if I was in intense heat. All my nerves left my body and flew wildly about the room, like feathers blown from a burst pillow. As much as I tried, I could not get them back in order.

I believed in the power of the Qur'an, so I reached for my copy and placed it on my chest. Though belief may be distinct from faith, as sometimes our fears threaten us beyond our faith, but perhaps what made me pick up the Qur'an was what made many other Muslims pick it up and hang rosary around their necks and in their automobiles; what made the Christians pick up the Bible, wear the crucifix and cuddle Mary's statuette; what made the Buddhists adore the statuette of Buddha, and perhaps it is what made the polytheists cuddle and worship their various gods. Perhaps it was the unacknowledged idea that God may be too far away to be reached, at least quickly enough when we desperately need Him. I did not fool myself that my faith in an instant delivery by the power in the Qur'an was not lacking. My faith was one stubborn thing that needed more than preachers' words to hang its coat upon and goes to sleep. I cuddled the holy book with a begging spirit, waiting for it to strengthen my faith by sample.

A few times I got a towel and mopped streams of sweat from my body, yet it continued to ooze out, as if I was a water-filled plastic bag with pinholes all over. I considered going out for help. From the boys' quarters of the house where I was, however, it was not easy to reach Baba in the main building at the time of the night. Besides, going out at this time was something of fear in itself.

Our house was in two pieces: a three-floor main building in front and an equally tall boys' quarters at the back, linked together as one house. The third floors of the two buildings were occupied only by our family, and the other floors below were occupied by tenants and a few family members. It was a huge complex structure that housed our huge complex family. A blend of traditional setting with a modern structure, it was built and used like a village family compound, with sections of closed dwellings like the huts in the ancient compounds. The main building was roofed, but the top of the boys' quarters was not. It was a floor left opened to the sky, with lines for drying clothes and a large space that served various purposes: praying, playing, fighting, hiding, and as love nest under the cover of night. Sometimes in very hot weather, people would go there to sleep.

The toilets, bathrooms, and the kitchens were built as sections joining the two buildings and the walkways that led to them were opened to the watchful eyes of the sky. Hence, passing through the walkway at night could be frightening, especially when one remembered the stories of ghosts in the house, and of weird demons in the neighborhood. For children and adolescents like me, this posed a problem. Some of those who were bold enough to sleep on the top open floor of the boys' quarters had told stories of ghosts encountered there. One night an elderly man ran down wildly in the middle of the night, claiming he was woken by footsteps he found to be of a ghost's. Earlier in the same night, my grandmother had had the same experience while she was observing her salats there. Repeatedly, she heard footsteps of someone while she had her head to the ground in worship, but saw only the shadow of someone walking back and forth in front of her when she raised her head to look. My grandmother did not tell anyone about her experience, but the man's age and the fact that it was not his first time sleeping there gave credibility to his story and strength to our fears. Surprise came the next day when the news arrived that one of Baba's wives had died in Lagos the previous day, some hours before the experiences of the ghost. "She had come ahead of her news," my grandmother would later tell me.

Although people still came out to use the toilets at night, and some brave ones continued to sleep on the top floor, there was no question about the reality of ghosts in the house. Everyone only hoped not to encounter them. We had intra-mural graves at our backyard and we believed it was the ghosts of those buried there that co-habited the house with us.

Wasiu and I also had a mysterious experience in our room one night. We just finished watching a late TV show in the living room and returned to our room at around midnight. The stairway that led to the open-floor on top of the boys' quarters was in front of the toilet, separated from the boys' quarters by a noisy door. We closed the door firmly behind us as we crossed to the boys' quarters. Adjacent to our room was another stairway that led to the next floor beneath us, with a noisy metal gate at its bottom end. We closed and put a latch to the gate. These were our routine every night to secure the boys' quarters. The people in the house had slept and, as usual, we locked our door and got into our beds.

Suddenly, we heard heavy footfalls of someone running from one end of the open-floor and toward the stairway. It was as if the runner was being frightened and chased by his fright or by a ghost. At least, this was what we thought at first. We listened as he passed over our room to the stairway. He ran down the stairs and, in a short time, he was in front of our room. He banged on our door, three, four, or five quick times, as if he needed help. We were poised to help, but the person said nothing and did not wait for our response. He immediately continued his race down the adjacent stairway on to the next floor and then further on to the ground floor, where the footfalls strangely died out. The footfalls died out not as if the runner entered a room, for we heard no door open or close, but as if he thinned away into the air, as it might have thinned in. We were confused. We stayed still in the darkness of our room, hoping to hear more of the drama.

Then the realization dawned over us and we became more confused: the noisy door from the toilet side to the front of our room had neither been opened nor closed during the race. And the noisy metal gate, which was harder to deal with, also had neither been opened nor closed. Yet, the runner had run through them. Then, we wondered what he could be - a runner not restricted by closed doors and gates!

Whenever I remembered this, I thought I had an experiential proof of the existence of ghosts. No normal being could breeze through walls like that. But, sometimes, knowledge brings burden. It would have been good for me, if I did not know this and had only believed as my brother's view. My fear of ghosts now prevented me from going outside for help. My internal organs continued to vibrate and my heart pounded, as if trying to break my ribs to its freedom.

Hours passed and there was no sleep in my eyes. As I tossed and turned in bed, afraid to step into the dreadful outside, my condition only grew worse. The panic increased further with time, and I feared being eventually consumed by the phenomenon tonight.

We did not have a clock in our room, but I knew it was dead of the night. Frantic, I looked up toward one of two paintings in the room, *The Mammy Water,* or Mermaid, done in oil on canvas. The second painting was of Ali, the in-law of Prophet Muhammad, seated on a mat and flanked by two handsome young men standing. The young men were Ali's sons, the twins of Fatima, the famous daughter of the Prophet. In the moment, the painting reminded me of a story about the twins and their father, Ali, who also became the fourth Caliph (successor of the Prophet) of the Islamic empire and the figure around whom the Shiite sect of Islam was founded.

The twins became sick, as the story goes, and after a lot of futile worrying and running around to find them a cure, Ali made an oath to God. He promised that he would fast for three days in gratitude if God healed his twins. The twins became well thereafter, and he fasted as promised, although with a lot of difficulties relative to the circumstance of the promise.

Two key lessons often taught with the story were that making oath with God ensures the answering of one's prayer, but that fulfilling one's part of the oath may be very challenging. Remembering the story, however, I quickly made an oath to God that if He helped me overcome these problems, not just the one of today, but all from the *evil-day*, I would fast in gratitude. I did not mind as Ali's three days' fasting had been testingly grueling, I promised seven days of fasting.

Ignoring the time of the night, I then rose up. The anxiety had become too excruciating that the need to get help overrode my fear of going outside. I carried my Qur'an in one hand and opened the door with the other. I was going down to the ground floor, the most dreaded floor in the building. Our Islamic teacher, whom we called Maleem or Imam, lived on the ground floor and I was going to him. In addition to preaching God, he also helped people with their problems. Once when my grandmother's money was stolen, he had done his spiritual work and pointed out the thief, who returned the loot to my grandmother. Now I hoped Maleem could do something to help me.

But was I going to make it down this night? With all the stories of ghosts and spirits now flowing through my mind, I clutched the Qur'an tighter and chanted *Ayat al-Qurisiyy*, a Quranic verse reputed to be powerful. I looked to the right and left, up to the open floor and the black sky of the night, and I stepped on. Terror lurked within and around me, but the strength of the one within pushed me on. I moved toward the left where the stairway was and continued chanting the long verse.

The house was so big that it housed over a hundred people. Now everyone was sleeping and it was as silent as if there was not a single person in the house. I reached the next floor, opened the metal gate and walked the long lighted balcony to the next stairway that carried me to the ground floor. It was partially dark on the ground floor, only a faint reflection of light from the second floor shone on it. Yet, I had to walk through its long passage to the turning that led to the basement where Maleem lived. At this point, the fear coming from outside increased.

As I took my steps gently, I fixed my gaze at a door ahead of me, hidden in the shadow and silently frightening. It was the door that led to the backyard where the graves were, the backyard where ghosts lived, and it was right in front of it that I had to make the last turning to Maleem's quarter. Here was the most terrifying part of my trip, as I inched toward it, eyes intent on it, with the fear that a ghost might come out through the door. At one time, I was engulfed in darkness. I increased my pace and my concentration on the chanting. I could barely feel my head on my neck by the time I made it. Leaving the door behind me, I ran to Maleem's door, looking repeatedly over my shoulder to be sure nothing was coming behind me.

"Who is it?" Maleem called out, almost immediately I knocked his door.

"It's me, Rahman. Please, open the door."

Maleem slept in a separate room from his wife's, so I was sure he was the only one in the room. He let me in without questioning me on what the matter was. He had a habit of saying little, making his little body more little, and his personality insignificant. He was unassuming.

"Maleem, please help me. I don't know what the matter is with me. I'm very frightened and I cannot go to sleep or stay calm. I'm afraid I'm dying. Please help me."

He was surprised, but characteristically unperturbed. "Sit down," he said calmly, as he offered me a position opposite to him on the only mat in the room. It was his prayer room and he slept and prayed on the same mat, surrounded only by his Arabic slates that looked like those Moses received from the mountain.

"How did it begin?" Maleem asked in his native accent. He was from Ilorin, Kwara State, the only Yoruba state where Islam was the predominant religion. After the Fulani Jihadists conquered it in the early 19th century, Ilorin became the Islamic education center in the Yoruba land, and its culture modeled after the Islamic culture. Even for economic reasons, the Ilorin people would rather go to Saudi Arabia than to think of countries in the West. My mother's residence in Ilorin became the factor for her migration to Saudi Arabia where she would live for several years.

Because I had been very active at Islamic classes and prayer, Maleem especially liked me, so I feared marring myself in his face. The story of smoking marijuana was too bad to fit my image in the face of this gentle teacher who had taught plenty to me. Yet, the fear of losing my life was more and I thought he might have a solution. I spilled up everything from the *evil-day*. He was inscrutable as he listened, taking in everything gentler than I was rushing it out.

Then he poured some water into a small cup and prayed over it for several minutes. It seemed to me like several hours. After I drank the water, he said I would be all right, and that I should go and sleep now. He promised to do what he could do about it for a lasting solution.

Taking the drink calmed me, but only a little, and perhaps merely suggestively. It was not like the other alfa's concoction and I was not relieved enough to trust going back upstairs to sleep. I asked him to let me sleep in his room and, after some time, I fell into sleep on one of his praying mats. My nerves settled back into my body, like when birds come back to nest.

V

I still had a trace of the illness the next morning and I promptly decided on what to do. The events of the last twenty-four hours had given me an attitude of hope for a solution, and now I wanted to look for it everywhere I could. I saw both the alfa and our Maleem for what they had to offer, and then embarked on a journey to my father at Oyo for traditional treatments. If it was truly the work of some evil people, traditional and spiritual treatments might be my best bet. It had been two weeks from the *evil-day* and a part of my mind thought that, if there was no foul play as suggested, it might not have taken this long if it would kill or run me crazy. Nonetheless, the part continued to struggle with the other that thought the *evil-day* still might have been the cause, and perhaps the only cause. Whichever the case was, however, traditional treatments might be a good choice of help.

Maleem did not say it was the work of any witch. Rather, he said it was the devil that deceived me into smoking the marijuana. By *devil,* most people mean Satan, the fallen angel who goes around the world casting the spell of deception to make more people fallen as he is. For some others, the humanist thinkers, they mean personal moral weakness. Which one Maleem meant, I tried to figure out, but I found it shameful to lump the *evil-day* on the fallen angel. Afterall, I had gone to take the weed by my choice.

Seated quietly on the bus to Oyo, my mind kept busy on my circumstance, with its distress and confusion. In some way, whether the story of the witches was true or not, the idea seemed functional: having an identifiable cause meant having a possibly identifiable solution, and it helped me partly from the surreality of my situation. However, Maleem's theory of the devil rather than of witches now threatened the quaint hope with a perception of conflict of theories, and I was not getting anywhere. Perhaps the idea of the devil also was only supposed to be functional, as functional as religion generally may only have been in the psychological demands of human life. Then, as the *civilized* people have been claiming, there might really not be anything like witchcraft, and the witches might have been as illusive or elusive as religion's devil. Then, I may only have been my own devil, my own witch.

Could this be true? It appeared logical, but it got me nowhere. In some way, I could not ride it out of the quagmire of witchcraft, hitherto hidden at the backyard of my mind, and now awash on my thinking. I was still confused, and, for the first time in my life, I began to give it a serious thought. These bad people might really be having hands in people's misfortunes. Everyday experience and media programs carried the bold placards. And sometimes I reasoned that if there was a reality for prayers to bring what we desired, as in religion, believed by most people in the world, then there might be other such reality of opposite nature to bring unwanted things, and which could be appealed to with a force opposite of prayer. Our world is one of opposites. The witches may have been the opposite of priests. Then, one might be indirectly denying the credibility of God and prayer if one denied the credibility of witchcraft and witches, and that of devil and evil. Yet, I believed in prayer. Perhaps, then, logically, there is witchery. Like the alfa told me, I remembered the tinker's divination, and also a man who had told me a few months back that an evil woman in my house was holding me down from progressing in my proposed trip to America.

To God, I still did not want to admit to such beliefs! I could not imagine myself as one of such characters in the movies haunted by witches. I listened to the man further only because I wanted to go to America and I was afraid of failure, instigated by anything or anyone. I thought myself civilized enough to not meddle in such 'superstitions' that cannot hold water in the concrete thinking of modern science. I could not even talk about such a thing too openly. Neither could I use it to convince the American immigration officers for an asylum – I would only be exposing my African ignorance in the civilized age.

Though I may only be pretending to know what civilization was supposed to mean, I could not imagine myself as not civilized – perhaps like most people in the world. Whether, by interposition, civilization was supposed to be the way of learning and living the Western way, in spite of all, or it was supposed to be an understanding and living one's own natural way, adaptively and improvingly to one's time and place, I could not face the question. Then, rather than a civilized person, I may have become a victim of what some called *cultural imperialism*, shackled with cultural ambivalence. I fancied jeans and Oxford shirts to *buba* and *sokoto* made from *ofi*; tuxedo was a better elegant dressing than agbada; salad, cheeseburger, and crackers were superior to *amala*, *fufu,* and *kulikuli;* Rock, R&B, and Country were better music than *fuji*, *juju*, and *waka;* and visiting traditional medicine men had become a stigma, too unfashionable where there were white-cloaked doctors with needles, tablets, and syringes. Yet, I was pursuing such folk medicine while thinking myself a civilized individual.

That there might be medical and psychological explanations for all or most of these things I was experiencing did not make my situation easy to bear. As I would later learn, many Western intellectuals believed that Freudian psychoanalysis has undermined beliefs in witchcraft. Moreover, if my problem, along with various others that people experienced in this part of the world, were happening to people away from these witchcraft environments, and known scientifically to be naturally caused, how could anyone say that ours, or at least some of ours, were caused by witchcraft? It was ridiculous, and I seemed to be living in a crazy world.

In a pre-Classical Greek myth, however, Pan, the Arcadian god, was known to instill anxiety disorder in mortal men who ventured into his domain. By this, any trivial cause would spark into a full-blown, groundless panic that would eventually kill the victims. Then, could my situation be a Pan-like example? Could our problems sometimes be caused by gods, goddesses, spirits, and supernatural humans, while we know the symptomatology of the problems? Could the natural events in our lives be caused by forces beyond our natural comprehension and control? Or is everything simply the result of evolution, of organismic adaptation and mutation, and we only ascribe meanings to random events from our evolutionary contexts? The world really does seem crazy.

Though still reveling in my 'civilized' paradise, my decision for pursuing the folk medicine may be seen as one of caution. Though I believed that, in their own way, the traditional medicines worked, at least as I had seen many times before, I did not think I was a subject for anyone to hate so much to the extent of bewitching, and my current decision was based on my effort not to leave anything to chances. The death of my friend Hagler had been in a mysterious circumstance and news spread around the city that he was a victim of such deviltry. My friends who escorted his corpse to his hometown for burial met with people who claimed they did it and threatened to do more in the family. It was an interfamily feud in the closely packed community of his hometown.

If we were to be dying in the reality of our environment, then one may wonder whether the civilization imposed on us was right, or entirely right. It had given us many conveniences and it had answered many questions, but there were still questions wanting of answers. Yet, the civilization wanted us to dump them in the garbage of history as ignorant beliefs of a blind period. If it was then wrong, was it deliberately wrong and serving us wrong, or was it just itself hoodwinked by its own senses in the intricate and subtle nature of reality?

I continued to wonder on what civilization was. We were neck-deep in its modern trend, its modernism, but now I must pause and wonder before I lived my life along. Is civilization a cultural state of selecting what to believe, or to understand and accept reality as it shows itself to us? Is it a cultural state of choosing to believe what we like and denying the reality of what we are ignorant of? The sun shines, the wind blows, sound hums and matter sits to be seen and touched; are these just all the reality there is? Even, all these are acknowledged in different ways and by different means. Then, is this civilization a culture of hypocrisy? I did not want to be a savage, but I did not want to be a hypocrite either.

But if the civilized people have truly been hypocritical, then, the so-called savages might not be all wrong. While there might be parts of the world that did not have this sort of things, perhaps in our own world one should not ignore it. They would spoil many good things. Most people thought that if Hagler had known and tried to "protect" himself, maybe he would have lived.

I remember the case of a white girl allegedly brought from Canada in the 1980s. She was afflicted with an incurable illness and was brought to Chief Yemi Elebuibon, a chief traditional religious priest and doctor. Through Ifa ceremonies,[16] the Chief used traditional and spiritual medicines to help her, as shown on television. Then, I thought that one might not be able to rule out traditional doctors in all these things. Maybe I was being sentimental, and maybe I was becoming too ensconced in a typical mentality. But also, I reasoned, as various experiences were showing me, that in many cases of physiological and psychological illnesses, including this anxiety stunt on me, they might be scientifically explicable when evil voodoo forces might really have caused them. Perhaps, then, our task would be to find the connections.

These were the questions on my mind during the one-hour journey to Oyo, but the most important thing I wanted was to get out of my present problem. However, whether death or something else, I had a strong foreboding something terrible was about to happen in my life. I had a feeling my life was journeying into a world I did not want.

---

[16] Ifa is the most famous African system of divination and it is the main traditional religion of the Yoruba people, around which other traditional religions revolve. Essentially, Ifa symbolizes spirituality, the ways of the Heaven; it is believed to be a god that came from heaven to teach humans the secret of medicine and prophecy.

My father sent me to a friend of his who was a traditional spiritual healer. It was encouraging that I was going to the man. I had known of him enough to trust in him. At least, if faith or positive mental attitude was what I needed, I had it.

We called him *Baba-elero*, because he ran grinding machines for business. That is what the name means: the man who owns (grinding) machines. He was in his mid or late 50s, short and thickset, and he had tribal marks which indicated his birth, his family, and compound in Oyo. When I explained my situation to him, leaving out the marijuana part, Baba-elero did not appear to be paying me attention. He was attending to a herbal preparation one of his apprentices was making and he was returning the greetings of every passerby in front of his shop. But this was his characteristic way of dealing with things and I was used to it. He rarely appeared serious with his work or concerned with the clients' plight, though everyone knew he was both serious and deeply concerned about them. That was why he was so loved and respected in the entire region of Isale Oyo, the region of the murdered Asipa of Oyo. Baba-elero had met my father through the struggle against the Alaafin and assigned himself to protect our family. Most of the people of Isale Oyo saw the king as the prime suspect in the murder of their leader. They sought justice relentlessly, vowing not to bury the dead leader until justice was served – the corpse would spend seven years in the mortuary before it was finally buried. For this fight, they saw their hope in my father's candidacy and both the family of the Asipa and the people of Isale Oyo rallied behind him. Hence, many medicine men from the region stood to guard my father and his family and cater for traditional medicine needs of our household.

As flippantly as he had listened to my complaint, Baba-elero gave me a specially made snuff. Sometimes, I thought he was as such careless in order to make the clients' problems seem unserious, perhaps to make the clients have a mental advantage over the problems. But this time, I knew my problem was serious and I was not going to think otherwise, unless proven otherwise. The snuff he gave me was medicinal, and it was often his first administration to his patients. He claimed it would abate almost any ailment, partially or completely, depending on the gravity of the ailment. I sniffed it, and for the next hour I sneezed so continuously and tempestuously that it was as if my nose would fall off. I felt my head lighter and lighter. He ignored me, or so it seemed. And after the long period of sneezing, he turned to me and assured me not to worry and that everything was under control. For the next twenty minutes, he gave me about two or more treatments and I left for home afterward.

I decided to spend the night at Oyo. I felt better, at least less tormented from within. My eyesight was still hazy, and my insecurity, though greatly reduced, still made me feel vulnerable. I was put to trial during the night's late show. It was a Nigerian-made evangelical horror movie about the battle between the power of Jesus Christ and witches. I had watched the movie several times before and it had never bothered a thread of hair on my body, but this night it bothered my entire being. Even in bed, where I had run to, its soundtrack oppressed me. I could not tell my younger siblings who were enjoying the movie to turn it off or lower the volume; I would have looked a freak to them. I could not sleep until the movie was over.

VI

Though I was remarkably better, three weeks after my visits to the three medicine men I still had some unignorable fear of going outside and I still thought I was living in a dream. Thinking that my poor eyesight might be the only remaining problem responsible for my present state, I decided to see an ophthalmologist. I could not register images in my eyes as I used to and my sight was still hazy.

After an exhaustive examination, the third doctor I visited also did not see any problem with my eyesight. He ran a reputable clinic, the most expensive in the city, and I had expected to have a good return for my money. He gave me some medicine to try for a week, after which he asked me to come back.

***

The following week was that of the 22nd of November 1993. I had an idea of what I thought should happen in the week, but I did not have the idea of what was about to happen. I woke up happy on the Monday morning, expecting Uncle Jibola's arrival on Friday, the 26th of the month. He was to stay for two weeks at my grandmother's house at Oke Ado and I had to spend the next few days to put one of its spare rooms in good condition for him.

The hope for my American dream was high on the rise. Everyone in on it thought something must be done, and would be done to make it happen. Uncle Jibola also put my mind assured. "When I come, we'd find something to do about it."

Nothing improved in my eyesight and I told the eye doctor when I went back to him.

"Do you sometimes or often feel tired?" he asked after various other tests.

"Yes. Sometimes so much that I would feel like sitting on the sidewalk on the street."

"Perhaps, you should see a medical doctor, then. All the tests showed that your eyesight is good enough. So, your problem may be medical."

That was confusing.

On Wednesday I went to Dr. Ishola's clinic. He was our family physician, and when one of his nurses asked to check my blood pressure among their preliminary tests, I quickly rolled up my sleeve. After all the troubles of the last two months, I was eager to know my blood pressure.

"It's normal," the nurse said to me. Though I was happy at that, I was a little disappointed. I did not expect my blood pressure to remain normal after all the stress I was going through. I hoped it would indicate the state of my condition and gave a red light for a medical overhaul.

"Rahman, how are you?" the doctor asked cheerfully as he always did.

"Not good," I replied bluntly.

"What's the matter with you?" he asked, professionally and brotherly.

"I think I'm dying, doctor." I wanted a very full and accurate diagnosis and treatment, so I told him how and when my predicament began. I did not tell him I smoked marijuana, but, to be close to it, I told him I had been smoking cigarettes lately.

Despite its concealment under his professional look, I could see his disappointment. "You have to stop it," he said, "It's not good for you."

In the next few minutes, he examined me and also re-checked my blood pressure. "You appear fine," he finally said.

"But I'm having this problem, and even the eye-doctor suspected it could be medical." I was bewildered and he could see it.

"Ok, don't worry yourself; we'll do a full check to see whatever it is." On a blank paper he scribbled some things in a typical cursive and handed it to me.

"Take this to Biomedics. They'll perform these tests, and when I see the results I'd know whatever it is that's bothering you."

As I rose to go, he asked about the well being of my grandparents and Uncle Tunji and I told him they were all fine. He was Uncle Tunji's college friend and that was how we got to know him.

"And don't forget, stop smoking cigarettes. It's not at all good for your health."

"Okay." I nodded and went out, realizing that he had registered it that much. I wondered how he would have taken it if I had told him I smoked marijuana.

Biomedics was a private laboratory. The nurses and technicians went through all the procedures of the tests, and after that, I was told to go. The laboratory would send the results to my doctor.

On Thursday, I woke up with a mild pain in my right arm. I did not like to go out with it and I thanked God I had completed the work on the room at Oke Ado. I took some analgesic pills and stayed in bed reading an African novel, *Black Maria.* The pleasure of the book was relieving, but not enough to take away the pain. The medicine was effective, but also not enough. The last time I used it a few months before, it had killed my pain in less than thirty minutes, but now I still felt a little pain even after the second dose.

Having slated the evening to meet the doctor for the results of my tests, I decided to ask for treatment for the remaining pain. Tomorrow should come quickly, I hoped, and without any more pain. I was eager to meet my uncle. I was eager to go to America.

***

I was the last in the line of patients waiting to see the doctor, and, after every one had been attended to, the doctor came out to sit beside me.

"I didn't see anything wrong with you. Your test results reveal that you are in good health. I think you only need some rest. Take one Folic Acid a day, relax, and you'll be fine."

He gave me the results sheet and I looked at it, as if I knew what all the jargons on it meant. In some way, I was disappointed, and uncomfortable at the circumstance making me look like someone with a factitious disorder – feigning symptoms to assume the sick role. Already, I was afraid of hypochondria, and now I appeared as a pathological fake. But I was relieved that I was medically certified as all right. I could now assure myself and continue my life properly. For the pain, he advised me to take another dose of the medicine and wait to see how it would work.

***

Unusually, the night's sleep was deep and sound. I did not wake up at all during the night. It was so pleasurable that I thought the pain might have not been there while I slept, because I never slept that deep with pain in my body.

The night's sleep was to be the last to Uncle Jibola's arrival. I expected it would be the last in this house for the month, at least until after a fortnight. Starting from the next day, I had planned to stay with Uncle Jibola at Oke Ado to make it easy to go around together to do what we had to do. However, I did not expect the night's sleep to be my last in this house in many years, perhaps forever. Although I did not think Uncle Jibola could round things up so quickly in two weeks and take me back with him to America, I did not think it was impossible. It was only that I did not expect it, and therefore did not think I might be having my last sleep in my grandparents' house at Oniyanrin, a house that had been my home for twenty-two years. I did not know that the coming *tomorrow* would bring a change to my entire life.

I enjoyed the sleep, and if anyone had said that it would take several months, perhaps even years, before I would be able to sleep as equally deep, sound, and pleasurable as this, I would take him for a mad person. I could not even imagine throwing myself into the well-known frenetic pursuit of life in America, at least not as much as to lose my sleep. But no one told me, and how could I have known? It was a journey into the unknown.

SIX

The Oath

I

The usual knock on our door woke me up for the early morning salat. I would have expected my medication and depth of sleep to make me feel better. Even though the pain was gentle, it was distressing. It had left my arm for my waist, a place I had never had pain before, and it fatigued me. The worst of its burden, however, was the realization of its coincidence with the day I had been waiting for in a long time. It was Friday, the 26th day of the month.

I felt the intensity of the pain increasing. By the end of the morning prayer, it had become considerably severe and the fatigue unignorable. To keep it from holding me down for the day, I decided to go to the hospital. I noticed that Baba was about to go out and I decided to use the opportunity and ride with him. Wherever he was going, he could be of help in my journey.

Brother Tahiru came out of Baba's room with the car keys. He was Baba's chauffeur. We did not like to call him as a chauffeur because he was more than that to us. He was like a brother.

"Would you follow Baba to the hospital?" he asked me. "Taofeek is going somewhere else today and Baba has to go for a check-up."

Baba always needed someone by his side wherever he went. Although, the duty used to fall on anyone who was free at the time he needed, but at some different, regular periods there was one person or the other assigned for the duty. This time it was Taofeek, an uncle of mine, who was supposed to be there for Baba.

“Very well,” I replied quickly - just what I wanted.

"All right, Baba is ready," he said as he walked away to get the car.

Baba did not know I was going to see the doctor; he thought I was only escorting him. We were half way to the hospital when I began to feel giddy. I kept to myself about it. At least, we were heading to the hospital, I thought.

At the hospital, I mustered all the energy I could to help Baba up the three or four steps to the doctor's office. There were patients waiting to see the doctor, but, customarily, they respected Baba's old age and allowed him straight in. This was a great opportunity for me, for I might not have been able to wait a turn at the end of the line to see the doctor. I escorted Baba in.

The doctor rose and bowed to greet Baba, and we sat opposite of him. He listened to Baba's complaints, examined him, prescribed some drugs, and gave him some advice on his health. When the meeting was over, Baba turned to me in a *let us go* manner.

"I think I want the doctor to examine me briefly," I said to him in the ears of the doctor. "I'm having some pain in my waist and I feel dizzy too."

The doctor walked around his desk to me. "Lie on that table," he said. He examined underneath my eyelids but kept what he saw to himself. He brought out his stethoscope. I flinched at the touch of the cold instrument on my body. With his sphygmomanometer he checked my blood pressure, and with his hands he pressed all over my tummy until he was satisfied.

"I'm afraid we'll have to admit you for a while," he finally said.

"Admit me?" I who had left here less than twenty-four hours earlier with a clean bill of health now have to be admitted for treatment?

"Not a big deal – it's just to make sure everything is all right. By evening you could go home." He turned to Baba, "Baba, you can go; I'll take care of him."

Baba was as confused as I was, but after the doctor assured him, he gently rose to go.

"I'll send someone to your mother (my grandmother)," Baba said to me, "she will bring all you'd need. Be strong, and you are going to be all right, okay?"

I nodded my head in reply.

Perhaps Baba was more confused than I was. From that moment on, he would be troubled by a question that would be quoted of him often: "How could a person who escorted someone to the hospital turn out to be the one hospitalized?"

The doctor called a nurse and ordered her to set me up. I followed her, and by the time we reached the room I had stayed in August, I knew the doctor was right in admitting me. I collapsed on the way and it was the nurse who helped me to a bed.

Within a few minutes, I had been set up with a bag of drip, given Novalgin injection, and was about to be overtaken by sleep when Uncle Jibola came to my mind. What a day. Is he going to meet me here on bed? I began to think. No, never. I would be better and I would leave this place by evening, just around the time he would arrive Ibadan. It was already about 11 a.m. and I was left to sleep.

By the time I woke up in the afternoon, the pain had left my waist and moved to my right leg, and it was more severe. Is this thing going to go by evening? The nurse gave me an injection and I prayed for it to work. I waited to see it work, but I did not know when the hurrying sleep swept me off into the world of blankness - not of dreams.

It was around 5 p.m. when I woke up again. Sheri was at my bedside. She was a live-in apprentice of my grandmother, learning the trade of cosmetics, which was now my grandmother's trade. She was a stumpy girl, about 17 years old, and she was gentle in her manner as in her looks. She had brought me a flask of hot water, something to eat, and other hospital needs.

"Will you eat your food now?" she asked in her gentle voice. Sheri was assigned to stay with me until evening when my grandmother would come.

I sat up. The pain, though reduced, had passed from my right leg to my left leg. I drew closer the table that held my lunch and tried at the food. But I was now too sick to eat. Sheri made me a cup of tea, instead.

The doctor came in and I told him how the pain had been moving around my body, from waist to the right leg and now to the left leg.

"Don't worry; it'll all soon go away," the doctor assured me, as if he was the one who put it there and was waiting for the time to take it off.

Other than the time I was admitted for a fracture in my arm as a kindergarten kid, I had never been admitted for pain before in my life. I had never been troubled by my characteristic pain to the extent of hospitalization. But whatever difference this had, I had no time to think of it. I lay back in bed, staring at the ceiling and careful not to disturb the flow of the drip. Re-adjusted by a nurse, it was now slow moving.

As the day went on, I realized I did not get better. Instead, I became sicker. The pain ate my strength little by little, and, by the time my grandmother came, I was worse than I had been in the afternoon. It dawned on me that I was going to spend the night at the hospital. I still tried not to worry. I re-focused my mind to accommodate the untoward development. Tomorrow is not too late, I told myself.

"Ayinla, *oko mi*,"[17] my grandmother said as she walked into the ward, accompanied by Brother Tahiru and Bayo, one of my cousins. She sat beside me on the bed and held my hand, staring into my eyes, speechless and worried. From the way she looked, I could tell she was thinking *how could you be sick at a time like this?* I could read all her faces and her moods, and she also understood me as I stared back. *I wish I could help it.* Then, I shifted my gaze to the other people in the room and tried to smile off my distress.

"Why today?" she finally asked, a question which would forever refuse

[17] Literally 'oko mi' means 'my husband', but in this context it is a phrase of affection mothers often use for their children and it means 'my jewel' or 'my precious'.

to go away in her mind and in the minds of many people in the family.

"Just today," I replied dismissively, "Nothing to it; it just came and it'll go away."

She was not comforted and she continued to stare at me, as if she would find answers in my eyes. She brought me dinner, but I could only pick at it. I still did not have an appetite.

For about an hour or more, there was not much activity or discussion in the room. Then I asked them to go, especially to prepare for Uncle Jibola. They left Bayo to stay the night with me and Sheri went with them. The nurse on duty gave me some injections to kill my pain and to induce sleep. But I did not get much sleep in the night. The pain now did not allow me.

II

It was about 6 am the next morning when Uncle Jibola walked in with my grandmother and two other people. He had arrived late the previous night at Oke Ado and could only call Oniyanrin on the phone. This morning, he sent for the car to take him over to Oniyanrin, but they came first to the hospital to see me.

He was bigger than he was five years earlier when I last saw him, and he had on a crimson double-breasted suit and a shiny pair of black brogues.

I welcomed him.

"How are you feeling now?" he asked.

"Better," I replied, as if truly better. But I was better in as much as I saw him.

"Where is the pain?"

The pain was in my right leg and I told him. He felt it with his hand, as if he was going to remove it. That reminded me of the old days when I was a little boy. Whenever he saw me having pain, he would bring himself down to my mat, like a doctor with a special healing power, and touched wherever the place I was having the pain, as he if wanted to solemnly call it out by a secret name. But, at such moments, I used to feel the pain less, for there was a magic in the touch that I was sensitive to: empathy, love.

Uncle Jibola was in the habit of talking little, the quality of which, however, showed deep and wide thinking, just like Baba's.

"I hope you get well soon and be discharged. And try to be strong."

"Yes. Very soon," I said. I expected to be discharged soon and I was determined to make it happen that way.

They stayed with me for a while before they rose to go. Bayo went with them. Uncle Jibola left behind some medicines that he brought for my doctor to see if any of them might be helpful.

I tried as much as possible to shake off the sickness. I was eager to discuss my prospects with him, and to know what and how to do with the opportunity of having him here in the country. I took my medications regularly and called the doctor's attention often. My mental attitude was in a state that psychotherapists would call *doctoring* to my physical health. I fell into a brief sleep and, by the time I woke up, people from our house were in my room to visit me.

Uncle Jibola came again the next day. I was a little better, or so it seemed. He stayed with me for some time before moving on to other places. He wanted to reach as many of his family and friends as he could within the little time he had. We could not yet talk on my travel plan; sick time was not a good time, and neither was hospital a good place. I hoped on the following day, Monday, to be discharged.

On Sunday evening, Bili came to visit me. My grandmother had notified Oyo about my hospitalization and Bili had come as my father's eyes.

In the next two days, the pain did not decrease or increase and I was not fit to leave the hospital. People came and went often. I was anxious to leave with them. Within myself I felt how bad my health was, but I did not want to admit it. I am going to be all right soon, I kept thinking and trying. Like a snake, the pain crawled from one leg to the other, and I slept less and less.

My cousins gave me the gist of how Uncle Jibola had given them clothes and money; how many trips they had enjoyed with him each day, and how he had paid for educational opportunities for them, including computer training classes for those who wanted. I admired them, though I did not envy them. I assured myself that I was going to get good things as well, and even before the year ran out, or, at least, at the wee days of the coming year, I would be in a school in America. What is more envious than that? The thought was pacifying.

On Tuesday evening, I felt better than before. The pain remained on the right leg for some time, crawling nowhere anymore, and it was already relieving me. I was able to sit and stand longer than before and the weakness in my body was diminishing. It was now a plausible hope that I could go home the next day.

The doctor saw me and was also happy at the improvement. But he told me, "not tomorrow, boy; Thursday. You'll be very better, and then you can go."

Thursday - that's another extra day! I consoled myself, anyway, that I will still have more than a week with my uncle, and I could draw out of him all I wanted in the period.

As early as 6 a.m. on Thursday morning I had prepared myself and ready for home. I was not any better than I was on the Tuesday evening, but I was eager to get out of the hospital. So I pretended I was better and ready to go. I had been acting out the pretense since the previous morning. I feigned the night's sleep so the nurses would not have any reason to keep me there and the doctor had declared me okay to go. Although it was not that I was deliberately deceiving them, it was that I was trying not to give myself to the sickness. I was trying to believe and act that the sickness was going, and must go.

Though less disturbing now, the pain in my leg slowed down my gait, but I thought it would be walked out. Even in the past experiences I had had with the pain, I had never waited in bed for everything to clear off. I always walked them out, as I always had something I was eager to do: soccer, basketball, break-dancing, and other neighborhood stuffs.

A painful and nagging nerve-pinch rendered my left arm almost unusable, but I tried to believe that it was a mere thing from the injections I had been taking through the arm. I had taken more injections than I could count, and all had been through my left arm. Even, the drips were passed through the same arm, where its needle had to remain throughout the period.

The car came and I rose to go. They packed my belongings to the car and I hobbled toward the section of the hospital where the nurses were officed. I wanted to sign out. The place was often busy, with the nurses moving in and out as they went about their duties. I felt weak and light on my feet. A mild wind could blow me off the ground. It was a feeling of sickness and I could hardly feel my head on top of my neck. Yet, I assured myself that all would be fine through activities. I only need to eat well and exercise well, I thought.

As I came into the open, a nurse came out of the office building and met me at the door. I greeted her, but she returned my greeting with a searching frown.

"Mr. Oladigbolu," she said, "it seems you are jaundiced."

"I am?" Whatever jaundice was, I did not know, but, from her look, I sensed it could be an obstacle to my going home.

"Yes, you are. I don’t think you can go home like this."

"That's what you think," I said, "It’s the appearance. I'm strong enough inside to go home now." I beamed, so she could think I was fine.

"But, I'm afraid, we can't discharge you in this condition. You still look sick."

I stood dumbstruck for a few seconds and allowed the reality to come over me. That was a professional judgment, and I could not argue. Reluctantly, I turned back, and she hurried to assist me back to the sick room.

I lay in bed. My sick needs were put back in place and brother Tahiru and his company took the report back home. I feared they would shock my grandmother. She had already been preparing a welcome dish.

The pain in my leg was dull and ignorable. I only wondered on what type of treatment I would now be given and, most importantly, how long it would take. I was later to learn that jaundice was typical of the body pain that characterize my genotype, but in the two decades that I have been living, I had never had anything like it. So, I had no idea of the gravity of my new condition. I hoped it would not take more than a day for treatment. Perhaps two, or three at most.

When the doctor came in to examine me, I searched his face, but could not see how trivial I had expected my condition to be. I could not see how serious either, but I heard something when Uncle Jibola came a short while later.

"We'll have to transfer him to U.C.H.," the doctor said to my uncle.

That was enough to tell me how serious my condition was. The doctor could not handle it alone any longer and he had to transfer me to a bigger hospital, that college hospital whose imagination terrified my psyche.

The doctor discussed with my uncle how the transfer would be done and they agreed on the following day, a Friday. Uncle Jibola asked me to come with him. We went to some private laboratories for tests, whose results I was to take with me to U.C.H. Then he took me home to be bodily and mentally refreshed for the journey ahead of me. He stocked the car with bottled water and urged me to drink as much as I could.

"You need plenty of fluid," he said.

At home, I had a warm bath. I was weak and had to sit on a metal chair while someone bathed me. This was strange. No matter how sick I was, once I made up my mind to bathe, I always did everything through by myself, and on my feet. Though I knew that things were not same with the life I had always known, I did not know it was the jaundice that was biting into me. Too many of *first time* circumstances were happening to me now. While it may be normal for such things to come once in a while in a lifetime, these did not warn me that I was in for a big ride. A ride that would drag me out of my present steps toward America and into one of the worst conditions life could offer. It was a big ride of a lifetime.

I ate a specially prepared dish and spent some time with Baba. I had changed into fresh clothes, from a black pair of jeans to a black soft pair of chinos, and from a blue Oxford shirt to a college shirt. I felt fresh. I tried to ignore all worries and prepared for the hospital. Though it seemed that Sonponna, the Yoruba god of disease and sickness, had cursed me, but like a demigod I was taking up my armor. Perhaps in the human spirit a god-like strength lies. I wanted to fight. I wanted not to be smitten.

"Be strong," Baba encouraged me, still confused over the events. "God will be with you. And everything will be all right."

As I climbed down the stairs, leaving the house on an unknown journey, an idea came into my mind. It was a special prayer that a Sheik taught us and I decided to do it. I put my right palm to the sidewall of the stairway and said: "*Lailaha ilallahu* (*There is no other God but the One and only God*); take care of me, God. Don't let me die where I'm going. Help me, heal me, and when I come back into this house, I will complete this statement."

It was a contractual oath. The Sheik said it would secure safety in journeys or precarious conditions, like the one I was in, and that one must not fail to fulfill the promise of completing the statement. It is a glorious statement in Islam, the fundamental testament of faith, recited as a solemn affirmation of one's belief.

Whether it would work or not, I did not have the vaguest idea. But, I had faith. In the much of God that I knew, I had faith. Perhaps this was all I could have now. Perhaps it was all I needed. Faith may have been a gift to us as a tool against the uncertainty of human destiny - a tool that humankind may have developed out of his realization of his limitation and fear. Our life on earth seems to have been born out of an indiscriminate union of fear and faith, and when one is not in the heart of a man, the other is. It was the last thing I could hold on to, whether it was strong or less.

III

The harmattan season had just begun, but the hazy atmosphere that my eyes saw was from my condition and not of the season's. It seemed as if we were in a dream scene of a horror movie. There were five of us in the Peugeot 505 saloon car. Brother Tahiru drove, Bayo was seated beside him, and my grandmother and Uncle Jibola flanked me at the back seat as we pulled into the premises of the college hospital.

I could not use my right leg properly, so I leaned on Bayo as I walked into the emergency hall, my gait short and slow. I was signed in and passed on to a hall that looked like a passageway, with benches lined up on our left side and doctors' offices, draped with curtains, on our right. We sat among the people on the benches and waited for my turn to see a doctor.

When I heard my name called, the curtain directly in front of us drew apart and I hobbled inside. The office was clean and small, containing only a small examining table and a desk with two chairs on its opposite sides. The doctor, a student-doctor, occupied one of the chairs and offered the other to me. She was a young lady in her early twenties. Her topcoat was as white as snow, her eyes suggested an admirable mental brilliance, and she had a grace to her speech as she offered me the seat. She looked like someone academically serious, sometimes too serious, with eyes weary from years of tedious studying. In school we called such students *efiko*, a slang that meant *the bookish*, though with an ironic mockery or derogatory tone that was usually used unconsciously to disguise our envy for them. Everything about her reminded me of my sister Toyin: her grace, brilliance, profession, and her large-brimmed eyeglasses. As it was not easy for me to see my sister as a doctor, due to the years of familial disrespect with which we had lived together, I felt the same way with my new doctor.

Nonetheless, she intrigued me. Doctors always intrigued me, reminding me of the premium I placed on being useful in the world. Also, one of the sayings of Prophet Muhammad I learned was that the "most beloved of people to God is one who is most helpful to others." In Islam, God is everything, and being beloved to Him is the ultimate goal.

"How are you?" the doctor asked with a smile.

"I'm fine, thank you." As if I was truly fine.

"What's your problem?"

"I had pains in my pelvis and was admitted into a private hospital a week ago. But yesterday, when I was to be discharged, they discovered I had jaundice and they sent me here."

"You don't have the pains anymore?"

"Only a little bit in my right leg."

I gave her the transcript results of my blood and ultrasound tests and she browsed through them. She examined me briefly and then continued to ask questions.

"Could you tell me how it all started - what you think caused the pain, and any preceding ailments you had, if there were any?"

It seemed this lady was looking for a corpse already buried. I had a nagging feeling that all these may still have a connection with the *evil-day*, and something in me wanted to tell her everything, thinking she might thus be able to help me better enough. You tell doctors the truth to stay alive. But I was ashamed of my truth.

I began carefully from the *evil-day*, how I had felt the strange sensation, and up to the moment I was in front of her. But I did not tell her I smoked weed. When I saw she was silent in the next moments after my narration, I quickly added, "I've been smoking cigarettes heavily in the past few months, and I wonder if it could be connected to the strange feeling I've been experiencing." I thought smoking cigarettes heavily in months could pass for smoking weed in one day.

"Just cigarettes?" she asked, staring into my eyes, as if to have them divulge their secrets, as a babalawo looks for answers in his oracle. But my eyes were accustomed liars, trained over the years by experience.

"Just cigarettes," I replied.

"Nothing stronger than cigarettes?"

"No, nothing stronger than cigarettes. Or do you think I smoked marijuana or heroin?" I replied with a pretended embarrassment and distaste.

"No, I was just asking. One can't tell, you know?" she replied.

"Just cigarettes. That's all. Only heavily." I still emphasized the word 'heavily'.

She further asked some innocent questions and I gave her the innocent answers. I took off my shirt and lay down on the examining table at her request. The cold sensation of her stethoscope moved around my chest. She applied pressure on my limbs to know how they hurt. Feeling for my internal organs, she touched around my stomach, as I held at my pants, afraid for her hand to stray into restricted areas. I was yet to accept the fact that no part was restricted to doctors, and I was yet to be sick enough to forget anything private or unprivate on my body.

After about a half-hour of questioning, testing, and writing, she asked me to go back to my seat outside the curtain. I sat up, put on my shirt, and buttoned up. Initially, I felt just as I did when I walked in there, but as I stepped out of the curtain, I felt as if life was going out of me. My lungs lost its energy and breathing became a task. Slowly, my eyesight dimmed, like a lamp burned out of its last drop of fuel. My legs buckled at the knees and I was falling to the ground without realizing it.

Someone had noticed my condition and ran to grab me before I reached the floor. I heard my grandmother scream and I felt the presence of more people as they settled me on a bench.

My eyesight went completely out. I saw nothing, while I did not close my eyes. I only heard humming murmur of the voices around me, with my grandmother's voice over the rest, screaming my name, utterly distraught, and trying to call me back to life: "Ramoni! Ramoni! Ramoni!" I moaned, as I tried effortlessly to clasp onto life. I tried also to respond to my grandmother's call so I could give her some hope to hang on to. She was aged and hypertensive, and I was afraid of her falling sick by my sickness.

Another voice came over, giving directions. My shirt was unbuttoned and someone fanned me.

"Ramoni, Ramoni, have pity on me, please!" my grandmother pleaded, "Have pity on me; answer me; don't leave me like this, please, Ramoni!"

I still tried to respond to her, but, for a while, I could only make it with my breath. Laid on the bench, my whole world spun around my head and I did not know whether or not I would lose it.

After some time, I mustered some strength for something like words, but it was still more a moan. Then, my eyesight began to come back, like the lamp refueled. A wheelchair pulled up by my side and I was carried into it. Though I now could see, I shut my eyes and left myself only to feel the motion. A hospital maid pushed me and my people followed us. My grandmother bent to look at my face, and she called me again. I opened my eyes and assured her I was all right now, though I was only a little better.

We took an elevator and emerged onto a floor of which I had no idea, and then entered a long ward where we stopped before an empty bed. My grandmother kept bending over me to ensure how I was feeling. My repeated assurance did not help her.

Some drugs had already been prescribed, mostly injections, and Bayo went to buy them. We were to buy most of the drugs I needed from drug stores anywhere outside the hospital, including the drips, and I had to wait until Bayo came back before a drip-pole was set up. That was one of the sad realities at the hospital I was beginning to learn.

Since my left hand had been ailing from the previous needles' experience, I insisted on my right arm for the drip. The right arm now began its own sordid experience. I was given some injections and I fell into a short sleep.

***

"How about food?" my grandmother asked me when I woke up.

"It's all right, you could bring it." I was not hungry, but I had not eaten much before. And the better you eat, they said, the better your chances of quick recovery.

She served me a wrapped *amala* from a warmer and okra soup from another. It was my favorite local dish. The okra was served with fresh fish. Other than *gbegiri*, the favorite Oyo soup, there was not a better soup for *amala*, unless a mixture of both okra and *gbegiri*. A nurse helped raise my head and inclined my torso with a pillow. And I fed myself, wishing I were all right so I could eat better. It was with my grandmother's petting that I finished about half of the wrap, one-sixth of my normal non-gluttonous ration.

The doctor came and talked to me. It was as if she was teaching me a school subject, and I listened like a good student.

"For the jaundice, you'll need to help yourself more than we can help you, Rahman," she stated. "You have to be taking a lot of fluid. Fluids - any good form of it; that's what you need. You can put powdered glucose in water so you could be able to drink well. You need plenty of fluid."

She checked the flow of the drip - the second or third bag of drip in the last few hours. Satisfied, she talked a little with my uncle before she left the ward. She did not say anything about my leg, though she prescribed Chloramphenicol, an antibiotic. But then I realized there was no pain in my leg anymore. That came to me as a relief, and I thought I would be all right and discharged soon.

Across the ward, directly opposite my bed, I saw a new patient settle in. On a second look I saw he was a friend of mine called Desmin. His eyes met mine and we waived at each other. We both could not leave our beds. Another friend, Emanuel, was with him, attending to his sick needs. He was Desmin's alter ego, and they both were students at U.I. where I knew them. Emanuel came over to greet me.

I did not talk or move until evening. I lay inclined in bed, dazed and weak. I had no will to do anything and I had a delusion that I was on the ground floor. I had forgotten all preceding events, including the elevator ride, and would only later realize that I was three floors up from the ground floor.

People came to visit me in the evening. They kept company with me, though I was not always with them. Often my mind wandered aimlessly. Dr. Ishola also visited me and he tried repeatedly to assure me that I would be well soon.

At 6 pm, a nurse announced that all visitors should leave. The hospital's rule did not allow anyone to stay beyond 6 pm. A little after 6 a nurse asked me to eat. All the other patients had been served dinner from the hospital kitchen and were already eating. Though we had paid in advance for the service, as we had done for all the other services I was receiving, I could not eat the food from their kitchen. My grandmother left me food in a warmer, but I could not eat any food at the moment. I was not in any mood to eat.

When a clock on the wall adjacent to my bed read 8, or something close, a gorgeous young lady walked into the ward. Even though I remembered the prophets say the first glance is enough, and that the next may be a sin, I could not resist the temptation, and I was not too sick to look. Perhaps I was doing justice to God's artistry.

She wore a light make-up, and was dressed in an exquisitely elegant African dress. I once preferred Western clothes on girls: the tight jeans, the mini skirts, and other varieties displaying the seductive parts of the woman's body. Now, Paris, New York, London, and Milan may be in for a battle with the increasing works of modern African designers, if only they could escape the local and international economic obstacles against African businesses. The attire on this lady could make one think that we have finally discovered the female trend that will make it to Paradise - by which all the unaging virgins of the aging Islamic promise would be dressed. But perhaps there is not going to be any battle. Modern designers seemed to be integrating, mixing up styles for the 21st century: African, Western, Asian, Latino - the liberalism and tolerance of fashion, the kind found in arts and science, but unfortunately lost in politics.

The lady paused by the two nurses on duty and talked to them. I could not believe my eyes when one of the nurses pointed toward my bed. I was the one she came to see! I did not know who she was, but seeing this, I was eager to meet her, even if only to say hello. She thanked the nurses and walked over to my bed, with a feline grace that befitted her image.

"Hello," she said. Her vivacious beam was invigorating.

"Hello," I replied, still wondering who she was and what she wanted with me.

"This is our first meeting," she said. "My name is Nike. Aunty Iyabo told me about you and I thought to stop by."

Aunty Iyabo is my mother's cousin who worked at the hospital. She visited me earlier when she learned of my admission. Perhaps, then, Nike was a relative or a family friend. I waited to know which she was.

We exchanged more cordial greetings and she drew a seat close to my bed. For the next few minutes we talked about my condition, and then she said, "I'm a student nurse here and I live at the hostel down there." She indicated the direction of her hostel. "I can always come and give you company anytime I am free, especially night-time when visitors aren't allowed in here."

"That's kind of you; thank you." Now I was uncomfortable that I had earlier stared at her shamelessly, as if she was Halle Berry taking off her clothes in a show I had paid to see.

When Nike learned I had not eaten, she served me and inclined my bed more to bring me close to a sitting position. Still, I did not feel like eating. My right arm was taking the drips and I had the nerve-pinch in my left arm. I did not yet know how I could go about eating like that. I gave her an excuse so I would not have to deal with the situation in her presence. But she did not buy it. Instead, she sat beside me on the bed and tried to feed me.

"Oh, no, no, don't do that; I'll eat when I'm ready."

"Never mind. I understand; I'll help you do it. Or are you shy of me doing it?" A spoonful was already knocking the door to my mouth. Reluctantly, I opened and she fed me. She mixed a new bottle of water with glucose and, as I had been doing all day, I drank until my stomach would not take anymore.

I was touched by Nike's caring. In one moment she was a complete stranger, and in the next she was my close friend. I had not yet known the kind of seed in the friendship or family plantation that brought us together, but with her beautiful mind, she had cultivated a full-grown flower whose splendor dimmed whatever seed into little recognition. Already I felt as if I had known her a long time.

"Thank you, Nike," I said to her.

"Never mind. Just get your spirit up and get well soon. That's what I want. And I'll always be here for you."

About two hours later when she was about to leave, she asked what I would like for dinner the next day. She wanted to make it for me. "Tell Mama not to worry about cooking you dinner tomorrow," she stated.

I did not know what to say, and I still had not known what to say when she asked again, "Would you like rice?"

"By God, you've already done enough."

"Never mind that - rice or beans?"

Still I did not know what to say. She had swept me off my balance and I must have nodded in acceptance, for she smiled and bid me goodnight. I watched her as she walked out, with the same grace she had walked in.

***

My doctor came to treat me for the night.

"You've not been taking enough fluid, Rahman," she said as she looked away from the report in my case file. The nurses had been testing my urine and noting the result each time they disposed it from the bedpan.

"I have," I replied. "In fact, this is the second bottle (about 3 liters in a short period)."

"You need to take more; the report shows that you've not been taking enough. And I told you, plenty of fluid is what you need."

Perhaps I would need a spare stomach.

"How's your leg doing?" she asked.

"It's fine. I don't feel the pain anymore. I think it's gone, or almost."

"Can you lift it up for me to see? Both of them, please," she demanded.

I had not lifted them off the bed since late in the morning because I did not need to. I did not think anything to it and I tried to lift them up.

But, alas, my legs were stone heavy, with the right one heavier. As much as I tried, I could not lift them off the bed.

God, what is this? I thought in utter dismay, realizing that the condition of the legs had become one I had never experience before. It was a completely strange phenomenon. No matter how my pain was in the past, I had always been able to lift my legs and walk with them. Now, even when I felt no pain, I could not lift them at all. I felt the problem around my right hip joint; it was a pinioning feeling I could not describe, but it was not pain.

The doctor asked for my medicines and gave me a Chloramphenicol shot before she left for the night.

Something transpired between my father and me on the day I last returned from Oyo. When I went to say goodbye to him, he asked, "Do you pray regularly?" I told him I did. He asked me what *sura* or *ayat* of the Qur'an I used, and I told him it was the *Ayat al-Qurisiyy* – the 255th verse of the second chapter. "Good," he said. Then he asked me to include *Ayudafiu*, a special prayer composed by venerated scholars. "It's good for everything," he said, "protection, healing, prosperity."

Since then, I had been offering the synergic prayer at bedtime over my condition. And on this night, with the fear of my unknown condition renewed, I offered it silently as I lay down to sleep.

***

When one cannot sleep in a night, the period of the night becomes an eternity. As much as I tried, I could not sleep until around 5 in the morning, as if cursed by Hypnos, the Greek god of sleep.

Tossing and turning have a way of reducing the torment of sleeplessness, though only a little, but my condition did not allow me the luxury. My torso also was heavy, almost as my legs. Like this, I could not lift myself up from the bed. To sit up in bed, I would have to drag my legs arduously to the edge of the bed, drop them off, and then pull myself up with my claws in the mattress. I itched to wriggle my body, but my limitation made it a trauma. To make things worse, the lights went out in the middle of the night. I remained in the pitch-black, still night, staring into the darkness for two unnerving hours before the light came back on.

All through the night there was always one nurse at a time to watch over us. There were two nurses for the ward, but they split their time to help themselves sleep. It was their regular practice. At 12 am one would go into an inner room to sleep until 3 am while the other would keep the watch. At 3 they would switch places for the period between 3 am to 6 am, but they called for each other's help whenever necessary.

My sleep was shallow and short. It was filled with disturbing hallucinations, which made me ironically glad to be awake again by 6 am, despite that I still longed for sleep.

The cleaners came in and the night nurses signed out as two other nurses signed in. I lay supine in bed, staring ahead and around with disinterest. My mind now was hazy, as much as my eyesight was.

IV

Harmattan was the coldest season in Nigeria, though students could still wear short pants and mini skirts to school. A few broken glasses in the windows and doors of the ward allowed the chills of the season to drift in. I covered myself well in my bed.

At exactly 6 am an old woman came into the ward. She had a son in the ward, who was always tied to the bed, as the pains in his body troubled him mentally. He was noisy for most part of the night, violently rocking his bed up and down.

The old woman was the first visitor in the ward and I guessed she was allowed in that early because of her deprived situation. I was to learn that she was so poor that she could not afford to pay for transportation to go home at night and come back in the morning. She slept outside at the hospital gates. She was also under pressure from the hospital; the authority threatened to throw out her son because she did not buy the necessary drugs for his treatment, and he was overdue in hospital bills. She begged for the hospital's patience to allow her some time to get money from the young man's brother, a soldier whom she had sent for, apparently from a distant state. Desmin and some other patients contributed the little drugs the young man was receiving at the moment, and I gave him my meal tickets.

That was the sorry story of a fellow human being, and emblematic of a nation in decline. The hospital, like most other public hospitals in the country, had changed for the worse. They seemed to contain no hospitality anymore. In the past, when the well-being of the human life was the priority, treatments would be promptly dispensed to save a patient's life, whether he had money or not. That was the period when U.C.H. was rated among the ten best hospitals in the world, a period when Nigeria was among the world's most prosperous nations.

Now, Nigeria was among the most economically and structurally depreciating nations and her hospitals were falling apart. A famous soccer player would later die at this hospital from a gun wound because the hospital did not have water supply at the moment to perform a surgery on him. If he died in this manner, one may wonder, in spite of his fame, social class, and wealth, what hope could the faceless poor people have?

Cynically, some people now called public hospitals as *mortuaries*, because it seemed that it was only the mortuary section that was working properly, especially when its rate of intakes was disproportionably higher from the failings of other sectors of the hospitals. But, if the dead in there could talk, perhaps they, too, would have complaints on certain unmet needs: repeated power outages, for one, making a mess of their cryonics - unless they left that to punish us through our nostrils.

While some people blamed the suspension of foreign aids by sanctions, some suspected all the circumstances surrounding the aids in the first place, both internally and externally. It was appalling that as wealthy as Nigeria was, rich in natural resources, she was far from self-sufficiency. Perhaps, material wealth is not the primary factor for self-sufficiency, but intelligence; whereas the successive Nigerian governments in the last few years had lacked intelligence. They had understood their Machiavelli reading backward and had only been selfishly cunning. Yet, like the proverbial ticks that lived parasitically on the dog, thinking they were killing only the dog, the Nigerian rulers blindly adhered to power, sucking out the nation's blood and oblivious to the fact that the ticks could not survive beyond the dog's life.

The hospital workers on their side had been so frustrated and made obdurate in their present condition. Perhaps, they could not do less, sometimes. I could never forget one night in August when, at the private hospital in which I was admitted, a dying patient brought in was turned back because his people could not pay the up-front fee for his treatment. And many good medical hands were fleeing the country for greener pastures.

My grandmother walked into the ward at 7 am. She carried a food warmer in her hand and her worries in her eyes. I feigned a smile to change her mood.

"*Oko mi*, how do you feel now?" she asked as she reached me.

"I'm much better this morning," I lied.

"Did you sleep well?"

"Very well."

A silent moment followed, in which she searched my eyes to be sure of what to believe, what I said or what my eyes revealed. I quickly found something to divert her attention.

"Nike came here last night," I said. The name was not pronounced as the sportswear maker's, neither as the goddess Athena's epithet, the Greek word for victory, but like 'nickel' with letter 'l' omitted.

"Oh, that's nice of her. Did you know her before?"

"No, it was my first time meeting her, but I figured that she's either a family friend or a relation. I did not want to ask her about it because she expected that I knew already."

I learned that Nike and I are second-generation cousins, and my trick improved my grandmother's mood. She brought out my food.

I could not like the sight of any food in the world at this moment, and I did not like the sight of the one laid down in front of me. However, if she knew this, she would know the truth of my condition. I dragged my legs down and pulled myself upright in bed. She wheeled the dining table to a position she thought comfortable enough for me, not knowing that there was no position in the world comfortable for me at the moment. I picked at my food while I tried to maintain conversation with her to obscure the betrayal my eating manner could give my condition.

"Have you talked to Uncle Jibola about getting you the car?" I asked. She had planned to ask him to buy her a car.

"Oh no, I'm not asking him anymore," she replied. "He has spent a lot of money in the few days he has been here. Not that he wouldn't want to do it, but he has impressed me too much than to ask him again for anything. He has gone to many places and reached many people that I hadn't expected. People have been coming to thank me for what he has done for them. Imagine, people I hadn't seen in years. I'm overwhelmed and I'm leaving the issue of the car for another time."

"That's true," I said. Uncle Jibola had always been like that, caring for everyone he knew.

I did not eat much, but I took a lot of water, enough to give me a potbelly, which must have looked ugly on my lean body. I was not getting better and I knew it. I did not want my grandmother to be with me any longer; I could not keep up the pretense for long. I wanted to lie down. I wanted to wriggle. I wanted to moan. I wanted to cry. But not when she was there with me. My eyesight now gave me only a surreal impression of the world around me.

"Why don't you go on to the shop?" I asked her, "I think I want to sleep some more."

"Don't worry about me; just sleep. I'm fine here. I came to stay with you for the day."

"No, no, you don't need to do that. I'm already recovering and I can take care of myself now. Besides, you know the shop is not safe without you there."

"Forget about the shop. I'm staying here with you. You get well and everything will be fine. What is the shop when you are down in here?"

That hit my bosom and I looked away for some time. I could not risk a teardrop now, yet it was close to rain down my cheeks. I was cautious not to tell her to go again; she might sense I was not at ease with myself. She knew her grandson better than anyone did. I lay back in bed and, haltingly, we talked on.

The doctor came for the morning treatment. She went through the urine reports, but still was not satisfied, even though I had drunk heavily throughout the night. She asked me to try to lift my legs. She spoke in English and that saved me the problem of letting my grandmother know exactly what was going on. I could not yet lift up the legs and I told her. But I could drag them, and I dragged them down to sit on the bed, like a one-trick magician repeating his only trick again and again to cover up his emptiness.

"Don't worry, everything will soon be fine," the doctor assured me. "Just keep taking plenty of fluid." She brought out some glass tubes from a small container and took samples of my blood before she left.

***

Next to my bed on the right side was the bed of a young man around my age. His name was Segun and he had never left his bed since I came. I later learned that he could not use his legs yet.

Next to Segun was another young man, Tunde, also around my age. He occupied the first bed in our row, closest to the only TV set in the ward. I remembered he was in my hair in the night with the late show on, loud. Tunde appeared to have recovered from whatever ailment he had. Unlike the rest of us, he did everything by himself. He hurried to the bathroom every morning, and, with Emanuel, he used his condition to help the rest of us, Desmin, Segun, and me. Together, we eventually became a kind of hospital fraternity. Emanuel always came in the morning and stayed until evening.

I did not bother to know how many beds were in the ward, but I knew there were many, perhaps twelve, and all occupied. There were about six student doctors carrying the primary responsibilities of the patients in the ward, with a few others helping them when needed. The only luxury I had throughout the weekend was to sit up on the bed, and only for a few minutes at a time. I was very sick, growing weaker, and I had no sense of location. I heard noise from outside and around the building, sometimes unsettling, as if there was a swamp of suffering people circling the ward and murmuring. Though, I never really paid attention, the truth was that there was no noise. I was on the fourth floor, far above anyone that could be around the building, and what I was hearing might have been sounds from the world trying to claim me, a world perhaps only within my head.

About twice during the weekend, however, we all heard outbursts of people weeping and lamenting over deaths of their loved ones at the hospital. As terrifying as this was, my only escape was absorption under the most immediate pressure of my own fate. I did not know of any reality beyond my bed. My personality, my history, and the entire world I had ever known were shut away, and my bed became the aperture through which I was being sucked into another world.

People came to wish me well, uncles, aunts, cousins, in-laws, and family friends, bringing different kinds of gifts suitable to a sick person. I only could smile and wink in acknowledgment of their presence. They all wore sorry looks, but careful not to make it obvious enough to poke my mental guard and worsen my condition.

I was given Chloramphenicol regularly and I was placed on drips most of the time. By the end of the weekend, I had begun to feel pain again in my right leg. Though not a severe one, and not my usual type of pain, it was enough to make me restless. The nerve-pinch in my left arm continued to trouble me, and it seemed to be growing beyond what I thought it to be. Above all, I did not sleep much, at least, not more than about one hour in each 24-hour day. I was given painkilling and sleep-inducing injections regularly, but neither worked. I took in and pissed out fluid as if I was some kind of figurine fountain of special art. Yet, most of the time my doctor was not satisfied with the urine test results.

"You need to do better, Rahman," she always said.

V

At around 11 on Monday morning, a huge man walked into the ward. Surrounded by student-doctors, he looked more like a researcher mistakenly blessed with the body of a bouncer, and less like a physician. My doctor had informed me about him and I had been waiting for him all morning. It had seemed a never-ending wait, as I had him in my mind as if he was going to be Jesus Christ - to come in and perform a miracle to take away my sickness. By this time, I had come to understand that my doctor had not found the control of my sickness. She had not even found the correct diagnosis.

The huge man was a professor of medicine and he was the young doctors' instructor. He was an elderly man with a thick voice. His disposition seemed to be saying, *I have no time to waste*, as if forced to make this visit from his research laboratory where he was about to hit the formula for an AIDS vaccine or immortality elixir. My doctor was one of the nearly twelve doctors around him, and one of the two females among them. They started the day's work at the first bed and eventually reached mine.

As they had done with the first and second patients, they draped my bed around and enclosed themselves in with me. My doctor unclipped my case file from the bed's frame and read out my case to their attentive audience. But I was not attentive. I was eager, expecting Prof, as he was called, to get busy and free me of my bondage. I had thought it was going to be a big doctoring session, with all the young doctors to help him fight my tormentor, but I was disappointed to see that they were holding a lecturing session with me. The Prof asked questions objectively after the case reading, and, as in a classroom, the young doctors answered their instructor. My doctor seemed the most brilliant of them. She answered most of the questions with a dazzling brightness, not only on my case, which was her only case in the ward, but on all the other cases into which I later lent my ears after they left me. The thought of being an experimental subject at this moment disturbed me a little; nonetheless I followed the session.

But the professor did not just lecture. He sought my complaints afterward and I told him of the pains, weakness, and sleeplessness. He advised my doctor on some drugs, of which I can only recall a drug called *Petidin* or something like it. It was in the family of the depressant morphine, a compound named after Morpheus, the Greek and Roman god of dreams, son of Hypnos (or Somnus) the god of sleep, perhaps alternatively to appease the god in the scientific way to give relieve from pain, tension, and sleeplessness.

I was given a shot of the Petidin. The nurses expected the drug to make me sleep and they kept visitors away from me, but for hours I did not sleep. I was only tranquilized. My eyes were wide open, as if they were surveillance cameras for a high-profile bank or Mafia fortress. I lay in bed, staring at the tall ceiling and hearing the muffled voices of people around in undisturbing murmur.

By the evening I felt better and I had my bed inclined to view the activities in the ward from a better angle. I remained in this position when Nike came around 8 pm. She brought me dinner again: a dish of rice, fried plantain, and fresh fish. After I fed myself, she helped me lie properly, supposedly for the night's sleep before she said goodnight.

The ward was still and silent, except for the sound of the late-night movie on TV. Tunde was enjoying himself. I waited for sleep to sweep me into the night as the ward ate into time slowly. By midnight, all the patients had slept, or so it seemed. The first-shift nurse was already dozing, but I had not slept, and it was not as if I was going to sleep anytime soon.

In addition, as if I had wronged the sleep-god and he was taking it out on me, I became restless. No position would comfort me. The stillness of the ward also unnerved me and I wanted to turn here and there. But I could not turn anywhere beyond the wriggling of my heart and chest. Tossing and turning became precious to me. When I looked at some other patients already sleeping and turning, I coveted their good fortune. I had wanted to sleep, but now my condition had so deteriorated that all I wanted was just to be calm.

Yet, my condition deteriorated further. I was still wriggling for comfort when, suddenly, I felt the presence of people around me, moving back and forth and across my bed. I did not see anything at first and I thought it might have been from my state. I closed my eyes and tried to shut off my mind, but when it did not help, I impulsively opened my eyes. Then I saw a shadow of a small creature jump over my bed. Simultaneously, I felt its pressure on my legs and the bed as it passed by and I immediately became frightened. What in the world was that? I did not know. I looked around, as much as my position could allow, but I saw nothing anymore. No one was around me.

I was afraid that my condition was now making me see things I should not be seeing. If this was a hallucination, then I better keep it to myself and try to get out of this sickness. I did not want anyone to think I was now going crazy. Even when I smoked weed, I had not seen anything.

Out of the torment of the fear and sleeplessness, I dragged down my legs and slid off the bed slowly. I stood up and realized that my legs could still carry me - although I had not expected them not to. I did not want to waste anytime. If I could not go to sleep, I could use the time for exercise that would help me improve quickly, and perhaps arrest the onset of any hallucination. I began to walk around my bed. I felt weak and frail, but I struggled on. I supported myself with the bed as I walked.

I tired out fast, having to sit and rest after each cycle around the bed. I tried on, until I could not do it any longer. I lay down, hoping now to catch some sleep after such a strenuous exercise. I was wrong. I still could not sleep. When the light went out, I stared restlessly into the darkness for the two hours. Though I had been accustomed to the blackout as a routine, my condition made the burden of the darkness heavier to bear. I remembered the Petidin and I called the nurse on duty. I wanted, at least, the kind of tranquility it had given me in the afternoon.

"It's addictive," the nurse said to me. "You shouldn't be taking it all the time, and we won't allow it."

"I won't become addicted," I argued. "I'm restless and unable to sleep; that's why I need it now."

I did not give a darn about becoming addicted; I just wanted to be calm and, if possible, sleep.

"I won't give you Petidin," she maintained, "I'll give you Valium injection instead."

She gave me the Valium injection and I waited to sleep. One hour, two hours, three hours, I was still wide-awake, as if I had not taken anything. As usual, I ended up not sleeping until about 5 am in the morning, and I was back awake at 6 am.

About an hour later, my grandmother arrived with my breakfast. This time I could not disguise my condition. Concerned, she asked about it.

"I did not sleep much, and that's why I feel this way now. I'd try to get some sleep after my breakfast." I still tried to control the ideas she received of what was going on.

I was hungry but could not eat much, not even half as much as she expected. She was worried, and, that morning, we prayed and hoped. I was given Petidin injection again and I was tranquilized for some hours.

Though my body was failing, my spirit was not. I still strove mentally to get well and out of the hospital. My doctor encouraged me and maintained my hope. She went about my treatment in what I saw as the best of her capacity. Day and night, she was taking care of me. However, it had become obvious that the control of the sickness still eluded her. I could see her confusion every time she was with me. She continued to take samples of my blood and sent me for x-ray photographs, looking for what the problem was. Even, weekend days, during which the laboratory and the radiology department were closed, she was not held up in her struggle. She opened all closed doors in her effort to help me.

After many days at the hospital, I was not sleeping much, and I went on Petidin more than the nurses' professional minds could negligibly contain. During some of the nights, I tried to get some walking exercise, but it did not help. Also, despite my drinking like a horse, the jaundice did not improve. I was gradually becoming weaker, but I could not help it. No one yet could help it. I was dying.

People continued to visit me. I tried to deal with them with flippancy toward my condition, so as to appear better to them. I did not like being the source of pity in people, and as a result, I tried to avoid taking or feeling myself as pitiable. My father also came, and, in his habit, he built an atmosphere of levity, concealing his worries over the sickness.

One of my cousins and her husband visited me for the first time one evening. Though she had wanted to wish me well, she ended up ruining my evening. As they entered the ward, I beamed as I always did to visitors, but I quickly realized that they were not returning my expression. They wore their sadness like facemasks and, before they reached me, she broke down in tears.

I did not know I was so bad as to cause anyone to cry. I had thought I was shielding the gravity of my condition successfully from everyone. On instruction unknown to me then, everyone had been careful not to let me have a mirror, despite my repeated request for it. They always found one excuse or another to put me off the idea. I tried to console my cousin as she wept uncontrollably into her husband's shoulders. After they had departed, I inveigled someone into mirroring my appearance, and I came to know that I looked every inch the dying creature that I was. I was extremely frail and pale. Even my sick eyes have been deceiving me and I had not seen the severity of my condition on my hands and fingers. They were so yellow that they could rub off on a surface.

I did not worry about the frailty of my body – afterall, no one expects to grow robust on the sick bed. I worried on the sick hue of my skin. It reminded me of how strange my condition was to my knowledge.

There was nothing I could do than to keep trying in spirit and obey my doctor's instructions. She seemed to know what she was doing, though what she was doing it on was not justifying her effort, or not yet. For this at least, I knew I had to be vigilant about things going on around me, even if she was an expert with years of experience, and not a student doctor. No one is a perfect master of all situations, and the highest diver is also prone to belly flops. I knew what a belly flop would mean in my current situation. For the diver, she could always try again. For me, the only advice would be that given to my friend Hagler, for my soul to choose a better destiny if given another chance. And it would be painful to me if I could have seen it coming - if I could have helped it. This was my life, and whichever way my destiny would turn, whichever destination it would reach, I had to be there. Because something must end this story, and my actions, consciously or unconsciously, will determine that end.

Something happened one early morning. One of the hospital cleaners, an elderly woman, said something strange to me, but it did not warn me of anything. She was mopping the floor around my bed when she paused, looked at me for a long time, and said, "You are in the wrong place, my dear. A golden lamb is torn apart by wolves, and its meat shared and taken back to their den. The shepherd now comes looking around the barn for the poor thing. Isn't he looking in the wrong place? Time is running out, my dear. Time - is running out." It was the first time I would see the woman and, as it turned out, it was the only time I would ever see her among the hospital cleaners. Who she was, I could not find out.

I was not disturbed by this, or weighed down too much by the gloomy cloud over my health, but I prayed that my family and friends were not seeing the last of me.

SEVEN

The Decision

I

"It was a week after my admission and two of my friends, Desmin and Tunde, had been discharged. The elderly nurses in my ward then advised my doctor to try the hematologists. Sometimes the experience of long-working nurses serve better than that of young doctors. Working with different doctors and patients over years, they would have seen plenty. Immediately, my doctor sent a letter to the hematology department. Hematologists are experts on blood and its diseases, and thus specialists on my genotypic crisis, suspected to be my primary problem. They came to my ward on Sunday, but things did not turn out in my favor.

The Sunday was the last day of Uncle Jibola's two-week visit and he came to wish me well and say goodbye. Even though he had been visiting me everyday, there had not been an opportunity to talk or do anything on my American plan. How events often mock at human foresight. Something I had been expecting for a long time was now slipping through my fingers.

Uncle Jibola stood by my bed and was studying my x-ray photographs. Being in the medical profession, he had been paying close attention to my condition and treatments. After working as a dentist for years, he had picked up the guts to go and start all over in the medical school, his goal ever since he was a little kid. I did not know many people with such fortitude, and I always wondered how one could do it. Now I guessed such a dramatic step in one's life takes not only the nerve to make the decision, but also patience to go through it. Uncle Jibola was an embodiment of patience, dedication, and care, which was the reason I always thought he was in the field perfect for him. It was as if he brought to the world all the patience my mother forgot to bring from heaven, when, perhaps, she was in haste to see the beauty of the world. "You're going to be her brother, aren't you?" God may have asked my uncle, perhaps in His famous deep bass voice. "Take all the patience with you, man; she might later have to learn them from you. Or her son might. 'Cause the way I'm looking at him now, he's got his eyes on the world out there; he might forget to take his too. Like mother like son." And I did forget, and from my uncle's life I was learning patience.

Uncle Jibola was still examining the photographs when three hematologists walked in. Two of them, a man and a woman, were probably in their late 20s. The third was an elderly doctor, their instructor, and he looked in his late 40s or early 50s. They stood at the foot of my bed and stared at me.

After a few minutes and they were still standing there, I asked if there was anything they still needed.

"He's the one we are waiting for," the woman said as she gestured in the direction of my uncle and as their chief walked away from my bed. She and her colleague promptly followed him and they went over to another patient.

Uncle Jibola was at the head side of my bed, and was absorbed in the photographs. He saw the hematologists all right, but we did not think he was in their way. The hematologists had said nothing and there was no way anyone could have thought what they needed. Besides, no doctor that worked with me had seen my visitors as obstruction, and my doctor always chatted with my uncle whenever she met him there. Nonetheless, Uncle Jibola immediately stepped out of the ward to allow them the freedom they wanted.

I did not like the situation. I was too eager for treatment than to be passed over like this. Yet, there was nothing I could do other than to wait for them to finish with the other patient and return to me.

But they did not return after they were done with the patient. They went to a few other patients, and after about a half hour, they walked out of the ward. I was not sure what was going on, but after waiting a long time, staring expectantly at the door, I realized that they had deliberately ignored me.

I called my uncle back in. I tried not to worry about it, hoping that they knew what they were doing and would return at the right time.

"There's not much we can do now," Uncle Jibola said, beginning the conversation about my plan. This conversation was important to me, and every cell of my body was attentive. "For now, you'll have to brace yourself up and get well. Your health is the most important thing now. Everything else would be fine as soon as you are well.

"About coming to America - since things are the way they are now, and I have to go back, there's nothing we can do right now. The best I can suggest then is for you to apply for a student visa when you are all right. I'll pay the tuition and all necessary fees and the embassy should give you the visa then. However, you'll have to wait until June (about six months from now). I'm just beginning a program, and it's taking a lot of my money. By June, I should be able to pay your tuition and you could come then." He fixed his gaze at me for my reaction.

"It's ok," I replied, solemnly. It was the reality and I had to take it. Besides, it did not seem too bad, if I could get well quickly and find something to do. We talked about taking computer classes and I thought it was a good idea. And if Chief Bernard's process yielded, I might not have to wait that long.

From his bag he brought out the current issues of *Ebony* and *Sport's Illustrated* magazines. "I'll leave you some money with Alhaja (my grandmother)."

I thanked him, and after some time, he lifted his bag and I bid him farewell.

***

Angry, my doctor came the next morning and accused me of keeping a visitor to obstruct the hematologists. I was upset to realize how they had interpreted it. I explained to her what happened and she eventually understood.

She went to them and came back to tell me they will come again. But the hematologists seemed to have their hearts at the back of their spine. Intended as a punishment for me, they would not come back until after a week. One may wonder whether they ever took the Hippocratic oath. A punishment of neglect by specialists for a dying patient? Nonetheless, this was a bad portent for me and it worsened my already degenerating condition.

I had spent two weeks at the hospital, but I had not slept more than an hour and a half in any day. I still always had my sleep around 5 in the morning, only to be up again about an hour later. Sometimes I would sleep for about half-hour more during the day, but most times none. Yet, many times, my little naps in the morning were without satisfactory depth, haunted by dismal half-dreams. Often, I would find myself in some kind of trance in which my environments would be horrifyingly surreal and in devilish darkness. Sometimes, when the scenes were sunlit, the sun would be bleary-eyed, as if it had been shedding tears of blood. It would make things seem unnatural and completely out of order, like a cosmic disorder in Greek mythology, perhaps with Zeus rending the sky and banishing the Titans to eternal damnation. If one thing was not chasing me about, another would be tormenting me. I call them dreams because they occurred as if in my sleep; they were much more than dreams, for they occurred in a state of my consciousness where I was neither asleep nor awake.

In one ordeal, I witnessed one of the most bizarre experiences I had ever had in my life - though the strangest thing about it would come years later when I realized I may have lived to fulfill its forecast.

I found myself in front of Bodija market on an afternoon. I neither knew from where I was coming nor to where I was going. It was a sad afternoon, perhaps toward the sunset. The sun was bleary-eyed and the sky wore a thick gloom that expressed its passive sorrow, drizzling things that looked like fire but smelled like something else unknown. It was as if it was doomsday. I knew it; God has promised He would not destroy the world with water anymore. Now it is fire, and the fire has come. The message was thick in the air, unspoken and unwritten, but loud and vivid: THE END OF THE WORLD HAS COME. Bodija market was one of the largest markets in Ibadan and the thousands of people there this afternoon scrambled for home in horrid fear.

The place was in helter-skelter and I found myself caught up in the haste. I wanted to get home before the "End" closed in on me. I wanted to die among my people, not in this disordered, burning market where everyone was tormented by the atmosphere. Yet, the picture of the home was lost to my imagination. Which home I was hurrying toward, I did not know, but I did not seem like I did not know. It was not Oniyanrin, not any place; it was just home, an unknown home, an unconscious home.

"Home" was only a concept in my head, but the impulse for the home was aggressive in me. I floundered to catch a bus, but all the buses had been struck by the fate of the day, some of them smoldering in the fiery downpour.

Then I woke up. I did not know how I got away from the market scene, but I woke up into the semi-darkness of the hospital ward, where I had fallen asleep only an hour before. Suddenly, I felt a jolt on my left knee as I saw the shadow of a creature jump off my leg and onto the bed frame. It was like the small figure I had seen in the previous week. I thought I was still dreaming and I rubbed frantically at my eyes. Then, I noticed that they were more than one; there were three of them as they moved into focus at the foot of my bed. They were the most dreadful creatures I had ever seen in my life. Less than three feet tall, they looked like overgrown infants. My heart raced and my body trembled. And after a few minutes, I woke up the second time.

II

There was no safety in my familiar wakefulness either. The physical and emotional trauma did not make me fair better than my trance-like dreams. My health was not yet improving, and I still was trying to cover the truth from my grandmother. I got up as quickly as I could in my snail manner whenever she was around, and lied to her that the drugs were working fine, especially a ridiculously expensive drug she had had to break into her savings to afford. Suggested to my doctor that it might perform wonders, it cost my grandmother about a thousand naira each day.

But my grandmother was not deceived about my true condition. In fact, one event gave me completely away. She came to visit me one morning and I picked up my act. With great effort, I tried to keep up a shrouding conversation and she seemed to be taking my intended impression.

"What would you like for lunch today?" she asked with a progressive air. She knew that if I could choose and eat well, then I was improving.

I thought for a moment, knowing that I was sick of anything that looked like food, and I asked for yam and fried egg. I hoped she would send the food back to me and would not be there when I had to do the chore of eating, but she went home to prepare the food and brought it by herself. As she walked into the ward, I struggled up to a sitting position and made myself ready to eat a meal I was not hungry for. I managed to start eating.

The first bite was enough. The second was too much. It made me feel sicker and I could not eat any further. She urged me on, but I could not go on. That informed her I was not improving as I had been pretending. She was disconsolate as she left the hospital with the remnants. Each of her sad steps out of the ward gave me the saddest moments of my life. Out of my sight, my imagination continued to picture her steps further down the building and onto the street. What a world in which mothers cannot feel safe over their children. Day and night she wept at home, depressed at her dream going sour.

Nike continued to give me company in the late evenings and she took up the responsibility of taking care of me, as I needed. As if a nurse working in my ward and solely for me, she saw to my regular treatments. She did my petty washing and bathed me. In the middle of one night she ran around the doctors' hostel, knocking on doors in search of a doctor to attend to my emergency need, and eventually dragging out of bed a young man who saw an opportunity of dating a cute lady.

People brought various gifts to encourage and aid my recovery. But in the midst of all the love and positive expectation, I continued to languish. The jaundice worsened, and the sleeplessness and restlessness persisted. I was given Petidin once in a while to enjoy some tranquility in my life. Whatever the god of sickness was, he still hanged around me, smiling and feeding on my health. I had been sacrificed for his pleasure, and I lay on his altar, bleeding. I prayed he did not kill me. I prayed he spared me for my family.

***

On Saturday afternoon, my doctor announced that I needed to be transfused urgently. Though my blood-count had been below normal since my admission, the rate at which it was dropping had frighteningly increased. A pint of blood was N400, and, according to the hospital rules, I had to produce four donors for replacement before I could buy the pint. Blood banks were in dire shortages and people were not donating. According to my doctor, however, my present need was so urgent that she secured a waiver for now, and I could produce the donors later.

I had never been transfused before and it was fun to watch the red liquid glide slowly into my body. But I could not savor that for long. For the process, I had to remain in a position, and that heightened my restlessness. I felt as if I was freezing up in the state. Then something unexpected happened.

A nurse came over to check the flow of the blood and she was shocked at what she saw. The blood had clotted, all the way from the blood-bag to the tip of the needle. Yet, I had not taken more than a quarter of the pint. From the nurse's reaction, I understood it was a rare and dangerous occurrence, by which she was momentarily lost of what to do. "Thank Jesus it was not in your body," she said. But it was close.

They did not see any reason for the blood-clot and they hurriedly sent for my doctor. It was mysterious and she could not understand either. But her worst fear was that I had to wait until the next day before I could receive another one.

I did my prayer for the night.

***

Sunday turned out to be a day I will always remember, with events meaning more than I could imagine at the moment. The whole of it could have been half of a single day, with the following Monday as the other half. It was a day of a crucial decision in my life, one so critical that it raised questions that I would deal with for a very long time into my future. And it was a day I did not die, giving back the future almost denied me.

I woke up as terrible as I had always been lately, and the normal routine of the hospital workers went on in my dismal sight. Christmas was drawing closer and today was for the hospitals' Christmas Carol. The ward was specially decorated with fresh flowers and white linens. The most beautiful ward was to be awarded by the hospital management. The nurses looked ceremonious and eager.

I wished I were one of the nurses, so I could feel the breeze of the moment - the scent and thrills of the approaching yuletide. But I was not. I was myself, and for myself alone I felt the smoldering fire inside my blood, bones, flesh, and heart. I wished I had been an insensate natural object - maybe Mount Everest, the Kilimanjaro, Mount Arafat, the Olumo Rock, a monumental statue, an ancient obelisk, a river, or part of the blowing wind - anything but the miserable creature that I was. Or if I had died at birth, I would not have had to go through all this and my family would have forgotten that I came at all into the world. Perhaps I would have been in Paradise, as Jesus says for little kids. Now, I had known plenty. I had known the world, known my family, known career and ambition, known the pleasure of sex, and I did not want to leave them just like that. Perhaps, these were the hell of grown-ups. Moreover, I was living through a kind of hell unique to me.

Around midday, I saw the three hematologists walk in toward my bed, but I did not see trouble walk in with them. I did not have a clear picture of what went on the moment they came. I was absent-minded, awry-focused, and my concentration had been disturbed by my growing sense of insecurity. The next thing I knew was that my right leg was bandaged and put in traction. They elevated my bed at the foot-end to make a slope downward to my head and about 40-pound metal weight was suspended from my ankle. It was the most uncomfortable position I had so far been at the hospital.

Simultaneously, my doctor set up another transfusion and my right hand was also hooked up, connected to the blood-bag through a rubber duct. Then the ward began to shed its skin, revealing itself now as the real underworld where, as God had angrily decreed, the most excruciating tortures and pains abounded. Trauma began to swarm my bed in the form of restlessness and pains all over my body. By early evening, the restlessness had reached a terrible level, and the pains persisted. Through my right leg, the traction pulled at my backbone, and it became increasingly difficult to endure. I complained to the nurses, but they only encouraged me to hang on.

I endured on. With all my dwindling energy, crackling spirit, and troubled concentration, I endured on. I had many visitors in the evening, but my condition was far from reception. I was going through the tortures of death and everyone looked somber. They muttered prayers under their breath, but it seemed it was my funeral prayers. I felt more desolate than ever. The blood flowed slowly into my body until there was none left in the bag.

The traction was my main trouble. Nike tried to help to make me feel better with it, but nothing in the world would make me feel better unless it was removed. Tension mounted on my existence and I could not see myself surviving the coming hours.

"Don't worry, everything shall be all right." Nike, distraught by my look, sat on my bed and held my free hand as she tried to assure me. "I'll come here more often, Rahman, and we'll handle it together."

I could only hope so.

She fed me what I could eat of my dinner and finally left for the evening. She promised to come the following morning after her first class. She could not wait for the regular evening time to see me again. I did not look at her in the eye and watch her walk out of the ward. I did not hold her tightly and thank her a million times. I did not see the need for it at that moment, since I did not think anything would happen that will make me wish I had done so. As she kissed me goodnight, we did not know that we would not see each other again until after more than a decade. Perhaps more.

III

I wished the hands of the clock would move faster. Increasingly, I became so distressed that I was afraid the morning would not come for me anymore. It was about 10 pm. The night nurses were already at their shift, so I called out for help. That night, there was a female and a male nurse, perhaps the first male nurse I had ever seen. He gave me a Valium and Novalgin injection, and assured me of relief.

Instead, things continued to worsen. The pains from my arms, legs, and spine grew more excruciating, and the restlessness more traumatic. My spirit writhed about me in anguish. Breathing became tasking. My body became the temple of the devil and I wished I could just walk out of it.

After what seemed like several days, twelve struck on the clock and the male nurse went into the inner room to sleep. I called for help and the female nurse attended to me.

"Please, could you help me remove this thing?" I said to her. "I cannot continue like this anymore."

"We've given you sleeping and pain-killing injections; you should relax and be patient for them to work," she stated. "I cannot remove the traction. It has to be there. Just be calm for the injections to work."

"That's just the problem; I'm unable to remain calm. The injections are not working. This thing has to be removed to relieve me, please." My voice was now faint and shaky. Then she offered to support the weight from the bottom, but insisted that she would put it back before morning.

A current of relief swept through my body as a small table held up the weight, and I thanked the nurse. However, the intensity of my torment had become too strong for that alone to satisfy my hunger for relief. I starved for more. I needed to move. I needed to turn. I needed to sit up.

After about twenty minutes, I tried to sit up, but the link from my leg to the weight posed a problem. It would not allow me to drag my legs to the side to drop down. Also, the sloped position of the bed would not make it easy for me to sit up. Raising my torso was difficult enough when the bed was leveled, and now it was more, as the whole weight of my body inclined toward my head. Yet, I felt I had to sit up. Then I needed all the strength I could muster. This was something I could not do ordinarily, but I was dying at this point and I had some kind of last life-saving energy to use.

For several minutes I tried and succeeded in moving a few inches. I rested, tried again, and moved a few more inches. Then the nurse saw what I was up to.

"What do you think you're doing?" she stormed at me.

"I want to sit up. I cannot remain in the lying position anymore," I replied. I had not been stealthy about my action, so I did not see any reason to be chided. Besides, sitting up did not seem too much for me to ask. But she became angrier and removed the small table. The metal weight dropped back with a jerk and pulled tightly on my limb.

"Now, that will stop you from being silly. I thought you could be treated nicely." She walked back to her seat, scowling at me.

I cursed my luck. The weight pendulumed and tightened on my leg and spine. I could not move anymore – not even half an inch. And in bits and pieces, the walls of life began to collapse over my head. Hot tears dripped down the sides of my head to my ears. I was not crying from the physical torment itself, but from what just happened: that I could not help myself while the person who should help me did not know what I was going through. I was dejected, completely desolate, and the tears gathered around my head and soaked my pillow. I bawled silently in the semi-darkness of the hall.

Would this thing be allowed to smother life out of me? I thought miserably. God seemed too far away, as deluge of pains swept through my nerves and every part of my flesh. Restlessly, I struggled against my fate, trying everything I could. I pulled my leg to pull up the weight, but it was too heavy. I raised my body a little on my elbows, and then went down again. I did it again, again, and again, but I only got worse.

After so much effort in different uncomplementary ways, I thought of a way and decided to take it. It was the last thing I could think of. The bandage of the traction was wrapped from my ankle up to my thigh. I reached for it at my thigh and pulled it loose. Then I began to unwrap it around my limb. This time, I was stealthy in my action. After so much time and effort, the metal weight dropped off and songs of praise echoed through my body and spirit.

Like a volcano, the nurse erupted and poured hot lava on me. She called me names, but I ignored her, like a statue in the rain. I did not care anymore. I tried to drag down my legs to sit up. That way, I hoped to feel better. But she responded with a threat.

"Don't you dare get off that bed," she barked at me. "If you try any nonsense to get out of that bed, I will get a rope and tie you to the bed. You think you've seen hell? It's now you'll know hell. Dare me."

That shocked me and made me tremble from inside. When I am not crazy! Even crazy people deserve a seemly treatment. I realized that she could do it. They had ropes. I remembered how they had tied the old woman's son and I knew I should not call her bluff. She had more strength than I had and she was mad enough to have lost her sense. Something told me that if she tied me to the bed in this condition, I would not see the morning light. And the twilight cockcrow, for the first and only time, would ring though the air but to the dead of my hearing.

I obeyed her, promptly. She looked a Jezebel to me now and I feared her. She went back to her seat and kept watch over me. My bed was now one of the worst in hell that the devil himself would not want to sleep on. It was so uncomfortable that I was almost going crazy. Yet, I tried to endure on. Even, the dead have to endure something in the mortuary; it is too cold in there. I prayed that the male nurse would treat me differently.

Time crawled, eating gradually into my body and leaving behind a trail of ailing cud. My situation had become such that I could not imagine myself convalescing. It seemed as if recovery would never come, unless, perhaps, by a stroke of miracle, like the cleaving of the Red Sea or the healing of Lazarus. I wished earnestly for such a miracle. Maybe I had had too many of the instant miracle stories of conventional preaching, but I wanted whatever God could spare - just something to help me out. It dawned on me, however, that this hospital could never do it for me, but my mind was bleak and I could not think of a way out.

Suddenly, out of somewhere within my heart, without premeditation, I said to myself: *I am going to Oyo in the morning*. Then I began to recall how I had been healed through traditional treatments at Oyo, sometimes instantaneously. I remembered one man, especially, who used scallions to take out body pains. I was a living testament to this. Out of pain, I had leaned on someone when I entered his house one day, but I walked out by myself after some minutes of treatments. Not even with a limp. Muttering out incantation, he used the scallion leaves to rub out the crippling pain in my leg.

My father told me the man could stop the recurrence of the pain, and that he had done that for many patients. But from my experience with various traditional treatments of the ailment, I had learned that ultimate stopping of the pain's recurrence is unignorably relative to individual patients. Why and how this is so, I did not know, but the episodic miracles that I knew the traditional treatments were capable of was what I now wanted, and it reinforced my decision.

I must leave for Oyo, I told myself again and again. Thus, I made a decision to leave mainstream medicine for traditional treatments. There had not been progress since I came here, I reminded myself, only retrogression and preternatural occurrences: blood clotting and awkward treatment effects. Sometimes the image and warning of the old cleaner flickered through my mind, though it was so strange that I could not imagine myself going through such unnatural event. And I could no longer be sure whether I had seen a real person or an illusion precipitated by my sick state, just like my hallucination of the little creatures haunting my bed. Still, I did not see any reason to remain at the hospital any longer. The thoughts of continuing to be under the hematologists also put me off - those who had punished me with a week of neglect. And then someone who was supposed to nurse me wanted to tie me down. Apparently, they had seen too many corpses, and one more would not make a difference to them. What a banality of death in the faces of hospital workers. The one death would definitely make a difference to my family, and, to prevent it, my mind had already left the place. But I was afraid they might refuse to let me go.

It was a miracle when I heard the clock strike 3. The nurse went into the inner room and came back with the male nurse. She showed him what I had done before she went back for her turn to sleep.

"Why did you do this?" he asked with a compassionate voice.

Gently and haltingly, I explained to him. He sympathized with me and allowed me to sit up. With his help, I dragged myself to a chair beside my bed.

I remained on the chair for some time while I went over my decision again. I could not point at what thought or chain of thoughts resulted in the decision in the first place. Although it had a logical correspondence to my bank of experience, as often people's ideas do, but the idea and all the reinforcements came into my head not as a logical sequence of thoughts, but as a gestalt, making a whole picture at once. It might be true, as I later learned from psychoanalysts, that sometimes ideas might occur to humans but which apparently could not have come about with preparation. But this, like the controversy over mainstream and traditional medicines, has been a problem for empirical psychologists, who did not think any mental act could come from outside human consciousness. In my prosaic thinking, my decision was a voice of God coming to my aid, though this poor old religious view had been abandoned as a senescent old man in the society of young elites, driven by their newly acquired knowledge – the modern knowledge of human science and psychology.

For my type of personality, willing to be attuned to my time, this was one question that would later plague my mind. Although I eventually saw no difference between the religious view and the psychodynamic view - except in the standpoint from which one saw it. That is, that ideas or decisions could come to humans like a strange anonymous parcel delivered at one's doorstep by the mailman, and found later to be of a distant, well acquainted and involved arrangement. Hence, sometimes in life, things happen as if by chance, by accident, but that actually have a cause and purpose, only too deep in the web of nature's ways to be ordinarily understood. But, at this particular time, I did not care for whatever philosophical validity the process of my decision had. The decision, to me, was one from a troubled soul, experiencing agony, failed by the system in which he was and hoping to try out in another system - perhaps to flounder for safety like I once did in the swimming pool at my recreation club. Whatever could be more valid, more justified in such a state.

This is what I am going to do, I assured myself repeatedly and prayed that they allowed me the freedom to do it. When I began to fall asleep on the chair, I called for the nurse's help to bring down my bed to normal position. I could not sleep in it in the sloped position.

"That wouldn't be appropriate for me to do," he explained after thinking it over. "I can only give you another bed."

It was when he tried to help me to the first bed on the opposite row that I discovered that I could no longer stand on my legs. Lifelessly, my legs dragged along as he moved me across the ward.

This was another degenerating turn in my predicament, and perhaps it would not have happened if not for the traction. But I did not put the blame on the doctors. The traction may have been the right thing for them to do according to their logics, the scientific logics. It was just unfortunate that my condition defied the logics. It was unfortunate that the consistence in calculations on human beings sometimes need more than that of the replicable scientific logics. Perhaps, human conditions are not as constant as determined mathematical conditions. The mathematics or logics of human experience, deep-buried in the unconscious, may at best be illogical. Even though the Enlightenment thinkers, the founders of modern science, knew mathematics to be the pride of human reason, they still recognized and respected its limitation in surveying and exhausting human reasoning, the prism through which human experience is made and perceived.

Hence, my intuition was telling me something different from that of my formal world, and I knew I must take heed from somewhere: from intuition within or from scientific experts without. But it was apparent that it would be from that which my sense of rationality agreed with. Nonetheless, I knew I must dance to whatever tunes my choice would bring.

Lying down on the new bed was a relief for me, and I was lucky to have the chance for my short sleep. I slept at around 5 am.

IV

As short as the sleep was, I enjoyed it, more than any I had had at the hospital since I was admitted. I had no dream or trance. I sat up as early as 6 am and waited for my grandmother. My decision still stood and I was only afraid of being prevented from carrying it out.

When I remembered my doctor, I shuddered. I wished she would not come until I had gone. She had tried so much that I thought going away like this would not appear complementary to her efforts. The other nurses also would not like it; they had been caring and expected only that I recovered to leave.

My grandmother came into the ward and her eyes went to my former bed. I tried to call her attention, but my voice was weak. At the sight of the vacant bed she stiffened, shocked by the interpretation of what she was looking at. Knowing the state in which she left me the previous evening, weighted to bed by the traction, she feared that I may have quieted and my remains packed to the mortuary. As the food warmer in her hand dropped to the floor, I quickly called out at her again, this time loud enough, as I was afraid of having her break down in grief.

She looked in the direction of my voice and gave a sigh of relief. "Why did you change your bed?" she asked as she walked over. I did not know how to explain. I searched for suitable words but finally said what came to me.

"That thing they tied to my leg was killing me and I removed it. And I've decided to go to Oyo." She was surprised and afraid again. "Don't be afraid, I'm getting better now, but the remaining problems would be handled better with traditional treatments, and that's why I've decided to go. There's no cause to worry at all; just help me get out of here."

"Have they permitted you to go?" she asked.

"They should let me go," I replied, though uncertain they would. "Would you please go to tell Baba to give me his car?"

She stared at me for a long moment, saying nothing. Perhaps she saw in my eyes that I was not going to be persuaded, or she felt the same way as I did about the issue. She did not bother to persuade me. "All right," she said, though she was not all right. She was not at ease with herself. No good mother would. My condition spelled uncertainty. But this is better than death, I thought, or, at least, better than easily giving in to death.

"Eat your food before we come back," she said as she placed the food warmer on the table and walked out with a lamenting gait, perhaps thinking *What kind of a thing is this, oh God*? Tears welled up in my eyes.

A motherly nurse came over to me. "Why did you do this, Rahman?" she asked. The overnight nurse had briefed her about what happened, but she was sympathetic with me and wanted to help the situation. "You know the hematologists would be very upset if they saw this."

She was so compassionate that I wanted to cry. But my dominant mood now was defiance and it still had sway over me. I was afraid, too. Would she force or persuade me to stay? She was an elderly woman, and, from my upbringing, I always respected elders. She then seemed to me an obstacle I hoped to overcome.

"I think I have to go home, ma," I said calmly.

"You think you have to go home?" she asked, surprised and worried. She had not seen that coming.

"Yes, I have to go home."

"You're not serious, are you? You don't know what you're talking about. Do you know the condition you are in?" She paused, as if waiting for me to reply, but I did not have anything to say. Then she continued. "Do you know the state of health you are in? Forget all that and bring N10 so I could buy you a new traction and set it up before your doctors come in. That's why I have come to you."

"I'm sorry, ma, but I have to go."

"Don't go and kill yourself, son. If I could give you a mirror, I'd be glad to let you take a look at yourself before you decide. Unless you want to go and kill yourself, your condition needs urgent medical attention and there is no other hospital you can get that."

"I'm sorry, but I need to go." I was still afraid of being persuaded to stay.

"Think again, Rahman. Think well, again and again. This is a good hospital in which you are. Have you discussed this with your mother?" She meant my grandmother.

"She already knows about it, and she knows where I'm going. It is to my father that I'm going. I've thought it over and I've resolved to go."

She walked back to the nurses' desk. Deflated and giving up, she sat down. "You are over 18," she said, "you can choose for yourself. But think very well before you choose; there's still time before the doctors come, and I'd be willing to fix that thing back for you."

Reminding me of my legal right to leave, I was relieved. I am over 18 and I am going to Oyo today! I was sorry I had to be recalcitrant to her age and experience, but my condition was pressing on me.

Then, my doctor came. They told her of the development and, surprised, she walked up to my bed. Disgust and anger creased her face. "What's wrong with you?" she said, " Why did you remove the traction?"

"Nothing. I just think I have to go home. I'm really sorry, but I think I've had enough here."

"What has come over you? You're going home? Do you think all these are a joke? You removed the traction and still have the gut to say you're going home?" I had never seen her as worried and angry before and I felt sorry for her. I was a job uncompleted. I disliked seeing people in displeasure, let alone for me to be the cause. However, my life was too big a compromise now.

"I can't stay here anymore. You've tried so much and I appreciate it, but now I have to leave."

Informing me of my critical condition, my tenuous breath that they hoped to maintain and improve, she spoke angrily, though concernedly. But in the end she gave up. "You have yourself and can do whatever you want with your life." Her voice and manner, though, begged for my change of mind. She still wanted to help me.

My grandmother, with a wan expression on her face, arrived back with Brother Tahiru and Sheri. Immediately, I asked them to pack my things to the car. My doctor saw she had no more choice; she brought out a paper for me to sign, that I chose not to receive treatment there any longer.

"Once you signed this," she threatened, "U.C.H. will not take you back if you come back."

The elderly nurse came again to persuade me for the last time. She held back the doctor and the paper. "Why don't you think again, my dear?" Referring to my grandmother, she added, "Consider the plight of this old woman who has been struggling for your good all these days."

That peeled at the scab of a wound, but I tried to bear the pain.

"Tell me, where do you plan to go now?" she continued. "I mean, how do you think to treat yourself in Oyo?"

"I'll go to a private hospital," I lied. I could not tell them what I had in mind; they might think I was more insane than they already thought I was.

"Private hospital? Wasn't it from a private hospital that they sent you here?" she asked, but I said nothing. "Okay, why don't you call your father and hear his opinion on this before you sign the paper?"

I hesitated, a little afraid that my father might listen to them and ask me to stay, but I gave her his phone number.

"Ayinla, what's the problem?" my father asked. Ayinla was the affectionate name he sometimes called me by.

"I decided to leave the hospital and come home, but they said I should seek your consent."

"Is that what you want?" he asked.

"Yes, I don't want to stay here anymore."

"Okay, I'll be expecting you. Give the phone back to the nurse."

I signed the paper and my things were moved down into the car. I said goodbye to Segun, my ward-mate. He had been watching the drama all the while. His mother shook her head, feeling sorry for me, and she wished me good luck.

As my wheelchair rolled toward the door, I said goodbye to my doctor and to the nurses. I did not look at them, but I heard them wish me luck, where they did not think there was any luck. I seemed to them a foolhardy, and they were sorry for a boy going to kill himself.

My grandmother had adapted to the new development and she suggested a herbal concoction she had used in the past for someone with jaundice, which, as she recalled, worked remarkably well. Immediately, she sent Sheri to the market for the ingredients.

The car drove out of U.C.H. I rested my head, closed my eyes, and waited for home. I was so sick that I hardly felt I was in the world anymore. I felt as un-terrestrial as I looked. Every small gallop the car made sent floods of discomfort all over me.

We stopped in front of the house at Oniyanrin and Baba came down to sit beside me in the car. He wanted to see me. He wanted to talk with me. But, worried and confused, he did not know what to say. For a long time he stared at me and ahead. Then he prayed and went back into the house. In his many years, he had seen many sick persons and many dying persons, he confessed that he did not like the way I looked and all the report he had been receiving. While I was still at the U.C.H., he called alfas to offer special prayers for me and he killed a goat as an offering to aid the prayers.

The "mothers" of the house, Baba's wives, also came to the car to pray for me, and so did many tenants. Everyone knew my life was hanging by a single hair-thread and was afraid. One of my aunts had been terribly shaken that morning when she was told at the hospital that I had left for Oyo. Aunty Ronke could not believe it. She thought the nurses had only lied to keep her from breaking down at the hospital, and that the truth was that I had died and been taken to be buried in Oyo. Hysterical, she rushed to Oniyanrin, but afraid to go near the house. She feared to see her mother, my grandmother, in tears. She feared to see the whole house in tears. She feared to see the lifeless body of her nephew. And for a long time she stayed at a building a few blocks away from the house until she saw someone who told her I was still alive.

As the car started to move again, I took a glimpse of the house. The verandas on the first and second floor were filled with dozens of people. They watched somberly as the car drove away. They were not sure they would see me again. I was not sure I would see them again. We were five in the car: my grandmother and I, Sheri and Brother Tahiru, and Uncle Biodun, my grandmother's last born.

***

Was I right or wrong to leave mainstream medical treatment for traditional ones? That was one question. For hundreds of years it has been the ground of battle between the old traditional ways and the modern scientific ways of treatments. To some people, it was like leaving the modern world for that of antiquity. But it may be too early to make a judgment at this stage, even though my decision was a child of circumstance rather than of reason. Perhaps the stronger the messages in one's intellect the better on could make reasonable decisions, but the stronger the messages from one's feelings the more likely one decides respectively. And the messages of pains and imminent death have a strength that is hard to surpass. For many thinkers, survival is the most basic instinct in humans. Even, Jesus Christ did not want to go on with the crucifixion, despite being aware that *so has it been written*. Pain and reason may not go together in our thinking, but for thousands of years that humans have been searching for the absolute rationality of the world, they have always been confronted by the irrationality of its ways.

From this standpoint, if my decision resulted in death, I would never have regretted it, unless I learned that the marijuana had caused it. And if time were reversed, I would still make the same decision in a situation as exact as this. On the other hand, if it brought goodness and benefits, I would thank my God. At this junction in my life, however, I knew I was in a precarious state, and all I could do was to drive along the road I have taken, and then hope and pray.

Really, at the time of writing this book, my experiences have shown me the rightness or wrongness of my decision. But, being aware of the relativity of judgments, I will leave to my reader the pleasure of making his or her own judgment. Unfortunately, or fortunately, I had made my own judgment by direct, painful experience of the subsequent events. Of course I did not die, for this book then would not have existed. But I hope my reader would not make a mistake of assuming the future events to be in my favor because I was alive to recount the story. There are other consequences that are as bad as death, sometimes even worse.

Like a long highway strip
lying in the bowel of the night,
is life to the vision of man.
He sees just where his lamp showers alight,
and where his feet are stamped.
And though he thinks into the dark ahead,
with lofty hopes of where his journey could take him,
but not by what he sees and knows for sure,
only what he's told and what he's promised,
by the littered signs along his road,
written down by the heels and wheels
of all those gone before.

"Life," Rahman

PART TWO

Awakening

You are sometimes wiser, more creative, and far more knowledgeable when you are dreaming than when you are awake.

But the time has come for mankind to take several steps further, to expand the nature of his own consciousness by trying to comprehend a more profound version of reality.

Seth.

(From *Seth Speaks,* by Jane Robert)

EIGHT

Apeta

I

"Alhaji wants me to bring you to Sabo; he has gone there to wait for you." That was Baami, and it was my father he referred to as Alhaji, a Yoruba variation of the Arabic title 'al-hajj' used for a man who has performed the Hajj to fulfill the fifth pillar of Islam. We just arrived at Oyo and met him and my father's wife at home. My father's wife, pregnant, had Bucky at her side, the youngest child of the house, then four-year old. My eyes, half-closed, could barely see anything, and my breathing had become erratic. Each of my heartbeat quivered the rest of my body. Realizing that if they could do anything to keep me alive, they had too little time, Baami hurried into the car to lead the driver to Baba-elero's place at Sabo.

I was placed on a chair at the backyard of Baba-elero's house. Swiftly, he took off his top clothing and began treatment earnestly. I had never seen him as ardent as this before. And even though I had an inkling about the nature of his work, it was now I realized that Baba-elero was more than just a traditional herbal doctor. He was a spiritualist, a witchdoctor.

He first washed my face with a local black soap. It was not an ordinary soap and he made sure the soapsuds entered my eyes. It hurt my eyes and I cried out. He went on to wash my head and mouth with it. He lighted up some incense sticks and arranged them in a way that the smoke engulfed me. In my front he placed a clay bowl, darkened with years of use, and he filled it up with blood directly from the slit neck of a fowl. In the next instant, the blood was aflame, strangely as if it was gasoline, and he moved it so close to me that I was afraid I would get burned. As my grandmother would later recall, someone from a distance might think I was being cremated alive, as ears of the fire rode up with the enshrouding smoke.

Then, almost in a whisper, Baba-elero began chanting incantation, with one hand on my head and the other swinging something up and down and back and forth. He sweated profusely, and once in a while I heard him call out the name of God, but in the Rastafarian word *Jah.*

The treatment went on intensely for about an hour before he asked for me to be taken inside the house. I was seated on the only bed in one of the rooms and he ordered that something be brought for me to eat. I did not know what it was, but I was forced to eat a little of it. After a while, he resumed work and concentrated on my right leg. He said that the first phase of treatment was to restore my life, and this phase was to revitalize the leg. He brought out a long snake fang and pricked on the leg, jabbing the way the snake that earlier owned it would have loved to do on a prey.

He called one of his sons and gave him another fang, and they both used it on the right leg, rapidly and continuously. It was painful, but I could only moan. After some time, they stopped. Blood dotted all over my leg, sometimes rolling onto the bed. He rubbed the surface with some black powder, apparently a burnt product of some herbal materials. It hurt. Then he gave me some sour concoctions to drink and laid me down to sleep. I slept off the moment my head touched the pillow - a first sign of change.

I did not know for how long, but the sleep was like a return into the world. When I woke up, I saw my environment and everyone in a different and natural way. It was then that I realized the strangeness of the whole event. From sometime in the middle of the night at the hospital, while wide-awake, my trance-like perception had caught up with me and I had been experiencing the world like in a dream. I wondered out to know whether I had been dreaming and they told me the day and time we were in, and confirmed that everything I recollected was real. But Baba-elero chuckled and said, almost to himself, "What is not a dream." Then he asked us to go home, so that my grandmother and the rest could be able to go back to Ibadan before nightfall. They had about 50-mile journey ahead.

At home, I was placed in the only bedroom on the ground floor. It was my younger brothers' room. For my comfort, they moved the ten-inch mattress from the bed to the floor and they laid me there. My father assured my grandmother that I would soon be perfectly well and that they could leave. If all he knew was one thing, it was to allay others' fears at times like this while he hid his own.

Reluctantly, my grandmother rose to go. I asked her to wait a few days before she comes back and promised her I would have been much better by then. I meant and believed this, as I could feel everything tending toward normality.

I remained on the mattress after they had gone. I did not sleep again, but I was relaxed, very much unlike I had been in the morning. I was as if three quarters of my life had been drained out of me in the morning, and the remaining one waiting impatiently to follow. But now I felt I had regained more than half of it back. My breathing and heartbeat had returned close to normal and my condition did not seem threatening of death anymore. Together with Baami, my father sat at my bedside for the rest of the day.

The Yoruba culture, aimed at close-knit social integration, tries to bind its people with love and respect. Thereby, it discourages discriminatory remarks, greetings, calls, or references among the people. It is this that first plants discipline in the Yoruba child. In this manner, we were to understand and refer to our parents' siblings as fathers or mothers, if older or about the same age with our parents, and not as uncles or aunts. Hence, the use of *Ba'mi,* or Baami, which means *my father,* for my father's brother. If aunts, we use *Ma'mi,* or Maami, which means *my mothe*r. And if in a polygamous home, every child would refer to every wife old enough to be his or her mother as *mother*.

The Yoruba culture - and its language - was richest in Oyo, with all the integrating elements, love, and respects contained still in use. In our home, as many others, our orientation in Western culture through Western education had led us to refer to our father as *Daddy*, rather than the Yoruba term *Ba'mi*. Therefore, we referred to his brother as *Baami* to distinguish between him and my father, though both words mean the same thing.

Baami offered himself to tend me to full recovery. He had been living alone in our family house since his wife died about ten years earlier. He ran my father's remaining scrap of business with him, and therefore came here every morning and went back in the evening. But now, he would stay here to nurse-sit for me.

Baami was about sixty years old and he had patience more than the vulture. He was wisely acquiescent and loving in nature. I could never have had a better person to nurse-sit for me. His knowledge and experience would later be a source of education and entertainment for me.

It was a long time before I fell asleep for the night. Though it was not yet much of a sleep, I slept better than at the hospital, and my restlessness and hallucinations had already disappeared. I was happy that a reliable treatment for my condition had begun.

II

It was still dark outside when Baba-elero arrived at our house early the following morning, accompanied by a middle-aged woman he called Sidi, his spiritual assistant. Even though I knew my treatment would not be taken lightly, I did not know it would be taken as much seriously as to make Baba-elero so eager, almost to nervousness. At a much later date, Baba-elero told me that the day I left U.C.H. was supposed to be my last day alive, and he was always amazed at how I came to decide to leave the hospital on the day. When he laid his eyes on me, he said he was looking at a dead man, and he could not believe I would live until I did.

They began the treatment ardently again this morning. They washed my head with the same soap he had used the day before, and they burned the same kind of incense. He went into his incantation in the same fiery manner as on the day before.

Being brought up with the idea of God so planted in my heart, I was comforted by Baba-elero's repeated mention of God's name in the incantations and his other conversations. He kept me at ease with my conscience, because I had been predisposed to religious preaching that condemned the use of voodoo, as his treatment form was. Islam and Christianity have been built into people's hearts as some kind of superego against traditional practices. While our Islam and Christianity were often syncretized with traditional beliefs and practices, most people did not realize this and were wary about the appropriateness of voodoo. They regarded it as devotion toward another and lesser god beside the God of Islam and Christianity, who was a "jealous God." Muslims called it *shirk,* or idolatry, and many Christians saw it as a pact with the devil, an idea inherited through the European witch-hunt of the past centuries.

Although, I had been exposed also to views that argued against these assumptions, but I was not really decided either way, and I did not concern myself with validity of beliefs at the moment. Spontaneously, I was only afraid not to wrong God, and I thought I was okay with the way the man was handling the treatment. Whenever he assured me of healing, he would say, "We are not healers; we only care and try. God is the Healer. It is to Him that we appeal. He is the medicine owner, and He will heal you. He will save our face and heal you."

This hints at another type of cultural ambivalence that plagued the hearts of many Africans - a spiritual ambivalence. While they were not aware which of their norms and practices were informed by African polytheistic traditions, they criticized traditional religious beliefs and did not want to be associated with them. Often at the peak of their human neediness, many of those who thought these beliefs as paganistic and evil still ran to voodoo practitioners for their various problems, sometimes clandestinely. The magical shrine of Bilikisu Sugbo, the Queen of Sheba, preserved for centuries by traditional worshippers, have become a holy pilgrimage site for many Muslims and Christians.

My father belonged to the other school that believed it was not *shirk* using these things when necessary. He was a man of intense prayer in the Islamic way, but he believed that our environment occasionally necessitated this kind of things, natural to our culture, and one would only be fooling oneself to think otherwise. Such a belief might not be necessary in places like Mecca, Jerusalem, or London, he always argued, as "their world in places like that has become different from ours." To keep the practices in cognitive assonance with his monotheistic faith, whenever I was taking any medication, medical, herbal, or spiritual, he would advice me to say "*Lahaola walaquata ilabillahi l aliyul Azim.*" It is Arabic for "*There is no other power beside the power of the only God,*" and saying it implied the submission of the treatment effort into God's Hands. This, my father believed was in the tradition of King Solomon, whose life scriptures associate with witchcraft and both good and evil demons. "All these things are God's creation, and they are for our use," my father would say, and he was never hypocritical about it.

I also received some indirect treatments in the manner of *etutu*, spiritual sacrifices or offerings. These, as Baba-elero explained, were to appease and employ certain spiritual entities or forces to be in our aid in what he called a battle between the powers of good and evil. Against such blatant acknowledgement of polytheism, some people sometimes asked, was God's aid not enough to call in such a battle, if this was not idolatry? But what Baba-elero and my father believed was that employing these entities was a relative way of imploring God, and which should be seen as natural as employing a physician in an illness or an attorney in a lawsuit. One might then ask, is God not enough to heal a sick person without a doctor? Or is He not enough to ensure justice without an attorney?

The entities, or forces, which may be seen as embodiment of ideas, energies, or forces of nature, were respected as participants in the creation and maintenance of the universe. As I would soon learn, even the gods and goddesses found in various ancient religions are, in the same way, symbolic representations of various contributory and constitutional aspects of Nature. They are parts of the thousand faces of the “Hero” called God.[18] The only problem with this may be the over-identification with any single one of the faces, or a few of them, by which one fails to acknowledge the liberating universal and uniting image or truth that they collectively represent. This was a corrective and preventive reason by which, I would later realize, the concept of monotheism eventually became imperative after centuries of polytheism in the world.

Baba-elero used this kind of spiritual approach because, as I learned, he had diagnosed my problem as not just physical or ordinary as it appeared. All the physiological symptoms we saw were said to be from spiritual causes, or had spiritual influences. Therefore, if the spiritual aspects were not identified and treated accordingly, all physiological treatments - including the traditional herbs - would be ineffectual. As one pharmacist friend of mine used to say, it takes scientific solution to solve scientific problem and spiritual solution to solve spiritual problem. By the word *spiritual*, we mean the supernatural, magical, voodoo, or plainly religious.

Although, I did not anticipate all these before I left U.C.H., all I wanted was to get well, and I thought traditional medicines would work better. But the decision brought me the benefit of an advantage of traditional treatment over mainstream treatment, which was its ability to detect spiritual causes or influences in illnesses and to treat accordingly. Health, they say, is an existential state of bioorganic, emotional, and spiritual harmony, even according to modern medical philosophy. It is a holistic state of well being at which the physical, mental, and spiritual states are

---

[18] *The Hero with a Thousand Faces*, by Joseph Campbell.

supposed to be in equilibrium. Hence, as spirituality in our world was seen as influential in human conditions, our traditional form of treatments was constituted to respect it.

However, the description of what spirituality is has been a problem in the modern world. By this, modern medical practice could not acknowledge spirituality, though its philosophy theoretically does. Even the mind-body nature of pathological conditions is only recently becoming unignorable in science. Yet, to those of us who believe or are aware of spirituality, the extent of reality that it covers still eludes us. In this part of the world, the idea of spirituality meant more than it does under Western view, and this was what events in my life now seemed entangled in. In addition to the spiritual constitution of humans, it is believed that every natural thing has a spiritual counterpart to which it is inextricably connected, including ailments and events, within which individual conscious forces and energy reside. And human beings, like sorcerers and witches, are believed to possess the power to influence the spiritual states of people, things, and events. When such a situation occurs, some parts of the problem may be explicable physically, while they may not be treatable wholly as such.

"These people do not inflict problems and sicknesses that are out of this world;" Baba-elero explained one day, referring to witches, "it is the same natural ones that we know that they use. In many cases their inflictions are diathetic, provoking a natural predisposition in individuals, or just accentuating its effects to naturally unreasonable or supernatural extent. But the fact that the natural elements exist always deceive extremist natural perceptions not to recognize the existing scientifically unreasonable extent - its supernaturality, or spirituality." This, perhaps, is one important message of the old Arcadian myth, from whose god, Pan, the word "panic" was derived.

The appearance of naturally detectable factors, or its possibility, is sometimes used as a feint, a sham attack meant to deceive victims and their caregivers, until the real insidious ailment does the expected damage. Really, for human physical consciousness, in which we are so engrossed, spirituality is an intricate and tricky phenomenon to deal with.

***

The rest of the week continued with activities toward my recovery. Every day, Baba-elero and Aunty Sidi came before dawn. The treatments they gave me varied, but the washing of my head, face, and mouth, and the pricking of my right leg with the snake fangs remained constant. They made incision cuts on my body to administer medicines, gave me concoctions to drink and to rub my leg with, and they made me exercise my legs.

Something happened one morning, to which we paid little attention. To Baba-elero, it was significant, but, to keep us calm, he pretended to ignore it. While he was using a snake fang on my leg it fell onto the bed and rolled underneath the leg. But when he lifted my leg to retrieve it, it had disappeared. At first I thought it stuck somewhere in the mattress, but, despite careful searching, it was never found.

***

Genuine traditional and spiritual practitioners believed in and respected the uniqueness of every condition. By this, such practitioners would not insist on a single line or source of treatment for their various clients. Even though they trusted their own medicines, they would leave room for other trials, as there was often no fear of overdose or adverse side effects as in modern medicine – perhaps due to the natural products and manner of preservation they employed. So when other traditional doctors were recommended Baba-elero welcomed the idea. Two of them gave me treatments specific for my pains, one of which was of the scallion leaves that I recalled at the hospital.

The most significant of the other treatments, however, was the service of a psychic woman, famous for her clairaudient ability and her impressive rate of success. She was an elderly Christian priestess, who used the opportunity of her gift to preach God to her clients. She was like Jesus, saving lives and preaching. One reason people were sometimes afraid of visiting her was her accuracy in telling them how much they were lagging in their respective religions. Hence, if not an emergency, people would try to be regular in their Churches or Mosques for weeks before visiting the octogenarian psychic. By tradition, we simply called her Mama or Mama Pakoyi, because she lived in a neighborhood called Pakoyi.

Though they did not tell me yet, Mama Pakoyi diagnosed my problem as basically spiritual, caused by some people with voodoo. "An imminent death had just been averted," she said to my father's wife the day she went to her on my behalf, unwittingly buttressing Baba-elero's claim. Still, she warned of renewed efforts from the witches, but she assured us that I would be all right again. Although I had been sleeping a little better than at the hospital, with no more restlessness, I still had not been sleeping soundly well. In daytimes I often could not sleep at all. When my father's wife complained of this, Mama Pakoyi's response was astounding. She assured her that the forces she was working with, the angels, whom she called "the Warriors of Heaven," have gone at that moment to improve the situation, and that my father's wife would meet me at home sleeping. I did not know how I fell asleep, but my father's wife met me sleeping that afternoon, the first time I slept in the afternoon since days before I left the hospital.

Mama Pakoyi's peculiar treatment style was nothing elaborate. She only prescribed special dieting, psychically communicated to her by someone she said was God. She would tell her clients or patients to eat one thing or the other at certain times of the day, for certain amount of days, and specially prepared in certain ways and sometimes with certain ingredients and proportions. Her prescriptions included a wide variety of food, and, as her legend went, they always worked. Some people thought that her style was a way of harnessing the spiritual potentials of the things she prescribed – since every object and phenomenon in nature has its spiritual counterpart and a mind of its own, as Africans believed and respected nature for.

All these treatment activities revealed how shaken my father and the entire household were over my sickness. They did not want to leave anything to chances. Various special prayers were offered in the house and outside. At the town's central mosque, the Chief Imam gave a prayer session for my recovery during the Friday Jumat prayer. And, as hoped, the downward spiraling of my health stopped.

On Saturday, my grandmother and Uncle Tunji came to visit me. My health was already improving, and it was so obvious that my grandmother was happy for the first time in weeks. The jaundice was fast disappearing and the pain was increasingly relieving me. Although, I could not yet stand on the legs, but I had got energy enough to allow me to fold and stretch my legs on the bed in exercise, something I had lost in the first week at U.C.H. Now, also, I could carry myself on my hands and I could toss and turn in bed. Everything was returning back to normal and they looked promising.

I began to plan my return to Ibadan, hoping to enroll in a computer class while I waited for the outcome of my American plans. In the coming week, I expected to see my complete recuperation and finally my movement back to Ibadan. I told my grandmother to come for me on the following Saturday.

At this time, my father did not reveal all he had learned about the cause of, or influences on, the sickness. I also did not bother to ask. I was comforted enough by the improvements. But he said something suggestive when I mentioned my intention to go back to Ibadan with my grandmother in the following week.

"You cannot go back to live at Oniyanrin anymore," he said.

"Why?" I was surprised.

"That's what Baba-elero advised," he simply replied. And, as I would later learn, Mama Pakoyi said the same thing too.

"Okay," I said, giving up.

"Where will you go to stay, then?" he asked.

"I'll go to my grandmother's house at Oke Ado."

He agreed and we ended it there. But the discussion was insinuating. Although I did not worry about it, I got the hint and moved on with my recuperation and planning. My spirit was up and my body was following suit. I struggled to get back on my feet, taking all my medications and doing the necessary exercises regularly. With a little help, I eventually began standing on my legs and taking some steps after a few days. One day, I walked to the living room from my room, and then around the house. As Mama Pakoyi predicted, I now slept well and for longer hours. I was recovering fast, and, finally, that chapter of my story appeared coming to a happy ending, like a Hollywood hit movie.

III

One night toward the end of the second week, I slept earlier than as usual, and I thought it was a good thing, a sign of improvement as every other thing I had been experiencing. It really should have been a good thing, but I missed something in the night. I forgot to say my regular prayers of *Ayudafiu* and *Ayat al-Qurisiyy* before I slept. Missing it like this might not have mattered, however, except for what happened in the night, which would change the course of the sickness, and change my life forever.

I would not have slept that night if I had known, but I did not know, as we sometimes do not know of certain things that later turn sour in our lives. In car crashes, airplane crashes, shipwrecks, earthquakes, terrorist attacks, muggers' attacks, victims never know it would happen; otherwise they would not have been victims. I did not know, so I fell for the pleasure of sleep and found myself in a dream. A dream that turned out to be no less real than my wake state, and one that casts a question on the nature of human consciousness.

In the dream, hale and hearty, I escorted one of my cousins to his girlfriend's house. It was a thing we often did for each other, so I did not see anything odd to it, even when the house was, in reality, someone else's house and I was left outside when he went in. Dreams have their way of been odd.

I was waiting impatiently outside when, suddenly, a shadowy figure sprang out of the darkness of the night. I sensed danger and tried to take cover in the house, but the time and place were too restricted to protect me. I took to my heel. The gunman, intent on executing me, chased me around the neighborhood, through a jungle of houses and trees, and eventually shot me as I dived into the Alawo River.

The bullet caught me at the buttock and sent a violent tremor all over my body. I wailed out in agony, feeling a sharp, intense, and shattering spasm of pain at the delicate muscles around my groin.

The puzzling thing about the event, however, was that I woke up to reality with the bullet in my body, and with all the pains and trauma of a real gunshot. As I tried to say something to Baami who slept on a mat next to me, I felt the pang, tugging at the extremely sensitive muscles of my groin. It was murderous, like a high-voltage electric shock, and it continued to shoot through my body at every stimulus, internal or external. The slightest move of a body part, a word or an attempt of a word from my mouth, a cough, or even a deep breath became a spark sending me gasping for life in the shock.

It was the strangest thing I had ever witnessed, worse than hell, and I could make an oath to God to live the rest of my life in the mosque, offering salats and scrubbing the floor twenty-four-seven, if only He would relieve me of the condition. But the condition did not have time for such freedom of the mind. It shot through my life repeatedly, like a violent thunder through a house, threatening the foundation upon which it was built.

The dream, as it turned out, had not been just a dream. Though it occurred in my dream state, the gunshot was a planned event carried out by a real person in another location scores of miles away from where I was, and they would later retrieve its bullets from my body. It was a dream, but real as every real thing I had ever experienced since I was born. And I realized that my life had now entered a phase in which coming out may be as difficult as coming back from death.

"God, God, why have you forsaken me?" my heart languished and cried. Was it not a tragedy for someone hoping and working toward a dream for his freedom to land in a gruesome situation as this? This damned destination was even free: no visa, no ticket fee. Misfortunes, it seems, are so free in the world; it is fortunes that carry prices. And high prices. Sometimes in life we think we know where our destiny is taking us, even when we do not particularly think we are in its control, but it turns and turns and we eventually find ourselves in a world we had not seen ahead. *Like a long highway strip, lying in the bowel of the night, is life to the vision of men. They see just where their feet are stamped.*

If a god could not help better my situation, as our fathers always say, maybe it would have been better he left me as he found me - and not make me worse. I was not given America, yet I was not left alone as I was. I was only more shackled and barred. My health has been taken away and there was nobody I could ask why. Shakespeare sometimes thinks the Heaven may be deaf, but, since it sends forth the rain, I think it may only be doing what it pleases, perhaps regardless of what pleases us. With the shawl of Heaven, God has covered Himself from the barrage of questions from human hearts.

Although I was too tortured to entertain thoughts or questions about my condition, my family thought of it to their sorrow. As a desperate grief cured with the languish of another, I only could hang on to the God I believed in for my life, even if I would think He had not been fair enough to me.

IV

The whole house was thrown into pieces by dawn. Baami was at the edge of his seat as he repeatedly tried to pacify me. My father rushed to Sabo to call Baba-elero and he sent his wife to Mama Pakoyi, the clairaudient woman. And to reduce tension in the house, the children were quickly sent away to school, hours before the school's opening.

Since the moment of the gunshot, the inguinal spasms continued to recur at intervals of two to three minutes and at any stimulus. At first, I kept still and silent to prevent the spasms, but later my voice lost its life and I could no longer talk. Whenever I needed something, Baami would put his ear very close to my mouth to hear the stretched words come out slowly one after the other. It was in this manner, taking several minutes to make a sentence, that I had briefed them of the dream. I became hypersensitive. No door must be knocked anywhere in the house, no cup or spoon must fall, and in my room no voice must be raised beyond a whisper. Even when the children returned from school, they all perched quietly in corners, moving gently around in the house, careful not to make a noise and afraid of losing a brother.

All I could do was to remain still like a statue wherever I was placed. This way, I could help myself from allowing extraneous stimuli increase the already torturous firing rate of the spasm. I was placed in a chair while I waited for help, if I could get any. My arms were placed at my sides and I stared straight ahead, almost sightlessly. I could be mistaken for an evocative masterpiece in a museum, sculptured to tell the ordeal of human suffering, and situated next to that of the Crucifixion.

Baba-elero and Aunty Sidi began their work immediately they entered the room. They filled the room with incense and went through the same process I had come to know well. They fed me a few concoctions and I was incited at the hypersensitive places of the spasms. This was the most painful part of the treatment. I could not remain at ease for anyone to drop a feather on the places, not to talk of having razors make cuts there. And a peppery brown powder was rubbed on the incisions.

The message from Mama Pakoyi was as strange as her system. Before my father's wife would say a word about the new development, she sent her back, quickly to tell my father to remove the clothes I had on at the moment. I should never wear them again, she warned, and I must eventually burn them by my own hands. It was the clothes I had on in my sleep during the mysterious dream. It became stranger when, after a few months, I had the luxury of remembering that they were the same clothes I had had on on the *evil-day*, on the day I collapsed at the hospital, and on the day I left U.C.H - the four crucial days of my entire predicament. Why I had been making the choice to wear the same clothes, I did not know.

Mama Pakoyi said the shooting was done from our real world, in the real time I had experienced it in the dream, and it was by a woman with a borrowed gun, not a man, as it appeared in the dream. But she assured us not to worry, that I was not going to die, no matter what, and that God's plan was to save me. She promised to begin an intense prayer and she prescribed certain types of food to include in my diet.

At a later time, my father told me that Baba-elero had said the same thing, that it had been the work of a woman who was responsible for the sickness from the beginning. He also said the woman, a witch, had a coterie of witches, who all knew about the deed and also had hands in it. He added that I had been under the spell for a long time before I actually broke down, but that God had taken control away from them, and it would only be "an experience of sickness and not of death as the witches had intended." They took the step of the gunshot when they realized that I was already recovering against their plan.

My father made me understand that they decided to tell me this much now so I would know what I was up against and be able to build up courage for the struggle ahead to help my treatment.

"Your will to get well is important at this stage. We need you to keep up your spirit and fight for your life, and that is why we think you should know this, and know that God has already won the battle for us. I've known about this since the day you were brought here, but I could not tell you anything because I was instructed not to. They revealed the identity of the woman to me, but you'll have to wait until all this is over before I will tell you. What you need to know now is that everyone is doing their best to bring you out of this."

There were a lot of things in this situation, but I could not really make anything out for sure. I was not sure of what I thought, but I lived on. The world seemed a disturbing mystery to me, especially because I was trapped in it. I loved mystery stories in books and movies, but direct experience of it was not the same thing as those. I loathed it. However, this supervening sickness was already making me a student of another side to life, while my peers were away in regular schools. Many things were explained to me, or just in my hearing, and many things I directly observed and experienced. Unfolding events of life, they say, are the stimuli for human consciousness and thinking, and the true system of education. This was now my school.

After the treatments of the day, I was again assured that all would be well. But it was not yet well - not even close. I felt the torment severely and unrelenting. It became difficult for me to eat, as I could not use my arms anymore. The poison of the bullet was spreading all over my body and I lost the control of my legs also. By evening, the walls of my throat and the food duct were coming through my throat each time I tried to squeeze out disturbing sputum. I always sent them back in place by swallowing back the sputum. I was afraid to see my intestines come out through my mouth.

Day after day, it was as if I was being consumed piecemeal. I had only one occupation, only one care in the world, and it was to stop my pains. All my effort was to try as much as possible to remain still, but it was the most difficult thing to do. One may be able to do it easily for a little time for fun, but when it becomes imposed and to be done for a long time, it becomes a predicament. And I had to do it all day and all night. I lost the improvements I had earlier gained in my sleeping pattern too. My sleeping degenerated to about one hour or less in each twenty-four-hour day. Sometimes, it was not that the sleep would not come. There were times that I would feel like sleeping, but I dared not sleep. If I lost consciousness to sleep in half a minute, as it sometimes happened, the concentration on my role as a statue would falter, the phenomenon would tug painfully at my groin, and it would wake me up violently. It was as if there were devils in my room, holding ropes tied to my ailing muscles, and which they tug to keep me in pain around the clock. The effects of the pulls were as if a Sumo wrestler gave me a deadly knee kick in the groin.

After some days, I began to get used to the normal two to three minutes interval pulls of the spasms. It now only distorted my face, with my eyes widening in grief, and a moan everyone was becoming painfully accustomed to. But the externally stimulated ones were still too severe to get used to. I never wanted anyone or anything to touch me or touch my bed. It was bad luck when I had to urinate, and emptying my bowel was worse luck. I chose not to do it on one occasion and held it for five days. On the fifth day, it troubled me so much that my bowel itself became a stimulus for the spasms, and, at one final time, before they could help me with the bedpan, it was all over my bed. And that was worst luck, because I had to be completely carried off the bed to have the beddings cleaned. Every hand that carried me was like an electric rod of an electrocutioner. This was the world I was living in now.

***

The gunshot was a confirmation that carried us beyond reasonable doubts over the events that would become part of my identity. However, it raised two crucial questions. The first was that, as innocent as I was, why would the Heavens allow this on me, and at this point in my life? The second question came later when I thought about writing the account. It was about explaining the evidence of such an experience to the increasingly Western, scientific civilization, which was already biased toward the African experience, both academically and religiously. It was a concern for intellectual legitimacy.

If the anxiety and the subsequent events could be explained scientifically, psychiatrically, I began to wonder, what about this dream-state gunshot, whose bullet wound I carried into wake-state? Could science or psychology help in enlightening me about this? Sometimes later, someone tried to use psychoanalysis to explain it, but it still left its all-important mystery unsolved. The most basic mental need of human life is validity of the self, of experience, and of all what one represents within the context of one's world. But I was now losing this, along with my physical health. The validity of my current experience, and of its contextual African experience, was blowing away with the wind. I was now an individual symbolizing the conflict of cultures, and, regrettably, my body and psyche were the battleground. Struggling with this, I later came to a conclusion: if I would know where I was going, I had to know where I was coming from. Perhaps somewhere in my journey lay an alchemist's stone to help transform my debilitating cultural ambivalence into an empowering sense of cultural complexity. Hence, without being overtly conscious of it, my soul began to quest for the true knowledge of my situation, individually, culturally, and historically.

For Baba-elero, and those with whom he shared a school of thought, the mystery of the dream-state gunshot was not in its explanation, but in the unpredictability of dealing with it. The event was a phenomenon they knew well, called *apeta* in Yoruba philosophy. It was associated with the art of witchcraft, done by magically conjuring the spirit of the victim and shooting him with a gun or bow, as he answered the call. It was like *image magic*, by which harm was inflicted on a victim through his effigy.

Sometime ago, a woman in my neighborhood at Ibadan found a piece of kolanut in her mouth, after waking up from a dream in which she was given the kolanut to eat. Spontaneously, she became sick and, a few months later, died of "an incurable disease" that they could not particularly diagnose at the hospital. This was how it was believed to work. Her spirit had been poisoned in the dream, and thus, all physical treatments given to her symptomatic manifestations did not reach the seat of her problem.

At this stage of my experience, though I might still be struggling with its scientific evidence, I no longer could shrink diffidently and hypocritically away from its reality as it corresponded to what I knew as my reality. I remember a small boy in a famous colonial-era novel,[19] whose freedom in his quest for freedom is barred. A Nigerian teacher warns him that he should stop inquiring about witchcraft in the classroom because of the white teachers in the white-run school. This was a typical story of how these things were treated in the colonial time, and which we have carried into present times. The white men said it was an illusion and the black men were afraid of the truths they faced in their everyday lives. And even though the white men have left our land, their ideas still controlled almost everything in our lives: what the white men say is the truth; it is we that are foolish, deluding ourselves with what is not real, the ignorance of our ancestors.

I had been hypocritical in the past for fear of being regarded as a fogy, a savage, a rustic. Though this was not the way of the *elite*, the *educated*, the *civilized,* I realized I had no choice but to open up to these voices in my blood, the echoes of my heritage. Anyone could call me an antediluvian, but I would never be happy to live a hypocritical life. After learning deeper into the phenomenon, it became surprising how anyone could regard something of such prominence and pervasiveness as an illusion. It became increasingly apparent to me that to disbelieve in this reality of my environment, I must be in stupor of something, of liquor or of Western education.

I came to understand that the Westerners, and their African counterparts, who denied the reality of witchcraft did so merely because almost no scholastic theory of Western education accommodated the phenomenon. Then, it became clear that such people had been so intoxicated by the Western education to forget that it is the natural events observable in nature that would constitute the basis for the legitimacy of any theory claiming to explain nature.

Regrettably, many Africans have adopted the strength of these theories and principles over the strength of the observable natural occurrences in their environments – some even becoming whiter than the white educators.

---

[19] *The Bottled Leopard,* by Chukwuemeka Ikwe.

If this whitewash had not bleached African civilization, perhaps I would not have been in this confusion, while stuck between two realities, two fields of activities of nature, and asking which was true. Perhaps, there would have been a consistence and harmony in our civilization, and in which conflicts of concepts were resolved, making it easy for people in my kind of situation to know what to do at the right time instead of wasting so much time searching for clues where clues have deserted.

By our experience in this part of the world, there is no doubt that many lives have been wasted by this confusion. Many people have died in hospitals under the doctoring of strict mainstream practices while their problems were spiritually rooted in voodoo. And many people have died under the doctoring of strict voodoo practitioners while they could have been easily saved under mainstream doctoring. On both sides have there been causalities, and these kept the conflict going on and on in our world today.

***

For the rest of the week Baba-elero and Aunty Sidi came regularly to treat me, sometimes twice or thrice a day. One day, they had to move me to the bathroom for a special bathing. Because of my painful sensitivity to touch, the day seemed my doomsday. I could only wish they did not touch me; I could not give a day-old baby's resistance. Although, they carried me so carefully as if I was a big brittle egg they did not want to squash or drop, still a painful pulsation developed in my body and it took several hours to abate.

My father called my grandmother on the phone and asked her to postpone her next visit till the following weekend, "when his treatments would have been completed," he lied.

She came the following Saturday, but my condition still remained the same. I hoped not to let her know of the real situation, yet my condition was worse than to be able to keep up a pretense. Then I wanted, at least, to cover the extent of my suffering, so she would think there was only a little to worry about. However, my appearance and my disposition showed her there was plenty to be worried about. She knew I was in pain.

It was more than keeping fire under one's garment. It was keeping fire hidden in my nerves and veins. I could not talk like I used to do when pretending at the hospital; I only wore a mask of hollow and mirthless smile. She brought her ears close to me; still she could not hear a word of the sick-stuttering sound coming from my mouth. And as faint as it was, opening my mouth triggered the spasms. My father took up and did the talking, telling her various lies to shield what actually happened.

All the time she was with me, I prayed in my heart that she would leave, not to see my truth. And I was so sad I burst out crying like a baby immediately she stepped out of the room. Crying also triggered the spasms, so I stopped. I ended up smoldering with grief only in my heart, non-viscerally, and with hot tears streaming down my cheeks. They did not tell me that she broke down when she got back into the car. Keeping her truth away from me was also a functional plan.

***

The New Year celebration was an ill one for everyone in our house. For me, it was pain throughout. The children were silently discharged to an annual party exclusively organized for princes and princesses of the Oladigbolu clan. My father did not want the new development in my story to spread beyond our household and to alarm anyone, so discharging them to the party was to keep the secret. The other relatives at the party would not have any cause to want to know why we kept out of the party, as they would if the children were not sent there. Adults could have many excuses, and so all the adults stayed home.

Everyone in the house perched in different corners of the house, hoping, praying, and waiting for what story every next minute would tell. With my condition still painful, sorrowful, and pregnant, 1993, the once hopeful year of my dream, died and was buried in history. A new year was born. And in the condition, which the past year impregnated in my life, I continued to go through the travail of labor as the new year marched on. What the pregnancy would bear, of which no one was sure, made everyone nervous, sorrowful, prayerful, and tenuously hopeful. The time it would also take to bear it all, no one knew.

Everyday was war, and my bed the warfront. Every morning was not only a sunup for the day's fight, but also the continuation of the night's battle. There was no time to pause to re-energize; I was always using the next inch of my life in the war. And I was dying. Every morning the people in our house woke up and anxiously came to my room to be sure I had not died in the night. As for me, within all I knew as my life, within all that remained as my life, I wanted nothing other than one thing; neither a career nor wealth, neither America nor anywhere, and neither to die nor to live, but for my pains to stop. In the condition, I knew no other world but that of agony. It was what my eyes saw, what my ears heard, what my mouth tasted, what my lungs breathed, what my mind thought, and what my heart and body felt. Pain was the blood that flowed in my veins, and for it to stop was all my mind craved and prayed.

V

I felt an itch on my left buttock, close to the place where the spinal bones join the pelvis. It was the spot where the gunshot had hit me. I was laid in bed, the way dead people are laid in the coffin, and I was almost in the same stillness. I spent my nights in this position, feeling a little of what those folks go through in the grave - perhaps a reason why both good and bad people are afraid to die. It is misery already in one position for eternity.

It was about three weeks from the night of the gunshot, and my mattress had been moved onto the bed. The process of carrying me off the bed in the morning and back in the evening was the curse of my everyday life now. It would throw the muscles in my legs into painful jerks, which put my whole body aflame. I wished I would not have to be carried, but it was ordered that I should not be allowed to remain in a single position all the time. This would allow regular flow of blood through my system and keep my muscles activating at least twice a day. Because of the additional pain, I did not like to have anyone stretch out my legs for me. Rather, with my toes, I would crawl them down over the bedspread as gently as I could. It always took time – sometimes about an hour or more – but I found it less troubling.

To reduce the troubles further, I later decided to remain in the chair from morning till evening once I had been carried in the morning. This cut down the carrying about to half the time. I would only go to bed to await sleep, which would not come until around five o'clock in the morning, and only to wake up an hour later. Sometimes when I became sleepy in the afternoon, I could not return to the bed to sleep. The physical process of being carried back to the bed would send the sleep miles away from my eyes. Life was a furnace and I was burning in it.

Baami slept on a mat close beside my bed so I could easily wake him up whenever I needed his help during the night. He tied an end of a long strip of cloth around his wrist and placed the other end in between my fingers, so I could pull as little as I could to wake him up whenever I needed him. Remarkably, my tenuous pulls always had him up quickly enough to attend to me, as if he never slept at all. He knew my condition; I could only move my wrists and fingers, my toes, my mouth enough to take in spoons, and my eyes to aim and rove, so he was always at alert for me, even in his sleep.

On this night, the itch on my backside persisted, but I did not want to disturb anyone. My younger brothers had wrapped a band-aid on the thick end of a broomstick, so they could use it to help me scratch any itchy spot without hurting me.

I endured the itch at first, though it was difficult. Then it increased and reached a pitch that eventually sparked off the spasms. The intervals between the regular spasms had increased to about ten to fifteen minutes from the initial two to three minutes, and the stimulus-intensity had slightly reduced. People could now sit and talk freely in my presence, but they yet could not touch my chair, my bed, or me without firing the spasmodic tremor. They only touched me when they had to, and it was usually for treatment and carrying to and from the chair.

I cried from the spasm caused by the itch and Baami woke up immediately.

"What is the matter?" he asked, and, as faintly as I could, I told him.

He reached for the broomstick and put it through the space between my bottom and the mattress. I had no clothes on. I was only covered with a piece of cloth, as I was often dressed now, day and night. With my direction he reached the spot. Gently, he moved the stick back and forth to rub against it. Scratching is sometimes pleasurable, and when I was satisfied I told him to leave the broomstick at the spot and go back to sleep. I knew the itching would come again, but I did not want to disturb his sleep anymore. The other end of the broomstick was at the easy reach of my right fingers, and, whenever I needed, I could push it back and forth to ease myself.

It was around two o'clock in the night. I was wide-awake, while everyone in the house was sleeping. I knew of time by my father's table clock that chimed at every half hour, piercing through the still night from his window to mine. The itch started again after a little while and I thrust and pulled gently and continuously at the broomstick. I enjoyed the sensation and I did not know when the broomstick strayed from the spot to explore new pleasurable frontiers, which also I enjoyed scratching. My problem was that I overindulged in every opportunity of pleasure I had, since it was always the only one to enjoy and engage my attention.

On and on the broomstick went, exploring further until it reached a part where I realized I had no sensation whatsoever. What? I was afraid. I did not even feel the broomstick was there. I explored the whole area with the broomstick and discovered that that part of my left buttock did not feel a thing. It was the side the mysterious gunshot had hit me and now it was dead. What this meant worried me. I was losing the leg; perhaps both legs; perhaps the whole of me.

The next morning I complained to Baba-elero and he examined it. He touched the place for sensation, but there was none, even when he used the snake fang on it. He used the fang down the other parts of the leg, but the sensation was little. I did not feel the pricking pain of the fang as I used to.

He realized that the gunshot was now ruining my leg, and he intensified on its treatment, making incision cuts and pricking more with the snake fangs. I had taken too many incisions to remember the number, and in this little period of this sickness, only God would know how many bites those lifeless fangs had made into my skin. The owner-snakes could not have made a third of it in their lifetimes.

***

One day late in January, Brother Akeem came home from Lagos where he lived, and, seeing me in the condition, he asked me a question.

"Don't you think daddy should call a medical doctor?" He had visited me at the hospital, and, though he acknowledged the disappointments I had there, he thought having a medical attention on me was still reasonable.

"Yes, I think so too," I replied, with the spasm still haltering my speech. I did not think of this before, but, when he mentioned it, I thought it was wise. At home, I could enjoy all forms of treatment, as I needed. Besides, I was in such a desperate state that I would do anything to get well.

Brother Akeem talked to my father about it and he agreed, but only after some argument. "Wasn't it from the hospital he had come?" my father had argued. He did not believe that mainstream medicine could do anything at this stage and he had his reasons. But, as Brother Akeem asked that we should have a medical eye on me anyway, he agreed. "What would we lose by having a medical expert have his eyes on him?" Brother Akeem had argued. "It wouldn't stop the other treatments but go alongside. And even if it does nothing to help him, we still wouldn't lose a thing; it's all for the boy's good."

Everyone was a bunch of intelligence in our house, and whenever there was an argument, one would hear good reasons fighting good reasons, and usually ours against our father's. He was wise in the old, natural way, while his children, with the opportunity of higher Western education, tried to be educationally wiser. In our various disciplines, we would argue with him that the modern sophisticated way was wiser than the old, crude one. At such times, my father would be proud of his children, but also angry at the situation. He had chosen and paid for us to be able to think the way we were taught in school; therefore, for him not to accept us as right might be as admitting himself as wrong for having chosen our way of life thus. However, many times he would think he was right both ways, in his arguments for the old ways and in his decision to send us to school. Going to school was the modern road to social and economic success, he believed, and he wanted us to be so successful. But he also believed that Western education was, to a ridiculous extent, empty of basic wisdom essential to life.

It was not that my father did not believe in mainstream medicine. He had children in the field: a physician and a pharmacist, and he always had a family physician that he consulted regularly. But for all what he had known in his world, from his various experiences in which the two forms of treatments had met, and from his knowledge of my particular condition, my brother's argument did not convince him out of his own opinions. And, to him, calling a medical doctor would only be a wasting of our scarce resources. Nonetheless, being someone who respected advice, even if only for the sake of the advice, he had agreed deferentially. *If it's not going to spoil things, let us expend the advisers' feelings and ideas.* This was his attitude toward strong instances of advice of which he was not really convinced.

One interesting thing about my father was that most of the times he won against his children, although not by the verbal argument – he often did not win in this – but by unfolding events, which he was always patient in waiting for. Many times, in our ambivalence, we would run back to him for assistance – just like I had done in this situation. He was the stubborn, ignorant old man, but whose ignorance was always needed – always valuable.

"What do you guys know?" My father would later often boast to me. With pride, he would tell me of how he had come to the rescue of many of us with his 'primitive' ideas. His most mentioned instance was when his physician-daughter was dying away in childbirth labor at U.C.H. while her colleagues struggled for means to help her. In a way strange to the physicians, she had recovered by the traditional help my father got for her, and even participated in an emergency surgical operation eventually performed on her a second time in seven days during the labor of her first child.

Though still confused at this time, I hoped that mainstreams' analgesic could arrest my pains pending the time that the traditional treatment would help heal me. I held this as a good point, and it is a point that suggests that mainstream and traditional treatments might be better allowed to complement one another, creating an integrated health system. This was an argument of some groups in the on-going debate over traditional and mainstream medicines in Nigeria, and, as I would later learn, all over the world.

As I found out, there were circumstances in which traditional treatment excelled mainstream treatment, but there might be something missed out that mainstream medicine could have supplied. This would be either the much important sterilization of materials, anesthetic aids, or any other. For example, in orthopedics, putting broken bones together was done better in traditional treatments in Nigeria than in mainstream medicine. These bone-wizards were so good that, in some parts of Nigeria, the government provided hospital-like structures to make their work easier and more antiseptic. Although, in modern medicine, orthopedics has admirably advanced beyond just putting broken bones together, the service of these traditional workers may still be ultimately valuable in the areas they could handle.

However, these traditional practitioners did their work in crude ways. They mended the bones in the full conscious feelings of the patients, without any anesthetics or analgesics, which mainstream medicine could provide. One could only imagine the pains. Nonetheless, people thronged their places because of the better results of their work. There were also many cases of patients who left mainstream hospitals for these traditional orthopedic surgeons after their bones had been wrongly put together at the mainstream hospitals. These traditional surgeons, as the nature of their work demanded, would re-break the bones in the full conscious feelings of the patients, pinned down by hefty men, and deftly put them back together. And this is how they still do. In this area, mainstream medicine could easily supply anesthesia, among other things, to make the treatments easier on the patients.

My father called our family doctor and asked him to examine and work alongside the traditional doctors. The doctor, also, had seen so much for him not to worry about such *alongside-ness*, especially in this town, and to make him careful. He examined me, but saw nothing particularly out of ordinary. Then he only ended up prescribing some drugs for the pains, hoping that if the pains were arrested, maybe my condition would be calm enough to reveal any fundamental problem or I would just need physical therapy to move on.

We bought the drugs and I began to use them, with high hopes for improvements. But the harsh reality showed me that my condition was beyond the drugs. The sleeping drug did nothing to help my sleeping, and neither did the painkillers kill a fraction of my pains. He asked me to double the doses on both medications, but they were still to no effect. For the sake of taking, however, I kept on taking the drugs, and still with hope.

NINE

In the Spirit of Job

I

February came in, as gently as people came into my sick room. My sickness continued, defying all treatments. The medical doctor came once in a while, mostly on my impatient request. But he always maintained that there was nothing he could do for now, and that when the pains and spasms were under control, using the limbs might come. He saw me move my toes, as he requested, and he said it was an assurance of a possibility of walking again.

Somehow, we had forgotten about Mama Pakoyi, and Baba-elero's visiting had slightly slackened. He came once in about five days and treatment was not anymore as intense as in the early days of the sickness. Although the excuse was that the sickness required no such intense treatment anymore, but my state of mind, influenced by my state of health, hungered for treatment attention. I later learned that there was something wrong in my relationship with Baba-elero, although I did not know what it was at the time. Nonetheless, he always assured me whenever he came. "You are going to get well by the grace of God. Do not worry; you are not going to die. Just try as much as you can to help yourself. Keep up your spirit and exercise the legs as much as you can."

Sometimes he told me stories of people he had known with similarly terrible problems, some of whom he had treated, and how, with time, they had overcome the problems. "Patience is what you need at this time," he always said, "You only need time to heal and for everything to return to normal."

Also, people who came to visit me told many astounding stories at my bedside. Stories of how different people had coped with situations of equal or more difficult degree in comparison to my case. The stories were often told to help me build up courage for the sickness.

At first, only a few people within our extended family came to visit me. Since the gunshot, my father had prevented open prayers at the central mosque to keep the development from the public. The mosque, like public media, was where the news of the sickness had been openly broken when I first came from the hospital. But because of my father's standing in the town, the news could not be kept as secret as intended for long. Through whispers and gossips it spread out like a centrifugal sea wave, only not yet an open discussion. Relatives and close friends who picked up the news from such mediums now rushed to our house to confirm it. And like this, more people came and more encouraging stories and testimonies were told at my bedside.

Baami and my father, at the incitement of one of the relatives, told a story I often remembered. It was about their father, my grandfather, who had a serious sickness at a critical stage in his life. The sickness reached its peak one night when he stopped breathing. His heart stopped and he was later confirmed dead. It was around 10 o'clock in the night and, for that reason, no burial arrangement could be carried out yet.

He was laid in a room and they kept incense burning in there to shroud the stench of decomposition. My father, my father's mother, and Baami slept in the room with the corpse. At around 3 to 4 am, they heard something like a cough, as if from the corpse, and they quickly got up to verify. The fume from the incense disturbed the corpse and he coughed again. They could not believe what they heard and saw at first, but when it dawned on them that their dead had risen, they quickly sent for a medicine man who treated him till daybreak, and finally until he fully recovered after some time. He lived for about two more decades before he died the second and the final time in 1984.

Many times, I was reminded of Job the man of God. I was always asked to take comfort in his story, how he had remained steadfast in God, and how he had eventually overcome his sickness and accompanying misfortunes. But sometimes when I wondered about the great man, it was more about how strong his fortitude must have been to live by such stoicism. As in my condition, suffering, alone, was demoralizing. How then could anyone have been able to bear such great misfortunes as his? He must have had some deep understanding of the ways of God and the world, which the taciturn world kept away from most of us. Perhaps, no one could do that empty-headed, unless one was a biological idiot, a complete opposite of what Job must have been.[20]

---

[20] In this case, I was reminded of the Islamic Job. He is slightly different from the biblical Job, in that he does not question God on his situation. This acquiescent Joban character, similar to the one in the original ancient Babylonian story, is a more matured Job who has learned the lesson of self-responsibility that the Old Testament God seems to be teaching him. He takes everything with stoic equanimity.

But I was not Job, and neither was I an idiot. Perhaps, I could have learned to be like him, afterall. Sometimes, I remembered something in the story of Job's sickness that closely related to mine and always wondered how poles apart we were in our thinking. Some bugs made his body their home and fed on the rotting parts of his flesh, yet Job was never disturbed. He even helped them find their ways back into their shelter – his sick body - whenever they were confused and lost. In contrast, when bugs flew disturbingly close to my face, I cursed and wished thunder struck them dead. If not for my incapable state, I would have crushed them till no part of them would be left as proof of their existence. What a polarity in our thinking.

A visiting Hausa priestess, one day, stated that people come to the world with different spirits; for example, with the different kinds of spirits of the prophets of God. She said those who have the spirit of Joseph would live a destiny similar in pattern to that of Joseph's; those with Jesus' will live one similar to Jesus', and she concluded that I must have come into the world with a spirit as that of Job. Hence, in religion, we have a personality catalogue that may be helpful in psychotherapy, and perhaps in the psychological study of the value of religion.

I would have preferred the spirit of Joseph instead, I sometimes thought. Though I might find it difficult to refuse Zuleikha, Portiphar's beautiful wife who constantly seduced Joseph, his destiny appeared least traumatic to me. I would not want to spend seven years on this predicament like the poor Job. However, I realized that I might appear not to have had anything as much as Job, but my dream and hope were as much everything to me as Job's children and wealth were to him. Hence, I may really have become a modern day-Job.

On one hand, this idea gave me an insight into the usefulness of religion; at least, all I had to do was maintain faith through the fortitude of Job, my spiritual model, and take comfort in his experience. On the other hand, the entire Joban issue incited unsettling questions in me, many of whose linchpin was the idea of God, the true nature of God. Realizing how real the art of witchcraft was, and seeing the wicked uses of it, I often wondered how God could be so loving and merciful, as religion preached, and still allowed and watched us suffer at the wishes of such evil.

Something was amiss in the whole picture and it sometimes made the situation appear unreasonable. People raised such questions out of confusions, and now I could not help but to join them. Some ask, "Why was Job not told why he was made to suffer, especially if he was so pious?" Merely for the devil's asking, and to test him? Perhaps this was not a reason good enough. And now that I was in Job's track, sharing his kind of fate, I could not help but ask, *why is it that I suffer?* I hoped that the Imams who taught me religion would not disown me for my straying mind, but I have entered into this climacteric period of my life with my heel unprotected like Achilles', and, though pain was primary in my life now, the questions were assailing my soul and leaving me hungry somewhere.

Some people may not feel insecurity in such a conceptual inconsistence of life in God, because many people think they could not question religion in terms of logic. Believing that faith is inherently irrational, they think religion is a different, separate, and unrelated aspect of life that must go only parallel to science and logics. Unfortunately, I could only wish I was such type of a person, living perhaps peacefully amid the ideological chaos of the world. I could no longer be comfortable with such a cognitive dissonance in my life; it would seem to me as living two contradictory lives without seeing the need to have them reconciled - if at all they were reconcilable. It was difficult to be at peace within myself seeing contradictions in life as this, and even seeing contradictions in my own life. I could not be at peace when I could not see a logical relationship between my yesterday and today. It made me see things as evidence of irrationality, whether it was in my perception, in life, or in God's actions. Yet, I liked to know which the irrational was, God, life, or I. Right now, a lot of things in my yesterday and today did not make sense together. I was born a charming prince whose life-promise many envied and prayed for. Later, I lost my Zamunda. A year ago I was an energetic young man, admired by friends and neighbors for my looks and the good I was trying to make my life into. Now, I was a withering, dying person in a situation nobody wanted to be. Although, if I discovered that it was God who was the irrational tyrant that made life go this ugly way, it did not mean I would stop believing in Him, unless I found out that He was not real afterall. I had crazy, irrational teachers when I was in school and I still respected them, anyway – despite their cruelty; it was for my own security. So even if God was irrational, I might still worship Him, anyway. As long as He existed, and I had no option, I would be afraid of Him making my situation worse than this. But I would feel better knowing what the situation of the world really was: the world of the Tyrant God, and I could go on and be one of His sycophants.

I still felt sympathy for my Imams and their invaluable teachings, and for all conventional religious preachers of the world; however, the infestation of logic and reason in the present world is giving such an irrational faith-based system of teachings a hard world to live in. If there is God, many of us want Him or His Idea to be accountable for all the chaos the world contains. This may not be too much to ask. We want to know why bad things happen to good and innocent people; we want to know why good things happen to bad and corrupt people; we want to know why those who work hard are not repaid as much as they work and why those who do not, and those who do not work at all, are enviously and disproportionately paid. We want to know why many things are the way they are and others are not the way they are supposed to be.

For me, I wanted to know why I had not been given what I wanted, while what I had had even been taken away from me. Hence, unquestioned faith disturbed me. I did not disbelieve in God and I did not stop praying to Him, but I could not defend my belief of His existence and ways to myself, and I could not protect myself enough with my idea of Him in the circumstance I now found myself in. If one cannot defend a God against all questions that challenge His idea in one's mind, perhaps the God may not be able to serve one beyond the defensible ideas of His that one has. I was poignantly conscious that I was still bound in shackles and fetters of questions as I was of pain, and I needed answers to be free. At this stage of my life, the conventional way of teaching was no longer enough for me, and my persisting belief in God may have become a wager, unconsciously betting on His existence along with the majority of humankind, and hoping to lose nothing if eventually I was wrong.

***

Eagles are known to frown at their eaglets as slothful whenever they refuse to fly after twelve weeks of their birth. To force them to fly, their mothers then throw such lazy eaglets from mountaintops. Now I feared my father being as daring as the eagle. I knew I was not a lazy son of the erne, and I wished he new this. It was true that I had gotten used to Baami and his full-time help, but my father appeared to think that I was becoming ensconced in the mentality of the sickness and, by indulgence, I was lagging in spirit to pull myself out into good health.

Maybe this, really, was my father's thinking, or he was only employing tactics to prompt the desired recovery early enough. Nonetheless, one day early in February, he warned me not to take myself as an egg, and that I should get myself together and put the sickness behind. He then threatened that if I did not get well by Ramadan, beginning by the end of the month, he would withdraw Baami's service and there would be no one to tend me.

This was a baffling development. I did not know where it came from. I did not know what had come over my father. But, unfortunately, I was an egg. I did not know whether I could say I was improving yet, but, if at all, it was like from fire to frying pan. I was still as fragile and susceptible as an egg, and I appealed to my father not to carry out his threat. My heart and mind had become so feeble by the sickness that any small threat would throw me into pieces, even when such threats may not be more than just threats, like a two-year old would feel when threatened to be thrown to TV monsters.

Yet, my father was not sure. From my appearance, I was in a bad condition. He had his fears about this, but he tried to make a man of it, and perhaps he now wanted to push me a little to be sure.

"Just get well before Ramadan; that's what I want from you," he concluded and left me in fear of my unknown fate.

But one day in the middle of February, something happened that made my father reconsider his view. I was eating in bed, after I begged not to be carried to the chair. The carrying to and from the chair had grown more painful that, after each carrying, I would remain shockingly still for a long time before the high-pitched pain would recede. This made me afraid of the chair when on the bed, and of the bed when on the chair. And the fear was a torment in its own.

Baba-elero walked in warily, as if he knew something was wrong with me, and without being sure what it was, he was shocked to see me being fed in bed, against his directive.

"Why are you feeding him in bed?" he asked. Baami told him about the increasing pain, but he insisted on having me seated for the meal. Then he carried my legs off the bed and put me in a sitting position. The pain was fierce and I was still crying out about it when he noticed a queer stench in the room. Immediately, he bent behind me to see whether I had defecated due to the pains of the exercise, but what he saw was many times worse: a discharge of pus from my backside. The discharge was thick, its stench horrid, and it took only their sense of necessity to remain in the room with me. It oozed out from the spot where the gunshot had hit me. It was like a bullet hole and, strangely, it smelled like the local gunpowder, by which I had been shot in the dream. The dead skin initially covering the hole had stuck to the bed when Baba-elero lifted me up, and now it left the hole open. The pus coming out of it was obviously from a putrefied inside, revealing that my left buttock was already decomposing. Finally, the bullet wound had come to physical reality.

He asked my father to have his doctor send a nurse to dress it everyday to keep it from infection while it healed. It was not too surprising when the nurse, who just saw me for the first time, asked, "This is a bullet wound; why did you leave him this long before you called for help?" No one knew immediately what to say to him, but my father finally replied: "We have been taking care of him." The sound of his voice told the nurse that he would not entertain any more questions. He looked into my father's face, looked around, suspicious, and then continued with his work.

Whether my leg or my life was decomposing, I did not really care; that I had to be carried up while the male nurse treated the hole was my problem. I did not feel the nurse's tools and everyone who had a look at the hole exclaimed at the depth and nature of the hole. I overheard my father commenting about it to someone that "I could see his bones inside."

I tired out fast, and, with the pains of holding me up, I had fainted by the time they put me back on the seat.

"Ramoni! Ramoni!" they screamed as they tried to bring me back. But my vision faded out as all the little energy in me left my body, leaving just a tenuous one that perhaps pumped my lungs. The nurse finally found a way of saying one more thing for the day; he warned that if care was not taken, the leg might eventually need be amputated.

***

My father was a persevering supplicant and he prayed more intensively during this period. He slept only half of every night and spent the rest supplicating, praying to God and into bowls of water. He cleaned me with the prayer water every morning.

In fear and pains only I lived, fear of carrying me about and pains of being carried about. Wherever I was placed, I could not help myself in any way other than to stare ahead, swallow food placed in my mouth, and grip the armrests if on the chair. And I could breathe. These were all that were in my power. There was almost no life in my arms, and when they fell off the armrests, I could not lift them back by myself. Also, someone had to constantly re-adjust my position in the chair, because I was like a collapsible air doll with a pinhole that let out air gently. Slowly, I always collapsed to one side of the chair. When flies buzzed disturbingly in my face, I only could pray they went away. I had lost the control of my neck and I could no longer move my head by myself to shake off flies. To keep my head from rolling backward or forward, as it often did, they folded a towel to hold it up, as with days-old babies.

One afternoon, I had a terrible spasm and my knees rammed into each other, like two rams fighting, and since then my legs could not stay independent of one another. A folded piece of cloth had to be forced between them to keep the flesh from eating into one another. Literally, I was now paralyzed from the top of my neck to my feet. I was dying piecemeal and I was not able to help it. No one was able to help it.

Treatment attention fell short of what could be enough to satisfy my desire. In such a condition one wants every moment to be of treatment until one gets well. Baba-elero was staying longer and longer away. My father tried to make me understand that it did not mean treatment was not going on, but that I needed time and myself more now. The medical doctor came once in a while, merely for visiting, and we had completely forgotten about Mama Pakoyi. Really, I did not know what was going on concerning my life; I only knew I was suffering, living one of the worst lives a human being could ever live.

II

The holy month of Ramadan began in late February and ended in late March, with a few but important occurrences in the period. The most significant event during the month occurred after the first half of the fasting month, and it deepened my father's fears and perhaps made Baba-elero to reconsider the situation.

My father, stricken with fear, rushed out of the house one early morning. I did not know what happened, but I sensed it was something grave when I saw Baba-elero ardently working through the kind of intense treatment he had given me the first day I arrived in the town. He had his agbada and buba cast off, and only in his pants he sweated as he went about his work on me.

I was placed on the chair and incense burned incessantly in the room. Everyone in the house was present in the room, chanting after my father the *Ayat al-Qurisiyy* and some other prayers in the Qur'an. They were terrified of what they thought might happen to me, but they told me nothing. It was some days afterward that my father explained to me what happened.

He was praying in the middle of the night when, suddenly, from a tree directly in front of the house, he heard a strange bird cry seven times in a certain way, and directed toward our house. This was a bad omen. Traditionally, the bird was known for this. It was a rare bird seldom seen in human habitation, and its presence and squeaks only came on purpose. It was like the *fenghuang*, the Chinese mythological phoenix whose rare appearances portended great events in Chinese history, as it did the death of the Yellow Emperor in the 3rd millennium BC.

According to tradition, the bird's crying was a warning, portending that the person under pressure in the house to which it was directed was going to die within the next seven days (the number of time it squeaked), *if proper care was not taken to circumvent the decree.* In this case, that person was I. My father knew this and it was the reason he had agitatedly rushed out in the morning to call Baba-elero. But Baba-elero needed not be told before he knew something was wrong. Strangely, through his own medium, he had known about the event, and before my father reached his house and missed him, he was already on the way to our house with all the materials needed for the rituals to ward-off the decree.

Yoruba tradition holds that animals, or most of the animals, have senses capable of perceiving subtle things and messages that humans ordinarily cannot. As spirituality is of a nature subtler than physicality, the people believe that, ordinarily, animals are more spiritually conscious than humans, and thus their subtle perceptions. The people, therefore, seize this opportunity in various ways to enhance their own spiritual understanding and capabilities for the improvement of their lives. And one of the ways is the folkloric awareness of messages from the animals, such as the strange bird.

The perceptive abilities of these animals vary as the animals themselves, though the dog is reputed to be the most spiritually perceptive animal, or one of the most. Among other things, spiritualists use the dog's tears and eye pus to enhance their own vision of things too subtle for ordinary human eyes. It is almost the way modern scientist aids his imperfect vision with the use of powerful lenses in microscopes, telescopes, and night goggles to see beyond the ordinary. Although more subtle than the scientist's are what the spiritualists look for. Like this, the spiritualists could see the various spirits believed to roam the earth with us, including those of the dead, which dogs ordinarily see.

Like the mysterious bird that squeaked on my sickness, the cat is another famous portending animal in sickness situations. A cat living in a house in which someone is sick offers a clue into the fate of the person. If the cat runs away from the house at some point, or stays deliberately away from the sick person, it implies that the sick person is going to die - and the cat ran or stayed away because it has perceived it. If it stays with the person, and even plays with him, the sick person will recover from the sickness.

But dogs are often preferred over cats as pets. Cats are known as favorites of witches. Usually, witches control cats and use them in transporting their spirits wherever they want to go and to perpetrate their evils. By this, cats are notorious for selling out to the evil forces of witches attempting to attack its owner or someone in its home. Black cats are more feared for this, whereas dogs, and pigeons, are famous as rectitude and faithful creatures. It is perhaps because of this that the dog was chosen as the traditional pet and symbol of Sango, the African god of thunder worshipped as the guardian god of morality and justice.

Realizing how distraught my father had been over this, I could not help but to feel for him. It was still less than a year that he lost a daughter to the great beyond, and now a son whom he had born around the same time with her was one leg here one leg there. Though he was always stoical, my father appeared pitiable as he talked to me, forgetting about the threat he had made at the beginning of the month. One of the stories about my sickness that went around the town was that I was a victim in the war over the crown, and that I was going the way the first victim, my sister, had gone. I could only imagine how grievous my father must have been inside. Although he did not believe I was a victim of the conflict, neither that my sister was, but this correlation put him under a sorry light in the town and tried his ego. He could not but remember an intimidating puzzle about the date that I fell ill and was admitted into the hospital. November 26th 1993 was the third in the consecutive dates that had brought him tragedy. November 26th of 1992 was the date Asipa, his most notable ally in the struggle, was murdered, and November 26th 1991 was that which claimed the mother of his only childhood friend. Though he still had his supporters in the struggle, and they were all fighting hard, all these suggested that he might not be up to the task he was pulling, and the opposing camp was already gloating. Yet, he was losing his children. He could not even tell me about the occurrence of the bird until after the gloomy seven days had passed and he had given a sigh of relief.

***

After the event of the bird, Baba-elero's coming was further slowed down until he finally stopped coming for me. Now, he only came on friendly visits to my father, and, at those times, he would only drop in some words of encouragement for me. My mind hungered for treatment attention and I neither understood nor liked the way things had become.

The last time that Baba-elero came for me, something happened, which perhaps indicated his decision to stop coming. For a long time he had promised to bring a medicine that he believed would help my situation significantly. It required a great deal of time and effort to get its scarce components together and to be prepared, and he had spent several weeks working on it.

When he finally finished it, he came over to our house to use the medicine for me. He placed it on the table and asked for a bowl of water and a razor. While someone went to get those, he chatted with the people in the room. But by the time everything was ready, and he proceeded to administer the medicine, it was not where he had placed it. They searched everywhere but were unable to find it.

I had not paid attention to the missing snake fang, but this occurrence was a different case and it raised my interest. We had all seen the bottle in which the medicine was contained, and it was not a small thing that could disappear in a junk of things.

Perplexed, my father asked whether Baba-elero had any more of it at home. He had been waiting and hoping on the medicine since he learned of it. But Baba-elero shook his head and replied him, insightfully, "Never mind, it can never be where I left it anymore." He had a wry expression on his face that was distributed from the corners of his mouth, but he was not smiling. He added that he knew he was being closely watched since the day he started preparing the medicine and that he was being followed as he was coming to our house.

My father could not say anything anymore about it, but he was afraid that Baba-elero might be losing the control of the situation he had once had.

The remaining medicine, made in a medium-size clay pot, was not where he left it at his house anymore.

***

Though I was constantly assured of an eventual positive outcome, all these events deepened my fears about the condition and my life. Alone, the thought of being trapped within phenomena difficult to perceive and deal with bedeviled me. Yet, my God seemed to ignore me as I languished. More often now, I lamented within on the nature of the creator who allowed this on me, and who would not, or unable to, help me from the clutches of these unseen evil.

However, being a person who often tried to see things from all its angles, my lamentations often got me nowhere close to a resolution. As I wondered on the nature of the God, whether or not He existed, and what His aims and ways were if He did, I could not help but to also wonder on the nature of the world itself, what its aims and ways were, and whether it was really real or not. Since the beginning of this predicament, my life has been traversing between wakefulness and dreams, between conscious and unconscious worlds, the seen and the unseen, between life and death, and without demarcation separating the worlds. I could not help but to wonder, as these now constituted the two conflicting realities between which I was now ensnared, and which were both confounding in their own ways. In this perspective, I looked at the success and failure of life and wondered what they all meant.

On the physical plane, what could be called the scientific view, I saw life only as an illusion, or something like that. If I was to fail in this battle for my life, or if I was to win, what would it all mean in the end? I mean, even if all scientific facts proved to me that God was an illusion, what could the facts do to cure or palliate this deepening hole in the history of my life? What could the facts have to comfort me that the world itself was not an illusion, including the science and my dear self – by which all my goals and my struggles would be nothing but a farce? The fact that I could touch and feel could not answer the question. Perhaps, then, I did not need to struggle for any victory anymore, if neither the victory nor the failure made sense.

I began to think long-term in terms of happiness, longer than I had ever done in my life. What power do the facts have to make my success and happiness worthy absolutely and eternally? Unless I would not age and die, as sometimes I had in my fancy, worldly success could never be worth what it claims, or what it seems to be. The best casket in the world could never do the trick, not even the loftiest grave, the best spouse and children, or high social status and laudable history left behind. Unless aging and death would not put a bridle to my success; unless I would not leave everything for which I was striving and go away into the unknown or nothingness; unless I would not go into extinction, life would not be anything but meaningless. And, then, it would not make a difference if anyone – like the witches – would take that life into their own hands and do as they wish. It would not matter if anyone would take up evil as a means to whatever sick ends they have. It would not make a difference if people find succor in evil or good or science or God. Nothing would make a difference, and the only meaningful thing would be whether one is lucky or not. Now I seemed to be an unlucky one, caught in the wheels of another creature's evolutionary vehicle.

Scientists were working hard to boost human longevity, but could that ever be enough to compensate our struggles? Many past kings of my ancestry were known for a magical power called *ajidewe* that they used to rejuvenate and boost their longevity. Yet they all died in the end, despite all the famous and controversial longevity. After all the centuries on his back, Noah is now no less gone than the thirty-three year old Jesus. If King Solomon had been privileged to spend 200, 300, or 500 years, with all his wealth and glory, he would still have died as he had done at his normal time. And today he would be no more, just as he really is.

Therefore, a span granted me like onto Sibyl[21] could not have been the perfect fill to the mental vacuum to which my condition was now exposing me. Longer life was not the answer, but eternal life, a life that would be worth all the troubles we encounter as humans, and in which all would be meaningful. A life that not only contains my failures and successes, my weaknesses and strengths, my sorrows and joys, my ignorance and knowledge, my ill-health and good health, my fear and faith, and my life

[21] The Cumean sibyl, oracle of Apollo, who was granted as many years of life as there were grains of sand in a handful of sand.

and death, but which is also worthy of them. For it would not make any sense if I would still die at any conventionally ripe age and leave all I did not want to leave now at age twenty-two, while in addition I suffered through this bewildering and demoralizing misery. Although, I might have achieved something then, if I was lucky, but it would all amount to the same naught. Stripped would I be then as I would be if I died now. The sun would rise the next day on a new world as it would tomorrow if I died today.

Yet, to die was not digestible to me. Despite all the beautiful stories of paradise, with all its promises of virgins and fruits, I still preferred my crazy world and its girls – the only place and fun I knew surely as real. And death may still not be digestible at such a conventionally ripe time. Many old people pass away, not because they feel comfortable to go, but because they cannot help it.

I remember a story of an Egyptian told by a visiting Imam at my grandparents' house sometime ago. The Egyptian saw life as a helpless situation of being born only to die, no matter what time or condition it is. He blamed his father for bringing him into the world to die and he chose not to have any children because he did not want to carry the blame of bearing children only to die.

Thought-provoking it seems, but, also, I still wondered if anyone of us afraid of aging and death could ever like to live youthfully forever if given the privilege, especially my kind of person who is prone to be blasé and bored with anything rhythmically regular. Then, I realized that backward or forward, life is a labyrinth. It is a big dilemma, a crazy maze with no way out. Then, what is the real answer, the real way, if we are not trapped in the game of some gods, or a God, and doomed to a fixed fate in which we are helpless? What is the solution to the puzzle of life?

To a psychotherapist, this wandering of my mind may present me as a classic example of someone falling into depression, especially in the condition of the sickness I was. My perception of life as a maze within which there was no way out suggested the symptomatic cognitive triad[22] within which the depressed sinks and is lost. Perhaps they would be right in making such an assessment of me, but it may not be all who wander that is lost. For me, this was the plight of my soul in the eyes of the stormy weather of life, which seemed a plague to kill human consciousness.

I did not think the right answers to my questions could come without my efforts, or that my efforts could be so good enough to discover the right answers. And I did not think I could get answers while alive. Even, maybe there is no answer, and life and death are simply a fabric of mystery masked over our face, deluding us into fear and faith. Maybe there is no question either! Perhaps the state of questioning, then, is simply or intricately a symptom of the questioner's condition, as high temperature is

---

[22] Cognitive triad is the representation of the thoughts of the depressed individuals as containing negative views of themselves, their world, and their future.

of fever. One interesting case point strikes me in the biblical version of the story of Job, however. After all his questioning of his Lord, the answers He gives Job are also questions, asking Job whether he is aware of the origin and workings of the universe, and implying the question whether he is aware of who he himself really is. Job realizes that he really does not know, or that he has only forgotten. Job realizes that he has only been ignorant, and that leads to the solution of his problems, at least to the extent that he becomes aware that as he has questions for God, so does God have questions for him.

Maybe this was my problem also, standing in front of a mirror and asking the image where I got my affliction. Maybe it is the problem of the world. May be rather than questioning God why He created evil in the world, may be we should be questioning ourselves. Afterall, I now do not see it good to live forever, while sickness, aging, and death are our ultimate definition of evil, and life and health as good. At some point we think it necessary to die, even if only to give room to later generations that we cannot help but to bring into the world. Perhaps, then, labeling my situation as evil and blaming it on God, witches, or anyone was a symptom of my ignorance, my cosmic depression of which the psychotherapist may see only an ephemeral reflection. Some analysts of the story of Job also put the blame of his predicament on Job himself, sometimes presenting him as mentally troubled. Hence,. I was really increasingly becoming a modern day Job than I realized.

In an old Indian Scripture I later learned, the question, rather to God, was asked man, "Why in this truth find sorrow?"[23] Also, at the entrance to the temple of the Pythian Apollo were the words "[Man] Know thyself!" which welcomed the ancient Greeks into the temple. How old the chaos and quest have been, I wonder, while the world still rambles around with no peace for her poor creatures. Our science has done a very good job of dissecting and explaining every bit of my apparent reality, but the question of who really I am has remained ever elusive and I could not find it in any science textbook. However, as my heart and body suffered, my mind asked and learned, and even though I still believed that the Lord was my Shepherd, my problem was that I still wanted.

So runs my dream; but what am I?
An infant crying in the night;
An infant crying for the light,
And no language but a cry[?]

Lord Alfred Tennyson, "In Memoriam"

***

The process of being carried to and from the chair went on despite my abhorrence for it. The pains did not reduce, and neither did my fear. After being carried to the chair in the morning I would be worried until evening

---

[23] Bhagavad-Gita

with the fear for the evening's carrying back, and after being carried back to bed in the evening I would be worried until the next morning with the fear for the next morning's to the chair. The pain was so much that only a fraction of it would be more than enough to make a hardened criminal confess to a crime he did not commit. Yet, there were no human rights organizations that could intercede for my relief.

Now I slept with my legs folded and supported by a pile of cushions mounted to my left side. I could not go through the demands of stretching them out on the bed anymore. With the spasms alluringly reduced in the folded position, it became irresistible for me, even though they said it might not be ultimately progressive.

When and how all this would go and leave me in peace, I did not know. I was only constantly assured it would go. Many evenings, I sat there, staring ahead like a statue, breathing through the pains in my muscles and veins and rummaging through the sorrows in my heart. And many evenings they gushed out hot tears, which, more unfortunately, I could not mop with my paralyzed hands. I only licked those that rolled to my mouth. My younger brothers who sometimes shared the tears with me cleaned the rest. Weeping for myself was a peak state of suffering for me, and my family knew it. To weep for myself, especially in front of others, was a rarity; it was to weed for others that I could easily slip into. Now it was a commonplace; I was often mixing my suffering with tears and having a sour drink.

But when I realized that my tears could not wash away my sickness, I began to take it as it was. I began to live it as it was, although not to stop my tears or give up, but to try harder to get well, if at all I could get well. I have been born with a considerable amount of concern for others that sometimes when I asked myself "Why me?" I got echoes reverberating from the walls of my skull, saying back to me, "Why not me? Why somebody else?" Then I began to wonder whether it mattered who it was – we are all humans, anyway.

God has been so much ingrained in me that I still could not help but be careful how I thought and talked, and I sometimes felt guilty at the kinds of thoughts that came in to my mind. Even though I felt bad that He could let these things happen to me, I still hoped on Him, as my father and all my religious consciousness encouraged. I often strengthened myself in the spirit of a Quranic verse that says, *If your stream be some morning lost, who then can provide you with clear flowing water*.

I lingered on. With all the troubles the Heavens heaved over my neck, I lingered on. To keep my mind away from dwelling all the time on my condition, Baami talked to me day and night on various issues of life, for encouragement and distraction. He talked about people, traditional issues, and stories from the history of our town and dynasty. Since the hypersensitivity of my condition had receded from the pitch at which I could not stand high voices, the children in the house also have been coming to give me company. They only had to keep their voices at a normal conversation level and not touch the chair or bed on which I was.

Soliu, Oladimeji, Akeem - not Brother Akeem, but a younger cousin of mine - and Gboyega, were four teenage boys whose room I now shared. In the house were ten other children. Four boys: Adekunle, Gbadegesin, Bamigbade and Bukola; and six girls: Joke, Temilade, Dasola, Peju, Fatima and Solape. They were always there, one or more at a time, to help their brother from sinking in his grief. And they always prayed for me.

Also, they ran my various errands, and I only sat as if in control of everyone. As painful as it could be, the period of sickness is a period for one to feel special. You feel the exercise of your will over your family members, friends, and well-wishers, and you see their sacrifices as proofs of their love. And ironically, like a king, I controlled everyone present around me, since they did everything for me, only that I lacked kingly majesty and that they could not help me of my burden of pains, not even for a minute or two, for me to flex my muscles before I took them back. From this I learned more how alone man is in the world. Even among those he loves and who love him, what goes on in his veins, bones, and nerves are all his alone to bear.

I was smoldering with tears one evening when Baami consoled me and said, "Take heart, Ramoni, and don't cry anymore. We all love you, as you know, and we always pray for your recovery. If this thing could be shared like a loan of money one owes, we would all have shared it in harmless pieces and you would have been well and gone about your plan for your life. Even if you owe a million bucks, our family is large enough to share it. But, regrettably, it cannot be shared. We don't feel comfortable seeing you in this condition, but we cannot help it. So take heart, it is only God Who can remove it, and we are all calling on Him to do it."

Sometime later, all my thoughts reached a state of poetic effusion, and having eventually learned to put my thoughts into verses, and having had an inspiration from a write-up with a similar theme in a Nigerian magazine,[24] I picked up my pen and put my thoughts into verses:

Alone and alone is man,[25]
all alone in the world.
Journeying through the harsh oceans
and deserts of life, alone is he.
No one tells him where or when,
or how long will take his journey.
Purpose or end, he knows not what.
From the beginning, in the lonesomeness
of the dark, watery sac,
which knows no sun, or any blowing wind,

---

[24] By Dan Agbese, Newswatch Magazine

[25] *Man* is used as a neuter noun in this poem, as it is sometimes used in this book, and it is strictly for convenience sake.

to the soft-walled little cradle,
man comes, alone, all by himself.
Even though blessedly circled around
by families, friends, and well-wishers,
who jolly and sadden at his feelings,
and even though despised by foes,
man lives but alone in the world.
In his thoughts and feelings, and in choice
of what path there is to follow,
alone, alone, and alone is man,
all alone in the world.
And when it's time to bow out -
though, for some, timely, gently, and happily,
but for some others, suddenly and too soon,
seemin' forced out of their show.
And still for some others, agonizingly slowly -
families, friends, fans, failures,
and all successes his life have furled,
all come to nothing else but naught.
Man finds himself absolutely alone,
dead alone, and in the six feet deep hole,
buried and left all alone.
"Alone In the World", Rahman

Now, I knew this truth and I was learning to come to terms with it. Although, I did not have a better choice, but I was not anymore so much afraid of dying and being buried alone as I was of dying agonizingly slowly. Already I was living agonizingly slowly. What I wanted, however, was for it to end someday, and not to end me.

***

This period made me realize how an interesting and an enlightening figure Baami was. His stories and discussions at my bedside were to play roles in my cognitive development. At the few times that I had less pains to hear him, his philosophies, in the context of Yoruba philosophy and the royal clan's, gave me so much knowledge and amusement about the world, and much later gave me inspiration.

Many of the Yoruba proverbs have interesting stories behind them, and sometimes Baami would tell proverbs and the stories accompanying them. At some other times he would go into the genealogy of the royal family, which, almost for the first time in my life, made me proud to be born of the blood of those great kings. Their philosophies were as amazing as their birth, and their stories fascinated me. The tale of the deification of one of them gave me a remarkable spiritual revelation. I was amazed to find out that the legendary god worshipped across Africa and the "African world of the Americas,"[26] whose story was as intriguingly fantastic as those of the Gilgamesh of Uruk, Babylonian Hammurabi, Sargon of Akkadia, the Greek Zeus, the Indian Rama, the Egyptian Thoth, and the Roman Jupiter, was actually a man from whose blood I was made. This gave me an epiphany to the understanding of the great religious heroes of the world, as I learned into why and how he was deified, in what ways he serves his worshippers and, especially, in what ways nature provides for these. Sango, "the god of the West Coast, hurler of thunderbolts and lord of the storms, render of trees and slayer of men, cruel and savage and yet beneficent,"[27] was a king whose story has been woven in global mythology. With an atavistic pleasure often said as characteristic of the children of the royal family, I felt thrilled to know myself as his ancestral son.

Although, I had known of many of the past kings before, but it was this time that I learned deeply about them and intellectually about the Yoruba culture which was most saturated in Oyo. I now began to learn the value of my hometown, appreciating its ancient preservations. I had lived in a sophisticated world for too long. Even when I was schooling at Oyo, I had not been exposed to this much. I was always surrounded by friends from West-African cities - big cities soaked in Western ideas and cultures. To my amusement, the quaint Oyo dialect of the Yoruba language also began to appeal to me and accustom to my tongue, something deemed as local by 'civilized' Yorubas, many of whom spoke a polished form of the language, often diluted with high volumes of English words.

In time, I would discover African philosophy, embedded in proverbs, folklores, legendary figures, symbols, festivals, myths, poetry, songs, and even in taboos much held in contempt in modern times - the various beliefs and practices of Africans that show the process of the African mind. And from it I would learn the universality of regional philosophies in general, even though many of them, like the Africans', had not been written down to invite universal celebration.

Perhaps, this unwritten philosophy had its advantage. Africans in ancient times carried all they learned in their hearts and their daily-life activities, especially as proverbs and rituals. This enhanced the intellectual and pragmatic values of the ideas in their lives. They immediately understood and wove every piece of knowledge as part of their lives, unlike the alienation of the written form of our values and wisdom today. Many of us today regard the scholastic philosophies as only of the book and for bookists, and we have found ourselves merely lounging in a philosophical limbo, interestingly, predicted by an African legendary king. Thamus, the Egyptian god-king warned Thoth, the mythological inventor of the art of writing, "... this discovery of yours [writing] will create

---

[26] A phrase used by Wole Soyinka to describe places in North and South America, to which African people and culture have migrated.

[27] W.E.B. Dubois' epithetical description of Sango.

forgetfulness in the learners' souls, because they will not use their memories [anymore]; they will trust to the external written characters and not remember of themselves. The specific, which you have discovered, is an aid not to memory, but to reminiscence, and you give your disciples not truth but only the semblance of truth..." Although writing has become an indispensable invention of humankind, as I really could not imagine life without the written word, I realize that Thamus has a good point.

III

One day, toward the end of the fasting period, I was laid back in bed after the dressing of my wound, and, as usual, I remained still and silent for a long time for the flame of pains to recede. Afterward, Baami began to talk to me. He sat on the chair by my bedside to be close enough to hear me.

One topic evolved into another until he came to the topic of the different natures and principles of the works of those who had been treating me. Then he mentioned a case of one of my cousins, Rafiat. He told me how an illness she once had had been cured through the *eat-this-eat-that* of Mama Pakoyi, and how the clairaudient woman had been widely known as a trustworthy psychic and spiritualist in the town. "She gets straight to people's problems," he stated, "and, she would tell them things they conceal only in their hearts."

Then, the idea struck me. After all these days, I realized everyone had forgotten about her in my treatment.

"I think I was taking treatments from her before," I cut in.

"Yes, you were."

"But why did we stop?" I asked, with a marsh of astonishment, pleasure, and eagerness.

In realization, Baami smiled and said, "I think we all just forgot about her."

As my heart had been yearning for more treatment attention, I decided to continue with the treatment from Mama Pakoyi. Coincidentally, Rafiat, who lived in one of our family houses in the town, visited me in the evening and she volunteered to go to Mama Pakoyi's place on my behalf.

From all I had known about the old woman, I felt happy for being onto something to improve the course of my recovery. It was not that treatments on my sickness had completely stopped; it was that my mind wanted all the treatments I could have to get well as quickly as I wanted.

Mama had also been worried that we had not been coming to her, as she said, and she had tried to contact us. On my condition, she said I would have to be patient. Because the sickness did not get into my body in one day or one month, I should not expect it to go in one day or one month. She noted again that I had been under the spell long before I broke down, and there had been complications that needed time and carefulness to deal with.

Then she said something strange. She said there were three unseen demons planted in my room, trying to spoil all the treatments I was receiving and worsening my condition. They have been influencing the turn of events in my sickroom in a long time.

"When you forgot about me," Rafiat reported Mama as saying, "you all thought it happened just like that… the truth was that those creatures put veils over your eyes so you didn't see the right things to do. I wanted to contact you, but the Lord calmed me, assuring me that everything will be fine."

This shocked everyone in my house. However, she added that we should not worry, and that by God's power they would all leave. "Everything has its time. Tell Rahman that no one can take away his time to heal and triumph."

Of course, I did not disbelieve her; a lot of things that had happened buttressed her claim, from the hospital to this moment. One of them was the disappearance of the snake fang and the medicine right under our noses. Without being aware of Mama Pakoyi's message, Baba-elero had later told my father that someone we could not see in the room had taken it. "Rahman was never alone," Baba-elero had said, "they always waited in there for the chance to finish their work."

Sometimes I wondered whether they were the creatures I had seen at the hospital, which I thought were figments of my imagination, precipitated by my sick state. About two to three times I had experienced the same thing here at home, seeing the childlike figures jump on and off my bed. Many times they caused my spasm, but I did not yet see anything clear enough to mention it to my father without raising suspicion of a psychological disorder in me.

Nonetheless, I could not imagine these things happening to me. It was like in the movies. I could not imagine such things as demons could go beyond the motion pictures screens and radio sets, as stories of fiction and fact often documented by our media, and I could not imagine myself as a character in one of them. I often listened to the famous radio program, *The Mysterious World*,[28] and I only thought it thrilling. I did no one any wrong, I contested nothing with nobody, so why all these? How could anyone so much wish me dead and go to this extent?

Mama Pakoyi prescribed a new diet for me, and required that Rafiat continue to come to her every alternate day. The treatment had to be persistent for consistent effects. First, she said she had to deal with the problem in my internal organs. The organs had been grossly affected by the gunshot and other charms and she would have to surgically clean and restore them. I did not ask how; I knew better than to think she was talking of physical surgery.

***

[28] *Iriri Aye*, translated as *The Mysterious World*, was the name of a reality based investigative program by Kola Olawuyi. Successful on radio, it went onto TV.

The carrying to and from the chair continued and I could not stop it. The wound in my back had to be dressed everyday. I asked for it to be done in bed one day, but it was so difficult I discarded the idea. Nothing was easy with me. Everything having to do with touching and moving me was done because it had to be done. Sometimes, I had to be forced. Now, I spent only about four hours of the day in the chair.

My sleeping improved and sleep state became the only desirable state in my life. I slept about three to four hours a night and I dreamed every minute of it, seeing myself as a healthy person going everywhere and doing everything I wanted. Sometimes I went about my chores like a superman, fluttering about for pleasure and escaping from unpleasant circumstances. It felt good to live like birds, and sometimes I wished to continue sleeping the rest of my life.

Most of my dreams, I realized, were significant, as they often had clear but mysterious relationships to my daily and future experiences. Sometimes they were precognitive. In some dreams I would see people I had not seen in a long time and wake up to have them visit me the same day. In some others I would dream of an event, which at the time would seem absurd, but to one day find it as a clear prediction of a later real life event. Literally, I began to see my future in my dreams. If I had been well enlightened on dreams, perhaps I would have known that the *end of the world* dream I had at the hospital was a vision of the erstwhile imminent death of my earthly life at the hospital, and the *scramble for home* was a warning to leave where I was and to go to Oyo, which eventually happened. And perhaps I would have saved myself early enough from the prolonged trauma that I was now going through.

Once in a while I dreamed of meeting my sister, Ganiyat, and it put me in fear for my condition. I often came out of the dream thinking it might mean I was going to join her, but my father always reassured me that seeing a dead person in dreams meant that one would live long. I was not sure whether he was stating an objective truth or he was only trying to pacify me to keep my hope alive. One night I had a dream that frightened me most. I found myself lain at one side of a large bed while Ganiyat lay at the other side. Though I would later realize this to mean that we were at opposite sides of reality, a glimpse of assurance that I would live beyond the sickness, but it frightened me so much at the time.

Living so close to death, I became curious about metaphysics, especially about after-death phenomenon. I hoped to survive the sickness to tell the story, but I feared it might consume me, perhaps by my choice to ease myself of my burden. They said suicide was a sin, so I wanted to know whether I would be punished for neglecting myself to death (I did not have enough health to actively kill myself). Or if I could reincarnate, for I did not want to go into extinction. The concept of reincarnation, thus, occupied my thoughts every time I had some freedom of the mind.

***

After Ramadan, we noticed something we hoped was a milestone of improvement. My bowel discharge contained and smelled of local gunpowder, as of the gun with which I was shot in the dream. Mama Pakoyi had said that my intestines had been damaged by the shot and it was this that would first be taken care of. If this was it, it was a smelly job, as everyone noted, though I could not smell any odor at this time. I did not smell the gangrene from my wound or the odor of death that people sometimes talked about. "Your nose has become accustomed to the odors," my father said sometime later, "You smelled like a corpse. It used to smell like a graveyard in here (my sick room). You were (like) already gone; only that you were still breathing."

Now I might be getting better and it gave me a glimmer of hope. Though the pains still remained as cruel as ever, and I constantly complained to my father and asked him to do something. Most of the times, the only things he could do were to pray and to try to console me. "... All will be well," he would say, "... it's not in a day it got there, and we shouldn't expect it to go in a day. Patience is all we need."

That was true, only that my condition was too pressing for the truth to comfort me.

After several weeks, the dressing of my wound was not getting anywhere. The nurse said it needed fresh air to heal quickly, but the position for it to get the air was a nightmare for me. Hence, I ignored any concern for the wound and only hoped it would heal someday.

One morning, I was carried onto the chair for the dressing. It was so painful that I burst out crying and could not allow any further touching for the dressing. They sent for my father to talk to me. About an hour later, after I had eventually been treated and carried back to the bed, I got into one of my lamentations, asking my father questions hurting my heart: "What kind of a thing is all this? Why is this happening to me? What is it all about and who is this woman you talked about? Who is she and what does she want from me?" I was frenetic, sobbing out my questions as my father stared at me. Even though he also clung to the hopeful sign of recovery, he had become so worried over my health lately that he could not stay a long time with me in his sight. I was too terrible for him to contain and he did not have anything new to say.

Though I questioned him this way now, it was not that I did not have a general idea of the situation. It was that my pain was at a hysterical height that I blubbered out anything disturbing in my heart. I cogitated on all I heard around me. When they warned me not to go back to live at Oniyanrin I understood what it could mean. Yet, Oniyanrin was a big neighborhood and I still wondered who there might be causing me so much anguish. And if it was in our house, as I sometimes thought, who could it be? There were about a hundred and twenty people living in the house, who could my enemy be among them? Now my desire to know the specifics stabbed at my chest and I insisted that my father say something.

"I wanted this to wait until you're all right," he finally began, "There's no cause for any rush, but if you insist, I'll tell you a little of it.

"This thing came from your house at Oniyanrin. Who and who, I'm not going to say now, but it is from someone close to you."

For a long time I wondered what to make of the information. The knowledge perhaps could not make a difference right now; it could not give me the only thing I wanted. Yet, I could not stop wanting to know. Almost spontaneously, I asked, "But why would anyone so badly want me dead? What did I do? What do they hold against me?"

"They've got this thing going in a long time - since you were born; perhaps before. First, there had been a longstanding festering over my choice of your mother in the house. There were certain persons who wanted me to marry someone else, and then someone else. They tried to divert my heart from your mother, and they even talked about it with me. This was the beginning of your troubles. One may then call it all a polygamal festering, but I think it is more than that. Though it had started from within your family, more people outside your family are now involved, for they (witches) work in groups. You have been delivered to a group and, collectively now, they see you as their target.

"Secondly, the current war was largely because of your plan to go to America. They see it as getting away from under their noses, where you have been all your life, and a step toward your success, and they don't want it to happen. They didn't want to kill you initially; they've placed a mark on you and they only wanted to know all your steps so they could be able to control and frustrate your life as they wished. It's now that you decided to travel out of the country that they want to finish you off.

"I've known this since you were a little kid and I've always wanted to take your eyes off the house. That's why I refused you to go there sometimes. It's your love for your grandmother that always made me give up and hope we could always protect you. Even if you had been vigilant, you would have known that something was wrong somewhere. Ninety-nine percent of the time you've fallen sick had been crucial moments in your life, mostly during school exams. Your first years in school, as much as you loved school and as bright as you were, you fell sick during every single exam that I was so worried I wanted to yank you away from the house.

"In both ways, however, their actions were deliberately made to hurt your mother. She has people in there who don't like her, and she herself is not helping her situation." I knew this in a long time. My mother also always said it, and as much as I loved to have her around at Oniyanrin during family occasions, I never liked for her to come. Every single one of her visits in the house, at least that I can remember, had ended in a fight with someone or another. Sometimes I thought she became so paranoid that someone would do something to her or me. She often warned me not to go to the house anymore and took me to various alfas, beseeching them to offer special prayers for my protection.

"For this sickness, you've been under the spell for some time," my father continued, "long before the sickness actually appeared. They were only counting down your days, waiting for you to finally be spent by their spell. At such a point, anything could have triggered it, anything as simple as a stress or headache, any natural phenomenon that people could blame for it. It was your characteristic body pain that did it." Sometimes, I think it was my crazy mistake of smoking weed that caused it. My father had known about the weed, but he pretended not to know because I did not tell him.

"But God is more powerful than they are, and, by what we can only call a special blessing, He does not want you to die. He wants you to live to tell the story. In their way of execution, you had been spiritually butchered and your body parts had been shared among the witches for a feast, but, by an extraordinary stroke of luck, not yet eaten. They were waiting for your last breath before they began the feast, which they were sure was going to happen. It was by God's love and permission that we were able to get help through a stronger intervention." This would flabbergast me at a later time when I remembered the story alfa Ibrahim had told me about the animal shared by jealous other animals, and which the old woman at U.C.H. also talked about.

"This is why I tell you that all your life you must be grateful to God," he continued. "In the extent that they had gone with you, your survival is a very rare opportunity, and it makes many spiritualists wonder. Many people haven't seen an occasion where someone whose spirit body has been shared as meat among witches would turn around to survive the spell. All of the witches were made to return their rations. If a small piece had been missing, it would have been fatal for you. But we got everything back. It is God who wants you that saved you. It is Him who wants you not to die. Don't think any medicine or medicine man did the magic. That's only an appearance of the world. It is God who saved you. He only used them as mediums through which you received His grace. Immediately this whole scheme burst open to us, I was told the bitter truth that no father would like to hear. I was told that if at all you survived this, it would only be that God has a special purpose for your life. But if He didn't, then we were only seeing the last of you.

"Your decision to come home from the hospital happened to be very instrumental in this. How you made the decision to leave on that day, no one can tell. Perhaps we wouldn't have been saying what we are saying now; the story would have been unfortunately different. The witches didn't expect you to leave U.C.H. alive, and that day was supposed to be your last in the world. It was because you survived the day that they quickly tried to use apeta (the spiritual gunshot) on you. This is also a terrible kind of attack that only a few victims have survived. In anger, they meant to finish you up quickly, because your survival beyond the *last day* had not only been surprising to them, it had also been shameful.

"But no one knows what's between you and your God, and I want you to know that there's nothing to worry about anymore. They can't harm you anymore. No one is as powerful as God, and no one can stand His fight. For your information, the member of the group who did the shooting died some weeks ago. In a backlash of the event, she had had to give her life for it, because the spell they used could not be merely dispelled; someone had to fall by it. It is God Himself who will fight them all. So, relax your mind, believe that you'll be well, and you'll be well, Insha Allah. I think you know how to read the Qur'an in Arabic, don't you?"

"Yes, I do," I replied.

"Then start praying with it, instead of crying and lamenting. *Suratul Qaf* is a good sura, the eighteenth chapter. Read it once or thrice daily, and your recovery will be sped up."

Although perplexed, I nodded as if in full comprehension, and he left.

The bug killing a plant is one that is living with the plant, as a saying goes, *and it is always someone who knows a man that does him harm.* I had not been entirely oblivious of such a close fact. I did not think the people called witches were the grotesque creatures described in folklores as pointed-nosed, raspy-voiced, and black cloaked old hags who live in deserted houses, caves, and in the woods, waiting for unsuspecting kids straying along their domains. This was only symbolic of the reality. I knew the witches were ordinary people living ordinary lives, only with an extraordinary power to exaggerate the evils of their ordinary human propensities – jealousy, anger, hatred, and so on. I had heard the idea at Oniyanrin from time to time but I had never taken any of them seriously. And every time my mother warned me against the place, she directly stated this sinister side of the house, though I always ignored it still. It was unimaginable to me that anyone would think of making me a part of such tragedy.

Yet, my grandmother lived there, someone to whom I was attached. Perhaps, then, all these could only be blamed on the polygamous setting of the house, which had led to intricate complication of relationships. Such things were most common in polygamous homes. I began to remember some events and I began to put pieces together in the puzzle. One day when one of my maternal uncles came to visit me and heard of the gunshot, the first thing he said was, "Your mouth must have been loose on your planning to go to America. You guys are so naive when it comes to handling of your affairs." He knew his home so well that he believed that keeping one's affairs away from people's knowledge there was a golden wisdom.

In this world, and especially in the world of polygamy, one could only be sure of whom one wishes well; one never could be sure of who wishes one well. It is usually the fronts, the outer displays of people, that meet the eye. Many people are bad inside, but, as a proverb goes, the skin-covering of the belly does not let us see the inside of a bad person.

Someone from other parts of the world may ask what a family this was, but it was not only a story of my family. It was a story typical to families in this part of the world. Because of the complexity of family structures, especially in polygamy, there was hardly any family or large family without, at least, a witch or a witch story. Except in some small modern families that are remote from the vicinity of their witch-cancerous large families. And even only in some circumstances where the modern families remain monogamous, as now often advocated.

Many of the families of such undesirable elements exist in ruins, while our home, Baba's family, was blessed highly with fortunes, successes, and virtues, the types that were the envies of families. The undesirable elements were, then, only a small sore thumb that people would like to keep distance from. In many other families it is rife.

The problems of polygamy begin from the weakness of the husband. Out of sexual insecurity or lasciviousness he marries one woman after another, making the women the first casualties. As their number increases, they become neglected, and, consequently, daring and venomous. When they are met with bitter rivalry among themselves, jealousy, envy, and conspiracy develop. Some, or many, start to visit voodoo practitioners in search of security and power in the family feud. Of these, some become so hardened and persuaded to join the society of witchcraft, by which they will not need voodoo practitioners anymore for whatever voodoo they needed. They will become voodoo authorities on their own.

Children suffer next. The wives, wielding the various powers in their possession, insidiously attack each other and each other's children. On the surface the wives pretend to like each other and love each other's children, but underneath rages wild fire. Loving façades fool the children into enemies' holes. Nettles blow around filling the house with calamities. Many children with promising future die untimely. Those who could have been doctors are doctored to their early graves. Others, supposedly future professors, lawyers, engineers, politicians, preachers, end up with their paths contorted. Many run out of their heads and litter the streets. They become figures of disgrace to their families and society. Healthy kids are reduced to vegetables and outcasts, moving the heaven to tears.

As many children ramble hopelessly with various afflictions, however, some are lucky to survive, though not without the spear marks of the war. They become morbidly wary of their parental home and many will not take their successes back there for fear of being fresh targets. I remember some of my uncles who would not come home in their fancy cars and clothes, and would not give anyone money big enough to turn spotlights on them.

The father, aging, suffers last. At a time when he needs his children most, he is neglected, and sometimes deliberately by his children. Successful children, cautious, secretly take care of their aging mothers, while the father is too conspicuously situated for them to give company or help. And the father suffers most. The burden of afflictions and losses of the victim-children of each mother are all his burdens and losses, and he carries them as he dies slowly, lonely, and bitterly.

Sometimes, polygamy may appear glamorous and enviable, as our house often did, but there is always plenty of troubles and strong endurance beneath. Polygamy brings out the worst in people. It is the most fertile ground for suspicion. Even the most innocent actions raise suspicion, and suspicion is the beginning of festering and feud. Perhaps, each subject in a polygamous home needs more patience in a day than a subject in a monogamous home needs in a thousand days. Now, many people prefer to make nuclear and monogamous families, admirably called "the happy family" in contradistinction to the troubles of the predominant, complex polygamous families.

Baba realized the origin of the problems in the house, though not early enough to rid himself of it. He knew it was not so much his own mistake as it was of his contemporary tradition's, and he did not want us to be deceived by any glamour in it. He always advised us about circumventing such malevolence within the family and on making better decisions concerning marriage. Talking about polygamy one day, he said, "if only I had known, I wouldn't have done it."

My father may not be someone with an admirable respect for women, but still I learned from him about women. Women are the center of polygamy games, and in this case women are like horses in an equestrian steeplechase, racing through the hedges, hurdles, and ditches of life, and men like the horse riders. If a rider was not trained well enough to select a good horse for the race, or did not understand and respect his horse well enough, the horse would sooner fill him in one of the ditches than he could fear. Yet, men, swooned by the tingling in their crotches, want to ride more than a horse tied together, while there may never be a possibility of a man getting well trained enough to understand the intrigues of even a single woman. Because, as men think they are playing games, so are women playing games. To them, men are at the center of the polygamy games. And hence we have all been caught in the big game of life, the conflict or struggles of the sexes, and by this have various civilizations been wrought.

For this reason, I realized that women are not only the vehicles that convey men into the world; they also convey men through the world. Overtly or not, they have being the strong force that dictates every action of men in this world, and the strong force that dictates civilization. An average Yoruba person with more traditional knowledge than Western indoctrination believes that the more powerful sex in the world is the female sex, socially, sexually, and spiritually. And even though they abuse women, as feminists now rave, they still feel themselves in some way enslaved to them. My father often said to me, "It is in the hands of women that God puts the world." Perhaps, then, men's abuse of women has only been an unconscious rationalization aimed at consoling themselves – a kind of defense mechanism. Afterall, it is a world fashioned by the conflict of the sexes – as of all opposites. Perhaps, then, our term 'abuse' in this circumstance is a relative word, valid only from certain perspectives.

I liked Oniyanrin, but this knowledge made me realize that things between the place and I may never be the same again. Ordinarily, of course, things do not remain the same again after being torn apart by time, but my liking of my past made me dream of visiting the house in future and relive it.

I began to pray with the Qur'an. The sura my father recommended was too long for me to read once or thrice a day, as he had said. I could not even finish half of the sura in one day. I was slow in reading Arabic. When I began, it took me four days to laze through the sura once.

"Not bad," my father commented, "your pace will increase by practice."

I had learned only to read the Qur'an. After I completed the traditional learning and had done the Walimah Khatmil – the completion ceremony - my Imam asked me to continue into the next stage by learning the Arabic language to understand what I read, but I thought that was not necessary. With my experience in this period making me think about God more than I had ever done, I would later wish I had heeded my Imam's advice, as I became curious to understand what I recited.

Really, the completion ceremony was the beginning of what was supposed to be a spiritual journey. This made me later to see that my Imam may not afterall be to blame for having my heel unprotected. Though many alfas only indoctrinated their students with their interpretations of the scripture, some were aware that different people had different capacities to understand the message. Hence, they hoped on imparting the knowledge of understanding the Arabic language, by which the lifelong journey would be made easier.

TEN

Physiotherapy

It is becoming more and more obvious that it is not starvation, not microbes, not cancer, but man himself who is mankind's greatest danger, because he has no adequate protection against psychic epidemics, which are infinitely more devastating in their effect than the greatest natural catastrophes.

C.G. Jung
Modern Man in Search of a Soul

I

One day early in March, Baba-elero visited us and noticed acute anemia from my appearance. My father also had been worried about this, as the nurse who dressed my wound had warned us. To receive transfusion, the problem was how to get blood from the General Hospital and set up the process in my room. For the hospital's patients, there was already not enough blood. Our family doctor came to assess the situation and promised to try his best.

But Baba-elero told my father to leave it to him instead. "Don't worry about it," he had said, "I'd bring you something for it tomorrow. Your blood will be restored as soon as you use it."

This was madness. The only logical remedy we were aware of was blood transfusion; what then could this man bring that would give me blood? He does not have I.V. materials or a blood bank. He does not even have a fridge to preserve his own food, not to talk of a refrigerator to preserve donated blood in his house. Or would he kill a goat and bring me its blood?

Nonetheless, I did not doubt him and I did not worry, perhaps because I did not even worry about the threat of the blood shortage. Stopping my pains was still more of concern to me than stopping my death.

On the following morning, Baba-elero came with something wrapped in a brown paper. He instructed Baami to make incisions all over my back, from below my neck down to my ankles, and rub the surface of the cuts with the content of the brown paper.

Using a brand new razor, Baami went to work, making the cuts as gently as possible. The only problem I had was that I had to be held up so he could reach my backside. A sign indicating the extent of the anemia became more apparent: the cuts were almost bloodless, appearing whitish, with only a few red films upon some.

The coarse particles of the grayish powder hurt as he rubbed it over the cuts, but that was quickly overtaken by its burning effect. It burned so much that I could swear the powder was made from hot pepper or salt or both.

"Tomorrow you'll do the same," Baba-elero instructed. "But don't let the cuts be as much as these, so the blood would not be too much in his body."

That sounded funny, as a 6-year-old boy who has seen Harry Potter too many times would sound when speaking to his friend during a pretended quidditch game, "Hold on tightly; in a second the broom is going to fly up into the sky and I don't want you to slide off." Yet, my mind did not falter on what I expected the man as capable of.

The following day, we did as instructed. I liked the idea of fewer cuts; it meant less time to be held up and less burning. But, astonishingly, Baami was not even allowed to do much cutting. The flow of blood was so much that he had to stop the cutting. Blood gushed out as if I was some kind of a blood bag with pinholes all over my back. Even though we were hoping for the medicine to work, and we were expecting to see something remarkable, we were still surprised at what we saw. My legs and slippers were bathed down in blood and the cushion of my chair had plenty to drink.

“This man is a wizard!” Baami exclaimed. When the nurse came for the dressing of my wound, he was amazed beyond words. He had never seen anything like this before and he shook his head repeatedly in wonder.

Among stories of Baba-elero’s prowess that were told at my bedside, there was one that I always remember, assuring me that God imbues the world with power in many different ways. The story was about a young woman who had a pregnancy locked up in her womb. Growing up, I had heard stories of witches locking up pregnancies like this, but they were so remote that I could not think of them as more than stories. But this story was different, in the sense that the woman was an identifiable member of our community, known through her predicament by people who came to visit me. The experience was partly the reason for the apprenticeship of Aunty Sidi who had been a midwife all her life.

The woman’s pregnancy was well over a year but the baby did not come out. One mysterious thing about her condition was that the pregnancy only showed up at around midnight and disappeared before dawn. That is, there was no pregnancy during the day, only during the night. Strangely, all medical tests confirmed it like this and she was transferred from one hospital to another, including U.C.H. Finally, a brave doctor decided to tackle the job as systematic as it appeared. He arranged to deliver the baby by caesarian procedure during the nighttime when the pregnancy showed up and he set a date.

On the appointed night for the surgery the doctor and everyone were ready, but, for the first time in the history of the pregnancy, it did not appear. A wonder. The doctor was pertinacious and he tried again. The following night, it did not appear. Funny. Then it appeared on the third night and the doctor hastened to seize the opportunity.

On the doctor's way to the operating room, an unlucky fly strayed into one of his eyes. He tried to remove it quickly like any other one, but it proved not as any other one. It proved the doctor unlucky, too. The fly did not come out and the doctor did not feel comfortable with it in his eye. It was more than endurable; it was painful. Then it became a trauma. He could not go on with the surgery. This was the moment in the story that one would wish he had worn a pair of glasses - perhaps such a misfortune could have been averted. But the fly did not come accidentally as it appeared; it was on a mission. While unable to perform the delivery, the doctor himself had to be transferred to another higher hospital out of town before the fly was surgically removed.

This may sound like a fable, but, in the end, this spiritual doctor who mysteriously gave me blood from a peppery powder delivered the pregnancy. And the art involved in the two treatments, hers and mine, often made people pause and think. While such procedures could do a lot of help in the world, my father argued one day, how could they be proved in our laboratory? In truth, the blood treatment could give blood to people without fear of contamination, genetic mismatch, or shortage in the blood bank. Yet we believe that modern scientific laboratory is the only test-house for all that is real. Here was I, a flesh-and-blood like everyone else, witnessing and enjoying un-laboratorial treatments. Then, one could say that our modern scientific techniques must be inadequate for capturing the whole of reality. From these, like many others, I realized that man in his universe is not an all-physical affair for mere physical techniques to fully grasp, define, and determined.

If man were only a physical entity, anything called spiritual manipulations or unphysical manipulations like these would never be able to affect him. Also, if the universe were only a physical dimension, spiritual manipulations would not move an atom in it. Yet, by what we see in this part of the world, spiritual manipulations move much more: rain, thunder, fire, diseases, blood, flies, life, death, and so on. Why then does our modern civilization deny the world of the understanding of spirituality? I could not stop wondering. Why do people in this part of the world accept such a partial structure over what is so obvious to them?

I became curious about the interactions between physicality and spirituality, and what I learned amazed me. They were discussing it in my room one day when Baba-elero said, "If a sickness is only of physical causes, it could be cured either physically or spiritually, but a sickness caused spiritually may not be cured by only physical treatments."

At some point in human evolutionary history a cataclysm may have occurred in our psyche, one as much or more colossal as the tectonic one that tore the continents apart, Europe from Africa and the Americas, and Asia from Australia. And this has left our psychic *continents* of physical and spiritual perceptions individually inadequate. This understanding would have a far-reaching influence in transforming my life. It would show me the total dependence of the physical facet of reality upon the spiritual facet, and the partial dependence of the spirituality upon physicality. It would reveal to me what witchcraft has in common with science and religion, and it would strongly suggest that gods, goddesses, spirits of the dead, and demons, may afterall have a hand in the natural phenomena we are experiencing – even in the function of the modern technology we are enjoying. Understanding this would only depend on how much we understand human nature and human experience, phenomena too intricately constituted than the simplistic explanation of modern science.

I did not become one of those who believe that only spiritualists should be sought when there is a sickness or a problem, as sometimes done by a lot of people. I believed that in our present world, with our achievements in science, one should seek mainstream medical care on sighting a bodily irregularity, but that one should not forget the other reality of one's being and of the world. And one could take one's steps respectively if there happens to be the need.

My body may be breaking down, but my mind was building up. For the first time in my life, this period of the sickness became one that made me begin to wonder about man, his soul and his world – about myself, my soul, and my world. From these, I realized that even though the two, physicality and spirituality, are dependent upon one another in varying degrees and at varying circumstances, spirituality is more important than physicality. And thus, technically, the spiritual part of the human being, or soul, is more important than the physical body. Although, we possess the body to work the cause of our soul in this physically oriented world, and therefore the body is not unimportant, but the soul remains the main reality on which *larger attention* is due. I began to realize that the world is a valley of soul-making, and an individual's soul is not something he possesses, but what he really is. It is the entity, the inner self, which, in a sense, co-determines the evolution of the physical and mental portions of the individual. And it is the entity of which the physical and mental portions are parts.

I became a seeker, by which I would end up with a new outlook on life. The philosopher's mind had something for me, so did the psychologist's, the scientist's, the religionist's, the witchdoctor's, though they conflict among themselves. I decided to step into the battle to find myself the perfect bride among them, with whom I would live the rest of my life. However, after eventually seeing the interconnectivity of the apparently disparage ideologies and practices of the world, I would only end up building a harem for a polygamy of views.

II

After about three weeks of Mama Pakoyi's prescriptions, the rate of the spasms reduced and a thin ray of energy returned to my arms. Now I could keep the arms from falling off the armrests, and my body from collapsing to the sides. This was a remarkable improvement, inasmuch as it induced hope of further improvement, or, at least, of an end to my health's degeneration. But the pains were still tormenting and, anxious for more attention, I often groaned and complained. One never has enough attention when one is sick. I would hire all the doctors in the world if I had the means: medical and traditional doctors, alfas, pastors, rabbis, babalawos, and even heavenly angels willing to be bought. That was the way I felt.

Because of this, I still worried my father persistently, and one day, in search of a way to respond to my need, he discussed it with his doctor during his regular check-up. Due to my father's repeated disapproval of medical involvement at this stage, this was odd. Baami thought that the persistence of the condition perhaps had pushed him to the wall, but we would later realize that there was more to it than the apparent frustration. Although my father was still jittery about the move, he claimed that all he was looking for was a palliative for the pain, while the traditional treatments were allowed to achieve their goal.

The doctor, now always on his toes whenever he dealt with me, still found nothing that would work. He ended up suggesting "physiotherapy," and he recommended a therapist to my father.

For me, I was happy to hear this, as I always was to hear of treatment suggestions, no matter what the treatment was. Once in a while we followed suggestions of *try this, try that*, medical and traditional. If they worked, they did not show or, at least, not immediately or not much. Baba-elero once said they all worked, only not yet to the surface, and that when they begin to surface, my improvement would be rapid. I could only hope so.

One medicine that Baba sent from Ibadan raised some eyebrows, yet I took it. A powdery stuff put together by a traditional doctor and to be drunk as a beverage. It was well packaged like a pharmaceutical product, but there was a strange aspect to it. I was required to drink a cup of my urine three times a day for it to work. My father inquired from Baba-elero and he confirmed that, even singly, urine is a good medicine. He advised me to take it.

Urine as a medicine was an issue of controversy in Nigeria. As some traditionalists were trying to respect scientific modalities, they conducted research on herbs and other medicine potentials. By such a research done on urine, they claimed that urine, among many of its good uses, was good for enriching the liver with necessary antibodies to combat diseases. Many medical doctors condemned this. The Nigerian medical association thought it was ridiculous, but said it would endorse it if proven by medical scientists. The traditional doctors, however, continued to prescribe it and many people used it.

I listened to everyone on the issue. It sounded ludicrous, and though it might be difficult to try when healthy, in my condition it was almost a pleasure. Really, I could not tell what I would not do to stop my suffering. I took the medicine regularly with the cup of urine three times a day and thought nothing of it. A few years later I learned that medical science discovered human urine to be sterile, only it was yet to find its medical use, if at all it has any. Cow urine, however, was found to be useful, said to contain a certain kind of hormone that is extracted and medically used for women.

Eagerly, I accepted and took all medicines suggested for me, but I soon learned that the physiotherapy was a different game. I had never seen how physiotherapists work, so I did not know of what form or how much physical the therapy would be. But when the therapist entered my room, I had a slight idea that the work was not going to be doctors-as-usual, as I had expected. A thin and tall man with a bushy head and a gentle face, he appeared toughened by studies, work, and Nigeria's economy, and he looked at me the way a butcher would look at a difficult bull. He had his stripped shirt tucked into a pair of chinos pants. The sleeves of the shirt were rolled up above the elbow in a manner that informed me that this was not a medicine man, but a labor man, who may have some labor to do with my frail body. A big travelers' bag hung across his right shoulder, and from the look of the bag I knew he did not carry medicines and syringes. It looked as if there were only boxing gloves and karate costumes in there. I became a little afraid.

I was on the bed and he outstretched his right hand at me for a handshake. I lifted my fingers. He expected my hand to come further at him, but when he saw I could not give more he came close to grab it and shook it with some firmness that cared not for my sick look. Something told me I might have bitten more than I could chew.

The therapist entered into a dialogue with my father, who was still a little uneasy about his decision. He asked questions about my condition and my father answered him. Then my father went into a long monologue telling him the story of the sickness. When he learned that the therapist had been Sister Toyin's classmate at the University of Ibadan, he became relaxed and they interacted cordially. This would become a problem for me, for he was now gaining my father's confidence.

One other thing that would later catch my father's sympathy for his work was that every time he came, he would go to the back of the house, somewhere behind my room, and stayed there for a while before starting his work. It was like a silent moment, clandestinely done, and appeared so ritualistic that my father assumed that he might be performing a spiritual ritual to aid his work. As people in our modern religions secretly went to the traditional spiritualists, many medical professionals also did so to aid the efficacy of their work and to protect themselves – especially from repercussions from cases they believed might not be as ordinary as it appeared, as in the case of the doctor and the pregnant woman mentioned earlier. My father believed that such professionals were the wiser ones. For this reason, he became completely comfortable with the therapist and thought he might have something to contribute as remedy for my condition.

"Can you straighten out the legs?" the therapist asked me, seeing that they were folded and inclined upon a set of cushions. This was my only comforting position, and which allowed me to sleep. Now I was always in bed for about twenty hours a day while the legs remained in the folded position.

"Yes, I can," I replied him, "but with some time."

"Okay, do it and let me see."

I did not think I could not do it and I began as gently as I could. Because all that was in my control were my fingers and toes, I tried to use my toes to crawl and drag the legs gently over the mattress. My muscles twitched and jerked, but I worked on. I was afraid to have the therapist touch the legs, which seemed to be what he was waiting to do.

"What's that thing there for?" he asked about the cushions.

"His legs are more relaxed resting that way," Akeem, my younger cousin, replied. He had noticed me tensed up with fear and he was afraid for me.

Swiftly, the therapist moved close. My heart jerked. And, unrepentantly, he withdrew the cushions. "Go on," he ordered.

For fear that the legs might fall to the side, I tried to hold them up. But my muscles were hell and the legs swayed painfully in the air. I was as slow as I could be, while the therapist watched impatiently until he realized that I could not do it. I was frightened to see him move forward in a sudden. He reached for my knees and, as loud as I could, I screamed, "No!" But he had no ears for me. He palmed my right knee and pressed forcefully. In pain, I cried out as the knee went down.

"This won't help you," he said as he released the pressure.

"Okay sir," I said, cringingly, as if he had asked a question.

He palmed the left knee as well and applied force to it. Again, I cried out loudly despite my will not to cry. The left knee reached the same level as the right knee, but they were a few inches away from the mattress. It was shocking to realize that the knees had become stiff. I felt the pains so intensely all over my body that it was my agglomerated fear that held me weakly from weeping. I stared at him as if he was a monster, watching him intently as if to mark down his next strike.

"Your knees are stiff," he said gentlemanly.

"Yesssir," I replied, trembling.

"I'll have to work on it for some time to get it straightened out and I'll need your cooperation."

"Okay sir." I did not know where the 'sirs' came from. I was not that courteous to address people like that, as if I was the most perfect gentleman in the universe.

"The way you're screaming won't help you; you're a man and you should act like a man."

"Okay sir." As if I was truly a man. Not even him could be a man in this situation. It is only someone who has not seen war, as the adage goes, that calls himself a man.

"Let him sleep like this tonight. Or, at least, he should be in this position until midnight," he said to my father.

"I'll come here every alternate day," he continued, "starting from Monday (today was Friday) but not on weekends, and I'll need eight weeks to finish with him. He's going to walk again. Tell the nurse to stop coming for the dressing of the wound; I'll take care of it."

I looked at him but not meeting his eyes. Now I had an idea what kind of treatment I was in for and I did not want to go on with it. But I could not say it. Instead, I assured him of my cooperation. I promised to straighten out the legs completely by Monday to make his work easy for him. Although I was saying all this out of fear, I meant it, because my hope was to make his work easy on myself. I wanted to help myself so he would not come and heave hell on me.

It was after the therapist had gone that I was able to know the extent of my present predicament. All the muscles in my body were extremely tensed, more than I had ever seen them before. They twitched and jerked, sending torturing messages across my body. The hypersensitive muscles about my pelvic joints stuck out as if they were going to jump out of my skin. I could not move, I could not talk, and I could not even breathe normally. My concentration was fully on the internal workings of my body, listening intently to every nerve cell in my body as if I could learn how to control them. Yet, I was ordered to remain in the position at least until midnight. I doubted it, even when my father made it a law in the room.

I remained in the position for a long time, perhaps for an hour or two. I wanted to ask for help to return the legs to the folded position, the only comfortable position I knew, but I was still afraid of being touched. I ended up asking only when the condition did not improve and I could not take it any longer.

I cried as Akeem pulled them up, and gradually it paid dividends. The muscles slowly and gradually calmed down.

"Do you think you can continue with this thing?" Akeem asked after allowing me time to return to what seemed normal.

"I don't think so," I replied, phlegmatically. "It's tough, and I don't think I need such forcing now."

"Then would you stop it?" Akeem was not just asking to know what I would do; he did not like what he had seen and he was telling me what he thought I should do.

"Your father won't agree," Baami responded, "I just got up from talking with him; though you can try, but I don't think he would agree." Baami understood my condition and what I faced right now, but my father had talked to him so much that he did not think he would agree.

I agreed. "I'd love to stop it, but I don't think I can," I said to Akeem.

"Tell daddy you don't want it; he has to agree. From what we have all seen the moment the therapist walked in here, it doesn't make any sense to go on with it. You have been dying since he left. Daddy won't have a choice."

"Let's wait to see how Monday would be first," I said to him, "And I want us to try to straighten the legs before then."

The next day was a day Rafiat was to go to Mama Pakoyi. She always went there from where she lived and came to me the same day to give me the report. In the afternoon she arrived to tell me the report of the day. First, she told me what to eat and what not to eat in the next few days. Then, as if she knew what was already going on in the house, she said that Mama warned that we should not force the legs, and that my case was not yet for that. Without anyone telling her, Mama had known what was going on in our house.

At first, I was relieved to hear the warning, but I quickly realized it would not be easy to sell it to my father. I had expressed my wish to stop the therapy and he had been persuading me with gentle but resolute words to continue with it. Even though he would believe the message, the circumstance had been too suspicious and he had been so inclined to continue with the therapy that we would have a hard time to reach an amiable understanding. Telling him of Mama's warning would seem to him as the proverbial fowl that died at the doormouth of the fox; how could the fox prove it did not kill the fowl, especially when it had been seen chasing the fowl earlier in the evening. For me, it was true that I only liked the warning because it might be a way out of the impending torture. Pain was still primary in my life and getting rid of it was still my only desire.

Over the weekend, I tried to straighten the legs gently by having me placed seated on the mattress, with room for the legs to naturally slide out. Baami and my younger brothers knew it was impossible, but they left me to find out because I insisted. I also was not confident about it, but the fear of the nearing appointment with the therapist goaded me on and I hoped to ignore the pain. My legs were now very thin, perhaps as thin as those of a two-year old child. One would fear they would break under the slightest force and my brothers were reluctant to follow my instructions in the attempt.

I soon found out that this was not the type of pain that could be ignored. My muscles tensed up and my breathing was constrained. When I looked as if I was going to stop breathing, they quickly carried me back to bed.

"I told you," Baami said, "You can't do it; you are not healthy enough to do that." I could only wish my father and the therapist knew this.

One sad story of it was that there was no pain medicine arranged for the exercise. Although I did not think any pain medicine could help, but it appalled me that the therapist did not even see it necessary to try to reduce the pains up-front. When my father, worried, asked him concerning the pains, he assured him that it would reduce by each day's work. That is, I would not feel as much pain in a day's exercise as the one before it. My father believed this and persuaded me with it, and, as difficult as it was, I tried to believe it as well. I hoped that by the time the first week ran out, the pains on the fourth exercise would have been greatly reduced.

III

At around 5 pm on Monday, one of my younger brothers keeping watch outside the house hurried in to tell me as soon as they saw the therapist emerge onto our street from afar. I did not want him to meet me in bed, because I thought the exercise might be less painful if I was on the chair. Baami and Akeem promptly put me on the chair as planned.

Fear, sometimes, is analgesic. My fear of the therapist reduced the pains of being carried to the chair. I groaned as usual, but I hushed up as he entered my room. He reached for my hand at the armrest and shook it.

"Carry him onto the bed, please," he said to Baami and Akeem.

That hit me like a fireball. It disrupted my stomach and I felt I wanted to move my bowel, though I knew I was not due for it. "Can we work in the sitting position like this, please?" I asked in a trembling voice.

"No, we can't," he replied curtly as he rummaged in his traveler's bag, as if he knew what was going on in my mind.

"Can I move my bowel, first?" I asked in a childish subterfuge. He looked at me, then he asked my brothers to get the bedpan.

Nothing came, and it became obvious that it was my fear that had activated my visceral system.

"I knew it was the therapy that made you want to shit," he said, "And I have enough time for you."

They carried me back to the bed.

"Would you please go on your side?" he asked, "Or should I help you?"

"I'll do it myself." The less the touching, the better.

My legs were in the folded position and I tried to go on my side by lowering the knees to the side. It was the only possible way I could turn, though it was difficult. Despite the fact that I took my time, currents of sharp spasmodic pain shot through my legs and body as I went about it, like electrical charges through the sky during lightning and thunder. After several minutes I managed to reach my left side and I lay with my muscles tensed up threateningly.

"If it were someone else," the therapist said, "I would have pushed him on his side. I wouldn't wait for anyone to waste my time like that." This further gave me reasons to fear him. I could worship him.

He removed the plaster on my wound to clean it. It was still a deep hole, almost as it was when it was discovered over a month ago. He had earlier told my father to get some honey ready, and, to the astonishment of everyone present, he poured the honey into the hole.

"Honey?" my father uttered, surprised.

"Yeah, it's very good for wounds," he replied and continued his work. He covered it up with a new plaster and started on my legs. He pivoted my right leg at the knee and forced it gently forward to exceed its limit. I screamed out loudly, but he ignored me as he worked it back and forth. Each stroke brought forth its interpretation of agony from my mouth. I was helpless in his hands, and miserable.

"Recite *Ayat al-Qurisiyy* instead of crying," my father advised and walked out of the room. He pretended as if he had an engagement, but the truth was that he could not stand the scene.

I heeded the advice and chanted the verse. The therapist also joined me in the recitation. He was gentle on me, but the pain was nasty, as if dismembering. Still, my recitation reflected my trauma; I wailed out the words of the noble verse in a manner that was funny in retrospection. It was like sound from a cow under strangulation.

After he had completed the exercise on the two legs he put them apart, the right in front and the left at the back, while I was still lying on my left side. He put something between them to hold them from sliding from the position he wanted, and he ordered that I be left in that position at least until midnight.

Every cell in my body pulsated with pain, and my head throbbed threateningly as if it would burst. Since I could not move any part of my body by myself, I remained in the position for a long time. Believing that the therapist's condition would in the long run be helpful, my father refused to let anyone help turn me around into my comfortable position. I cried at my pain and my helplessness, until my father could not take it anymore and allowed me back in my usual comfortable position before the therapist's required time.

***

Everyone was amazed when the therapist uncovered the wound on the next appointment day. The hole had closed in about halfway up. "Just in two days!" my father exclaimed.

This was a medical benefit of honey I never knew before. I only thought of and used the substance as a sweetening substance for my meals. One of my uncles was fond of mixing honey with his locally made bathing soap (black soap), claiming it was good for cleansing the skin effectively. The traditional doctors also believed that it was good for various health-related functions in the body, including the care of diabetes. A traditional doctor argued that honey contains fructose, and is absorbed into the cells easier than glucose otherwise obtained.

Fortunately, the improvement in the wound was an achievement that might have taken the previous conventional nursing more than two months, but, unfortunately, it deepened my father's confidence in the therapist.

The therapist worked forcefully on the legs again, but, unlike the last time, he left me on the chair. However, the pain, this time, was more than the last time. It struck me temporarily dumb, with all the nerves and muscles in my body vibrating like water pipes when high-tension flow of water ran through them. Possessed with lives of their own, they seemed to have a mission of torturing me to death.

Words are inadequate to express the experience. I sat there, staring ahead at nothing. Breathing was as difficult as eating, and I feared to be carried back to the bed, just like I feared the physical therapy. Baami repeatedly asked to carry me back after he had tried to feed me. Out of the fear, I could not agree until after about an hour later, and only when I realized it was unavoidable. If at all I was going to get any sleep, I could not do it on the chair. And when I was eventually carried back it took an unusually long period to be calmed physiologically, and more to be calmed psychologically. Unlike in recent days, I could not sleep until five in the morning, and I had only about an hour of sleep. The pains were supposed to diminish by each exercise according to the therapist's logic, but they were increasing and my whole health was degenerating again. It was enough for me to cry out, and I did.

"Don't worry," my father still persuaded, "endure it a little bit longer and you'll then see that the pains would eventually diminish. That's what the therapist says."

But it did not. Instead, it increased. The wound was improving, however, though not in the rate it had sped up in the first and second treatments. The therapist was working toward his goal of walking me in two months, but my body was lagging, and, by this, my spirit also was lagging. He worked on me throughout the week as he scheduled, but in the weekend, when I saw that it was going nowhere good, I continued to persuade my father to stop it.

One day the therapist tried to stand me up, but my knees had no life enough to hold me up. Then, he stood in front of me and placed his knees directly to mine to keep me standing for a while, but I fainted in his hands and he quickly put me down and left me for my people to revive me.

Although it was not as if he did not care, he was only too careless about it than to make me comfortable. He did not have a single idea of what my problem was; he only knew that sometimes physical therapy was so painful that patients would try to avoid it, and he thought that was what I was doing. Then he brought some plastic braces on the next appointment day to force my legs into a standing position. He ignored the increasingly apparent sign that I still needed to have life back into my system before I could face such rigorous exercise. I needed health to be able to sit up by myself in the chair and to be able to feel my hands and legs before I could walk. Something was my main problem before walking became the problem, how then could the aim of helping me out dwell on walking alone at this period? I was afraid the therapy would eventually kill me. I feared I might fall silent in the midst of the high-pitched pains one day, and silent forever. If I had not been imprisoned in my body by my total paralysis, I had reached a point at which I would rather kill myself than to maintain hope or let myself be smothered by these pains. If I had a choice, I would choose euthanasia. To hell with life if this was all I could have. Then I knew I had to stop the therapy rather than linger on and let it consume me piecemeal. That was a worst form of death.

I explained to my father but he became angry and stood the ground that I must continue with it. "You'd only be postponing the evil-day if you don't do it now," he said, but I tried to make him see that we would only be making an evil-day - my end - come too soon instead. Yet, he remained adamant.

I was confused. I saw my world closing in on me, squashing me, and I did not understand what was going on. Aunty Sidi told me something about the situation and I tried to give a thought to it. Although I found, perhaps, a weak explanation to my father's reaction: I thought he was still thinking that I was being indulgent and he wanted to force me. However, Aunty Sidi advised me that I should not dispel an idea that my father was being acted upon, that he was being made to be such daring and obstinate. She claimed that there was more to the situation than met the eye, and that it was not just on the issue of physical therapy, but on the general situation of my condition. Though he still sympathized with me, Baba-elero did not want to have anything to do with my problem anymore, Aunty Sidi had said. But my father would not recognize this, and his trust in Baba-elero made him take all questions and problems to him. I was yet to see Baba-elero's reason for his apparent avoidance of my case.

"This case needs as much help as we can get on it," Aunty Sidi explained to me one day after I beseeched her not to ignore me, as she seemed to have been doing along with Baba-elero. "But your father just doesn't understand this. It is not my pleasure to come here and see you like this, still in such a condition, and do nothing about it. But what could I do when your father is taking things irrationally. I have gone out of my way to introduce some other people to him, but whatever they wanted to do, your father would take it to Baba-elero. And Baba-elero couldn't be as dedicated anymore as these people would be. Every good spiritualist that we can get has his or her unique power to bring into this – and you need it. I work with Baba-elero and I know everything going on about you and him. It is not that he does not want to continue to help you, but you will not understand his reasons now. Yet, Baba-elero shouldn't know that I was leaning out for you while my feet are in his house. He's my master, and I am torn between his plight and your plight. So what do I do? That's why I sent other people to your father, but he blinds himself to the reality.

"I know the people behind your sickness are now using your father to worsen your condition, but your father would never agree to such a suggestion if someone told him – even though he was also aware that some of the witches are still trying to get you. (Really, I think my father believed he was too strong spiritually for anybody to bewitch.) They have put a veil over his eyes. And now he is relying on a medical doctor; what could such a therapist do in this?

"But I believe that one day God will uncover the veil they put over his eyes. That is one of the ways that witches work, and it is in this kind of situation that they employ it. They will try to isolate their victim, make him like a plague, a menace, or a nuisance to the people around him, so they could weaken and cut off his help supports and so they could get him more easily. This is what they are trying to do to you now. I've seen it done to people many times before. And all I can say to you now is that you yourself have to be careful. Until you get cleanly out of this, you have to be careful so you don't aid their aim by your conduct. You need not to add to your predicament by getting your father angry with you in this situation. And know this as very important. To some extent, he is your cover, and because of his position here, this town has been made a sanctuary for you. The elders behind the fight to save your life wouldn't do for anyone half as much as they are doing for you. Most of them are concerned more on the larger society than on individuals, and it is more because of your father's position that they are doing this. They love and respect him; out of all the princes in this town, he's their favorite. If you get out of his favor and out of his cover, things might be difficult for you. So, you need to handle your father with care."

Aunty Sidi assured me of her continuing assistance and she offered to appease Sango and have him involved in this. "Sango is your father and the god of your family; he wouldn't harm you and he wouldn't let anyone do it if he's initiated into this. That's one good way to maintain a shield over you as things are going this way. But, most importantly, keep praying to God."

During the weekend I called my father's wife and asked her to persuade my father for me to let us stop the forced physical therapy. She did, but he still did not agree. So much the worse for me, I thought and wept over the queer development. Before the gunshot, I had been wholeheartedly involved in physical exercise, with no fear of the pains, even though the pains were also intimidating then. They all praised me for being brave at the time, but now I did not know why my father could not think that I was still the same person they used to praise. He was now so hot about the issue that everyone was afraid to touch him.

The following week the therapy continued. The hell continued. I did not feel any improvement in my condition. I only felt more pains, more fear, more traumas, and I still cried in protest every moment I had energy to do it. I passed out two times during the week while the therapist was trying to put me on my legs, but my father instead chose to focus on what he saw as improvement in the knees. He claimed to see the knees improving but I argued that, even if they were, my body was not, and that my overall health was deteriorating.

"Of what good would the knees be if my life was smothered in the process?" I asked him, bitterly.

"You're not going to die," he persuaded with a strong tone of voice.

"You got to understand; you need this. Or do you want to be confined to the wheelchair for the rest of your life?" he added heatedly and I replied:

"It would be better than to be confined to the grave. If this is the only process to prevent the wheelchair, I'd rather have the wheelchair then."

He became furious by my words and he stormed out of my room.

On the following Saturday, I sent for one of my aunts, since no one in the house was anymore willing to face my father about the issue. She was my father's younger sister whom we called "Alhaja Alliance" because she lived opposite a hotel called Alliance Hotel, in the house my father built for their mother. I explained the situation to her and asked her to talk to my father. However, by this time, my father also seemed to have been thinking it over. Everyone except him in the house was opposed to the physiotherapy and he had been realizing how difficult the situation was. My younger brothers and sisters frowned whenever he was in their presence. His wife told me that whenever the therapist was working on me he deliberately stayed away under one of the trees outside. And when he saw anyone of my younger brothers coming out of the house, when the therapy session was still on, his heart would skip and race for fear of a problem, and he would not be all right until he knew there was no problem. They had gone for him each time I fainted in the course of the therapy. Though the physical therapist still did not think much about it, but it registered in my father's mind.

My aunt talked to him, and - thank God - he agreed. He talked to the therapist when he came on the following appointment day, and the therapist wished me luck.

"I pray God heals you," the therapist said to me on the last day of his visit. "There is nothing God cannot do, but please try and keep the legs straightened out so it would be easier for you to walk when you are better." I nodded my head in acknowledgment and waited almost impatiently to see him walk out for good.

***

Now, what I wanted was to be left alone in bed. I did not want anything or anyone to trouble me as I enjoyed the little peace I could get in this condition. However, it was not all that good for me, as they claimed. My father insisted that I should be carried to the chair for every meal, as Baba-elero warned, to allow my body systems to activate, and that I should stretch my legs while in bed, as the therapist. All these were to make my muscles lithe in readiness for walking someday.

But all that sounded good and easy only in theory; practically, it was impossible for me. As I saw it, the process of activating my body systems also activated the pain systems, whereas the pains would peter out only when left undisturbed. Carrying about only recurred the trauma and invigorated the agents of the pains.

Baami felt with me, as he always did. He was the one closest to me and he knew the true condition I was in more than any other person. He would have ignored my father's order, but he wanted that I should manage to sit on the chair once a day so we would not be doing the complete opposite of my father's directive. He wanted to be able to tell my father without feeling guilty that we were doing what he wanted. So, secretly understood in our room, he allowed me to be carried to the chair only once a day.

Mama Pakoyi remained the only person tending regularly to my treatment needs. Her medications were easier and I went on regularly with her instructions. She directed that I rubbed the limbs constantly with palm oil and I used in a day an amount enough to fry a big fish. She also prescribed another medication for the wound. Honey is good, she said, but my case now required powdered groundnuts, something as odd as the honey treatment. She said honey was good for wounds, but better for scalds and burns. She ordered that we bake the groundnuts until there was no oil left in it before grinding it to powder.

Surprisingly, the wound healed very fast, although the improvement in my general health was slow. However, without too much complaint, she constantly informed us of improvements from within, and occasionally that we should not be hasty in our expectation of the general health improvement. Slowly and patiently does the sun move, but by the end of a long and gentle journey we measure the progression of time: days have gone by, and a year has ripened. "Rahman will walk on his legs again by the grace of God," she always said, "but he has to be patient. His problems didn't start in a day; he shouldn't expect them to go in a day."

Mama also urged me to pray with the Qur'an to bring and strengthen the help. Without knowing the Qur'an, she assigned a particular chapter of it for my reading. She claimed the Warriors of Heaven informed her that I should be reading the chapter for my prayer, and strangely it happened to be the sura my father had suggested. Interestingly, I eventually learned that the sura, called "The Cave," contained some of the puzzling stories of the Qur'an by which the nature of time, good, and evil are mystically addressed. This amazed me, especially because the woman was a Christian priestess, while our society was sprinkled with religious discriminations. As a Muslim I had grown up typically in the idea that all Christians were on a wrong path, as most of my Christian friends grew up typically in the idea that all Muslims were on a wrong path. And we often argued over it.

Like a Christian friend of mine, though, I had begun to wonder whether God would really put Christians in hell, as he also wondered whether God would put Muslims in hell. While it was inconceivable to me that more than a billion Christians in the world, and the four more billion people that even belonged to other religions, would not see the truth, it was not intelligible to imagine that such an amount of people would be thrown in hell. The numbers were so huge, for God's sake! Yet, many of us were in our religions by birth, what seemed an accidental stroke of nature.

Sometimes I wondered that if, at the end of time, God finds only half, or even less, of his creation unqualified for His beautiful paradise, would that not be His own failure? Would that not show that He must have been an imperfect artist all the while? Then I realized that I had simply been breastfed and grown into my religion without questioning or being able to question it, just as the Christians with whom I argued had been breastfed and grown into theirs. Hence, we all basically had in our heads ideas that have become as natural to us as the tissues of our brains and we all had them to protect. This was how I was beginning to see many of us in the different religions of the world. We accept our religions because we were born into them and we discriminate against others who were also *coincidentally* born into theirs.

Then, the question that troubles our lives becomes, who is right and who is wrong? The purpose of religion, evolved or given to humankind, had been to give meaning to human life amid the chaos of the natural world. Now it has become part of the chaos, and intensifying the disorder of the world. We hate and kill ourselves over it, whereas someone, or some people, may have pre-programmed our conflicts and assigned us our roles in it even before we have a taste of the breath of life. Could paradise, then, be a game of chance? Like the gambler's throw of the dice? A chance by birth? As Muslims, God warns us in the Qur'an not to play games of chance; yet, it sometimes seemed to me to be the favorite game He has been playing with our lives, and the chance of paradise and its beautiful virgins waiting for us there have only been favoring those born in Islam.

In this part of Nigeria, however, we have enough sanity to refrain from physical conflict over religion. The only thing common here was occasional verbal expressions of fear and trespass from both sides. Muslims often charged Christians with trespassing by their cornering of Muslim youths for conversion, hunting into houses for conversions and undue social influence and intimidation, especially through the largely Christianized press and schools. Because of the largely Muslim federal government, Christians charged Muslims with attempting to Islamicize Nigeria, especially through the once alleged attempt to join the Organization of Islamic Council and later the declaration of the Sharia law in some states. Some other times they challenged one another on authenticity and supremacy. An interesting aspect of this was the public debate program often held to question one another's scripture, rituals, and faith, and it was often fun and educating to both sides. Although not enough to disabuse them of their prejudices, these have been creating a ground for better interfaith relationship. No one in the Yoruba land seemed willing to die or kill for Christ or Mohammad. Whether a curse or a blessing, the emerging world perhaps would find many Nigerians multi-religious. And some people have been using the term "Chrislam" for the anticipated union of Islam and Christianity, though currently facetiously.

These are the two major religions in Nigeria. The traditional religions have been reduced to extreme minority and now had almost no voice in the country's religious affairs. Regrettably, the traditional practitioners were even regarded as pagans in the national census, a term by which they meant heathen, the dictionary meaning of the word and idea ridiculously created by the Roman Empire. Many traditional spiritual healers also now belonged to either of the two major religions, Islam or Christianity, while they practiced their vocation in the traditional ways. Like Mama Pakoyi, all the traditional doctors who worked for me during this period belonged to one or the other of the two main religions, except for one man who was an outright Ifa priest, whom Aunty Sidi charged with the appeasement of Sango.

Mama Pakoyi also sent reports about the demons alleged to be in my room contaminating any activity or medication supposed to help me. Initially, there were three of them, but after a long time she said they had been reduced to two, and now to one. She assured us that the remaining one would also soon find it uncomfortable to remain there and would leave.

The carrying to and from the chair faltered. I began to allow one, two or three days intervals between the carrying to suit myself. I would not even have allowed to be carried at all if Baami had not insisted on it. But it became increasingly difficult on me and he also knew it. Then the days' intervals began to run into a week or two weeks' intervals. I could not help it. Though we still kept it a secret, but my father knew it; only that he also could not help it anymore. My knees became stiffer with time as I was expecting my health to become better enough for me to be able to exercise them. Without the fear of carrying about, however, I could focus on keeping my spirit up. And I did.

Despite the little improvement, my condition was still terrible and it was too apparent to ignore. Friends and relatives who came to visit me mirrored it, though unintentionally. They entered my room, gaped at me, ossified with fear, prayed, and walked out shaking their heads. Many looked hopeless, with only a thin strand of thought that "*Well, there's nothing God cannot do.*" That was how they saw me, as someone who could survive only by a miraculous stroke of luck. Yet, many of them thought they were seeing the last of me.

I always lay in bed with my legs folded, knees towering above my head level and leaning on the pile of cushion on my right side. That was my jail. I remained in a spot, with no desire but to move, and no movement but stillness. I feared God. In the miserable life of the time, the miserable time of my life, I was chained down with my own nerves and muscles, caged by my own bones, frightened still by my own brain, and drowning in my own breath and blood. I always raised my voice: "God, save my life. If these things were a punishment for my sins, please forgive me and set me free."

IV

The Ileya festival of the year 1994 was on a Saturday, the 21st day of May. On its eve, my father's wife gave birth to a baby girl. She was named Tolani, after my father's mother, and her birth and life would become an extraordinary phenomenon in the history of my sickness. It changed the treatment pattern and the course of my sickness' journey.

First, on the fourth day of Tolani's birth, Uncle Remi, one of my maternal uncles living in America, came to visit me in the company of my grandmother and Uncle Tunji. He was in Nigeria to celebrate the Ileya festival.

According to him, Uncle Jibola informed him of the protracting sickness and they had been discussing what to do about it, perhaps fly me to America for treatment.

"In America," he said, "you'd be given a very good treatment. You'll be exposed to many options, and the one best for you would be chosen."

He wondered why I had been kept here, in a "hidden corner of the world," as he put it.

"That's how we've had to do it; the sickness is more spiritual and the hospitals wouldn't let us deal with it that way," my father stated. Because Uncle Remi, an obstetrician and gynecologist, was a scientific professional, and who had lived in America for so long, about twenty-three years, my father did not think he would still believe in witchcraft.

"I don't think they know of such things in America?" my father added, out of curiosity and not necessarily in relation to the current suggestion.

"Some people do. In places like New Orleans, for example," Uncle Remi replied, and further talked about witchcraft in America.

It was interesting to learn that there was witchcraft in the Western world, and not just in their fairy tales and history. Sometimes I wondered whether it had only been eroded by the industrialization and urbanization. Even in Africa, urbanization had its effects on witchcraft. But I learned that Christianity had dealt it with the most devastating blows prior to the industrial revolution, and modern urban dwellers need no witchcraft to express their antisocial tendencies. They have guns and other weapons like that.

"It is likely that his hip joints have been damaged," Uncle Remi explained, "and in that case he wouldn't be able to walk unless the hips are replaced."

I was bewildered. He saw this and he added: "There's not going to be any problem about that; you will walk well again. They do it everyday in America. Even that's what Pope John Paul uses now."

Then Uncle Remi asked us to look for a specialist hospital where they could assess the problem. If they could do it there, he and Uncle Jibola would send the materials needed for the treatment from America. But if they could not, then I would have to be flown to America.

Events have shown me that having a dream may be a luxury that life offers, a gift of God to those who are free. I hardly remembered America in the past months. Even when I learned that Chief Bernard had stopped the visa process due to the sickness and had returned my money, I had not cared. What worried me now was the thought of carrying me around. I wanted any treatment that could quickly help me out of this condition, but I was afraid. Although I did not think of any spiritual aspect of the sickness to frighten me from going to the hospital, I knew that would be attended to if I had to be taken there. It was the pains of carrying about that I feared could kill me before they even touched me with a scalpel. To be carried outside the house to the car was enough; then the joggling of driving motion from the bad roads, the carrying into the hospital, and the carrying about for the various tests. My condition was still such that if a day-old baby kicked at my bed, as if in a torture, I could confess to the murder of Abel, allowing Cain to be exonerated, just to prevent further kicks and be left alone. I did not think I could go through all the troubles of carrying about, not even for America.

My father still believed that what my treatment needed might be more spiritual than medical, and he might not want to leave me in the hands of medical doctors, unless the spiritualists assured him to release me. Although he did not think hospital could not help me out, but from his general experience, and especially of the latest physiotherapy's, he only believed the spiritual aspect must be allowed to go on. Nonetheless, he did not argue against the proposal. He figured that since I was not going to be carried away right there and then, he would have enough time for consultations.

My case file would have to be obtained from U.C.H. first to process my case for another hospital. My grandmother decided to secure that, and she promised to come for me when all is set.

It was a good place to end the meeting and they all left for Ibadan. But what everyone did not realize was that the mystery surrounding my predicament from the beginning was still playing a central role. First, even though I was afraid of being moved around, I was uncomfortable with my father's conclusion as well, because of the fact that he, as Aunty Sidi had counseled me, did not realize that he did not have the house of spirituality together for good consultation. Baba-elero was the only witchdoctor in his purview, yet Baba-elero was already avoiding me. Then, came the news about my file at U.C.H. My grandmother went there several times but could not get the file. We were later to know that it had disappeared from the hospital, and this was to delay the American process until it dropped into oblivion.

***

The eighth day of a child's birth was the traditional day for the naming ceremony, and often greeted with festivity. Though I was sick and dying, Tolani's eighth day happened to be memorable for me.

For my father's position in the town, hardly could any event in our house be done in a low key. Two years earlier, when my grandmother died, my father planned to have a quiet prayer session with only a few relatives, but the event ended up with almost half the town's people gracing the occasion. As much as he tried this time as well, there were many relatives, friends, and well-wishers at our house for Tolani's naming ceremony. Though they had all heard about my sickness, most of them had not seen me. The most convenient thing to do concerning my presence in the house, then, was to shield me from the crowd. Neither my father nor I wanted anyone to be reminded of me during the occasion, or to poke into an affair that did not concern them. I did not like to be a drop of bile in anyone's soup, as my condition was enough to be to the joyous mood of the party.

I asked my younger brothers to shut the door and windows to my room and, as I often did whenever visitors were at the house, I avoided activities that could bring me pain. Someone was visiting in the house one day and while she was having fun with my father's wife and the children at the backyard, the nurse came to dress my wound and I had to be carried off the bed for the exercise. As usual, I wailed uncontrollably as they lifted me off the bed and the agony in my voice ruined the visitor's day. She came into my room afterward and could not help but to cry for me.

On the day of joy and glory, oh God, let me not be shut away from participation. On the day of pride and happiness, let illness not lock me out of sight. This was a favorite song on many occasions, expressing a fear and wish important to the people. Today, I could not help but to stay out of participation. I could not help but to be locked away from the joy and fun. And for the first time in my life, I realized that I was experiencing a condition so much abhorred, so much accursed, that no one would kneel down in prayer without asking God to keep it away from his or her destiny. For this, in the old traditional religions, people made offerings to Sonponna, the god of sickness and disease, so he would not afflict them. They feared him so much that they deemed him a god whose name it was not propitious to mention during the dry season, and, euphemistically, they called him *Hot Earth*, the god who made life hot for anyone he visited. The dreaded Sonponna now dwelled in my room and slept with me in my bed. I now represented an image most unwanted by the people. I often remembered how our Imam at Oniyanrin always prayed that God should not tie us down with our nerves and muscles, but now I was living to know what he meant. For whatever reason, God had not granted me that prayer at this period of my life.

Only a handful of the few people who had seen me before were allowed to visit me. Among them was my father's uncle, my grandmother's brother, whom we called by his professional name as Baba-bricklayer, or, more accentually, Baba-brikila. Seeing how little my condition had improved over the months, he called my father aside for a talk.

Baba-brikila had a son living in Kano, a northern state in Nigeria. During a time of petrol scarcity in the country the boy met with a fire accident in Kano, which almost roasted life out of his body. This was how it happened:

A cab driver had a container filled with petrol in his trunk and was driving through a busy street. Suddenly, the car had a problem and caught fire under its hood. Knowing how inflammable petrol was, the driver stopped the car and rushed to remove the container first, to prevent the whole car from burning. He grabbed and flung it forcefully away from the car, but he was a little late and was only lucky not to bear the brunt.

The container was not well covered and its content dripped as it flew through the air. The fire from the hood found its way to the container through the drips and flew with it to its unfortunate destination. It landed on the head of someone walking by, a young man who happened to be the son of my father's uncle. The petrol sprinkled over him and the fire torched him. He was given a glimpse of hell while walking the street on earth. The only places on his body that the fire did not scorch before it was extinguished were the soles of his feet and a small patch on his head. He was rushed to a hospital and had severe burning pains around the clock.

I do not need to go deep into this story, so I will only tell how it came to affect mine. But first, there was something about how people in this part of the world looked at such events that is noteworthy.

Physicalist philosophy or science could easily explain the event logically in relation to its obvious causes: petrol and fire, and a natural coincidence upon the young man. Simple. Of course, someone, something, or nothing must be there to take the fire; mathematically, the eventuality would then depend on individual ratio of probability.

A good sociologist may extend the causal relationship to the administrative neglect of the Nigerian government who put the oil-rich nation through the unnecessary suffering of fuel scarcity. Also, a good judgment.

However, in environments in which people were so conscious of endemic witchcraft, they would not wait for such forensic evidence to know what was going on. The question that would come up in their minds would be, "Why the particular victim?" "Why did it have to be him, especially in his particular circumstance?" The particular circumstances of such victims usually lent more strength onto the suspicion of an insidious foul play somewhere. It could be a time that such eventual victim was at a threshold of success, or any desirable change in his or her life, like the situation with my late friend Hagler and like my situation when my problem began. It could be when he or she had bitter quarrels with some people, or certain persons, who may already have been suspected of voodoo practices. It could be at any time or on any reason, reasonable or unreasonable, but apparently reasonable enough to elicit suspicion.

As I have said, physicalist philosophy was the quickest way to arrive at an answer, though perhaps only a theoretic, even if valid, answer. Its practitioners would simply say it was merely a coincidence. And they would be so stubborn to speciously argue themselves out as right, even though they might be relatively wrong. But the people of environments of profound witchcraft awareness always thought more in their own cognitive world. They knew that pieces of chicken could not just be missing in a pot of stew by mere coincidence, especially when there was a stray cat in the neighborhood. It was as a homicide detective, in his own cognitive world, smelled foul play in a death that appeared strictly natural when the particular circumstance begged for attention. Though, sometimes, such suspicions were misplaced when truly there was no foul play, but seasoned detectives always knew it was worth the while to follow the suspicion through. And statistically, perhaps they might find only two in a hundred to be truly natural and merely coincidental. Perhaps two more could be too difficult to crack and thus passed on as coincidences as they were meant to appear by the smart culprits. This is modern environment with modern causes, and even though it may be as the thinking in witchcraft-endemic environments, there was always more.

In these African or witchcraft-endemic environments, people's idea of causality was not as simple as in Western-oriented environments where it had to be on the same observatory dimension with its effects. No, it did not have to be. And it was by this African view that my father's uncle was thinking when the unfortunate event befell his son, especially in his awareness of his own extended family that was notorious for witchcraft. There had been many unnatural occurrences in his extended family, many youthful deaths and many confession-preceded deaths of old women. A young man belonging to their family came to visit me one day while on this sickbed and he promised to visit me the following month, but he never made it. Before the "following month", he had to be buried in his nearly completed new house, a house that he only recently had money to complete after years of abandonment due to economic constraint. And an ugly confession followed the event.

As psychological study is advancing in the modern world, perhaps physicalist thinkers could learn to understand the insubversible dualistic interaction of mind and body, of the mental and physical world, and of the preponderate capability of the mental world in relation to the relatively static physical world. Perhaps they could learn to understand the epigenetic or multi-layered nature of causality, rather than their current linear idea. Then they would be closer to understanding the African concepts of the spiritual constitution and interaction of human beings, human affairs, and of the universal process in general. Then, they might be closer to understanding witchcraft by principle, by which it might even enhance the understanding of physical science.

A few weeks after his hospitalization, Baba-brikila realized that the treatment's effect was too slow while the cost was too high, and that the young man's burning pain was still too much. He came to my father for help and my father introduced him to a traditional-spiritual doctor here in Oyo. The spiritual doctor's family compound was named Akinnu, and by this they called him Baba Akinnu, meaning Baba from the House of Akinnu.

After making rituals in appeasement of the tense situation, Baba Akinnu assured the young man's father not to worry anymore, that his pains had stopped right at the moment of the appeasement, and that he only needed some time for the wounds to heal. The father thought Baba Akinnu was bluffing; he had seen enough spiritual bluffers and boasters and could not stop worrying. He quickly traveled back to Kano to see what was going on at the hospital, and, truly, he found that his son's pains had stopped.

The young man narrated to his father how two gentlemen had come to pray for him – which happened to be at the same time the appeasement was made hundreds of miles away in Oyo. The strange visitors were of the Fulani tribe, whom the young man did not recognize. Mysteriously, he said, his pains left his body immediately, walking away with the visitors as they walked out of the hospital ward. The nurses on duty did not see any visitors, even though the visitors passed by their side, the only entrance, as they entered and exited the ward. No visitor, the nurses claimed, and as also obvious, could enter or leave the ward without their awareness. It was the nurses who had to receive and direct visitors to the specific patients they wanted to see, among about twenty patients, and thus they thought the young man had only been hallucinating. But whether these two men were figments of the patient's hallucination or not, the important thing was that the event inexplicably stopped his pains. And in a very short time his wounds were completely healed, all in a period within the time I had been bedridden.

This kind of marvel that Baba-brikila experienced made him wonder why my father, who introduced him to the spiritualist, had not taken his own son's case to him before or after his son's fire incident. And also, when another person in his family fell seriously ill, my father had advised him to go to the spiritualist again, and he even provided a private room in one of his houses in the town for the boy to be secretly taken care of, away from their dreaded extended family. Baba-brikila asked about it from the spiritualist, who was more surprised that my father did not inform him of my situation. Although the spiritualist had known about it almost immediately I arrived in Oyo, and he had seen me twice when he visited my father on their normal friendship level, he warned my father's uncle not to discuss the issue with my father. The spiritualist never mentioned it during his visits to our house, as my father also did not. If my father would not raise the issue and call him to it by himself, he had maintained and stated to my father's uncle, he would not come onto the case. He even stopped coming to our house after the two visits, so as not to appear as if soliciting to take up my case.

My father's uncle, though uncomfortable, had also kept mum as warned. He was afraid not to break any traditional and spiritual etiquette. But on seeing me again during Tolani's naming ceremony, seeing how my condition still was, he could not heed the warning any longer and he asked my father about it – why he had not taken my case to Baba Akinnu.

My father, disillusioned and bemused, had no reason for it. He did not understand why he had not. "I guess I can only say it just didn't strike my mind," he said regretfully, and he ended up resting everything on a notion that God must have a purpose for it that way, lest he would not have not thought to do it. This was his repeated statement. "If you are sitting by a river, you would not be able to drink thereof unless as God wants; someone miles away might come by and drink while you remain by it."

"Let's take it that this is how God wanted it to be," he said apologetically to me. "It was like I had been walking with a veil over my eyes, which now fell today."

He quickly went to Baba Akinnu on the same day, leaving all the visitors at the party. When I heard this, I wondered over what Aunty Sidi had told me about him: had the witches put the veil over his eyes so he would not see the right thing to do?

***

It was no longer surprising how the various reports on the root and nature of my sickness were the same. Baba Akinnu also did not tell me the particular person or persons involved, though I was not curious about that and all I wanted was to get well and clear of the mysteries.

Baba Akinnu was an elderly man with gray hair all over his body. He would be in his late sixties or early seventies. He was tall, broad shouldered, and slightly muscular. His physique said plenty about him: he must have done tough physical jobs in his early life. He was once my father's employee, driving one of his commercial trucks in the flourishing old days, and this was how he and my father came to be friends.

The first time I saw Baba Akinnu was sometime in the eighties. It was early in the morning and he was at a well in front of our boys' quarter, drawing water for his day's trip on the truck. I was staring at him when one of my brothers walked closer and said to me: "If you've never seen one before, that man you are looking at is a wizard – no kidding." Baba Akinnu was a regular guy working hard at a regular job for his daily life; he did not wear a black, tall, and pointed hat, so I could not have known he was a wizard.

"The first time I came here," Baba Akinnu said, as slowly as his age allowed, "I found three demons in this room with you. They stood at different corners of your bed, and they were hamstringing all your medicines. They were there on a mission to ensure that you did not get well. They saw me, and they knew I saw them. They stared at me in the eye. It unnerved me, but I could not do anything since your father did not say anything to me about taking up your treatment. Yet, that was the reason I was sent here on that day.

"From the first day you arrived in this town we had known of your condition and I had come for you because of the kind of person your father is to me, and how much loved he is to the people who sent me. They were the ones who sent me to your father years ago when I needed a job. They said, 'Go to him and tell him we want him to give you a job.' Your father did not know them – nobody knows them – yet he acquiesced. That impressed them. Nothing goes on in this town without their being aware of it. But we cannot be asking to take up any work, not even from the king. Afterall, there are many works out there begging to be done. I was ordered not to say a word of it if your father did not mention it, so I kept silent. I don't work alone. I do only what I am told to do.

"The second time, I came purposely for you again, because I knew you were still here, and that your condition was still terrible. We could see your pains and traumas and we itched to help you. That time, there were still demons present here, though they had been reduced to two. They took up strategic positions, but still your father said nothing, so I kept silent and went away. Then I was ordered not to come here anymore."

He sniffed from a snuffbox as he talked. We were all surprised when he talked about the demons. And I remembered that the second time he came, when he said he saw the demons reduced to two, was around the time that Mama Pakoyi also sent word that the demons had been reduced to two.

"But today there are no demons in here anymore," he continued, "that was the first thing I looked out for when I entered here. And that's good news for you."

This was one of the statements I had become interested in. Mama Pakoyi had, of late, said there were no demons in the room anymore. Though it was not that I did not want to trust them, I needed that agreement of vision to fan my faith in their works. Then I realized that if all these were true, as all seemed strongly to support, then the damned demons must have been around all along from U.C.H. and before, messing up all the treatments I was receiving, amplifying my physical ills beyond the reach of medical treatment and pushing me toward the edge of the cliff. Perhaps, they were the ones who even stole my file from U.C.H. And when I remembered what Baba-elero and Mama Pakoyi had earlier said about the sickness, I wondered how much more I could believe these things. "You've been under the spell for sometime," they had said, "long before the sickness actually appeared to begin; they were only waiting for you to finally be smothered by the spell." It seems to me that it is only a plan like this that could necessitate such a serious arrangement for such demons to follow up and see the plot through. I could not figure out what my life meant to these people so much for them to go to this length.

Like Mama Pakoyi, Baba Akinnu could be said to possess psychic abilities in the sense that Western people understand, but he was a witchdoctor. Generally, however, we called them spiritualists. Psychic works in the West seems as just investigative and directive; there were such here as well, but the art of witchcraft here made many others more than just that. Many of the witchdoctors usually or always worked with a kind of people called *agba*, or *elders*. The elders often stayed in the background while the witchdoctors were the ones that interacted with people. These elders, although also witches and wizards, were usually more powerful than ordinary witches in the art of witchcraft or, generally, in spirituality, and they were mostly for the good of the society. As a witchdoctor, these elders were the kind of people Baba Akinnu referred to whenever he used "we" in his conversation. They were the ones he meant "sent" and "ordered" him to do whatever he did. They were the ones behind him, using him, helping him.

"There is something you must know," Baba Akinnu said to us. "By the grace of God, this boy will get well and he will walk again on his feet. Exactly how that will come by, I do not know for sure. But it is something you need not hasten for. The case, as it is now, is like a dried folded fish, which, if we hasten to straighten, would break. But also, if we leave it too long in water to soften, so as to be able to straighten it easily, it may become too soft for good. So, we have to be patient and careful. The people who have been taking care o f him have been doing a great job and God has been accepting their efforts.

"You will get well, no doubt," he turned to me. “We don't have the power; it is God who has the power. We just care; He is the One Who cures. But we have been assured that you will get well and up again. So be patient and be rest assured. When we give you medicines, don't think they are small or insignificant; our treatments are not just basically direct medicines. Whether we give you something or not, we are taking good care of you, and I want you to believe that. If anyone gives you anything to use, take it and use it, you are under our watch, and we won't let you use wrong things."

This was a characteristic of Baba Akinnu that is worthy of note. In principle and practice, he attached importance to mission getting accomplished as desired by the clients rather than seeking self glory for himself for doing it. He never objected to medicines from elsewhere to be used by his clients. As long as it did not interfere with his treatment, or the client's progress, as he usually had knowledge of, any other suggestion was allowed. Whenever my father showed him medicines from any other traditional or mainstream doctor, his remark always was "If a man sees a snake and a woman kills it, there is no ill-feeling about it, as long as the snake is dead. That's what matters." Also, I learned that he sometimes sent some patients to hospitals for medical care, if he thought necessary, and he would assure them of his *background* work, if he thought the problem was of witchcraft conspiracy. But he did not approve of medical injections for me at this time. He said too many injections had contributed to my present condition, and if I would need more medical treatment before I regained my legs completely, he would let me know at the right time. Physically, the only thing he gave me was a locally made ointment, and he began to visit me every weekend.

ELEVEN

The Soul's Story

I

They call it incubus, an unseen force that held me down in my sleep. Like someone twice my weight lying on me and choking me, it was so common at this period that it became one of my major concerns.

Many times it would appear as if I was awake and looking at something or someone in the room, usually at Baami, but I would not be able to alarm him until after a little struggle which would bring me fully awake and screaming his name. Sometimes my frightened voice would tear through the night, reach up to the top floor of the house, and have my father and his wife scurrying down to see what was happening. And some other times, the struggles were so strenuous and the asphyxiation overbearing that it was my choking sound that would wake Baami.

One thing intriguing about it was that I always felt and saw that I was moving my arms during the experience, but to later realize that I was moving another set of arms, and not really my physical arms. Some other times I might want to take off my cover cloth, and after several attempts of taking it off but finding it back where it was, I would cry out and wake up. As often depicted in ghost movies, it made me seem like a ghost trying to move material things but finding it difficult to do. This made me conscious of at least one unphysical body alongside my physical body, and both having the same image and, perhaps, the same life.

One day, I made up my mind to recite *Ayat al-Qurisiyy* or *Ya Allah*, a mantra-like prayer, whenever it happened again. When, afterward, the phenomenon began, I would not struggle as before. I would just remain calm and recite whichever one of the prayers I chose. After a while, the incubus would slip away and I would wake up gently without disturbing anyone. I conquered the incubus.

Something curious to me in this was that my determination to recite the prayer was done consciously in my wake-state, yet I remembered it in the supposedly unconscious sleep-state and recited it as if consciously. In some way, this brought down the apparent barrier between my wake-state and my sleep-state, between the conscious process and unconscious process of my mind, and it kept me wondering on the nature of human consciousness.

I was also aware that, during the events of the phenomenon, I was aware of myself as awake, only not yet in the everyday physical wake-state, and I was aware that it was not in the physical wake-state that I was awake. In other words, I was conscious in the unconscious. It was like the trances I had at the hospital, only that I was more conscious and active in it. Though fascinating, this was all strange to me.

There were some explanations by which people tried to explain the incubus, but which, all together, could be misleading. Some people said evil spirits that tried to annihilate their victims in their sleep caused it. Some said spiders sometimes caused it. When asleep, and a spider at the ceiling came directly in line with one's heart, it could result in an incubus. This latter explanation seemed more like a moral taboo to get people to clean their bedrooms. Scientifically, on the other hand, some claimed that a low blood pressure was a factor causing the incubus.

Interestingly, I experienced the phenomenon in self-studied circumstances that I was sure that neither of the last two was the cause of my experience. And after some time, I so much played with it that I thought no evil spirit would cause it and allow me the fun, unless my spirit overrode the evil spirit. Sometimes I would consciously lift the unphysical hands for fun to see how they were, and sometimes I would wriggle the entire unphysical body, while my physical body still remained in bed – like a new ghost thrilled to see his new capability. Since the sickness had held me so captive that I could not move my physical body, my ghost body became my citadel and I often wished for the phenomenon to occur so I could have fun and experiment. It became something of so much fun and interest to me and I was increasingly realizing that human consciousness has capabilities more than ordinarily known by modern science and psychology, and more than the physical body could determine or participate in.

But I had understood a little enough of the world that I would not dispute any of the above speculations on the phenomenon. There could be different cases of it, and each one could be caused by each or more of the explanations. Moreover, I learned to know that, in this world, things are not always caused by one thing rather than another; there are always more dimensions to life and everything in it than the human mind can ever imagine. In ancient times, the incubus was known as a male demon that sought to have sexual intercourse with sleeping women. Its female counterpart was called succubus, and that was where the modern scientific term *incubus* came from.[29] Perhaps there are more possible circumstances responsible for the incubus than now recognized. Sometimes, the apparently simple world is really too complex for specific assumptions to be made, lest we fall into error of oversimplification of reality, as often scientists and most other people do.

It was by these events and my thoughts on reincarnation that my inquisitiveness into spiritual science widened, making me hungry for rational relationships between both physical and psychic aspects of our lives and our world. Because of the limitation on my life, however, my inquiries largely took the form of self-study, taking me deeper into my own life and seeking meaning therefrom.

Thinking is partly reminiscence, and learning into higher understanding is partly a correlation of present experiences and ideas with past experiences and beliefs. Though desultorily lived, I began to recollect my past experiences and see their actual integral places in the reality of my world and the larger world. Past experiences such as the old-time folklores we used to tell as little kids, the nighttime stories, religious lore, radio and television programs, various accounts of other people's lives that I had heard, traditional lore and ways, taboos, superstitions, myths, and my childhood fantasies and apparitions, all which I had carelessly experienced in the environment since my childhood. Even experiences that seemed unimportant and silly became meaningful and were coming to take their places in the larger picture that reality was portraying itself to be. I realized that, in life, there is no experience that is a mere and useless one. It is only when we do not understand them that they appear to us as useless. I began to see the true meaning of proverbs, songs, plays, myths and stories, and I began to see the underlying reasons and meanings of various so-called real life experiences of mine and others'. My consciousness was expanding and nothing became meaningless anymore.

Oftentimes, however, I still found contradictions and obstacles in these correlations of my past, present, and future, but I took them as challenges necessary for better understanding, of which someone who fails to correlate fails to attain. Sometimes, such a failure may be due to a lack of courage by the individual to go beyond the boundary of old and grown-into ideas that may sometimes be necessary to be dropped or transformed. Courage, because ideas or beliefs are like parts of oneself, and having to drop them may seem as dismemberment of oneself. Yet, it is when old fronds are discarded that new ones spurt, and it is then that the palm tree grows.

Cognitively and experientially, all these would soon change the course of my life, especially relatively making me less innocent in the cause of my predicament and my entire human existence. It was poignant to

[29] In medieval Europe some people believed that sexual intercourse with an incubus was responsible for the birth of demons, witches, and deformed human offspring.

imagine, but the recollection and correlation were revealing a consistent order beneath my existence, and which created my predicament for a purpose. I was finding it hard to blame God or anyone else for my circumstance. I began to see my sickness as part of a pattern toward who I was and who I was to become, rather than an injustice or neglect of my creator. In spite of the witchcraft, I began to see my sickness more as an instrument deliberately but unconsciously wielded by myself – perhaps mystically to assume the sick role.

***

"When a person is fallen by a big problem," as an adage goes, "small ones take the advantage and plague him." The more I stayed in bed the more difficult it became for me to be carried out, and the more bed problems arose.

I was fed in bed, treated in bed, bathed in bed; I did everything in bed. But doing anything other than feeding in bed gave me problems. I wished I would not have to sneeze or empty my bowel. Sneezing was so violent that it would shake me to the bones and leave me in pain for several minutes afterward. I had to learn to repress it, and for an unbelievably long period I kept myself from sneezing.

My knees and my heels also created more problems. The folded towel in between the knees ached my legs by contact, and then caused blisters. The blistered sides of the knees wanted fresh air to heal, but I could not allow it because I needed to have something to keep the knees apart. Yet, it was also painful to keep the towel there because of the blistered surfaces. It was a dilemma on its own, a problem that disturbed my daytimes and kept me awake many nights. The same went for the heels to keep them from touching one another and to reduce the pressure of their contact with the bed. As with Job, bedbugs built mansions in the crevices of my body and the mattress, and around the frames of the bed. They fed on me all the time, having their Christmas everyday. All these plagued me in bed. Though they may seem as trifles, they were worse enough to make me sick of living, and once too often I still found myself weeping for the life I was living. I was like a dilapidated building falling apart and only held by patches of stuffs here and there.

However, after several weeks of doing things my way, I had enough relief to allow my head to be raised for short periods during the day, with a pillow carefully tucked under my head. This allowed me to feed better and see the room at a better angle.

Gradually, my pains reduced and, after some months, I was able to move my legs forward little by little, as the physical therapist had advised. This gave me more room to raise my torso and, thus, more comfort. My hope was unfolding. My health was improving. The sickness now appeared to be pulling its stakes, though it had only just begun and it was not in a hurry.

Loneliness crept in to fill the space the pains were leaving behind.

Although, Baami was always there with me, the age difference limited the scope of our discussions less than my spirit began to demand. The age difference was also between my younger siblings and me, and yet, they spent more of their after-school periods outside than inside the house. Nonetheless, they still provided enough company to keep my blood from freezing up in the increasing loneliness.

I did not want my ailing body to jail my mind. So, since I got back some life in my hands, I started to read omnivorously, devouring every book I could lay my hands on. From kindergarten stories to university texts, recommendable books to long-forgotten ones, and many that, as a young boy, I had hated to see on my older siblings' shelves. Many of my sister's medical schoolbooks became my staples. I discovered many subjects and intellectual problems that scholars have been dealing with for centuries. My curiosity about the world and its intricacies increased. I found interest in literature, psychology, and philosophy.

Every month Wasiu came to visit me. A few people came once in a while to visit me from Ibadan, but Wasiu was the only one who kept it up as a duty. My sickness created a fear that ostracized me from the people at Ibadan. Everyone knew about the strange circumstances surrounding my sickness, and they did not want to visit me for fear of being roped in by the witches. This made my place seem a kind of quarantine station. Most of my friends also stayed away from me.

Wasiu looked beyond this and came monthly as his school schedule allowed. I was always happy to see him, and whenever he came we spent the whole day talking. With him, I shared my worries and woes, and the kind of things we talked about was so intriguing that I always looked forward to his next visit. He was now studying philosophy at the University of Ibadan and had relevant topics to discuss and debate about life.

Really, my cousin introduced me to philosophy as a discipline simply because of his being a student of philosophy, but he has always been somehow philosophical in nature since our early years. He had possessed idealistic traits, by which he often made choices that reflect deep thoughts. When I and my other cousins poked around pleasure joints where fun and girls could be found, Wasiu spent his times at home thinking and writing essays and poetry. He kept a serious relationship with one girl while we sampled girls around. Too entrenched in the idealism of adolescence, he was known in the house for taking radical principled decisions to which he had a kind of religious devotion. Sometimes they earned him a good reputation, but oftentimes they made him look foolhardy in the house, as his decision to keep visiting me did.

Wasiu's visits also brought me the awareness of a secret that my father had been keeping away from me, the secret of Baba-elero's avoidance of me. After rounds of discussions and debates during one visit, Wasiu, concerned, inquired about details of my current state of health. I told him all there was about it, and then he told me of a spiritualist at Ibadan, to whom he told my story. The man did not know me and I did not know him, and Wasiu had only met him as an errand boy for an elderly relation for whom the spiritualist worked. Through this relation, Wasiu had been convinced of the spiritualist's genuineness and capability. For this reason, with my condition burning on his mind, he asked the spiritualist if he could help his sick cousin. For the fear going around in Ibadan, that was dangerous for him to do. It was his sense of family duty that overrode that of danger.

The spiritualist made his divination and checked on my case in his own way and honestly told Wasiu what he found out, that the case was beyond his abilities. I had used the word 'honestly' because there were many spiritualists who would not say that to their clients. They would want to keep an appearance of a powerful spiritualist and make money off the clients. Instead, he explained to Wasiu that the people responsible for the sickness were powerful witches with whom he or many spiritualists would not dare to combat. But he assured Wasiu that I would survive it, because the people taking care of me were also powerful people who could meet such an evil force, and that "God has taken control of the situation in my favor."

Then came the bombshell.

In the spiritualist's explanation of how serious my situation was, and how powerful the witches were, he told Wasiu that the struggle for my life was so tough that one of the men taking care of me had lost one of his children to the battle. The witches had attacked his household because of his involvement in helping me, and they had killed one of his children in vengeance.

This was a shocker to me. I wished it were not true. But at my inquiry after Wasiu left, my father confirmed it. It was Baba-elero's child that was killed. At first, my father wanted to stop Wasiu from coming to the house. He was puzzled at how he came across a secret known only to him, Baba-elero, and Aunty Sidi, and angered by its revelation to me at this stage. But because of Wasiu's loyalty to me, he let him be. My father explained that Baba-elero had been forewarned not to be involved before I reached his place the day I left U.C.H, but he offered to help me because he thought he could not turn me back and watch me die. He took up the treatment as a responsibility of a healer.

I was overwhelmed with confusion. God, what a life I am living! I shuddered. What force in the world is then keeping me alive at the expense of others' lives? I cried bitterly and fell into a turbulence of emotions. I felt so much for Baba-elero, and I felt with him. He did not need to continue to be around me anymore, not when the witches threatened further calamity over his family. I wanted to live, but I did not want someone else to lose his or her life for me to live mine. I did not want a mother to cry only to keep my fingers at the hook of my life.

By this, I knew more the gravity of my situation and I trembled within. But I would not stop thinking that this should not have happened. What a cost to a man who was helping to save my life. What a people so wicked, so heartless, so diabolic. In the middle of the night I remained awake for hours, wondering about my situation and all the troubles it was causing, and I ended up crying late into the morning. What force in the world continued to keep me alive? I could not help but think about the mother of the child; how miserable her life must have become. Forever will I feel for Baba-elero and the mother of the child. I will forever respect them. I will forever pray for the soul of the innocent child who did not know me but had her life sacrificed for mine. It is a horrible world we live in, and I was afraid.

When Sister Toyin came home one day from London, where she now lived, she gave me some inspiring words that I henceforth kept to my heart. "Keep up your spirit, Rahman," she had said, "if they cannot defeat your spirit they won't be able to defeat your body." Thank God they found my spirit undefeatable, and now I was waiting, hoping they really would not defeat my body. If only I have to live to justify the little girl's life, I wanted to fight on.

II

As time crawled on, the pains thinned out of my body and loneliness thickened in. I thought about having friends to talk with. I had only a few friends in Oyo, but none of them regularly stayed in the town.

Because Wasiu, before the sickness began, had always advised me on settling down to one girlfriend, he now sometimes raised the issue about how helpful a love relationship might be to me at this period and it slightly hurt that I had not set the stage for it. I missed the intimacy such a girl might have brought to my bedside. One does not know the value of something until one needs it. As the god of sickness fed on my health, the goddess of love mocked me.

I had fallen in love twice before, but both were ruined at their budding stage by my immaturity. The first time I had acted stupidly and on the second time I had talked stupidly. Although on both occasions I had wanted to fertilize the love, I had instead burned them out. Since then, I did not fall in love, careful not to break anyone's heart because of the abroad career I embarked upon. I had girlfriends only to stay in tune with the sensuous songs of our time, to which my subconscious shred of pride and determination strove to dance. Although I did not feel deeply comfortable in the practice, but my lord was my ego, subliminally indoctrinated, and to which I was sensually enslaved.

Now I thought seriously about love. Sometimes I thought I was becoming softened by the weariness of sickness to worry about love, but I always realized that I was never hard against it in the first place. I had only been acting according to my orientation and reasoning. Perhaps as many adolescents do, I had interpreted my inner desire for love as for lust, my desire for intimacy as for sex. My second experience with love seemed a metaphor for this interpretation. I had misunderstood the word *lust*, newly found in a dictionary, as another and intense word to describe love, and I had used it to express my feeling to the girl. And I lost her. She knew the meaning of the word better than I did, and she must have had a dose of smart players, while my malapropism presented me as another.

I wished I had someone to love and to love me back. My thinking of love as soft, while I did not want to be soft, may be another misunderstanding of love. Now, I realized that beneath my participation in the game of sexual conquest typical of boys, I had a desire for intimacy, but which I may have been using everything to repress or silver over. By her repeated rejection of me in my early years, my mother, the first woman in my life, might have left me wanting. With all the anxiety with which I used to think of her whenever I wanted to get close to her and make use of her position in my life, she might have left me almost incapable toward the women I cared for, and thus, vulnerable. Every time I had been in love I had failed; I only conquered when not serious. Thus, I may have been using my feelings of not wanting to break girls' hearts for two reasons. First, consciously to prevent them from pain, because I have always been considerate of others; and secondly, unconsciously as a defense mechanism to prevent myself from anxiety and pain – for fear of my love being rejected, like I had been rejected by my mother. However, finding myself in the loneliness of the sick room, a situation vulnerable to an individual's primitive emotional needs, I became desperate to fill my vacuum.

The need to have friends to talk to made me inquire about some of my friends in the neighborhood. The compound next to ours was of a large estate that belonged to the father of two of my friends, Tunde and Yemi Adelakun. Another one, adjoining the Adelakun's, was owned by Banji Akinboye's father, another of my friends in the neighborhood. And less than a mile away lived Dotun Aruna. We had been friends since I moved into the neighborhood in 1984, and we attended the same secondary school together. There were other school friends of mine in the town, but all or most of them were in out-of-town schools and only came to town during the holidays and the often-repeated closure of schools due to administrative problems. When Tunde and Yemi Adelakun came home one holiday, my younger brothers told me they saw them around and I sent for them immediately.

Boredom had become so thick in my room that one almost could touch it. Many times I only stared at the ceiling. Sometimes I watched spiders play, fight, stalk, and trap their preys. Their live movies gave me their own quota of amusement. I hoped to see them make love to confirm what I heard that female spiders eat up their male mates as refreshments after the energy-consuming mating period. Perhaps a metaphor of the true sexual relations between the human sexes, but it appears on the surface as if the female spiders were taking it out on their males what feminists claim of males' chauvinism in the human world. I was curious to watch this happen, but I did not get the opportunity. Perhaps spiders are also afraid of leaving witnesses.

Everything in the world seems to have an educational function and sometimes I had lessons from the spiders. I often became so much absorbed enough to empathize with them, and one day I saw an event that got me into an emotional and intellectual confusion. This was what happened:

One spider caught a butterfly bigger than itself. The spider must have been very hungry, as it had keenly stalked and gripped the catch with extreme caution. Maybe it had a family to feed. One could imagine how the spider's throat must have been watering for the feast that would follow. But the butterfly, in its pains, fright, and struggles to escape, did not make it easy for the spider; it flew desperately about while the spider gripped tightly at its head. It knocked about on the wall, windowpane, and glass, knocking the spider's head along on all the hard surfaces. This is a catch too much, I mused, and I was already giggling at the spider's predicament. “You bit more than you could chew, fella.” Even daily bread is not easy for the *low lives*.

The spider gripped tightly and tried to subdue its troublesome prey while the butterfly struggled to escape the fate of becoming someone’s dinner. However, the strength of the butterfly seemed to outweigh that of the spider. I did not know when the spider painfully let go and the butterfly slipped out through the opening in the window. It became a sad story for the spider. A cartoonist would have painted rings of aches and sorrow around the spider’s head like a string of halos, because its head must be aching from the knock-about and it must be sad for the loss of its lunch. What a sense of humor God must have, I laughed.

But I soon felt pity for the spider for losing a meal and enduring such a painful adventure. I imagined the miserable countenance a person would wear if it were to a human it happened, and by this I was able to empathize with it. Yet, at the same time, I was happy for the butterfly for its freedom and the narrow escape. Of course, the butterfly was out on that day for its own daily bread, to which it was entitled by nature, yet another creature wanted to make it its own daily bread, to which it was also entitled by nature. Then I became confused over which my sympathy should go to. I did not know whether to feel happy for the butterfly and mock its enemy, or sorry for the spider and curse its lost prey. One could not feel with one and not hurt the other.

What a contradiction of nature? Yet, such is the case among humans, sometimes. With humor, perhaps, God also teaches. "While you laugh, lad," He seemed to be saying, "learn."

I wondered whether we were inevitably trapped in a world in which we cannot help but to feed on one another for survival, perhaps as Sigmund Freud thinks, that “men are wolves onto men.” Out of my developing social and human conscience, I could not find this digestible, but it stared at me in the eye and I could not look away. Yet, those of us who think we could make judgments about life tend to look at stories only from the side nearest to us.

With this and many like it streaming into my consciousness, I sometimes wondered whether humans could really make objective judgments about one another. Perhaps humans are only poor souls who find themselves in a world so dimensionally restrictive, so strange, so cold, so taciturn. But rather than waste so much time of our lives judging one another, compounding our misery, then it may be better to be trying to understand one another, personally, culturally, politically, and religiously.

Whenever I remember the story of the spider and the butterfly, I muse at how God's humors are so rich in knowledge. Often, events that seem to have no sense at all may be microscopic and telescopic clues to larger and more important events that closely affect us, and whose puzzling sense troubles our ideas and beat our thinking. Perhaps in every event in life is a metaphor for another. Perhaps everything is a story written with cosmic grandiose.

***

Yemi and Tunde Adelakun walked into my room, unsuspecting of anything. They had come to meet a friend who probably just came from Ibadan and sent for them, as I used to do. But, like Job's friends, they were stunned osseous by what they saw. Our eyes were never enough to take in the shocking sights that life sometimes presents to us, and our mouths often assist us. As they gaped at me, their lower jaws dropped, almost to the floor. The bag of bones on the bed did not look nice; he was so different from their friend. The extremely pale skin, the clean-shaved head, and the unusually long goatee made me seem like an extraterrestrial.

As my friends had not expected to see me like this, I also had not expected such a reaction from them. I had waited for them as if things were normal. In the euphoric expectation of meeting old friends, I had forgotten my condition. Now, I was stuck in the moment, conscious of myself, a wraith-like figure, with my skin thinly laid on my bones like the centuries-old mummies now exhumed by today's nosey folks.

I must have inherited some traits of levity from my father. I tried an attitude of frivolity and greeted them like in the jolly old days. But they had been moved to a degree of surprise and horror that my frivolity did not find a place.

"Jesus Christ!" Yemi exclaimed. "What's the problem with you?"

"What has happened to you?" Tunde also asked.

"Just one of those things," I replied, "What's up?"

Their mood was too far away from *what's up* stuff. They just wanted to know what the problem was and I briefly told them how and when I had been sick.

"I've been in this town since December," I smiled.

"But I was home for the Christmas and New Year and no one told me anything," Yemi said.

"Yeah, it was a top state secret then, kept only within the house because of its initial gravity. But now I'm getting better, as you can see. It had been terrible in the past."

"You're getting better like this?" they exclaimed. My words had sounded to them like a big joke.

"That's why I could send for you. In the past I was in a different world and it couldn't occur to me that you guys existed. I wouldn't even give a damn if it did."

"But the last time I saw you," Tunde commented, "you told me you were going to America soon, so when I didn't see you around I thought you had gone. How did things change this way?"

"Yeah, that was what I saw coming and was expecting then, but this is what happened; it's how God saw it and it's what I got." I replied. "Life is always His way, isn't it?"

We talked about it for some time while I tried unsuccessfully to get them over their fallen moods. They asked about the cause of the sickness and I tried to be evasive. But they were Nigerian enough to get some hints. At the end of the visit Tunde asked Yemi to pray for me and we all closed our eyes for the emotional prayer. They walked out of my room shaking their heads.

Banji Akinboye was also in town and they told him about me. He came in the evening and had his own share of the drama, though with less of a surprise than that of Tunde and Yemi, because he had been told what he would meet.

Yemi was now a devout Christian and in our subsequent meetings we discussed more of Jesus than any other thing. As he told me, he had a vision of Jesus Christ and had become an evangelical mouthpiece. Sometimes, he gave me Christian books to read, kindly hoping to save his friend's soul, and not only his body. I found the books edifying, especially those written by evangelists who were also psychologists. There was something about psychology and religion that made psychologists better preachers to me, something that I learned made St Augustine's teaching relevant sixteen hundred years after he had done us the service. Yemi was an Electrical Electronics Engineering student at Ladoke Akintola University at Ogbomosho and we talked computers too.

Tunde was a Pharmacy student at the University of Jos, and when he came in the subsequent times - they often did not come together anymore - we discussed everything, from films to girls, guys, and politics. We also discussed religion, but not as Yemi and I did. Tunde was also a Christian, but he was a latitudinarian, as I saw myself becoming. Our stances saw religion from similar views, only that our languages put us in occasional discord. He spoke Christian; I spoke Islamic. Tunde was my earlier-mentioned friend that wondered whether God would put all Muslims in hell for being non-Christian. It did not seem to him as fair.

Banji was almost like Tunde. They went to the same school and were doing the same program. Together, all three of us, we discussed our worldly concerns. Sometimes, we would go into debates on various issues, local and international politics, metaphysics, African magic, science, religion, history, technology and so on. We were young men developing into the world, and curious to know about what went on in our world - if not yet able to participate directly. We raised and expressed our doubts and confusions, our satisfactions and prides, and we pooled our thoughts to analyze meanings and values. Whenever we talked, I forgot my predicament, and it never limited my participation.

One day Tunde asked me, "Don't you think there might be some kind of foul play behind your sickness? It worries me. I mean some kind of insidious cause by some evil people." He came together with Banji and Banji also gave a tacit agreement with him.

I did not want to go into this but they were so close on me and I did not know how exactly to handle the situation as I would have preferred. My manners had become slightly rusty and I had lost touches of tactful behavior. I went roughly about it as I often found myself doing now.

"So, they say," I eventually replied, calmly.

"I knew it," he said, "But why don't you arrange to beg the person behind it?"

"I don't really know for sure, but I don't think that will be necessary. Daddy knows what to do and he's doing it."

"Do you know the person?" Banji asked.

"No."

We dropped the topic after a while. They all were friends indeed who were there for me when in need. But they could not stay in town for long. They soon resumed at school and had to go back. I was to wait six months until December to see them again.

Some of my other friends who heard about the sickness also came to visit me, but for one reason or another they could not keep coming as I wished. A few years later, some of them told me that they had stopped coming because they could not stand the sight of me lying in bed, as I was, and looking the way I looked. One said it was only the spirit with which I talked, as if nothing was wrong with me, that kept him from crying in the room. Although I did not like to see people sad because of me, I talked that way because I did not want to be felt sorry for, and because I did not like to miss the fun of having friends around. Such an opportunity was extremely scarce in my life at the moment. By eventually keeping away they had even made it scarcer for me. But I understood them; it was not only because of me but because of them as well. I represented one of the worst conditions a human being could ever be, and seeing me would remind them of it. It is like people feel when they hear of the death of a relative, friend, or acquaintance; they are not only faced with a sense of loss, they are frighteningly faced with a sense of their own mortality. Our fathers used to say, "When death goes around claiming of our peerage, an important proverb is death telling to us." My condition reminded them of their insecurity in a world that seemed arbitrary.

***

The sickness was further pulling its stakes, though still not in a hurry. My grandmother hoped that when I was relieved enough to be carried out of the house it would be better to be flown to America to complete the treatment. She discussed it with everyone she thought could help and waited to see what would come up.

III

Human beings are better to live in love and harmony among themselves. So says the old preaching of love. In relationships where these are lacking, suspicion, real or imagined, becomes the reality. But the edifice of life may have been underlain with the stones of chaos, and perhaps it is natural for differences to occur among people. Then, the next question will be how we handle our differences.

As gradually as my health appreciated the relationship between me and my father's wife depreciated, and I began to lose some of the warmth that I had enjoyed in the house. There were petty details, real and imagined path-crossings probably amplified by both of us, but it was merely food that started it all. The issue of feeding may not be a little one, especially in my situation, but in a polygamous setting, with its typical potentials for suspicions and distrusts, things that cause quarrels are usually trivial. And although she was the only wife at the time, there were children of ex-wives in the house, and such a house could still only behave as a polygamous home. The development was thus predictable from the circumstance.

For normal feeding, and especially for health restoration, I began to need more food than I was receiving. But she no longer cared as much as before, and she did not think I could have more, even though there was often more from which I could get. She was the wife of the house and, therefore, the mistress of the kitchen. And that kitchen was her only way to directly exert power over her oftentimes adversarial stepchildren.

I leveled the allegation against her one afternoon. The situation bred and we eventually had a brief quarrel. It was a quarrel that was as gentle as my sick state could allow, but it said plenty and promised plenty. My father did not say anything over it, but I knew he was stuck in the middle. The tension soon cooled off and we got along together again. However, it was like we laid down our spears, not buried them. The air between us was still inflammable. She did not help matters, and I did not help it either.

While not an excuse, I would later blame it on my puerile simplicity. I embraced life and humans as innocently as I idealistically saw them, ignoring the chaos that our egos forced on us – the psychopathology of living. For my father's wife, she was as well a victim of the circumstance as I was. The polygamy of the house was too complex for her young and inexperienced temperament to easily endure. She was so young that I could not call her my stepmother. She was about the same age as my older sisters, and only a few years my senior in school when my father married her.

Nonetheless, I would come to be bruised by the development, perhaps more than the bruises of my physical health. In life, there are many kinds of suffering, but I do not think there is any kind more troubling than one incurred in relationships with others. Perhaps, human beings could even deal with the wrath of God directly from heaven than through relationships with other human beings. Businesses with intermediaries are always more complex and exacting than with business-owners. This was the contribution of my inter-personal relationships to my ordeal.

My grandmother tried to alleviate the tension of the circumstance by sending money and food stuffs periodically to run a separate kitchen in the charge of my younger siblings. For my need for a healing diet, this worked for me, but not for the relationship between me and my father's wife. Having the separate kitchen heightened her anxiety and allowed for the persistence of our suspicion, which would seek expression in another way.

***

One afternoon on an August day I had an august visitor. I just came violently out of a short afternoon nap. One of the problems that still remained with my sleeping was that I woke up with violent shakes from within, as if my soul jammed back into my body from wherever it went in my sleep.

As I woke up this afternoon, there was nothing to read, so I stared up at the ceiling and watched for the Spider's Show. In many ways, they could be inspiring if one had eyes and mind for inspiration. They exhibited patience and carefulness and skills in stalking and capturing their preys, something one may need to learn in the game of life. Sometimes, I would turn the watching into a game, taking sides with either the hunter or the hunted and enter the suspense for the gladiatorial event.

As I was becoming absorbed in this afternoon's show, I heard a woman's footfalls coming toward my room and I looked away at the doormouth to see who it was. One of my younger brothers appeared, directing my mother to my room.

"Mommy," I heard myself say, unwittingly. I expected to have outgrown the baby word, but it seemed my unconscious mind still held on to it, perhaps as a need for being mommied, something men later seek in marriage.

"Ramoni," she said gently, also unconsciously. Conscious, she would rather call me AbdulRahman, as she had become religiously accustomed to in Ilorin, or Demola, for her occasional fondliness.

In the next instant she broke down into tears and bawled. I had never seen my mother like this before. She slumped into the chair facing my bed and wept into her hands and laps. My father had been informed that she was around and he entered at that moment.

"What's all this?" he asked. He did not want anyone to cry about me, and especially to my face. Though often unsuccessfully, he had always tried to shield me from visitors whom he knew would break down at the sight of me. With my mother crying uncontrollably, I did not know when I started to cry.

"Why should this happen to me?" she lamented, "... Who have I offended? I never wished or did anyone bad; why should I be treated this way?" And she cried on.

"This is a time to thank God, and not to cry," my father cut in. "He's now recovering and crying days are over. What you need now is to give praises to God."

My mother had heard about my sickness only a few weeks back in Saudi Arabia, where she had been for months, deliberately hiding her whereabouts from the family. She had since been struggling to get back home.

"I have never been the same since I heard and I had been going to the *Kaaba* to pray over it," she explained. "But I just wanted to get home. It surprised me, because I thought you were in America and that someday I'll hear from you."

Kaaba is the black-draped square house at the center of *masjid Al-Haram* at Mecca, the central mosque where pilgrims go for worship. It is the great house that tradition tells to have been built by Abraham, the father of the three major religions of the world, and Ishmael, and it is a place that Muslims believe that prayer is guaranteed to be answered. My father sometimes told a story about the Kaaba and Sister Toyin, when he took her and Brother Gbola on a holy pilgrimage in the period before her admission into the university. She had always wanted to study medicine, which had the highest JAMB admission "cut-off" mark. But when her result came out she was a few points short of the "cut-off" mark. The process of the admission was still on when she went on the pilgrimage and my father urged her and my brother to pray for whatever they wanted at the Kaaba. Though she knew she had not met the admission requirement, she still prayed for admission into the college of medicine. The miracle happened by the time they returned home: the educational board had lowered the "cut-off" mark for medicine to exactly her JAMB score and she was accepted into the college. Hence, learning that I had been prayed for at the Kaaba was encouraging, strengthening my faith to overcome my problem.

My mother was surprised to learn that I was better now. All the muscles in my legs were atrophied and the legs seemed as thin as broomsticks. My butts, too, had flattened out like dried-out pizzas, and she could not believe I was getting better. Terrified, she asked my father, "Do you think he's going to walk with these legs again? They are too thin and frail."

"Why not? By God's grace he will walk again," my father replied, confidently as if he had received a certified mail from God to the effect, and grinning to stifle a speck of pessimism in his heart. In my heart also was a struggle against my fears. While I constantly prayed for the complete recovery of my health, I harbored a fear of never being able to walk again in my life.

"Move your toes and let her see," my father added, "He can control them and that's a sign he's going to walk again."

I moved my toes to let my mother see. The underneath of my feet crackled. The top skin, about as thick as 5 millimeters, had dried up. They had not touched the ground in several months, and now they cracked and peeled at any movement. They looked like something discovered by the paleontologists; the toes drooped and the nails were like animals' claws, which would make such a discovery seem like in a monster movie. Humans are horrible in death, as a saying goes.

"What needs to be done now?" My mother wanted to know.

"There's nothing to worry about," my father replied, "those who have been taking care of him are capable and only need encouragement. Go to them and thank them, and give them whatever you can afford to show your appreciation."

My mother went to each of them and did as my father bade her. She took up part of the finances and tried to make up as much as she could for the past times she had not been around. She also consulted a medical doctor who prescribed some medicines that she brought for me. One of them was an imported beverage that took more than half of my weekly expense.

My mother hoped to stay and see me through to recovery. She expected that, with the intensified treatments, her son would get up soon. But it was not like that; the sickness was not in a hurry. She realized this after some months and her hand already touching the underlining of her purse. She was not making money in Nigeria; she was only spending.

One day, I called her and advised her to go back. I did not want her around anymore. She came from Ibadan regularly and expected to meet improvement, which often she did not see. This always disappointed her and I did not like it. It gave me a sense of haste that I had learned I did not need. Also, if she did not have money, she would not be able to do much for me, and she herself would be in a mess. She was already digging into financial holes.

She had to go back and she agreed, hoping to go and make money to bring back home. "I wouldn't be long before I come again," she had said, "Pray to God, and I'll do it over there as well. Let me meet you well when I come back."

She left me with some money and a computer brick game. Once again, I became a little kid, staring into the tiny screen day and night, and watching the bricks fall in innocent excitement. If only life could be simple as in computer games.

***

I had a dream one day. I was riding in a taxi and I encountered two nomadic Fulanis. They looked at me and then to my legs. Then they shook their heads, expressing doubts over my legs being able to bend and walk again.

"Do you think these legs would be able to bend for use again?" they asked.

"By the grace of God, they will," I replied them. "It is God who helped me to this stage and I believe He will do it completely as I want." That was my father's common statement that found its way into my dream mouth.

They asked again and again to reinforce their pessimism and register it in my heart. It appeared as if they wanted to influence my spirit negatively, but I maintained my stance and reinforced my optimism. Finally they left me and I woke up.

Baba Akinnu said it was not an ordinary dream, and I should thank God that I did not yield to their suggestion, for it would have affected my reality. I wondered over this and I remembered that the two visitors who visited the son of my father's uncle in Kano had also been two nomadic Fulanis. They had been instrumental in Baba Akinnu's work and I was to later learn that he knew who they were.

From this, I learned further into the nature of dreams, and especially my dreams, which contained meanings than I had ever realized. I remembered many of my past dreams and I realized that each one of them had had something to tell me. I had only not paid attention. One of them now stuck out on my mind, sometimes bringing regrets for my neglect. It was said to have foreshadowed this sickness, by which I might have averted it if I had understood and taken necessary steps.

In the dream, about a year before the sickness, I had traveled from Ibadan to Oyo in new clothes. In the Yoruba tradition, the dead are buried with new cloth. Hence, for someone to wear new clothes in dreams was a bad omen, usually portending death. So, the dream, a warning from my soul, had forecast my being carried dead to Oyo.

Being aware of the scientific claims against the mystery of dreams, I could not help but to confront this with the questions of science. Some assume that people determine or prearrange their dreams and fail to recognize them in the distortion of the dreams. Using a Freudian psychoanalytical concept, someone once tried to explain my gunshot dream as a psychic response to an impending physiological event. But I could no longer accept that a person's night dreams are merely projections of what he thinks and does during the day. This may only be true in some cases. In some other cases, it would only be a near-truth, and far from true in many others.

Nonetheless, if I could consciously determine or prearrange my dream by myself, it still does not take away the wonder on the nature of the human consciousness, for dreams and everyday life are two different realms of activity. Neither does psychoanalytical interpretation of the gunshot dream could take away my wonder, because it only would suggest the power of the human mind being aware of impending physical condition, an idea that would still formidably uphold the idea of precognition, a non-scientific notion.

My dream experience with the Fulanis may be rightly interpreted as a psychological representation of my inner struggle between fear and hope on the issue of my walking again. However, although it did not abnegate Baba Akinnu's interpretation, such a psychological representation still contained a sense of mystery and wonder that science cannot throw away. And this is also because, as I was to later learn from life, my struggle of hope and fear may also likewise be an emotional representation of the dream experience, as the dream experience was of the emotional state. Which one was truer, or which one actually represented the other, may then become the question.

As I realized at this period, most of my dreams were not figments of my imagination. Sometimes they were so precognitive that their consequent real life events had turned out almost exactly as I had dreamt, with little or no symbolism. One night, when I was still a little boy at Oniyanrin, I was dreaming of our house burning when my grandmother suddenly woke me up and dragged me outside onto the street. Fire had erupted in one section of the house and the people were being evacuated.

With increasing curiosity, I learned that dreams are of the activities of our souls not consciously available to our human or daily consciousness, and from which the true meaning of our experience may be obtained. In his psychoanalysis, Sigmund Freud saw the interpretation of dreams as the royal road to the knowledge of the unconscious activities of the mind. With clinical confirmations, he believed this was the clue to curing mental illnesses. Hence, from the temple of Aesclepius, the Greek god of Medicine, where the sick slept to receive dreams that would heal them, to the Freudian couch, where dreams are analyzed for therapy, dream have manifested itself as a numinous part of human reality. Really, the understanding of these unconscious activities of our mind may be clues to solving life problems, which may not be but mental illnesses.

I learned of this unconscious part of our mind as a section of the consciousness of our souls, of which our conscious mind is also a part. Sometimes I saw the soul as the "Unconscious" itself, the large phenomenon that Freud may have discovered only its exterior part. Sometimes I call that "Unconscious" as "Consciousness", though a transcendental consciousness far beyond the mind that modern psychology currently deals with. And this made me understand how vast human reality and potentials are, as unknown to our ordinary senses and thinking.

Interestingly, by all these, and a closer study of Freudian psychology, I always thought Freud, through his psychoanalysis, had discovered the human soul, which ironically he did not believe as existent. Really, the Austrian-born doctor had discovered more than that, only that the scientific limitation of his discipline kept him from realizing it.[30] His friend, Carl

[30] From my later study and reflection over the psychoanalysis of Sigmund Freud and various other psychological and spiritual ideas, I discovered that the idea of the Unconscious leads to the ideas of paradise and, eventually, of God. I came to see that even though Freud did not believe in God

Jung, also a psychoanalyst, discovered that the reality of this inner, larger Unconscious is a logical inference. Today, psychologists have discovered that the unconscious database of a human being is larger than his conscious database in a ratio of about ten thousand to one. "The Brain," says one of the greatest poets that ever lived, "is wider than the Sky…deeper than the Sea…The brain is just the weight of God…"[31] Though we only use about 0.01 percent of our brain in our daily activities, as studies have shown, it is both instructive and inspiring to learn that the brain is equipped far more than enough to allow the channeling of this larger potential.

In my later learning into Asian religions, this larger part of the soul was what I found some of them call *oversoul*, and what some others call *inner-*, *higher-*, or *super-self.* And the spiritual realm in which it dwells is a place I learned to call, for my convenience, the *superverse*, as it may not be a realm separate from the physical universe. It is a realm that contains the universe and its infinite variations now discovered by physical science.

By all this, I began to see life as a deep and intricate psychological phenomenon that I hungrily wanted to explore. It is this great transcendent human consciousness that I later realized creates everything in the human world: the science, the religion, the witchcraft, the materials, and every single experience in the world, individually and collectively. Everything is a function of the great Consciousness, and it is in this understanding that I would lose my innocence in the cause and course of my sickness. Sooner or later, I would realize that, despite the natural and magical causes involved in my condition, the ultimate responsibility for my predicament lay at the feet of my soul's great consciousness, the summary of who I am and the purpose of my being. My sickness may have all been a mystically factitious condition, an unconscious design to play the sick role toward a goal I did not yet understand. It seemed a function or an enactment of an interaction between my soul and the individual consciousness of my body parts and of the specific ailments that plagued me. My sickness, thus, may be a metaphor for a world more exciting and enlightening than the world of my physical manifestation. Then, the purpose - perhaps also the process - behind all these may elude me if I concentrated too much on my ailments, sorrow, and the physical manifestation of my general condition.

Following from the dream about the Fulanis, my health continued to

---

and religion, he has discovered God, unintended and unaware by him, and has laid down a reasonable psychological platform to bring religion and science together. It appears ludicrous to imagine Freud a prophet, but perhaps he was a prophet of what can be called the atheist's religion or the atheists' God. The curious thing is that atheists have a God, only that both atheists and believers do not realize it. And sometimes, or all times, it is the same God of the believers that is of the atheist, only wearing different masks and perhaps playing hide and seek with his creatures. For the idea of God or gods in religion, Freud has only perspectively represents it as the Unconscious or the forces therein respectively. Now I see psychology as religion, and religion as psychology. This is because, as I came to realize, religion is about life, and life is a state of the mind, a deep psychological process that started in the symbolic "Garden of Eden," of which our birth and death are only a part. Curiously, Jesus' "prodigal son" may roughly be a mythopoetic personification of the phenomenon Freud later discovered as the id.

[31] Emily Dickinson

improve, now remarkably. The pains in my joints gradually reduced and one could now sit on my bed without hurting me. I began physical exercise, trying to fold and bend my legs, and to sit up in bed. The knee joints were stiff and painful to bend, but since my general health was improving, I had more strength to try on.

***

After a few weeks of relentless exercise, I was able to bend my knees about thirty degrees. It was inspiring and I intensified my efforts to soften the muscles of the legs and increase the bending angles further.

One day, following Baba Akinnu's direction I tried to sit up on the bed with my legs touching the floor. It would be the first time in about a year that I would attempt to sit up without being carried. If possible, the position would make it easy for me to exercise my legs better.

It was a half-day's job, with my younger brothers assigned to different roles. I spent all the morning to prepare my mind, and, around 2 to 3 in the afternoon, we began. It was like moving a huge statue made of glass. We had a carefully created plan and a lot of resting intervals, but at the end of the day, we did it. The muscles around my groin still jerked now and then, only not enough anymore to keep me from the exercise.

This was my first step toward getting out of bed. It was around November and I began to sit up on the bed everyday. The first day my legs touched the ground, I felt very unusual. The floor was strange and hard under my feet, and my feet had been so deformed that I could not have them evenly flat on the floor.

Nonetheless, the feeling of the regained experience was refreshing. I further worked on my legs. One day, Baba Akinnu nudged me to move completely away from the bed and sit on the chair, stating that it had to be done by the New Year. This would be a great step in my improvement. It would mean freedom from my confinement to the bed and I tried to do it. I spent a few days to muster up my determination, and, on the 31st of December, I finally attempted it. With only a minimum help, I moved myself from the bed to the chair, without pain or spasm. Everyone in the house was happy. My father gathered them in my room and had us chant *Alhamdulillahi* a hundred and one times on the rosary. It is the Islamic way of thanking God.

I was remarkably happy during the transition into the New Year. I had survived about fourteen months of total paralysis. I could not have believed I could live through such an experience. It was a miracle of my life.

TWELVE

David Alegbeleye

I

Bili came from Ibadan in February to spend Ramadan with us. Seeing the improvements in my situation, he was encouraged to join in my efforts and he offered to give the physical therapy needed. I still feared force on the legs, but I agreed. If I would walk as quickly as I wanted, I knew I had to allow it.

Bili suggested that we buy a herbal ointment from an old woman in the town. Sometime when we were in the primary school, Bili broke his left arm and had been helped by the woman who was said to be an expert on muscles and broken bones.

That was an understatement. This woman was a bone witch. Really, as I later learned, she was a real witch, an elder in the rank of those Baba Akinnu worked for. Though there was always suspicion of witchcraft about women practicing traditional medicine, people often looked at her just as a medicine woman whose prowess had been proven in both famous and ordinary cases in the town. Her witchcraft, a non-malefic family heirloom, was thus not an open knowledge.

When Bili was taken to the woman, she scheduled him for physical therapy, and, using a special ointment, she had returned the arm to normal. The ointment was the mysterious story behind her orthopedic success. It was a unique product of her family and only a single person in every living generation knew its secret formula. This time, it was the woman, and, like any other person of any generation to be in the position, she was never to teach it to anyone else. More strangely, the choice of the next person to inherit the secret was not of anyone alive, not even of the incumbent bearer, and only after the death of one was another selected and taught in a dream.

As Bili now advised, we attempted to contact the woman, to purchase the ointment and receive counsel on treating the legs. But she had died. Her family was still waiting for the next person to be chosen and was only selling the leftover from the ones she made before she died. We bought some and, remarkably, it reduced the morbidity in my joints. It strengthened the muscles and allowed for relative ease in my exercise.

Overall, my health improved and increasing energy returned to my legs. Though my hip joints were not responding to therapy, and it sometimes frightened me to take further steps in the on-going progress, I stubbornly continued to try. If a baby refuses to stand because he is afraid of falling when standing, he will not be able to walk. I wanted to walk, so I must learn to stand.

One day in March I attempted to stand on the legs. I was eager and I thought I could do it. I held on to the backrest of my chair and started with a lot of effort. Both Baami and Bili stood close to me, where they could quickly help me if needed. Little by little, I tried. I crawled and climbed my hands on the backrest of the chair. It was energy-consuming. Sweat streamed down my forehead, but I progressed gradually. I leaned back on my arms, supported at the top of the backrest of the chair, and I finally stood on the legs.

I finally stood on my legs! And almost in the twinkle of an eye, the whole house was in my room to see the development and share the excitement. Again, my father had us chant *Alhamdulillahi* a hundred and one times.

It was such a pleasure to level eyes with people when I talked with them, as if I had never before in my life had the opportunity of standing. The fear of not walking again faded in my heart. Once I can stand, I can walk, and once I can walk, I can make movies. I was so happy and I looked ahead and tried on. It was like a fleshy bone at one end of a tunnel, and I a hungry dog at the other end. I tried on.

Everyday, I stood on my legs for longer and longer periods. The trick was to put more and more weight on the legs and make them resume their responsibility. With time and persistence, it became easier for me and I eventually began to stand directly on the legs while I held onto a four-legged walker in front of me. I kept at it until it became monotonous and I pined to surge up the improvement scale. I now wanted to take steps, at least with one foot. This would be a giant step in my recovery, and one day I made up my mind on it. I transferred my weight more on my arms and the walker. I was a right-side user and I tried the right leg first. It was heavy. Yet, I tried on, sitting down to rest and returning. By the end of the day, I took not just a step but six happy steps. My joy was great.

That spurred me on. I kept on trying. I was like a new baby learning to walk. I walked with the walker back and forth in the room. It was fun, and it reduced the boredom that had grown in my room.

One disturbing awareness, however, was that my hip joints still did not respond to the exercises. They were stiff and could not move apart at all for walking. I only carried each leg as a whole and swerve-walked as if I was made of wood from my hip downward. "That will change for better too," my father assured me, and I continued my exercise.

On the 14th day of April, I woke up with some determination. I wanted to walk to the living room. It was Good Friday and I hoped to enjoy the festival's special shows on TV. The television set was in the living room and I had not set my eyes on it for months. I only heard its sound from my room. It was like a miracle that I could endure the smell of movies all these months whenever my brothers and sisters were watching. Today, I wanted to watch with them.

The Good Friday turned out to be a good one, indeed. Coincidentally, the first movie I saw was the same Christian movie that I saw the last time I watched TV. It was the evangelical horror movie that shook my heart on that November night in 1993 when I could not remain in the living room to finish it. Though the movie was scary, it did not frighten me this time. Rather, the joy of having an opportunity to watch it pleased me.

Since I started to use my hands, I had begun to keep a journal of my experience, and when I returned to my room I gladly picked up my journal and wrote into it. From that day on, I began to walk to the living room at least once a day.

Initially, all the programs on TV fascinated me, because sitting down there and watching the moving images had become novel. But after some time, I became selective. Then later I became bored of the channel, the only one our TV could pick.

***

I began to look forward to walking outside the house. I had glimpses of people passing on the street and it stirred my curiosity further. I wanted to see them better. I wanted to get closer to people outside my house, the only world I have come to know. I wanted to meet new people in the outside world.

Perhaps the day a man's hopes furl, the day he ceases to be. One day early in May, I took a further step in my struggle for recovery. I walked outside the house. Though still within our compound, it was out into the open, my head directly under the sky. The daylight was too bright for me. For a long time it hurt my eyes, but it did not kill the joy of the day. I sat there for hours until it was dark, reveling in the pleasure of seeing both old and new faces. It was so fascinating to see people going about their daily life, as if I had never seen people like this before.

The girls were the most spectacular to betake. In their appearance I could see the passage of time, the transformation of culture. They looked prettier than before I fell sick, more sophisticated, and apparently more conscious of their appearance. I saw the reason my grandmother switched from selling medicines to cosmetics.

I could not have enough of my new world and, every evening before sundown, I went outside to watch people pass back and forth until everyone retired to their homes. I greeted everyone. This was a cultural element I had to adopt in Oyo. The sense of community was so strong that people had respect and concern for one another, at least overtly. Greeting was like a duty and I would be committing a social sin if I did not do it. The first time I lived in the town, I had been too young to be concerned about this, but now I had to begin to learn to blend in. Like in Lagos, urbanization had been eroding this culture from Ibadan and I had been used to the careless attitude of the city, or at least of some parts of the city.

After some time, I began to walk outside the compound and nearer to the street. A tree next to the house offered a good shade and the opportunity to come out earlier in the day. It was at the side of our mosque and it brought me even closer to the people.

The people of Oyo were as gentle as the town itself. It had become a school town, and there were a lot of teachers living there, along with farmers, traders, and transporters. There were many religions, among which Islam and Christianity dominated. There were many churches in our neighborhood, as there were more Christians than Muslims. Most of the church leaders visited me often, and they prayed for me every Sunday at the churches.

Sitting under the tree, I faced the main road that linked the north and the south of Nigeria. The fence of my alma mater, Olivet, was about twenty feet from my seat. It was a distance that one could call 'next door,' though it did not make me punctual when I was in school. Built during my first year in the school, the fence blocked me from directly walking into school and I had to walk about a third of a mile around it to get to the school gate, at least on days I did not feel like jumping over it. It was built for various reasons, but primarily to prevent truancy and keep the boarding house students from wandering into town. I remember sometime before the wall was built, when Brother Akeem was in the school. There was still money in the family and he always had parties every weekend in the boys' quarter. Many of the boarding house students would sneak through the dark farmland to reach our house for the party.

The land was so vast that the school made a good farm of it. The school's founding fathers, Reverend Pinnock and Reverend Locket among others of the American missionaries, met a generous king who gave them such an amount of land than they knew what to do with. Alaafin Siyanbola Oladigbolu gave the land free of charge to the American missionaries. They also founded the Boys Baptist High School at Abeokuta, the school that produced national leaders like MKO Abiola and General Obasanjo, who would rule Nigeria both as a military and civilian president.

Our neighborhood was more reserved and modern than most part of the town. It was named Agodongbo, because it was the part of the town, an outskirt, where the ancient kings' horses were bred in a small house called Ileko. The historical house was still there, a few yards from our house.

The word *agodongbo* in ancient and almost forgotten form of Yoruba language means a stallion. However, the neighborhood only bore the name officially. Many people called it Labamba, by the famous Labamba Hotel situated along its main road. The neighborhood was a projection of the residential district called Araromi, most of whose inhabitants passed by our house going to work or school and coming back home. By this, I had a lot of people to greet and sometimes to chat with.

I had lost my social bearing. My ability to discern people's attitudes and personalities had been dewed by my long period of ostracism and my manners were as rusty as my legs' joints. Naturally, I had not really been socially smart, but I was now socially confused and I had to begin to learn again. Sometimes when people greeted me with phrases other than "sorry", which was the only greeting I had known for months, I became confused and did not know how to reply. Some other times I took ordinary symbolic greetings very literally. For example, when they asked, "How are you?" I wanted to tell them how I really was feeling from my toes to my head, as if they were my doctors who wanted every detail. And when people introduced themselves to me, I did not know how to handle it, and I would not even remember to introduce myself back. I would only nod my head comprehendingly, as if I was being instructed in item identification in a kindergarten book. Sometimes, I replied "good evenings" for "good mornings", and sometimes I smiled widely to cover my loss of what to say in conversations, as if I was just learning the language. In a way, I was like someone who, having lost the faculty of language and was learning again, expected to see dogs and cats from the sky when he heard someone say "It's raining cats and dogs."

Oftentimes, I stuttered and got lost in the middle of my sentences. Though I appeared quick in clearing the rusts and bouncing functionally back into my manners faster than I could on my legs, this problem would persist for years afterward. The most hurtful thing to my psyche, however, was my constant fear of sinning against etiquette by inadvertently saying wrong and hurtful things in conversations. I often thought I did in afterthoughts and it disturbed me.

The sight of girls made me lovelorn. I wanted someone with whom I could share my heart, but I doubted myself able to make a relationship. I did not see myself as possessing the fun that the girls wanted. I had become a kind of idealistic person while they were socially conventional. I had lived too much in my room, in my books, and in my mind to be exciting. Their spirits burned for activities. They wanted to enter the world and go through the motion as they feel the heat of their moments, and not to sit down in a room and under a tree all day. When, eventually, some girls came to give me company, the only thing I could use to induce fun was to talk. Yet, I had very little contemporary topics to talk about, as I was practically new to their society. The current music and musicians they knew were new to me, both Nigerian and American, and the growing trend of video-movies – soon to be known as Nollywood movies - were also novel to me. I knew almost none of the current movie stars. I did not know the current slang-language spoken at the time. I had been completely out of the show and many things were not the same anymore. Although sixteen to seventeen months did not seem much of a time, but these past ones had seen a lot of changes, and, thereby, making me a stranger in my own world.

People in the near and far neighborhood began to notice me. They talked about me everywhere, about "Alhaji's son who has been sick and cannot walk." I was always surprised at places wherefrom the talks filtered to me, and I sometimes winced at people's searching and pitiful eyes. Now I had a new identity; most of them did not know me as the energetic and motivated young man that I was; they knew me as this frail and unhealthy person that they felt sorry for.

II

As I continued to see improvements in my health, it became apparent that the problems in my joints were graver than I thought. Working on the knees and hips was still frighteningly painful. Bili tried hard to improve their condition, but, in the knee, we could not get further than the little room we had achieved early in the year. In the hips, there was no room at all, and the left hip, directly affected by the gunshot, was worse than the other. I feared it might become a job for professional physiotherapists.

After all the past suffering, I wondered why I still had to go through so much pain. Despite all efforts to put them apart, the legs were stuck to one another. I could not stand erect and I could not walk normally. Standing up, I had the shape of an ape-man. A creationist might be tempted to believe in the evolutionary theory and see me as a modern example of how hominids must have been. And when I walked, I looked worse. It was as if my hips were welded together.

Nonetheless, I continued to exercise the legs. If it was exercise that would solve the problem, it was better we did it by ourselves than to have a physiotherapist do it for me. I had developed some sort of phobia for physiotherapists. I devised ways of achieving better results and I doubled the time of my exercises.

Adding to my condition was the disintegration of my relationship with my father, which consequently disintegrated the mutual understanding between us. My father's attitude became so hurtful that it amplified my other problems and tried my filial sensibility. This became the new temptation in my life as I struggled between hating my father and respecting him. Yet, he had always been a loving father, to whom I had especially become indebted.

Attempting to figure out where things went wrong, I suspected two things as responsible: primarily my degenerating relationship with his wife, and then my mother's prolonging absence. I thought both bothered him, though I still thought there might be more to it.

This problem in our relationship affected my treatment and I longed for my mother to come. I hoped I would be able to take care of my situation better with her around. There were treatment bills that my father left carelessly unpaid, and decisions that he ignored, making my treatment hampered and slowed in some way.

I was preparing to walk outside to sit under the tree one day when my father walked into my room to play draft with me. It was a game Americans call checkers, but with 20 pieces of players instead of the 12 pieces in checkers. Before, he often played with me to kill my loneliness and enliven my spirit. Now, he played with me whenever he was not feeling good, and it was to enliven his own spirit instead. But his attitude had poisoned my mind against him, and the events of the past months were demystifying him from the status of a god. I did not like to play draft with him anymore, though I could not overtly refuse him. So, I chose to get back at him through the game.

Against me, he was not a good player, and after I had beaten him in the first few matches, he wanted to leave. But he changed his mind and asked for more matches. I could see that he was worried over some problem and he wanted to use the game to help his mood, but I was not helping him. He became desperate to win just one match before he went out. Sometimes, I wanted to let him win the one match he needed, but an angry part of me would not let me. I was sulky and I intentionally beat him in every match. I used some matches to deliberately worsen his mood. I let the game appear as if in his favor in the beginning, giving him hope of beating me and be happy before he went out, but turned it around to beat him.

Before he picked up his recent attitude toward me, I was always mindful of his feelings. Whenever I saw him in a bad mood and playing draft with me, I would feign seriousness but deliberately let down my moves so he could win and feel better. This had made him believe he was my match, or that he could defeat me if he tried hard. Now that he had worked me in a sour mood, I did not find it easy to take a dive for him. Besides, I wanted to beat him to a frazzle so he could be frustrated and leave me alone. Sometimes, the more he won the longer he stayed, and I did not want him around anymore.

My father was still looking for that one winning match when my mother walked in. She had come again. I was happy to see her and my father smugly waited for what she brought. I saw a new hope for the betterment of my condition and we began a new gear swiftly. However, the gear did not turn out favorably. My father's initial comfort that she had come back quickly faded when he saw the game was not as the first time. This time, she did not agree with my father anymore, and she went by herself in search of treatments for me. Although she paid all the treatment bills I had incurred while she was away, but her new attitude toward my father was "do your part and I would do my part."

Because of the situation between my father and me, I did not mind. I even encouraged my mother. But that was only a first reaction. I did not realize that this was a bad omen for me, and which would make my relationship with my father even worse.

Strangely, when I complained about my father to Mama Pakoyi and expressed my wish for my mother to come, Mama Pakoyi had warned me not to expect a difference. She foretold that things would not be the same whenever she came back, and that she would come back with a problem of her own. My mother had come back to Nigeria with a bad wound on one of her feet, and because she had an illegal immigration status in Saudi Arabia, she got into immigration problems and lost almost all her investments. This frustration influenced her attitude this time around.

My mother went to different places and got me different treatments, medical, traditional, and spiritual, and she burned her money as fast as one would burn paper in flame. Yet, she burned it almost to nothing, as paper to worthless ashes. My father saw this as an unwise defiance, and after about a month or more that she had come, he talked to me about it. My mind softened and I sympathized with him. I discussed it with my mother, but she disagreed with me. Although it was not that I wanted her to stop looking elsewhere for complementary treatments, I only wanted her to cooperate with my father so there would not be any more trouble for me. But the trouble continued to brew. They eventually stopped talking to each other, treating one another like mere acquaintances, and I became stuck in their game.

"It wouldn't cost you a thing to do it, yet it would help me a lot," I had persuaded my mother. But she refused obstinately. And when I tried to persuade her further, we ended up in a loud argument over it, and, in anger, she stopped coming to see me.

It was so unfortunate that my father and mother took up this kind of attitude toward me at this crucial stage of my life, and toward one another. Of course, there might be more to it than met the eye, but I could only look at what met the eye and had more burden on myself. Though I did not want to blind myself to the insidious activities often suggested in my problems, I could not help but to link the events to her disappointment from her early relationship with my father. She did not seem to get over it. To her, I was the only good thing she had come to accept from the relationship, and she was so confused she did not know how to handle her relationship with me. And now, events in my life turned this way.

Something happened in my mother's search for treatment that suggested the possibility of the *more to it than met the eye*, but I did not have eyes enough to see them then. Before my argument with her, she arranged to bring a witchdoctor that someone advised her to try for me. She had been bringing traditional medications from different practitioners, to which my father always called Baba Akinnu's attention for sanction before I would use them. Baba Akinnu never stopped me from using any of them, despite the fact that my father always did not want me to. "She's his mother," Baba Akinnu would say to my father, "Allow her to try her own best too." But there were peculiar differences in the arrangement of this particular witchdoctor that appeared suspicious to Baba Akinnu. First, he asked to come to Oyo to perform some rituals in which he would kill a ram for offerings, and that he would take the intestines back to his place at Ibadan for special use. Baba Akinnu smelled an evil plot, but he warned my father not to object to the plan, that he should give his permission for the man to come. If he was honest, Baba Akinnu stated, he would come and do whatever he wanted. But if not honest, he would not be able to make it.

My father gave the permission, but, surprisingly, the man did not come, despite all the much ado about it. And since he did not come until my quarrel with my mother, he could not come anymore. I learned that my mother had trusted and paid the man heavily, and the way the events turned was a frustration to her, adding to that she let out on me.

Several weeks after, Baba Akinnu explained to me that the man could never come into our town with the intention he had. "He was not coming with a good intention," he had said to me. "He wanted to come to spoil all we've achieved so far. The people behind your sickness were the ones who wanted to use him. The ram was meant to be you; killing it was meant to be an attempt to kill you, and the intestines he would have taken away would only have been yours."

I remembered the earlier disruption of my intestines that had been their modus operandi and I shuddered. It was the primary problem that Mama Pakoyi had tackled, and now these people wanted to take me back to the hell days. I was shocked.

"What about my mother?" I asked, confused over her involvement.

"Your mother is at risk. This was what she did not know as she went about the treatment's stuff the way she had been doing. I appreciate her efforts as a mother, but she was taking advice from people involved in the plot against you without realizing it. She was vulnerable. In some way, your whole sickness and the intention to kill you was partly a war against her, and partly against you. It was a shot for a double goal.

"Now let me tell you something. Don't ever be angry with your mother for any reason." Baba Akinnu continued, "She's being troubled by this same people. Your recent misunderstanding with her was not unconnected with this whole thing going on. Even the wound on her leg was deliberately planned. It was meant to prevent her from coming home at all. They were hoping to isolate you in order to get at you better. Yet, your mother is so impatient that she trudges around carelessly. She thinks she knows those behind it, and she thinks she's avoiding them. But she doesn't know anything and she is only avoiding those who know nothing about this."

True to this, my mother did more disturbing things afterward. She went to Oniyanrin and accused one of her father's wives as the witch behind my sickness. This saddened me. I did not want to think or hear whether the accusation hit the mark or not. Personally I condemned the act as wrong. I thought she should have been patient even if her finding had been true, but that was a word that was far away from my mother's spirit. She was hardly patient. Because she did not like to sulk or keep grudges with people, she was always hasty to straighten out whatever seemed to her as irregularity, always hasty to correct what she saw as wrong, and always going about them wrongly. This was her way of life. Although she was usually not guilty in the circumstances, she often overplayed her cards to turn around to become guilty.

I wanted to ask her and rebuke her for what she had done, but she was so frustrated with the whole situation and angry with me that she never came back to me before she left back for Saudi Arabia.

One day, I called Oniyanrin on the phone and talked with the person she accused. I knew she was just unlucky with my irate mother and I apologized to her. Even though my father had offered to tell me the mastermind behind these problems, I wanted to be objective in the way I handled it. I thought it paid my soul better that way. I was increasingly realizing the complexity of such circumstances, and the ambiguity within them. Knowing and believing that someone did it - even if one was right - might turn around to be inadequate or erroneous if one did not take into consideration certain other elements of our world. Despite my undeniable belief in witchcraft now, the kind of spiritual unfoldment I was having was already influencing my thinking and I could not ignore these elements. Good or bad, God is behind everything that befalls a person, as I have come to understand, yet God does not inflict evil on anyone; He has a purpose for everything.

III

When Bili went back to Ibadan, I became lonely again. I continued my exercises. First thing every morning, as I observed my salat and supplication, I tried to bend and straighten the knees, and to force the hips apart as safely as possible. After this, I would walk outside for my walking exercise and pleasure, and within a short time I would walk back inside to interchange sitting on the chair and lying on the bed until evening. In the evening, I would go back outside for pleasure. I spent hours on every spot I stayed, the same thing every day, and it increasingly became a boring routine for me.

I wanted to make new friends but, somehow, the people made it uneasy for me - though they were unaware of it. The problem was that they were always sorry for me. They looked at me with a *poor boy's* look and that ruined the dignity that I needed to make friends. Although I was later to succeed in overcoming this, and I was even to get many people look up at me, but it was not enough. My desire was to walk as normal people did.

I remembered my libraries often and I missed them. I did not know their value enough when I had access to them. Now in my memory, they became something like an intellectual palace. I surfed through the halls of bookshelves and I was always tantalized by the stockpiles. I was lonely and they teased my thirst.

One day, in the process of my self-education, I became curious about concepts in the Humanities and asked Tunde Adelakun for a volume of their twelve-volume World University Encyclopedia. As a little kid, seeing the books in his father's library, filling up a long row of the shelves, I always wondered why in the playground of a world would anyone waste his money on such big piles of papers with infinite amount of boring words. Now I knew why, and I hungered for the infinite amount of words.

Tunde borrowed me a volume, but rather than have that satiate my curiosity, it only increased it and made me a glutton for more information. When Tunde left back for school, he instructed one of his younger sisters to collect the book from me whenever I finished with it. Instead, however, I used the opportunity to collect more volumes until, without realizing it, I had all of the twelve volumes at my bedside, sleeping with them, waking with them, and reading them back to back. They became the only friends I could turn to, reducing my loneliness and enlightening me as the months rolled by. They informed me on a wide variety of subjects. Everyday I learned about the evolution of civilization from ancient Egypt and Mesopotamia down to the twentieth century world; the history of the slave trade, the American Revolution, the French Revolution, the Russian Revolution, and the African Revolution. I learned about philosophy, science, psychology, and literature; about the human mind, religion, and society; and about the similarities and differences of ancient men and modern men. Scientists, philosophers, and writers became my heroes, and many of my everyday thoughts were about inquiries, discoveries, and intellectual dialogues and debates.

The books greatly helped in the making of a new personality in me, although they could not replace my need for human interaction, and they could not satiate my learning hunger. Rather, they opened my awareness to more and more books that I could not lay my hands on in my present circumstance. It seemed to me that the encyclopedia was one of the greatest inventions of humankind. It was only regrettable to find that the version I had, an American encyclopedia, did not give enough respect to Africa. I did not see in it the name of Sango, the lover king who plaited his hair to show his love for his wife.[32] I did not even see the name of any of the African kings, while it contained the entire European royal lineages. I thought this was an abuse on African history, as I had thought when, in the Guinness Book of World Records, I did not see Abami Eda's unprecedented wedding to 27 wives in a single day and in a single ceremony.[33] The entire amount of words used to discuss Nigeria in the encyclopedia was so paltry and not more than one would use to describe

---

[32] Sango was the known originator of hair plaiting in men. He had surprised his chiefs one day when he appeared at the palace's meeting room with his hair neatly plaited like his wife's; she had done it on him. After his death, his worshippers retained the fashion and it survived to this day.

[33] Fela Anikulapo Kuti, sometimes called Abami eda (a strange being), was an African musician wed to 27 wives in a single wedding ceremony.

the stub of a cigarette. World Encyclopedia, indeed.

Through the process of receiving the books, I became a good friend of Tunde's younger sister, Bola Adelakun, whom he instructed to collect the first book from me. She sometimes came to give me company and overlooked the fact that almost half her father's library now resided in my room. At around this time, also, Wasiu introduced me to a vocation. He was on one of his visits one day and we were outside the house betaking an evening scenery that reminded me of my desire to capture its beauty. I expressed my wish to paint it and my regret at being a poor hand at painting.

"I wish I could paint," I said to Wasiu, "I would have been doing a lot of art works now that I have plenty of time." Then he suggested that I tried poetry. Though I had been reading about poetry, I had never thought to write a poem.

Now, as Wasiu suggested, I tried it, but with many failures. They either did not satisfy him or me, but somehow I arrived at a point at which I liked my work, though at which I could not show it to skilled eyes. I started having a strong liking for poetry, trying to memorize every good one I came across. I learned of fine timeless poems and poets and I developed a taste. I loved mystic and philosophical poems, perhaps vestigial of my first encounters with poetry, the African types, whose enactments were part of normal events of life. In wedding and funeral proceedings, for example, women cried out their joy and sorrow in inartificial poetry. From these, much deep thought flowed. Also, for years after we moved to Oyo, the royal troupe came to our house once every lunar month to sing. In peculiar poesy, the accompanying griot would recount the history of the kings, their heroism, opulence, and their indulgences, while the band beat and danced. Because many of the kings were interestingly philosophical in character, the poetry often offered things to think about.

IV

The month of November changed things remarkably for me. My grandmother left for the United States early in the month to visit my uncle who had twins about a year and half earlier. She came to say goodbye and encouraged me to continue with my exercise.

One day, late in November, I went outside early in the morning to feel the fresh air and to get closer to the world. I loved going out first thing early in the morning to watch students and workers go to their schools and workplaces. Seeing people was better than the mute walls and furniture of my room.

As usual, I greeted everyone that passed by, and they greeted me in return. Then, David walked up the street from Araromi, as all others had been doing. He was dressed in his school uniform and was going to school. Alegbeleye was David's last name, which he pronounced with his British accent as 'Aleblai'. He could not pronounce the consonant 'gb', as also in Oladi*gb*olu, and he misrepresented the last three letters *e-y-e* as the English word *eye*, instead of being pronounced with the 'y' as in *yet*. This was one of the comedies of foreign-born Nigerians when they tried to pronounce their Nigerian names.

Many Nigerians abroad liked to send their children home for 'Nigerianization'. They thought the culture out there was too extreme to be the only one their children were exposed to, and they thought to give them a Nigerian experience would help them a long way. David was one of such children. He was born in England and sent to Nigeria in his mid-teenage to go through his secondary school and be nigerianized. He lived with his family friend, Alhaji Aruna Elewi, an uncle to my old school friend Dotun Aruna. David also called him as 'Uncle'.

David was in his final year at the Saint Bernadine's Grammar School. He had been in Nigeria for five years and, of course, was already eager to go back to London, as most people in his kind of situation felt eager to go back to where they were from. He was the most popular student in the town, a figure of envy to his mates in every school in the town, and of delight to the younger students. My younger brothers often talked about him at home, too.

David lived about half a mile away from our house and we greeted each other as he passed by our house every day on his way to and from school. But today he stopped by to chat a little with me before going on to school. It was our first time talking beyond passing greetings.

"I finished my exams, so I could stay some time to keep you companied before I go to school," he said. I could always do with a company and I thanked him. Then, after the usual talks, familiarizing with one another, he inquired about my health, wanting to know the actual cause and nature of my sickness.

I did not yet feel comfortable talking about my condition, but, for the offer of friendship, I found something to tell him. "I really don't know. The doctors didn't tell me at the hospital, but I later saw it develop into some kind of system breakdown. I lost the use of all my body parts except my eyes, mouth, and fingers."

" I heard it has to do with the *Air Force,*" he pressed on.

How people hear things, I wondered. *Air Force* was a colloquial term used for witchcraft, because the notion was that they work unseen through the air, and some of them fly, incarnated in birds. Sometimes it is said that it is only a place where the wind does not blow that the forces of witchcraft cannot reach. I did not feel comfortable still to talk of my sickness in this sense, but word had gone around the town and people had formed ideas about it. In this environment, people could put two and two together and arrive at an answer, sometimes blinding themselves to the fact that two and two could exist in various forms to make their easy answer wrong. Every culture has its extremities. How such stories begin to circulate, one may never know. Rumor is always an orphan. I did not want to lie to my new friend, but I did not want to pursue the topic either.

"You seem to have heard a lot," I joked and then answered him with a tone of finality. "Somehow, it appears so, but I don't think I know for sure."

He felt pity for me, and that was the only time he was unable to hide the feeling. We dropped the discussion about the sickness and went on to other things. He knew enough about sorcery and he liked to hear about it and experience it as real rather than as in fairy tales, as he had often heard in England. To many people outside our world here, it was something of a fantastic wonder, a kind of wonder upon which the likes of Harry Potter thrive, and among whom were the skeptics. But, even though David was still a British boy, he was no longer the type that would be too thrilled by Harry Potter. In the little time he had been in this town, he had had direct experiences and has known the real thing from its fiction. As one story went, he had been struck with a voodoo ring before, and the experience was enough to make him believe and fear it as real.

Of course, that was too much an experience for someone who had only been in the country for five years. Even here in this environment, many people live full lifetimes without having such a close encounter with voodoo. They would only hear stories about witchcraft, of which many might be inflated or not true. As David's story went, he had been fighting some boys who cheated a small girl at a students sports gathering at the local stadium when it happened. Because David was a legendary student among the body of students in the town, the news spread and I heard the story from my younger brothers on the evening it happened. They had narrated that the boys were many, while David was the only one heroically fighting them. He was said to be beating them and the crowd was cheering him, until one of the boys, with the voodoo ring on, hit him on the shoulder. Then David fell into spasmodic seizure, sprawled on the floor and made foams from his mouth. Everyone thought he was going to die and the crowd screamed and got into a pandemonium.

This part, David himself explained to me one day:

"I knew I couldn't afford a slack among the guys. I didn't know how many they were; they were a gang and were just coming from different directions. So I put a lot of energy behind every blow, and that put anyone I hit out of the fight. But they kept coming, though I wasn't afraid. You know, everyone was cheering me – that gave me more strength and I just went on. One of the guys hit me with a big stick. I wrenched it out of his hand. I was so mad that I didn't feel the pain. I used the stick to put more of them away until it broke. It was like in a movie. Then one guy just appeared right in front of me. I raised my fist to punch him in the face, but he just tapped me on the shoulder and I felt my whole energy leave my body. I didn't realize I was falling and I had my fist up until I landed with my back on the floor…

"They said the boys were *oja* boys (boys from a market neighborhood called o*ja*, literally meaning market). I feared them from that day on. Really, they don't know how to fight; they rely only on voodoo... There was a guy I knew there who used to have head butts with real rams! He used voodoo on his head to toughen it to fight. I was there at *oja* one day and I saw him knock down strong rams with his head... Believe me, I have seen things in this town."

On that day, David fell and shook violently on the floor with foams coming through his mouth. People thought he was going to die, and, in fact, the news later spread around that he had died. He was rushed to a hospital, but the doctors could not save him. He was eventually revived with an *ero*, a de-charm, brought by another guy from *oja*.

The event, however, added to David's fame in the town. During the next public event in which he first appeared to the people after the fight, he came out to mime to an R. Kelly sexy song at a public schools gathering. He came on the stage, holding the microphone, and said: "The ghost is back." He had them all thrilled, the girls screaming for him as usual.

On the morning of our first meeting, we talked about a lot of things: girls, movies, music, and novels. I had been reading some James Haedley Chase's novels around the time; captivated by his spellbinding storytelling, I hoped David could get me some of his books. But I did not know yet that David did not have much time for pleasure reading. His sister read the only Chase's novel he remembered to him at bedtime when he was a little boy in London. He promised, instead, to bring me magazines.

Throughout the time that we spent together in the town, David did not bring the magazines. But he brought me plenty more important things, and that made us forget about the magazines. David changed the way I was living at the time. He brought me a new era. He enlivened the dull sick corner of the world that I was, as he brought there to me all what constituted his world at the time, both his reality and his legend. That was for a friend he saw in need. He took me as his best friend and older brother, giving me respect more than anybody in his world, and I thought I owed plenty to him.

V

My place became David's second home and he only went to his apartment to sleep at night. He leveled me up to date in movies and movie news got through the satellite TV hooked up in his house by his wealthy uncle.

David had many friends, men and women, and he began to invite them for me to meet new people. He did not want me to feel I was sick and incapacitated, and he was successful, as no one else could surpass. Although not entirely, because nobody but myself could really make me not feel sick and incapacitated. I continued to long to walk. For my career, I pined to walk, and sometimes, rather than take comfort in David and his friends, I envied them, as they did everything on their legs while I could not. They played basketball in the front yard of our house, they went to school, they went to parties and - I had not forgotten – they dated girls. All these reminded me poignantly of my present incapability and I wanted to overcome it. I often remembered bitterly that I used to do all these in the good old days, when even I took them for granted. They were now precious to me, almost like it would be to an old man who is so much enamored with his fancy of being a youth again. Mine was sadder, for I had not yet had much written on my youth's slate.

Envy, they say, is an agent of evil. Though I sometimes envied David and his friends, I was never green with it. I had come to believe that sometimes envy was normal, and perhaps necessary. The envy that I felt never raised the slightest ill feeling toward anybody; it only added vigor to my desire and effort to walk again. It spurred me on and David also helped me on, oftentimes giving a hand in my physical exercise.

One Saturday morning, David suggested that I take a longer walking exercise. "Maybe it's more walking exercise that your legs now need," he said to me. "You never know, maybe by long walking exercise all the tight places will loosen up and you'll get back on the block again."

With the aid of my walker, we set off toward Araromi. It was a very sunny day and I felt frail on the road. After having been hidden away for several months, the sun was glad to have a taste of me. Everyone we met greeted me in a poor-boy manner and prayed for me. They had an ample opportunity to see me walk. Before, I only slinked out and into the house when no one was passing by, embarrassed of how I walked.

Little by little, we ate the road, stopping at short intervals to wash it down with a drink, until we reached a row of shops at the gates to the Adelakuns' compound. It was about a tenth of a mile from our house and I thought it was enough. Walking with the walker, I rested heavily on my hands, and my shoulders and arms were already aching. And I had used up more energy within an hour of the exercise than I used to do in about five or more days.

The next day, David brought me his video player. I was overwhelmed. I had not watched video in two years. There used to be a video recorder in every living room of our house, but since they had broken down, my father had not seen any need to replace them. The only movie David had was "The Black Rain", with Michael Douglas and Andy Garcia. I watched it first, and then we turned to a video club, renting about two to three movies a day.

David soon realized that I was lovelorn, and one day, he asked me, "Maybe I should get a girl for you, Rahman. Do you mind?"

"No, I don't want one." I surely wanted one, but I was used to getting my girls by myself and my ego would not take for someone to look for a girl for me. It would seem to me as if I was admitting to a state of personal weakness, by which I could not get a girl for myself. Moreover, I thought that any girl that followed David home would want him, and not someone who was just learning to walk like a baby. Many times he repeated the offer, and, at each time, I refused and we laughed it off.

David was handsome and strongly built. Like a model sculptured in the fashion of Michelangelo's *David*,[34] he looked like someone contesting for Mr. Somewhere. He was light in complexion and had a grace to his walking, all which attracted girls toward him, and among whom he had a steady rectitude girlfriend. I was in my room watching a movie one afternoon when David came with the girl. She was light-skinned, petite, and stunningly beautiful.

"Meet Rahman," David said to the girl, who shyly genuflected to greet me. "Rahman, meet Ruka."

He had talked about the girl several times and I needed no further introduction. Besides, I could see in her face a copy of her father's face. She was one of the daughters of the incumbent Alaafin. This was not the first time I met Ruka. I attended her birthday party held at the palace three years earlier, but because of the war between our fathers, and the fact that I did not live in the town, we did not have the chance to know each other well.

David left her with me so we could get to know each other better. He hoped that, with my relationship with the girl, I could influence her to reinforce her feelings toward him. Undoubtedly, David loved her. But by my getting closest to David, and eventually close to Ruka, I could see the natural incompatibility between them, at least for the moment. David had enough of youth-liberty and exuberance to see Ruka's rectitude as too straitlaced, and she had too much of love to blind her from David's restless heart. She was a Juliet, but David was too out there to be a Romeo, although he appreciated her true love and wished it was always there for him. Nonetheless, I tried all I could to keep them together, with his flightiness making it difficult.

In December, David went to Lagos for a three-week holiday. He told two of his school friends to visit me regularly so I would not feel lonely. My old friends were also in town for the Christmas and New Year holiday, and I had a nice time.

***

Nineteen ninety-six began, like 1995, with the hope of being rid of the sickness in the year. Some old school friends came to visit me during the transition holiday, many of whom I had not seen since I left school six years earlier. They were all surprised and embittered to see me in my condition. Those who had seen me just before the sickness could not believe I was the emaciated figure they were looking at. Though I had gained some flesh and looked better, it was still unbelievable to them that I could not walk. Not only did they feel sorry for me, they realized they had to thank God for their own situation. For whatever trying situation they were in, as life is wont to create, they knew that what they were looking at was far worse.

---

[34] The Renaissance artist Michelangelo Buonarroti rendered a sculpture of David, the slayer of Goliath.

Although they would not say this in my face, I saw it in their silence and manner, just as I saw it in the face of everyone who visited me at this period. I was a symbol of one of the worst things that could happen to a human being, and only a fool would see me and not thank God for his or her situation. Perhaps, this was one of the reasons the Heavens put me through the travail: to stir people out of their indulged vain pursuit of the material world, and into thinking about themselves beyond the deluding limits of their ego. Perhaps it was to make people humble themselves, think, and accept whatever condition they were in and appreciate the truer nature of reality. Perhaps this was true, but what I did not yet understand was why I had to be the Grecian 'scapegoat' to symbolize this ignorance of humanity. Why I had to be the Jesus crucified for the sins of the world, I did not know; I only could hope I resurrect for another opportunity.

Some of my friends were born again Christians and we often ended the visiting sessions with prayers, vigorous prayers as their minds felt, as if for their friend's tragedy to be miraculously transformed in the instant. "Youth time doesn't come twice," one of them prayed one day, "God, let our friend get well quickly and use the prime time the way it should be used, and not as chained down as he is now."

And chained down, really, was I, like the poor dog missing the bones and the bitches. Only I wished I was not like those waiting for slaughter. I was already missing a crucial social participation and development of my youth time, and I might later have difficulty fitting back in. This was supposed to be the period between my late adolescence and early young-adulthood, a transitional period that is so crucial in the development of a human life. But I had been made different, and, fortunately or unfortunately, different for life. I was no longer like every other kid, and perhaps I would never be like every other man.

I was hungry, very hungry to get back on the social block. It was a paradise of its own and I craved for it. My quiver was still full of arrows, and I needed to go to the field to make the shots. I watched friends and other people come and go, and I envied them, while my arrows seemed to be rusting away.

I had lost track in the knowledge of social development, especially of my generation and the successive one, a development that seemed to have taken a jump while I was on bed. It is a good knowledge of life to keep track of the cognitive development of, at least, one's own generation. I was now alien to the current fashion of language, clothes, and mannerisms of my generation. In only two years hiatus, teenagers have become worldlier than they had been in the past. I was stunned, almost out of my mouth, when some teenagers surprised me with their sexual, interpersonal, and environmental affairs; it seemed so immoral that it seemed to me a psychological complex. It was a kind of affairs that was characteristic of old uneducated women and men of my understanding before the time of the sickness; now it was something common in their lives. Rape, love charms, extortion charms, sexual intrigues, and many others of such were all what teenagers' affairs were now made. And these were mostly students under eighteen. It was like I had been away for 30 years.

Also, before I fell sick, the manners of dressing would clearly distinguish the educated youths from the uneducated ones, but now there was hardly any difference between them, and an alien like me had to begin to learn to distinguish between them. But it was more difficult to do because our failing educational system had made their languages and mannerisms almost indistinguishable as well. Except for a few university students, many so-called educated youths now spoke and behaved like their uneducated counterparts. With money prominently becoming the only goal of their pursuit, there was hardly any difference between the school and the street. Whenever I spoke in English with some of them who claimed to be in school, I had to carefully select my words, lest they would be lost.

Stories of advanced cultism on campuses seemed to me as in American mafia movies. I could not help but to wonder how our future political and economic scenes would then be like. Perhaps, like the old-time Sicily. The campuses were already near Sicilian replicas.

Interestingly, as typical of any remarkable period in history, Renaissance to Enlightenment, Romantic to Modern eras, these extreme behaviors retroactively produced a new religious attitude on the other end, though sometimes as if equally extreme in the other end. The universe is an interesting phenomenon; it seems always trying to keep itself at a balance. In spite of the government's secularist expulsion of God from schools in the 1970s, which many blamed for the decadence of subsequent times, God had inevitably been springing back from within the walls of campuses. More often one would see born again Christians and the new Muslim Brothers and Sisters dotted around the schools - the chagrin of the illusion of the sociological world we create. The Enlightenment[35] leaders of the world who separated religion from the state, of course, may have been commendably smart in bringing the attention of the world to the despicable running of the state in the hands of religious leaders, but they also had not created a perfect world. They have only run to the other extreme. Perhaps, then, the truth that needs be realized is that God and man, religion and the state, faith and reason, are too much interrelated than could be separated as such. In this case, it is only our misunderstanding of them that must have been misleading us over the centuries, blinding us from one extreme to the other. I wonder whether there can be anyone in the world who would not live by one faith or another, in God or humanity, theocracy or democracy, sentiment, intuition, or reason. Rather than be something characteristic only of religion, faith seems elementally psychological, basic to life, and perhaps its absence would only be the absence of life. Then, in the name of something else more fashionable to

[35] European intellectual movement of the 17th-18th century by which celebration of reason was used to revolutionize religion, art, philosophy, and politics. It was a period that produced secularism and led to the separation of Church and State.

the time, the leaders of the Enlightenment period and their modern secular successors may have been doing the same thing of which the religious leaders had been guilty. I wonder whether secularity or the state is not only another form of religion competing in the conflict for religious or ideological supremacy in the world.

Every conflict, however, is a challenge for development, an opportunity for synthesis of the good parts of the conflicting sides. In this case, the beauty of this God-state conflict may be for us to realize that we are in control, whether in our religious affairs or state affairs, or in control more than we think we are. Perhaps we are responsible in the creation of the world more than we realize. Afterall, we create our sociological world. Perhaps, then, those leaders in the past should have learned better before sentencing God to exile for the misdeeds of His so-called followers. Perhaps we need to learn that humanity and divinity are two sides of a coin. No wonder, in all these years, religion has not gone away in the affairs of the states, even in the West, and their conflict has persisted. Perhaps we need to learn better to understand that we may not need to eliminate God from public life. At this stage in my life, it was interesting to begin to see that in most arguments, when the sides are conflicting, it is not really because they essentially differ, but because they do not understand themselves enough to understand one another.

I craved to be up and have direct experience of all these activities and phenomena going on in the world. My cut off from the media also worsened my situation. My radio set had long broken down, the only channel on our TV set was of a zombie station, and I saw newspapers and magazines once in a blue moon, after their news had long become history. It was in bits and pieces that I heard of the state of affairs in the country's political scene. The kernel of all the news being that Chief Abiola, the winner of the last presidential election, had been locked up and Nigeria was now being ruled by Abacha. They often said he was a potential Idi Amin,[36] throwing fears into people's lives with spates of bombings and assassinations. Many human and political rights activists had fled the country, while many others in jail and on the streets lived with uncertainty of their tomorrow. Apparently, it was the worst chapter in the history of Nigeria and I was shut away from keeping adequate track of it.

But I always shook the pressure off my mind and took my life as it was. This way, I could keep track of my own unitary life, so as not to lose my head along with the time I was losing. This was my destiny and I had to keep track of it. If you do not stay ahead of destiny, or, at least, alongside with it, it drags you along, and it could be disagreeable at times. This was my philosophy. I saw destiny as a dynamic phenomenon; it has to be in constant motion, and sitting down and worrying about life without acting toward something positive would only aid its viciousness. It would not even take "*I've been sick*" for an excuse. It is no respecter of anyone,

---

[36] Reference to the evils of the Ugandan regime of General Idi Ami.

except those who respect it and run along. This is Nature in its non-sentimental nature.

Sometimes, however, as I ran to stay with my destiny, I could not help but wonder whether this was really my destiny, or how this came to be my destiny. Though I thought I was understanding the flexibility and dynamism of destiny and the fact that God is good; still, from my reasoning, the sickness seemed to be a preordained destiny. It seemed a fixed fate already waiting in time for me. Afterall, I often thought, there had not been much difference between my character and the characters of most people in my age group. There had been no failing in my character to the average character of people in my age group, and yet I had this destiny that showed a vast difference between my fate and the average fate of people in my age group. By this, I pondered over the old concept of destiny I had always believed, that everything had been predestined. Although I also used to believe that prayer changes destiny, but I seemed to be facing a possible fact that my prayer had not changed this waiting sickness. If all had been predestined by God, then I am afraid certain innocent people are perhaps doomed despite any effort they make – innocent people like Job, like me. In such a direction of thought, it is obvious that even Judas could not have helped the situation but to be the unfortunate betrayer and to suffer its damnation for some 'Word of God' to be proved true.

If this was my destiny, how come I have such a destiny? I still asked. Is it God that just imposes this on me, as a dictator imposes jail terms on his antagonists? But, in my own way, I have always been a lover and worshipper of God. Even though I had been seeing myself as a deliberate contributor responsible in my experience, I still sought to know how it all fit together in one world and in the context of our conventional religion.

With such a perceived disparity and arbitrariness in destinies, God's much-preached quality of impartiality would be shaken in one's heart. One day, during a bitter argument with my father, I accused him of being unjust by partially attending to the needs of some other children (his wife's) and ignoring mine. He looked at me and said: "Even the God who made us is not just." This was his belief and, rather than a disrespect to his much adored God, it was meant to stop me from questioning his judgment. He was the father; God was God, and neither had to be reasonable. That was the message; although, immediately after he said it, he regretted being that blunt. Most people feel this way, only too afraid of God to say it, or even to think about it. Some would rather blame it on life and say, "life is not fair," while on the other hand they believe it is God who creates and governs the life - perhaps an indirect way of placing the blame at His giant feet.

I always remembered something I read in the "Time" magazine during the 1990 Gulf War. An Arab woman, in condemnation of what appeared to her as the Western view of destiny, was reported as saying: "They in the West, they believe their destiny is in their hands, but we believe our destiny is in the Hands of God." This was a dynamic reflection of the conflict between the two intellectual schools I learned about called determinism and indeterminism, between the fatalistic religious devotees and the modern rational or scientific liberals, between the *ways* of the East and the *ways* of the West. Although Yoruba tradition seems to have a solution between these, claiming that a person's destiny is what he had chosen for himself in heaven before coming into the world. Thus it gives determinism an interesting indeterministic cloak, and fatalism a free-choice ground. But this view has been diminishingly influenced by the way the modern Muslims and Christians view destiny since the advent of Islam and Christianity in our culture. This way, we have been torn between the two famous religions of the world, between the East and the West, and we are left to pitch our tents in the conflict, widening and perpetuating the conflict of two apparently different civilizations.

Finding my life on such a critical pedestal, the conflict of these worldviews worried me. And, seeking for which would explain my experience consolatorily enough, I found that they might not really be conflicting. The truth of many things in our natural world might not be as they appear, and sometimes not exactly as they appear.

Many people are in doubts, too many people than could be imagined. Many of us are only sweeping the questions under the mat, and the attitude of *you-question-too-much* is not helping. For me, in the situation that I now saw myself, of my soul as partly or wholly responsible for my circumstance, I saw this attitude as a fear of looking into the mirror, a fear of finding the truth about oneself.

These, of course, are not new questions to the universe, and God must have been well acquainted with them, perhaps even before He created us. We only tease and beg the questions, evading them with our smattering religious doctrines to ease ourselves of the burden of proof. But we hurt our souls that yearn to let us become aware of the truth. The angels must have been sick of the hokum movies that we play on top of the soil, in which our heroes and heroines run away from battlefields. An interesting dramatic irony, they may be saying.

At the end of the day I always continued to believe in God and have faith that one day things would go my way. This comforted me. Doubting the 'Word of God', which many people and preachers color with their own sentiments, was no longer a question of sin to me. Experience has made it my culture, and a path that may eventually show me the truth, or a clearer truth. Abraham began his religious career by doubting the polytheistic doctrines of his time, and so did Prophet Muhammad. Like my father, Abraham did not even think his Lord as perfectly just when He planned for the destruction of Sodom and Gomorrah; only he did not quietly accept it as my father did, and he engaged his Lord in a catechuic argument over it.

Even though the concept of destiny was not yet clear for me to strengthen my faith for the better, I had enough hope to forge on. As I thought about those whose lives appeared arbitrarily better than mine, I thought about those whose lives appeared arbitrarily worse. And from all I have learned about my predicament and survival, sometimes I thought I did not have a cause to feel unhappy. God had juxtaposed the circumstances closely enough that I could not help but to consider the good part of my story as I did the sad part, and at the end of the day this was where I often got my consolation.

I became unsatisfied with just my Arabic recitation of the Qur'an. I wanted to know the meaning of what I read, with the hope of learning the ways of God better. I borrowed an English version of the book from a friend and embarked on the spiritual journey. I read first the chapter prescribed for prayer by my father and Mama Pakoyi, and it was surprising to find the story of three men who had a brief nap in a cave. As with my hiatus, they had woken up three hundred years later in real time, and to a world they did not recognize anymore.

VI

My friends went back to their schools and David returned from his vacation. We filled my time with activities that kept boredom away. The priority was on my exercise, and David produced a part of the motivation. He always urged me to step up onto a higher stage of walking. When I walked, he would hit his shoulders against mine to challenge my balance for a stronger balance. Sometimes he would throw obstacles in my way and ask me to walk over them. "Don't be lazy. Walk over them. Conquer them." He would say and hurried to my assistance whenever I had difficulty.

We often joked about the way I walked. "Like something in a robot movie," David would say. Whenever friends were waiting outside for me, he would escort me from my room, but would quickly run ahead to announce my arrival. Bowing and gesturing in my direction, he would say, "Ladies and gentlemen, it's a great honor to present - the Robocop."

With an increase in the rate of my exercise, I eventually dropped the walker and moved on to using a walking cane. The prospect looked bright and we were happy. But an unfortunate event occurred in February that influenced my situation in the house. Because my grandmother was away, I was absolutely at the mercy of my father's wife's kitchen. I got into another quarrel with her and it led to a clash between me and my father. Everyone blamed me, and, learning from it, it became the last time I would ever quarrel with her.

"You need to be very patient," Baami said to me. "You are a man and you should behave like a man. There are times in life that you'll have to overlook what you see as irregularities and injustice and learn by them... If you had listened to my words, this wouldn't have happened. I've been telling you in a long time that sometimes patience is simply foolishness. But that foolishness, at such a time, is wisdom. You have to act foolish to get yourself through this predicament, and not be judgmental. Judging will only get you into more problems, and you already have more than enough."

This had me burning inside. I found it objectionable to be blamed for what happened and I sent for my father's sister, whom I had sent for during the period of the physical therapy. Baami's words were not enough to calm my temper. Though I was an emotionally hot person, ready to steam at the slightest friction, I thought her wrongs were too obvious for anyone to blame me for. I thought everyone was only afraid to confront my father and his wife with the truth because they were the master and mistress of the family.

I told my aunt everything as it happened, how I saw I had been offended and how I had reacted. I expected her to see the wrongs clearly and vindicate me. But she only spoke to me as Baami had done, enjoining me to be patient.

"Patience is what you need," she said, "And patience could seem as foolishness at times, but it is the only thing that pays. When necessary, you stoop to conquer. You act foolish to get what you want. It would only be for a short time. Endure everything that appears to you as wrong. Concentrate on your recovery and your freedom. Don't burden yourself with this kind of things, and by the grace of God you'll get well and move on with your life."

Then, it sank into me and I accepted gratefully. My temperament was undergoing the toughest trial so far in my life, and I was faced with a tough task of taming it, as done with wild animals to be domesticated. It was as if all these were a trial for me. I had made the confrontation so that things could be smoothened, so that my father or Baami could iron things out. I saw my father's wife as a friend who was only misbehaving and needed to be brought back on the right track, so our innocent relationship could remain and improve. Now I realized that I had been too naive to expect perfection, too naive to expect such ironing out as the only right thing to do. It is now I realized that such ironing out is so simple a remedy in such a circumstance that it could result into complex troubles, because our home was not a simple home, but a complex one.

Nonetheless, our relationship could not continue to be innocent anymore, because we were no longer innocent to one another. She saw me as someone making things difficult for her in the house, and I saw her as someone making things difficult for me in the house. We were both inexperienced and the difficulty continued, though only for a short time. Even though patience was a difficult thing for me at this stage, I realized I needed it for my inter-personal relationships. I needed to suppress my ethical perfectionism, and I began by being insouciant. Sometimes foolishness is wisdom, and I realized I had to be patient. Really, anyone in a polygamous home needs more patience in a day than one in a monogamous home needs in a thousand days, and anger may be terribly destructive if unbridled. Simplicity led me into the fracas, but this simplicity, as I later came to understand, may be ignorance.

With this new attitude, I learned to see my father differently. I saw him as someone in a difficult situation whenever there was a fight between his wife and his child, as it often happened between her and many of us. Although it was a difficulty that came with the lifestyle he had chosen.

***

I began to feel my grandmother's absence stiffly. The people in charge of her shop were supposed to send me food supply, as she had arranged for, but things had not been the same with the shop since she left. My feeding became erratic and far too short of what I needed, and it affected my exercise. Mutual understanding increasingly degenerated between me and my father, and he now dealt with me as if I was partly independent, having little to do with me.

A few people in my neighborhood sometimes offered me money, which I was always hungry enough to want to take, but proud enough to reject. Two of them were a compassionate couple who also wanted me to accept Jesus Christ as my Lord and Savior along with their money. Although I always thanked God that they always forced the money on me, but I always asked myself, "Do I look hungry?" That was how bad my situation was.

I tried to hide this from David at first, but he saw it and offered to share his own supply. I eventually took myself as partly independent, as my father took me, and, to stay alive, I turned to pawning my possessions.

THIRTEEN

Nike

I

My grandmother called on the phone one day and told me of how remarkably good medical treatment was in the United States. She had the opportunity of witnessing it and she was so impressed that she wished for me to be treated there.

"If you would have to go to the hospital for the rest of the treatment, it would be in America," she had said, "The doctors are so good and there are good facilities." She encouraged me to remain patient and hopeful.

"Keep on exercising the legs and let's see how they would be over some period," Uncle Jibola also said to me, "Whichever way, don't worry, we'll find something to do about it."

Though there were many opportunities in this, what came to my mind most was beginning my career in America. My relative freedom had granted me the freedom to dream again. I tried harder on my exercises, hoping the legs would improve and even make the plan easier. I concentrated on the hips. They were my main problem now. If I could have a little free movement in the joints, I hoped it would be easier to improve upon them. I increased the time and effort for the walking exercise, and, rather than go outside to just sit down, I constantly walked around. And it was during one of these walking exercises one afternoon in March that I met a young girl passing by our house. I had seen her a few times before, but she had never looked toward my side, as if I was never there. This time, however, she took a glance at me as I was stealing one on her. Our eyes met briefly and she greeted me. Though surprised that she did, I returned her greeting and she walked away toward Araromi. This encouraged me to try to talk to her.

In the evening, I saw her coming back from afar and I turned to face the road so I could greet her again. I prinked myself up. My heart lurched as she approached. This time she ignored my side. Perhaps she had greeted me mistakenly at first, but I decided to greet her then.

"Hello," I said to her. She had already left me behind on her way.

"Oh, good evening." She stopped and walked back to me as she continued talking. "You see, I've been seeing you sitting here but I didn't know there was any problem with your legs until I saw you walking with a cane this afternoon. I'm so sorry. What caused it; automobile accident?"

Spontaneously, I salted my language with some grace. "Oh no, not an accident. I have only been grounded by a small illness and I'm just getting over it. It kept me on bed for some time while my legs were out of work in the period. So, I now have to take some time to re-activate them to return to their normal state. It is nothing much of a problem anymore (as if it wasn't). How are you, by the way?"

"I'm fine. Each time I passed by here, I wondered what this cute young man is doing at this same place all the time. It never crossed my mind that it was something like this. I'm so sorry. My name is Nike."

"I'm Rahman, and it's very kind of you to have wondered about me."

We got into conversation for about half an hour before she left. Her name was Nike Babatunde. She had just finished secondary school at Ibadan, and came to Oyo to prepare and re-sit for her school certificate exams that was about three months away. She had been here for about four months and she lived with her sister's family, about a hundred yards away from our house. Their apartment was part of the Akinboye's Estate, owned by Banji's father.

Proportionally, I told her a few things about myself, and she closed the meeting with a promise to visit me the following day. I watched her walk away. She was slim, dark in complexion, and attractive. The nature of the meeting forecast the kind of relationship we were journeying into and it filled me with pleasure. She was very effusive and her eyes sparkled at me, making me feel I had a strong impression on her. And she had a good overture that was to welcome me into her world.

David was eager to meet her, and as we sat under the tree waiting for her the next day, I felt happy that I would have a balanced family - a good friend and a good girlfriend. When one has a good partner, one has a degree of confidence, perhaps. I was already feeling the confidence - the sense of a more completeness. I had known the value of a *good* girl in the life of a man and I was ready to treat this opportunity right.

Nike arrived just a little before 4 o'clock in the evening. Clad in a black mini skirt and a blue blouse, she approached us in a careful elegance, typical of first dates. It was like a date for us. I took a furtive side-glance at David to see what he made of the sight, but he was inscrutable.

Nike greeted me warmly and, as she sat beside me, gave a brief 'hi' to David. It was condescending, the way a class-conscious lady would say to her little sister's boyfriend when she passes by them in the living room. David did not like it, and he replied in like-manner. I hoped it was only a first meeting bashfulness between strangers and I quickly introduced them to one another. She managed to say "hello" in a manner a little better, but with a smile that was reminiscent of the religious sermon that teaches that it is "good to give in charity what one has, even if only a smile." David did not return the 'charity' smile; he only nodded in acknowledgment, with an invulnerable countenance now deliberately worn to belittle her presence. Then he rose and announced his leave.

That was the beginning of friction in my friendship family. David, a princely figure who saw his worth in the eyes of girls, and his command in the response of boys, could not be more hurt. Girls had turned out a star-like ego enough in him, many of them filled with crushes for him. Nike, on the other hand, was a city girl, hoity-toity, and somehow discriminatory against the “local” culture of the town. Hence, it was a clash of egos, and as they contended, dishonoring their first meeting, I knew it was an ill omen for me.

Our relationship leapt from flirtation and into a blossoming love affair, despite their disapproval of one another’s friendship with me. Some good news was that Nike often visited me in the morning when David was in school. Nonetheless, I sometimes lamented on my luck. How fine would it have been if these important persons in my present life could be friends? Perhaps, it is hard to have a perfect situation in life events. I tried all my best to make them like each other, but it was all in vain.

Things became difficult for me when they began to express their dislike for one another whenever they met at my place. Though I tried to make their hatred for one another not sully my relationship with either of them, but when David bordered on extremity, it tried our friendship. He would burst out into scornful laughter when the girl was talking with me, and some other times he would gawk at us, make teasing eyes and smile sarcastically.

"Stop this nonsense," I would say to him after the girl had gone, more of an appeal to him than a warning.

"Can’t I laugh because some bitch is here?" he would say to me. "Besides, she was lying to you all this while. I can't help but laugh when she fills your head with lies like that. She’s not the kind of girl she’s pretending to be.”

One day, after an argument over the girl, David added, “Do you want me to stay out of your room whenever she’s here?"

"Yes, stay out for her. Do all your laughter outside when she’s here," I replied angrily. I did not know whether this was right for me to do or not, but it was painful having to shut my best friend out for my girl.

"Okay, I'll do just that,” he replied, “But I'll keep telling you to forget about that bitch. If you want a girl, I'll bring you a decent girl. And even if you just want to fuck, I'd get you a pay bitch. A hundred naira would be enough and she'll give you a run for the money. Pay bitches are better than this girl."

The only time they said any word to each other was that first day they met, when they greeted one another dishonorably. I needed both of them, so I tried to play on with blinders on, though my blinders was weak. My household had no problem with Nike and I thought that was enough.

***

I continued to make more friends in the neighborhood, from near and far. Although most of them could not come around regularly, I knew no loneliness anymore. I was only eager to walk. I met the rest of David's family, his uncle's children, nephews, and nieces. It was interesting how I made friends now: rather than have a close friend or two in a family, everyone in the family became my close friend, including the parents and the little children. I met and knew many families like this and it also gave me a broader opportunity to get more books, even more than I had time for. I became choosy, browsing through blurbs to select which book to read now. Subject books, plays, and novels all littered my room, and I in turn became a source of books to other readers. I became a middleman, like a librarian, receiving books from around and circulating it around. And, like in a book club, I sometimes had discussions with my friends.

My relationship with Nike blossomed, and it gave me its own degree of satisfaction and happiness. She sought assurance of my love often and I gave her more often. I was head-over-heel in love with her. Although Cupid did not need to waste his arrows, as I was prepared to love almost anyone, but I still thought that Nike loved me enough to make my affection strong for her. And she knew it.

II

Someone broke into David's apartment and looted his belongings, amassing into thousands of naira loss. He suspected a boy in the neighborhood, but he had no proof against him. He went to the boy's house, found nothing, yet he believed, as most people did, that it was the boy who broke into the apartment. They believed that the boy had taken everything to Lagos, where he sometimes lived, so they would not find it on him here in Oyo.

This troubled David so much that he wanted to give all he could to have his property back. But David's orientation had changed; he had adapted to the African way of thinking. He reported the theft to the police, but he did not think that to rely solely on the police was wise enough. He might have to wait till Judgment Day before he would ever see a trace of his stuff. Apparently, there was no sector in the country left unscorched by the misadministration of the country. The police force was cash-strapped and demoralized, and David knew he would have to part with bribes but with nothing to show for it. So, he hoped to get his possessions back by another means: by voodoo.

David had been so influenced by his experiences with voodoo in the town that he believed he could get his things back if he went to the right people. There was an experience that stood out in his mind. His uncle ran a movie theater, and one day some people stole one of its film projectors and some other property from his house. When his uncle raised an alarm, someone offered to help him get back the stolen property without involving the police. Of course, his uncle did not intend to rely on the police; after all, he had a police station in front of his house, while his house was still robbed. A voodoo charm was set up, casting a spell over the unknown thieves, and within a short time, the thieves brought back the loot with their own hands.

This amazed David, and now it sparked his hope to look for the person who did the magic for his uncle. But the person was no longer in town. This disappointment did not stop him, nonetheless. He searched further and got into the hands of a voodoo man who collected two thousand naira from him. But he did not see his property and he did not see the thief. There were so many quacks among the voodoo makers that sometimes they did not fare differently than the Nigerian police. The suspect also moved temporarily to Lagos, where people claimed to have seen him living large on the stolen stuffs.

One day, David asked me to implore Baba Akinnu to help him expose whoever stole his things. He had been seeing Baba Akinnu coming to our house and he had asked me enough to know about him and his work. But I was reluctant. Not that I thought Baba Akinnu would not help him, or that I did not want to help him, but I did not want to mix anything with my treatment, and I feared my father might not like it. Also, I had not been involved in voodoo activities beyond my treatment, and I therefore had disinclination toward employing it this way. Although it was not that I thought it was sinful, as our Christian and Islamic preachers claimed, but because it was not of an open acceptance, and people who used it often would not admit they did. Hence, I did not feel comfortable getting involved in it beyond my treatment. However, David's concern over the stolen things was troubling enough to him and I was aware that I owed him more than what he was asking me to do for him. Eventually, I persuaded Baba Akinnu to help him.

"If he could get three hundred naira to buy the materials for a preparation, he'd see his things back," Baba Akinnu said to us.

Beneath the primary motive of retrieving his belongings, however, David wanted to have another direct experience with voodoo, especially in which he would be at the other end to experience it work - and not worked on as in his first experience. He wanted to have a chance to wield the power - to be Harry Potter.

Baba Akinnu prepared the charm and gave it to David to cast the spell from his house. There was a Yoruba incantation that he had to recite when using the charm, and that gave me concern, as David's tongue was British. I taught him to say the words, but his recitation was still a bunch of howlers. I wondered what effect it would have on the spell and hoped it would not make him like one of Potter's friends whose magic spell backfired.

David did the voodoo as he was instructed, and we waited for the result.

***

Nike stopped by at our house one morning, intending to spend only a few minutes before going for her lesson. But I knew she would spend a lot more. Whenever we were together, we experienced time differently from the popular time. The popular time raced and flew by the rungs and wings of seconds and minutes, whereas ours flowed by the pulses of our hearts. And in the face of the popular time, it was unimaginably slow, making us feel that we had spent too little time together when the hands of the clock had run incomparably too fast. When lovers talk, everything else ceases to be. Not even the wind blows. I used to be like Adam and she Eve, both in our timeless Garden of Eden, waiting for the devil to offer us the apple one day.

About an hour later, she was preparing to leave when we heard some footsteps coming toward my room. It was Banji.

"Wow! See who's here," I exclaimed. "When did you come into town?"

"I just came right now and I thought to drop by to say hello."

"That's so nice of you. By the way, she's Nike Babatunde," I introduced Nike to Banji. "And he is Banji Akinboye." They greeted each other warmly.

Banji sat down and we picked up issues from my health to his school. When we saw that Nike was feeling left out of the discussion, we switched to general issues that allowed her to contribute.

"You live around here?" Banji asked her out of apparent curiosity. She nodded and indicated in the direction of her house's location.

"How is your brother in Jos?" he further asked, a wry smile lined his tired face as he enjoyed himself with the question.

Nike looked surprised. "How did you know I have a brother in Jos?"

"Clairvoyance," he replied, grinning widely as some parentheses enclosed his mouth. "Do you believe in extrasensory perception?"

"I try not to," she replied.

"She's not the gullible type," I added.

Banji asked more questions about her brother, questions that were so related to him, and he surprised her more. Her brother had never been in this town and she did not know how anyone here would know him. Though she had told me about the brother, the things Banji asked were unknown even to me. After some time of confusing her, Banji rose to go. He greeted Nike warmly and left, leaving her no clue into his psychic revelation.

"He's the son of your sister's landlord," I said to Nike to diffuse her bewilderment. "He collects rent from the tenants whenever he's around, so he must know your sister very well. You're your sister's split-image, and immediately you told him where you live, he knew who you were. He goes to school in Jos, and that's where your brother lives. So tie up the rest; he has no magic; just common sense."

"He looks a nice guy," she said, "He's not like David."

In the few days that followed, Nike and Banji met at my house. To my delight, they became relaxed with one another, and Banji played the role of her boyfriend's friend, a role I had hoped for David. Because of my present condition, I thought that role was important and I was glad that Banji filled it.

My other friends came around, both boys and girls, and though they all got along with Nike, it was with Bola Adelakun, Tunde's sister, that she became close friends. She often visited Bola at her house. She was friendly, and it was just unfortunate that she and David met at the wrong sides of their spirits.

III

Shortly after David cast the spell, it delivered. However, in a twist of events that followed, we did not retrieve the stolen goods. This was what happened:

About one or two witnesses alleged that they saw the suspect go into the house around the time of the theft, but it was only their word against his. After he left town, some people claimed they saw him in Lagos with some of David's clothes and shoes. But whenever he came to town, he was clever enough to keep himself clean of David's stuff.

Now, after David had cast the spell, he came back to town again, and this time with David's clothes. Although he did not hand them back to David; maddened perhaps by the voodoo, he wore them around. Whom the gods want to destroy, they first make mad. First he tried to avoid our place, but people who saw him with the easily identifiable clothes reported to us. We evaluated the circumstance and agreed that since the magic had done thus far - the boy had come back into town and he had brought the loot - then, maybe its time David go to him. Curiously, as we were figuring out how to take on him, he showed up in front of our place, and with a pair of David's jeans pants on him.

Promptly, David stopped him on the road and asked to check the pants.

"What do you mean?" the boy retorted.

"I mean I want to check that jeans you're wearing; it looks like mine."

Though the boy was older, David was bigger and stronger, and, realizing this, fear jumped into him. He began to tremble and he could not stop David from inspecting the pants.

"This is my jeans," David finally said and indicated a sign. "I mistakenly tore this tag like this when I was washing it sometime ago. It's mine. You stole it. You were the one who robbed my apartment."

The boy's fear increased. He did not know what to do or say, and he knew he had walked into trouble. He stepped back a little, as if David was taking too much space on him. He wanted to say something, but it was incoherent. Then David grabbed him by the pants, the way cops grabbed thieves that tried to run away.

"I'm taking this off you, right here and now."

"This is not your pants, and you can't take it off me," he protested. Though he tried to be firm, his voice shook with a mixture of fright and regret. "You can follow me home to confirm. I bought this with my own money."

"I'm not following you anywhere. I'm taking this off you right now."

Out of confusion, the boy walked closer to me. He wanted to buy time, and probably to talk me into saving him out of the calamity that was about to befall him. I lent him my attention. While their first argument was going on, I had called two of my younger brothers to guard me in case they started a fight, and the boys were firmly rooted as my shield as the boy spoke to me with prudent honor. I could have been a king right there and he my page.

I made no sense from what he was talking about, but I listened. In fact, it had little or no relevance to the accusation on him. I did not want him to walk out of the trap; at least, I wanted that we get the stolen things back. But his coming and talking to me seemed to be an appeal for me to intervene to his safety. I was still thinking of what to do when David blew up in anger at his gibberish, grabbed my walking cane, and clubbed it on his right arm.

"Take off the pants, you thief!" David yelled fiercely.

Fear jumped into me. I had never seen David this mad before. His jaws grinded tightly into one another, as if they were going to pulverize, and one could almost see steam streaming out of his ears and nostrils like an angry cartoon horse. He could not have hit more if he was the best baseball player and was hitting a record shot. I became afraid that he might slaughter someone. My walking cane was about twice the size of a baseball bat, and I saw a big bulge pop out immediately around the boy's elbow.

Strangely, the boy did not act as if anything hit him at first; then he took to his heels, attempting to run away. David pounced on him and tried to remove the pants forcefully. The boy struggled in resistance and it seemed a terrible fight as one of my neighbors called DDC ran up to separate them. DDC had two friends with him and they all tried to hold David from the boy.

David was so strong and mad that the men found it difficult to hold him. It became a struggle between them and David, and the boy saw this as an opportunity to run when I quickly ordered one of the men to stop him.

The older men asked for the cause of the fight. David told his side of the story, but, as the boy claimed that he bought the pants, the men had no proof to support David's claim. David tried to explain, but it was difficult to convince them, because he could not argue his case by telling them he had used voodoo to expose the thief of his property, by which the boy had been there with us, dressed in the pants. The argument of voodoo did not hold water in the law court; it did not even hold air. This was a problem that some African philosophers had with our legal system fashioned by the colonialists. They argued that the legal system did not provide a platform to handle the nuances of our society, especially to tackle the problem of voodoo. How could a mother whose child was killed by witchcraft from her polygamal rival prove to the Western court that her child was murdered?

It was hard for me to pitch my tent with those philosophers, however. I believed that the whole situation was far more complex than they thought. In court proceedings during the pre-colonial era, when such peculiar circumstances were often well contained and justifiably dealt with, it was because the people had everything necessary to deal with it. Today, due to the Westernization, the entire structure of the society had been changed and things were now different.

Then, David suggested that they all go to the boy's house to look for the rest of the clothes, but the men could not go and they feared leaving the boy to go alone with David. They tugged at the case for a long time while the older men still maintained their stance that there was no evidence that the pants belonged to David.

I did not like the obstruction. Although I did not want David to fight, I wanted him to have his things back and I had thought this was an opportunity. Now it seemed to me that there was no way other than to let the guy go at this moment. We would get him again, I thought and asked David to let him go for now. But that was a big mistake and David did not like it. I could see the weighty effort it took him to agree with me. He could not even look at me in the eye. He seethed with frustration and anger as the boy walked away.

Then I regretted letting the boy go. In the next moment after he left in a taxi, a policeman emerged onto our street. He was the one David met at the police station on the day of the robbery when he went to report.

"You shouldn't have let him go," the policeman said when David told him of the incident. "He's a thief; we always have him brought to our station for one theft or another. You should have removed the pants and left him butt naked."

David looked at me, his eyes saying, "See what you did." Many times after the day, he would say to me: "No one else could have made me let go of him like that." I realized that it was as if I had failed him. I had been wrong, at least, to our aim and hope. If only I had remained quiet for two minutes, the policeman would have met the boy with us. The boy left town surreptitiously that night and was never seen again.

We had expected for David to get his stuff back, but, by the way things had gone, we found ourselves wondering on whether this situation had not been one of seeking something God did not want to give, but through a medium He did not want to fail. That is, a situation of using a valid power for an invalid desire. Perhaps it was a revelation of how much our personality, who we are, influences the things we do, and those done on us, especially in situations of such unmeasurable things like voodoo. I tried to apply this to my situation, on the validity or non-validity of the witchcraft used on me and the desire of the witches behind it. So far, their ultimate goal had been thwarted, though I could not ascertain it until all this was over. For a long time, we seemed only to have been concerning ourselves with whether voodoo was real or not. But whether it was real or not, one thing I now realized was that voodoo was not just voodoo by itself; there was a whole lot of universal principles and prodigious intricacies underlying its reality and function, and whose understanding might be lost if not paid due attention. Part of it may seem like fate, but concluding thus may end up being an oversimplification of the reality and function of voodoo.

There was a story that I sometimes look toward in this consideration. It was a widely publicized story of four men who went to a voodoo man to make voodoo money. I cannot tell how accurate the story was. It was common to hear stories of voodoo money-making in our part of the world, but whether they were true or not, perhaps only direct witnesses could tell. Here, I tell this story because of its theme relative to my attention.

The voodoo man, the story went, was famous for his successes in making voodoo money for his clients. The method used in voodoo money-making varied by the practitioners, and sometimes relative to individual circumstances. Some killed humans for it while others used less damaging methods. In this man's method, the clients would have their heads turned into vulture-heads. They would be left in the forest for seven days, after which rituals would be performed to turn them back to complete humans and consequently make them rich. But on this four men's case, events turned out differently.

On the eve of the seventh day, the voodoo man traveled to a nearby town to buy the materials needed for the final rituals. On his way back, he had an accident. When the vulture-headed men did not see him at the necessary time, they took the ignominious venture of going to his house to look for him, but only on time to meet his funeral service. No other person knew the voodoo man's method, and the clients were turned over to their families, vulture-headed.

Perhaps, one may say that the four men sought what the higher determining force of the universe did not will to give them, and even mapped themselves a sorry fate. The voodoo man's work could not be said to have failed; it was the circumstance that failed.

To most ordinary people in our environment, witchcraft was no longer a theoretic issue whose validity needed to be confirmed; it was an experience they encountered everyday, and the questions now on many minds were about its morality. Is it right or wrong to use voodoo? If right or wrong, how much right or wrong is it? Or what aspects of it are right or wrong? Sometimes, Western educated people who believed in the validity of witchcraft wanted to know how it fitted into the scientific structure of life they had been taught. However, to understand these, one may need to understand of what fundamental and constitutional nature witchcraft is. Languishing in the quagmire of witchcraft now, I strongly wanted to have a scientific understanding of its nature, its relativity to individuals, circumstances, and environments. And especially in the face of scientific explanations of the afflictions and events ascribed to witchcraft. This way, I thought one might be able to explain why one occurrence in one part of the world might be validly explained by voodoo while the same occurrence in another part will be validly explained by another means. As many Africans may be doing in the face of intimidating reality and application of science in our modern world, I did not want to run away from attempting to understand the mystery of witchcraft.

Today, a major goal of anthropologists studying so-called primitive societies is to derive values from them to help modern societies, and also to help the primitive societies by values from modern societies. But, as few philosophers, psychologists, and anthropologists have long discovered, events in modern times have shown that contemporary societies probably have more to gain from primitive societies than the other way round. For example, contemporary societies are seriously in need of their preserved natural health clues while the primitive people probably have no need for the synthesized products of contemporary times. They do not even need the money that contemporary societies have to pay for the help they get from them. They need no automobile, no computer service, no Machiavellian philosophy to govern themselves, and no nuclear warfare to threaten one another. They are closer to nature and to spirit, living simple lives, and they are happier.

We may have acquired various kinds of things improving the physical situation of humanity than they had, but, in the euphoria of our resourceful adventure, we have left certain useful things behind, among which are things most important to the existence of the humankind. The primitive people have contentment and peace of mind, which is the first thing lost in the pursuit for utopia by our modern societies. The mentality that created and sustains modernity is hunger, hunger for the fruits at the horizon. And while one cannot be content when hungry, the horizon runs as it is pursued.

When I cuddle this primitivism,[37] however, I do not do it to chagrin modernity; I do it with the hope that perhaps the best of the primitivism and of modernism could meet to produce a better civilization. And witchcraft, I discovered, is one of the natural ways by which primitive people make their lives what it is. The old scope of witchcraft may have become too old-fashioned in modern times, but we may learn a lot to improve the understanding of ourselves and enhance our society.

A larger part of Africa, though still a traditional culture, is by no means

[37] *Primitivism* is the term given to the philosophical and artistic idea that primitive or chronologically earlier cultures are qualitatively superior to contemporary ones.

primitive anymore. Centuries of foreign interactions have changed the physical and psychological landscape of the continent, but within the current African culture still lay many ancient elements that contrast with modernity. The problem now is that the contrasts bring confusion, making many Africans stuck between ancient and modern times.

FOURTEEN

Witchcraft

I

Witchcraft is an art that has been a backbone in the culture of primitive societies, traces of which exist in traditional societies today. In their perception, the people see themselves as part of the natural and supernatural environment they live in, and while they try to understand the environment and use it to their good, they try to function respectively and along with other creatures.

In all their endeavors, especially in religious rituals, the primitive people believe in the existence of hidden impersonal power that looms in all mysterious and dynamic things and creatures. They are aware of ethereal entities such as genies or spirits of the dead (not necessarily souls of the dead). Through these, they are able to discern, a realm of unseen forces in and beyond the world around them, where also they believe gods and goddesses dwell.

Believing that their gods are essentially good, they see spiritual forces as neither good nor evil, and which a person can manipulate by certain rituals to make natural things happen as wanted. Everything in the physical world, material or event, has its spiritual or unseen counterpart that interactively affects and sometimes controls it. It is the deliberate process to influence natural events through the manipulation of the unseen forces that we now know as voodoo, magic, or witchcraft, and it is used strictly to the benefit of their communities.

It is believed that the ancestors and ethical divinities jealously guard the societal morality and code of conduct. This has contributed greatly to the upright morality of African societies before the incursion of the white men.

Although there are excesses in some areas, which may be said to have led to over-identification with idols and ideas, but the truth of the world known to these societies are there, valid and verifiable. Up until present times, the spirit of Sango is used to expose or punish anyone who has committed social ills, and throughout Yoruba history, after his reign as the Alaafin, the dispatch of his symbol was sufficient to impose peace among quarrelling Yoruba states.

However, there are some people, perverts, as we have in all human history and times, who use these magical forces, not only selfishly for their personal benefits regardless of others' well-being, but also with the intention of injuring other people. This perverse use of the art is condemned as antisocial, immoral, and ungodly. It is outlawed, and in most tribes death is the penalty for the offense. Hence, as understood in these societies, the art of witchcraft is not the crime, but the selfish and immoral use it. That is, the evil is not witchcraft; it is the personality of the practitioner that is devilish. The world is beautiful and good; it is humans who are sometimes ugly and bad.

It is this negative part of witchcraft that the Christianity imported into Africa capitalizes upon to decry the entire art of witchcraft as evil, and it is this negative part that most people now have in mind when they talk about witchcraft. Following the Protestant Reformation and the Catholic Counter-Reformation of the 16th century, the vestiges of witchcraft in Europe became associated with Devil-worship. The art was decreed heretic and the notorious witch-hunt was institutionalized. This ended up blurring the difference between good and bad practitioners, and the Western view was thus carried over onto the African continent.

Coupled with the scientific notion of witchcraft as unprovable and therefore unreal, these are the questions that witchcraft faces in the modern world, and it puts the cultures of primitive and traditional societies to the same questions. Hence, the African man is not only suggested as an ignorant, his experience is suggested as a delusion. Whereas, all these do not mean that witchcraft is less real than science or any other thing in the world; it is only different from science in that it is predominantly a psychical or psychological phenomenon while science is predominantly a physical phenomenon. This is a reason that modern psychoanalysis may be able to provide some insights – though limited – to events like the mysterious gunshot I had, while physical science cannot. To modern science, psychoanalysis is a heresy, a heresy as witchcraft is a superstition, because it borders on the unseen, the intangible, the unmeasurable, the physically unprovable.

Thinking about all these, I came to understand something crucial about life: life is a deeply psychological phenomenon, and which physical science may make us miss if rigidly focused in the physical dimension. Perhaps all what we are doing in the world, from our most mundane activity to our most sacred one, is to build natural (earth-compatible) matrices, or *practicable constructions*, within which we could phenomenally live our series of years with sanity and happiness, and to be able to achieve whatever it is we need after the life is spent. Therefore, everything is a creation of the mind, of our mind, of the collective human consciousness. And everything, from witchcraft to science, politics to art, religious systems to social systems, is also for the mind. We only need to understand the human mind enough to understand this and the world. The intangible mental world, rather or more than the physical world, is the clue to the knowledge most needed.

In other words, in a way more subtle and mystical than our ordinary perception, everything in the world is a product of human consensual validation, regional or universal. For this reason, in no way is witchcraft less real than science or any other thing in the world; it is how much attention we give to each of them that determines how real it appears and functions to us. As much as we construct the infrastructure of our physical world - its roads, buildings, parks, and its laws and norms - so also do we construct the infrastructure of our psychic[38] world – its beliefs, its expectations, and its perceptions. As much relatively real our physical world is, as much real our psychic world is. Perhaps even more, for it is the indispensable interface through which we experience the physical world. And as our environments differ by place and time in the world, so do our physical and psychic constructions differ, and none is more real than another. This is why we experience things differently in the world. And perhaps why and how the same problems happen to different peoples in different places and times, while the problems are caused by as many different things as the different psychic infrastructures of the different peoples of the world. A migraine headache ailing an African is morphologically the same as that ailing a European, yet the things responsible for each case *sometimes* may be as different as the different psychic worlds of the two.

Hence, as the Western thinkers have been regarding African beliefs and practices as superstitious and nonsensical, they are the ones who have been arrogantly irrational and ethnocentric. It is the self-limited orientation of their approach that has been blinding them from seeing African beliefs and practices as intelligible. They thought that we knew nothing and that it was them who knew everything. They brought a religion whose basic truths their restless spirits misinterpreted; they brought a science and technology whose essence they have misunderstood and overemphasized; and they brought a government whose motive of imperialism they disguised as humanitarian concern. And all these clog their sight from seeing us aright.

The present cultural problems of Africa began with the slavery and the subsequent colonization of the continent. The long-term usurpation befogged many Africans to take the whitewashed view of their culture. This was the cultural and intellectual colonization that has led to our cultural and intellectual slavery. What greater harm could be done to a

[38] The term "psychic" denotes the mental and spiritual faculties.

people than taking away their natural character, the idiosyncrasies of their spirit, culture, and language? Perhaps, then, all these songs of 'superstition' were deliberately composed as a tool to discredit the African culture and to subdue the people. Afterall, the obliteration of the history of the Africans enslaved in America and the rest of the West, and the withholding of education from them, have been the tool to confuse their self-identity and to subdue their spirits, effects of which still remain today.

As scores of millions of Africans were shipped out of Africa, scores of millions of African intellectual potentials were thus shipped away. And they were not shipped away to be realized, but to be smothered. However, the intellectual slavery of the colonized Africans was as devastating, enough to cause the present confusion that the continent is in. How could families that have lost fathers, mothers, brothers, and sisters to oversea slavery be strong enough to produce inquisitive minds like those of the contemporary West? How could members of families that have been so disoriented and culturally confused see any reasons to look into the outer space, the human cells, or into the nuances of the mind for answers and cures as the modern times demand? How could children from families that have been dehumanized because of the color of their skin and the ways of their culture see motivation in their world to make meaningful impact in it? By this plundering of Africa, both Africans on the continent and in the Diaspora have only been thrown into a state of anomie, a condition of social instability and personal unrest resulting from a breakdown of standards and values or from a lack of purpose or ideals.

Studying the present economic situation of the world, one would not be surprised to find that the nations in the ridiculously low-income stratum of the world, insultingly called third world nations, are predominantly the nations of Asia and black Africa, the nations that suffered slavery, colonization, and imperialism the most. The most crucial thing to the sense of freedom, self-reliance, and productivity of an individual or people is the mental (and emotional) stability that these people have lost. And one would not need to squint to see how crucial the way they see themselves - which is usually influenced by the way they are looked upon – affects this mental stability. From my personal experience, the confused and ambivalent consciousness of the African man and woman is quite too obvious. The low economic rate among the African Americans is another example. Within the wealthiest and most productive nation in the world, many African Americans have been wasting away because of the cultural and historical confusion they had been grown into, like their brothers and sisters here in Africa.

If Africans had been left alone, perhaps they would have demystified this perplexing issue of witchcraft for an adequate understanding and use for the modern world, rather than try to walk around it as the West had done. Africans have always been more spiritual than to flip away the concept of witchcraft for an evolving civilization. It is a philosophy that they understood enough to adapt with changes of time and place, and they would have developed an equally valuable and defendable substitute to the Western materially oriented system. Perhaps, this would have created a situation of mutual collateral checks and balances to the extreme tendencies of one another, and lead to a healthy competition and synthesis of the two civilizations. Perhaps, it could have grown to douse the centuries-old bitter rivalry between the Western and Islamic civilizations, which was caused and fuelled by ideological paranoia on both sides, and which also divides and threatens to destroy Africa and the entire world. Sudan is already like a ghost of her old self, and the clash between the Islamic Sharia Law and the British-bequeathed Common Law is currently threatening the unity of Nigeria. We have not been left alone; we have only been required to bleach out the color of our skin and culture before we are considered for a tentative inclusion in the human race.

Even, the witch-mania that pervaded Europe and America in the medieval period and that led to brutal killings of real and imagined witches did not infect Africa. In most cases in Africa, as also done in ancient Babylon and written in ancient laws like the Code of Hammurabi, bad witches were dealt with through the same medium in which they caused their harms. This left little or no room for the victimization of innocent lives as done in the West. But now, we are ridiculously halfway out of our old system and halfway into the new Western-imposed system, bringing us into confusion and making us vulnerable to Western abuse.

One of the major problems facing the health sector in Africa today is the shortage of blood in the blood bank. The blood banks in Africa are far too under-stocked to help the many ill and war-wounded Africans to get transfusions in the Western scientific way that we have been taught. Many Africans are under-oriented into such a system of blood-donation; while, as a consequence of colonization and imperialism, many are hungry and have not enough blood in them, talk less of enough to donate into blood banks. In this case, if there was such a blood-replenishing traditional medicine, as the one used to save my life, why could it not have been so developed and sustained to reach a state of mass benefit? There would be no need for the pain of matching blood for patients and less risk for error as in mis-transfusion of infected blood into patients, as is now common in Africa. Blood transfusion has aided the spread of Hepatitis and AIDS across the continent. This is just an example out of the potentials in the endangered African culture.

Witchcraft was not just a practice, the narrow definition that most people see and talk about, but a philosophy and a culture, of which the practice was only a part. It was a philosophy that created and bound African cultures. It was their religion; it was their life. It was an imaginatively and creatively constructed culture that embodies all aspects of life, and whose truths and meaning modern science and philosophy have only been reestablishing in their own ways rather than disproving.

Some of us are now whitewashed into disliking our culture, some are threatened into fear of opposing formidable Western principles, and others are lured into greediness, making even political and economic administration in Africa difficult. Everybody now talks of Africa as a place of ignorance and diseases. The most heinous crimes and the most dreadful diseases of the modern world are cried to be of African origin and dwelling. One may wonder, sometimes, that if all the beliefs and practices of Africans had truly been superstitious, nonsensical, and useless, the white people might not have met anybody on the continent when they came. All the dreadful diseases would have wiped them out. And if their religions were so 'paganistic' and hateful to God, God would have destroyed them long before the foreigners found them. Afterall, the Bible and the Qur'an talk of how swift God had destroyed generations of unbelievers and perverts. Or had He exhausted all the rain and brimstones in the periods of Noah and Lot?

Now, most of their practices no longer help them as they used to do, and Africans are dying of diseases and are killing themselves in political and religious conflicts in alarming rates, and with firearms flushed in from the West. Why now, one may ask, after Western incursion, and not before, are all these happening to them? The number of lives that imported firearms have destroyed in the last few decades in Africa, evil witchcraft has not done a fraction of it in the last two thousand years. The Nigerian civil war alone was tantamount to the destruction of Noah's flood, and, ever since, many others across the continent have midgeted its magnitude. Have not the white men really put a knife on the things that held us together, and have we not been falling apart? This was the question many are now asking, wondering whether it is not time to stop thinking the gods must be crazy. It is we humans who have been insane, as it is only a narrow-minded ethnocentric person that would define reality in his own terms and project his own experiences and limitations on others. And it is only a like-minded person that would accept the definition over his own experience.

FIFTEEN

Love's Irony

...Some there be that shadows kiss
Such have but shadows bliss.
There be fools alive, certainly,
Silvered over, and so was this.
William Shakespeare

I

David came back from town one evening and said to me, "Just sit down there and watch your spiders while a richer guy bangs your girl for you."

"What are you talking about?" I asked, confused.

Wearing a mischievous smirk that I could not quite decipher, David said, "Your girl's already going out with the guy with money and cars – Banji. He takes her everywhere now."

"How could you say such a thing? Because you don't like her doesn't mean you should discredit her and spoil her relationship with me."

David said nothing more. His grin only widened, and I thought he was really being mischievous.

Nike and Banji met at my place often and they became closer friends by virtue of their relationships to me. It was nothing that I saw as more than friendship. Although I could not say I trusted Banji, but I thought that a friend who was that close to me, who knew my condition and how soothing Nike's love was to me, would not do a thing like that to me. A friend who had the freedom to date as many girls as he wanted, like the biblical rich man, would not take my only sheep to feed his guests. A friend, especially like Banji, with whom I shared issues about my relationship with the girl; Banji, from whom I got advice whenever I was having rough times with the girl; Banji, who would assure me ten times in a day that I had a good girl and should try very well not to lose her; Banji, who stood with me to ensure that I did not lose her.

But I was wrong. Banji did betray me. He reminded me that even the biblical rich man went ahead to take the poor man's only sheep, and that the covetousness in men was still as fresh today as it was thousands of years ago. I had been foolish enough to allow my 'good' friend to drop my girlfriend at school with his car, and I had been foolish enough to talk with him and seek his advice on my girl.

It was a well agreed-upon affair between both of them, so it was not only Banji that played a fool of me. They had been carrying on with it long before David even knew, and I hated myself for being that naive to have trusted them. This was how I came to know about the affair:

One Saturday afternoon, Nike asked me, "Rahman, do you think we can get any good thing out of this relationship?"

"Don't be pessimistic at this point," I replied, "We love each other and it's been good so far."

She looked at me with eyes like that of a doll that needed a new battery. "I just don't know. I worry all the same. My mind tells me strongly to discontinue with this thing. I can't help but to think you'll dump me for a better girl when you get well. I don't think there is anything good in it for both of us. Believe me; my mind never alarmed me falsely."

I became worried when she went this far. We did not have any quarrel and I was at loss of what could have caused this. For about half an hour I was on my feet while I tried to persuade her. I assured her of my love, but she was not swayed.

"Think on it, Rahman," she had said on her way out of my room, "I'll come for the reply tomorrow."

This jolted me. Yet, I still thought what she needed was an assurance, and I planned for an effective way to talk to her. I remembered how I lost my first teenage girlfriend when I failed to assure her of my love by dialogue. I did not want to fail again. I had loved Yemisi with all my heart, and in like coin she had requited. But I had been poor in orientation to keep the relationship alive. Although I was still inexperienced in bed plays, and I did not really go far in our games, but I thought that bed was the only wonderland where love was expressed and fulfilled. Accordingly, I took Yemisi to the ever-ready bed every time she visited me.

This was the legacy of our famous house at Oniyanrin, while I did not realize that it was only a game of lust. Many of my uncles were different kinds of players, Casanovas, and Don Juans, but I was a Romeo. I did not know the difference, or how else to act other than like I knew my uncles play their games. Nobody even cared to know how my relationship with Yemisi was doing; all they did was hang around in the house whenever we were behind closed doors and ask me afterward, "Have you done it?" "Did you do it?" And they would advise me to quickly do it, and as many times as possible, if I did not want to lose her to bigger boys who could really do it. They pressed me so much that I eventually started to lie that I had done it to save myself from the embarrassment, though the girl did not let me do it. Although she liked to get into bed with me, and liked to fondle with me, but she was afraid to do it, and we never did it.

Yemisi's refusal, however, saved me from another embarrassment, for I did not know exactly how to do it. Although I had been exposed too early to the environment and feeling of sex, I had learned little of the act itself.

The prostitute figure[39] was no longer an honorable woman to midwive men into civility, there were no streams of sex movies to teach me so early, and no internet service dangling under my puerile noses. We only had a few pages of pornographic magazines hidden underneath our beds. Because the pictures in the magazines were still images, they did not reveal the motion involved. So, if Yemisi had allowed me, perhaps I would have just gone in and parked myself there, like a damned car parked in a garage after a long and longing journey for the spot, or just run around in naive ecstasy amid the shrubs of the drive.

I was playing the overtures to bed one afternoon when Yemisi stopped me, looked at me straight in the eye and asked, "Do you think you love me?"

I looked at her with a *see-what-you-are-talking* smile on my face. You are dribbling away from the goal, girl. “I wouldn't be doing all these if I didn't love you.”

The next thing I saw was that she was crying like a baby and I had a complication on my hands that I did not know how to handle. I tried to calm her, but not assure her by conversation. When she walked out of my room, I did not know I was seeing the last of her in our house. And that was the end of the relationship.

My relationship with Nike was my next big love affair since then, and I thought I was not going to fail again. This situation was slightly different from Yemisi's. I did not make any mistake or ruin anything to require reparation, and I was older and more matured. All I thought I needed to do now was to assure her of my love.

But Nike seemed to have made up her mind. In spite of how much I tried, she did not change her position. Nonetheless, I still did not think I should let it go like that. Afterall nothing reasonable was the problem, and she might just be playing her game still this far. Nigerian girls were famous for saying "no" when they did not really mean "no" but "prove yourself" or "try harder", or even, sometimes, "yes".

Nike’s exams were commencing and she had a busy week ahead. I decided to wait until the end of the week to talk to her again. I planned to seek Banji's advice and probably have him talk to her, if need be. I did not like having others talk to my girlfriend in such circumstances, but conditions are sometimes unique, and I intended to respect that.

The following Monday was a bad day for me. Though I always tried to prepare myself for such unexpected in relationships, there was nothing to prepare me enough for what was coming. I sat under the tree with some friends. They talked, but did not know that there was little or no hearing from me. I was all mind, lost in though, thinking of what and how to do next. The time was around 4 pm and, because Nike was supposed to go to sleepover at Awe, the neighboring town where she would take her exams, I

[39] Reference to the ancient role of prostitutes in boys’ passage into maturity, as alluded in the Gilgamesh, the ancient Mesopotamian epic.

expected her to come to say goodbye as she always did whenever she was going out.

Just then, I heard a Volkswagen Beetle accelerating noisily. Spontaneously, I looked up to see it, knowing by the increasing pitch that it just took off from around Nike's place. Automobiles from the area always hit the main road from that point which I could only judge by the sound. I was not expecting to see anything but a distracting car, as usual, but I saw much more.

It was Banji's car, with Nike beside him as he drove toward downtown. She was not seated like an ordinary passenger given a help-ride; she was indulgently comfortable. The picture told me many things and reminded me many things at once. It was like an electric shock as the reality unfolded in my awareness. The car had sped past, but its image remained in my heart. My eyes were fixed on the road and I still saw them drive past again and again, like in a motion picture effect. The worst of the picture was Nike's image, laughing merrily as if on honeymoon, and not caring to see me before leaving. It was like a fireball hitting my unarmored heart; it almost stopped its working.

Could Banji be doing this to me? I asked myself. Could David have been right all these days? Why should Banji be taking her to Awe without me know about it? Is this why she's thinking we can't continue anymore - to get me out of their way? Or are all these merely my imagination?

Then I reverted into the past for answers, remembering many times she had gone to visit Bola Adelakun at odd hours while she gave me unreasonable excuses. I was so besotted by love that I did not suspect anything. It was now I realized that she had been lying all these days to cover her coquetry. I remembered many other circumstances and it made me feel stupid to have fallen for their intrigues. Love is suffering; love is hell. My heart ached in flames of lovesickness. It was an inferno. An arson by persons closest to me; by the object of my love, one precious to me. An arson by my love, the love I give. "O ruthless fate!" my heart screamed, "Why am I made thy mark of hate? Why must my heart thy victim be?"[40]

I also remembered a question that Banji often asked me, while not aware that I was dining with a traitor with a short spoon. "Have you laid her?" he would ask.

"No," I always replied. "It is not easy for me to do."

"You should do it, if you don't want to lose her," he would advise me. "Sex is the key to wield control over a girl; once you have done it, she respects you. It's like she would feel you have *known* her secrets, and sees it better to stay with you than go elsewhere."

At my age and experience, I did not need him to inform me this; my uncles had rammed it enough in my head, but guys still give advice anyway, even if they themselves have no gut to practice it. Yet, I was

[40] *Joseph and Zuleikha*, by AbdulRahman Jami, a Persian poet in the Middle Ages.

beginning to learn that this might not always be so with all girls.

“I would have done it if I could. But I can't.” I told him the truth the first time he mentioned it.

“Why can’t you?”

“I cannot climb the bed up on her; my legs won’t allow me."

He laughed. "You should try, I think. This girl isn’t for lovey-dovey."

“Banging is not everything.” I responded, “I haven't done it all these years and I haven't gone insane and my thing has not rusted. Sometimes, sex is something nothing." I explained to him, but only trying to put myself on a graceful side. Not that I had heeded preachers' vehement warning against what they called fornication; that was still a wild beast yet to be tamed for me, only now trapped in a cage. In a way, I believed my words made sense, but it was difficult for me to completely admit them to myself and I knew it was my condition that forced me to look at it this way. I had tasted the forbidden fruit at a ridiculously early age and I had been ensnared into the superficial mentality of sexuality. Shamefully, I had not even outgrown the delusion of perceiving women lustfully, as sexual objects, perhaps an ineluctable burden of manhood. Although this may be one of my foibles; yet, by the women’s own delusion of the increasingly provocative sexy culture, they had also not been helping me. They have not been helping many men. The modern world is becoming increasingly ‘hot,’ burning us up, so much that one may begin to wonder whether most women really know what they want. They want dignity and respect from men, yet they like to be seen as sexy, presenting themselves provocatively as sexual symbols. This, first a confusion of the womenfolk, subsequently confuses the modern Cyclops,[41] the men, further in their already one-eyed narrow, foggy vision; we only see one thing at a time, and always the one pleasurable. Perhaps the Bible was right that one fault of the woman is her inability to make up her mind.

Not that I think sex is the problem, however. Sex is good; I have known that in a long time and, unlike Mahatma Gandhi, it would be difficult for me to give it up even for the Lord. Sex is good; the problem, then, may be our overindulgence in it, and this is the characteristic of our day, overly stimulating and feeding that crazy urge of our id. Many times I could not help but wonder how lucky Adam had been, having no other woman around to distract him. I wished I was the first man on earth.

Nonetheless, even though I liked sex, I was never a sex glutton. Sex voracity sickened my nerves, sometimes. But in this circumstance, I was forced to take the position that I took. My legs were so rigid and awkward that they would not allow me to climb the bed even if my health would. As if that was not funny enough, it was not until I began to shut myself in the room with Nike that my father began to exhale about his son’s sexual potency. He had been afraid that it had been blasted off in that devilish

---

[41] Used in Homer’s epic, ‘The Odyssey’, the Cyclop is a one-eyed giant in Geek mythology seen as a phallic symbol, usually of uncivilized manhood.

gunshot and rotten away in the prolonged sickness, especially when parts of my pelvis decomposed. He did not know that I did not do anything behind the closed door.

Banji repeated this question often, and I always replied in the same way. "You better try and do it," he would finally say to close off the conversation. But by these conversations between Banji and I, and all other reminiscences, I began to ask myself, "Am I getting more answers to the puzzle?"

I was so distraught that I could not do anything anymore. I did not know what I had done to deserve this. Our story had gone from the revelry of Adam and Eve in our timeless Garden of *Eden* to one of Adam and *Evil* in the garden of *heathen*. *Eve* and *Evil*, who ever coined the two names, whether God or man, I hope was not pulling a fast one on humankind, especially on the sex of Eve. Yet, we, men, are fond of saying that women are evil, from the first story in the heavenly garden through to the likes of mine here.

I was not prepared for this kind of development. The sense was no more of a girl merely leaving me because of her unreasonable feelings; it was a consuming sense of my girl dumping me for another guy, and my own friend, taken to be better than I. It was a sense of a double-barreled shot of betrayal, from my friend and my girl.

Although I had an idea how terrible such a situation could be, but I had never directly experienced it before in my life, and it was only now I knew how painful a situation it was. Added to it was my feeling of being taken advantage of in my condition. I felt strapped to the seat on one end of a seesaw, teased to ride up high and had the weight emptied out on the other end. I crashed down, and now I lay in my crash spot, left alone to bleed.

Hearing about David's disparaging comments about Nike, Banji had even advised me to take stiff and angry measures against David so he would not spoil my relationship with the girl! I had only refused to do it because of how much David meant to me. Now I was appalled that Banji was even pushing me toward an edge where I would lose my girl and lose my friend, leaving me in a dry land, cold and lacking. I scarcely slept in the night.

***

I sent for Nike immediately she returned the next day.

"So this is the way you want to play me," I said calmly as I leaned against my tall bed.

She pretended not to understand what I was talking about. "What do you mean?" she asked.

"I introduced my friend to you and now you are *chasing* after him."

"What are you talking about? What friend?"

"You know what I'm talking about." My voice began to rise. "Do you want to tell me that you are not fucking around with Banji?" I was talking with the severity it induced in me.

"Me? Banji? Aren't you funny, Rahman? Is it because I go to his house that you think I'm dating him?" She was bold, dramatically pretentious.

"Yeah, all the cars and all the property you see in their house have got you out of your senses and you run about after him. And you come here to tell me that we cannot get along anymore. How can we get along, when you've sold out yourself for a cheap meal?"

"Rahman, I'm not going to stand here and look while you accuse me of what I did not do and still have you talk to me like this. I told you I'm not going out with Banji, and if you're not satisfied, you can call him here and ask him about it." Her voice was now a little shaky.

"Listen, I didn't call you here to argue with you. I've got all the evidence to know that you are messing around with that bastard. I only wanted you to know that I'm not at all fooled and that I'm through with you. Not because of the stupid *yarn* of yours that we can't continue and all the shit, but because of your lechery. You stink too much for my pleasure now. So, please, get out, and never come back into this house again."

I sat back on my bed and pretended as if awaiting her exit, but, as I had hoped for, she did not go. She threw down her pretense, went down on her knees, and shook like a water plant.

"Rahman, please... it is not like that. It was Banji who started it and I can swear nothing has happened between us. I had never let him touch me... Please Rahman, forgive me... I'm confessing it's true. It just started this week and I promise you it has ended at this moment... Please, forgive me." She very well appeared to be pretending on another level.

"You don't need to beg me for forgiveness. You've not wronged me, you've only shown me the type of person you are, and that dog has also shown me the type of person he is. Whether or not you quit, I don't care. Just leave me alone and get the hell out of my room."

"Please, forgive me, Rahman. I was forced to give in to his pressure. I didn't know you would know about it. It's the devil's work. Please forgive me. I assure you it has ended right away. It's all the work of the devil."

It is always the work of the devil. Isn't the devil a poor creature? He carries the blame for every wrong thing we do, only that he cannot carry the pains it causes. In my pain, I continued.

"You figured that my present condition wouldn't allow me to see the back of my head?"

"No, I didn't think like that, but, please, let's just forget it all. I admit all the guilt."

"You have to. It's tailor-made for you. You did it - you and that bastard."

"Let me carry the whole blame; don't take anything against Banji," she pleaded, "It's all my fault. If I had not accepted, he wouldn't have been going out with me. So, please, don't hold anything against your friend. And forgive me, please. Let us bury it here."

The plea disturbed me. Why should she care about Banji? I would be glad if she could truly quit with him and feel responsible to me, but now she was acting as if responsible to Banji as well. I reacted in my anger. "That's none of your business. Just get out and leave me alone."

Slowly, she walked out. I lay down and pondered over my new predicament. I had always been careful not to break girls' hearts because of the torment in it. Now my heart was broken. Could the law of karma be blind? I wondered.

Happy that I had known the truth at last, David told me more stories about them. The truth hurt me more, however. It over-burdened my heart, but I did not have the courage to hold back from hearing more. I wanted to hear more and David was eager to tell me more.

As the night grew older, I tossed and turned in my bed. I did not sleep until early in the morning. I was depressed.

II

On Wednesday, I sat under the tree waiting for what would happen next. I still wanted the girl and I still hoped the coming events would be in my favor. Along with my heart, my pride was on the line, and I wanted her to come back and say she loved me and wanted me. I was under an illusion that she would come back and all would be settled. Sometimes a person in love is half blind and half insane.

What I saw was not in my favor. They drove away again in Banji's Beetle, and even in a somewhat elated mood. It dawned on me that I had lost the game. The sweetest thing in the world of a man may be a woman, but she could turn around to be the bitterest. I could not help but worry that they were only taking advantage of my condition. If the string had not cut, the archer's bow could not have been so dishonored to be turned in to a mere walking cane.

Who said love was blind? Who said there was unconditional love? Love must have eyes that see clearly more than human eyes. For if love was blind or unconditional, Nike might not see any other person better than I was. Perhaps it is what love looks for that varies, and Nike did not see in me what her love wanted. Every person in the game or business of love seems to want in his or her object of love what he or she wants in life. The lover's priority, that is, is represented one way or another in the loved, whether directly perceivable by the lover or not. Perhaps this priority, usually or always, is essentially *security*, an unconscious need for security against the unpredictability of life. Perhaps this *security* is often misunderstood and misleading to many who cannot figure out what they essentially want in life; yet it is the way the individuals see it that inevitably determines their choices in life, and how they behave.

Then, may be I could not blame Nike. She saw someone just graduating from one of Nigeria's prestigious universities with a degree in pharmacy, someone whose father owned a large estate and a fleet of about eight cars. How many people in Nigeria if today would see these and still stay with someone who was just graduating from the University of Sickroom, with a degree in pains, boredom, and unrealistic idealism? This was a time I would wish I was the prince of Zamunda. I felt I was less of a man. I wished I were someone more capable. And for a little while, I could do anything to be that someone more capable. Whether moral or immoral, all I wanted was to be the man that made Nike's heart beat.

It may also be true that men do not know what women want only because women do not know what they want. Many women are of confused and misplaced priorities, especially as influenced by the misplaced and confused priority of our time. With due recognition that many men's love is but lust, love now seems a materialist in the flesh of women, and a ruthless one at that. Hence, even though love sees, it may have been blinded in its own conceit.

Sometimes, thinking this far did not help my situation, because it tended to exonerate my object of bitterness and give me nothing to fight. But perhaps I really did not have anyone or anything to fight, except myself – my psyche. Our problem seems to be all about control, the need to be in control of the other, and it is a natural obsession intrinsic to humanity in general rather than to one gender group. Women may have been historically placed on the passive side of relationships, whereby men feel in control and women are expected to behave in a certain way acceptable to men's ego. When things go wrong, then, men blame them for things men take liberty in doing. The way we behave is always a function of our evolutionary history. The good thing about the feminist movement is that it is disillusioning men of their sense of 'natural control' over women, and that of emotional control in man-woman relationships. Though feminism has its down side; most importantly, deluding women with the opportunity of assuming the control, but the movement seems to be nudging us to realize that it is both sexes that need and seek the security equally in life. The angle from which women see and desire life may often not be the same as that of men; women are seeing and seeking the same thing as men are, only in different ways, only in different psychological pathways. Thus, our crises may have been buried too deep in our genes than could be easily changed, and we may together have crafted the materialist flesh of women.

Deceiving themselves, men like to think they are invulnerable in relationships. If daughters of Eve have been evil, sons of Adam seem to have been ridiculously adamant, as adamant as Adam had been, refusing to accept responsibility in the eating of the forbidden fruit.

Yet, this ruthless materialist in the flesh of women has had deeper hands in crimes in the world. It is the kind of thing that makes victims like me so desperate to wish to strike back, to even up, and protect themselves against the oppression of such situation, pushing men toward behavior that women would wish they did not do. It is the kind of things that makes men go all out through all sorts of crimes to enrich themselves materially. It exposes a weakness spot in our psyche, in men's psyche, and, because of its material undertone, it makes us pursue our security and weapons in materials, by which women consequently pursue theirs in successful men. Life, then, seems all about wealth and women; it is all about wealth for women; it is all about women.

Like my father always told me, whether on the passive side or not, the womenfolk control the world and the world of men. Hence, I see feminism as a movement not only to free women, but importantly to free men. The woman is a goddess, perhaps sometimes a brutal goddess as symbolized in the image of the Hindu goddess Kali, at whose feet man's blood is poured in libation. Men reduce women down to "pussy", though still often encouraged by women. But, even though it is disrespectful to womanhood, the irony of it is that men lock themselves up in the ecstasy of the "pussy" and live all their lives in the pleasure-stuffy, suffocating room. This is where our intoxicating sense of 'natural control' may have led us. An incredibly large percentage of what a man thinks and does thus becomes influenced by his "pussy consciousness," whether he has the real thing or not. Although, the force that binds and attracts man and woman toward one another may be more than sex, the force that is structurally functional in the process of the universe itself; it is our obsession with the sexual aspect that ruins us. Perhaps, then, the evilness of the woman is men's misunderstanding of her: men's over-identification with her thing. Perhaps, it is the misunderstanding by both men and women, and not just the men: our over-identification with the interaction of our private parts. Thus, when I look at the world through the prism of social conflict, taught by Marxist sociologists as playing a role in civilization and social evolution, I cannot help but to see the conflict of the sexes as part of it. It is a complex conflict deep-rooted in the mysterious struggle for balance between the male and the female – like in the Chinese concept of yin and yang. A paradoxical struggle for control and harmony. This may be the hidden truth of pansexualism, a Freudian theory of sexuality as the basic instinct underlying reality, determining every human action.

Do all these mean, then, that Nike was not wrong, like many unfaithful men and women? There has to be a bad guy against the good guy for a story to be fun – at least, in the context of the world we have set. So, the event troubled me for a long time and I hated Nike and called her all the names for such a bad person. Sometimes I thought of getting to even up one day, but I realized that while it may not do me any good, it might still be fanning the flame of gender suspicion and conflict. Our ego exaggerates things to our consciousness, and this may be the reason we feel so hurt in circumstances like this. The ego is not only a jealous and indulgent god; it is a tyrannical and often unreasonable god. It loves and runs after vanity, the Devil's favorite sin. In any condition, life may not be worth a blind struggle, for a blind struggle is like a struggle in the quicksand; it only sucks you more and more. I eventually decided to let things go, seek comfort within my heart and move on with my life.

Nonetheless, the event rendered me almost incapacitated. Mama Pakoyi sent a message to me that I was worrying too much for the good of my health, and Baba Akinnu also visited me for the same reason. They were monitoring my biological and emotional states, and they knew whenever anything was wrong. Though they only thought it was the condition of my legs that depressed me, it still amazed me how they did this while not present with me. I promised to try and be happy.

I picked up the pieces of my heart and made a steady and hoping whole again. Something great about the human spirit is that it has the potential for being stronger and more focused than before a crash. I tried to sublimate my emotions into creative and progressive exercise. I intensified my physical exercise with the strong dream and hope of giving myself something better than any girl could offer. *When life lows and crawls, clouded upon by flameless smoke, dreams are the tufts of wings that make men borne as pretty aves.*

***

This experience with Nike eventually became a contributory part of my intellectual development at this stage of my life. Sometime much later, I reflected that I may have fallen that much in love simply as a love weakling that the psychosexual fixation of my early years had made me. Maybe my falling in love as I did was crazy and blind, but it got me thinking philosophically about love. I came to discern three types of love, among which I may only have fallen into one of the low ones. There is the material love, the romantic love, and the spiritual or philosophical love, and I see them as three stages of love, respectively as pre-conventional, conventional, and post-conventional stages of love.[42] The people in the pre-conventional stage are those with material love, whose love is nothing but lust. They love other people simply to fulfill their need, or what they thought to be their need.

Those in the conventional stage are those with what I call *classical infatuation*. They are the ones with mindless romantic love; they love with their heart, but have no knowledge of their true heart or of what true love really is. They love only because the society or their situation conditions them so, and thus the fate of their heart is in the hands of the relationship. In this type of love, the lovers worship one another, because their happiness is at the mercy and sanity of each other. And if things go wrong, they look outside at the society for consolation – where really there may be no consolation. Attachment misconstrued as love, it is at this stage that love is suffering; suffering from the anxiety created by either the intimidation in acquiring the desired love or the fear of losing it after acquiring it, both which characterize the attachment. Even in the pre-conventional stage, the suffering seems less to this stage's, although this is because the pre-conventional love is brutish, uncaring.

---

[42] An adaptation of Lawrence Kohlberg's psychological model of moral development.

Those in the post-conventional stage are self-discovered independent people who are in love because they know the true nature of themselves and of love, and because they know the function that love is meant to perform. From the appreciable understanding of oneself, one is able to understand one's partner as like oneself, with the same basic purpose and means in life. And by this one will be able to respect and love the partner as one loves oneself. Although, perhaps, only an extremely few percentage of the world's population gets to this stage, it is a stage that subsumes the pleasures of the two other stages, and that seeks and enjoys far greater pleasure than the two combined. It is a stage of love that is strong, fulfilling, and secure. Since love is supposed to bring freedom, post-conventional love is the stage that frees the individual from the threats of desire, the fear of disloyalty and misunderstanding, and the various other things that plague the other two stages of love.

The true love is an alloy of understanding and trust; an understanding and trust of one another, but which only comes from an understanding and trust of oneself. My love for Nike, I realized, was a conventional love. Like most love affairs in the world today, it was ironically a symptom of my condition, more or less than something I willfully shared. It was like a sophisticated tasty wine drunk to silver over an emptiness in my life, a weakness, an unsecured consciousness, whose existence I was not aware of. It was a relationship I had unconsciously sought to obscure the vacuum in my life. My heart had been broken and hurt only because Nike's betrayal exposed me once again to the vacuum and I could not stand its intimidation, even though I still was not conscious of it. Thus, even if she had not betrayed me, my love had in some way been a romance with a mirage, a romance with a shadow, and I might have missed the real heavenly essence that casts the shadow. Those who kiss the shadow, have but shadow's bliss.

However, this might not mean that one should not fall in love in the conventional manner, because at some stage one might not be able to help but to be whatever one is, even if made superficially by circumstance or the society. At such a point all one's happiness would be dependent upon it, and even if the happiness is also as superficial as the self, it might not be wise to deny it – because one does not have anything to replace it. Sometimes it might be fatal to deny it. It is like looking at all the things that make a little child happy. An adult knows they are trivial, and that there are better things to make a person happy, but in the world of the little child, they are all that make sense, and placing him in the world of the adult will never substitute. The child has to grow into it. Therefore, one could, and perhaps should, do whatever seems fitting at any particular time. The best thing then might be to be mindful and seeking to achieve the better, the real, and not leave oneself to the superficially created life. Because, even if one falls blindly in love as such, by being thoughtful one can eventually develop the true love of understanding and trust. Sometimes, perhaps, the conventional stage of love may be seen as a stepping stone; if not accepted and respected, one may not be able to climb to the higher rung. For some of us, it may be the best way to learn, though for others it may not.

By this understanding, I lived on without regretting any of my love experiences. Aphrodite may have been turning her back on me, and my relationships may have ended up as stories of loss, none of them I saw anymore as a failure. Aphrodite may not have been the goddess of real love, anyway; from the Trojan War to the sinking of the Titanic,[43] all she has been causing was trouble. To her chagrin, all my relationships have really been stories of successes, because, though failures they had seem, inspiring they now are.

III

I was in my room one Monday afternoon when David came in, apprehensive. It was exactly noon and I was surprised to see him that early.

"What's up, aren't you supposed to be in school?" He was in his final year and it was the period of preparation for the school certificate examinations.

"I finished all I got to do early today."

"But you look worried; what's wrong?

"Uncle's room was burgled and there's a problem about it."

"Burgled? How?"

"I don't know. When I was going to school this morning I saw his windows thrown apart disorderly, whereas he didn't sleep home last night. He slept at is office at Plaza. I was a little suspicious, but I thought it might be that a carpenter was working on them and I hurried off to school. I was surprised when Baba Dotun (his uncle's younger brother) came to me in school to ask me questions - cop-like. You know he was once a cop. The burglary looks phony and they thought someone in the house knew about it."

"They thought you knew about it?"

"That's what they thought. Although Baba Dotun realized that I didn't know anything about it, but I still feel embarrassed."

"If you think the burglary really looks phony, then you should understand his questioning you. And afterall you've been found clean."

"Yeah, maybe. But I feel embarrassed all the same. It bothers me why they would think of me like that in the first place."

In some way, I was not surprised that they suspected David. It was a common thing, even though wrong, for young boys to pilfer from their parents or guardians to make fast bucks. But I was surprised that such magnitude of the act was suspected at him. Breaking into a room through the window is no longer a petty pilfering. What young boys used to do was

---

[43] Reference to the Hollywood adaptation.

lift some quick cash materials that they could sell, and which in most cases would elude detection in their house.

"They've called in the police," David said as he rose to go. "I should be around them in case they need me. I don't want anybody to think anything funny or suggest anything funny about me. I knew uncle couldn't have sent anyone to question me like that if someone had not made such funny suggestions. And Baba Dotun trusts me so well that he wouldn't have come either."

If David would do some lifting, I thought I would somehow know about it. I might not be able to stop him from doing whatever he wanted to do, but he could not successfully hide things away from me. Even though he had a lot of respect for me, and he knew I would not approve of such things, I knew he would still have done it if pressed for cash. He would assume that I was too straight to understand that he needed the money, but he would later tell me about it. That was what I thought, though it never happened between us and I could not have thought anything more to it.

Actually, I could not have made any stiff disapproval of such lifting in the house. At this period of my life I had become a big brother to many teenage boys who, despite my restricted condition, looked up to me as a role model in the neighborhood. Sometimes, also, teenage girls. Often they came to hang with me and seek my advice about their school and social life. And when such an issue came up between us, I often would not stiffly disapprove of it. I had my way of disapproving and, at least, it worked once in about three cases. For me, that was success, for I believed that stiff disapproval could not have worked once in ten cases. When children have reached the late teenage, and are under peer pressure, iron opposition from parents or guardians may do little or no persuasion to stop them from doing whatever they think they want to do. What I always did was to enlighten them on such circumstances and allowed them the freedom to make their decisions.

I reckoned by the fact that I had done it before, and how difficult it had always been for me to refrain from doing it, even in the face of stiff disapproval. Disapproval often was challenge for me; giving me the chance of rebellion, it was the strongest motivation for me to do it. It was fun trying to beat authority's detection. I had pilfered from my father, my mother, and my grandmother. It was now, in retrospect, that I thought that I should not have done it. I realized it was not worth it. It was a vice, juvenile delinquency. However, I knew that if time was to be reversed and I was under the same condition, I would do it all over again, unless I had a good and effective counsel. This was what I tried to make available to my younger friends.

All day, I waited for David to come and tell me what was new on the case, or, at least, come around, but I did not see him until the next day when he branched at my place on his way to school.

"I've got the boys who did it," he said.

"You did? How?" I was amazed.

"Yesterday, as I left your place, I went straight home and I heard the detail of the burglary. I heard all that was stolen and something struck in my head: an audio cassette player with a built-in TV. I remembered that Kazim had said in my ears that he would soon buy a cassette player with a built-in TV and I became suspicious of him. You know he has a bad reputation for such behavior."

Kazim was David's neighborhood friend, and I asked how he knew what was in David's uncle's room, if David did not tell him. But I later learned that David had met him in the house when he came from London. Kazim's father was David's uncle's former chef and both father and son were always in the house all day. "He knows the house so well and he knows everything in there," David explained.

"Then, what happened?" I asked, anxious to know the rest of the story.

"I didn't want to alarm uncle because I might be wrong. I decided to check on him, so I went to his new school at Fiditi (a neighboring town). He stays all weekdays in a rented apartment over there and only comes home during the weekend. I was directed to his apartment and, to my surprise, I found Kunle and a big guy there with him, and I found all the loot right there in his room (Kunle is a boy that lives in their neighborhood, too).

" I was pissed off. I shut the door behind me and asked them to pack the loot and come with me. I warned them not to make any stupid move, but the big guy wouldn't let me take them without a fight. I injured him so bad he couldn't get up. Both of them became frightened; they saw I was damned mad and I could hurt them. I tied their hands together, got a help and chattered a taxi that brought us all home with the loot."

"That was impressive," I remarked.

"Yeah, my hat was up yesterday. Uncle was proud of me. He has his goods back, and the thieves."

It sounded like one of Steven Seagal's movies, but it was true it happened and I was also proud of David. He hurried to school and promised to come in the afternoon. But, strangely, it was not until after two weeks that I would see my friend again.

The following day, his uncle's nephew, Dotun, who was my schoolmate, came to tell me that the boys had incriminated David and he had been locked up as well. I did not believe it. I thought Dotun must have confused the story and I argued with him that it was David who caught the boys at first. But by the time he told me that it was his father who picked David up at school, and many other things about it, I realized that his story was accurate. The boys told the police that David knew about the theft, and he had been locked up in a cell at Durbar police station, the central police station at Oyo.

I became worried. "Do you think David knew about the burglary?" I asked him, curiously. Considering the fact that he was the one who captured the boys in the first place, I became confused.

"I don't know exactly, but Uncle now thinks he did, and he is taking steps accordingly."

"Okay, let's look at it from all angles and see whatever could be seen there. Do you think David would know about it and still bring them home that night?" I asked, troubled about the events.

"That's part of the story that seems to muddle up the case. David wouldn't be dumb to do that. But there was a point raised to David's disadvantage: Kazim is free in the house, he knows all the nooks and corners of the house and David had colluded with him in the past to lift stuffs from the house. Kazim now used that to glue him to the case. If they had done it together before, Uncle thinks they could do it again. To make things worse for David, Kazim said they would find an empty case of gun in David's room. It was Uncle's gun's case and it was found in David's room, while the gun was in uncle's room. How David got the gun-case was the question raised, since Uncle's room was always locked. That was enough to convince Uncle."

"Could David then have colluded with them again to bring them home with the loot in the first place, assuming he knew about it?" I asked.

"That's part of the confusion. The guys couldn't be foolish enough to come with him. He genuinely subdued them and brought them home."

The story was foggy and I decided to leave it until I saw David himself. The issue about the gun-case made his situation worse. Even though he claimed he had only taken it out of fascination, some people in the neighborhood did not see it that way. They were convinced by Kazim's story and thought David might be planning to get the gun to rob. Most of them did not hear the distinction between the gun-case and the gun; all they assumed was that he had a gun. This problem, of course, was also due to the difference in mentality between the people and David. To them, a young man needed and possessed a gun only because he was an armed robber, an assassin, or a virulent cult member. To David, someone who grew up in West, it was different; he grew up knowing people owning guns.

David also did not help himself. He became irate and threatened to kill someone in their house and two people in the neighborhood, implying his uncle's wife, Kazim, and Kunle. He had always been in a fight with his uncle's wife and he thought she was responsible for the earlier suspicion of him and the incarceration. He thought that, otherwise, his uncle would trust him more than to throw him in jail. Because of the threat, however, his uncle did not want him to be released from the cell, as was about to be done in a few days. His uncle feared he might carry out his threat and that would be trouble for him. He was the one who brought David from London and that made him responsible for his actions.

Due to David's fame, the story spread throughout the town. Elderly people in his neighborhood took it with mixed feelings; some with fear, some with contempt, and some with both. And these feelings were already mentally ostracizing David, even in his absence.

I began to count the days of his imprisonment: four, five, six, seven,

David was still there in the prison. I was worried, but I tried to remain calm. There was little or nothing I could do. I could not even go there to see him. So, I waited. I tried to calm Ruka as well; she had been worried over all sorts of rumors about the event. I told her the stories were untrue. Although I did not know the truth, I hoped none of the stories would be true. That was one thing that troubled me most. It would be too bad for him if he was really the one who asked the boys to do it. I waited for the truth.

People already knew that my house was his second home, and they came to ask me about the case. I tried to convince everyone to his sympathy. One thing I believed was that, even if he was as such involved, the people should not treat him this way. But I could not blame anyone because his threats were also doing more damage. David was only unequivocally popular among the youths, but not among the elderly. Many of the elderly did not understand his language, and the message from his body language was often taken in a stereotype. His fancy clothes, things of envy to the youth, and often sent by his family from London, were, to the elderly, too expensive and un-homely. The only young man in the neighborhood who could afford the kind of David's wardrobe, and who dressed like him, was generally distrusted as a scoundrel whose business was believed unclean. Now, they heard of David threatening to kill, while they believed he had a gun.

There was a problem that this could cause, and I was carefully poised to prevent it from happening to my friend, regardless of his involvement. David was in the prison where criminals were. He was intermingling with them day and night, and this could have a bad influence on him. Most Nigerian prisons were criminal-making institutions, and many parents made the mistake of locking their wayward children in there for punishment and correction. Little or nothing did they know that they were actually locking them up for more corruption. Growing children are quite impressionable, no matter what stage they are, and there was no good provision for juvenile delinquents in this part of the globe. They mixed with the rotten fruits in the prisons and they contracted the criminal germs.

Yet, for David, as it was for most others, the environment outside was chilling up for him. Many people were already mentally ostracizing him. Of course, very easily, the criminal world would not only throw its gates wide open for such children, it would also be enticingly promising at such critical points of their lives. By this understanding, I knew I had work to do; I had to rub out all those kinds of germs out of his mind if they had begun to breed, and I had to stop him from thinking of revenge. I prepared myself for it. Though David was no longer a little kid, he was not yet an adult, and his developmental stage may be the most crucial.

Nigeria did not yet recognize dual citizenship, and one either had to be a Nigerian or foreigner. For this reason, David was booked as a British citizen and the police, at first, wanted to deport him to England. They dropped the idea when they found no proof against him, and especially because they could not do anything his uncle did not like. His uncle was a man with muscle in the state. Although, he was yet to become a minister in the president's cabinet, he had once been the chairman of a local government and a gubernatorial candidate, and he was a fairly successful businessman. In Nigeria, men with muscles were laws in themselves, laws often respected and protected by the police. Because they did not find anything against him, the police also could only keep him in prison because his uncle said so. His uncle wanted him to be there, perhaps until he could get him out of the country by himself. He was angry and afraid he might carry out his threat.

After two grueling weeks, David was finally released. But because his uncle was still afraid of him, he still tried to keep him restrained. He placed him in an apartment house he built as a police quarters to have his neighborhood under police protection. It was directly in front of his house and some of the apartments were occupied by a few police officers. Although it was not a major police station, and it was not the one in which David was initially held, a section of it was used as a police office, and another as prisons. And although David was now a free man, as the apartment was a free place for him to live, but the idea that he was living with policemen made him seem under police surveillance. His uncle did this especially because he was about to go on a business trip out of the country, and he did not want to keep David in prison or leave him at home with his wife.

David met me under the tree the day he was released. He was gaunt and unkempt, which made him appeared wretched. His body odor revealed that he had not bathed in a long time. A heavy bandage wrapped around his right hand made him look mean and desperate. It was a wound and it smelled worse than his body.

I started smiling at him before he got to me, more a twitting smile than an ordinary one, and it relaxed him as I intended. He did not want to be felt sorry for.

"You're lean, man," I said as I ran my eyes conspicuously over him.

He smiled soundly. "You don't know what it's like to be in that hole."

"I know. I only didn't expect you to be this affected. I heard you were the president of the prisoners, is that true? You must have spread your tentacles a great deal."

"Yeah, who told you?"

"News - always spreading around." Then he told me the story. He fought the president in the prison and won the title for himself. The guy had a knife and cut David's thumb in the fight. The thumb later became infected, and then a whitlow.

"I was just lucky. The policemen ignored it at first and it grew malignant. Then they took me to the hospital when my whole hand swelled up. The doctor said if it had been left a little longer, it could have led to an amputation of the hand."

"That must have been a hell of a pain." I empathized with him.

"A very bad pain."

He told me all about the prison experience, how he had fought on more than one occasion to defend his title; how he had suffered pain, hunger, and other inhumanities; and how he had always had to sleep with his backside against the wall so he would not wake up to find somebody's dick up his ass. I listened to him and I only asked a few questions. I was cautious. I wanted to divert his mind from any anger, tension, and any threat of which he could have been made. Though he became relaxed on the threats eventually, he was still angry and bitter. Then he got to the issue of the stealing and we both became serious.

"But did you do it, David?" I asked him. "Tell me the truth. I don't expect you to look at me in the eye and lie to me. You know how we are - you and I. It is not of immediate importance whether you did it or not, but it is very important whether you'll lie to me or tell me the truth. Did you do it?"

"I didn't do it. You would have known, wouldn't you? I was just a fall guy. They set me up and that's why I shouldn't let those guys go free. It's now I realized that when I came into this country I didn't know anything and I made too many friends than is good for my reputation..."

"...than is good for your entire welfare. How do you think people will believe you didn't do it?"

"I don't care whether they believe me or not. I know it within myself, and I'm going to kill those rats for it. Look at it this way: do you think I'll know about it and still bring them back home after they'd been successful? When I can make money from them and when they were not fools? Think of it. I went out all the way to Fiditi to bring them back here. I was helped by a policeman who lives in that town to put them in a taxi. The policeman works at the Durbar police station and he saw me there and testified. How could I have known about it and still do that to myself?"

"But have you lifted in the house with Kazim before?"

"Yes, I have," he replied, "He's not new to the house and we've done shit like that together. But this was robbery and not lifting - I didn't do it with him, but I don't care anymore. I don't care what anybody thinks, except for Uncle. That's what's hurting me. He trusted me. He couldn't have locked me up like that if not influenced by someone. I only wish he knew I didn't do it."

"You and your threats influenced him, not anybody, or at least more than anybody you think. First, you pissed him off by being dragged into the whole thing, and then you're shaking him out of his pants by your threat. They found his gun-case in your room, didn't they? You have to cut all that threats out and get serious with yourself. You've told me a lot about him and you know as well as I do that this whole thing disappoints him. How much careful you can be is the only remedy now."

Our discussion over it was all right for me. I had to know what I was involved in and where I was going. I was ready to run the neighborhood gauntlet with him rather than desert him, and we surely ran one. We endured humiliating looks and remarks. Some people have a way of over-blowing such situations, and we had to endure their exaggerations and pseudo-moral displays.

When a middle-aged woman saw him at my place one day, she stared embarrassingly at us for a long time, and shook her head pitifully, as if she was acting in a sad drama. I did not know that her impudent head would not fall off. One man came to my father, as if he was a neighborhood special goodwill officer, and advised him to stop David from visiting me. But I was proud of my father's reply at his effrontery: "My son knows right from wrong. I don't need to tell him what to do or pick his friends."

My father did not ask David to know whether he did it or not, neither did he ask me. In fact, he would be hard to convince if he asked, because he also thought David knew about it. But he did not think it was right to ostracize him as the older residents of the neighborhood were doing. Some of them even wanted him to be cast out of the neighborhood; they only could not pursue it for fear of losing his uncle's support in the community.

IV

I could stand for longer times on my legs now, I could hobble for longer distance with my cane, and I could manage to walk a few feet without the cane. But the pelvis joints still held together and the knees also remained the same. My father still believed the exercise would one day loosen the holds in the joints, but my hope in it was now dwindling and I was becoming bored with the exercise. Yet, everyone advised me to be patient and persistent.

I tried to be patient, but several things made it difficult, including the fear of an imminent war in the country. One afternoon someone broke a news report to me: Alhaja Kudirat Abiola, the vocal wife of the jailed president-elect, was murdered in broad daylight on a Lagos street. It was obvious that it was a political murder and the fear in the country was that it might lead to a civil war. In the past, there had been several civil disturbances over the annulled presidential election and the prolonging lock-up of Chief Abiola, but now no one could tell how far any next one would go. I did not want war, especially when I had pictorial reports of the humanitarian catastrophes in war-torn African nations and other nations around the world. It was bad enough in news and I was afraid of a direct experience. Yet, if war broke out, I might not be able to survive it in my condition. I was a lame duck.

***

Life did not return to normal for David. His uncle was out of the country and was not expected back until the end of David's final exams. Although his uncle arranged for an ample allowance for him and there was no financial problem, but he had emotional problems. Out of them all, he pined for London. That was where he saw as home. "That's my freedom," he always said, but he was afraid his mother might force him to continue his education in Nigeria. She still hoped to continue the Nigerianization process, even though she did not know how much David had learned.

David may have really been nigerianized in some way. He lived among the people and had learned some things about the culture, but he was not as nigerianized as would be commensurate with the number of years he had spent in the country. For one, the majority of the people among whom he socialized hoped to improve their spoken English, and they saw him as an opportunity. They spoke to him only in English and David now could only speak a few words in Yoruba, and mostly curse words. Also, his Western culture, especially dressing fashion, was admired by the people of his social group, and therefore they got better on him more than he did on them.

Part of this failure to learn enough may have been David's fault, nonetheless. He enjoyed his oyinbo status and he always tried to maintain it.

David finished his exams in June and his uncle came back into the country in July. He sent for David and asked what his plans were.

"I'd like to go back to London," he replied.

And without question, his uncle said dramatically, "Your wish is granted."

In September, David left back for London. And that marked the end of an era in the story of my sickness. The time coincided with the time I wanted to recover myself from the trauma caused by Nike and Banji, and David's presence would have helped me toward my recovery. Loneliness and worry crept back into my life. It was as if he left me as he had met me, except for the memory and lessons of our experience.

Ruka now came frequently to give me company. Our relationship had grown to be the opposite of the one between our fathers. Even though my father liked her, and was very fatherly to her, he was never comfortable whenever she was with me. He always kept an extra eye out for her to ensure her safety. An accident to her in our house would definitely be misinterpreted in the town.

By the time David left for London, the natural incompatibility between him and Ruka had created a mental gulf between them, but they still loved each other. Nature, in her non-sentimentality, was now to make the gulf physical, and we saw it begin on the September day as I watched David walk away from me, as he reached the door and turned back to take a last look at me, and as he smiled and raised his two thumbs up, complimenting our good old days and wishing me good luck. But this was not only significant to Ruka's relationship with him; it was to mine as well, and I hoped our four eyes would meet again someday.

SIXTEEN

Journey to Ibadan

I

A hungry man, they say, is an angry man. I should have known this for myself, for anger is nothing but hunger for something - for food, for freedom, for love, for recognition, for attention, for rights, for fantasy, or for any other thing. As a result of my hunger for many things: food, attention, love, health, independence, freedom, and career realization, I became someone about to blow up from anger. I was angry with myself and angry at the world.

I tried always to suppress the emotion, but, on few occasions when I could not hold it, it made me difficult for my father and the rest of my family to deal with. I knew how problematic anger could be to health. Yet, whenever I was angry and could not let it out, I worried and I seethed. I boiled within like hot water on a flaming stove, with my composure threatened and my blood pressure threatening.

Even though humans create language by their ingenuity, language seems a phenomenon that possesses a life of its own, sometimes playing on human folly. It was interesting to realize that the word "anger" was only a letter short of the word "danger," while really anger is a step short of danger. Sango, the warrior king who fought and won many wars, conquered and subdued many lands for the glory of his kingdom, fell to the battle against his own emotion. In Sango's brittle and uncontrollable anger he had brought destruction on his own palace with his power of thunder and consequently led to the end of his life on earth. This was the counsel my father often reminded me of whenever I burst like a volcano.

For a good part of my time I gave myself freely to my emotion to rule me. I wanted every wrong righted, every command obeyed, but my problem was that I did not understand the nature of the world, and that what anger wants, it buys at the price of the soul. This was no longer the issue between my father and me; it was between my emotion and me. It was an internal war.

Periodically, Uncle Tunji now sent me foodstuffs that helped me in taking care of my hunger for food, but the flood of other emotional troubles in my life kept me hungrier for food than I had ever been, and I often remained wanting. That was a sign of depression.

My grandmother returned to Nigeria late in September. Now seventy-one years old, age had taken its toll and she could not continue her business anymore. She wanted my legs to be operated in America because of how good she had seen medical treatment there. But Uncle Jibola had to be given time to be financially ready, as she said. Hence, it was now all about patience - waiting patiently. For my composure and my goal, I had to exercise patience. I tried, but the burden that I had to go through to uphold the virtue was heavy, and it soon became too heavy.

Several months passed while the condition remained the same. I knew Uncle Jibola would stand by his promise, but I wondered whether the time he would finish school and be ready, as now planned, would not be a time too late for me. I began to think on how to struggle to achieve a relative freedom, wondering if I could find help for my legs in Nigeria. I pondered on what to do while I went about supplicating to God with increasing fervor.

Concentration during salats became difficult for me, however, as my mind strayed repeatedly in many directions every minute of the day. I was slipping into depression, forgetting myself in things I was doing. Many times during a prayer, I would catch myself lost in other thoughts or reveries and would have to start all over again. After several failures at observing a prayer one afternoon, I finally got it right and was about to complete it when I realized that I did not have any clothes on. I had to start all over again.

Many a night I slept too little than good for me. My mind was always too saturated with dismal thoughts and my heart too clogged for my eyes to get a blink. I resorted to taking sleeping medicines almost every night, bringing me closer and closer to its addiction.

Sometimes I would pick up my journal and write down accounts of the day. And sometimes I used the journal to talk to God, though unsure whether He would read it. On the 28th of September I wrote:

> God, why was I born into this world? Why? With this problem of my barred freedom, I still feel abandoned (by You and my father). How can I continue like this? Who am I to turn to? At this juncture, life doesn't seem to worth continuing. But I believe in You, God, I believe in You. If there is still light at the end of this

hellish tunnel, please let me see it now. And if there is not, please let me die now. Don't let me suffer any further, please.

Oct. 5th '96: I feel despondently about life. I feel detached from the future; I feel it might never come. But when I think about God, I feel may be it could come, but I also feel ready for death, though at the bottom up my heart, I don't want it. I prefer to live, but...

Oct. 31st '96: I don't know why God would make forbidden the only door that seems open when the rest are closed. The only way out I see today in my life is through suicide. I wish I hadn't heard about the preaching; it would have been my excuse on the Day of Judgment. I see myself in the midst of an ocean, with my boat stuck and my oars broken, perhaps reparable. I see no one close by. Some other boats were around, those whom we took off at the same shore, but they seem not to see me or hear my call for help. Is there any breath of heaven? Or is it just too bland to help? I looked up at the sky, in search of stars to direct my journey. Rain fog depressed the sight of the sky. My belly is twitching. I'm hungry. How long will I last?

The persistence of my condition seemed to have frazzled out everyone in our house. They just watched on and awaited a miracle. I was now like a burden, and the house became an uneasy place to endure. By these, I became so edgy that I found faults everywhere, perhaps unconsciously seeking attention. With my father's wife, it was an unpleasant story, deepening the rift between me and my father. Though I always tried to reason that my father may be stuck in the difficult situation, but I carried the brunt of his attitude. I was confused and distressed about it and I always wondered why this would be happening to me at this period of my life.

My suffering marked a height one evening when I fell down while trying to take a shower. I was the only one in the bathroom and I had absent-mindedly shut the door before I remembered that I always kept it slightly open to hang my towel and to be able to call for help after I had bathed to the knees where I could not reach beyond. Then, I reached out to open the door. It was a few feet away, but I could not reach it. I stretched further, perhaps because it did not seem unreachable from where I stood, or perhaps my mind had strayed away into something else. All of a sudden, I lost control of myself. The sense of danger swept over me and I shrieked as I crashed to the floor.

I was lucky I did not break a bone to add to my problem, but the emotional pain that resulted was traumatizing. I thought my heart should not be left to burn anymore. I thought it was high time the Heavens sent down rain to quench the flame devouring me and wash away my tears.

II

"The tough witch days are over," Baba Akinnu said to me when I told him about the American plan, and he advised that any medical aid at this point was workable, because "the hip joints may now require their (medical) help." Baba Akinnu was in a position to know that such a war could not simply be said to be over like that, but he wanted to keep me positively assured about the process. Talking to my father, he instead promised to keep a strong watch over me wherever I went to prevent any renewed attack.

With my mind in this comfort zone, I decided to check out my condition at the hospital to see whatever they could offer me. If medical treatment could now help on the remaining problem, I might as well see what Nigerian hospitals could do about it without having to wait uncertainly for America. I was desperate. Though I wanted America so much, I needed to get out of this condition by any means possible.

I contacted our family doctor to determine what problems remained with the legs, and if they could now be easily treated medically. The doctor thought it was a good idea, but, from what he had seen trying to help me in the past, he was reluctant to tackle it. Doctors like him who had experienced witchcraft were often cautious when dealing with suspicious patients. Besides, I had gone to him only a few months after one of the famous doctors in the town died in such a mysterious circumstance. Nonetheless, he sent me for x-ray photographing of the joints.

I sat nervously in front of the doctor, waiting for him to decipher the photographs. Behind him was a poster with an absurd inscription, to which my eyes strayed: YOUR HOSPITAL BILLS ARE A FRACTION OF YOUR FUNERAL EXPENSES. That was a cold truth, Doc. Our physicians, then, are our brokers, helping us make practical investments toward the last harvest. Life is one huge alligator, and its most reasonable appeaser may be one who feeds the animal, knowing it will eat him last.

"The good news is that we can now see something to deal with," the doctor finally said. He saw some mal-formation in the bones and he thought that orthopedic surgery could take care of it. He gave my father names of three hospitals where he thought the surgery could be done, all government-owned, U.C.H. inclusive.

Then the reality of surgery swept over me. How much money would it cost? I began to wonder - N20, 000, N30, 000? These were lots of money. How much time would it take? How much pain? I shuddered at these thoughts. Would there be physical therapy in the treatment? I hoped not. What about the overall success of the surgery?

When Sister Toyin heard about it, she promised to help in the financial part whenever it came to that, but warned us not to do the surgery in any government hospital. She had worked at U.C.H. before she left for England and she knew about the dwindling condition of the hospitals. She emphasized that this kind of surgery needed keen attention that only could be got at a responsible hospital, now usually private hospitals.

Once again, the doctor gave my father the name and address of a 'good' surgeon at Ibadan. He was a chief orthopedic surgeon at U.C.H. but had a private clinic in the city.

But my father relapsed into his lackadaisical attitude. For the rest of the year he sat on it, allowing procrastination to steal into our time. I became angrier with him than I had ever been in my life, and I became so edgy that for a few times we clashed in the house. Sometimes I could not help but to remember what Aunty Sidi had told me about him, that he was being used to stall my progress. Other times I wondered whether I had caused it by myself, or it was just the complexity of our home, or both, or all.

In February, two months after the doctor's suggestion, my father finally attempted to do something. He asked me to go to Uncle Tunji and tell him to take me to the hospital. This was a bad idea. Suddenly deciding to send me to Uncle Tunji who had not been informed about the new development and my coming was a way of trying to ignore his responsibilities. But because I wanted to get out of my predicament, I did not have any choice.

It was my first trip to Ibadan after all the years. I did not know what I would meet, so I was not at ease with myself. I prayed as the bus gobbled up the road, and as my eyes delighted at seeing the road and its sidelining forest once again in my life. The last time I traveled on the road, I remembered, on the cold December day in 1993, it had not been certain that I would travel back on it in my lifetime. I thanked God that I was alive.

PART THREE

Family Matters & Self-realization

The Lord is my shepherd; I shall not want.

He maketh me to lie down in green pastures:
He leadeth me beside the still waters.
He restoreth my soul:
He leadeth me in the paths of righteousness for his name's sake.
Yea, though I walk through the valley of the shadow of death,
I will fear no evil: for thou art with me;
Thy rod and thy staff, they comfort me.
Thou preparest a table before me in the presence of mine enemies:
Thou anointest my head with oil; my cup runneth over.
Surely, goodness and mercy shall follow me all the days of my life:
And I will dwell in the house of the Lord forever.

Psalm 23

SEVENTEEN

Coming to America

I

Three years have told little or no new tale on the city. I could have been away for only three weeks. Unlike on humans, time seems sympathetic on the inanimate occupants of the earth. Perhaps, then, events and effects are the real babies of time, gradations by which it could be measured, rather or more than the movement of the earth.

Uncle Tunji had moved into his new house. It was a beautiful architectural piece singing its own song, as Goethe might think, amid the hoarse cries of the old buildings that made up the neighborhood. But it was yet unpainted, and that hinted that Uncle Tunji must be broke. With a mixture of joy and surprise, I was welcomed by the family: Uncle Tunji; his wife, simply called Mama Lanre; Lanre, the first son; Sunkanmi, the second son; Bisola, the third child and only daughter.

Without wasting time, I delved into the reason of my visit. And just as I had envisaged, Uncle Tunji became angry over it. First, it was over the idea of putting me on the road without an escort, in spite of all the troubles and years of the past. Next, it was about my father's apparent neglect of his responsibility.

"What does your father think he's doing?" he said. "Sending you to me to take you to the hospital? What is he doing himself? Or is he not your father?" Uncle Tunji knew all the languages that responsibility spoke and he had ears that heard them more audibly whenever he was broke.

I said nothing. I knew my father had played it too frivolously to be right, but I did not know what to say. After all these years in my condition, he really should not have sent me out like this, in this circumstance especially. He should have come here with me, or first come alone for discussion about it. He should have acted earlier. He should have acted in any manner better seemly than this. But I knew my father enough to know that this was part of his nature. His levity sometimes went a little excessive to displease a few people concerned. Although financial hard times may have contributed to this, but he was a man who was smart enough to know how to eat his cake as well as have it. And he always did. Even during our draft matches, when his friends mocked him at my beating him, he would say he was not losing the matches, since it was his son who was winning. “My son’s victory is my victory,” he always laughed last.

No doubt, he would have his cake here as well, whether they let him eat it or not. He knew that before he sent me here.

Uncle Tunji’s first reaction was, “You'll go back to him and he'll take you to the hospital by himself." But he was confused at the same time. Considering my condition, he found it difficult to send me back to my father. That would also make him less considerate as he thought my father was. He sent for my grandmother, instead.

Though my grandmother also became angry that my father sent me there without an escort, she took me to the clinic immediately. She is my mama, and nothing made sense to her other than my welfare.

The clinic was at Ikolaba, a section of Ibadan increasingly inhabited by wealthy people. I was stunned to hear the registration fee. Thirty, forty, or fifty naira was the range I had in mind, or at most a hundred naira. But we were in a private specialist clinic and I had stayed too long in a hidden corner of the world, shut away from everyday life, to know the current state of things.

"Eight-hundred naira," the smart looking nurse said. It did not surprise my grandmother and she paid.

Doctor Akinyemi’s appearance was impressive enough to encourage someone into the medical field. He was wealthily cut, light in complexion, and handsome. He would be in his late '30s, perhaps early '40s. My eyes may have been too accustomed to the common Nigerian condition in which poverty withered people’s looks beyond their age. Even many doctors were not spared. But Dr. Akinyemi practiced in England as well as in Nigeria, and was not touched by the Nigerian condition.

He clipped the x-ray photograph of my hips to a light board and examined it thoroughly. He had read the case note put up by his nurse before my grandmother and I came into his office and he already knew fairly about my condition.

"These are fusions," he said, his eyes still fixed on the photograph.

"Fusions?"

"Your bones have grown into one another," he said confidently, and almost lightly, as if it was my hair that had overgrown and needed a cut. "See, there are no joints here and here anymore." He pointed at the two hip joints in the photograph. Then he asked for more detail of my sickness and

I explained the medical history.

"Come over here." He beckoned me to his examining table so he could examine my hips. He tried but in vain to move them. That confirmed his theory of fusion. He reached for my knees and found them stiff as well.

"We would need x-ray photographs of the knees, too. I don't know exactly the extent of their problem right now, but I think they are fused as well."

"I think so, too. They give me so much trouble that I think the bones must have been seriously affected."

He returned to the photograph and said to me, "What you have is septic fusion at the hips."

When I heard the word 'septic', I cut in. "Does that mean this condition has been going on since the beginning of my sickness?"

"Yes," he replied, "From the history of your sickness, it may have been going on since the beginning."

"Could that mean that I should have allowed the tractions then?" I had told him about the traction in the detailed history I gave.

He thought for a little while before he answered the question. "Okay, let's put it this way. If I were to be in charge of your case then, what I would have done was to drain all the blood in your system and give you another one. Your blood had been poisoned and that was a critical condition. It didn't mean the traction would not be there, however; it would only be for a secondary concern."

I nodded in comprehension.

"Probably, the same goes with your knees," he paused and stared at me, "although we're not hundred percent sure yet. But looking at you from this point," he paused again, "I'll say your treatment is going to cost a fortune."

"How?"

"There are two different types of treatments for the hips. One, called *gird stone*, involves cutting the heads of the femurs where they join the pelvis. You would move about functionally, but your height would be about four inches short.

"The second one is a total replacement of the hips. In this case, you will walk better than the first, but you will not have the freedom of doing some little things like wearing your own socks or tying your shoe laces. The joints may pop out in such circumstances and you'll have to go back to the hospital to have them restored. And you would even have to replace the hips in, say, periods of ten years."

This seemed to me a dilemma, even a trilemma, considering the choice of remaining fused up like the hips of a mannequin. However, I was equally concerned about cost and I asked the only question that came to my mind.

"Which one of them is cheaper?"

"The gird stone is cheaper," he replied, "Far cheaper."

"And am I going to walk all right again with that?"

"You're going to walk all right, but not hundred percent as you used to walk before the sickness. It's a treatment that is better for old people, so the total hip replacement may be better for you."

"Money is a factor to be reckoned with, doctor," I said, "Let's have the cost for the cheaper one."

He pulled out a blank paper and calculated from British pounds to naira.

"For the hips, the cost is N100, 000."

My heart sunk. I could not imagine where I would get a hundred thousand naira.

"And for the knees, to make your treatment complete - as I figure they are fused too, the only treatment I can give you is to cap the heads of your knees with rubber replacements, and then we can achieve about 120 degrees room for your movements." Calculating again from pounds to naira, he added, "That would cost N200, 000 each. And that makes the entire treatments about N500, 000 altogether. Our hospital charge would be N30, 000 for six weeks stay; that makes it all N530, 000."

I blew it out unconsciously, flabbergasted. "Five-hundred and thirty thousand?" That was more than three times what the country's president *legally* earned in a year. I first shuddered at the cost, but then the feeling disappeared. It deflated me of any expectation. I was waiting for a cost to split up among my people, but this was just too much. I did not think I could face any single person and ask for N100, 000. I did not think I was worth that much to anyone with the money. It was too much for me to worry about and I saved myself the troubles of worrying and prepared for whatever life now held in stock for me. Once it cannot be changed, it is fate, the fate with which to continue the struggles of life.

I explained everything to my grandmother in vernacular and she did not know what to say either.

"What do you think?" the doctor finally asked.

"If I'd do anything, it would be the cheaper one." I replied. "But, we'll have to go home first." I asked him why he calculated from pounds to naira, because I knew it was what made the cost that high.

"We would have to import the materials from England; they're not available in Nigeria."

I nodded in comprehension and rose to go. He put everything in written form for me and I shook hands with him. The prince of Zamunda would not have been sad over such an amount. Although I was not thinking of him, but if I did remember him, this was a moment I would wish I were he, or like him. Different strokes for different princes.

It was already dark and I could not go back to Oyo. On our way back to Uncle Tunji's house I began to imagine the walking manner I would get if I were lucky to have the surgery done. I tried to picture it the way the doctor had said. I did not mind four inches shortage in my height – afterall, I was not hoping to replace Akeem Olajuwon at the NBA. Even, if it was possible, I could sell four more inches to pay for my surgery and passage to America; I would still be taller than Danny Devito.

Walking functionally to me meant being able to function as a movie director. If I could become healthy enough to live my life in my career as I wanted, then that makes me as healthy as a sportsman with enough health for his career. In some way, mind is health and health his mind. It was assuring enough to know that Spielberg did not have to jump over any tree to make a movie a winner. I would only not dare think of becoming a Jackie Chan or Wesley Snipes. Two types are the fighters in this world: if you cannot be a lion, be a fox; if you cannot be a fox, be a lion; there is always a prize for everyone to fight for.

II

My grandmother did not say much about the new development. She only prayed. All she wanted now was for me to be flown to America for the treatments. I liked the idea, but I was afraid that this might now be too long a shot for me to take. Yet, gathering such an amount from people here in Nigeria seemed a longer shot. It was only the power of strong currency from abroad that could solve my problem.

Uncle Tunji arrived from a party and I realized that he had been to the hospital. That night I heard the longest speech he had ever made to me in my life. By nature, he was taciturn, but, coming from a party, he was high on liquor and he poured out his mind on my situation.

"The doctor has told me everything," he cut me short as I tried to tell him the events of the day. "I don't think there is anything to worry yourself about, however; the best we could do for you is fly you to America. That's what we've already been hoping for, and now it's the only option reasonable. They would do it better in America, and the cost would not be much different. The cost that the doctor gave you is the cost of the treatment abroad. So, why spend all that money here instead of where we are going to get its worth. All we have to do now is to push on it to be done, and I'll try and see to it.

"Although I don't have money enough to tackle it alone, and I don't think Jibola is ready to carry it all alone now, but I'll try and we'll do something for you about it. If we can get more people in America to be in on this, we would get you there sooner. So, Baba is our resort to tell the necessary people to have it done."

I stared at him in wonder. This was interesting news to me. I could see the conclusion in his eyes, but I could not say anything. In the family, Uncle Tunji was a strong voice that could not be ignored. If he could be serious on it like this, and Baba could pick up steam to drive it, I might not really be far away from America.

Uncle Tunji went on and on, and I listened. In the end he turned to my father's issue. "The way your father did was not appropriate, and that was why I was angry at first. Now, see what has turned up from this. Would he give you five hundred thousand naira to do the surgery?

"What I want you to do now is not to tell your father about this plan. Just give him the doctor's report and let him find all he can to contribute, and then we'll join it up with some money to send you to America instead. And I mean it, don't tell your father about the plan. You know he would relax and leave everything to us. Tell him to get any amount that he can in the N530, 000 and that we'll do the rest. That's the deal. He has children in England and he could raise money from them if he wants to. Tell him to do it."

That speech was long, but far from boring. I enjoyed every bit of it. It made me feel being responsible to, after all these months that I had been thinking of myself as neglected. I thought I could rely on what he said. My major problem had been the uncertainty of how long it could take Uncle Jibola to be ready to help me, and sometimes whether I could really get such a magnitude of help from him alone. But raising it like this and having Baba talk to my other uncles in the U.S. could make it come quickly. Due to the complex nature of our family, Baba was the only one in a position free enough to talk to anyone about such a contribution of funds, and I knew that now that the problem had been known, Baba would be more than willing to do that.

However, one thing worried me: my father. How could I keep the idea away from my father? Morality, seemliness, and filial responsibility stared at me in the eye. Morality in this sense was not only about dealing morally with my father, as African tradition required, but also prudence in navigating my own life rightly out of this situation, so that I would neither hurt my filial obligation nor my destiny. The modern world is one of romantic individualism, perhaps selfishness, justified only by its personal gains. But Africa was slow at becoming modern. The sense of family and communal respect still played roles in many people's lives.

My father would like the idea, but the question of whether he would leave the whole responsibility for my maternals or not was a real question. Knowing my father as someone who would try to eat his cake as well as have it, and from what had been going on between us in the house, I knew this was a problem, and I decided to take some time to think about what to do.

Uncle Tunji drove me back to Oyo on the following day. My grandmother came with us. They intended to drop me and turn back; they were still indignant over how I had been sent to Ibadan and they decided not to discuss the matter with my father at all. But after meeting with my father, Uncle Tunji could not hold his anger, though he tried to be polite about it.

"We were surprised to see him yesterday, and he explained that you sent him to me to take him to the hospital."

"Yes," my father replied, "I thought we shouldn't wait too much on his condition anymore, and during the Ramadan like this I'm always busy, so we decided that he should come to you."

"You shouldn't have done it like that. That was not the right way to do it. However, we have taken him to the hospital and he has the report. We just came to drop him off."

He walked out and my grandmother followed suit. My father was shocked at this attitude. It appeared as disrespectful of him and he was surprised that my grandmother turned back on him as well. But he bore it philosophically.

As without words my father and mother fell apart, he and my maternals also did. It was the last time they would look each other in the face, the last time they would ever see each other, the last time they would ever talk to each other.

In 1993, when I decided to leave U.C.H., Uncle Tunji had refused to let me leave, thinking it was not reasonable to send me to my father in the sick state. So, he was justified to blame my father now. But, justified or not, this was not a good sign for me. As sick and in need of help as I was, I found myself in a mud of family matters, struggling lamely to get out of the problem. In the coming months, the lack of harmony between them would tell terribly on my prospect. I tried not to look at these as anyone's fault. I took it rather as God or Nature's way of creating stormier path for me to sail through. Though a disappointment, I had had too many disappointments that it now appeared teleological, and more of it were only more hurdles to jump over to reach the end of the race. Nonetheless, it was a difficult situation for me. Hurdles are no mirages that disappear when you are near, they remain real as ever and they need your sweats before they are washed away.

"Five hundred and thirty thousand naira!" my father exclaimed when he saw the hospital report. Then he rose up and went to attend to a visitor.

The situation from the day's event made it more difficult for me to decide whether to tell him about the American plan. I thought that if I did not tell him, I might not be doing the right thing to him, but if I told him, I might not be doing the right thing to myself. Bili was in Oyo at the time, so I discussed it with him. Two heads, they say, is better than one. We jogged the matter up and down and arrived at a conclusion: to keep it away from my father. Baami also agreed with us. Yet, my conscience continued to perturb me over the idea. Despite all odds of the past, my father was big in my heart. But expediency, we decided, was the watchword. Sometimes it is the most reasonable - if done with adequate concern of all reasonability.

A few days later, when my father finally came to talk about the situation, he told me of an idea he had. "Someone suggested a surgeon at the Baptist Hospital at Ogbomosho. He was the one who operated on the NEPA[44] manager who had an accident last year. The manager now walks fine. So I think we should give the surgeon a try. Or what do you think?"

The NEPA manager's case was a sad one. He had an automobile accident over a year earlier and had multiple fractures in his legs. He was admitted at the State General Hospital at Ilorin, about 70 miles from Oyo where he lived and worked. But things went awry for him. One day, three

[44] National Electric Power Authority

members of his family who were traveling to the hospital to visit him met with a fatal accident. All of them died, and that made his life worse. He stayed for a long time at the hospital but did not get well. Then he heard about the surgeon at the Baptist Hospital at Ogbomosho and he went to try him. The surgeon fixed his fractures, and now my father wanted me to try the surgeon.

After I have been betrothed to the opportunity of going to America for the treatments, I could not fall in love with such an option as this. Now, I either had to accept his idea or tell him of the American plan. But if I did not want him to suspect that I had kept it away from him at first, it was already too late to tell him of the plan. So, I accepted his idea.

For him, the situation was now one of rivalry between him and my maternals. If it would not cost him too much, he now wanted to get the remaining credits for my recovery. He was enthusiastic about the option and he arranged the trip for the following Tuesday.

My attitude to life now was to try to look and take things objectively. It was an attitude that I was growing to believe could cater rightly for the concern of everything in my life. I believed there was no mistake or chance in the works of God. Though I realized that my case was different from the NEPA manager's case - the manager had fractures; I had fusions – yet, I tried to take the disturbing suggestion objectively.

None of my father's cars were working anymore, so he arranged for us to go with Mr. Oseni, a banker friend of his. Most of his friends did not like the idea of him taking public transportation, so they often volunteered their cars for him whenever he had to travel. Mr. Oseni even offered to drive us, but my father took the wheel first.

We had a dangerous beginning. My father hit the road when a dreadful tractor-trailer was speeding down behind us. It was about a hundred yards away from us and my father figured that the speed of our small car would get us away before it came near. But he was wrong. The small car's speed had been worn by age and it could not do the job. The tractor-trailer's driver, whose temperament turned out to be more dreadful than his threatening vehicle, became angry and violently increased his speed down our trail to teach us some lessons for not giving him the way.

We saw him closing the gap between us unrelentingly. His was a huge vehicle compared to the small old Toyota Carina we were driving. It was like the one the Terminator used in chasing the pregnant Sarah Connor, and for once it felt as if we were being chased by a Terminator. Fear gripped me. Mr. Oseni screamed with fright. Then my father swerved off the road when he saw he could not beat the tractor-trailer in the run.

More than bad roads, sometimes anger and impatience were the causes of accidents on our roads. Instead for the driver to go his way, he displayed some madness at us. He also swerved his wheels and aimed to smash our car. But my father was fast enough to swerve further into the grass verge and averted the impending crash. Angry that he missed us, he cursed as his vehicle sped by.

The road between Oyo and Ogbomosho was not a good one. It had too many hills and corners that people often called it a death trap. And it was a single carriageway, which made it less worthy of the immensity and variety of traffic using it daily. The road recorded hundreds of accidents yearly and claimed several scores of lives along. It was the road on which the NEPA manager had his accident, and the same road his three family members died. The little experience of hitting the road for the journey reminded me of all these and I harbored a lurking fear throughout the journey. To add to the terror, we saw a new fatal accident on the way, with fresh human blood all over the scene.

III

The surgeon, Dr. Alex, listened attentively to the history of my sickness. He examined my joints and the x-ray photograph. Then he went into a monologue. He appeared as a busy man who did not have time to drag issues or window-dress. He knew all he thought he could do and he went straight to the points.

"I'll need x-ray films of your knees. Your hips are fused, but I'm not yet sure of the knees. It's until we have the x-ray films of them that I can be sure what their problem is. Besides, there's nothing we can do about them, unless they were not fused like the hips. If they were not fused, then physical therapy could help you out.

"For the hip joints, I'd cut off the head of your thighbone to loosen one hip for you. That would give you some freedom to be functional. I'll do nothing for the other one; it will have to remain as it is. I'll operate only one. It'd become about a few inches shorter than the other and you'd walk like this." He demonstrated, limping. At best, it was depressing.

My father looked at me for my reaction, but I kept my face inscrutable.

When Dr. Alex later saw the x-ray photographs of the knees, he advised us to try physical therapy, since there was nothing he could do to them. He pulled out a plain sheet of paper and wrote on it.

"You'll take this to the physical therapy department. I want them to work on the knees for three weeks and after that you'll come back here for the surgery. The physical therapy is going to be a little painful, but you have to endure it. If they tell me that you are not cooperative, I'm not going to work on your hip. So be a good man and endure the pains, okay?"

I nodded, fearfully and sadly. After all the pains I had gone through, the best advice I still got was to endure pains. We headed to the physical therapy department.

"You see that this doctor knows what he's doing?" my father commented on our way. I did not say anything because I knew he was engaged in salesmanship. He wanted to condition my mind to accept it as the reality, the best option I could get, and he exaggerated every thing about it.

Of course, I could go for the treatment if I had not known what I had known, which he did not know and did not know I had known. My goal now was to pursue the best I could get, even if it was the least some other person could get. Perhaps, a man should only come to terms with what he cannot change. I thought I could get something better, and I did not want to live with a situation that I could have made better. It would put me in regrets for a long time, perhaps as long as the rest of my lifetime. The way the surgeon demonstrated how I would walk was a difficult way to walk. It horrified me: having one leg sickly shorter, and the other fused.

As we approached the hall of the physical therapy, cries of agony greeted us. It was like a war infirmary, with wounded soldiers screaming at the blades cutting off their injured arms and legs. The Hall of Terror, I thought, remembering my last experience with physical therapy. I wished Jesus Christ would just descend right there and heal my legs before the physical therapist's hands tightened around them.

My therapist, one of the two therapists in the department, was a dark complexioned born-again Christian who went about her duty slowly and gently, and with a mind also intent on soul therapy. She had a female nurse whose official duty it seemed was both to nurse and to preach to patients, and she faltered in neither.

The pain was too much for me. Though gently and kindly, she bent my right knee forcefully, I cried out loudly, throwing my machismo out the window.

She let down on the force and said, "Sorry, but we'll do it again." She genuinely felt sorry for me, and I liked her for her kindness. I did not want to cry out like a baby anymore, so I buried my face in a pillow and cried into it.

The therapist and the nurse found a good friend in me. We always talked as friends and they did their best to help me. They set my appointment dates at three days a week: Monday, Wednesday, and Friday, and the therapist promised to try as much as possible to achieve 90 degrees movement room in the knees.

My father arranged that Bili and I would go on every appointment date on public transportation. This was now a dilemma. It was either I tell him about the American plan and risk whatever would come, or I go on with the surgery at Ogbomosho. I chose to tell him.

At first, he was indifferent, but I tried to convince him. I turned his attention to the difficult life I might end up living as a result of the surgery. "Dr. Alex only believes that this is the best we can achieve by the standards of the Nigerian economy and public health services," I added, "But since I have people beyond the Nigerian standards to help me, why couldn't I opt for it? This is an opportunity for me."

He pondered over it and then said, "Okay, let's do it this way. Go on with the physical therapy and follow up things at Ibadan. By the end of the three weeks' therapy, let's see where the situation is to make our final decision."

This sounded understanding and cooperative of him, yet it was not. A new game began in the house, a game I did not like. He wanted me to do the surgery at Ogbomosho and he had misgivings about me. I did not want to do the surgery at Ogbomosho and I also had misgivings about him. Also, we were both aware of the worsening friction in our relationship. He looked at me as a fool because I did not want to go along with him, and I looked at him as disingenuous because I saw his attitude as selfish and unsympathetic to me. Hence, there continued a psychological hard time for me, a time so painful that I thought it was worse than my physical pains.

IV

The thought of traveling on the road between Oyo and Ogbomosho three times a week for three consecutive weeks terrified me. The accident we saw on the first day we went to the hospital rubber-stamped my cause to fear the trips. Although we did not see the victims, as the place had been cleared by the Road Safety Corps before we reached the spot, but anyone who has witnessed an automobile accident before could imagine how gory the situation must have been.

An accident that I witnessed in March of 1993 stuck to my memory. It was a grisly experience that, at this point, formed a specter in my imagination. It was enough to make me a road advocate.

I was going to Shagamu with Uncle Tunji to pick up an allocation of building cements at the cement factory. The Lagos-Ibadan road, along which Shagamu was, was a better road than that of Oyo-Ogbomosho. It was a double carriage highway with a wide grass section between the to and fro roads.

We had driven for about half an hour when we came to the area of the accident. The place was hilly and we ascended toward Lagos. At the peak of the hill, we began to descend, still toward Lagos. Just then, we saw a man sitting on the side of the road, groaning. He was trying to move. Behind him, into the bush, was a small green car that looked as if taking a pee as passengers often did when they had to go. It was an accident and the guy was a victim. It was a single car accident. Perhaps the driver lost control of the car and found himself in the bush. Whether the man was the only victim or there were others in the car, we did not know at the moment. To find out and to help, we joined the line of cars already slowing down and searching for places to park.

About ten yards from the spot of the accident, we found a space to park, from where I was able to see that the person, or persons, involved in the accident had been extremely lucky. Just three feet away from the car was the edge of a steep cliff from which the car would have dropped hundreds of yards into a ditch. The cliff extended to where we parked and beyond, and it was frightening to look as I came out of the car.

We had to roll up the windows and lock the car, because thieves often robbed in situations like this. By the time I finished rolling up the manual window and got out to lock my side of the car, there had been a long chain of cars parked in front of our car, and a longer one slowing down from the top of the hill. Some were finding a space to park while others just wanted to go on with their journey. But this had created a traffic go-slow.

At the other strip of the roads, conveying traffic in the opposite direction, a white commercial bus had also parked to see what happened. It was the only vehicle at the other side, and two of its passengers, a man and a woman, seemed quicker than the rest of the passengers in crossing to the grass section between their road and ours. They paused there for a while, looking for opportunity to cross finally to our side – the side of the accident.

Suddenly, a 30-foot long tractor-trailer traveling at about 60 to 70 miles per hour appeared at the top of the hill on our side. Its driver was shocked to see the long line of slow-moving cars in his way. The road was too steep and he was traveling too fast and too close to the cars for him to step on the brake. Stepping on the break at that point would have been like an act of mass-murder, wiping out the multitude there, including my uncle and me. Trying to avoid that, the driver swerved onto the middle grass section.

But his new path was not devoid of obstacle. The man and woman from the other side were still at the grass section, waiting to cross to our side. When they saw the vehicle coming toward them, they ran back for their lives. The tractor-trailer still could not stop. Their escape, then, depended entirely on how fast they could run out of the grass section.

It was like a scene from a Hollywood movie and I wished it could just be that. Except that it was bigger than Hollywood's biggest screen. This was the large screen of harsh reality, far from make-believe, and, in fear for the lives of the poor fellows, I was already trembling on my spot.

In the end, the woman had the opportunity of being a leg ahead of the man, and, with a gap as thin as the thread of a cobweb, she had an extremely narrow escape. The man, running fast in her trail, sweated for the life race – or, rather, death race. He had on a white native buba dress, perhaps made from cheap Guinea Brocade. I could not help but picture him with sweat trickling down his face, a face which terror may have distorted beyond recognition.

He only almost made it. It was gruesome, as the 18-wheeler monster devoured him right in front of our eyes.

The atmosphere was horror-stricken. A swamp of dust swept up into the air, embittered dust, making the scene awfully ghastly. And a heavy silence descended upon the place, a silence so powerful that even the roaring sound of the tractor-trailer was engulfed: the momentary aftermath of death.

I was dumbstruck, too terrified to move. A nasty angel that would have tugged life out of me along with several others' had just taken one instead, and in the full gaze of our eyes. It was like a sacrifice for all the lives present at the scene - Jesus Christ at Golgotha, choked in his own blood, and swept up into heaven. Momentarily paralyzed, humbled by the presence of death, everyone watched as the tractor-trailer hit back the main road, dangerously beside us, and continued its cruise toward Lagos. The driver did not stop.

Something horridly poignant about the event that would also stay with me for a long time was my wondering about the victim's circumstance. If the man and woman had not run back, the man might not have died, unless if in a movie in which the director wanted the character killed like this. This was because the vehicle did not reach the spot where they had initially been waiting to cross. In the sight of death in the most vicious garment, they had followed the first reaction from their hearts. Really, hardly is there anyone who would not have run in such a situation as they did. In that time and place, it seemed the most reasonable course of action, especially when it was an instinctive first reaction.

This event often reminded me of an assertion by the prince of Zamunda, that "the first reaction is usually the correct one." The man's first reaction had not been a correct one, unless the prince defends his claim by stressing the word 'usually', or by appealing to some unconscious motivation. Perhaps, then, there was a Director somewhere, hidden in the depth of the human psyche or under the cover of the Heavens, who wanted the character killed thus.

Whether the Zamundan prince was right or not, nonetheless, something about this man's death in itself raised curious questions in my mind. Considering the loss and the circumstance, I always wondered, had Mother Nature made a mistake? Had she committed a culpable error against her own?

Sometimes, also, I thought nature might be hinting at our helplessness, our limits under her government. But are we truly placed in a world within which we are helpless? Prophet Mohammad once said, "Know that what missed you could not have hit you, and what hit you could not have missed you." Could the tractor-trailer truly not have missed the man? And could it not have hit the woman?[45] By this also the wise prince of Zamunda could not even have found an escape out of his word 'usually', for Mother Nature would always - and not usually - be the authoritarian ruler directing our affairs.

I remembered this accident and many others like it, and I developed a phobia for the road I had to travel thrice a week. What could miss me and what could hit me beat my judgment, and I feared for my unknown fate. For the three-week period, we witnessed an average of two accidents a week on the road, gory and fatal. We got to the hospital one day to find a large crowd mourning new victims. And on another day, a victim was wheeled into the physical therapy hall to register. She had her left leg in a cast and she was in haste to witness the burial of one of her relatives who had died in the accident in which she broke the leg.

---

[45] I always note that what the Prophet says is not "whatever is going to hit you *cannot* miss you, and whatever is going to miss you *cannot* hit you;" they are two different statements with two different meanings.

The three weeks were tough ones for me. It was a period of physical pains and fear. The physical therapist could only try to make the exercises less painful. When I was not in pain, I was in fear of it. But I had a hope to achieve something during the period, even though I did not want to do the surgery there. I hoped that if the knees were made better, the overall cost of my surgery would be reduced. To observe the exercises at home, I improvised makeshift materials like those used at the hospital, and even after the three-week period, I still continued to use them. I wanted the fate of the knees to change. Although they improved a little, we discovered that the knees, too, needed a surgery. But the surgeon said there was nothing he could do about it.

V

Uncle Jibola inquired and found out that there was opportunity for me to regain appreciable use of my legs better in America, but at an intimidating cost of $50, 000. Because he was still in school, and taking loans to pay his tuition, Baba promised to talk to my other uncles there to split the cost and make it easier to bear. Besides Raymond who was in Canada, I had three uncles in America. Even so, the amount was still daunting, but Baba asked me to be patient.

In the meantime, I was asked to get my father to produce whatever amount he could, even if it would only be enough to purchase the flight ticket. This was a nice deal that I thought my father should accept. Money enough for the flight ticket was nothing compared to what the treatment would cost, even in Nigeria. However, the tension in the house between me and my father waxed so strong that it became almost impossible to get his cooperation. The house was now so frosty between us that my room already seemed hanging icicles on the roof.

This turned out to be one of the toughest endurances of my life, one of the toughest tortures my heart ever had to live through. Yet, I still tried to look at it objectively. Objectivity helped in talking to myself for comfort in the difficult situation, which, as I could not ignore, may also be a problem for my father. Sometimes when I blamed him, I still realized that to blame him might be a judgment too simplistic for the complexity of our family. I saw a conflict in him, between the condition trying to bend his parental principles and him trying to hold onto it, especially when it involved his wife, as it often did. A major part of his problem was how to be a good father and a good husband at the same time when his child and his wife were in discord.

Perhaps, he was aware of this conflict, and only did not want to admit the reality he felt. Many men in this part of the world would not admit that, in a way, their wife was more important to them than their child. Though largely due to their machismo, this may be partly because it was easier for men to multiply or substitute the wife. And especially in a culture in which polygamy may have persisted beyond its ancient procreational motive, and only to become a defense mechanism for men's weakness in the tussle between the sexes. The more the number of a thing the lesser its value, and the lesser its value the easier to control. Perhaps, then, the truth is that the wife is more important only in some circumstances. The attitude of the extended family to the wife did not help men to realize the importance of the wife, either. The extended family usually saw the wife only as a commodity, a machine to produce children, which they saw as more important because they carried the family gene into the future.

Whereas, naturally or ideally, a man has a half-life, which is completed and strengthened by the wife's half, while the child's life is a new half to be aided in the life's journey. He or she would have to look for its other half, which would become more important than the parents. This is a truth that people often are afraid to look at.

This situation now became a problem for my father because he was not familiar with sharing his life with a woman. In the good old days, he always had more than a wife waiting on him, and he was always busy and away on business, only to come home and spend time with his children more than with his wives. Now he could only afford one wife, and, more than he had ever realized in his life, he knew the value of the wife, especially one with whom he had been for thirteen years so far – the longest marriage of his life. Perhaps, then, I should pity him rather than blame him. But I was languishing in my own pain and I could not afford to do that.

Within my father, his wife's interest had now been conflicting with mine over the scarce resources in the house – which included both money and his attention - and I was unfairly carrying the brunt. Moreover, a wife's interest includes the interests of as many children as she has. Hence, the interests of seven people came unfairly before mine in the house, despite the fact that our conditions were not equal and I was in dire need. To my admiration, however, my father struggled to be a good husband and father at one place – to the wife and her children - but to my repugnance, he compromised being a good father at other places – to me and other children in the house. Like this, he ended up creating a nuclear family within our *expanded*[46] family. I became angry one day and accused him of being unjust in his dealings. To my surprise, he admitted, though with an understandable but blasphemous grace (this was when he told me that even God was not just).

All these taught me another side of life. People often or always have children not because of the children, but because of themselves; they are only not aware of the real motives. Hence, in a way, children are tools in

[46] The term 'expanded family' was coined by one of my cousins, Jelili Oladigbolu, a teacher of Social Studies, when he realized that the division of family structures into 'nuclear family' and 'extended family', as described in our Western education, did not account for the various kinds of African families. Expanded family is meant by a family more complex than a nuclear family, but not as complex as extended family. Often, it is polygamous.

the hands of their unconscious motive, a motive that may be nothing more than the desire to be who they think they are. What was going on in our home was simply a lopsided polygamy in action, but this situation was not peculiar to our home. It ran through millions of polygamous homes and all kinds of homes around the world. It was not just a problem parents found themselves in, but one in which children also found themselves, and by which they become similar parents. It was not just a problem of homes, but of all situations of life. Life, unfortunately, is woven with threads of chaos; we are all individuals with interests conflicting with one another's. And this strengthened my belief that man is alone in the world; the parent and the child, each is alone. We are all evolutionary tools in the hands of the universe, procreational tools for the universe to perpetuate itself, and to satisfy its desire to be what it thinks it is. Perhaps, like us, the universe is also not aware of the real motive to perpetuate itself. This is the junction where the best a philosopher could do is to leave everything and hang himself.

While I accepted that this might be the root of the problem between me and my father, I did not disregard the possibility of other contributing factors, of which future events would soon make obvious. One that currently disturbed me was his strong belief in his struggle for the crown to come to fruition "soon", always "soon", and he now hanged my goals upon it. While I did not disagree with him on his ambition and hope, as all my older brothers and sisters did, I always told him that this was his own dream and life and he should not bring mine into it. I saw his heart as that of strong and admirable courage. He was even so actively persistent in the struggle that in the last one year or so he had actively started an effort, in his own way, to have the president-elect of Nigeria released from jail. Because of a connection between them, he believed that Chief Abiola's success would bring about his own success sooner. However I had my life to live and I would not wait for his to live it. But he never wanted to hear this. To him, it was pessimism, a lack of support for his cause.

***

Baba continued to try the best on his part. Although he was aware of the difficulty of raising money from everyone, as he planned, especially because many of them would be afraid of appearing wealthy in the house to keep the spotlight of polygamal jealousy away from them, he believed that with his unwavering insistence he would get them to do it. Because he was the only person in a position to talk to everyone in the family like this, he was the one I looked toward most.

I wanted to get my brother and sister in England to join in, but, with my father in the way, the task was not as easy as it appeared. He held back on any assistance for me to reach them, and he did not move a finger to find the contribution he was asked to make.

One thing that everyone now knew in their hearts was that if I would ever regain the use of my legs appreciably enough, I only could get it through treatment in America. However, whether I will get there or not, almost no one was sure; they only hoped and prayed. Once again in my life, coming to America became my cardinal goal, but in the way toward it lay various kinds of obstacles I could not imagine. If I could regain my health as much as I now knew I could, I wanted it, and I hoped strongly on getting to America despite the odds.

EIGHTEEN

Reincarnation

It may be that I shall fade, fade and die,
I, the young corn stalk.
A green jewel is my heart, but I will see gold,
I will be content once it has grown ripe;
The warrior chief is born.
A song of the Aztec god, Xipe.

I

I was glad to see Wasiu come down a bus and walk up to our house one sunny afternoon. It was late in October and I was under the tree outside the house. Held up by schoolwork, he had not had the chance to visit me in the past few months.

I asked him up into my room immediately. I wanted him to see my new room and judge my new poems. He once told me that my words were good but the poetics was not as good. Now I believed I had improved. I knew we would also discuss or debate philosophical issues and I wanted us to have a better place. I did not know which topic we would stumble upon, but I was eager to broach on any. Thinking and reading, I had been uncovering a lot of interesting ideas in the last few months and I could not wait to talk with him about them.

On the first day of October I had moved into the boys' quarter, called "The House of Lords." It was the name my older brothers gave the house, for which it was famous in the early eighties when it served as a regular weekend party venue for the "who's who" of the town's student-body. The name was written boldly across its façade and it was still visible now.

The house was the first building from the main road and it was detached enough to relieve me of the pressures of the main house. It also offered me a comforting view of the neighborhood without the trouble of the stairs to go under my regular tree. So, I went downstairs under the tree only when I wanted to get closer to the people of the neighborhood, most of whom I had come to have close relationship with. In the room, I gave Wasiu my poetry journal.

"I think these ones are better," he remarked on the first few poems, "but you should now start varying your rhythm. All these ones have the same rhythm, and such regular verse forms make a boring reading. Also, you need to be flexible with style."

He continued through the rest. While being polite so he would not discourage me, he commented on the other poems. He liked them, but I could see that only a few impressed him. He suggested for me to try natural words for the technologized ones I had in some poems.

"I think natural words make poems sound natural," he said to me. "Take this poem for instance: *Row, row, row your boat / Gentle down the stream / Merrily, merrily, merrily, merrily / Life is but a dream*." With the common lilt peculiar to the kindergarten poem, he read it two more times. It was not until then that I realized the wisdom in the poem. We discussed it for a while and it led to the concern of my present condition, about the suffering and frustration that I was still going through.

"It's almost over," he said with pity in his eyes, and I felt a little embarrassed. I did not want him to pity me, and this brought us into another discussion that we found interesting. Every one of his visits had its major topic of discussion, often with one of us talking more, championing the topic. Today the topic was reincarnation, and I talked more.

"You know what, Wasiu?" I started when I realized his eye of pity on me. "I think I see the world in a different way now. I now don't blame anyone for my sickness anymore, or not entirely, and I don't see why I should be pitied."

"How do you mean?" he asked.

"Let me put it this way." He listened intently. "A young lady met me sometime ago. She had heard a lot about me and about my sickness and its circumstances, and on that first meeting, with pity in her eyes, she asked to confirm the story. 'This kind of a thing shouldn't be happening to you..." she went on to say, "… a cute guy like you... I heard you were about to go to America when it began... people are so wicked in this world... as innocent and cute as you are...' She went on and on and got me to a point where, embarrassed, I found myself telling her, dismissively:

"'If time were reversed back to the time before it all began, and I was made to see in advance the intellectual and spiritual benefits that I have now found, and I was asked to choose to either fall into the sickness for the period and gain the understanding or go on to America, achieve the typical "American Dream" but without gaining such an understanding, I would choose to fall into the sickness if I was wise.'

"That was what I said to her and I meant every word of it," I said to Wasiu. "Although I was dragged into this, as it was against my expectation," I continued, "and so far I have been forced to remain in it, but so far it has been the best thing that has ever happened in my life. God has used this period to do me priceless favors that I might not have been able to achieve otherwise. It's like He called me to a corner of the world to teach me things about the world, as a special favorite of His, and to enable me to live it better. That's how I feel.

"In my suffering I can see things that had been obscured to my self-centered ego and the indulgence of my senses. I have always been somehow critical about happiness and I have always seen people pursue one thing or another for happiness only to later become unhappy again. I myself would have become such a victim of life if I had not been shown what I can see from this standpoint now. Now, I may not yet be completely happy, but I know I'm on the ladder to true and lasting happiness."

Wasiu stared at me, almost lost in pondering over my words.

"Or what do you think?" I tried to shake him out. "Sicknesses and misfortunes may not afterall be evil as people normally see them to be? Of course, I've gone through physical and mental tortures, and I'm still going through them right now, and I don't say some witches don't have a hand in this, but, surely, all these are only for a little time. If one doesn't leave a sickness, it would leave you alone one day, even if only in death. But the truth of God and the world that my soul feels now is eternal, transcending life and death. And that is an everlasting achievement for my soul."

"Fine," Wasiu finally commented, "I think it's fine. I'm glad you can see it this way. Many people don't and that's why they don't thank God. There is always a purpose behind everything, and a reason to thank God."

We talked on and on and my spirit was lifted, as I always felt during his visits. He introduced some philosophical perspectives that were germane to the discussion, and we talked and weighed things together. Getting to the core part of the discussion, I went on to add:

"You know what I realize now about this?"

"What?" he responded.

"I now believe that whatever someone does, good or bad, he does it for himself. And one way or another, it will come back to him. Therefore, any misfortune that befalls an individual is a product of his handiwork, regardless of the contribution of any evil-minded person that hates and hounds him."

"You've been reading Socrates." Wasiu laughed.

"I didn't know Socrates talks about that."

"That's like the epicenter of his teachings."

"I haven't read Socrates; I've only been having a strong sense of self-responsibility for my condition, and my various learning has been revealing things this way to me. It's called the doctrine of karma in oriental philosophy and I've been reading a few books on it - even the Qur'an. The most dramatic rendering of the idea, however, is in a book called *Erewhon.* Do you know Samuel Butler?"

"No, who is he?"

"A 19th century English satirist - he wrote *Erewhon*, a story that described the doctrine satirically. The title is an anagram of "Nowhere," written backward with the transposition of "w" and "h", and it is the name of a fictitious European country. The book was aimed at mocking the institution of European civilization and its corruptions. Everything in *Erewhon* - customs, manners, and beliefs - is as backward as its name is, and opposite of those in Europe. Crimes are treated as diseases in hospitals, and misfortunes and diseases are treated as crimes in law courts. Do you get the symbolism?"

"Sort of."

"Butler was a man you would like to know. I wish he had named the book as "*Erehwyreve*", because the truth of his book is actually *everywhere*, and it transcends the ignorance of the then Europe that he was literarily understood to have used it to mock. The truth is, in reality, you get what you deserve. Misfortunes and diseases are results of our earlier ignorant choices, to which we are responsible, and crimes and misdemeanors are the choices born out of our current ignorance of these causal relationships. Hence ignorance is a disease of the mind, one that needs be cured as physical diseases do."

"Can you direct that instrument at yourself?" Wasiu asked - a very good question. Even though it was like a harsh truth, I was not afraid to handle it. I believed that all was not gone, and that this realization was good for me to handle my present condition toward my future. I replied Wasiu:

"I wouldn't be telling you this if I had not directed it at myself. I no longer think my condition was arbitrarily thrust upon me, of course. Look at it this way: if we use the premise of the witchcraft story, do you think God did not know when the witches were at it? Or did He not have power enough to stop them? And if He did know, why did He allow them to do it to me? Or has He done a wrong thing for not stopping them when He had the power to - a culpable error in His actions?"

Wasiu believed very much in God and he replied, "I wouldn't think so."

"At this point in my life, I wouldn't think so either. While it's difficult to think God knew and didn't stop them, it's also difficult to think He did not know of it. Neither fits our idea of God – the merciful, all-loving, all-powerful, and all-knowing God. Yet, we think the sickness is evil and wrong. I did not pray or work for the sickness. I did not bewitch myself with voodoo; all I wanted was to improve my life by my dream. Then, God must have allowed it because I had deserved it, because it serves His justice. As the witchery had been secreted, so was something secreted about me that must have corresponded to let it happen. The Qur'an says, 'All things (good and bad) are from God. But whatever good happens to you (o man) is from God, and whatever bad happens to you is from your own soul.' What a paradox.

"The knowledge of this has satisfied my curiosity better. Since I do not see anything in my life so far that has made me deserve this, I have come to believe that in the present life, an individual is purged of stains from a past life. That's the point. The witches' attacks were just instrumental, and it is more their own problem than mine. It is their current ignorant choices. Life is largely subjective, and their handiwork is their problem."

"Does this mean you believe in reincarnation? You believe that you have lived before?"

"It gives me a sense of balance and fairness to believe so. It makes life meaningful. In this way, I can say nothing happened to me, but that I myself happened. One life, I believe, sometimes follows another, and the former affects the latter. When things appear naturally unreasonable to us in this life, it's not because they are unreasonable, but because their reasons are buried in past lives. If not, suffering of the present life won't be understood, especially those of innocent people, like children born into various forms of disability and adversity or another. Something must make it make sense. This has been in my destiny all along; I only hadn't understood enough to see it."

"But I don't think I believe in that reincarnation stuff."

"Then you wouldn't be able to explain many conditions in life, and you wouldn't be able to find (consistence of ideas and) peace within yourself. Why do you think God allowed this on me while the world seemed to pass me by? Look at you; look at our other mates; look at my juniors in age and school, all climbing the ladder of success the way we know, while I'm here, suffering. So far in my life, have I been a bad person more than any of our mates? Then, why me? Or has God been arbitrary?

"There is reincarnation, no doubt about it. I must have set the stage like this in a past life. I don't see God as unjust or wicked. He gives to every man his due. I don't disbelieve that the witches are involved in this, but it took their acts to afflict me because I had deserved such a thing. It's a principle of correspondence: it takes one to fit the other. If reincarnation is not understood and believed, one cannot understand reality enough."

"I have heard a lot about reincarnation, but I'm yet to be convinced."

"I could make you see it, if you give me the chance. If you believe in the Qur'an, for example, you could see reincarnation suggested in the Qur'an. Although conventional Islam, like Christianity, doesn't recognize it, and most preachers have not been teaching it, but I could give you the numbers of the verses where you can find it and I'll leave you to think about them."

"Okay."

"I'll recommend you use the Qur'an translated by Yussuf Ali. It is a very good one. As a conventional Muslim, Yussuf Ali himself was not fully convinced on reincarnation, at least while he was writing on the Qur'an, so it is not going to be a case of a writer trying to persuade you with his ideas. You are going to reason for yourself. Yussuf Ali seems to me to be confused about reincarnation: he was undecided. There is a place in his eighth appendix (of the edition that I used) in which he is pressed very near declaring reincarnation, but because of Islamic conventional silence over reincarnation, he became hypothetic and assumed that 'if we live more than once.'"

I also advised Wasiu to be ready to accept new ideas if they convinced him. My father and I always debated the issue of reincarnation, but his problem was that he did not want to give way for new ideas about the Qur'an and he always missed the point. From his traditional knowledge, he believed in reincarnation, but he thought Islam does not preach it. He then believed it was an esoteric knowledge that could be misunderstood and abused by the common people. By this, he thought it should be kept away from the masses, and that this was why the Qur'an was silent about it. For me, I did not believe that the Qur'an was silent about it, but, whenever I showed him the relevant verses about it, he always saw them in literal and different ways.

II

This was how Wasiu and I left the discussion on the day. However, I later realized that my explanation had been an answer comfortable enough for my disposition, but too rigid an explanation, and I may have been too harsh on myself. Perhaps, there were some ends left too loose.

Questions about fundamental truths of life as this are not always as straightforward and matter-of-fact as I had presented it. Sometimes our answers may be oversimplification of the truth. Sometimes they really are oversimplification of the truth. For years, human affairs have been explained on the one hand under the paradigm of the theory of God's will, mercy, and punishment, as taught especially by the teachers of modern monotheistic religions. On the other hand, they have been explained under the paradigm of the theory of reincarnation and the function of the principle of karma, as taught especially by the teachers of ancient and Indian-originated religions. The former, shared and taught by both Muslim and Christian preachers, is the objective paradigm under which I had been brought up, and under which I had been seeing the affairs of my life. The latter is the subjective view that I just learned at some point during this predicament of my life. However, I later came to see the two doctrines, while not wrong, sometimes as oversimplification of human affairs, especially when seen and taught as independent of one another. I later learned deeply enough to see the reincarnational and karmic concepts in the Islamic and Christian scriptures, and to see the mercy and punishment concept in the karmic teachings of the ancient and Indian teachers.

Nonetheless, I do not see the oversimplification as that of the religions themselves, but of the various interpretations of the preachers teaching them. Such a view of the principle of karma as I had given to my cousin, though it is the most common, may not see the all-important compassion and grace of God in human affairs. In some way, the grace may even be all that was there – the teleological warmth within which the system works – and there may be nothing like punishment and reward as the religions preach. Hence, we may have oversimplified the concepts of God's justice and human condition.

NINETEEN

Hands of God

I

Though Oyo was my spiritual safe haven, the emotional burden of my father's attitude and the frustration to my efforts choked so much at my life that I decided to take a break and leave the town for a little while. I thought I needed a vacation. Life is like a game and there should be 'time outs'. It was like opening up the windows of my head for clean ventilation. Right now, I felt damp and clammy up there.

I decided to spend a week at my grandmother's house at Oke Ado and I took with me a spiritual subject book and several past issues of Time and Newsweek magazines.

The vacation was short, but it served me well. At the end of the week I was relatively happy, relieved of my pressures and I was ready to continue with the struggle. On the day I was leaving back for Oyo, my grandmother looked at me closely and said: "You know you are happy now, so please remain happy at Oyo. Do not worry yourself over the problem. I know God will help you out soon."

She made another remark that I found ironically interesting. "Was this the jacket you bought sometime ago?" she asked. I had on the big, black corduroy jacket I had bought years earlier to wear to America. Instead, I had been using it on the sick bed and it was now becoming worn out.

"Yes, it was," I replied.

Remembering the reason for which I bought it, and feeling pity for me, she said, "Don't worry, *oko mi*, it will all be a story to tell."

One great thing that made me happy about my vacation was my trip to Oniyanrin. It was the first time in four years and I was delighted to meet

Baba and everyone else in the house. Almost all of the people in my peer group had left the house for further challenges in life, and a younger generation had now taken over our place. That was what the house had been doing for ages: nurturing one generation after the other.

As I walked through the passageway, the walls seemed closer to me on both sides, and the roof seemed nearer to my head. I remembered the oath I made with God when I was leaving for the hospital on the last day I was in the house, and I realized He has kept His side of the oath. He has brought me back into the house alive as I asked. I was happy for this and I stretched out my right arm, touched the wall with my palm, to fulfill my part of the oath. In a low voice, I uttered, "*Muhammad Rosulullahi – Salalaw alei wassalam.*" It was the completion of the statement of the oath.

When I entered the living room I tried to feel comfortable in the house as before. But the experience of the past remained indelibly between the house and me and it was no longer the same. This was the house in which I was born, but now I felt as if I was only a stranger. I was no longer a naïve child running around the house with bared torso. The paradisiacal innocence was gone and I had suspicions inside me. This was the kind of experience that often ruptured the communal love and cooperation for which the African family was famous.

I was eager to meet Baba. I had been carrying in my mind his picture as he was before I left the house, and he remained almost like that when I saw him rise in his massive frame, full of years and experience, to welcome me. I knew he was not the same health-wise, however. Internally, he was more senile, only that he would not want to show it. He would not even want to admit it to himself. This was the body he used to slam his older brothers in childhood wrestling and bullied them around; it was the body he used to handle heavy planks and hammer in construction jobs as a young carpenter; it was the body he used to breeze through shores across African continent in the course of his earthly sojourn. Nothing had ever restricted him. Now, age was taking its toll. This was Baba, known to many simply as "Baba Ilupeju." All his life he had been the conductor of his environment, and I knew he would never like to be conducted by the environment. He rose briskly toward me, as if he was still as healthy as I had last seen him.

When he sat beside me to talk with me, I had a relive of my past, but it was a painful awareness that it could not go on for long. All his actions were reminiscent of the past and I felt as relaxed.

The physical reunion was marvelous. He sent everyone out of the living room for him and I to enjoy some private chat. We talked about my health, his health, and some of the private family matters we often talked about in the past. He was one of the best listeners I had ever known. He had a silence to his nature that, during conversations, seemed to probe the heart and mind of whom he talked with, and which seemed to weigh every word he heard for more noble understanding, as the goldsmith weighs his metals. It was a silence of thorough attention that made the talker feel worthwhile and encouraged. I felt like I wanted to live with him again.

He stuffed my pocket with money before he called everyone back in for a special thanksgiving and prayer to God. The session was long, strong, and intense. His chief request was terse, however, and oft-repeated. "By the grace of God, you will go where you want to go," he prayed, "You will be thoroughly healed; you will walk as fine as you used to do; you will achieve your goals in life; and you will live the glory of God for the whole world to marvel at. And God will give us (himself and our mothers) life and health to see appreciably of it."

"Amen!!!" everyone chorused.

Baba promised to continue to do the best of his capacity to get help for me to get to America, and he wished for it to happen in his lifetime. But, by his awareness of his age and senility, he was not sure whether he would live to see it as he wished. I wanted him to see me go to America and walk on my legs. I wanted to call him from America. When I began my struggle, he had been the only person in the world who understood me. I wanted him to watch at least one movie directed by me. If anyone told me that this was the last time I would ever see him, I would not feel as relaxed and happy as I felt when I was leaving the house once again. Baba held my hand for a long time; it was hard to say goodbye. He took a long look at me. His famous metaphor for life was *war*; for him, life was a battle. Now I seemed to him a warrior who had been fighting the toughest of all wars, and he said to me, "You will win by the grace of God. You will win."

***

Since I was in Ibadan, I arranged to see Dr. Akinyemi, the surgeon, to have a check-up, but I could not make my appointment. He had gone to spend some time to practice in England and it was another doctor that I was booked to see. The new doctor did not have respect for the famous, sometimes notorious, African time concept. I missed him only by a few minutes. He had left as the exact time of the appointment struck and I was not there. The nurse on duty called him a man of time. I decided to come back from Oyo and I scheduled another appointment.

***

My trip back to Oyo was remarkable. I was happy as my grandmother observed. I had a lot of money to assuage the pressure of my physical needs for a long time. However, more remarkable was what was going on in my mind. I relied on Baba to do as he promised, but I realized that the process might take a long time to unfold and I would need a lot of patience in the mean time. My thought now centered on how to be enduring enough to bear it through.

On the glove compartment of the public bus in which I was traveling, I saw a sticker that bore some Arabic words. It read: *Inallaha maha sobirina.* Although I was not yet able to understand the entire language, but I understood what the inscription meant, and I thought it was a message for me. In translation, it read: *God is with the patient.*

I wondered what I could do to keep my ailing body from jailing my mind while being patient. Sitting down and waiting idly could make things difficult. I remember a discussion I had with the preacher-nurse at the Ogbomosho hospital. I told her that in spite of my awareness of the debilitating effect of worrying, I still worried over my problems, anyway. “You are giving yourself more problems," she had spurted with concern, and then asked, "Why do you worry when you know it is detrimental to your health?" With a deliberate humorous disposition to prevent her from feeling pity for me, I had replied, “I have the time,” and everyone in the room burst out laughing.

Yet, this was true. It is difficult not to worry over such a pressing situation when one has the time. Then I knew I had to find something to do with my time if I wanted to maintain enough patience. I had to find something interesting to absorb my attention and fill my time.

A few minutes later, an idea struck me. “A book,” I muttered to myself, “I think I should write a book about my experience.” Though I shrank from writing about myself at first, I thought what I had been through might be interesting in a book and people would read it. I had lived the past years like in a random but now it seemed to have an interesting order, one which I had never seen on the few occasions when writing it was suggested. One woman heard my story and came to visit me sometime ago. It was a period the sickness was still frightening, but rather than pray or do anything consoling, she only stared at me for a long time and finally said: “You should write a book on what you are experiencing.” My father later told me that she was a high-ranking witch, and he had let her in to visit me because she had no evil-intention toward me.

While I was not thinking of these suggestions now, I was being increasingly consumed by the need to render what I was experiencing. I thought the story was more important than myself, and I could undertake the sacrifice of writing it. The full story was there in my head, already written by itself, and all I had to do was to copy it down - although it turned out to be more than that. All my subsequent thoughts reinforced the idea. By the time I reached Oyo, I could not wait anymore to start writing. I began without a formal writing education, without knowing exactly how to write it, without knowing how wide and deep it would go, without knowing how much time and nerves it would take, without knowing how much it would stretch and sweat my intellect, without knowing a quarter of what the book would eventually say, without knowing how much doctoring it would give my psyche, how much reinforcements it would give my character, and, of course, without knowing how much it would shape my destiny. It was a journey into the unknown. The truth was that I had an idea, and I thought I knew what I wanted, but many times during the journey, I was to form an opinion that it was probably the idea that had me.

When I now think about the circumstances leading to the decision to write the book; when I think about the subtle conditions leading to these circumstances in themselves; when I think about my entire experience and its voice in the book; and when I think about how my dream to be a filmmaker had been born at my mother's place – something essentially responsible for my present condition, I cannot help but to wonder whether we really freely choose what we do in the world, or the things we do choose us.

II

Charles Okoh was the doctor substituting for Dr. Akinyemi. He was younger than I expected, and truly a man of time. On my second appointment, he walked into the hospital at exactly the time appointed, not a minute before or later.

"Do you understand English?" The handsome self-confident doctor asked me in English. I had never been asked that question before and I was at loss of how to respond. In a way, it sounded insulting.

"Little little," I replied in broken English, the way people who did not understand English talked. "Talk, I try," I added.

He screwed up his complacent eyes at me. "You look intelligent; one would expect you speak good English."

"Perhaps appearance is deceptive."

He shrugged, realizing that at least I would understand the session. He asked what the problem was and I explained to him. I told him the types of treatments I had been shown and the one I wanted to do – "gird stone."

"They call it *girdle stone* and not *gird stone*." He corrected me. I did not realize I was there instead for a tutoring session. I wondered who was right between him and the two earlier doctors, except if I did not hear them well. But what does it matter, anyway; what I wanted was my treatment.

He read through my case file, which the nurse had deposited on his desk, and then looked up at me.

"Do you know what caused all this problem for you?" He meant my legs. I wondered what kind of question this was, and what kind of effrontery was in this man's character. I had been feeling impressed by his apparent aplomb, but now I thought it was blowing him too fast and too big for his clothes.

"What?" I asked, with a little disgust.

"Ignorance," he said smugly and waited for my response as he twisted jauntily in his chair.

I became more disgusted. No wonder he was asking me whether I could speak English. He would have counseled me on the value of education and advised me to carry my butt to school. Everyone likes to be the wise counselor. He seemed to think he was good counseling as well as doctoring. Perhaps he was, but I thought he did not know when and how to start his counseling vocation. If this was what I wanted to know, I thought of saying to him, I would not be here. But I realized how my angered voice would hit him, while I did not want to work with an angry doctor. I chose my words carefully.

"I don't want to talk about that; it is too complicated a case. Let's get to the main business that brought me here, please."

But business was not as expected. We could not complete it until the next appointment, which fell into January of 1998, the year's month of Ramadan. He asked for a new set of x-ray photographs because, he said, the ones he had at the hospital had been taken almost a year earlier and there might have been changes in the joints. When I gave him the new ones, he observed them and told me that the hip joints had been damaged more than they were a year earlier. And, because I had been walking on them without treatment, one of the knees had bent a little more inward too.

This worried me, but not as much as what he said about the treatments. He said the complete replacement of the hip joints would not be perfectly right for me, that with time and use the metal sockets would chip at the head of the femurs. According to him, it could only be suitable for people over 40 years. This was a contradiction to what Dr. Akinyemi had said.

I was later to know that he himself had been ignorant on the current state of medical technology in his field. As a substitute, he suggested that I should do what he called "bipolar." The bipolar, he said, was the cutting away of the head of the femurs and replacing them with metal heads, and after about ten years, or a little more, I can go for a total replacement of the hips. In short, he confused me more than I had been. Which was which in the treatment options, I now could not tell. I left the hospital with plenty on my mind, plenty enough to confuse me, and I was depressed to learn of the further damage in the joints. I could only hope they would not be too damaged for treatments by the time help came.

***

Do you know what caused all these problems for you? The doctor's words rang in my head on my way back home after our first meeting, and I wondered whether he knew what he was talking about. If only it could be as simple as he thought. If only life could be as simple as its modern scientific explanation that had besotted him.

My case had been such a convolution that the word 'ignorance' may be mystically right, but Dr. Charles's idea of it was such an oversimplification that it has made him the ignorant. Unfortunately, he was educated to be such an ignorant. I would not have been his ignorant if I had let pain kill me. He had not seen all I had seen, he had not known all I had known, and he had not gone through all I had gone through; hence, such an answer was so easy to come out of his white-polished lips, as easily as 'love' comes out of the unctuous mouth of an infatuated young man making sexual advances on a pretty girl.

Sometimes, when I thought deeply about it, I did not want to blame anyone who argued against the reality of witchcraft, because I realized that if someone did not possess the power, fall a victim, or have a direct experience with it, he might find it difficult to believe. The phenomenon of witchcraft is, no doubt, confounding. Even sometimes, to those who experience it, the search for its culpability is like a search for a pin in a stack of hay placed in a dark room. You may think you know what it is, but you often have less than enough proof. So how could I convince the young doctor what my problem had been?

In spite of my experience, of which a lot was so clear, I have had deeper considerations of the two explanations conflicting for causes in my situation and the mystery they elicit intrigues me.

Writing this book, I did not forget the educated views my experience was up against, but I did not want to selfishly defend my experience about witchcraft. I could have taken the easy way out by writing the book the other way round, blindly confirming and glorifying modern science by telling the witchcraft aspect as a crazy superstition inherited from our 'ignorant' ancestors. This is what the vanguards of Western culture want to hear, and many Africans have been dancing along to seek the nods of science and escape into the romantic arms of Western acceptance. But I was a kind of person who could live his life as anything except as a hypocrite.

As with many others, Dr. Charles may have only had too much of a particular diet. Perhaps unable to accommodate complexity of ideas, people tend to believe one line of reality and blind themselves to other lines or possibilities of reality, especially when the other lines appear as if contradictory to theirs.

In this part of the world, some medical practitioners have spiritualists to whom they carry mysterious cases for spiritual guidance and protection on insidious cases. I only hope that such doctors with unbalanced diet of understanding, as my dear doctor, do not fall into situations where they would be forced to deal with the strange reality. In a world in which a person like Baba-elero could suffer such a punch that was struck at him, how much more would a mere physical doctor suffer? The white man's world may be different in some way, but this was a black man's country. This was Africa, the cradle of the world, where all or many of the crude knowledge of the world still remains.

Someone made a preparation for the treatments of sickle cell anemia in my town some time ago, and a confused pharmacist friend of mine confirmed that it worked when tested on some patients. But when it was examined in the laboratory and structurally adjusted according to pharmaceutical guidelines, it did not work. My friend was confused because he realized that it had not worked because its rules and system of work did not correspond to the scientific rules of pharmacy. But who says the modern scientific test was the only and ultimate test of reality? Who says its rules were the only rules for what was real?

This is the question I would ask myself again and again, and everyone with which I discussed it. It is the reason there has not been a stable explanation of reality in the science world. Many conclusions had been assumed and taken for granted, of which were later found as not true or not entirely true, and causing reconsiderations of the rules. Now, in search of stronger medicines, the health sector is sending scientists to nooks and corners of the world where science had earlier derided as savage. And seeing the huge perplexity of the task on their hands, the researchers are now increasingly relying on the tribal medicine men and witchdoctors of the places for the success and quickness of their endeavor. A science correspondent once reported that, "No longer do scientists simply dismiss witchdoctors' bat-winged remedies. [They have now discovered that] potions that call for toadstools plucked from a graveyard, or the blood of a black rooster may indeed have some scientific basis beyond superstition."[47]

Hence, we may be asking the questions again: do gods, goddesses, angels, demons, and spirits of the dead have anything to do with natural conditions? Could things that appear so natural to us be influenced by forces yet unnatural to us?

I have a great regard for science, and I have great commendation and recommendation for it, but I have become defensibly aware that it may have not been telling any new truth under the heaven that the old legendary and mythical traditions had not known. It has only been telling it in a different way, its own dignified way, and it often becomes an oversimplification when it denies other interpretations of reality. Yet, we need to know it both ways to have them complement one another, balance our understanding of the world, and optimally better our lives in it. We need to understand the truth of the world in all possible ways. Life exists in many dimensions, and the physical scientific dimension is only one of them. Because we can scientifically prove what causes lie behind thunder, earthquakes, and diseases does not disprove that they were results of the wrath of gods and goddesses. Rain may be explained as the precipitation of liquid water in the earth's water cycle, and diseases as introduction of microbes into the body, but to think, then, that rain has not been sent down by a god or goddess, or that microbes were not physical representations of demons and spirits, is to miss a truth also crucial to our humanity. This point of view may sound ridiculous, but it is like questioning that because the universe came about by the "big bang" and the process of evolution, then it was not made by some gods or God, or a self-consciousness that knew what it wanted by the creation. What lies behind the "big bang" and the evolution, empirical science does not know, and this makes the scientific theories no less mysterious than creationism.

When I looked at the conflict of scientific and spiritual explanations in my experience, I was amazed and amused by the fact that each side may have been relatively right in their claims. My history, including the details of my sickness, apparently revealed precipitating factors that they could count on in their different cognitive worlds. My preceding physical

[47] Time Magazine's Tim McGirk.

condition had obviously been walking in the valley of such a sickness for someone who is solely or largely physically oriented to disagree to any spiritual cause or influence. My genotype and the preceding month to the sickness are there for them to cite. I was stressed over my pursuit of America; I smoked weed and had a drug-induced anxiety. Likewise, with the fact that my preceding spiritual condition had obviously been walking in the valley of such sickness, someone who is solely or largely spiritually oriented would not want to agree to the physical cause, or as the only cause. They have all the witcheries and mysteries to point at; I went through them plenty enough.

With this in mind, I sometimes mused that skeptic philosophers would have some fun here. Their fundamental principle is that nothing had truly one quality rather than another; it all depended on the conventions and customs of the people, and no one could claim an absolute truth - using one quality rather than another. And this is always or usually the truth when two parties conflict. Many times in this world, scientific or spiritualist disciples have made wrong claims and thus caused unnecessary errors in people's lives by rigidly following their relative conventions to face specific problems. Hence, it became obvious to me that science has only been seeing reality through its own conventions and customs, and ignoring the other conventions which it is not oriented to understand. At its best, science is only strictly a literal interpretation of life, of the language of life, and which remains the same in any scientific experimentation. The moral, metaphorical, and allegorical interpretations, which are fluid in nature, are thus beyond its lenses. So, even though scientists may have been finding explanations to the natural things of our world, they have not really been refuting the old legendary claims of gods, goddesses, and spiritual events as forces behind the natural phenomena we are experiencing, claims based in another set of conventions. Perhaps everything we do in life is simply or intricately an experiment in mythmaking, from science to religion, art to society. "Superstition sets the world in flame; philosophy quenches it."[48] So says one of the poster men of the 18th century Enlightenment that has bequeathed to us this amazingly empowering scientific outlook. But how much quenching or none this philosophy or science has done, we are in flame of its superstition. The scientific explanation of a natural phenomenon is not the same thing as a scientific un-explanation of other claims for the phenomenon. Because the conventions of these other claims are as relative to them as science's conventions are to science. And, thus, scientists have been denouncing the so-called superstitions in a manner most unscientific – as if using a ruler to measure the size of water. The gods and goddesses of science, wherever they are, must be ashamed of this scientific escapism of their terrestrial counterparts.

Finally admitting the reality of witchcraft, the questions that now

---

[48] Voltaire

motivated me into further inquiry are on how the entire phenomenon operates. How do they go to their meetings without leaving their individual homes physically? How do the evil witches inflict harm without physical contact with the victims? How was I shot in a dream and carried the bullet in my body into wake-reality? What are the processes, or potential processes, of the universe that accommodate these unphysical activities? What does it all mean to the overall understanding of our world? These are the questions I think our scientific approach should be interested in, rather than denying witchcraft. As my experience and many others in the world have hypothesized, the human mind plays an incredibly substantial role in all these, and understanding the connections and processes will, no doubt, have a practical function in the way we henceforth perceive and live our lives.

For the overall understanding of my case, I have examined all scientific and witchcraft possibilities and found them individually inadequate to explain my experience. Through persistent searching, I have come to believe that the sickness was a product of both natural and supernatural correlation. Yet, it was more than the sum of the two. Having consequently become spiritually conscious, so to speak, I saw a staggering and enlightening transcendence manifested through all natural and supernatural phenomena. Hence, above all, I saw my sickness as a product of what I could call God-spirituality. It was an expression from above; a language of the mysterious world no one could quite fathom, telling a tale of goodwill and good purpose for and with my life. Now, this is an understanding that is beyond and more important than both witchcraft and science.

My inquiry into the phenomenon of reincarnation became the most important inquiry I made during my sickness. It threw light upon the fundamental things I needed to know about life, and it rid me of the burden of proof that came with the conflicts. Life was presenting itself as a simple whole, with none or fewer contradictions, and sometimes even revealing the contradictions as part of its harmonious structure. In bits and pieces, its various branches of knowledge were becoming sewn up into one, and within it I realized that life itself is a chaos, a challenge, an opportunity, and a trial, all woven in a silk of cosmic peace, compassion, and joy. And it is with this fabric that every single condition in it is clothed, for which neither science nor witchcraft could adequately account.

Through reincarnation, I began to see events as teleological rather than random. I realized that life and the goal of religion might not really be about punishment and reward, as I had told my cousin during our discussion on reincarnation, but about learning and coping in a difficult world. Understanding all these, I wished my mind had been built strongly enough to know them in the earlier days of my sickness, to understand the superficiality and symbolism of human pain and pleasure, sorrow and joy. Though I later realized that I enjoyed the ride like the biblical Job, I wished I had been like the other Job. This was the ignorance I may have been guilty of, and not Dr. Charles' superficial interpretation. The ignorance of the knowledge of who I was, of the world I lived, and the goal and grid I had set for my self.

This goal, I realized, superseded the intellectual conflicts I had been dealing with. Rather than scientific ignorance or a karma punishment, I now saw my condition as a condition for me to suffer, to suffer physical and mental tortures, physical and mental abandonment, loneliness and idleness, privations, frustrations, depressions, desperation and humiliation, so as to be humble, learn, recoup, equip and go on with my life in the real rather than vain way. This is the way that will be of utmost good to me and to the humanity of which I was a part.

It was all about self-discovery, the only antidote to all human problems. Adversity makes men wise, a proverb says. I found it interesting when I heard that in the Chinese language, the word 'crisis' is spelled with two characters that mean 'danger' and 'opportunity'. This dangerous crisis in my life has become an opportunity for me. It was so dark in my life that it was now I could see the stars clearly more than when things were sunny. It was an opportunity for me to look inward, discover the light within me, and appreciate its connection to the sun above.

At this point in time, I believed I had reached a crucial point in my life, and which may not be but positive. I have learned the truth that the only problem in the world is the idea of problem itself. Someone who is seeking to achieve something - be it freedom, children, wealth, health, career success, or any other - is having a problem as much as someone who has the thing and is trying to maintain it so as not to lose it and to keep it increasing or improving. The bottom line of the two sides is "problem," and this means that, in this sense, it could never be eliminated from a person's life, for when one overcomes the problem of *seeking to have*, one enters the problem of *seeking to maintain or increase*. Although cloaked in various desires, this is the sense of insecurity, real but imagined, to which we seek security. Therefore, the solution is in solving the very problem called "problem," the idea itself, which may be unrelated to the subject of our desires. *The problem is in oneself; the problem is oneself; one only needs to realize it.*

In this world, there is a joy in being who one really is; it is this joy in who I am that is now my goal in life. "A green jewel is my heart," and I have been born again. I have seen gold.

For thousands of years the Joban question has been asked, "Why do bad things happen to good people?" "Why do good people suffer?" As my life has been playing out on the stage of life, I have lived my own part of it. Although I may not have been said to be a good person, I could not be said to be a person bad enough to deserve half of what I was experiencing. But from what I have now come to realize, perhaps bad things happen to good people because we do not know what is good or bad – because we misunderstand who we are, our true circumstance in the world, and we misinterpret what happen to us as bad. Therefore, we suffer because we do not know, a reason why some scholars of the scripture put the blame of the suffering on the depressed Job himself. This is self-discovery. When God prods him to remember who he is in the holy Bible, perhaps this is what he comes to realize: that, in cosmic perspective, he might be assuming the sick role toward the realization of himself.

By all these, I have come to see that without the adequate understanding of the concept of reincarnation, one may not understand reality adequately, whether by modern science or witchcraft. Perhaps there can be no adequate understanding of reincarnation. Perhaps the best word I could use is 'appreciable', that is, *appreciable understanding* suitable to human nature. Many people sometimes think that by the principle of reincarnation they have a second chance. By this, many people indulge and wait for the second chance, which was a reason conventional religions do not want to mention reincarnation. But one truth I have also come to realize is that, even though we live more than one lifetime, there is no second chance. The concept of reincarnation known and believed by most people in the world, even though not wrong, is simply an oversimplification of the true phenomenon. Partly because of the placeless and timeless nature of place and time, as known from Buddhism to modern physics, there is no second chance, and this is where the walls of science, religion, and witchcraft meet.

We live in a symbolic universe, a world that, for a purpose, interposes itself in front of reality. This does not mean that it is an illusion, however; at least not any more or less than the pseudo-limbs of an amoeba, for example. It would only be an illusion when it is taken to be the only reality. It is a symbolic world all right, but one which should not be taken more or less for what it is, lest there be a detrimental disproportion in our knowledge and ethics, in our lives' achievement of purpose, and a disproportion which could range from simple to complex detriments, depending on how more or less one took it. Everything we do in life may be an experiment in mythmaking, in symbolism, but it is unwise to trifle with these symbolisms. Life, perceivably, is perfectly mathematical, determined by measurements of all things, thoughts, actions and events, but perhaps subtly mathematical in a way that is unintelligible to our everyday mathematics.

***

Baba became ill and was taken to the hospital. People who went to see him feared it was his time for the inevitable. This was depressing to me. Not only was he a substance in my past, he was a joy in my present and a hope for my future. I prayed for him to survive the illness, even if only to see me walk on healthy legs again.

TWENTY

Patience

I

Back at Oyo, I kept thinking on my worsening joints, and furious at my father for how things had been going on in the house to the detriment of my health.

"If he had been serious, we would have been through or almost through by now," I complained angrily to Baami while I was waiting to give my father the hospital report.

"Just talk softly to him; anger won't help your situation," Baami counseled me.

At first, my father showed concern at the condition of my joints, but he quickly readjusted himself and looked blank. He was in a real kind of game with me and he did not want to show any weakness to my advantage. Because I was no longer sitting and waiting according to his advice, I had become a stubborn boy in his view, and I needed to be taught a lesson in a cold way.

"So you can see that we have to be serious and quick about this thing," I said to him.

"Okay. But what do you want me to do now?" he asked, still looking as if unconcerned.

"Get some money to help me toward the realization of my treatment. The more we wait now the worse the situation becomes."

"But there's no money now."

I recognized the attitude with which that came and I became disgustingly angry. Yet, I suppressed it, and said to him, "If you want to get the money, all you have to do is make it top on your priority list."

"Then we shouldn't eat anymore in the house? Because you want to get your own money we shouldn't eat anymore?" He paused a little, and then continued, "Love thy neighbor as thyself is what Jesus says, and not love thy neighbor than thyself. Even if you don't think so, I think I deserve a commendation already on your treatment at this stage."

This made me angry still, but I remained calm as I spoke to him. "But I'm not your neighbor. I'm your son."

"You are a separate entity from me; everyone in the house is an individual, and whatever comes in should be equally distributed." He said that as if it was as the case had been in practice.

"You know that's not what you do in reality. You don't deal fairly with me."

"Then leave me alone and look for who would deal fairly with you," he uttered with an increasing anger. "Go look for who's fair. Your mother is fair, so go look for him. Where is she all these days? She abandoned you and you can't do anything. It's me you'll strangle despite all I am doing."

That hit me badly. I had always been trying not to face the truth of this matter about my mother, but my father's words knocked hard on the sore area of my psyche. Although I knew that she had some problems about herself, and I was not really angry with her, but she had neglected me too long than could go unnoticed by people. It was my shame, and I did not like to remember it.

Angrier now, but still keeping myself under cork, I replied, "Don't tell me about my mother. You are not the one to tell me that. You both put me into this, don't you? Whatever happened to me, you are both responsible. So…"

"Who is responsible? You think I'm responsible for your condition? You are crazy. If you think I'm responsible, go and find out who are the people behind your condition, and you'll learn to make your father's house as your house. And this is the only place where you can get help. They don't have anything to give you; you are just wasting your time."

"Listen, whether they have anything to give me or not, they are my family. A child cannot be born by only one parent; they are the other half of my parentage, whether my problem started there or not. Afterall, you fight your own war, and may be I am a victim of it. It's your dream; it's your choice, but now I'm suffering for it. And you know it."

That was the only way I could get back at him, and it hit him hard too. Despite all the evidence that suggested the root of my predicament as from Ibadan, this was a notion that my father was always afraid to look at. Many people in the town and some of my father's friends still believed that part of my suffering was a consequence of the battle for the crown, and I may have been attacked by some people loyal to the opposing camp. He rose up angrily and stormed out of my presence.

There was no food in my stomach, yet I had no appetite. I could not sleep in the night. I was filled with anger and hatred toward my father, and I felt wretched in the world, so wretched that I began to entertain the idea of walking out of everything in my life and away forever. I was less afraid of the uncertainty of life now, no matter how wretched. I was only afraid of doing a wrong thing that I would later regret, here or hereafter. Even if my leaving everything would be a wrong step against the good of my humanity, I would be afraid to take it, but not for fear of any more suffering. Thus, I chose to consider it deeply before I decided what to do. I had never before hated my father in my life. Sometimes, however, I could not help but think I had grown beyond being his responsibility. I was twenty-seven years old already, only I was handicapped and still needed to be someone's responsibility. Then, it was depressing to think the person who was supposed to carry it did not want to touch it. Yet, more depressing was the thought of Baba lying unconscious on a hospital bed, with less hope of waking back to life.

At this stage, it was hard to see what to do anymore to help myself. I was tired of planning and I could not plan or look ahead. Baami tried to pacify me. He was also confused and I could see sadness all over his face whenever he looked at me. He agreed with me that my father was wrong in behaving as he did, but he did not know what to do anymore either. He kept advising me to still exercise more patience.

I continued to be more patient, and now adding silence to my patience. For several weeks after, my father tried to pick a fight with me, but I always remained silent. On one occasion under the tree, everyone passing by could hear him using unspeakable words and threatening to disown me. Yet, I rose up and left him. Now we did not talk anymore in the house. I always tried to avoid meeting him.

I was in my room one day when Baami came to tell me that he wanted me. This surprised me. In this cold era of our relationship he never called me unless it was necessary. It was a war between us and I knew that whatever he was calling me for would only be for him to score a point.

And that was what he wanted to do. With him in his living room were two of his friends, Baba-elero and Mr. Oseni. I became uneasy, and a little afraid. Having known my father so well, I knew he would call for this kind of a sitting only when he knew he had enough aces to win a battle. All the air around me tensed up and I became restless.

Never before had I seen my father stoop so low. How circumstances influence human behavior. He had always been a god whose mystery I awed, but now he was charging so desperately at me that all the mystery was blown away from him. He had been so unnerved by my patient conduct that I had become the deity shrouded in mystery. With the patience he taught me, I had got him into a corner and he was desperately trying to find his aces. He had called me in the presence of these people to have them sympathize with him against me. He had called me to subdue my individuality, in all its understanding and desire, under his less concerned and less fulfilling authority. He was no longer sure whether he was justified in his actions toward me and he wanted to rationalize himself by selling a favorable story to his panel of friends and brother. But not all of them agreed with him and it turned out a travesty of his.

In an argument that may best be described as sophist, he accused me of not respecting his authority. He accused me of going back to my mother's family for help, forgetting that he was the one who sent me there first. He accused me of being a beggar, "begging around" for help from my mother's brothers and sisters. By the time he finished his litany, I was crying. In place of being a beggar in my mother's family, he offered an alternative for which I should have waited for, an alternative of a "possibility of being helped" by any one of his wealthy friends who might wake up one day and decide to help Rahman. And that was the most ridiculous thing in the whole charade. It depressed me to see him placing my life on such contingency. As a little kid, I never even believed life could be as cheaply coincidental as in Indian movies.

Mr. Oseni did not see any reason in his argument and he used a tactical way to blame and accused him of being unfair. In the end he implored him to take my situation as seriously as he had in the past.

Conversely, Baba-elero put the blame on me. He did so because he assumed that my present actions were neither mindful of how critical my condition was nor appreciative of my father's role thus far. He went on to remind me how critical my situation had initially been; how no one had had the freedom to think I would survive, how much sacrifice had gone into my survival, the money, the time, the efforts, and the innocent and non-innocent lives that had gone for it. "Many times we would walk in your room only to be sure you were still breathing," he had remarked.

I shrank at these comments. I knew them to be true, but I had hardly looked at them this way. I did not like to think of it. Baba-elero believed that I was a living miracle and, therefore, should not be found in such an ungrateful situation. "Now you have survived the grave dug for you by your enemies," he said in his long monologue, "You can see by yourself that it was by miracle that you live now. Therefore, all you need to be doing now is to be thanking God and thanking your father, and not get angry with anyone. For the rest of your life you should always be striving to be patient, good, and to make life easy and happy for people to live. You should have learned that God is doing such a miracle in your life so you can be His representative and contain humanity to make the world a better place, and not add to its troubles. You may be thinking that you are suffering, but indeed you have been blessed with a very rare of God's privileges. It is not from you then that we should be seeing acts of impatience or disrespect - of anyone in the world, not just of your father. I would have said that I'm disappointed in you by what is happening now, but I hope you will learn by it.

"I hope you were just being childish. Someone terribly sick and confined couldn't know how much efforts and running-around were being made outside for his sake. He could even think no one is doing anything for him. So, I don't blame you – I'm only advising you. You need to calm yourself down, and everything will come out well for you. It may take some time, but you'll always get what you want in life.

"From your experience we've all learned as well - we've all seen that God is talking to us. Please don't always get into anger. Don't always go into haste. You represent so much to us than that. That's my advice for you."

The discussion went on for a long time, but we were only circumnavigating these two main views. Baba-elero's words went straight into my bloodstream and knocked off my anger.

***

I was embittered when I re-lived the moments of the meeting back in my room. I agreed with Baba-elero, but, in confusion, I wondered whether I had not been right to be seeking a final way out of the whole problem. I wondered whether my father had not really been wrong, as I had been thinking. I remembered Mr. Oseni's speech, supporting my contention that my father had not always been right. I remembered many things in the past, asserting how wrong he had been in dealing with me, but I still remembered that Baba-elero had not been wrong.

Ruminating late into the night in bed, I ended up thinking that maybe I should always let things go. Maybe in my life I should always let everything go; judge or stand against no one, no matter what he or she does; and judge or stand against nothing. Maybe in my life I should just live and experience. Yet, I thought I could not be passive. I had to fight. I had always been fighting. But I could not fight if I did not see anything against me. I could not paddle my boat if I did not perceive the tide against me or have nowhere to go. Then, I began to think, maybe for the rest of my life my fights should be against myself. Maybe for the rest of my life the wrong I see in anyone or anything should be seen as a projection of myself, and I should fight against it only as thus. The world is too complex for haste to win the battles.

Privately in our room, I discussed it with Baami. He advised me to be calm over everything, and to go and apologize to my father, even if I thought I had not been wrong. "Sometimes you have to stoop to conquer," he had said, "You have to pretend to be foolish in other to get what you want. Several times I have told you this. You will take all that comes, and gently and humbly go after your goals." I agreed and I went to my father. We ended the night smiling at one another. Although I knew our smiles were superficial, and that the struggle with him was not over yet, but I was happy that, at least for now, I had beaten him in the game he taught me: the game of patience.

TWENTY-ONE

Hands of Death

I

My situation worsened during the few months following Ramadan. They were the months of loss. As I feared, Baba died. He passed away on the 9th day of February and was buried at Ejigbo the next day. Every cell in my body knew I had lost a gem, and my edifice of hope had been shot at. One of the questions that came to my mind was "Why this time? Why did he have to die now?"

Baba was the first great man I knew in my life. I respected him and everything I knew of him, even his weaknesses. No man has lived without his own weakness; I respected him for his because of the way he handled them. He would have loved to die from a small fever that would have not required him being carried out of his house, something symbolic of the independent life he lived. The day I heard that he was carried out of the house to the hospital, I knew things were turning out the way he did not like. As old as he was, he was not even ready to die. Most people are always not ready of course, but his was of the noble thought that he still had more missions to complete in the world - more people to help to independence, including me.

On the night I heard that Baba had died, I stayed awake late in the night to pray for his soul. Although I reflected from his death that I might not anymore be free to gather money from my uncles, I did not lose hope in everything. "What God wants to do, He will do," Baba had always counseled me. And my hope was essentially in God. As Mary the mother of Jesus says in the Qur'an, I believed God is the One who helps man from where man thinks there is help, and from where he does not think there is help. Therefore, for my hope I could not falter, but for the irretrievable loss of Baba I realized I had to learn to live with it.

***

On the 16th day of the second month of the year, I went to Ejigbo in the company of my father's wife for the eighth-day funeral ceremony. It was the first time I appeared to the whole family in my condition. It was not time for me to be going to social gatherings, but for Baba, I thought I had to be there, regardless of anything.

On this day, the family house saw a heavy flood of people. Family, friends, and well-wishers came from all over the country and from neighboring countries to greet the occasion. The crowd was so huge that it spelled out what many people believed to be the meaning of Baba's name. 'Ilupeju' sounds as 'gathering or assembly of a nation,' which then connoted Baba as the father of the nation.

And Baba was a man of that magnitude. I have never seen a single man control and brace together a family as extensive as ours before, especially without loads of bucks in the bank or official social position to do so. He had no enemies; all were friends and children. Imams and religious groups of different societies were at the ceremony to pray for his soul. He was a full-time member of the Ansar-ul-deen Islamic society, but due to his eclectic attitude to religion, he lived his life to pledge loyalty to many religious groups and he was favorably disposed to all he could reach.

The occasion was a big and graceful one that made everyone wish for such an eighth-day. By the colorful procession of the children, grandchildren, and great grandchildren, such an eighth-day could make one want to go into polygamy, while blinded to every other thing in the game. Life is a place of trial for humans, and Baba was not an angel. But he met with all the downs and ups of his life with fear of God in his consciousness. It took only a strong man to hold a polygamy together, and Baba was no doubt strong. Nonetheless, he was still bruised, as perhaps no one could ever escape. He was like a warrior shot in a war, but who still pulled his troops through to victory before he fell. As much as I knew of him, in terms of justice within the family he tried to wash himself clean, and that could be seen in the way his wives disposed toward him. Although she did not have to, my grandmother would not do anything without the knowledge and permission of Baba, and even though she was doing it with her own money. She owned the house at Oke Ado, a big house in itself, but she never lived there or away from under her husband's roof.

For his children and grandchildren, Baba was a honey that could never stale in our mouth, a mark that we are proud to wear. In one of the sessions he used to tell us stories of his experience in life, giving us light needed to tread the darkness of the world, he had said to me and others, "All those you call rich people (referring to the rich and famous in the city), we started together as youths. We knew each other and even had organizations together. Today, I am not called a rich man like them, but this is because I spend my money on my children, as you all know. However, who is richer than one who richly does his duty to his subjects? Therefore, I tell you that it is good for you to know your duties to God and to the people around you and thus ensure that you fulfill your part, no matter the cost."

Baba had been a helmsman from an early period in his life, as he was until his death, but he could never stand being helmed, even though old and sick. He was strong enough to have people lean on him, as he was always willing to help people carry on. But from a principle that must have stemmed out of his understanding of the selfishness of the human world, he never liked the idea of leaning on anyone in any sense, and he taught us to always try to be independent and enduring. "That is where your freedom and dignity as a human being is?" he always said.

***

The final ceremony of his funeral was set for the traditional 40th day of his death when, as expected, children, grandchildren, and other relatives and friends who were far away in distant countries would have the opportunity to honor Baba's transition. My uncles in America were also to arrive for the occasion. It would be good to meet them after a long time, but, on one hand, I did not know whether this was good news toward my goal. There was no Baba anymore to talk to them on my behalf. Nonetheless, I made up my mind to do as much as I could to get as much as I could from this apparently last opportunity.

II

Saturday the 14th day of March was the date I set to travel to Ibadan. The coming week was to be full of activities. My uncles were to arrive from the United States, two days of special prayer were to be held, and the 40th day ceremony was on the Saturday the 21st of the month. The week was also to bring me a forecast of my destiny; whether my uncles would have an agreement to pick up responsibility for my treatment or not, I wanted to be around to see. However, something happened that almost stopped me from going: Baami became ill.

Because Baami seldom fell ill, whenever he did, it was something that would keep everyone at seats' edges. His last remarkable illness had been about ten years earlier, and, since then, he had not been grounded for even a day by any ailment. He only sometimes had the typical stress headaches and fatigues. Besides, he had an exceptional endurance, even more than his physical capability. But this time he was very sick and had been visiting the hospital in the last one week that it began.

The eve of my journey to Ibadan was a frightening one. Baami was virtually not his usual self. He heard and saw nothing of anyone. To get food through his mouth evoked events of the bad old days when he fed me. I could not sleep. I tried to believe that it was the injection that he was given that made him so far away in himself, because he had been like that the previous day when he first got the shot. All day, after the effects of the first injection had worn off, he was all right and like himself, showing good signs of recovery, but only too weak to stand up.

Now, after another injection, he was no longer with us. I became so worried that I could not but remember some words of wisdom he had said in my ears at those unscheduled lecture periods he often gave me. He would say that there are three things in life that people should not trifle with. "We should not trifle with fire (whenever it breaks out anywhere); we should not trifle with conflicts (between individuals, peoples, or nations); and we should not trifle with sickness (whenever anyone falls sick). All these are dangerous and precarious situations, and no matter how small they may seem to be, we should always give them a full and due attention until we are sure it is over." This is an old Yoruba saying, and in modern times, lawsuits have been added to the three, due to the complexity of lawyers' casuistry, perhaps.

By our relationship in the last few years, I now could not imagine life with Baami sick or, at worst, without him at all. I loved him and I had been hoping so much about him, wondering how I could repay the priceless sacrifice he had been making for me in this critical period of my life - at least, if ever I get the opportunity to do it. Life does not always offer such a luxury as I received from him. I had become a career of his, which he hoped and always prayed to see to fruition. And I was determined to make the success, if achieved, complementary to his dream.

I was happy on the Saturday morning when I saw him feeling better and on the way to full recovery. He saw and heard us now, and he was much part of us. To shake away my fears, he affirmed that it was the injection that made him the way he had been in the night. He thanked God that he had completed the dose and that he was already recovering. He only needed time to sleep off the residual effect of the medicine. By the time the bus arrived to pick me, he had gone back to sleep, but all fears had been allayed. He was eager to hear what forecast the coming events would give about my destiny, and he prayed for me before he went back to sleep.

***

One after the other, my uncles arrived from America. Uncle Jibola stayed at Uncle Tunji's place, where also I stayed. He came with Aunty Dupe, his wife, and their three-year old twins, a boy and a girl. It was nice to have a reunion with the couple and pleasurable to meet the children for the first time. Farid was a replica of his father, while Faridat was of her mother.

Uncle Sheyi also stayed at Uncle Tunji's place, and he came into my room the night he arrived to talk with me about the situation. He was the youngest of my uncles living in the United States. He brought me information full of assurances of the excellent treatment I could get in America: the state-of-the-art facilities, the surgeon's burning spirits for achievements in the face of complementary incentives, and how I could benefit from the opportunity.

"Although things are not all that easy over there," Uncle Sheyi said to me, "you earn what you get in America, and tax and other bills are waiting to take the larger chunk of your money at the end of each pay day. But when you talk with the others and they split up the cost of the treatment, I assure you that I will run around and do my part."

I had a clear plan of how to talk to them, and I thought this discussion was a good start. But events turned out not as planned.

On Friday night, one of my cousins who had been at Oniyanrin in the day came to tell me what he overheard there.

"One of your brothers from Oyo came to Oniyanrin today," he said.

"To greet Alhaja?" I asked. I had expected that my father would send someone to greet my grandmother and represent the family, but I had thought it would be on the 40th day ceremony when I would also be at Oniyanrin.

"I don't know - maybe I shouldn't even tell you this," he replied. This made me anxious and I pressed him to tell me what it was all about.

"I overheard your brother telling Alhaja that one Baba that used to take care of you in Oyo has died."

For a moment I searched stupidly in my head for who it could be. My mind went to the traditional doctors and I was wondering which one of them. Perhaps, I had momentarily lost my mind.

"They said it was the Baba who used to sit with you all the time and tend to you," he added.

My heart seemed to stop working, and I stared at the boy, waiting insanely for him to say it was a joke. But he said nothing more; he only stared back, and my inner sight began to grow clearer than the outer sight of my eyes. Baami's image came out from the depth of my heart and I saw him more vividly than I saw the boy in front of me. I remembered his statement and I saw him repeat it to me: "We shouldn't trifle with sickness; not until it's over."

I asked to be left alone in the room. I turned in bed, slumped on my back and stared at the roof. But I saw not the roof. It was a large screen of darkness with Baami's images fading in and out. I saw him laugh; I saw him look serious; I saw him in many different positions as he took care of me while I was on the sickbed. He was feeding me when my arms were dead; he was cleaning my bed of my various sick dirt; he was cleaning me on bed; he was responding to my cloth-pull in the middle of the night; he was wiping my tears and encouraging me on; he was telling me stories; he was doing everything again and again, right in my absorbing vision. I remembered the day angry bees stung him as he tried to protect me from being stung by the bees. I could see him as he ran about like a mother fowl scurrying to protect its chicks from a hovering hungry hawk. I remembered and remembered and remembered and I burst out crying, silently and streaming hot tears. This was someone who sacrificed his freedom and all he had to tend my physical and mental woes when I most needed. How could life be doing this to me? How could life be taken away those who loved me at this critical period of my life? Literally, I broke down.

Baami's role during my sickness was unrivalled, unquantifiable. It was the most difficult role in the difficult situation. Still, in spite of this, he was never perturbed while it lasted. His hands were always gentle on me. His face always carried the message: *no problem, everything is going to be all right*, and it always calmed me. Even in his one-week sickness, he had allayed my fears of the unexpected. "There's no problem anymore," he had said in his last words to me, "I'll be here waiting for you."

I had walked out of the room without suspecting that death was just hiding behind the door and waiting for me to leave. I left without knowing that I would never see Baami again in my life. The goodbye greeting I gave him was now forever. I was later told that he died less than 24 hours after I left Oyo, but my father deliberately held back the news from reaching me, hoping not to add to my already heavy heart. But he later realized that, at least, I would not like to have every honor for him in his transition done in my back. Already, he had been buried in my absence, and the eighth-day prayer was Sunday, the day after Baba's 40th day ceremony. Hence, my father sent the message so I would not miss it.

***

The all-night ceremony was the final in the long traditional funeral process. It was to be a grand and merry party to give Baba the last honor. The ceremony tried hard to uplift my heart from the abyss it had fallen into, but the hole was too deep and its darkness too thick. I met with many old-time people, relatives, friends, and neighbors, and I met with a few new faces. There, I became a center of attention. I was crowded upon and all the old-time people in the neighborhood had me to watch, especially when I hobbled and wobbled through the street. They marveled, they pitied, and they prayed. They showed me so much love that I felt the world was lovely. I loved love.

However, I would have appreciated the occasion better if my mind was free. There was no moment I did not see Baami's face. In everything, everywhere, and all through the day and night, Baami's face kept popping up at me, smiling as he always did in life. One facial expression I never could imagine him in was of worry, either of sadness or fear. Even in the worst moments of my sickness, when every other person in the house was in pieces, Baami was always calm and collected, and his demeanor encouraging, anchoring me to hope rather than fear. The next morning, I went straight to Oyo for his eighth-day prayer. I did not sleep a wink in the last twenty-four hours, and even though I was sleep-laden, I went through the day's event with determination and sorrow. Though he had been buried the day after his last day on earth according to Islamic tradition, but to bury my sorrow could not come as easy. It is the human bodies, the object, that are buried, and not the memories and spirits in our hearts.

And thus, in two consecutive days, I went from funeral to funeral, burying the last of two of the most important persons in my life.

***

Uncle Jibola promised to help me out. With Baba gone, the complexity of the family now took toll. Though he welcomed any helping hand, Uncle Jibola could not ask anyone to contribute, so he looked at the responsibility as his own. But, as he said, he did not have that big chunk of money to pay the treatment cost at the moment, and this meant that he would not be able to formally ask me to come to the United States through the normal visa procedure. For the cost of the treatment, around $40,000 to $50,000, the consulate would not consider him able to foot the bill; at least, not until he completed his residency in six months and got a job.

On the alternative, however, Uncle Jibola suggested that if anyone could help me procure a visa, he would pay for my flight ticket to come ahead of time and wait until his financial situation becomes ripe enough for him to wheel me into the theatre. Aunty Dupe added that if I got to America now, I could enroll in a school while I wait for the "ripe" time to go for the surgery. In America, going to school in this state of health would not be a problem, she had said, as there was adequate provision for handicapped students.

This was good news and I thought it would be perfect if I could get a visa now and not have to wait in Nigeria. If I had all the help I needed, getting a visa might not be too difficult. So, I promised to get in touch with my uncle and aunt as soon as I got the visa.

III

The tree by our house towered slightly above the roof, dancing but somberly in the bland air. I saw the two houses, the main house and the boys' quarter, erect in their graces, but far from happy. I saw my room, my bed, chairs, and everything, arranged as they had always been, but dull in their voiceless welcome. And I saw my father and everyone in the house. But I did not see my other father; I did not see Baami, in whose chest I had a pillar of support, in whose throat I had a well of wisdom, in whose face I had a shrub of courage, and in whose presence I had an extra spirit of endurance. I was afraid. I did not know whether I would be able to continue my struggle here.

Without Baami, Oyo was now an empty place. He was not there to welcome me back home and to hear the good news he had been praying for in years. Although there was still much to pray for, we already had enough to thank God over. But now he was not there to join me. He was not there anymore to listen to my concern. He was not there anymore to teach me how to take my steps with my father. I found myself all alone. It was this moment that I realized I had lost not only a father; I had lost a part of me.

The irony of death perhaps is that it is not what happens to the dead, but what happens to the living. *Seth Speaks*, a book that became my staple during this experience,[49] revealed life to me as a state of becoming, and death as part of the becoming. For the *Bhagavad-Gita*, the ancient Indian religious scripture, death is like changing costumes. As an individual gives up the body of childhood and grows into that of adolescence, and then into that of adulthood, so does the soul gives up the physical body at death and accepts another. Then, the dead's dying is not the tragedy, but the living's forgetting, living with the loss from death. Loss, this is the pain of death, loss of parts that make up the whole in one's life. Even, the fear of death in the living is simply the fear of loss, a possible loss. It is the fear of leaving a world to which we have become so much attached. It is the fear of leaving a world in which we have been so emotionally attached to so many things, events, effects, places, and persons. No wonder, it is we who own things in the world that fear death, we who own a self-identity, family, friends, pride, property, dream, aspiration, and hope.

For a long time I worried over Baami's death before I finally brought myself to realize this. I could never have him back to mend my wound. I could only accept the reality. I could only let the dead bury the dead, as Christ says; life is for the living. Mysteriously, Baami himself later passed this message to me. I saw him in a dream, in which I was crying like a baby about him leaving me. He did not say a word; he only laughed heartily in his characteristic worry-free attitude. He appeared to be in a happy state, and he laughed in a way that implied that if only I understood how happy he was, I would not be crying childishly. And he urged me to go on with my life and toward my dream. He informed me that I have a life to live and I should not bog down myself with an event of the past, especially one I did not understand life enough to understand. From this, I realized what Jesus means: *the dead are taking care of themselves; the poor living folks only need to see and move on with their lives.* To the dead, it seems, death is an epiphany, transforming them to the consciousness of the larger world, within which our world is a small part.

Resignedly and painfully, I went back to the various places in my manuscript where I had referred to Baba and Baami and changed the necessary tenses to past forms. Christ is right, I agreed. Sometimes, when I look at all the troubles of the world, all the spreading wars and the threats of war, all the nuclear and biological weapons waiting for crazy men to unleash; when I look at all the chaos in the world, the threats of terrorists' bombs here and there, the threats of various gun-totting maniacs, the threats of virulent diseases and epidemics, the threats of natural disasters, the threats of racial, national, and individual discrimination, the threats of poverty, the threats of starvation, the threats of life and of death, of losing relatives and friends; when I look at all these troubles of the world, I give a deep sigh and say to myself, *Broken pots no longer feel the scorching heat of the flaming stove; saved are they of the trauma of cooking.*

Ecclesiastes congratulated the dead rather than the living, though I did

[49] Jane Roberts

not see his point that the situation of those yet to be born is better than of those living. For me, their situation seems worse, because all the turmoil of life still lay ahead of them. Perhaps this is the reason the poor unsuspecting creatures want to cry out their eyes at birth. I see with Montesquieu,[50] who thought that humans should be mourned at birth rather than at death. However, one thing also true is that it is only someone "that dies in earnest pursuit [that] is like one wounded in hot blood."[51] Really, to him alone is death a murder, one ignorantly committed upon himself, for both life and death have values intrinsic only to them.

Looking back at this period of my life, I often did not miss a realization that all these awareness were changing my perception of life, and thus changing my life. Unlike in the old days when I would be plunged into fear and insecurity at the general news of death, now when I learned of old people's death, I sometimes had a feeling of envy. I now believed that there is a world out there, not void, sordid, or grim. Really, only he is wounded in hot blood that dies in earnest pursuit.

Baba and Baami had not died in hot blood and I took comforts in that. Baba was a well-accomplished man who had God in his blood, always keeping it at room temperature. And so was Baami. I remember a comment about Baami made about eight years earlier by the Hausa alfa that lived with us. He often said: "I've never seen a man like him (Baami). He is a sinless man in the Face of God, and a blameless man in the faces of men. If he was hungry, no one would know. If he was fully fed, no one would know. If he was angry, no one would know. If he was unhappy, no one would know."

Truly, that was Baami. Never had I seen him strive to assert an ego; always was he playing a nobody while he enjoyed the ride. Never had I seen him claim to be right in arguments or counsels, nor had I seen him take pride in a justification of his claims. He believed in helping and letting everyone form his or her own decision. Baami was never bothered by anything. He cherished nothing more in the world than for him and everyone to have something good to eat, warm community to live in, values to share, and jokes to laugh about. This was the reason that every time I remembered him, I could not but see him laughing. He was a man who came and went as if he had not come at all. Yet he left behind marks too indelible to miss.

One thing I did not fail to notice in the experience of this period also was the contrast in the lives of these two great men in my life. Baba had been so great because of his strong hold on the control of his life and environment; Baami had been great because of his relinquish and mockery of life and his environment. Alexander the Great once made a remark that inspires me. “If I were not Alexander,” he had said, “I should wish to be

[50] Charles de Secondat, Baron de la Brède et de Montesquieu, was a French law philosopher, and an ideological co-founder of the American Constitution along with John Locke.
[51] Francis Bacon

Diogenes." Diogenes was an ascetic philosopher who claimed and owned nothing in the world, a complete opposite of the Macedonian conqueror. In these, were great lessons for me, and I held tightly to them.

***

Several months after the 40th day ceremony, I still found myself in the maze of my life, without the slightest clue for the way out. My situation even seemed more muddled than it had been. In the period of two months, I had run about, up and down, physically and mentally, trying to find a visa, but I had recorded no progress. As handicapped as I was, I tried more than could be convenient for my state of health, and the frustration sapped my health and the little finances I had.

Things did not improve between me and my father, and this also contributed to my situation. I expected him to take steps toward finding me the visa, but he only left me to my fate. My frustration was an opportunity for him to chagrin me - afterall, he seemed to be thinking, I now had money to run around, yet I was not getting anywhere.

My situation reminded me of a Yoruba proverb: *Difficult things are as difficult as what God does not do, and easy things are as easy as what God does*. I wondered whether God was on my father's side of our conflict. But I wished to remind God that whether I win or he wins in our situation, it is the same thing to my father, while my loss would be painful for me, and would do him no good either.

All these were forcing depression back on me, though I struggled against it. I tried to focus my attention on my writing and readings, but my effort was threatened when, out of the blues, I became stricken with panic attack. It was as serious as the one in 1993; however, it strangely brought an end to the estrangement in the relationship between me and my father.

This was how it happened.

As I have made known so far, my experience had taught me that, in this environment that we lived in, natural occurrences might not afterall be simply natural, or simply naturally caused. Physical illnesses might not altogether be innocent as simply physical as they looked, especially for me at this period of my life. So I decided to tackle the problem in the multilayered way that I believed.

First, taking control of the contents of my thoughts, I arrested the situation by myself, keeping the panic attack under control while I functioned seamlessly in my daily activities. Secondly, I consulted a psychiatrist who prescribed an antidepressant. Thirdly, I told Baba Akinnu about it and he promised to do something quickly. And finally, I laid the rest in God's hands, something that enabled me to see my affliction in a healthful context rather than focus negatively and solely on the symptoms. Postmodern psychotherapists would call it prosymptomatic, a process of embracing a psychological symptom, by which it drains out the energy that sustains the symptom. Moreover, I increased my prayer and considered fasting.

Then I decided to tell my father about it, to let him know what was going on with me. This was difficult to do because the situation between us had grown almost colder than ice. Nonetheless, I forced myself to go and talk to him, and he forced himself to listen to me. I expected the discussion to change his attitude for better, but it did not. The meeting ended up in a noisy fight. He flared up and vituperated me as badly as he could. It was one of the worst moments in my life and it plunged me further into my hell. His words were so weird that it seemed to me that my father had long died in his body and it was another person beneath his skin.

A few days later, however, I was in my room when a gentle knock on my door interrupted my sleep. It was Aunty Sidi. It had been a long time that I saw her and I greeted her warmly. She came to see my father and was directed to my new room when she asked for me.

"Your father told me some time ago that you were going to have a surgery in the white man's country and I expected you would have gone. So I was surprised when he now told me you're still around. I hope there's no problem."

I intended to shroud my problem away from her at first, but I thanked God I did not. I told her how the problems had bred until the last quarrel with my father.

"He already told me about it," she said calmly, "I only wanted you to raise it first. You see, what I want to tell you is for your own sake." She had already prepared to talk to me. "Though it disheartened me to learn of your difficulty with your father, it did not surprise me. I've always told you to be careful with him, lest they use him against you. And your father is ignorant of it; he always thinks he's in control, you see, while he puts all the blame on you. Now he claims that it's because you are visiting Oniyanrin at this point that you have the return of the panic attack. He said that he had warned you that it was [that woman] who is behind your entire predicament, and still you go there to meet your grandmother when she's around."

She paused to hear my response, but I had been ossified with shock at learning the name she just mentioned. It was true that my father had warned me about Oniyanrin, but he had never mentioned anyone's name as Aunty Sidi just did. I had never heard the woman's name mentioned before, and it brought to my mind a stream of memories and thoughts.

I could not believe what I just heard. This was the woman the alfa, Baba's friend, had sent me to in 1993 when this whole thing began, but it was now I remembered the queer circumstance of his message and wondered whether it was true. Is it really true? I realized what message the alfa was trying to get across to me and to the woman. I was not a kid then; I was only kidding myself. I tried to link her reaction over the message with the meaning of the message and I realized it was a common reaction to hide a secret, especially of such secret power, as I have seen quite often on TV. Maybe I had seen too much TV, but it became apparent to me that the alfa knew she was involved in my predicament, and she knew he knew, and he knew she knew he knew. And thus the sarcastic smile that lined the alfa's face when I reported her response back to him, which I mistook for a lecherous one. Although they said there were others who simply collaborated in the evil, this woman was said to be the boss of the villain group.

I dug out the grave of the past in which she had featured and I was sobered and embittered. I almost cried. She had been such a kind woman, apparently sympathetic and helpful to me. If she was the one involved in my problems, the world's appearance must have been ridiculously misleading. "The nose is a wicked organ," as our fathers sometimes say, "it doesn't smell the evil of wicked hearts." Yet, "the thin covering of the chest prevents us from seeing the stone the wicked one calls her heart." If the woman was truly the one, then my nose and my eyes had been betraying me all along. Neither had I smelled evil nor seen evil.

At a time when I never cared about witchcraft beyond watching its fascinating mystery in movies, someone had said in my hearing that she knew the woman was into witchcraft, but I was more conscious of the fear and suspicion in complex families than to take it seriously. Even if I took it seriously, I did not think I was anything for anyone to bewitch. Neither, also, had I heard evil.

On another occasion, when I witnessed an open accusation of witchcraft against her, which she turned into something else, I had not noticed or thought anything. By this, I knew that it is what a man's mind is interested in that his senses perceive. It is the state of our mind that determines what we smell, hear, see, and feel.

I was too shocked and confused at the moment to be able to say anything to Aunty Sidi. She advised me to be more careful, especially not to run against my father anymore. If God is protecting you, you do not climb palm trees with banana fronds. She warned me never to raise the issue with my father again, and that, though our relationship may have added to my predicament, but overall it had helped me more than it may have hurt me.

Lastly, she promised that, right from the moment, my father's attitude would change for better toward me.

And, really, it changed.

***

This revelation meant all the reality my mind knew at the time and I tried to be careful not to over-identify with any single one explanation. I sought equilibrium in my soul, in my consciousness of God. Perhaps this revelation meant to me that it was not yet God's time for me to get completely out of this whole thing. Perhaps it meant that my spirituality was not strong enough to be beyond the evil attacks. Perhaps it meant that all my steps needed more coordination and that I was receiving the tunes of the keys I had unconsciously been striking. The truth was, it was the expression of an inner reality, and it meant to me that all were for the good.

A few months later, the woman would come personally to apologize about all the events of the past, when then I assured her of my forgiveness. For me now, we were both victims of the general circumstance, transcendental in scope, and she needed most importantly to understand and forgive herself. Yet, I knew I had to be mindful about my safety. Life is wealth, they say, and so is its well-being. A war foretold, as a proverb goes, does not conquer or kill the cripple – but only if the cripple is wise. I was like the Israelites walking through the path in the parted Red Sea; the water-wall danger on both sides were real, the anger of Pharaoh coming threateningly behind was real; relenting or increasing my efforts along the sea path would definitely be real for my destiny. But, above all, God was the only Savior to Whom I looked. The final battle is what matters most in any series of battles. No matter what, light will always triumph over darkness. And it was for light I lived.

I decided to fast to aid my prayer. If it was this same God that saved Abraham from the burning flame of the idolaters, that saved Prophet Mohammad by sleeping off his enemies when he was fleeing his birth city, then He should be able to save me here as well. Every morning, I prayed God opens up the way for me to America and leads me through, as He opened the way for the Israelites in the Red Sea and as He led them through. I had hope in Uncle Jibola's promise, in his concern and kindness, and I prayed that God strengthens him as my Moses. The tougher aspect of it all, however, was not knowing when the fruits of my prayer and my efforts would come, and if at all it would come as prayed. But I kept struggling to be patient and to have it whenever it came.

IV

I needed to keep my mind from the brink of insanity where it trod. In addition to my writing, I bought an aerial wire for my television set. With a fifty-foot bamboo pole, my younger brothers sent up the antenna to go flock with the birds and my television came back to life. It was in time for the 1998 FIFA World Cup. I had been on bed during the last championship in 1994, languishing in pains as sound of soccer on TV and of thrilled audience around the neighborhood ripped frequently through the air. This time, I wanted to share in the fun.

As the tournament approached, my friends and I became political about it. We cursed our team because some of the players participated in one of the greatest political sellouts the country had ever witnessed: the inglorious "Two-million Man March" for the dictator General Abacha. But we did not want to chase out a stubborn child for the tigers to feast upon; we backed them, anyway. However, they preferred to be feasted upon. They crashed out ingloriously when trounced silly by the Danish team.

Individually, the Nigerian players were among the best in the world, but they made up one of the worst teams in the tournament.

We did not want the Nigerian loss to spoil the fever of the championship for us, so we became political again in choosing which team to transfer our support, as most people consciously or unconsciously did.

This was a moment to see that in terms of international politics as it affected Nigeria and Africa, the superpowers, America and Britain especially, were unpopular with most people. They were of Jekyll and Hyde reputations, often seen as wolves in sheepskin, a prism through which their sports teams were seen. Though often with ambivalent feelings, many Nigerians nonetheless liked America. American culture was admirable; it has conquered the world where American politics have failed. The movies and music, clothing fashion and sports, Coke and cheeseburger, and the perceived American consistent and efficient internal democracy were seen as the key to the doors of modern civilization. Hence, deciding against America was not always easy.

Something I have long realized is that the people of a nation are usually different morally from the government. Such a difference is obvious in politically troubled nations like Nigeria and most African nations, but in nations where the system of government is accepted by the people, the difference is not as obvious. The acceptance of the system of government, and the apparent ideals of the accepted system of government, often obscure the morality of the components of the governments from the general people. Therefore, when looked from outside, the people of the nation may be seen in the lights of the misdeeds of their governments, because it is the policies of their governments that reflect and touch the outside world, and not the true feelings and humanity of the people. This is a reason many people outside America might not like Americans. Americans are often forced to be seen in the light of their government's foreign policies, which foreigners do not see as a goodwill light to help illuminate their world as ostensibly intended, but to blind them while the government takes advantage of them. However, the people of such a nation as America may be culpable for indulging in the façade of the government. Many often feel too comfortable than to make efforts to see the realities in the government and its relationship with other nations of the world. To many Americans, they have only inherited the "white man's burden"[52] and cannot understand why the people of the world would still hate them.

At last, we chose to support the French team. Although not because of their politics, as that was also in disrepute, but because of the efforts and determination of the players, and especially because of Barthez, their goalkeeper. The little kids and teenagers in my neighborhood called him by my name because they thought he looked like me, and, because of that, they all gave him their supports – symbolic of the supports they had for

---

[52] Title of a poem by Rudyard Kipling, it is a phrase used to justify European imperialism in the 19th and early 20th centuries, and it implies that imperialism was motivated by a high-minded desire of the whites to uplift the people of color.

me. Like I always had my head and face, Barthez had his head skin-shaved and his mustache and low beard circled around his mouth in a fashion we called "Teddy", perhaps after Teddy Riley.

The French team eventually won the tournament and we were all excited. God had not let my spirit disappoint the kids.

In addition to the TV, I repaired my radio and, with access to local and foreign channels, I was always informed up to the minute about events going on in the country and around the world. The situation in Nigeria had worsened down to a dilemma in which the fear of a second civil war was heightened by General Sanni Abacha's self-succession bid. Ahead of us now in the country, it was either war or a continuing Abacha rule. No one could tell which was better. The man now seemed worse than the Ugandan Idi Ami.

It was depressing to hear of the various sad stories from country to country. There was great injustice and disturbance of peace around the globe. Everyday there was war in various places in Africa and the world. The threats of AIDS, natural disasters, and human hatred and anger kept shaking the world violently. Earthquake today, airplane crash tomorrow, train crash the next day, and then the embassy bombings in Kenya and Tanzania. Among those of many others, the fate of the little Kenyan boy blinded by shrapnel hurt me to my bones. Yet, the perpetrators of the evil invoked the name of God that we all prayed to for peace. What an irony of life to think about. Whose invocation was God taking?

The irony struck again in Nigeria when the prayer of the people was answered and General Abacha dropped dead untimely, only to be followed by the fulfillment of his wish. About a month afterward, amid the relief from the dictator's death, Chief Abiola's death was announced, leaving the country confused over its fate.

***

Because I had not seen an opportunity to get a visa, Uncle Jibola did not hear from me as I promised. But I heard from him. Late in June, he asked for my medical transcripts and my grandmother tried to obtain it from U.C.H. After a long search at the hospital, they discovered that my case-file was nowhere to be found. What they found was a 1975 report of my hospitalization when I broke an arm in my school's playground. We sent X-ray photographs of my legs instead to Uncle Jibola.

I kept on trying to be closer to God. Everyday and every night, I prayed, and secretly fasted. My father warned me not to fast in my condition. "Even God," he said, "permits persons in your condition not to fast during Ramadan." But I wanted my prayers to be answered quickly, very quickly, and I went on fasting without my father's knowledge.

TWENTY-TWO

Rain of Blessing

I

One of the first signs that good times had arrived was that my father was no longer lackadaisical about me anymore. He had considerably changed and now had enthusiasm toward my struggle. I found myself a little slow in accepting the new situation and feeling comfortable with him after the sour experience of the past. But he drew me into the old good state of mutual friendship, and I felt that my father had reincarnated into his body, chasing out my rival who had earlier dwelled there. When someone offered to help me obtain a visa, my father sold his last private car, a grounded Peugeot 504, to raise money. For him to be doing this for me was in itself enough to please my mind. The car was worth much more than he sold it, but he had let it go to meet a deadline for the prospect we had.

Then, a few days afterward someone sent N10, 000 to my father to help us in the pursuit. Professor Adedoja, often called Provost, was a good man in the minds of everyone. He had exercised a lot of humanitarian acts in his power since he came into the town about a year and a half earlier. A gubernatorial candidate in the state, he was the provost of one of the two Colleges of Education in Oyo, and he lived close to our house where he passed by me on his way to and back from work every day. A few months before, the professor had stopped his car beside me to inquire about my condition. He had been seeing me in the same position everyday and he had been wondering what could be holding down a young man like me to one spot. Then he offered to give any assistance that I might need anytime. However, this money came as a surprise because I had not talked to him in about six months and I wondered how he knew I needed money at this time. I thought the Heaven must be ready to blow my way.

***

Really, the Heaven was ready to blow my way.

I was in my room one February afternoon when Wasiu walked in unannounced. After exchanging greetings, he said to me, "Congratulations," and he extended his hand for a handshake, beaming with joy.

The particular action and its words were strange to me and I did not know how to respond. I could not remember the last time I was congratulated before. 'Sorry' was the greeting I had been accustomed to and I was already sick of it. A little impatient, I inquired what it was all about.

He brought out a large envelope from his backpack. It looked familiar. It was the kind of envelope in which I received magazines from Uncle Jibola about a decade earlier: the large orange-colored American envelope.

"Uncle Jibola has sent the documents for your visa," he said with a gleeful smile.

I looked at him for a moment, not sure what to say. Then, I said, "You mean the end of the tunnel has finally come?"

"Yes, it has. By the grace of God, it has."

I had not been as happy in a long time. Uncle Jibola had finished his studies and had embarked upon the process to save me from my troubles. I hurried to share the joy with my father.

Things changed sooner than I thought. Everyone looked at me as America-bound, with the degree of admiration typical of such a good fortune, and they gave me more 'congratulations.' It really felt good to be congratulated, I realized.

Uncle Tunji filed an application for the visa at the American consulate in Lagos and an interview appointment was set for the 8th day of March 1999. I moved my belongings to Ibadan two days before the date. I expected to come back only to show my father the visa and to say 'thank you' and 'goodbye' to everyone in the house and in the neighborhood. The neighborhood has been like a big family house for me; the churches roared with songs of praises to God. God has answered our prayers.

II

With Uncle Tunji, I arrived at the consulate at around 6 am on the Monday morning and we still met hundreds of applicants already there. Before the consulate changed the system from first-come-first-serve to service-by-appointment, it was worse. People would sleep overnight outside the place in order to make it into the consulate building in the morning. Some of them were true applicants who wanted to have the opportunity of getting an interview, but many others were jobless individuals who struggled to secure a spot in the line for the purpose of selling it to desperate applicants. Now things have changed; the consulate gave out dates of interview to applicants and you did not have to show up until your appointed date.

People now only struggled to get there as early as possible because there was a time limit for checking in.

At around 7 am, or a little before, the security guards checked us in and about two or more hours later I was called in for my interview.

There were thirteen windows in the long and curved hall, and an interviewer at each window. My interviewer was a young Asian-American lady that must be about my age and we greeted her with respect due her position. Perhaps even more, because sometimes the consular officers seemed like gods and goddesses. She looked disinterested as I gave her a calculated smile attempted to disarm her of her stern countenance. I exuded some confidence based on my arms of documents and my visa receipt. All applicants had to pay the non-refundable visa fee ahead of the interview, even though only a tiny fraction would be granted visa.

"Who's traveling?" she asked, refusing to be persuaded out of her official countenance.

"He's the one," my uncle replied, indicating at me.

I gave her all the documents I had with me. The first letter was written by Uncle Jibola, stating my situation and how and why he had had to send for me to ameliorate my suffering. He stated the establishment he was working for, Anesthesia Associates of Massachusetts, and the four hospitals in which he offered his services. As one of their anesthesiologists, the establishment expressed willingness to waive the charges for the anesthesia service for the surgeries at any of the hospitals (I was expected to undergo three major surgeries). He further stated categorically that he was going to defray all the other costs of the surgeries. To back up, the next letter was from his employer, confirming the waiving of the cost of the anesthesia service and stating how much he was paid annually to prove that he was capable of defraying the cost of the surgeries.

The next letter was from the surgeon, Dr. Aldo Beretta. He stated the complexity of my case, the careful step-by-step process by which he would tackle it, and how long the process would take. The first surgery was to be on a hip, after which I would be on rehabilitation for several months. During the rehabilitation, the two knees would be done in a second surgery, and after the three joints have grown strong enough, the third surgery, which would be on the other hip, would then follow and also be followed by months of rehabilitation. The surgeon then asked for a visa valid for minimum of a year.

The next papers comprised of completed affidavits from the Department of Justice with so much information on my uncle and his household: his tax information, his pay slips and some other relevant documents.

The consular officer browsed through the papers. She hardly read any of them, and then she asked me a question. "How much is the treatment going to cost?"

"My Uncle knows," I replied, careful not to use any negative form of speech.

“That's not what I'm asking,” she responded sternly. “What I'm asking is how much the whole treatment will cost.”

"I don't exactly know that but of course he does, and he has indicated his capability to defray it."

"I'll like to know the cost," she said with the full air of her authority. “If it’s going to cost $200,000, your uncle wouldn't be able to pay for it."

"But it's nothing that much. From all the information that I have the cost of the whole treatment would be around $40,000. It could even be less, but never more. There are indications for some wavering in the costs; you can see it there in the papers."

"That couldn’t be much; it's just for the anesthesia."

Uncle Tunji tried to explain to her but she put up her hand and said, "Let me tell you this: I don't know about surgeries; what I know is figures. So, I’ll like to see a letter from the surgeon stating how much it would cost and an evidence of payment or arrangement indicating that your uncle is sure to pay." Then she made some notes on some papers and gave one to me. "Take this to one of the four hospitals stated there. I want you to be examined by our medical panel and have them send the report stating that it is you who is in the passport you're holding and that the treatment you are seeking in the U.S. cannot be done here in Nigeria. I also want you to be medically examined and vaccinated, or to be proved as vaccinated against those diseases listed there.

"Take this (she gave me another paper). I want to see those items on it: your uncle's statement of account, a photocopy of his Green Card, and evidence of a deposit of the cost of treatment. Also, this affidavit form is a wrong one, so quote this number (she indicated on another paper) for him to obtain the right form, to fill it and send it back to you. When you have all those, bring them back. That's all I want."

These disturbed me. There was enough proof that the treatment and its costs were under control. However, we gave her a forced smile, thanked her and left her window, unsatisfied, though hopeful.

She gave us a maximum of four weeks to get the papers ready, but, by the third week, we had had all the documents ready and set again for the consulate. We had the right affidavit form, stating my uncle’s alien number, bank account, and owned stocks. The formal arrangement of his installment payment plan was made and I had a document to that effect. The cost was no longer as much as I had thought. Dr. Beretta was my uncle's colleague and he had indicated his willingness to waive the cost of his services. With the waiver of the cost of anesthesia and of the surgery, the cost remained only for the hospitalization. This, my uncle stated in a letter, in which also he stated the contact numbers of the surgeon and other concerned people for verification by the consulate.

After waiting for a long time on the outside bench, we were called into the interview hall. Today, there was about twice as much people waiting to be interviewed than the first day we were there. It was very difficult finding a place to sit. Anxiety ruled the place; everyone was quiet and intent, praying perhaps. We were all in the palace of an "almighty."

The period between the first interview and today's had begun for me with heavy worries, but which had thinned into a kind of stoic calmness before the last day of the waiting period. I had always been more alone than not, and thus lonely. There was a great vacuum that was then filled by anxiety over the visa, and once very often it was depressing. I tried very hard to concentrate on my writing, but still I often thought on how this next interview would be. I feared one imagined obstacle or another. This strictness to rules by the consular officer, mirrored by her indifference, was amplified in my imagination. Because of the notorious stringency of the consular officers I had never thought of going to the embassy for visa. I abhorred such a situation when my fate would be at the mercy of someone who did not understand me. The famous idea in Nigeria was that the consular officers were so trained that they could see beyond applicants' eyes and documents, and that they were officially disposed to denying the visas, unless convinced otherwise well beyond all doubts. Something interesting about this was that most applicants, whether legitimate or illegitimate, were always already afraid of the consulate before they reached the officers' windows. Therefore whatever these officers were looking for beyond the applicants' eyes and documents was already there. It was like using lie detectors on suspects; lie detectors are made to detect signs of fear in the breathing and blood pressure, while anyone regarded as a police suspect already had enough to be afraid of. At this time it was stated that the consulate granted visas only to less than 2 percent of Nigerian applicants in a year.

Over the past three weeks, while I was waiting for today, I prayed, I fasted, I deeply considered my case, I soliloquized. Often in my mind I rehearsed. I put myself in the role of the consular officer, with a toughened heart to deny the visa application, and, on the other side, I explained to her why she should give me the visa. I kept all these in my heart and waited for the real event, careful not to sound cunning while being convincing in my argument.

***

"Good morning," Uncle Tunji and I chorused warmly and she replied us with an official politeness. I gave the documents to her and waited for her to go through them.

She coughed. Quickly and eagerly, I said sorry to her. She could have been the queen of England at that moment and I her page. Queen Elizabeth would have smiled and given what I wanted for being that eagerly reverential, but my consular officer remained deadpan as she had ever been. She took the documents and browsed hurriedly through them while I waited in vacillation between fear and hope. Then she began to talk.

"What about the deposit of the cost?" she asked.

"The arrangement has been made and there's a letter in there to that effect as you requested." Uncle Tunji replied and indicated the exact letter. She had not read the documents in detail.

She pulled out the letter and read through it. Then she said, "Your uncle doesn't have the right to tell me this."

"But you can see all the evidence of his position and his inclination to settle the entire bill by installment. They are all in your hands, check them," Uncle Tunji explained, trying to urge her to read the other documents of the contract between Uncle Jibola and the hospital. "The contacts of all the parties are also there."

"No. What if he doesn't pay?"

"If he's not going to pay, he wouldn't send for me in the first place," I answered. "There is no cause for him to lie to you and lie in all those papers with his employers. He knows what the law requires and that is why he has waited this long until he's able to handle it before he called for me. There is absolutely no cause and condition for him to lie to you. He's not even such a person."

"Because he's a good Christian?" she said with an irritating sarcasm and I did not know what to say anymore. From her demeanor one could see that she was only taking us through the motion, and not ready to grant the visa. But I wanted to try as much as possible to get this visa and I tried more to persuade her. I still was hopeful.

For a few seconds she paused and gave us an inscrutable look, and then said, "I'm going to deny you the visa."

Like a fireball, that hit me terribly at a delicate spot.

"That would not be fair," Uncle Tunji said. "You can see this boy's condition; he has been like this for years and has not been able to do anything because of the condition. He would have completed his studies and started a life like every normal person, but he could not. This is the last hope for him and you should consider that."

"I'll refuse you," she said dramatically, ignoring my uncle's pleas.

"Then what would you want us to do?" Uncle Tunji asked. "This is our last hope. We have been running up and down to get all you asked for; we've been sweating and spending about all these days, and it wouldn't be fair on us if you denied us."

I could not finger what was going on in my mind. Many meanings of the situation were hotchpotch in my thoughts. It had dawned on me that she would not rescind her decision. She was a young girl and she still had the stubbornness and carelessness of youth written all over her. I did not think such a person could turnaround from negative to positive, although I hoped she would, and I wanted to press on the hope. I hoped, at least, that she would give another appointment and tell us whatever more she wanted us to bring. But she did not want anything anymore; she only wanted to deny the application and she took it somehow personally.

"Why don't you go to UK?" she asked, taunting us and deepening her sarcasm. "Or Germany? There are other places around the world where you could do the surgery; why don't you go to one of them? Why America?"

I had heard of angry American immigration workers bark things like this at prospective immigrants. Some would say, "Why can't you people stay in your country?" But I never knew I would encounter one. Unfortunately, such arrogant officers did not know how ignorant the questions were. This is the human world, and from time immemorial have humans been migrating from place to place across the world for one reason or another. And because a nation is richer than another and attracting immigrants does not mean the people are better and should treat others with contempt. It is all about conditions, for which no single person in the world can claim non-responsibility.

How the world had turned around only in a few decades. Siyanbola Oladigbolu did not ask the American missionaries who came to seek residence in his kingdom for any reason they had wanted to, not to talk of drilling them to prove it. Magnanimously, he blessed them with land so large that they did not know what to do with it all. Now, here was I at the American consulate, with the same name as his, the same blood as his, booted out like I had no soul, and in spite of my debilitated health. Wherever Siyanbola was in the firmament of heaven, I was sure he would not be happy to see his son treated this way. Neither, of course, would the missionaries, the American emissary of the time, from which this current embassy evolved. Perhaps, in the emerging world, anyone who sees him or herself as only a citizen of one nation would only be a simpleton.

I knew I was losing the game, but I still tried on. "America is where I have a relative who would help me, not UK, not Germany, and..."

"Where you can do it for free?" she cut in insultingly.

This was too much on us and I did not know what to say anymore. Yet, we continued to persuade her, though she stuck to her gun.

She returned my passport and the other documents and beat the air a little, insulting us more, before she finally said "Good day" and left the window for us to keep on talking to an empty seat.

I looked at Uncle Tunji. He was confused. His eyes met mine and I could see the regret in his heart. I pitied him instead of myself. He had abandoned his work to run around in the last few days to meet all the necessary requirements, all with the hope of helping me obtain the visa. Now, nothing. For some time he stood there, staring at the empty seat, looking at the structure of all the efforts torn down by someone's insensitivity, and he was temporarily paralyzed of what to do. "Let's go," I said to him.

We gathered the documents. Uncle Tunji walked in front and I hobbled behind him. Everyone stared at us. I could not look back at them. It was shameful going out like that. I spotted an applicant I had made friends with earlier on, and with whom I had discussed the prospect of the visa. He dropped his gaze as I looked up at his face. He could not meet my eyes. He seemed to be telling me he was sorry, and he was afraid of his own fate. When people cry at funerals, it is not really for the dead but for themselves, especially for their unknown fate. He was the next person to meet the same consular I had met, and now he was afraid.

It appeared as if the kingdom of God was easier to enter than the kingdom of America. While not being blasphemous, the truth is that, to enter the kingdom of God, as often preached, all you have to do is face the obstacle or the devil in you and overcome it. But to enter the American kingdom the obstacle is not in you, or sometimes not only in you, but mainly in the possessors of visa decisions. It is easier to take care of your own devil than someone else's. I have known many people who have submitted their lives to Jesus Christ, or to one religion or another, but the U.S. embassy did not care who you submitted your life to, not even if you did to their White House. How many pastors with their tunic as white and long as may seem convincing to the angels of God have been treated by the consulate as if they were criminals. Not to mention Imams, whose beards and turbans would even remind the consulate of Osama bin Laden. It was too much to think of, unless the God of the heavenly kingdom intervenes, twisting their minds to come in one's favor. With my mind I looked up to the sky in search of Him. Though it seemed clear enough, but at this time, He had left their minds in my disfavor.

"Why this, God?" I asked as I walked out of the embassy building. Sadness clogged my mind's eyes and I thought: God, is this what You want to do to me? Is this how you are going to treat me, still? After all the hell I've been through?

III

Sometimes a battle is fought many times before it is won. I made up my mind to focus on the situation as I believed it was: a challenge for tougher efforts.

After about six weeks, Uncle Jibola sent another set of documents and we quickly filed another application. But, to my utter dismay, the consulate set my appointment at a date about two months away, the 9th of August. This became funny, however, when I heard of the appointment date given by the consulate to the supporters club of the Super Falcons, the Nigerian female soccer team slated to participate in the Women's World Cup championship in the United States. It was also set at a date in August, while the championship they wanted to attend was to begin an end in July. I knew the consulate was up to a game of its own.

***

One significant thing that occurred during this waiting period was the restoration of democracy in Nigeria. The great day was the 29th of May 1999. It was a day of vivid restoration of hope in the people of Nigeria, a day of new beginning, a day of germination, a dawn of a new era. By so much of our bones we have tilled the soil; by so much of our thoughts we have sown the seed; by so much of our sweat, tears, and blood we have watered the plant, now the seed has germinated, the bud has sprouted, and this day we danced at the festival in joy of the favorable weather and in gratitude to God, the gracious Cause of the weather.

But the sprouting of the bud is not directly the harvest of the labor. There is a lot more work to be done. By more sacrifice and patience does the harvest come, and by more and more does it continue. The price of freedom, they say, is eternal vigilance. Presently, our foundational infrastructure was the major problem facing the nation. After the birth, resuscitation, or resurrection of a nation, this is always the first problem to be well determined and constituted for the eternal labor and growth to be well and ever guided. However, this new government seemed insensitive to the criticality of this problem, and subsequent events after the inauguration highlighted it bloodily upon the nation. The various ethnic groups and the two major religions felt unassured and unsecured in the current dispensation, and ethnic and religious crises blazed the nation.

IV

One afternoon late in August, Wasiu came to visit me and turned to his philosophy to console me over the bungled August 9th interview. In spite of the additional documents I took with me, the officer refused the visa the second time. I had the signed agreement papers of the installment plan between my uncle and the hospital, and the receipt of part of the cost he had already paid. But the consular now insisted that he should pay the whole amount before she would grant the visa.

"Listen to this," Wasiu began, "Sometimes one just has to take things as they are. We are all agents of God – what the Qur'an refers to as the vicegerents - and everyone is playing his or her own part. If you know that you are playing your own part, in that knowledge you would find comfort."

That was an idea of the Qur'an combined with that of the Jewish philosopher Benedict Spinoza whom Wasiu was working on for his Bachelor's final project, and now he thought it could benefit me. Something interesting was that my cousin and I had taken our debates from the academic platform and we now applied them directly to treat our various problems. We gave breath to the ideas we learned and let them hang with us. As he had repeatedly argued in the past, by practice, he had made me realize that philosophy is not just something about abstract speculations as people sometimes think, but a way of life, a religion. That was how we now practiced it.

I agreed with his Spinozan idea, only I was also aware that it was not something as easy in practice as in thought.

"A poor man that was beaten to death by poverty had no loss when compared to a rich man who lived in affluence until his death," Wasiu continued relentlessly, "The poor man simply had a kind of experience which the rich man did not have. It was all about doing your part, your experience."

I agreed again, but I wanted to drag him all out on it. It was a kind of fun I had not had in a long time, and I could do with a little of it if the American consulate was not going to give me fun.

"But the rich man also had a kind of experience which the poor man did not have," I countered.

"Yes, that is true. But it only makes it square." In a Shakespearean way he added, "We all end up dead, won't we? And that makes it squarer. We don't know what transpires beyond that, but both are dead and buried. So the poor man loses nothing special if he understood this while he lived, and the rich man gains nothing special (in that sense)."

"What if the poor man did not understand this?" I asked, "Instead of going through the experience as you say, he was dragged through it with thorns' cuts and all the rubbish; how square would he then be with the rich man who went through his own life with the pleasure of his wealth? The pleasure of yesterday might not be here today, but its memory is, and it might be something."

"So much bad for him, then," Wasiu replied. "The better it is for him to understand it, and that's the work of the philosopher, whether under the hat of a religious preacher or an academic scholar – let people realize this. And that's why I ask you to look at it that way. But, nonetheless, everyone is just playing his or her own part of the game, and it all ends in a square, whether we are conscious of it or not."

We went on and on, confusing and clarifying the discussion at the same time, until we became hungry and left it for the pressing need of our belly. Perhaps the proverb is right; there is no room for anything else when hunger dwells in your belly.

***

Blessed be thou who has wit to learn;
how the favor of fortune may change and turn,
whose head is not raised in his high estate,
nor his heart in misfortune made desolate.
AbdRahman Jami

Meditating on Wasiu's discussion brought me to an intriguing conclusion, that success in life may only be the integrity with which one lives the life. Any condition in life, rich or poor, able or disabled, leading or following, the success we are essentially after is the same: integrity, the food of the soul.

By this realization, I now always believe that no one is essentially in a place of superiority or inferiority to another, as Wasiu's idea implied. The rich, the poor, the prince, the pauper, the king, the servant, the slave, the slave-owners, the oppressors, the oppressed, the superstar, the unknown fan, all are equal entities gaining experience one way or another in the world. Therefore, if one learns to understand the world enough, no one needs to see him or herself as superior or inferior to any other person. As this world is a symbolic reality interposed in front of Reality, so is every situation in it. One only needs to know that whatever situation one is in the world, it is the role that one has to play in the cosmic drama. Although these roles are flexible rather than rigid, one may be better by willfully understanding deeply enough to play it as fully fulfilling and complementary as one could honestly and creatively play it.

This is one of the paradoxes of life: taking life as it is and (trying) changing it at the same time. It is like accepting a situation and not accepting it at the same time, for to try to change a situation seems to mean not accepting it. But there is no contradiction in it. As a result, any situation one finds oneself is simply a unique situation for playing one's role of integrity and creativity. Living is an art, scientific and artistic; it is an art of creativity. And, being fluid and changeable, the freedom lies in oneself to change, modify, or improve the condition within its natural limits. Therefore, I could accept my present condition, maintain its integrity and creativity, and proceed to modify it as I wanted, or I could sit down and worry myself to depression and death. This was the choice I had to make as I grappled with life in my current situation.

Life is a story, a huge multidimensional story, and the world, in all its times and places, is the huge set. The themes, parts, and plots are so varied, perhaps infinite, that a single person, people, race, sex, generation, or ideology cannot tell it all, even though each may broach or represent the main and essential plot for general remembrance and recapitulation. This is why the roles are variedly and mutually shared among ourselves: for us to learn from the mistakes and successes of one another, since we cannot individually live long enough to experience them all.

Developing this concept, ancient Greek thinkers created stoicism, a philosophy of accepting variable fortunes with equal equanimity. For conventional religion, the idea of teleology is the pillar: God has a purpose for everything. Like the Quranic *vicegerents* and the Biblical *children of God*, we are taught to accept our situations and rejoice – or find solace – in God's absolute wisdom. For the Bhagavad-Gita, perhaps a more mystical scripture, the question to us is "Why in this truth find sorrow?"

All this, I realized I needed to know to achieve creative contentment and peace of mind. It is a culmination for all the ideas I had been progressively dealing with since the beginning of my predicament. I wished I had known these in a long time, in all the years of the sickness in which I blinded myself to my own screenplay in my hands and was suffering myself in my act, looking elsewhere for what I thought I wanted. I wished I had known that the true nature of sorrow and joy are no more than they are to an actor in a Hollywood production. Sometimes in literature, the concept of dramatic irony is called *Sophoclean irony*, due to the dramatic ignorance of the actors in Sophocles' plays. Now I think it is this irony that we have been enacting over the eons, but only a few people periodically realize it.

This made me appreciate my life and love my career path more than I had ever done. Film is as complete a metaphor for life as life is for film. As observed by Elie Wiesel, the Jewish Nobel Laureate, God may have created the world out of His love for stories. Really, without our tragedies, comedies, tragicomedies, and farces, I do not think the engine of life would have any fuel to run. So much does God love drama that He cannot help but to come down to play a role – the thematic hero sadistically crucified to redeem us from our miserable sins. Perhaps, then, the ultimate pleasure a movie or stage director could ever pursue is to see his story acted out by real people, by which he would have become like God. The universe is one huge acting stage, and God is the big Director. Plenty of actors have passed through, playing their parts in His cosmic story: Adam and Eve, Noah, Job, Abraham, Oduduwa, Sango, Moses, Mohammed, Jesus, Judas, Buddha, Krishna, Zeus, Osiris, Isis, Odysseus, Pharaohs, Plato, Sophocles, Shakespeare, Darwin, Freud, Einstein, and so on. Now, it is my turn. It is our turn. We only need to see it, learn and play our roles as honestly as we can.

So far, my life has told a story in the world, as a symbolic mythology for humanity, and I am proud of it. My mother, my father, brothers, sisters, my entire family, friends, acquaintances, and everyone in my neighborhoods and entire world are but characters in my *True Man Show*.[53] Every life is a story; every story is a myth; every myth is a reality; and every reality is a life.

If I had known these long ago, perhaps I would have helped myself from suffering as I had done over the years. But I was always consoled by the fact that I was only human, and perhaps our temporal nescience is part of the thrill that life holds. Christ, forgetting his role on the eve of the Crucifixion, makes the Passion more touching and liberating.

Therefore, the success in life is far more than what it seems. And the degree or grade of the success depends upon the degree or grade of the integrity, which in turn depends upon the degree or purity of the discovered self. How conscious one is of oneself and one's role in the play is essential, lest the Director calls for more and more retakes. Perhaps, even throws one into lower roles, if one still refuses to wake up to one's acts.

***

With all these in my consciousness, the consulate's game could not deject me. I tried to remind myself of what it was beyond what it appeared to be – a role in the drama. I became a happy person with an inexorable dedication and spirit toward my goal, and with no sense of intimidation of failure. Sometimes momentary hands of depression tended to grip me; life

[53] Reference to *The Truman Show*, starred by Jim Carey.

really seems to always be a constant struggle between the opposite emotions. But when I took a recourse to my awareness of the profound depth and transcendence of Nature, when I took a recourse to my spiritual reality, remembering myself as a spirit soul, created not to suffer but to experience for the ultimate good, it illuminated and validated me with the better meaning of my situation, and I became mentally free of all the troubles that appeared to wrap me up. I became fearless of whatever the world may offer. Though I had always been thinking long-term in terms of happiness, and accordingly waiting, I had come to realize that happiness is really in the moment. And if the happiness is true, it is the moment that lasts forever.

Experience, this is perhaps all we are doing in the world, in any condition we may find ourselves, and its understanding is the dynamic road to the ultimate goal of freeing oneself of the world's trifles and reconciling oneself with one's true or higher self. Every circumstance is a potentiality, and I was now being driven by this transcendental awareness.

Then, life is not a mad do or die affair. And neither is it an issue of compromise. The point is to find and see happiness in the immediate rather than hope and wait for it. Now I was hoping for the best, while I was preparing for what ordinarily may seem as the worst, because, sometimes, in that worst seems to be the home of the best.

Before this time, I had been having a strong feeling from deep within me, that my life has been so wonderful, and I always thanked God. This condition from the sickness might be as it was, but I knew it has helped in advancing my life.

One afternoon, when all the seeming realities of this condition swept waves of momentary depression over me, I began hobbling about the empty house, and later into the bathroom, recalling all that God has done for me so far in my life and saying it out to myself. The miracle of my survival, the miracle of my healing, my un-waned and, even, growing respect among my peers despite my physical condition, my new intellectual awareness, or what I prefer to call my new ‘spiritual becoming’, and so on. I walked out of the bathroom with a different mood in place of the depression, and a song in place of my soliloquy. It was Bobby McFerrin’s, telling myself not to worry but to be happy. “In the world there is so much trouble / If you worry you make it double. Don't worry, be happy.”

It was the chorus, "Don't worry, be happy" that mirrored my heart and filled my imagination, especially as I saw in my mind's eye the funny face of the clown-singer as I had seen in his music video. I kept repeating the words and it moved me to make such a face at my obstacle - what seems to be my problem.

I had no cause to worry. I have known that to have a cause to worry is the only real problem in the world and not the natural conditions themselves. To the song, I danced around my room, dressing up and remembering a poem by Jelaludin Rumi, the 13th century Afghan sufist.

Dance, when you're broken open.
Dance, if you've torn the bandage off.
Dance in the middle of fighting.
Dance in your blood.
Dance when you're perfectly free.

Truly, life has been so hot in the furnace, but it has been so much fun with its ace. After I made the decision to write this book, I made an important decision about the book. I wanted for the bones of my hips to be given to me after the surgery. I intended to carve it into a pendant and wear it as a necklace for the cover of my book. The message is to tell my readers that even though misfortunes befall us, if we learn to see them rightly, we could see them as fortunes in disguise and we could turn them around to be beauties of life. The bones of my hips have been the bane of my life for so long; now it is time for me to wear them to adorn my African figure and make my story a beautiful one to remember.

Now I could see that my consciousness, though still naturally susceptible to environmental vicissitudes, was becoming invulnerable to their intimidation. "There is a war that opens the doors of heaven..." as Lord Krishna says to Arjuna in the *Bhagavad-Gita*, "Happy the Warrior, whose fate it is to fight such a war." I have been fighting the war, and now I have a better faith, that "the Lord is my Shepherd," and "I shall not want."

PART FOUR

Good Morning America

Not like the brazen giants of Greek fame,
With conquering limbs astride from land to land:
Here, at our sea-washed, sunset gates shall stand
A mighty woman with a touch, whose flame
Is the imprisoned lightning, and her name
Mother of Exiles. From her beacon-hand
Glows world-wide welcome; her mild eyes command
The air-bridged harbor that twin cities frame.
"Keep, ancient land, your storied pomp!" cries she
With silent lips. "Give me your tired, your poor
Your huddled masses yearning to breathe free,
The wretched refuse of your teeming shore
Send these, the homeless, tempest tots, to me,
I lift my lamp beside the golden door!"

"The New Colossus" - Emma Lazarus

TWENTY-THREE

The Holy Pilgrimage

I

A bad dream can make the night seem hopeless, but if one can make it through the night, there is always a bright day.[54]

At five in the evening, I was the first passenger to arrive for the 10 pm flight. The airport tout that helped me to the departure hall wondered why I had come that early and remarked that I had a long wait ahead. "Other passengers may not come until about 8 or 9 pm."

Only if he knew how many years I had waited for the flight. I dipped my hand into my hand luggage and brought out a book. But I had not read for more than an hour when my mind wandered off in humbling reminiscence. A deep evocation washed over me. All the terrible and significant moments of my sickness came flowing onto my mind's screen, while I was there in the departure hall of the airport living through a scene which had for years been only a piece of my imagination and hope. Dreams do come true, I believe.

It was overwhelming to imagine myself in the horrible days of the sickness, when it appeared too long a period to wait for America, and now to see myself here on the bench, with a valid "almighty visa" in my breast pocket, waiting to embark on the twelve-hour journey. It was as if I was dreaming and I did not find it easy to believe it as real. May be it was really a dream; it had dwelled long enough in my imagination to make it seem so. Almost ten years of war, of solitary struggle. I did not know how I still remained sane. But it was enough to overwhelm me in joy and

---

[54] Paraphrased from songs by Tupac Shakur, "Better Days" and "Dear Mama."

adoration toward the Heavens. I have made it through the night; here at my door knocks the dawn of a bright day. That was a miracle in my life, a miracle of my life. The past, a story told.

I put the book aside and left myself to the free flow of images and thoughts in my mind. I looked ahead into the welcoming hands of America and I saw the new challenge: living the rest of my life measuring up to the values I have learned. Though discovering a deep and dependable self-identity may be a periodic achievement that I have been lucky to discover so early in my life, a deep and dependable self-actualization is a constant, lifelong process of bringing the self and one's experiences into harmony. Yet, it is one thing to sail your boat on a calm sea, and another to sail in a storm. The future, a story yet untold.

For many reasons, America, no doubt, remained the most important place in my life, but especially for the encompassing reason that it was the land that has symbolized my ultimate spiritual liberty. From the moment I thought about going to America, I did not realize I was making a holy pilgrimage. The Promised Land was not only a geographical destination for the Jews; it was a symbol of their spiritual liberty as well. The most important things in life are abstract, but perhaps the only way to them is through concrete steps, physical symbolisms. This is what America has been to me; it is my Mecca, my Jerusalem, my Varanasi, my Bodh Gaya.[55] I have sailed and I have reached the horizon, the land where, as I discovered, no land exists.

As I went on and on in my mind, from parts to parts in my thoughts, and as I admired the minds behind the Jumbo Jets that sprawled around me, peeping through the windows to say "congratulations" to me, other passengers arrived one after the other, until finally we were all ready on the seats. We boarded the plane at about the struck of the time.

***

One of the scary things about the American consulate visa handling was a notorious rule that required applicants denied twice within a period of twelve months not to re-apply until after a hiatus of another twelve months. But Nigerians were one of the smartest people in the world, and no matter how and how much the consulate said no, many of them would not take it for a final answer, and would rarely take conventional lifeline against their obstacle. They always came again and again to the consular officers' windows, only with different identities and passports.

On the other hand, my case was now in a stage different from most other cases. I was in a desperate need of medical treatment, and it was by this thought that I applied the third time in November 1999. I had a copy of a letter from Mr. John B. Day, the President of St Luke's Hospital at New Bedford, Massachusetts, telling the consulate that the hospital has been

[55] Varanasi and Bodh Gaya are holy sites of Hinduism and Buddhism, where millions of pilgrims visit every year.

completely satisfied with the payment arrangement for the treatment I was to receive, and was expecting me at the hospital to begin the treatment. The original copy of the letter had been sent to the consulate.

So, when the consulate refused to reply to my application, I, at first, did not think there was any other option but to wait painfully for twelve months for my next interview. No one would imagine that the consulate would bend its rules.

On the second thought, however, I decided to try harder. I asked uncle Tunji to send another application and include a photocopy of the president's letter in the application. Uncle Tunji did not think it could move the consulate to change its decision, but he filed it to satisfy my eagerness, which seemed to him an unreasonable stubbornness. And, to prove him right, the consulate refused again to call me for an interview.

When I asked Uncle Tunji to send another application, I shot off his lid. For me, my thinking was only like that of a man cornered by a wild beast, and who thought it better to take the beast through a fight for its next meal, at least. Who knows, such a fight might re-write destiny. Usually, success is not a surety, but not trying at all is always a sure failure.

Though angry at my request, Uncle Tunji filed the third consecutive application, nonetheless - perhaps because he wanted to be firmly proved in his stance. But after waiting long enough with no reply, I also gave up all hopes of getting the visa appointment through the applications. I thought of trying other possible means. Although I could wait through the period of the penalty, and I had even been preparing my mind for it, but I still did not want to make such a destiny a surety.

I thought of going public with my case to instigate the embassy. I wanted to go on the national television, private televisions, and a few radio stations to bring my experience to public awareness. I hoped to motivate people from all the corners of Nigeria to join me in the struggle and publicly ask the American consulate to review my case. My father contacted the king of Ife, the spiritual father of the Yoruba people, and, concerned, he invited me to his palace. However, before any step was taken, an appointment letter came out of the blues from the consulate.

This was unbelievable, and I thought that the consulate had gone through my case again and realized that I should be granted the visa – thus, the bending of their rule. But this was a self-delusion. The appointment letter was a mistake, a mistake that eventually became my miracle.

By all I encountered at the consulate on the twenty-fifth of February of the millennium year, I realized the letter had really been a mistake. The first thing I saw was the refusal from a protocol officer, a Nigerian man, who refused to take my passport to pass me to the consulate on the same ground that, by law, I was not supposed to have an interview until after twelve months. I showed him the letter from Mr. Day, but, instead of being persuaded, he threatened to throw me and my uncle out of the building if we would not walk out by ourselves. Whenever they are drunk of their positions, men like to flex their muscles. Everyone there hated him. He seemed like one of the black men aiding the capture of their brethrens during slavery, and, secretly, people called him a sellout.

He was still swearing by all his dead ancestors not to let me in for an interview when, unexpectedly, a young lady came to relieve him of the post. When I presented my case to the lady, also a Nigerian, she reasoned and finally took my passport, though she said it was unlikely for me to receive an interview.

My next challenge was at the consular officer's window. She was a different officer from the earlier insulting one. However, though she decided to grant the interview, the visa had been denied before the interview commenced.

"Sorry, sir," the interviewer said after the usual greetings, "I won't be able to give you the visa." My heart almost fell through my bottom. "Before I called you in I had taken your case to the director (of the visa section) and he asked me to advise you to withdraw your application and collect your application fee. If you did not, and you went through this interview, you wouldn't be able to collect your money back. So the only choice you have is either to lose the money or collect it back right now, because I've been advised not to grant you the visa."

"But why?" I asked out of confusion. "Why won't you give me the visa?"

"Because you're not qualified for the visa."

"And why am I not qualified?"

"Your age. The U.S. immigration law requires for anyone about your age, applying for a visiting visa, to provide proofs that he or she will return to his or her country at the end of the granted period of being in the United States."

"But I'm not going on visiting; I'm going for medical treatment!"

"It's the same thing; the law doesn't see any difference between the two."

"It should!" I responded.

"But, unfortunately, it doesn't. And that is what I have to follow now. I'm sorry."

I was visibly worried, as I realized I was no longer up against one consular officer; the whole consulate was now up against me. I tried to give her the hospital president's letter, but she kept shaking her head. When I stubbornly presented the letter to her she said, "I'm warning you; if I read the letter, it means I've conducted the interview and you would lose your application fee."

Although, I did not think the decision of the American consulate could be overturned; it was like a hope of turning stone into bread, but I did not see any wisdom in backing out now just because of N4, 500. Already, tens of thousands of naira had gone into this, and a lot more in time and energy. At this time, my people were praying that I would come home with the visa, and the pressure of the prospect of being completely denied and thrown out of the system was unimaginable. What application fee could now be my concern? I decided to gamble on the money. Really, it appeared as a gamble, for it seemed a game of chance now.

But it only appeared so. I was now a staunch believer in the principle of teleology, believing that whatever hit or missed a man could never have missed or hit him. And, along with this, as necessarily as they go, I knew that whatever action or inaction I took here would not be left out of participation toward whatever would hit or miss me.

"Go ahead, conduct the interview," I said to her, "The money is not what matters now; what matters is my condition - you can also see it."

Fighting the battle uphill, I did not know how much chance I had. I remembered that the consulate should even have seen the original copy of the president's letter before I came in here, but she claimed they had not. That was another thing that showed that the consulate only looked for ways to deny the visa. One of the blue collar workers at the embassy had one day warned us not to let any of my documents be sent to the consulate directly from America, "They would put it away and pretend they didn't see it," she had said.

The consular took the letter and went through it, beginning the interview. In her mind, she was just going through the motion; the fate of the matter had been sealed by the higher authority.

"I still don't see how enough this is to qualify you for a visa," she said after reading through the letter. "This is not enough to comply with the law. It is not that we (consular officers) don't want to give you the visa, but it is the law that we follow. As I'm looking at you, I can feel with you. I understand your problem and I pity you. But the law doesn't pity you. The law doesn't see you; the law doesn't know you. And it is this law that decides."

And, truly, she felt for me. She was a middle-aged white woman and I could see the waves of compassion flowing from her toward me.

"But what can you do to help us about it?" Uncle Tunji asked.

"I wish I could do anything, but I'm sorry I can't. It's left to you; the proof of his ties to his country is what the law requires."

"What sort of proofs?" I asked.

"Proofs of employment, bank statement, deeds of property, all proving that you have something important tying you to your country and you are not going to take up employment in the United States, but return after the granted period."

"That's rather funny. I've been grounded for about seven years now, ever before I could get an opportunity to do anything with my life; how do you think I can get all that? But let me tell you this; it's all the proof I got. I'm a career person, hoping to go into filmmaking. To continue my life in the career, I need my environment. I cannot perform in an environment strange to me. This is where I grew up and, therefore, whatever story I would make would be in the context of this place. And, to prove that to you, I have a screenplay here." I brought out my only screenplay, *Dispossession.*

"Don't bother, that's not convincing. In America there are a lot of black people in the industry and it won't be hard to mix up. Besides, people are coming from all over the world and are making movies in the U.S. In Hollywood, where you are from doesn't really matter anymore."

"I'm an author and I also have a project I'm currently working on." I brought out the manuscript of my book. These were all the possessions I had in the world and I was just floundering for survival. "Here, this is the manuscript; it is a very important project in my life and I cannot abandon it just to live in America." And this is true. Although I hoped to publish it in America, I had become so attached to the manuscript that I would forego anything in the world than to lose it. At this time, it seemed the only thing I have to preserve myself in the world, the only thing to preserve my thoughts and experience forever.

"There are publishers in the U.S.; you could get it published there, too. It's not a reason good enough to give you the visa."

That seemed to want to spend me up, but I still tried some more persuasion, because I could see the compassionate flame of human feeling in her eyes as she kept a long look at me. I had a hope the flame would cook my meal and I persuaded on.

After some time, she said, "Alright, go and have a seat. It's no longer in my power, but I can go and talk to the director again. May be he'd reconsider your case. If it's in my power, it wouldn't have been difficult for me to give you."

I was relieved that I had a benefit of time, but what that time would bring, no one could be sure. I was not sure what this was going to lead to; success or failure, I waited. But I did not just wait, I prayed in my heart. "God, take control of that consultation and bring this event in my favor."

These were all the fog that I went through before I finally got the 'almighty visa', and they were part of what made it seemed to me more like a dream when I saw myself among the passengers heading for the United States of America on the fateful night of the seventeenth day of the fourth month of the millennium year. The consular officer had returned to tell me they have overturned the decision and would give me the visa. My hobbling out of the building on that day was a dance of joy.

We took off at around 10:30 pm and, for the first time in my life, I saw myself fly away from Nigeria. I had a window seat, and from there I looked down at the busy Lagos city: spots of golden lights lain on a dark velvet of the night, moving and still spots, all diminishing into the depth of space, deepened further and further by the climbing distance of the airplane.

The carrier was KLM, and, including an eight-hour stop over in Netherlands, the entire journey was to take twenty hours. I enjoyed every minute of it, so much that I did not sleep a wink.

II

I was not as lucky as many immigrants. I flew in through the Bay State and missed the pleasure of viewing the Statue of Liberty from the horizon. However, I did not miss the imagination, and it was as real as physically seeing it. Though permanently situated at the Liberty Island, the Mother of Exile welcomes all good-willing immigrants through all shores of America. In my mind's eyes, I saw the imprisoned flame, burning sacrificially in captivity to mark the grave of bondage and to symbolize human freedom - my freedom. In her mild eyes, I saw a warm welcome. Towering among the skyscrapers she sings, telling my heart that I am free at last, from the bars of flesh and bones, and from political oppression and repression. "Free at last," she sings, in tunes soaked in spirit, voice free from seal of lips. My heart filled with joy and my soul with happiness. It had been a long journey in time, but liberty always stands, patiently waiting for those who are bold enough to take the trip, those fortunate to make the trip.

***

It was intriguing to see for the first time the landscapes of "God's Own Country." As I waited for a wheelchair I fixed my gaze through the window and at the vast land that made up the Boston Logan Airport.

The famous New England weather greeted me as I emerged from the airplane. "It's cold here," I said to the African America skycap wheeling me out.

"This ain't cold, men. It's nothing. This is spring. If you'll be here long enough you'll see real cold weather."

My uncle knew that the weather would not be 'nothing' to me and he had brought along a long overcoat. I exhaled as we drove out of the airport and into America.

Like most newcomers my neck could not keep from turning around in fascination. I wanted to see everything on my way: the roads, the buildings, the people, and every other thing I could see. I wanted to feel the scent.

Suddenly, I remembered something and I turned my eyes promptly to the sidewalk to amuse myself. A white American young man, born and raised in Nigeria, wrote in a newspaper sometime ago that the sidewalk in America was not made of gold. Wiebe Boer so much loved Nigeria as his home that he called himself a Nimerican, and he had written this as a Nigerian nationalist trying to disenchant many Nigerians from unreasonable, wild ambition of going to America. To him, there were so much potential in Nigeria and he was unhappy with the chills of the cold water Nigerians fall into abroad.

Already, I knew that the sidewalk in America was not made of gold, and many Nigerians also knew this, yet America was a wild fire burning in our dreams. There may be no place like home, as often said, and thus many of us might like to live with the people among whom we were born. Only less than three decades ago, Nigerians were an admirable bride of the world, courted with free foreign visas, expected to lure them to spend their money in the foreign lands. Yet, to live outside the country was inconceivable to them. But now we aspire to come to America simply because America was presently and essentially different from Nigeria. America is a dreamland, rich and fertile to make dreams come true. The distance between a man and his dreams is far shorter in America than in Nigeria. Years of misrule have left Nigeria's gold in a position almost unattainable to ordinary citizens; it has left the distance between dreams and actualization, ideas and completion, plan and fruition to a state of eternity or near-eternity.

At the time when I read the admired gentleman's article, which, though, I applauded along with the far-end conservatives, I wished to say to him that the sidewalk in America was made of gold. The gold of a man's heart is really the realization of his dream, rather or more than *aurum* metals, and the means to it is freedom: adequate freedom in the system and in the accessibility to resources. When I later corresponded with Wiebe, he from Connecticut, I from Massachusetts, we agreed that we are both right. There is an enormous amount of potentials in Nigeria, but the government needs to help the people to it.

As my uncle drove out of Boston and toward Randolph, the suburban neighborhood where he lived, I could smell freedom in the air. Now I wished I could say to the leaders of our new government, who were presently too concerned about inviting foreign investors than building a strong foundation for the country, that this is the kind of gold Nigerians need. We want freedom and strength to compete with foreign investors in the land and anywhere in the world, rather than freedom to choose under which foreign investor we are to slave. I hoped the one-sided prospect of economic relief would not delude the leaders to turn them into modern-day counterparts of the old-time collaborators who helped the slave traders capture their kinsmen for slavery.

As the car pulled into my uncle's garage, I gave a sigh of relief and of gratitude to my uncle and to God. This is the land where I had been dreaming to begin a new life, a land to begin to realize my dream, a land whose dream and promises in me have sent me into intense agony in life, whose dream and promises in me have sent me into tears and sorrow, whose dream and promises in me have sent me into one of the worst of situations in life, but whose dream and promises in me have helped me through to victory at last. I was happy and, in my mind, I saluted America. I saluted her great sons and daughters who have toiled day and night to make it a land of that much promise; her sons and daughters who have sacrificed so much of sweat and blood to make it a land where dreams come true; her sons and daughters who have toiled so much to make it a human crucible for all the people of the world; her sons and daughters who have fought and suffered immeasurably to make it easy for my black skin to find life here, giving me hope to make my life better; her sons and daughters, black, white, and all races, dead and living. I was happy to be here at last.

***

The next morning, I woke up to a bright day and said "Good Morning" to America. I did not scream "Good morning my neighbors"; growing up in Nigeria was different from growing up in Zamunda. I never was like Akeem, and now I really did not wish I was like him. On the drama stage that is our world, every character is unique. I am happy with the part I have played so far. At least, I have told a story Akeem could not have told. God, using his vassals, so-called gods and spirits, has tried me so intensely, but has also strengthened me through the predicaments and has told me as a story of the strength and triumph of the human spirit. In the Yoruba tradition, the most potent weapon a warrior uses against his obstacle is his knowledge of its name; that is, the knowledge and understanding of what the true nature of the obstacle is. Often in his incantation, the warrior says, "I have known the (true) name of the snake; no longer can it bite me. I have known the name of the gun; no longer can it kill me. I have known the name of the enemy; no longer can he hurt me. I have known the name of evil; no longer can it touch me." Like this has God revealed to me the true name and nature of the god of sickness and disease, of the goddess of love and desire, of the god of misfortune, of the goddess of fortune, and of the god of suffering. I have known the true name of life, and if I do not forget, never again would it burden me.

By my past experience I may have been a symbol representing the ignorance and suffering of humankind, now I represent its success, its spirit of success, and its success of spirit. Not only have I achieved what I have always wanted, I have achieved much more. God has turned my suffering into an adornment, one I will proudly wear for the rest of my life. At this stage, I have been successful as a human being. Though new challenges lay ahead, I have achieved a better status in human ignorance, a status of enlightened ignorance, and by this I am prepared for the next phase of my journey. Perhaps the best thing a person could ever achieve in the world is to discover his or her ignorance. "One does not become enlightened by imagining figures of light," Carl Jung says, "but by making the darkness conscious." This is the ignorance that is bliss, one freely chosen, and not the one nature imposes on us, and in which we tend to indulge.

This is an interesting irony of life, and of knowledge. At the beginning of our pursuit we are looking for 'God'; at the end of our pursuit we are still looking for 'God'. The true progress is from ignorance to ignorance. It is like taking an expedition across the globe. If you travel long enough, you will only get where you started. The happy story, however, is that you would have seen places around the globe and there is nowhere else in the world to go. The horizon has collapsed. Yet, the purest of knowledge does not satisfy the seeker from looking for 'Him'. This is the mystery of knowledge, and only he or she who feels this that really knows. For, even though, once and again a pilgrim may wander off, the footprints that carried him to the horizon will never be erased.

Every life is a story; every story is a myth. A modern myth has my story told in the world, and as a mythological hero, I have conquered the monsters that threatened my life. The only problem I may now have is in keeping them in the captivity, in forgetting that I do not have any problem anymore. However, a mythological hero is always a myth; he remains real only as long as the story lasts. Now I am a rat in the rat race, and no matter how fast ahead I run, I will always be a rat like every other rat. The success of it is not to forget this. In ancient Japanese tradition, it is believed that witches or evils get you only by taking away your name (your identity) from you; they harm you only by making you forget who you are. I have known who I am; in the evanescent world, the new challenge is to always remember this, to always remember the footprints of the pilgrim.

I wrote this story because God has blessed me and I want the world to know. God has blessed me and I want the world to know how. God has blessed me and I want every human being going through the storm of life to know how a blessing it is for them - if only he or she can see it, grab it, and not let it pass by. This is not just my story; it is my story, it is your story, it is our story. We can dispute over the science of our experience and we can dispute over its mystery, either in witchcraft or religion. What we cannot dispute is the humanity of it all: the hope, the loss, the weakness, the suffering, the strength, and the hope again. This is the story of the human spirit.

THE EPILOGUES

I

Tolani

Gently, the breeze blew at the branches and combed its way through the pine trees a few yards away from my window. It made a hissing sound, one common during the cold dry season of the year. But the rain had just returned, with all the leaves green and luscious. It was a time the vegetable farmers of the tropics had less time to sleep.

A deep tearing sound tore through the sky. As little kids, we would say it was God walking through His garden; others would say it was the angels running their errands loudly, or the African god venting his anger. It was the sound of thunder, heralding the coming of a heavy rain for the day.

No one could tell what time of the day it was. Whether it was morning, evening, or nighttime, no one had the need to tell. It was about three or four months into my sickness, a period of heightened physical and mental trauma. Across from me, a strange visitor was calmly seated, facing the bed in which I lay half alive. She was my grandmother, my father's mother, whom we simply called "Mama" during her lifetime. She had died about two years earlier, but now she sat quietly in my sickroom, staring at my dying body, as if brooding what in the world she could do to help me.

To have mama and me in view at once, Baami and my father sat adjacent to my bed. From the way they were raised, they believed the dead were always alive in a world beyond human perception, sometimes watching over the living, and sometimes visiting into the human world for one thing or another. Yet, they did not know of a possibility of an ancestor visiting in the manner that Mama was currently doing. Though lying buried in the backyard, she was now here with us in flesh. Save for the sound from the trees outside the window, the room was still and quiet, until another visitor walked into the room.

Mama Fatima was the widow of Mallam Ali, my father's Imam whom we called Alfa, mentioned earlier in my story. She was called Mama Fatima because Fatima was the name of the child she had for Alfa. After the death of her husband, she had turned to deep spiritual life, as her husband had been, and spent her time studying and reciting the Holy Qur'an, meditating, praying, and educating her child in the way of the heaven and the earth. Although she was surprised to see Mama in the room with us, the situation did not appear to her as strange. She greeted Mama warmly and asked why she had come.

"It is this boy I have come to see," Mama replied, with a deeply worried voice. "My heart has not been at ease since I heard of his sickness. I'm praying for him and I know he will get well by the grace of God. But I cannot be away from him any longer, and I have come to stay with him for sometime, to take care of him until he gets well."

"How is everyone over there?" Mama Fatima changed the subject, asking about other relatives that had passed away, as if it was a normal situation and a normal conversation.

"Everyone is fine," Mama replied.

This was a dream Mama Fatima had one night in the month of March 1994, and she had rushed to my sickroom the following morning to tell it. The interpretation read into the dream was that Mama had really heard about my sickness and was being with me in spirit.

In the pre-colonial era this was one of the channels that witchdoctors liked to pursue. They would continue to make appeasements to the spirit of the mother to make her keep the suffering child in mind for recovery. People in the great beyond are believed to have a better understanding of and control over our temporal world. It was one reason that made Aunty Sidi offer to make a sacrifice to Sango over my sickness.

That morning, the discussion continued about Mama's motherliness when she was alive, and everyone in the room believed that this was what she still continued to do in her death. I took confidence in this interpretation, hoping that the spirit of my grandmother was aiding me in the battle for my life. However, God cast forgetfulness upon everyone of us and in a short time no one had the freedom to remember the dream, perhaps because there were a lot of mind-boggling events going on in the course of my sickness.

A few months after the event of Mama Fatima's dream, my father's wife had a baby girl. In the Yoruba family, whenever a child is born after the death of an elderly person, the child is named to suggest it as a reincarnation of the dead person, if of the same sex. If a male, the baby would be named Babatunde, Babajide, or Babarinde, meaning "Baba has returned"; if a female, she would be named Iyabo, Yetunde, or Yejide, meaning "Mama has returned." It was according to this tradition that the new baby was named Iyabo after Mama, and, in addition, my father specially gave her the name Tolani, originally my grandmother's name, because he and everyone thought she amazingly looked like Mama.

Tolani grew very fast and learned how to talk and walk with remarkable progress. Everyone in the near and far neighborhood adored her. She was so intelligent that people often marveled at how much she knew and how much she could think. However, the purpose that brought Tolani into the world was not one that anyone could imagine.

One remarkable thing that Tolani often did was to talk and dispose herself toward my father as if she was older than him - really, as if she was his mother. Some of us thought it was a bad behavior that my father should not let her develop. Yet, my father, seeing his mother in her, loved her so much that he often found himself indulging her.

Four years after she was born, Tolani fell ill and died a week afterward. This saddened everyone in the house and for a long time it troubled my heart. But one day, after the whole temporal dust of her death had calmed, my father and I were talking about the memorable things Tolani had done in her brief lifetime and he eventually mentioned something about her that I had not thought of, something that made him feel guilty over her death.

"There is something about that child that amazes me," my father said, "She didn't seem like she was an ordinary person like every one of us. I've been told about this in a long time but I did not pay much attention to it. I did not think it was something that could lead to her passing away like this. But now I realized it was, and it hurts me to think that I might have been able to save her."

Using a common Yoruba term, he went on to tell me that, ever since she was born, Tolani had been not a child but an adult, and she had been conscious not only of this world but together with another. He cited many events that suggested this and I also came to see it from his point of view. At the end of it all, I tried to console him and myself that we should not really be mourning that we lost a child, but be happy for the time she spent with us. Why the events happened that way, neither of us could think at the time, but we were awed by our awareness of the mystery that shroud Tolani's life and death.

Baba Akinnu came to commiserate with us on her death, and when he got into my room he also told me things about Tolani that was like what my father said. He went further to describe her in certain mysterious ways and he concluded by telling me that Tolani knew consciously that she was going to die at the time, and it was not surprising to her, only to us who had not known anything about who she was.

"Who is she?" I could not but ask.

"I wish I knew," Baba Akinnu replied, but added that Tolani had set her own death to the time it eventually happened, and that, for a purpose, she had deliberately come to live only for the small period.

What this was all about, neither Baba Akinnu nor my father could tell; they only knew that Tolani's life had not been ordinary. However, recollecting all these one day, I remembered Mama Fatima's dream and I began to tie the pieces of information together and wondered about the unbelievable picture it revealed to me. Had Mama really come to spend some time with me to take care of me? I remembered how Tolani had been very fond of playing in my sickroom. Many times she would be alone with me and, now appearing strange, she would sit at the same spot where Mama had sat in Mama Fatima's dream. That was her favorite spot. As little as she was, Tolani would sit quietly and calmly, as if brooding what in the world she could do to help me. Sometimes she would ask questions about how I felt or whether she could get me something. And sometimes we would just play together. The most intriguing elements in all these are the facts that Tolani was born shortly after the sickness began, as Mama had appeared in the dream, and she died when the sickness was over. Also, my treatment took its positive turn at her birth, specifically during her naming ceremony, when, coincidentally, Mama's younger brother talked to my father about Baba Akinnu.

Again and again, I wondered at the relationship of these events in my life, and, again and again, I still wonder. How can I explain the logics and sequence of this? Or how can I unexplain it? Life is a mystery, and even though we have a sense of reason to throw light upon it, there is only so much it can lighten up. Beneath it is always the staggering depth of opaque darkness. As Albert Einstein discovered, the best thing humans can experience in the world is the mysterious. Out of this realization, I hope never to lose my sense of wonder. I want to be able to go one wondering, dwelling in the possibilities of events in the human world.

Humbly, I believe. Tolani was the one. She came as my grandmother and she left me. She came as my sister and she left me. When next she comes, I hope she comes as my daughter, so I can show her how much I appreciate what she has done for me in both the lives she has spent with me, so I can show her how much I love her.

I dwell in Possibility-
A fairer House than Prose-
More numerous of Windows-
Superior-for Doors-

Of Chambers as the Cedar-
Impregnable of Eye-
And for an Everlasting Roof
The Gambrels of the Sky-

Of Visitors-the fairest-
For Occupation-This-
The spreading wide my narrow Hands
To gather Paradise-
Emily Dickinson

II

Time is one of the problems for people living in America. Sometimes I joked that we should petition God, asking Him to give us twelve more hours in a day. But I was not thinking of the problem this way on the 25th of April 2002 when my desire came up against the reality of the human limitation. I had spent my first year in America going through medical treatments and convalescing, and now I was finally in the stream of everyday life.

First, on this date, I wanted to be at Randolph Community Television station (RCTV) to help record a community show. In the past twelve months I had been volunteering for the RCTV, with which I had the great opportunity of shooting and broadcasting live the South Boston section of the July 4th Independence Day parade.

Secondly, I wanted to be at the Boston Neighborhood Network (BNN) television station at Roxbury to record the second part of a business program that TFPAA was producing. Television and Film Producers and Artist Association, or TFPAA, was an organization founded by Debra Shariff, a film educator from Boston University, and I was lucky to learn of it early enough to help give it birth.

And finally, I wanted to be at a reception party in honor of fifteen students of Quincy College published in the annual school journal. Currently a student at the school, some of my poems were published, and this was my first remarkable literary shot at the public. All these were to happen at the same time, on the same day and in different cities, but I did not think to be granted three bodies to be present at the occasions would be a solution. I only wished they had been scheduled at different times to allow me the opportunity to grace the occasions. Nonetheless, I laughed off the problem and went to the reception party.

"What are you going to wear?" I asked Lima on the phone. She was a Somali-American model featured many times on the cover of the school brochures, and with whom I had been going out in the last few months. Until I was writing this piece, I did not realize that I was fulfilling my vanity of dating a cover girl.

"I already have on a pink shirt and a black pant; would that be ok?"

"That's fine. I'm also dressed casually; I haven't been to a party like this before and I don't know how it's going to be like."

I stressed the word "casually" because I did not want her to have a high expectation of my dressing. Modeling after Iman, the famous Somali-American supermodel, Lima had a high taste in fashion and I did not want to disappoint her. Although I had not cared so much, but in the past two years that I have been in this country I had only been working as a volunteer at different places and I had not been able to purchase outfits for special occasions like this. First, it had been the problem of my legs, and then it was the problem of the law, finding legitimacy to work. I took some computer classes about a year earlier, and when I completed the certificate exams that qualified me as a ComptIA certified computer technician, I was not able to go for the job offers that came my way. The reason: I was not authorized to work and I did not have a social security number.

I later got an opportunity to work on campus as an English tutor, but I eventually lost it because, as an international student, I was not enrolled in enough classes to continue the privilege. Nonetheless, I continued to tutor, but for free. I had acquired a large number of loyal students and I did not want to disappoint them simply because of money. Their education was worth more to me, and I was happy to keep on helping them. While I do not disregard the need for the costly sustenance of life in American society, I disdain having to work just for money. Besides, I have fallen in love with teaching, and it was my way of keeping my sanity.

The moment I walked into the party hall, I knew I was in the place I should be. I went with my uncle, my seven-year old cousin Faridat, Lima, and Trey Nguyen, a Vietnamese-American friend of mine. All over the wall, I saw marble plaques hung at strategic locations, and, by the time I realized what were imprinted on them, I was looking at my name under one of my poems, "Dream", both stanzas of it.[56] The school published four of my poems, and the others were hanging around on the walls, engraved on the marble plaques. I felt deeply flattered. The feeling was more than just that of being published, which was great on its own; it was of feeling honored and respected by the high-class guests in the room. There was the school's president, the deans of faculties, professors, and a myriad of guests. Massachusetts is the heart of American intellectualism and I was now in the midst of some of the players, all celebrating my mind. Seeing my works and name on the walls was like seeing one's name engraved on a Hollywood walk of fame. While the school was feeling proud of me, I was feeling grateful for the recognition, and all I could say to everyone congratulating me was "Thank you."

At first, I could not help but to search in my mind for a connection between the image appraised with eyes of honor, and the dying one on the sick bed in Oyo, groaning under the wrath of sickness and unfit to show up at social gatherings. Now, many people in Oyo could not imagine me walking on my legs; here these people could not imagine me as having being a crippled miserable creature, hanging onto life only by something thinner than a thread of hair. I wished my family and friends at Oyo were here to witness this.

---

[56] Only the first stanza of the poem is at the beginning of this book.

Rahman obtained his Associates in Liberal Arts at Quincy College, and now studies at Harvard University in Cambridge, Massachusetts, pursuing higher degrees in Neuropsychology and Liberal Arts. He continues to write and actively purses his filmmaking career.

You can make comments or discuss your ideas about the book at: **www.onholypilgrimage.com**